One Disease One Cure

Ending Our Multi-Millennia Catastrophe

William Randolph

Table of Contents

Words of Gratitude 1

Important Notes on Sensitive Topics 3

Introduction 9

Part 1 - Healthy Nations: Remembering Who We Really Are 12
Chapter 1: This Is Who We Really Are - Healthy Nations Do Exist 13
Chapter 2: Discovering Three Core Spiritual Practices of Healthy Nations 20

Part 2 - The Core Infection: Rulers Forbid Solidarity and Accountability 28
Chapter 3: Shared Agreements vs Imposed Laws 29
Chapter 4: Shared Accountability vs Abusive Law Enforcement 35
Chapter 5: Encouraging Healing vs Discouraging Healing 46
Chapter 6: Blind Belief 1 - When People Ignore Reality to Maintain Safety and Comfort . . . 53
Chapter 7: When Children Learn to Take Responsibility 68
Chapter 8: Blind Belief 2 - Multi-Millennia Misunderstandings 75

Part 3 - Gift Economy vs Profit Economy 85
Chapter 9: Gift Economies 86
Chapter 10: Profit Economies 94
Chapter 11: Cascading Generosity vs Cascading Selfishness 109

Part 4 - What Defines a Person's World? 118
Chapter 12: The Family and the Burglar 119
Chapter 13: An Endless Nightmare Descends on a Healthy Nation 122
Chapter 14: Same Planet, Different Worlds 126
Chapter 15: Unhealthy Nations Shape the Worlds of Millions of People 135
Chapter 16: Courageous Solidarity in Action 151

Part 5 - Heart-Opening vs Heart-Closing 156
Chapter 17: Heart-Opening vs Heart-Closing 157
Chapter 18: The Great Scam of Heart-Closing Cultural Narratives 170
Chapter 19: Creating a Culture of Remembering 179

Part 6 - Unhealthy Nations Impose Division 188
Chapter 20: Imposing and Maintaining Racism vs Generating Unity 189
Chapter 21: Training People to Adopt Authoritarian Ideologies 198
Chapter 22: Imposing and Maintaining Hatred 210
Chapter 23: Addressing Shared Challenges With the Sacred Circle 228
Chapter 24: Sexual Discrimination vs Sexual Equality 233
Chapter 25: Sexual Freedom vs Sexual Repression 245

Part 7 - Creating Deep Division Through Privilege and Entitlement 261
Chapter 26: Privilege 1 - Lift-and-Turn 262
Chapter 27: Privilege 2 - Social Class and Promise Keeping 270

    Chapter 28: The Three Integrities 282
    Chapter 29: Privilege 3 - Going Through the Motions 292
    Chapter 30: Privilege 4 - Entitlement 313
    Chapter 31: The Story of the Peacemaker 319
    Chapter 32: A Study in Privilege and World-Shaping - the Police 331

Part 08 - Unhealthy Nations Prevent Deep Cultural Healing 343
    Chapter 33: It All Starts with Justifying or Ignoring Exploitative Rulers 344
    Chapter 34: Who Controls the Land? 351
    Chapter 35: Guerilla Gardening - Generating Abundance Without Permission 365
    Chapter 36: Sabotaging Efforts at Deep Cultural Healing 368
    Chapter 37: Culture Jamming 382
    Chapter 38: Endless Predation When the Root Disease Goes Unhealed 396
    Chapter 39: Even More Propaganda Techniques 407
    Chapter 40: Enough! - The Zapatistas' Deep Revolution .418

Part 9 - Spiritual Healing: Recovering from Our Multi-Millennia Catastrophe 424
    Chapter 41: The Deepest Lessons From Thousands of Years of Spiritual Leaders 425
    Chapter 42: Training Children to Give or Withhold Love, Part 1 433
    Chapter 43: Good Contact vs Poor Contact 448
    Chapter 44: Training Children to Give or Withhold Love, Part 2 460
    Chapter 45: The Spiritual Impacts of Physical Deprivation 471
    Chapter 46: Embracing the Sacred Feminine 488
    Chapter 47: Embracing the Sacred Masculine 492
    Chapter 48: Bravery and Cowardice 505

Part 10 - What Can I Do? 515
    Chapter 49: What to Keep and What to Let Go 516
    Chapter 50: What Can I Do? 523
    Chapter 51: We Are the Promised Land 535

Appendices 537
    Appendix 1: Acknowledging Contradictions 537
    Appendix 2: Healing Practices 543
    Appendix 3: Healthy Nations Discussed in this Book 546

Image Credits 547

Citations 548

Bibliography, Copyright, and Further Reading 561

Index 562

Words of Gratitude

Thanks to the nonhumans who helped me write this book. I often had moments of sadness, anger, and other hard feelings while writing, and sometimes I had no humans to share this with. But I kept going outside and sitting with the tulip poplars and oaks and dogwoods, and I listened to the carolina wrens and robins. I felt the sun and wind. I practiced feeling grateful and walking in a sacred way even on concrete and asphalt, and I always felt better.

I wouldn't have known to seek connection with nonhumans this way if I hadn't found the Kamana program. I thank Jon Young for producing it, and I am grateful for his mentors and other contributors, including Ingwe, Jake Swamp, Tom Brown Jr, Gilbert Walking Bull, and all the others. I especially thank Mohawk man Jake Swamp for sharing the Thanksgiving Address.

Thank you to Mike Paul for your quick friendship and trust. When you invited me to meet the Ashaninka, you changed my life forever and made this book possible. Thank you to the Ashaninka for showing me what a healthy nation is like.

I stood on the shoulders of so many giants to write this book, and I am grateful to each one. Some of these people know me, and some don't, and some died before I was born, but all of them made a big difference in my life. Starting with the people of healthy nations: Nancy Basket, Robin Kimmerer, Ohiyesa/Charles Alexander Eastman, Pretty Shield, Black Elk, Martín Prechtel, and others.

I also thank people who have seen the beauty in healthy nations and written about them in respectful ways, including Weston Price, Wilhelm Reich, Jean Liedloff, Derrick Jensen, Tom Brown Jr, Anne Cameron, Howard Zinn, James Nestor, James Loewen, Jared Diamond, George Grinnell, James Prescott, and others. Thank you to Liedloff, Reich, Prescott, and David Mantell for helping me see children's perspectives in ways I never had before.

I thank the people of unhealthy nations who model what it's like to give one's deepest love even in very trying times, especially my heroes Harriet Tubman, Martin Luther King Jr, Jesus Christ, and Malcolm X.

I am also grateful to all the journalists, whistleblowers and researchers who stand for the truth even at personal risk, including Chris Hedges, Yves Smith, Julian Assange, Caitlin Johnstone, Edward Snowden, Chelsea Manning, Gary Webb, and more. I sometimes felt afraid writing this book. But surrounding myself with the words and energy of brave people helped me carry on.

I thank my editor Cindy Spitzer. You were full of kind and encouraging words for a year before editing started and all the way through publication. You were often much-needed wind in my sails. Your editing made this a better book, and I am especially grateful for your help presenting the most sensitive material in a good way.

Thank you to the illustrators Chelsea Spitzer and Sophia Mueller. And thank you to Caelyn Vandermeer for assisting with research.

Thanks to my friends whom I anonymously interviewed. Your perspectives and experiences added a lot to this book.

I also thank everyone who joined my newsletter and sent encouraging words and constructive feedback, or who reviewed early drafts and helped me make connections I did not see on my own. And special thanks go to Tod, Lindsey, Bob, Nina, and Owen for your continuous support and good cheer.

The danger of listing people's names is that I may accidentally leave someone out who had a major impact. I've spent my whole life trying to understand the world around me and how to walk a good path, and so this book has influences from every mentor, friend, family member, and author I've ever encountered, and plenty of strangers too. Thank you to everyone who has helped me develop the perspectives I share in this book.

And thank you to everyone who works to make important information freely available online, including Internet Archive, Anna's Archive, Sci-Hub, ratical.org, and Wikileaks.

Important Notes on Sensitive Topics

Recognizing the Patterns Behind the Words

Many people throughout history have recognized that unhealthy nations are unhealthy, but it wasn't always clear exactly what made them unhealthy or what the root cause of the trouble was. Thus, sometimes people's descriptions of the problem are ambiguous, and interpreting their words takes special care.

For example, many people have complained specifically about white people or Americans, and certainly these groups have caused a lot of harm. For example, Sioux man Ohiyesa said, "while Indians unqualifiedly say what they mean, the whites have a hundred ways of saying what they do not mean."[1] Sioux man Sitting Bull said, "The life of white men is slavery. They are prisoners in their towns or farms."[2]

One could easily read these words and think that the problem is with white people specifically. But I believe skin color is irrelevant; what matters is that many white people have been trapped in abusive, unhealthy nations for millennia, and they have developed many cultural and individual pathologies as a result. A key message of this book is that *any* group of people – of any skin color, ethnicity, religion, or region – trapped in an unhealthy nation will develop similar cultural pathologies, including racism, sexism, selfishness, and so on.

This book is called *One Disease One Cure* for a reason. It makes the case that all unhealthy nations, including the United States, China, Russia, France, Spain, and others, past and present, show many similar problems. And while they differ in their customs, governments, etc, they all suffer from the same core cultural disease: where a few people rule over the rest.

In presenting the vast evidence in support of this view, this book contains many quotes from people who express negative feelings towards white people and Americans. This is because many of the healthy nations that I studied have faced abuse by Americans and western European unhealthy nations.

While I strongly sympathize with the negative feelings, the point of this book is that the problems are not unique to white people or to Americans. Sitting Bull, Ohiyesa, and many others I quote were only speaking of the problematic nation they saw in front of them – in their case, it happened to be white Americans. But unhealthy nations have existed around the world for millennia. That's why the Yuracares faced similar troubles with the Bolivians, as did the Mosuo with the Chinese, and the Arawaks and Nootka with the Spaniards, to name just a few.

White Europeans have conquered much of the world at various times over several centuries, but the point of this book is to diagnose the core disease, not just one manifestation in one unhealthy nation. To identify the fundamental problem, it helped me to look deeper than people's skin color, and not focus on just one or another nation, but to really look for the deeper patterns across nations.

Any place, any time, and with any group, when rulers impose laws to exploit, dominate, or otherwise control people, the results are predictable: racism, sexism, selfishness, inequality, pollution, forgetting, and more. Only when people clearly see the core underlying disease can they seek meaningful cultural healing within their unhealthy nation.

On Sharing Others' Stories

I gave a lot of thought to how best to honor the stories I share in this book, and how best to honor the people to whom these stories belong. I tried to reach out to some people of healthy nations with mixed results. I'm grateful for the interviews I received, but sometimes I was not able to make contact, and I had to decide whether I would use stories from nations I could not contact directly.

I decided that if someone had published their stories in a book available to the public, I would include some of the stories here with attribution and a respectful retelling. Whenever I directly received a story or perspective about healthy nations in private, I asked permission to share and invited the speaker to give me feedback on the final presentation to ensure the story or perspective was presented as they intended.

I did my best to quote or summarize all stories and cultural practices correctly. I did my best to distinguish between my own beliefs and those of others. I accept responsibility for any mistakes or misinterpretations I may have unintentionally made.

On Healthy Nation Names

This book explores the history of hatred and racism towards people of healthy nations embodied in terms like "savage" and "barbarian." Unfortunately, even the English names for many of these nations sometimes indicate disrespect or confusion.

For example, the people who call themselves "Lakota" or "Dakota" were never collectively called the "Sioux" until Europeans arrived. Lakota and Dakota refer to distinct groups presently united in the Lakota Dakota Nakota Traditional and Spiritual Government.[3] It is not certain where the word Sioux came from, but one story is that European colonists asked the Ojibway people about them and heard the term "Nadouwesou," which they shortened to Sioux. However, in the Ojibway language, that word means "little snakes."[4]

Colonists often decided on a nation's name by asking their neighbors or even enemies. For example, the people who call themselves Bzitsiistas are known by most Americans as Cheyenne because colonists asked the Sioux and heard they were called "Shaiena," meaning "people who talk differently."[5]

In this book, I avoid obviously racist labels like savage and barbarian except when discussing these terms directly or quoting someone who uses the term. I have chosen to use widely recognized English names of healthy nations to make the book accessible to a wide audience, and with that limitation, I generally use the names that authors or speakers used to refer to themselves. For example, Ohiyesa commonly referred to himself and his people as the Sioux in his books, while Black Elk referred to his people as the Lakota. In some chapters, such as *Who Controls the Land?*, I share stories from both Black Elk and Ohiyesa. I refer to them as Sioux to simplify the discussion, as Sioux refers to both Lakota and Dakota people.

For these reasons, the book references both "Sioux" as well as "Lakota" and "Dakota." I mean no disrespect by using Sioux and Lakota or Sioux and Dakota depending on whose stories I reference. Given that so many people use each of these terms in various ways in their books, stories, and quotes, including people from these nations, I generally chose to use the names that each author and speaker chose to use.

I considered using only the traditional names people of healthy nations call themselves, and thus avoiding words like Sioux entirely. However, doing so would have created many problems because of confusion that might result if, for example, Ohiyesa referred to his people with one name, and in the next sentence, I refer to his people with another name. This trouble and related troubles existed for multiple nations.

Ultimately, I had to balance many competing concerns in choosing how to present healthy nations, including clarity, accessibility to a wide audience, accuracy, and other factors. While I always prioritized accuracy and never intentionally sacrificed it, some concerns, such as which name to use for a particular nation, sometimes had no single obvious best approach. This book represents the best balance I could achieve after discussions with many different people.

On Healthy Nations Past and Present

One way that unhealthy nations minimize or dismiss healthy nations is by propagating the incorrect belief that they all died out long ago.

This is not true. Millions of people around the world either live in fully sovereign healthy nations or remember ancestors who lived in a good way and maintain much of their healthy nations' wisdom and practices. This book references the recent history of healthy nations, such as the Lakota and Nootka, including their environmental activism as well as how their children were forced into authoritarian schools.

In order to contrast unhealthy nations and healthy nations, I sought out stories from when each healthy nation could fully embrace their traditional practices and way of life.

The Ashaninka continue to live in a traditional way today while many nations, such as the Okanagan and Cherokee, have been unable to fully embrace their traditional ways of life since the unhealthy nations imposed their laws. The same is true for many other healthy nations around the world.

In this book, I refer to many traditional practices that were fully observed in the past, and I use the past tense to describe these, especially when a speaker like the Crow woman Pretty Shield, Okanagan Jeannette Armstrong, or Lakota man Black Elk spoke about them in the past tense. I also acknowledge that many of these nations continue to exist and embrace attitudes and practices from which people in unhealthy nations can learn a great deal.

Okanagan Jeannette Armstrong described this when she said, "I'm not saying that [the Traditional Okanagan decision-making process is] there today, that it works today, but elements of it are still present and have been carried forward because we are only two generations since colonization began."[6]

Unhealthy nations encourage forgetting, which is why so many people have forgotten that their ancestors lived in healthy nations. This book acknowledges traditional practices from the past and present, the efforts of many brave people to preserve ancient wisdom and practices for the future, and the present-day gifts of healthy nations.

On Not Capitalizing the Words "black" and "white" When Referring to People

In recent years, some American writers, news organizations, and publishers have begun capitalizing the words "white" and "black" when referring to people.

I chose not to capitalize either term. Ethnic terms like Haudenosaunee or Yequana have clear meanings, as do geographic terms like North Americans or Asians, religious terms like Jew and Muslim, or political terms like Brazilian and Russian. The meanings of black and white change over time, and mostly seem to exist as arbitrary categories that authorities use to divide people. Humans are not black and white, neither in skin color nor in any other way.

Even the US Census recognizes that no one is inherently white or black, as it says its standards on race "generally reflect a social definition of race recognized in this country. They do not conform to any biological, anthropological or genetic criteria."[7] In other words, race and skin color mean whatever people of any particular nation say they mean. I do not want to dignify these arbitrary divisions by capitalizing them.

On Not Capitalizing Titles

I chose not to capitalize anybody's title in this book, including president, chief, king, doctor, or anything else. This book makes the case that healthy nations, unlike unhealthy nations, maintain a baseline of mutual respect for everyone, and people of healthy nations consistently describe the importance of keeping everyone on the same level. For example, the San consistently remind their hunters of how much they depend on their neighbors, and not to feel superior in any way.[8] Tzutujil Mayans expected new chiefs to ritually give away all their things so they were on the same economic level as everyone else.[9]

Every human is divine, and no one is inherently more worthy of respect than anyone else. Making people's titles lowercase helped remind me that no one's title makes them special. And people without titles are not less worthy of respect.

On the Use of the Words "Slave," "Enslaved," and "Enslaver"

In recent years, many writers have begun using the words "enslaver" and "enslaved" rather than "slaveowner" and "slave" to refer to people during the time of US pre-Civil War chattel slavery. This newer language is used to make it clear that slavery wasn't inherent to the people trapped in it; rather it was done to them – that is, they were enslaved.

I support this perspective. A person's slave-status isn't inherent; it's given by the unhealthy nation they live in. However, there are many problems with using this language. In this book, I used "enslaved" when that seemed most appropriate, and "slave" in other cases. I would like to explain why.

The United States propagates a belief that Americans live in "the land of the free." In this view, people who aren't enslaved are free, and so once chattel slavery ended after the Civil War, black people were supposedly free too. This was even called emancipation. And while chattel slavery was absolutely terrible for black people, and in many ways what came next was a major improvement, they still weren't free. The rulers of the United States had simply raised many black people's privilege level so that, instead of being chattel slaves, they became impoverished laborers and remained second class citizens. This is explored in many chapters.

So long as there are rulers who can control people's privilege levels and arbitrarily enforce laws as they wish, no one is free. In fact, people who have actually lived in freedom recognize that all of the United States is a slave society.

Sitting Bull said, "The life of white men is slavery. They are prisoners in their towns or farms."[10] Sitting Bull referred to white people as living in slavery, but white people often at least owned a farm or house. He wasn't even referring to black people or immigrants who often owned even less than that.

A collection of Mohawk writers said, "Property is an idea by which people can be excluded from having access to lands or other means of producing a livelihood. That idea would destroy our culture, which requires that every individual live in service to the Spiritual Ways and The People. That idea (property) would produce slavery."[11]

The Mohawk writers are correct. Unhealthy nations have economies based on property ownership and profit, and these economies produce slavery at all levels, even among the rich who also submit to the rulers.

"Slavery" simply means coerced labor. Regardless of how one person forces another to work, it's slavery, though some slaves have been abused much more than others. This book explores many kinds of slavery:

- wage slavery: where people are kept in financial desperation and forced to work for others to live

- military slavery: where governments force people into the military and punish anyone heavily for avoiding the draft or disobeying orders

- chattel slavery: where people are owned by other private citizens

- prison slavery: where governments imprison people, with or without a good "reason," and then find ways to make prisoners even more miserable if they don't work.

When soldiers are forced to join the military and forced to obey orders or be severely punished, are they enslaved? If so, who is the enslaver, the commanding officer, the draft board, or the president?

When people who committed no crime are imprisoned after plea bargaining and forced to work for pennies an hour or face severe punishment, who is the enslaver, the guard, the warden, or the judge? Or is the enslaver the government or corporation that benefits from prisoners' slave-labor?

Pretending that chattel slavery is the only kind of slavery, and that everyone else is "free," only reinforces the myth that people live in freedom in the United States and other unhealthy nations around the world. People of healthy nations know better and see the whole profit-based economy as a system of slavery.

I don't want to propagate this myth that Americans live in freedom, and so I chose not to use "enslaved" and "enslaver" every time I wanted to refer to people involved in chattel slavery, as if these were the only people involved in slavery. To make it consistent, this book would need to refer to prison-slaves as prison-enslaved, laborers as wage-enslaved, and military slaves as soldier-enslaved, and the text would quickly become unreadable.

Instead, this book calls out slavery in all its forms. When referring specifically to chattel slavery, I used "enslaved" or "slave" as seemed best at each point in the text.

On Gender and Name Changes

When someone changes their name and gender, I use the current name and gender to refer to them for any activities after the change.

For any stories that occur before the change, I reference the name and gender they had at the time. This honors the experience of everyone involved in the story by relating it as it happened.

All Profits Donated

Initial revenue from this book will go to paying the book's expenses, including editing, copyright, and website costs. All remaining revenue will be donated to support people or groups who stand in solidarity with the Earth or help to protect people from exploitation. Examples include forest protectors, water protectors, and whistleblowers. In this way, the book will be part of a gift economy, moving money to where it's most needed. Thank you to everyone who donates or pays for this book for being part of a gift economy with me.

Preface to Chapters Containing the Word "Nigger" (Audio Version Only)

In this chapter, I quote people who use the term "nigger," a word closely associated with centuries of racist abuse. I believe strongly in telling stories as they happened and quoting what people truly said. In this audio book, I have decided to convey these racially sensitive quotes accurately.

Pronunciation in the Audio Version

I have not been able to confirm the pronunciation of words with each healthy nation reviewed in this book. Thus, I may not pronounce words the same as a native speaker would pronounce them. Readers who wish to learn the true pronunciation should seek out native speakers.

Why Call them Healthy Nations? Why Not "Native," "Indigenous" or "First Nations"?

I've struggled to have productive conversations when I speak with other people about healthy nations. For years, I called them native people or indigenous people, but this caused many different misunderstandings. One problem is that *native* and *indigenous* have different meanings to different people.

I commonly encountered people who believed they were native because they were born where they lived, or because their family had lived in that area for several generations. I found myself trying to define what I meant by native, or debating whether or not the other person was really native and this was never productive. If some people want to consider themselves native based on their definition, I've never found it helpful to disagree. But I am very willing to debate whether a nation is healthy.

Indigenous also has multiple meanings. For example, economists and war analysts talk about a country having an indigenous weapon system if they can manufacture it from start to finish in their own country.[12]

Furthermore, indigenous can also refer to people who've lived in one place for a very long time. But how long is long enough to be indigenous? Are descendents of early European colonists indigenous after being in North America for 400 years? Are the Chinese indigenous after living in China for thousands of years? Sometimes indigenous refers to people who lived somewhere before Europeans arrived. But some of them were unhealthy nations too, such as the Incans and Aztecs. So calling people indigenous can also be confusing.

I find *First Nations* unclear too, as it commonly refers to people who lived in particular areas immediately before European colonists arrived. But what makes "being first" special? Weren't there migrations, wars, or other pressures in many areas long before Europeans arrived, and other nations that lived in some places before the ones now called First Nations?

All these terms have different meanings to different people, and none get to the heart of why these nations are worth learning from. And of course, people called native or indigenous face centuries of racism and hateful misunderstandings, as explored in Chapter 22. So, I made my own names: healthy and unhealthy nations (defined in Chapter 2). This helps bypass the racist tropes and opens a dialog on what a healthy nation is even like. I have found this makes conversations much more clear, so I use the terms healthy and unhealthy nation in this book.

Introduction

I grew up in a middle-class family in the United States. Even though my life had always been pretty comfortable, by my mid-20s I had the sense that something in my nation was deeply wrong.

A few years ago, I picked up a book on the history of financial fraud, opened to a random page, and started reading about wealthy bankers who engaged in huge scams that made them richer while hurting many people. In response, people took to the streets in protest, many of whom had lost their jobs and livelihood due to the economic fallout of the bankers' illegal behavior. They demanded the government prosecute the criminal bankers and support the people in getting back on their feet. Instead, the government sent the police to suppress the protesters and protect the bankers.

I thought to myself, ah hah, I must be reading about the 2011 Occupy Wall Street protests. I know that story well.

I was wrong! It turns out that part of the book was actually about something that happened way back in the 1800s… but it was the same story!

This hit me hard.

I had spent years studying the financial frauds leading up to the 2008 crash, the resulting protests, and the government repression, and I wanted to work towards changing my nation so those problems would never happen again. But if this fraud and repression were simply part of a repeating pattern, why would present-day activists be any more effective at ending it than activists of the 1800s?

Upset at this revelation, I opened to another part of the book and started reading about ancient Rome. Once again, the details were different, but the story was the same: rich people using their wealth to take advantage of huge numbers of impoverished people in their own society.

Now I felt really disturbed. I was starting to see that these same stories keep repeating throughout history. What was going on? Why has it been so rare for so many societies to finally put an end to this kind of exploitative behavior?

I wanted to help change my own nation, but I knew so many people have fought for change in the past, only to see terrible patterns of exploitation repeat, seemingly endlessly. If I wanted to see profound change, I knew I would have to uncover the fundamental dynamics enabling the exploitation and then work to dismantle them.

What was the core problem that has apparently been going on for thousands of years?

Pattern recognition requires searching for common conditions, not just focusing on individual details. I started to wonder: What do ancient Rome and the United States have in common?

Well, for starters, both nations are characterized by relatively few people owning a huge percentage of the wealth while many people live in poverty. And, the wealthy people control the government that makes laws designed to support them in maintaining their vast wealth and social control.

In other words, a small number of people exploit a large number of people.

This fundamental pattern also describes China, Germany, Egypt, Australia, Russia, India, Ecuador, Peru, and every other unhealthy nation, past or present, that I could think of.

While all these nations seem so different, under the surface they all are basically exploitative. Suddenly, nations around the world with differing food, clothing, architecture, climate, and skin color started to look very similar to me. Some nations may identify as socialist or as capitalist, and some may be mostly Christian or atheist, Muslim, or Confucian. The nation's most influential people may be billionaires, kings, prime ministers, premiers, comrades, emperors, popes, pharaohs, presidents, or many other titles. But underneath all these differences, exploitative nations around the world have been dominating and manipulating their people, in some cases for thousands of years.

Thousands of years! How in the world have these exploitative nations lasted so long, up to the present day?

What are the most common ways that a few wealthy individuals trap huge numbers of other people in exploitative relationships over centuries, even millennia? And if I wanted to help heal these core exploitative patterns, what kind of change would I seek?

Was my desire for a healthy nation just some wishful pipe dream, or is it really possible for humans to live in a way where nobody dominates the rest? And if such healthy nations really do or did exist, what could I learn from them to begin healing the deep troubles of my own unhealthy nation?

As soon as I began to ask these questions, I realized I did not even know what a healthy nation looked like. Thinking back on all the unsatisfying political conversations I had had, and all the political conversations I saw on TV, I realized nobody else I'd talked with or watched on TV had any idea what a healthy nation looked like either.

Eventually, it dawned on me how ridiculous this situation is. Imagine if doctors only encountered sick people, and never encountered even one healthy person in their entire careers. What if, even after a decade of rigorous study of various diseases, doctors could only speculate on what a healthy person was like, and could only give diagnoses and cures based on their theoretical idea of "healthy?" Each doctor might have their own hunch about what makes a person healthy, but none of them would actually know, and so, not surprisingly, a lot of their "cures" might not be very helpful.

This is essentially what happens when most people try to diagnose what's wrong with their unhealthy nation and suggest fixes. People who have never even heard of healthy nations, much less experienced one, are trying to diagnose the social and political problems of their unhealthy nation and promote various cures.

People may argue for fewer taxes or more, less government or more, or more but only in certain ways. Like imaginary doctors who can only speculate about what makes a person healthy and then guess at possible "cures," most people can only speculate about what a healthy nation is like and guess at how to heal the unhealthy nation they live in.

Is it any wonder so many political, social, and economic problems recur endlessly, year after year, century after century?

Figuring out what makes a nation healthy isn't just an intellectual puzzle. This is more important than any election, because it gets to the heart of whether elections can address our deepest troubles. It's more important than any trial, because it gets to the heart of whether a nation can have a trustworthy justice system.

If humans can only have unhealthy nations with sexism, racism, pollution, dishonest leaders, rich and poor, child abuse, and so on, then there would be no point in trying to transform or end these nations because deep healing would be impossible. On the other hand, if it is possible to have a nation without racism and all the rest, then effective social activism really could make a difference. But in order to seek that deepest cultural healing, activists would first need to know what a healthy nation looks like so that they know what to work towards.

So, which is it?

Are humans only capable of creating and maintaining nations with discrimination, dishonesty, selfishness, and pollution? Or can we do better and potentially live in profoundly beautiful, generous, honest, egalitarian nations? And if healthy nations really do exist, what can I learn from them so I can help heal my own unhealthy nation?

After much study and exploration, this book is my answer to these questions.

Part 1 - Healthy Nations: Remembering Who We Really Are

I knew something was wrong in my life and in my nation. I could see a lot of problems, but I couldn't see a way to live differently.

It occurred to me that I needed to find something I had never encountered before: a present-day, fully functional, healthy nation that modeled how I wanted to live.

I went looking, and amazingly, I found one.

Chapter 1: This Is Who We Really Are - Healthy Nations Do Exist

I used to work in the so-called "defense" industry (more accurately, the war industry). The more I realized how my job supported wars that do not make the country safer, the more I wanted to quit.

And in February 2014, I finally did. I had no idea how I would find a more meaningful and satisfying life, but I was ready to start figuring it out.

I started my journey already upset about so many problems – pollution, poverty, dishonest politicians, wars based on lies, the rich getting richer, racism, sexism, and more. I was only beginning to understand how truly horrifying and insidious these cultural problems were, spanning around the world and across centuries.

I also had no idea where I might find a healthier, more caring nation – someplace where a handful of powerful people did not dominate and exploit the rest.

Did such a place even exist?

A year earlier, I had met a woman at the Age of Limits conference who invited me to join a worktrade program at her shared home at a large intentional community deep in the beautiful Appalachian mountains of Western North Carolina. I decided to go.

At the community, I suddenly was surrounded by people willing to question conventional narratives and to live in alignment with their values. We might disagree about some things, but at least we could talk about our concerns. What a relief to feel so free! Whether or not this community was my final home, I knew I had made the right choice to embark on this journey.

At first, everything seemed great. I studied organic gardening and natural building. I worked in the village's dairy and gratefully attended the village council meetings as a silent observer. Over time, I made friends and got to know several village elders who had been in the community for a long time.

Much about life in the community felt satisfying. But after a few months, I started to notice that some things were not working so well.

Unfortunately, they unintentionally created a culture of haves and have-nots. The village had created its own currency. People could work to earn village money to pay village taxes or buy things from each other. This was a key part of their plan to create an independent village economy. However, one class of people were exempt from paying taxes and had an abundance of village currency while the rest were constantly looking for jobs serving the well-off so they could earn enough to pay taxes. People would fight over a job, not because they wanted to do the job, and not because the work necessarily needed to be done, but because they needed village money to pay village taxes.

I noticed that the have-nots seemed uncomfortable discussing their concerns with the haves. Instead, people just generally put up with it, sometimes selling food or handmade items to each other for money instead of freely sharing as they may otherwise have done.

I saw other problems too. When people acted or spoke without integrity, I commonly observed that others would simply ignore it or pretend it hadn't happened. Many long standing troubles never got resolved.

In late spring 2014, I had a private early-morning conversation with a village elder. By her third cup of tea, she opened up and told me something I'd never heard from her before. As the sun sparkled on the dew outside, she said she had lived there for almost 20 years and yet felt disappointed. She was unable to leave because she couldn't afford moving costs. She still loved the physical environment, but village life was not what she had envisioned when she arrived decades ago. Sadly, I heard similar disappointments from other elders, including some who had decided to leave the village.

This hit me very hard.

Such a beautiful community – with hundreds of acres of land without debt, residents of all ages, ample space to garden and farm, clean water, streams and forests, and more – was, unwittingly or not, actively reproducing aspects of the unhealthy American nation so many residents told me they wanted to escape.

Listening to these elders' private concerns, I imagined myself in their shoes, filled with the same "go for it" energy of the original founders. The idea of "build the path as you walk it" seemed deeply wise to me. I could imagine working with others to found a village someday. But what if I founded a village with a group of friends and we also subconsciously manifested the same unhealthy cultural patterns that cause so much harm?

How could I even know what subconscious patterns I had?

It was then that I realized that I had never actually seen a culturally healthy village that I wanted to emulate.

So I had a crazy idea: I would go searching for a truly healthy nation living in a way I wanted to emulate, and I would learn from them. I had just read *Black Elk Speaks* and for the first time, I learned of the Lakota and how different their traditional culture seemed compared to mine. I hadn't yet thought of the term "healthy nation," but in November 2014, I set off looking for one.

I spent almost a year searching for such a group in Ecuador, Bolivia, and Peru while studying Spanish intensively. I got robbed a few times and I almost died a few times. Once someone told me I would be killed if I kept searching, making a gesture of shooting me with blowdarts and my body then floating down the river. Along the way, friends joined me and left again, and I had various adventures, but through it all I was always looking for a nation living in a way I wanted to emulate.

By July 2015, I was worn out. I decided to rest and do an extended water-only fast in Satipo, Peru. Eleven days into that fast, I finally gave up my search. Every hope had been followed by disappointment. I still wanted to find a healthy nation, but I had no ideas and no leads.

Exhausted, I had done my best and I had failed.

I felt a great relief. I imagined what else I could learn with the remaining time on my travel visa. That night, I fell into a more relaxed sleep than I had had in a long time.

The very next day however, I discovered I was wrong!

I met a tall thin Englishman named Mike, and we became quick friends. Each year for the last 35 years, Mike had been visiting a nation called the Ashaninka, and he had a profound respect for them. He invited very few people to join him on his visits. But when he realized that I would honor them too, he invited me to join, a gift for which I will forever feel grateful.

A few weeks later, Mike and his friend Jillian and I entered the first Ashaninkan village.

Before we got to the Ashaninkas' constellation of about a dozen villages containing 2,000 people, Mike told me two things I will always remember. Here is the first:

> *Bring them gifts. They are such kind and generous people that no matter how many gifts you bring them, you will wish you had brought more.*

Mike was right. These loving people constantly shared their food without asking for anything in return. They taught me their language, how to spin cotton, and how to make friction fire. I danced with them, participated in ceremonies with them, laughed with them, sang with them, and played games with the adults and children. They gave me so much and were very welcoming.

Even though I rarely understood what they were saying, I have never felt so deeply comfortable and at home with anybody or any group in my entire life. This relaxation itself was an amazing gift. I couldn't believe it when one night, a group of ladies sat in a row singing and the men got up to dance. They invited me to join. Eventually the other men sat down again, and so I began to sit down. Then someone gestured that they liked my dancing, and they invited me to dance again. I said ok, and got back up, but no other men got up with me!

Growing up, I'd had lots of anxiety around dancing, but not around the Ashaninka. The women sang for me, and I danced for everybody, several times. I mostly didn't think, but when I did I just noticed my total lack of anxiety or concern. I felt comfortable and at home dancing in front of them in a way I had never felt before.

This sense of relaxed comfort was a recurring theme. One of my favorite memories is of an older woman spinning cotton into yarn on a drop spindle. I sat with a few other people on the edge of a clearing, and she sat on a handwoven mat on the ground by herself 10-20 yards away. At first she sat upright, rhythmically working the drop spindle. Over the course of perhaps an hour, I watched an amazing transition. After a while, she leaned over onto her elbow and worked the drop spindle from that position, and then leaned all the way over and took a nap with the spindle resting beside her. Eventually I glanced over again and saw her back in her original upright seated posture, working her spindle as she had at the start. She was the picture of relaxation the entire time.

I believe I witnessed a few things here:

- *Meaningful work*: Ashaninka women commonly wove this yarn into bags and clothing for each other and the men. She wasn't weaving for someone else (such as a boss) to make money to pay bills which would keep uncaring people away (such as tax collectors or landlords). I never got to interview her about this, but I believe the work was directly meaningful to her in a way that paid work often is not.

- *Satisfying rhythm*: She was free to work or rest as she decided. I've observed managers in the United States shame people for not being a "hard worker" and threatening to fire people who didn't work hard enough on the boss's schedule. And so I'll notice workers (including myself) will work when they really don't feel like it, or when they're sick. This woman's grace showed me what it would be like to work when it's time to work, and rest when it's time to rest, and find satisfaction throughout.

I found this same graceful relaxation with the men, too. Several times, a group of older boys and men would want to travel from one village to another, and Mike and I would join them. On the way, we would stop and sit in a circle and rest. One thing really stood out: they laughed a lot! Even though I was studying their language, I never understood anything they said, but I always felt deeply at home and part of the group. Everything about them was so warm and relaxed. Once they looked at Mike and me, and someone made a comment and they all burst out laughing, and I had a moment where I expected to feel anxiety or distress at being laughed at. But then I noticed: there was nothing belittling or othering in their laughter. I never stopped feeling at home. Mike and I sometimes glanced at each other, and he would give me a knowing look as if to say, "aren't these people amazing?"

The children were just as relaxed. As I entered one village, the first person I encountered was a boy I estimated at 10 or 11 years old. Without any adult interaction, he was putting the finishing touches on a new arrow. I watched him carefully split a feather down the middle and attach each half to the rear. Soon the arrow was complete, and he'd apparently made an entire arrow by himself with only local materials. With sign language, he invited me to do some target practice with him. We walked over to a little clearing and we passed a handmade bow back and forth, shooting at a little log buried upright in a hole in the ground. I could see adults from where we were, but I never saw anyone try to control the boy or impose any time restraints, or warn him about safety. He seemed relaxed and very capable, and the adults seemed to trust him to take care of himself. And he was a good shot!

I wanted to learn to spin cotton into yarn, and I asked the woman I lived with if she would show me and let me learn with her cotton. She seemed a little skeptical. I only ever noticed women spinning cotton, never the men. When I asked again a few days later, my hostess brought me some cotton and a drop spindle. It took me a long time to make a strand longer than an inch! I later learned that cotton is one of the most challenging fibers to spin because the fiber length is so short. I started feeling frustrated as I eventually got strands of 2-3". I heard giggling nearby, and I noticed several little girls were laughing at me!

One of the girls, about 5-6 years old, came and took the spindle and cotton from me. With grace and confidence, she spun that cotton as if the drop spindle were an extension of her body. She looked at me and smiled and handed back the spindle and cotton, and then she ran away without saying a word.

I thought, "Wow, it's like she's been spinning her whole life!" Then I realized that was true. I had watched mothers spin with infant children on their laps, and so the little girls learned the motions even before they could lift a spindle. No wonder this girl was an expert at the age of six!

I never observed money exchanging hands while I was there. I heard from Mike and also saw signs that they had only recently encountered money at all, and most didn't seem to use money or have any. I never saw any transactions where people traded with each other. Instead, people just shared everywhere I went. It was common for the men to leave home each day to hunt, fish, or work in the large gardens. Women commonly stayed closer to home, often working together to weave mats, make food or drinks, care for the kids, or take care of other needs. I never noticed any disrespect towards the women or any extra burden on them. Even though men and women seemed to contribute to their family and community in different ways, everybody seemed to have the same respect for each other.

Whenever guests came to visit, they would commonly sit in a circle on the ground and the woman of the household would bring out a large gourd full of peorentsi, a very pink and mildly alcoholic drink made from yuca and other root vegetables. Sitting on the liquid would be a smaller gourd they used as a cup.

My main host was a man in his early 20s named Andre. One day, we had planned to walk several miles to a village and he asked, "Would you like to go there directly, or would you like to take the long way and stop several times?" I asked to take the long way, and I'm glad I did. Every so often, the trail through the woods would open up into another household area and we would sit in a little clearing. Without any prior conversation, a woman would bring us a large gourd of peorentsi to drink. Sometimes we would talk, and sometimes we sat in silence. There was never any payment or trade. These women just shared with their guests as a normal practice. When we had rested enough and finished drinking, Andre and I would move on, only to find another home a little while later and repeat this again. I felt grateful every time for their warm welcome as if something miraculous had happened. They seemed to relate to this generosity like a normal thing.

They had a beautiful practice for sharing peorentsi. All the guests would sit in a circle on the ground, and the hostess would set the large gourd with peorentsi in front of somebody. It would only contain a single cup no matter how many people were present. By the time a woman gave me the drink one day, I knew what to do. I dipped the cup-gourd into the peorentsi and passed it to the person to my left. Then he passed it to the person to his left, till the cup traveled all the way around the circle. The last person would drink as much as they wished, then pass the cup all the way back around to me. Then I refilled the cup and passed it around, and the 2nd to last person would drink. Only after everyone had enough would I fill a cup for myself. It was the most social and connecting way of sharing a drink I had ever experienced.

When there were many men and women or many boys and girls, we would commonly break into two neighboring circles, one circle of men and one of women. I never saw anyone eat or drink alone though. If there were just one or two men or just one or two women, then we would all dine together in a mixed-sex circle.

Amidst all their generosity, I was also amazed at their patience. It was as if they knew everything had to happen at the right time instead of rushing things. Early in my time there, Andre invited me to a distant village. We walked for several hours without stopping. After descending a long steep hill and crossing a river, we arrived. Our hosts invited us to sit under a pavilion with a thatched roof to block the sun. I had no wristwatch, but I suspect I was there for about an hour. There was no idle chatter. One or two people sat with Andre and me, mostly quietly. Every so often, a host would bring another piece of fruit. I still remember a very juicy papaya and how good it tasted after the long hike. They brought fruit faster than Andre and I felt like eating, so the fruit piled up a little. I welcomed the rest after a long hike.

Eventually I noticed someone come up to our host and whisper something and leave. A while later they returned and there was more whispering, and the person left. The person returned again, and this time the host talked to Andre and Andre translated into Spanish for me: a neighbor had just suffered an eye injury that morning, and they heard I had healing experience and wondered if I would help. I immediately sprang into action to gather my first aid kit and water before we hiked off to the injured person's home. I was able to help and the person healed ok. As I reflected on it later, I was amazed that they didn't immediately interrupt my rest to ask for my help. I would certainly have been ok with that. But giving visitors quiet time and food to rest after a long journey was clearly a normal practice for them, and they let me have that time fully before letting me know of the person's injury.

Even their leaders surprised me. When we arrived at their most distant village, Andre introduced me to the village's leader. He was a very unassuming man, with a small frame and a very warm smile. This leader never told us any rules or gave any orders. He showed Mike, Jillian, and me where we could sleep, make a cooking fire, and poop. Once we had no more questions, he went to his home. I sadly never learned his name, but I learned a great deal by watching him.

This village leader did not seem at all different from anybody else. His home was the same as everyone else's: a pavilion with 6 posts and a thatched roof. No homes in this village had walls. Some possessions like mats were kept on the ground, and items like fire making kits were kept tucked under the thatch in the roof. Thus I could tell that this village leader also did not have more possessions than anyone else; that is, he wasn't materially richer. He dressed the same as everyone else. He played games with other adults and children and me in a big clearing, including a big game of soccer one day with a ball of rags tightly wrapped in cordage. There was nothing imposing or threatening about him, so he wasn't a leader because he was a bully. Nor did he seem like a fool who was only a leader because of his possessions or parents. We never had any trouble, but I knew that if we did, I could bring it up and we would work through it. I felt just as comfortable around this leader as around everyone else.

In other words, he seemed like a normal man who took on extra responsibilities to help the village run smoothly but had no extra authority or power. Years later, I realized this was what it was like to have a community with strong leaders and no rulers.

I noticed another moment of leadership. The Peruvians had been overfishing the nearby river for some time, and fish were becoming more and more scarce. My hosts told me that they'd had some hungry times recently. On my last day, I witnessed a large circle of 15-20 Ashaninka men and women leaders sitting in a circle discussing the trouble and what to do about it. I did not understand any of the words they said, but I could tell in their eyes and body language that they were treating the issue with the gravity it deserved.

I also had two amazing experiences with water. The first came when I learned I could drink straight from nearby streams. I didn't use any filter or iodine tablets, not even a cup. I just dunked my head in and gulped down the freshest water I'd ever tasted. I loved it so much that I made a special point on my last day to visit a river I'd crossed many times. I jumped in naked and thirsty and savored the sweet water. I knew I was going back to the United States and I didn't think I'd be able to drink water this way again because of pollution in the rivers.

The second amazing experience with water started with a humble suggestion from one of my hosts: "would you like to go on a hike and see a special place?" After a steady walk through the rainforest, a group of 10-15 of us entered a clearing and I saw the most beautiful waterfall I'd ever seen. It fell down the side of a sheer cliff at least 40 feet high into a pond. On both sides, vibrant green moss shimmered under the water spray and golden sun. I walked through the falling water to see the cliff while little children played in the pond. There was no trash, no graffiti, no concrete or safety railings, no sign that humans had ever been there except the little dirt walking trail we'd arrived on. The waterfall's majesty left a big mark on me. It also showed me that humans could honor such a beautiful place, essentially indefinitely.

The villages were very peaceful. I never saw any conflict or upset feelings, including among children. However, they were also very willing to use violence to protect themselves. I learned that the Peruvian drug wars in the 1980s had cost many Ashaninkans their lives. Several times when we walked between villages, young men brought along shotguns to protect the traveling group. I wished I could help them protect themselves somehow. At least I was able to buy them some shotgun shells from a distant market!

The whole time I stayed with them, they never asked me for anything. I never paid them anything, whether in money or bartered food or anything else, although I did share the food I brought in with me. But I sure felt a continuous desire to give back to them.

Luckily, I had trusted Mike when he said I would want to give them gifts. Before leaving Satipo, I'd asked Mike for a list of all the items the Ashaninka might value. I went to the market and filled a huge sack full of knives, fishing equipment, sewing equipment, cloth, food, and every other tool or material they might want. I was not going to show up unprepared!

And yet… Mike was right again. I still wished I had brought more. After a few weeks living inland, several men, women and children went with Mike and me back to the Ashaninka river-side village where we'd left our sacks of goods. Nobody counted time in hours or minutes there, so I don't know how long it took to give out everything. They smiled warmly and nodded as they pulled the gifts out of the bag. I could tell they approved and welcomed all the gifts even though there was little emotion and they did not say much. By then I was so used to non-verbal communication with them that I knew everything was going great. I felt sad when my sack was finally empty and I had no more gifts to give!

Even this experience amazed me though. There were about 2,000 Ashaninkan people spread over about a dozen villages. Some had never used money, and some sold cacao to traders at a river-side market. I estimated that the highest yearly income of any Ashaninka person was less than what I'd spent on the gifts in my bag. Yet my bag sat in a home with no doors or locks for weeks, even while I was multiple days' hikes away. When I returned, nothing was missing. The bag was untouched. Mike had told me these people were extremely honest, and I could trust them with anything. And he was right.

Mike had told me something else before we arrived at the Ashaninkas' villages:

You will spend the rest of your life figuring out lessons to learn from these people.

Mike was right about that too. A few months later, when I was talking with my father in Los Angeles, he asked me what I had learned. I teared up, as I still do today whenever I think about my time with the Ashaninka. I told my dad, "I don't know everything I learned. I'm still figuring it out. But I know this: people can live differently. We can treat each other well. I know it is possible, and I will never doubt it again because I saw it with my own eyes."

Since then, I have learned: *This is who we really are!* We are not our unhealthy nation of racism, sexism, child abuse, worker abuse, domestic violence, unjust war, environmental destruction, poverty in the face of unthinkable financial wealth, ruling class laws, prisons, soul-crushing schools, and all the rest that we endure, and sadly also perpetuate.

I also learned this: The Ashaninka show how humans can live together when *everyone stands for a culture of mutual respect, and nobody rules over anybody else*. The Ashaninka have strong leaders and no rulers. No individual and no group imposes law on the rest.

The Ashaninka and others like them show us who we really are and who we were born to be. Every young child, before she is trained into thinking otherwise, expects to grow up in a healthy nation like this.

Since then, I have been honored to find many beautiful stories that show us who we are as humans. When we know who we are, we can also see the same repeating patterns of unhealthy nations – around the world and across time – that keep us from the world we want. We can see the trap we're in, and we can decide what to do about it.

I don't have all the answers, and I am no guru. I am a man who no longer works for the "defense" industry because I want to defend us from our unhealthy nation – before it kills us.

Chapter 2: Discovering Three Core Spiritual Practices of Healthy Nations

After returning to the United States, I wanted to connect more deeply with the Earth. I wanted to live like the Ashaninka and build a similar community with my friends.

I returned to the Appalachians, and a friend invited me to a very strange and magical place on the edge of North Carolina's Pisgah National Forest. Flowing water was safe to drink, and I drank straight from the stream as I had in the Amazon.

My new friends and neighbors taught me how to make herbal medicine, tan animal hides, and tell whether a dead animal was still safe to eat. I learned to cook over fire, preserve fruits and vegetables, identify wild edible plants, and preserve meat and fat, all without electricity.

Living in the forest had its challenges and lessons. For example, when sleeping under a tarp or pavilion with no walls, I soon discovered it was pointless to get upset every time my things got soaked in the rain. Instead, I learned to dry my belongings in the sun again to prevent mold. This simple transition – from suffering with a problem to seeking effective solutions – gradually started to soak into everything I did.

I kept finding more stories of nations that reminded me of the Ashaninka, such as the Yequana, Apache, Haudenosaunee, Lakota, and others. These nations had their differences, but people in these nations all live or lived in a beautiful way with each other and the Earth. After a while, I realized that while I was having fun and learning useful skills, it wasn't enough. I still didn't feel very connected with the Earth. I wanted to go deeper.

I kept thinking back to a self-study program I had heard about called Kamana. The program promised to help people connect with the Earth using similar practices, stories, and attitudes as in many of the nations I was reading about. The lead author, Jon Young, had received mentorship and guidance from sub-chief Jake Swamp of the Mohawks within the Haudenosaunee Confederacy, Ingwe who was raised by the Akamba people in Kenya, Gilbert Walking Bull and Tony Ten Fingers of the Lakota, and Tom Brown Jr who'd received extensive training from Stalking Wolf, an Apache man. The Kamana program seemed like a synthesis of what Jon Young had learned from people of all these nations with the goal for the student to develop a deep, personal connection with the Earth.

That summer, I began the Kamana program.

The First Core Spiritual Practice: Practical, Aware Gratitude

One early assignment involved finding a sit spot, a place I would go to every day, rain or shine. Instead of hiking all over and seeing many places for a few minutes each, I would spend hundreds of hours in a single location. Sometimes I would sit still, and sometimes I would go wherever my curiosity took me.

Often I fidgeted and my mind wandered. The Kamana program noted that many students have this trouble. I followed Jon Young's suggestion to "lose your mind and come to your senses."[1] The more I paid attention to quiet sounds and subtle smells, the more my mind quieted, allowing me to notice all manner of birds singing around me, or an edible plant or animal trail I hadn't seen before.

All these things were around me the whole time. I just hadn't noticed before because I was in my head. It was a weird experience to suddenly notice everything that I had not seen, even though it was all happening right in front of me.

I also studied the Haudenosaunee's Thanksgiving Address that Mohawk man Jake Swamp had shared with Jon Young. Growing up in a Christian family, I was used to praying to God, but this Thanksgiving Address was very different. Instead of thanking God for the trees, I learned to thank the trees directly for their shade, food, firewood, and the good company they give. I learned to thank the water for quenching my thirst, the deer for their meat, and the birds for helping me become more aware of my surroundings. I gave thanks to the stars, sun, moon and wind.

Potawatomi woman Robin Kimmerer got to visit the Haudenosaunee when they gave this Thanksgiving Address. She described how it is part ecological lesson, part civics lesson, and partly a reminder to feel grateful for the gifts of life.[2]

For a long time, I really struggled with the Address. I felt anxious and bored. Unable to finish it, I would go to my sit spot and fidget. Eventually I realized I didn't feel very grateful in general. It took years before I could consistently find that place of gratitude and finish the Thanksgiving Address. Luckily, I discovered that gratitude can be practiced, just like bravery, patience and thoughtfulness.

Eventually I recognized the deep truth of the Thanksgiving Address. Everything is a divine being with sacred gifts to give. Trees give gifts of food and home-making material for humans and other animals. They hold the soil in place so it doesn't erode, and cast shade so the forest floor remains moist. Individual species give different gifts. Basswood trees give wood which is useful for starting fires easily, and oak trees give wood that allows fires to burn a long time which is useful for cooking dinner.

Just as each person is unique, I started to notice each tree and bird as its own individual being. I felt grateful to a particular chestnut tree for dropping an abundance of edible nuts, or a particular buckeye tree for stabilizing the edge of a stream where I liked to sit.

Nobody makes the sun shine, but it gives its warmth and light for free. I can plant an apple tree and water it and even pollinate it, but I cannot make it bear fruit. Apples are just an apple tree's gifts. I didn't make my mom nurture me as an infant, she just did. That was one of her sacred gifts. Rivers give us water for drinking and cleaning. Trees give firewood, building wood, food, and shelter for many critters. Animals give meat and if we watch carefully, they can alert us to what's happening all around.

That's all life is – every being giving its gifts and receiving the gifts of others. And it's not just the Haudenosaunee who practice this gratitude for life's gifts. The Thanksgiving Address is unique to the Haudenosaunee, but developing deep gratitude is common in every healthy nation I've found.

Tom Brown Jr described how his Apache mentor Stalking Wolf helped him honor all the plants and animals as gifts from Creator, and to feel a deep sense of reverence as he practiced his survival skills.[3] Okanagan woman Jeannette Armstrong described how they love other species as brothers and sisters.[4] Potawatomi woman Robin Kimmerer described how humans are the "younger brothers of Creation" and our older nonhuman siblings can teach many gifts of wisdom.[5]

I'll never forget my first clear lesson from a nonhuman, a hunting lesson from red-shouldered hawks. I was walking through a forest and observed a single hawk flying and screeching overhead. Red-shouldered hawks like to hunt small animals like mice and shrews, so I knew they all would be acutely aware of the predator flying above. I assumed the hawk wasn't interested in hunting, since otherwise, why make so much noise?

I looked up through the forest canopy just in time to notice a second, silent hawk fly to the first one. Once they were together, the loud hawk flew in one direction screeching, and the silent hawk flew in the opposite direction. If I were a little mouse, I might feel relief at hearing the loud hawk fly away, and if I relaxed my guard I might not notice the silent hawk flying right over me! The hawks taught me a way to use deception while hunting. They also taught me to question my assumptions.

Hawks hunting

Every day I practiced developing this practical, aware gratitude for all the gifts I received from people and the nonhumans. Once I understood that all beings have sacred gifts to give – that is, special ways they contribute to making life better – that raised the obvious question: do individual humans have sacred gifts to give too?

The Second Core Spiritual Practice: Giving My Sacred Gifts

I kept observing the birds and trees and other nonhumans around me, and I studied lots of field guides. I learned so many ways each creature contributes to the web of life, but I had never wondered what my contribution could be. No one had ever told me this before, but I learned that each human also has sacred gifts to give. It only makes sense, since we're divine creatures like everything else in Creation.

Once again, every single healthy nation I studied recognized this to be true. Tony Ten Fingers described a Lakota phrase, "mitakuye oyasin," loosely meaning "everything is my relative." Ten Fingers' elders also taught him a deeper meaning: "I have a burning desire in my heart to know how I fit into the Creation which is one living being."[6]

Each person has sacred gifts, a life purpose, a way they make the world a better place – and only they can do it! All of Creation is simply divine creatures giving their gifts. That includes humans cultivating and giving our sacred gifts too. I believe that giving one's sacred gifts fully is how a person gives their deepest love. "Giving my sacred gifts" and "giving my deepest love" are the same thing. Thus, training a person to give their sacred gifts trains them to give their deepest love in life.

Some people have a special calling to enrich the soil, find food during lean times, or mentor children. Others are fighters who protect their people, or mediators who resolve conflict, or historians who keep ancient stories alive. I learned that it's up to each of us to find our sacred gift or gifts and our own unique way of making the world a better place. The Haudenosaunee noted that it's each of our responsibility to help each other find their gifts, since sometimes a person can struggle to discover them on their own.[7]

The Cherokee likewise see how important it is for people to help each other walk that sacred path, giving their divine gifts fully. Nancy Basket, a woman of Cherokee descent, described how traditional Cherokee recognized that they would keep reincarnating until everyone was living their purpose fully:

> Cherokee people anciently believed that we come back over and over again, like 144 times until everybody gets it right and nobody's left behind.
>
> Isn't that cool? … Reincarnation until you achieve what you need to be doing. Each lifetime you come with a medicine, a purpose that only you can get done. If you don't get it done, it won't get done.
>
> That's how important each person is. What is it that you love to do?[8]

Like the Thanksgiving Address and cultivating a practical, aware gratitude, I had a hard time with this practice too. I had never thought about my life purpose or what I deeply loved to do. In college, I wondered what sort of job I would most like, but I only considered decent-paying jobs that would let me have a life of safety and comfort. I never thought about what I would do or give if I didn't feel constrained by needing a job. When I thought about it, I mostly felt stressed or anxious.

Over several years, I sat with the stress and anxiety enough to notice that I actually felt angry. I felt angry that so many people, including me, are polluting the Earth. I felt angry with the sexism and racism around me, angry that prisons treat inmates so abusively, angry that politicians keep enriching the rich while so many people suffer. And I felt helpless to do anything about it, so every day I went through the little life I'd built trying to ignore an anger I didn't know how to channel productively.

Tony Ten Fingers noted that it can take years to recognize one's gifts and fully give them, especially in a nation that encourages people to walk a comfortable path, or live in a way that pays the most. But Tony Ten Fingers, Nancy Basket, and many others helped me get on the right path with the question: What do you love to do?

I knew I had a passion for learning and teaching self-defense even though I hadn't practiced in many years. While continuing with the nature connection training, I enrolled in jiu jitsu martial arts classes. It didn't address all my frustrations, but I knew I was on a good path, and I felt better.

I had found two big spiritual practices: a practical, aware gratitude for the gifts of others, and cultivating and giving my own sacred gifts.

I was fortunate to find the third core spiritual practice, one that tied them all together.

The Third Core Spiritual Practice: Living in Reciprocity

Many healthy nations like the Ashaninka, Lakota, Cherokee, Potawatomi, and Apache remain alive around the world, even if they're not all able to live in a fully traditional way still. At one point I noticed something interesting: they keep showing up in the news. Often when some environmental catastrophe occurs or a selfish corporation threatens to pollute the Earth, I notice people of healthy nations standing in solidarity with the land.

The Sioux led the Dakota Access Pipeline protests in 2016 in North America, seeking to protect the water from oil spills.[9] In 2010, the Indian government evicted many Jenu Kuruba people from their ancestral land, supposedly to protect local populations of endangered tigers. The Jenu Kuruba noted that the tiger population was so high where they lived precisely because they worship the tigers, as well as the other nonhumans. The Jenu Kuruba demanded to return and that the Indian government stop giving mining companies leases on their homeland.[10,11]

In Africa, the Mbuti likewise rejected a government so-called "conservation" effort that tried to force them off the land even while companies came to dig for gold. One hunter named Mapenzi said, "We know how to protect our forest because nobody knows it the way we do. We know where the animals give birth, where they sleep and during which periods one must never kill them… The animals that the modern law wants to conserve are already under our customary protection. These are the laws our ancestors established."[12] The Gumbaynggirr in Australia and Sami in northern Europe work to prevent logging the old-growth forests.[13,14]

In South America, the Yuracares, Tchimanes and other nations work to prevent the destruction of their forests in the TIPNIS region of Bolivia, where the government wants to allow illegal road development, monocrop farming, and deforestation.[15] In northern Asia, the Evenk, Nivkh, and other nations work to stop destructive Russian oil and gas extraction activities.[16]

Everywhere I looked, I noticed these nations were standing in solidarity with the Earth, even putting their lives on the line if need be. Eventually I understood this as the third core spiritual practice: living in reciprocity. This means I have a responsibility to give back to all the beings who give so much to me. It is not merely a nice idea; it is a core practice for individuals and groups who take responsibility for giving back to all the beings who give humans so much.

In her book *Braiding Sweetgrass*, Robin Kimmerer noted how any culture of gratitude must incorporate reciprocity too, saying, "Each person, human or no, is bound to every other in a reciprocal relationship. Just as all beings have a duty to me, I have a duty to them." If I receive meat from an animal, I am bound to support the animal or its family. When I eat corn, I have a responsibility to take care of the soil it grows in. When I receive a river's gift of clear water, I am responsible for caring for the river. Kimmerer noted that learning and practicing these responsibilities is "an integral part of a human's education."[17]

I grew up Christian and then became atheist when I found that so many religious leaders fall short of the ideals they preach. But when I noticed people of all these beautiful nations consistently putting their lives on the line to protect the land, to honor that responsibility for living in reciprocity, it showed me that they walk the walk. I believe this is normal in healthy nations. This explains why the Western Shoshone man Corbin Harney said, "native people are not separate from the environment. We are the environment!"[18] It also explains why Cherokee woman Rebecca Adamson said, "tribal people worship the sacredness of creation as a way of life, not as a philosophy or religion." She pointed out that no languages of healthy nations even have words for religion. The nearest word for "belief" translates to "the way you live."[19]

As a Christian, I grew up learning that pagans were bad or misguided people who worshiped false gods of the Earth. But Nancy Basket noted that "to worship" simply means "to respect."[20] When the Jenu Kuruba said they worship the tigers, that means that they respect the tigers. Tigers are divine beings with sacred gifts, just like humans and trees and everyone else. I believe the Jenu Kuruba simply honor that each creature has a special purpose or sacred gift, a special role to play. The Jenu Kuruba live in a respectful way so that there is room for everybody, human and nonhuman.

I believe that Creator and Creation are not separate. Creation is a manifestation of Creator. In other words, all of life is a manifestation of God or Goddess or Allah. Creator is like a woman. Women are life, and women also create life: women are life creating life. In the same way, Creation and Creator are the same. And that means that people who stand in solidarity with the Earth are standing in solidarity with God.

After studying many different religions, it seems like humans keep looking for words to describe the indescribable. It may be called Allah, Goddess, Divinity, Creator, God, Yahweh, Spirit That Moves Through All Things, Holy Spirit, Great Mystery, and so on. And of course, some people are agnostic or atheist like I used to be.

I don't have any more insight about divinity than anyone else, but I know this: every single person has a voice in their heart that tells them how to walk a good path if only they'll listen. This is true whether a person is Muslim, Christian, Buddhist, atheist, pagan, or anything else.

And it's not just humans who have an inner knowing. Every being has a special role to play in creation, and part of relating to life in a good way is learning how to respect not just ourselves and each other, but all the life around us. Christianity, Islam, Buddhism and other religions have aspects of these ancient understandings. The goal of this book is not to impose a particular religion. The goal of this book is to distill essential attitudes and practices that anybody can embrace to live in a good way with other people and the Earth.

Solidarity Together

Even after visiting the Ashaninka, I didn't realize how beautiful life could be until I understood how people who base their lives on living in reciprocity also stand in solidarity with each other.

Nancy Basket described how, when traditional Cherokee towns got larger than 600-700 people, they became too big because hunting and foraging became difficult. The town needed to split into two. After agreeing on the new town site, often about seven miles away, everyone would go build the new buildings and homes regardless whether they were planning to move or not. They even made sure all the gardens were planted.[21]

People would go back and forth between the new and old sites as they prepared the new town. They did not create winners and losers, where the winners stayed and the losers had to go off and fend for themselves. Instead, everyone took responsibility for their neighbors' wellbeing. Following the golden rule, each person treated the others the way they would want to be treated.

Okanagan Jeannette Armstrong grew up in British Columbia, Canada. She described the en'owkinwiwx collective decision-making process which explicitly includes several components: minority views, the land, human relationships, and creativity. She said that "the minority voice is the most important voice to consider… [it] expresses the things that are going wrong… if you ignore this minority voice it will create conflict in your community and this conflict is going to create a breakdown… This conflict will endanger… how we think of ourselves as a cooperative unit…, a unit that knows how to work together… and loves one another."[22]

Armstrong described how she was brought up as a *land speaker*, someone trained to speak on behalf of the land in their councils. They also have speakers for children, mothers, elders, water, and others. Armstrong described how she was "trained by my Elders to think about the land and to speak about the land." She does not represent people or consider herself an expert. Instead, "[I] must continuously be responsible to my community." Every time the community considers a decision, no matter how small, "my responsibility is to stand up and ask, How will it impact the land… our food… our water? How is it going to impact my children, my grandchildren, my great-grandchildren, what's the land going to look like in their time?"

When a community includes the perspectives of human relationships and the land in their decision-making, "community changes… the material things don't have a lot of meaning… material wealth and the securing of it or being fearful and being frightened about not having 'things' to sustain you, disappears… The realization that people and community are there to sustain you creates the most secure feeling in the world… When that happens, you're imbued with the hope that others surrounding you in your community can provide."

Healthy vs Unhealthy Nations: What is the Core Disease?

For years, I wondered what all these beautiful nations have in common. In traditional stories from all these healthy nations, just like I had seen with the Ashaninka, their children seem so capable and confident, both men and women have positions of real leadership, and they have leaders that people actually want to follow. It's normal for people to accept deep responsibility to treat each other and the Earth in a good way. Why do some nations have these qualities, and others seem really unhealthy?

And what do all these unhealthy nations have in common, with their racism, sexism, self-serving political leaders, pollution, and more?

Do nations become unhealthy when the population gets too large? Some academic literature states that humans can only maintain tight knit communities of up to 150 people, a limit called "Dunbar's number."[23] I commonly hear people claim that humans start behaving inappropriately towards each other in groups larger than 150, as accountability mechanisms supposedly start to break down then.

But that doesn't make sense. The Ashaninka number 2,000 and maintain a culture where everyone is treated respectfully. The Cherokee in 1674 CE numbered approximately 50,000 and likewise maintained that internal baseline of mutual respect amongst themselves.[24]

Do nations become unhealthy when they cover too much area? That doesn't make sense either. As of the early 1700s, the Haudenosaunee Confederacy covered over 38,000 square miles.[25] This is comparable in size to Switzerland, Bhutan, or Taiwan. If the Haudenosaunee were a US state, it would be the 38th largest, between Kentucky and Indiana. Before extended European contact, the Cherokee covered approximately 40,000 sq miles.[26] Clearly humans can maintain healthy nations that cover huge distances and include many thousands of people.

Did the trouble happen when people started farming? No, the Huron gained about 75% of the food they ate from crops they grew. They still shocked French missionaries who couldn't understand how people could get along without police, prisons, and authorities imposing law and order.[27,28] Even prior to contact with European colonizers, the Haudenosaunee relied more on farming than hunting for food.[29]

Sometimes people of these nations are called native, indigenous, tribal, indian, or first nations. I call them healthy human nations. And I have found one root difference between healthy and unhealthy human nations:

In healthy nations, everyone stands for a culture of mutual respect, and nobody rules over anybody else.

Healthy nations have strong leaders and no rulers, so nobody imposes law on anybody else. That means everyone agrees on their rules for appropriate behavior. And when someone behaves inappropriately, anyone may take initiative to ensure that the misbehaving person is held accountable. Such healthy nations may fight with each other, but within the nation, they maintain a baseline of mutual respect.

In unhealthy nations, one person or a few people rule over everyone else. Whether the rulers are kings, billionaires, imams, priests, prime ministers, or presidents, they impose laws that everyone else must follow or face severe punishment. The rulers choose how to enforce the law, and forbid everybody else from taking initiative to hold misbehaving people accountable.

Another way of putting it is this: in unhealthy nations, a small number of people trap a large number in exploitative relationships. Rulers use all manner of tricks, traps, and childhood training to convince everyone to accept the legitimacy of their rule. Other names for an unhealthy nation include "authoritarian nation," "unfree nation," "low-accountability nation" and "abusive nation."

Having rulers creates all the other problems that anybody can see. Racism, sexism, dishonest leadership, pollution, disconnection from nature, selfishness, widespread child abuse, forgetting, and poverty are all merely *common symptoms caused by the root cultural disease where some people rule over everyone else*.

No nation is perfect. Any nation can experience trouble. Any act of disrespect is a cultural wound, and disrespect can occur in any nation. However, healthy nations are able to address disrespect when it occurs so that it doesn't happen again, and the people can return to that respectful baseline as a normal way of life.

In unhealthy nations, when disrespect occurs, especially by authority figures, it is extremely difficult to address. Thus, it is common for disrespectful behavior to just keep happening. Unhealthy nations are not able to remediate problems and return to a baseline of mutual respect. Unhealthy nations are not able to heal their cultural wounds.

Living in reciprocity with each other and the Earth is who we are as humans. Living in deep gratitude and giving my sacred gifts, or living my life purpose, is who we are as humans. Different healthy nations may recognize different gods, have different creation mythologies, or different ceremonies, but I see these three core spiritual practices in every healthy nation that I have studied.

I believe these core spiritual practices (gratitude, gift-giving, and reciprocity) are universal. In healthy nations, people encourage each other to live out these practices every day. In unhealthy nations, authorities make this very difficult.

How do healthy nations create effective systems of conflict resolution and accountability? And how do authorities use the law to disrupt solidarity, discourage deep responsibility, and prevent people from holding each other accountable for inappropriate behavior?

To explore how humans can have real solidarity and accountability, and how these can be blocked, I invite you to *Chapter 3: Shared Agreements vs Imposed Laws*.

Part 2 - The Core Infection: Rulers Forbid Solidarity and Accountability

What makes nations with rulers so fundamentally unhealthy?

There are so many significant differences among unhealthy nations around the world, including social customs, architecture, clothing, food, political system, religion, and more.

And yet, every nation with a ruler or ruling class seems to have similar problems, including racism, sexism, corruption, pollution, and inequality.

Why?

Chapter 3: Shared Agreements vs Imposed Laws

In healthy nations, everyone agrees on how to live with each other. And when someone breaks a shared agreement or behaves disrespectfully, anyone may take initiative to ensure that person is held accountable.

In unhealthy nations, a few people impose laws on the rest. When someone breaks an agreement, only designated law enforcement is allowed (at their discretion) to hold them accountable. Anyone else who attempts to hold people accountable for inappropriate behavior is punished. And when someone behaves inappropriately and law enforcement refuses to hold them accountable, there is no legal recourse. Exceptions happen, but this is the norm.

In theory, the law might apply equally to everyone, but because the vast majority of people are forbidden from holding others accountable, including law enforcers, in practice the law is not applied equally.

Every unhealthy nation tries to justify this disturbance with some story.

- Kings often pretend that God made them king and thus it's appropriate for them to impose laws to control everyone else.

- Capitalist democracies, like the US, pretend that the majority of the people control their government through elections, therefore the laws must be what most people want.

- Communist countries, like the Soviet Union in the 20th century, often pretend that the people are collectively creating a workers' paradise.

This is all make-believe. The small groups of people who make the laws, and those who are hired to enforce them, commonly prioritize their own authority, social status, and keeping their jobs instead of maintaining a culture of mutual respect.

Abusive Laws and Unaccountable Law Enforcement are Divisive

In healthy nations, the purpose of shared agreements is to ensure everyone can get along, know what to expect of each other, and live in solidarity.

In unhealthy nations, rulers pretend that the law serves this function too, but actually they use law and law enforcement to disrupt solidarity and discourage people from taking deep responsibility for each others' wellbeing.

Here are a few examples.

Laws to Prevent Solidarity

The most fundamental act of solidarity is for people to come to each others' aid when anyone is threatened. However, in every unhealthy nation, only the police are allowed to enforce the law. Exceptions happen and authorities may enforce this law inconsistently for various reasons as this book will explore. In general, people are legally forbidden from coming to each others' aid if anyone is attacked or mistreated by authorities, and instead people are expected to report crimes to the police. When only police are allowed to protect people from threats or abuse, and the rest risk imprisonment for collectively standing up against illegal behavior by political, legal, corporate, or religious authorities, the law effectively outlaws solidarity.

Authorities may also explicitly outlaw solidarity. For example, Saudi Arabia outlaws labor unions.[1] The United States outlaws solidarity strikes, making it impossible for one union to legally strike in solidarity with another.[2] Others carefully manage people's solidarity, as when Nazi Germany only allowed government-approved labor unions.[3]

Rulers may impose curfews to isolate people in their homes after work hours during social unrest when people might otherwise meet with each other and achieve real change. Egypt did this during protests in 2011, making it difficult for activists to coordinate, recruit, and support each other.[4]

Honeypot Laws

Authorities also use many other techniques to discourage deep responsibility. For example, they may design and use laws as a honeypot, pretending to support whistleblowers but actually using the law to target them. For example, when Thomas Drake encountered illegal behavior in the United States National Security Agency, he dutifully reported his observations through officially-approved reporting channels. Authorities then arrested him, accused him of crimes with long prison sentences, ruined him financially and professionally, and scared his family deeply. Authorities themselves broke the law to persecute Drake.

When Edward Snowden chose to blow the whistle on illegal programs in 2013, he deliberately went public because he witnessed what happened when Drake mistakenly trusted the honeypot whistleblower law.[5]

This honeypot dynamic is acknowledged by the National Whistleblower Center, an organization that helps whistleblowers. They note that "Turning to the internal affairs or compliance department of your employer may seem like the logical first step to reporting violations, but such channels can be dangerous for whistleblowers… employers often promise to protect anonymity or confidentiality but fail to do so. Remember that internal reporting channels exist to benefit the agency, not the whistleblower."[6]

Of course, whistleblower laws are sometimes enforced for the whistleblower. In one case, an air force maintenance technician complained that managers were allowing airplane maintenance to lapse. The managers retaliated against him, and the whistleblower law ultimately protected him.[7] However, the general pattern is that if the highest-level authorities ordered the illegal behavior, whistleblower laws can become a trap.

Declaring "Habitual Criminals"

In another variation of using laws to divide and conquer, after the British took direct control of India in the mid 1800s, they legally identified certain tribes as "habitually criminal." All men of the Maghyar Doms, Kunjurs, Khangars and many other tribes were required to report to the police weekly. Thus all the people who were most likely to be warriors willing to stand against British imperialism were marked as habitual criminals from the beginning and carefully monitored.[8]

Vague Catch-All Laws

Authorities may use "catch-all" laws to silence critics. A "catch-all" law is purposefully designed to be vague and outlaw normal behavior so that anyone may plausibly be violating it at any time. China's law against "picking quarrels and provoking trouble" has been used against citizen activists like Zhang Zhan, who independently traveled to Wuhan in 2020 to publish video reports about the authorities' responses to covid. In an interview later, she said, "Maybe I have a rebellious soul… I'm just documenting the truth. Why can't I show the truth?"[9] She was sentenced to 4 years in prison for her efforts to share stories that authorities would not allow the news to publish.

Likewise, the United States has laws against "disorderly conduct" or "disturbing the peace," commonly recognized by lawyers as catch-all crimes.[10]

The Soviet Union enforced laws against "hooliganism."[11] These laws were commonly so vague that activist Harvey Silvergate said, "Even if you wanted to be a slave, you couldn't figure out how to be a slave, because you don't know what you should refrain from doing."[12] This intentional ambiguity further encourages passive obedience.

Optionality and Selective Law Enforcement

The most common dominance display in unhealthy nations occurs when authorities disobey their own laws and do whatever benefits themselves. When Russian Sergei Magnitsky accused Russian state officials of stealing $230 million through tax fraud, he was arrested and then died in prison. A Russian human rights council found that he had likely been beaten to death, but president Vladimir Putin claimed Magnitsky had died from heart failure and had not been tortured. The official investigative committee found no evidence of a crime in Magnitsky's death and closed the case.[13] Like other dominance displays, authorities' obvious disregard for the law can scare people away from taking a stand for what's right.

Private citizens may use the law abusively, and even this can help authorities by scaring people even further into obedience. Only about 15 percent of Nazi German police investigations began due to surveillance; the rest were due to private citizens alerting the police, and one estimate is that 40% of these tip-offs were personally motivated attempts to hurt the reported person. One man reported a prostitute after he received a venereal disease from her. One wife reported her husband so he would go to prison and she could more easily continue her sexual affair with a soldier. A very common way of snitching was to claim the person illegally listened to foreign radio programs or made anti-Nazi statements.[14]

Although police complained that many leads were false, the investigations had the desired effect of training people not to trust strangers or complain in public. In the city of Augsburg in 1933, 75% of cases began after a neighbor reported overhearing an anti-Nazi comment in a bar, while in 1939, only 10% of cases started this way.

Corporate bosses may abuse the law as well for their benefit. When a person is released from prison, they often face very strict parole requirements. Requirements often include getting and keeping a job, avoiding any illegal activity, staying in a particular region, and more. People on parole who violate these rules may wind up in prison again, making them very vulnerable to abuse by anyone who would falsely report a broken rule.

American labor organizer Bernard Callegari described how some corporate bosses abuse the parole system: "We've had stories of companies unhappy with a worker and literally contacting that person's parole officer to report that they're being insubordinate or showing up late, or some other lie, just to get the person in trouble. Those stories resonate throughout the job sites. Other parolees hear those stories, that's part of the coercion. The body shops use the parole system to discipline their workers."[15]

Authorities commonly embrace the unfair practice of "optionality," meaning that they have the option to enforce any given law or not as they choose. A police officer described this dynamic to law students:

> Are any of you guilty of anything? How many of you drove here today? Anybody go above 55 [miles per hour] on the interstate? [Students raise their hands] ... If you drive 55 on the interstate where it's 55, the only thing you're going to do is meet the person behind you because they're going to rear-end you and you're going to get run over.
>
> So, that's a fact, but everybody does something they can get in trouble for... when I was uniformed, I could follow a car, however long I needed to, and eventually, they're going to do something illegal. And I can pull them over.[16]

This illustrates how police themselves recognize that they can always find a plausible cover story – a harmless but illegal act – for detaining someone if they want to. They can enforce a law or not, as they wish, and they can detain someone with plausible justification or let them go, as they wish. This is optionality. In unhealthy nations where the vast majority of us are forbidden from holding others accountable for inappropriate behavior, this is the norm.

Beyond unfair laws and unfair law enforcement, these stories have something else in common. They show how those in power discourage people from taking responsibility for each others' wellbeing. We're discouraged from standing together for a culture of mutual respect.

What would a nation be like where, instead of authorities imposing law and law enforcement, people have shared agreements and everyone stands for that baseline of mutual respect?

The Nootka Stand in Solidarity

In *Daughters of Copper Woman*, a Nootka storyteller described a cultural technique the Nootka used to help people see their own foolish behavior: clowns.

These weren't clowns with big noses and bright costumes, and they didn't just act silly. Clowns were like magazine opinion writers who commented on all sorts of things. If a clown thought that the council was about to do something foolish, they might show up at council and imitate one of the leader's every moves so that "every little wart on that person would show, every hole in their idea would suddenly look real big."[17]

If a person were vain about their clothes, a clown might follow behind them wearing tattered rags and their hair would be like a bird's nest full of mud and sticks, all looking similar to the vain person. If a person had a bad temper, a clown might follow and have fits, hitting the sand with a rock or insulting birds and generally looking foolish. If a person became self-important, the clown might follow along babbling like a baby, "until you finally heard what an ass you were bein'." And if a clown started being mean or pushy, a second clown might follow along and let the first clown see how they were showing up.

The Nootka storyteller noted, "nobody would ever dare blow up at the clown!" Anyone who did would be shamed. Clowns did not make fun of people or act hurtfully. They helped people see what they looked like to others and how silly it was to put so much emphasis on unimportant things like clothes or jewelry, "instead of what counts, like bein' nice to people, and bein' lovin'…"

Christians arrived and started dividing up the land. They set up a church, and began trying to get the Nootka to attend, offering mirrors and other trinkets as enticements. At church, the preacher told them what to wear, how to live, and what to do. He insisted that men shouldn't wear kilts, and women should only have long dresses that covered them completely. He kept saying that everyone should live and dress like the white man.

One day, a clown from a nearby community arrived at the church. Like the white man, she wore a big black hat and a black jacket. She even wore old rundown shoes someone had thrown away. Unlike the white man, she wore nothing else. She moved to the front and waited for church to start.

The preacher got very upset, but everyone else looked at her respectfully. No one mocked her or looked away to avoid her nudity.

The preacher started ranting about nudity, naked women, sin, and respect for God. Then he came down from his pulpit and grabbed the clown to throw her out.

Acting violently towards a clown was absolutely not allowed, and the storyteller said, "The people just about ripped him apart." But the clown protected him from the crowd, went up to where the preacher had been, and addressed them in their own language: "She said we were all brothers and sisters… And she said different people had different ways of doin' things, and that didn't mean any one way was Right or any other way was Wrong, it just meant all ways were different."

The clown encouraged empathy, asking people to imagine how a stranger might feel, being away from home, surrounded by people who looked and acted differently. She added, "there was more than one kind of mirror. There was the white man's mirror that you got if you went to church, but there was the mirror in the eyes of the people you loved…" The clown walked out of the church, and all the people followed her, leaving the preacher alone. That church still exists and remains empty to this day.

This clown was very brave. I feel impressed that she invited her neighbors to have compassion for a stranger and see his perspective even after he'd acted rudely. I also feel amazed that the people quickly recognized who was in the right and acted in support of the mostly-naked woman instead of the self-righteous man. This story showed me that whole communities can act in solidarity and stand for a culture of mutual respect when conflict arises.

This story showed me what it's like when everyone in a nation upholds the rules for how people treat each other. The Nootka didn't have police; everybody took a stand to protect the clown when she was attacked. They had rules that worked for everyone, and everyone upheld them.

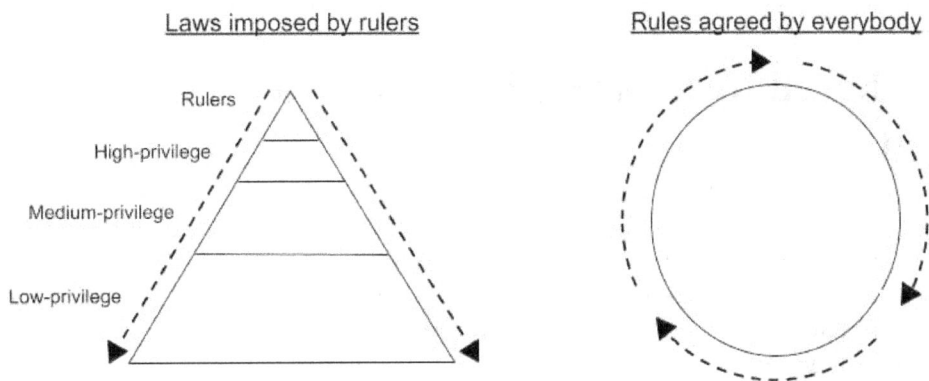

How does the nation set boundaries?

The Golden Rule of Healthy Nations

I used to wonder if it was possible to make rules or agreements that apply the same to everyone so that there are no favorites. I now believe the answer is clear: shared agreements can apply equally when everyone is willing to stand for that baseline of mutual respect.

The golden rule states "Treat others as I would want to be treated." I believe real solidarity comes from *the golden rule of healthy nations*: "stand with others as I would want them to stand with me."

When a Cherokee town grew too big, the Cherokee didn't have to worry so much whether they would leave or stay because everybody stood for the needs of the movers. The Okanagans don't need to worry about whether they were in the minority and try to form alliances, as everyone stands for each others' needs through the process of en'owkinwiwx. The clown stood for a peaceful culture where people could feel unashamed of their bodies, and when a preacher man behaved disrespectfully toward her, the Nootka stood with her.

This solidarity, stemming from the responsibility for reciprocity, is healthy and natural. It is who we are as humans. This solidarity and deep sense of responsibility for each other is exactly what authoritarian laws are designed to discourage and forbid, making it challenging to end the abuses of authoritarian nations.

And the problem goes beyond the laws themselves. When only authorities choose how to enforce the law or not, and when authorities forbid people's natural desire to hold others accountable for abusive behavior, it creates an environment in which passive obedience is rewarded and effective attempts at deep accountability are swiftly punished.

What does it look like when authorities block attempts to hold them accountable? And how do healthy nations succeed at holding everyone accountable so they can maintain a baseline of mutual respect? To explore, join me in *Chapter 4: Shared Accountability vs Abusive Law Enforcement*.

Chapter 4: Shared Accountability vs Abusive Law Enforcement

During my time with the Ashaninka, it was obvious to me that they had clear standards of behavior, respect for each other, and respect for their shared space. Nobody had to tell me this; I could clearly see that everyone acted respectfully. I asked a few questions, like where to poop and not to poop. But besides such practical matters, there wasn't much to discuss. Their expectations for each other just made sense and applied the same to everybody. It was easy to get along.

I believe this is a core, defining pattern among healthy nations: everyone agrees on their shared standards of behavior. And to ensure their shared standards of behavior apply equally to everyone, anyone in the community can seek accountability if someone violates a standard.

Shared standards of behavior and shared responsibility for holding each other accountable eliminates the need for imposed laws and designated law-enforcers. Everyone agrees on standards of behavior and everyone has the responsibility to hold anyone else accountable if those standards of behavior are violated. Different healthy nations have different procedures for responding to misbehavior, but it would be unthinkable to ignore the trouble if these procedures weren't being followed or if they weren't working.

The shared standards that allow mutually respectful relationships don't just apply to people, but to nonhumans too. The third core spiritual practice is living in reciprocity, and thus standards of behavior include how people treat nonhumans too. Shared standards of behavior are grounded in spiritual practice and a larger natural truth. I believe this is why Mohawk man Mike McDonald said, "That's where our laws have always come from. That is where our ceremonies have come from. They've always come from those people who learn to listen, who learn to see, who learn to be close to the natural world."[1]

Healthy nations may have widely varying standards of behavior. For example, nations with little access to water take care not to waste a single drop, while others have so much water that they seem less concerned with using it efficiently. But at a fundamental level, everyone collectively agrees on how they are going to live with each other and the land in ways that work for everyone, humans and nonhumans.

Stories of Healthy Nations Addressing Unwanted Behavior

If healthy nations do not have police or prisons or judges, how do they address trouble when someone behaves inappropriately?

I have observed all kinds of responses to hurtful or disrespectful behavior, from gentle to extremely firm. In general, I believe each group does what they believe would help them return to and maintain a core baseline of mutual respect within the group.

Priscilla Settee, a woman of the Cree people, described their reconciliation process where elders would consider how to bring a person "back into a balanced life" and help them "focus on what is important in life." Instead of believing that a troubled person is bad and deserves punishment, this more loving approach recognizes that the troubled person is basically good but off-balanced or missing something important. The goal is to help them recover their balance.[2]

Megan Biesele and Ju/'hoan San man Kxao =Oma (these punctuation symbols refer to sounds that don't exist in English) described the Ju/'hoan San healing dances where "they try to put these two people next to each other so that they can come into harmony by dancing together… What people have told me about what's going on in these beautiful dances is that it's a technology of opening the heart so that healing energy can enter and so that people's hearts will be revealed to each other and any problems or enmity will go out from between them."[3]

While the response is grounded in love and respect for the individual, maintaining the baseline of mutual respect within the group is paramount.

Depending on the nature of the misbehavior, temporary or permanent banishment has been used in a number of communities for certain troubles. Potawatomi woman Robin Kimmerer explained how anyone who took too much, to the detriment of the community, was "first counseled, then ostracized, and if the greed continued, they were eventually banished… It is a terrible punishment to be banished from the web of reciprocity, with no one to share with you and no one for you to care for."[4]

The traditional Cherokee also used banishment if someone behaved very inappropriately. First the troubled person would receive counseling from clan and spiritual elders and the gigau, meaning beloved woman. If this did not address the trouble, they would be shunned outside their home, then ostracized in their town, and if needed, eventually banished for a year from the whole community. If they were willing to make amends after this time, they would be welcomed back, and no one would speak of their past troubles again.[5]

People of healthy nations may also choose to kill individuals who refuse to get along, hoard wealth, or show severe disrespect. For example, the Huron would threaten to kill people who continually insisted on hoarding great wealth rather than sharing, especially while neighbors were suffering.[6]

Nancy Basket noted that traditional Cherokee would kill a Cherokee person for two offenses: killing in anger and incest. The Cherokee did not have prisons or jails. She said, "if you tried to run away, you would be found by the warriors and thrown off a cliff. That was the coward's way to die. The brave thing to do was own up to what you've done. And you would be killed in a ball game. You'd be allowed to play one more time. There were seven men chosen, one from each of the clans. Stickball is pretty harsh. One of those seven men would strike you hard with no one knowing who delivered the final blow and you'd die during that game, but at least that was honorable."[7]

Basket described what would happen if a man accidentally killed someone: "If you accidentally killed somebody, you'd be expected to become as the person you killed, providing for that family for the rest of your life."

Violence can be productive or unproductive. Productive violence in service of the group helps maintain that baseline of mutual respect, whereas unproductive violence leads to endless cycles of disrespect, retribution, and divisiveness.

It takes a deep wisdom and collective effort to decide when and how violence may be used productively. If people act violently out of ignorance or selfishness, it does not help. When the American general Harney convinced Ogallala chief Bear Bull to force his clan to submit to American dictates, the clan refused. In a drunken rage, Bear Bull angrily fired at his own people and killed Red Cloud's father and brother. Red Cloud calmly faced Bear Bull and his son who tried to defend him and he killed them both. Ohiyesa noted that "He did what he believed to be his duty, and the whole band sustained him. Indeed, the tragedy gave the young man at once a certain standing, as one who not only defended his people against enemies from without, but against injustice and aggression within the tribe. From this time on he was a recognized leader."[8]

Red Cloud did not kill the abusive, corrupt chief to take power for himself. He killed the corrupt chief to reestablish the baseline of mutual respect, and his neighbors recognized this. This is how a nation can have strong leaders and no rulers. Red Cloud became a leader because people recognized him as someone who stood against injustice to his people wherever it came from.

I was surprised at first to learn that exile or death could be the response to someone who insisted on selfishly hoarding wealth even after many requests to share. How bad could wealth-hoarding really be? Then I saw the wisdom: they saw how dangerous it becomes when some people hoard their wealth while their neighbors suffer. Eventually, everyone might feel the need to hoard whatever they can just to survive! Unhealthy, abusive nations would naturally result, and we see the consequences all around us in the United States, China, Russia, India, and elsewhere.

Based on my time with the Ashaninka and all my interviews and reading, I believe that these severe responses like killing or banishment were and are rare. After all, who wouldn't want to live in a nation that maintains a baseline of respect for everyone, where sharing is the norm?

In fact, many visitors to healthy nations have noticed that they do not have prisons and police, yet they seem unconcerned with crime. I noticed this when I stayed with the Ashaninka. French Christian missionaries visited the Huron in North America in the 1600s, and were shocked that thousands of people could get along so well without police and prisons.[9] Weston Price, an American dentist, visited many healthy nations around the world in the 1930s and wrote, "few impressions can be more vivid than that of the absence of prisons and asylums."[10] Benjamin Franklin observed healthy nations of eastern North America in the 1700s and noticed the same thing: "All their government is by Counsel of the Sages. There is no Force; there are no Prisons, no officers to compel Obedience, or inflict Punishment."[11]

All these observations showed me that healthy nations really are able to maintain that baseline of mutual respect as a normal way of life. Troubles may arise, but they're able to address them to so that respectful relations are the norm inside the nation.

There is no single "right" way for people to maintain that baseline of mutual respect. Every healthy nation has found their own way. Any group wanting to generate a healthy subculture must ask, "how are we going to maintain a baseline of mutual respect among ourselves?" Once that is established, they must follow *the golden rule of healthy nations: Stand with others the way I would want them to stand with me*. I believe that when everyone in a group lives in solidarity with each other and the Earth, a healthy nation or subculture is the result.

Legal Abuses When Solidarity is Lost

All humans want strong norms of appropriate behavior and systems of accountability and conflict resolution. In healthy nations, people all agree on those rules, and anyone can hold anyone else accountable when they act hurtfully or selfishly.

On the other hand, in unhealthy, authoritarian nations, rulers pretend that laws created by a few people and enforced by special law enforcers can maintain a baseline of mutual respect.

History has proven they cannot.

When a king rules over a kingdom, the law is whatever the king and his enforcers say it is, and they enforce it as they wish. Whether the head person calls themselves a president, premier, king, prime minister, or anything else, it works the same. It also works the same when the visible political leader is a figurehead fronting for a small number of oligarchs who own most of the nation's assets and income. This is why the Saudi Arabian monarchy, capitalist democracy United States, and socialist Peoples Republic of China all have similar troubles where authorities use the law and law enforcement in manipulative ways.

Manipulative Law Enforcement

When there is no law prohibiting some inappropriate behavior, such as polluting the local rivers and soil, it's simple for people to agree that something is wrong and should be changed. It is much harder, however, to galvanize people to seek change if a law exists but is only rarely enforced. When there is no law, a social movement can have a clear goal: getting a new law passed. When the law already exists, but unaccountable law enforcement routinely fails to uphold it, what are people supposed to do?

Two vivid examples come from poorly-enforced environmental laws in China and the United States. In China, poorly enforced environmental laws have led to over 450 "Cancer Villages," towns situated next to factories that have much higher than average cancer rates and cancer deaths.[12]

In the town Yanglingang, villagers could safely drink water and fish straight from the local river until the early 2000s when a paper mill and power plant began polluting both their water and air. Dust from the power plant smokestacks landed on their crops, making them unsellable. Xie Zhengqiang said, "Everybody here has some form of illness." Government officials refused to hear their lawsuits and resorted instead to intimidation. The Chinese federal environmental ministry once acknowledged a pollution-linked cancer problem but later retracted its statement, saying it was a mistake. The ministry was even reprimanded for it. The local courthouse wouldn't accept residents' cases, and the local environmental bureau denied that their cancer rates were a problem.

The US equivalent is called Cancer Alley, the length of the Mississippi River between Baton Rouge and New Orleans with a high number of petrochemical plants and also much higher-than-normal cancer rates. Local residents estimate that in more than one in 10 households, someone has died of cancer.[13]

One study found that one in three pregnancies resulted in a miscarriage. Residents no longer sit outside at night like they used to due to nighttime chemical releases that sometimes are so thick they appear as a golden mist. One resident said, "It'd look like raindrops but yellow. We'd have to hose our yards clean." Roadside ditches fill with blue fluid, birds die on people's lawns, and air can smell of nail-polish remover and rotten eggs.

Residents of one unincorporated area were able to stop new factory production by incorporating into a town called St. Gabriel and then consistently voting not to permit new construction. Company owners responded by fighting other town incorporation attempts, eventually obtaining a court injunction making it illegal for residents to take further steps to incorporate their towns. Thus company owners outlawed the one legal strategy that had successfully stopped the pollution in the area, and construction continued just outside St. Gabriel city limits.

Mirroring the Chinese example, the United States Environmental Protection Agency (EPA) began to investigate after several advocacy groups filed a complaint together. In a preliminary statement in October 2022, the EPA found "significant evidence" that the state's actions or inactions had had negative effects, especially on black residents. In June 2023, the EPA suddenly closed the investigation before completing it.[14] I wonder if this US environmental agency was reprimanded like the Chinese ministry was.

So long as people remain stuck in unhealthy, authoritarian nations, unfair law enforcement persists in many different forms. It takes tremendous amounts of time and money for workers to organize and get politicians to finally pass a law that addresses their needs. The US Supreme Court in 1938 showed how easily court officials could nullify all that work in the case NLRB vs Mackay Radio & Telegraph Co. The law at the time prevented employers from "discharging" workers on strike, but the Court decided it was legal for employers to "replace" them permanently. This decision, where the Supreme Court played word games to ignore the clear meaning of the law, remains in place as I write in 2024.[15]

In other cases, courts demand precise obedience to the law, deliberately ignoring any possibility that illegal behavior was appropriate. By the early 1320s, France had passed laws requiring physicians to obtain licenses and study at universities to practice medicine. Since women were forbidden from studying at universities, they could not legally practice medicine. In 1322, Jacoba Felicie was put on trial by the Faculty of Medicine at the University of Paris on charges of practicing medicine illegally. Accusations included that "she would cure her patient of internal illness and wounds or of external abscesses. She would visit the sick assiduously and continue to examine the urine in the manner of physicians, feel the pulse, and touch the body and limbs."

In other words, Felicie's crime was being a competent and caring healer without a license. Six witnesses testified that Felicie had cured them after licensed male doctors had given up. All this testimony ended up counting against her because it simply proved that she had broken the law by practicing without a license. Her medical competence, success rate, and care for her patients were all irrelevant. Felicie was banned from practicing medicine, heavily fined, and threatened with excommunication from the Catholic Church. Legal officials did not care whether she'd served her community; they only cared whether she'd broken the law.[16]

This pattern continues today, where judges commonly only consider whether a law was broken, not whether the person behaved inappropriately.

For example, Tim DeChristopher, an environmental activist in the United States, was put on trial for bidding inappropriately in an illegal government-run oil and gas lease auction in 2008. Activists outside the courtroom handed jurors pamphlets explaining the rights of juries, jury nullification, voting one's conscience, and other things. The prosecutor complained bitterly to the judge, saying, "This notion of voting your conscience, it's out in space!" The judge told the jury clearly they did not have that right, and had to follow his instructions. DeChristopher saw the results: "The discouraging thing was…you could see it kind of breaking the spirit of the jurors. You could see it in their minds when they made that switch of accepting the fact that they weren't allowed to use their own conscience, and they had to make a certain choice, even if they thought it was immoral, and that's a really dehumanizing thing."[17]

The judge then forbade DeChristopher's lawyers from acknowledging all the government's illegal activity in the auction or that the auction itself was illegal. They were forbidden from acknowledging that DeChristopher had offered the government the initial payment for the bid, and that the government had rejected the payment. The judge required the jury to focus only on some of DeChristopher's actions, and he was convicted and imprisoned for 2 years.

Sometimes even the judge acknowledges they're trying to avoid the most important questions. In a 1968 trial, Howard Zinn testified in defense of the Milwaukee 14, a group of nuns, priests, and others who had gone into an American military draft office, taken thousands of documents, and burned them to protest the Vietnam War. In his testimony, Zinn noted how the US Declaration of Independence says that when the government begins to destroy people's rights, "it is the Right of the People to alter or to abolish it."[18] He started giving a brief history of civil disobedience which the judge interrupted by pounding his gavel and saying, "You can't discuss that. This is getting to the heart of the matter!"

Nonetheless, the defendants' lawyer tried to stick to the heart of the matter, asking Zinn, "Can you explain to the jury, Dr. Zinn, what is the difference between law and justice?" After each such deep question, the prosecutor objected and the judge agreed. Eventually, Zinn loudly asked the judge, "Why can't I say something important? Why can't the jury hear something important?" The judge angrily responded, "You are not permitted to speak out like that. If you do that once more I will have you put in jail for contempt of court." Zinn said, "An IBM machine could make this decision if the question is only did they do this."

The judge refused to allow the jury to learn about the war in Vietnam or why the defendants had acted disobediently. The jury never learned that the Vietnam War itself was illegal, as US presidents sent the military to fight without the Constitutionally-required declaration of war from Congress. The jury convicted the defendants, and they went to prison for several years.[19]

Why would voting one's conscience in a jury trial be so terrible? Inevitably, the conversation would get to questioning the very legitimacy of the law which would then threaten the legitimacy of the rulers. Such questions might include:

- *Is it legitimate for some people to impose law on others regardless how they feel about it?* – If a juror accepts responsibility for voting their conscience – that is, doing what they believe to be right and appropriate even if the law disagrees – they're implicitly answering, "no, it's not legitimate for someone to impose law on me."

- *Are some laws legitimate and some illegitimate?* – If a juror got to choose which laws to follow, it would threaten authorities' legitimacy. Every authoritarian ideology boils down to "authorities impose laws for the good of all, and law enforcement keeps people in line so society can operate well." If a juror were allowed to think about whether a law was truly appropriate, and cast their vote based on that, it would threaten the ability of authorities to impose law on everyone else.

- *Is it ok to break the law, especially if it's done to hold authorities accountable for illegal or inappropriate behavior?* – Any discussion of civil disobedience would yield a conversation about the legitimacy of American rulers who had ordered an illegal war. Instead of allowing such deep conversations and allowing the jury to decide what was appropriate, the judge forbade such conversations and threatened Zinn with imprisonment for trying to acknowledge the defendants' motivation.

In a Selfish, Unhealthy Nation, Even if Laws Were Perfectly Fair and Perfectly Enforced, the Outcomes Would Still be Terrible

Shared agreements and strong accountability are crucial to creating and maintaining healthy nations and sorely lacking in unhealthy nations. However, without a willingness to share and take care of each other, even perfectly fair agreements could lead to unhealthy nations.

To illustrate this, let us consider what would happen if a nation had only 3 laws:

- Anyone may own property.

- No one may infringe on others' property ownership rights. Thus, no theft or property destruction is allowed.

- No one may kill, injure, or threaten anyone else.

This sounds perfectly reasonable, but imagine this scenario: what if 1% of the people owned 50% of the land, including all the good farmland, water access, hunting grounds, mines, forests, and more? Under these conditions, even perfectly fair laws that are perfectly fairly enforced would make the majority of people servants of the few who owned almost all of the valuable assets.

Thus it's not enough to ask, "Is this particular law fair?" or "is this law being enforced appropriately?" The fundamental question is: *are we collectively generating the kind of nation we want to live in?* If not, what's missing, and what can we do about it?

When the Potawatomi threatened to exile people who hoarded wealth, or the Huron threatened to kill them, I believe they were putting the *long-term health* of their nations over any abstract ideas about legal fairness.

Many people in unhealthy nations hold tightly to their property rights because they worry about selfish people taking their things, and because profit economies don't provide a safety net of support for everyone, as do gift economies (reviewed in Part 3). The legal regime around property rights exists to protect people from others who would selfishly take from them. But there is no need for property rights in nations that avoid selfishness at all costs, and instead offer the deeper protection of a way of life where everybody cares for everybody else. They have no need to worry if they can "enjoy the fruits of their labor" because no one would be allowed to selfishly take without permission what anyone else produced. Instead of selfishness, healthy nations encourage deep sharing, as shown in Chapter 9.

I believe these nations had norms where people could expect to use the tools and homes they made and the food they brought in, so people could enjoy the fruits of their labor if they chose, as long as they did not start hoarding more than they needed. They would not let an abstract ideal of fairness allow anyone to accumulate excessive wealth, something that would eventually lead to selfishness and greed taking hold in their nation.

There isn't any one thing that keeps unhealthy nations stable for so long. Abusive laws, manipulative law enforcement, and unequal wealth all combine with many other factors to sustain unhealthy nations and strongly discourage deep cultural healing. Unfortunately, the people who selfishly benefit the most do everything they can to keep things as they are.

What Defines a Nation? And How Could a Group of People Create and Maintain One?

In general, nations are created and maintained when people decide on three things:

1. *External boundaries*: The nation decides who is allowed inside and who is not, protecting against theft, attack, or exploitation by outsiders.

2. *Internal boundaries*: Shared rules and systems of accountability that ensure everyone is treated with respect by everyone else within the nation.

3. *How people live within the boundaries*: All the ways people choose to live within their agreed boundaries, including how to share, gather food, account for collective needs, account for the Earth's needs, honor individual autonomy, and more.

Most people in unhealthy nations do not have much experience with boundary-setting at the scale of a community or nation because authorities are the only ones allowed to set these boundaries. Authorities make and enforce the laws, which are the internal boundaries everyone else is supposed to live with. And authorities command the military, which establishes external boundaries to protect the nation from outsiders and protect the rulers from revolutionary movements.

Many subcultures form in unhealthy nations, and often the subcultures' external and internal boundaries are not chosen by the participants, but rather by authority figures.

For example, consider the subcultures of a child's soccer league team or a business.

A child's soccer league team has external boundaries that define who is and who is not on the team and internal boundaries called *rules* that define how people should treat each other. Usually, instead of the team members deciding for themselves who is allowed on the team and how to treat each other, the league organizers decide who is on the team and the coach often sets rules and adjudicates conflicts.

Likewise, each business is its own subculture with an external boundary that defines who is and who is not an employee and internal boundaries that define how people treat each other. Most employees do not decide who is allowed to be an employee or what the rules will be. Instead, the chief executive decides who is allowed to be part of the subculture – that is, who is allowed to be an employee – and how people are allowed to treat each other. Thus, these business and soccer team subcultures mirror the broader unhealthy nation, where authorities control the external and internal boundaries and systems of accountability.

Militaries

Militaries offer a vivid contrast, showing how differently boundaries are set in healthy nations compared to unhealthy nations. It all boils down to a simple question: do people set the boundaries for themselves, or do authorities set the boundaries for everyone else?

In unhealthy nation militaries, each soldier is assigned to a regiment with clear boundaries that define its members and rules about how they treat each other, but soldiers don't generally decide who else is in their unit or what their rules will be. Military authorities assign soldiers to regiments and decide on the regiment's rules.

Geronimo's description of his Bedonkohe Apache warrior council shows how differently the Apache warriors set boundaries compared to authoritarian militaries. Youth were not automatically admitted to the war council, but had to participate as servants on at least four expeditions. After this, the youth could only be welcomed as a warrior if every other warrior agreed to it. If any warrior doubted the young man's humility, courage, or knowledge, the youth was required to continue as a servant in future expeditions until he fully proved himself.[20]

While Apache leaders might give orders to other warriors, these leaders only led because other warriors valued their leadership. Whereas authoritarian militaries expect soldiers to obey their commanding officers no matter their competence or integrity, it worked very differently in Geronimo's nation. He said:

> When [the youth] has proven beyond question that he can bear hardships without complaint, and that he is a stranger to fear, he is admitted to the council of the warriors in the lowest rank. After this there is no formal test for promotions, but by common consent he assumes a station on the battlefield, and if that position is maintained with honor, he is allowed to keep it, and may be asked, or may volunteer, to take a higher station…

There was no risk of leaders appointing officers whom the soldiers didn't trust; in healthy nations, warriors decide whom they trust and choose their leaders "by common consent." Because the leaders were chosen by consent, the Apache warriors ensured that the leaders upheld boundaries that worked for everyone, not just the leaders.

Healthy Nations Create and Maintain Boundaries Based on Mutual Respect

In healthy nations and subcultures, everyone agrees on the internal boundaries (rules and systems of accountability), allowing the culture to have a baseline of mutual respect. What are the rules we're going to live by? And how do we hold each other accountable when someone breaks a rule? The healthy-nation systems of accountability explored in this chapter are simply ways of maintaining healthy internal boundaries so that everyone can enjoy respectful relationships with everyone else.

A healthy nation also has external boundaries that protect it from disrespect by outsiders. This is the role of warriors: when one group wants to attack another, and words won't stop the aggression, defending warriors use violence to establish a boundary, protecting their people from external threats.

Often boundaries are energetic, not physical. A physical boundary blocks a person, whereas an energetic boundary blocks certain attitudes or types of behavior. For example, an energetic boundary might block attitudes of selfishness or racism, or behaviors like lying, theft, or taking more than one's share.

Energetic boundaries can be as firm or flexible as people choose. For example, a nation might decide they don't like selfishness, but different acts of selfishness might lead to different responses. If one person sexually attacks another, the attacker may be banished immediately instead of being allowed to grow and get a second chance. On the other hand, someone who takes a little more food than they need might be counseled and offered a chance to grow without being forced out.

When a healthy nation upholds strong energetic boundaries, it evicts anyone who shows unwanted attitudes or behaviors and refuses to change. In other words, the attitude or behavior is the problem, not the person. Later chapters explore ways to set external boundaries with collective self-defense.

Geronimo hinted at an energetic boundary when he told his biographer that he felt free to either be kind to strangers or rob them, but once a person had been accepted as a guest – that is, once they had been welcomed inside the nation's energetic boundaries – they would be treated just as respectfully as everyone else within the nation.

No matter how much the nation's physical boundaries moved – say, because they traveled to a new region – within the nation's energetic boundaries, everyone was respected by everyone else.[21]

Likewise, when a Potawatomi or Cherokee person began acting selfishly, the group didn't instantly banish the person. I believe they commonly wanted the person to stay; they just wanted the selfishness to leave. The behavior or attitude was the problem, not the person, which is why they first received counseling and then light ostracizing. Only when the person insisted on acting selfishly did they finally remove the selfishness from within their nation by banishing the person.

This shows the power of holding energetic boundaries that allow a group to maintain an internal baseline of respect no matter what. Instead of judging a person as good or bad, judge a behavior or attitude as good or bad. This gives a wayward person a chance to grow and learn better behaviors. This way, only people who refuse to grow get banished.

Strong leaders uphold both these internal and external boundaries to ensure people can live in a respectful and peaceful way with each other. When Red Cloud killed Big Bear after he became aggressive toward his own people, Ohiyesa described how Red Cloud's people supported him because he "not only defended his people against enemies from without, but against injustice and aggression within the tribe." In other words, everyone took responsibility for deciding what was appropriate, and I believe the people respected Red Cloud because he upheld both the internal and external boundaries, ensuring his people were safe from disrespect no matter where it came from.

The third aspect of nations involves how people live within those boundaries. How do they share? How do the live in a way that takes everyone's needs and the Earth's needs into account? How do they support themselves and enjoy life?

Both healthy and unhealthy nations around the world show a huge diversity. There are countless ways of choosing leaders, raising children, gathering food, and everything else that humans do.

Of all the differences between healthy and unhealthy nations, I believe the most important is how they set boundaries. In healthy nations, everyone agrees on the rules and anyone can hold anyone else accountable for breaking the rules. In unhealthy nations, rulers impose laws and enforce them as they wish, ensuring that some people won't be treated fairly.

There are other major differences between healthy and unhealthy nations. For example, healthy nations emphasize reciprocity and sharing as a norm, whereas unhealthy nations emphasize profit. Healthy nations have an intimate, mutually enriching relationship with the land, whereas unhealthy nations exploit the land. These differences are explored throughout this book.

But I believe that the most important, fundamental difference is how healthy and unhealthy nations set boundaries. If people can successfully set their own boundaries, they can decide to have a culture of sharing and close connection with the Earth, as every healthy nation does. As long as rulers and other authorities set the boundaries, it is very difficult to fully take the Earth's needs into account as a normal part of life.

Energetic Boundaries = Agreements + Integrity

For a nation to have healthy energetic boundaries, they need to set clear agreements and each person needs to uphold them with integrity.

Let's imagine a scenario where a group of bullies is picking on smaller kids at school, teasing them, taking their money, and sometimes hitting them.

Suppose some of these smaller kids don't want to tolerate this abusive behavior anymore, and they talk together to decide what to do. They want to set energetic boundaries, where disrespectful behavior is not allowed towards anyone in their group. How could they do this?

First, they would *set agreements*. How does each child agree to respond when they see someone in their group being bullied? They have many options here – perhaps they could all walk over and stand with the kid being bullied and collectively tell the older kids to back off. Perhaps one of them could document the bullying on video so that adults could intervene. Whatever the kids decide, they must somehow agree to support each other so that collectively they don't allow any disrespect towards anyone in the group.

The second requirement is that the kids have *integrity*. They have to keep their agreements. Without agreements, the kids won't know how they can rely on each other for support. And if they don't have integrity, and they shy away from the bullies out of fear, then the agreements are worthless. Thus the kids must hold each other to a high standard of integrity to collectively protect themselves from bullying.

Starting a Healthy Nation

What would it take for a group of people to create their own nation? I believe any healthy nation or subculture must agree on three things:

1. *External boundaries*: Agreements about how we are going to protect ourselves from disrespect by outsiders.

2. *Internal boundaries*: Agreements about what rules and systems of accountability we want to have to ensure that, within our group, everyone treats everyone else respectfully.

3. *How people live within the boundaries*: Agreements about how we want to live together and take care of each other, accounting for collective needs, the land's needs, and individual autonomy.

Any group of people, whether a family, village, or a nation, can make their own agreements for themselves to create the kind of culture they want to have. So long as they hold each other to a high standard of integrity, they will hold healthy boundaries and be able to relax into a deep trust of each other.

Disrespect can happen in any culture at any time. Healthy nations commonly address disrespect in a way that feels deeply satisfying to everybody, whereas unhealthy nations do not. This is a fundamental difference between healthy and unhealthy nations. Healthy nations respect everyone's boundaries and encourage healthy boundary-setting, whereas unhealthy nations do not. After all, in order for rulers to exploit the rest, they have to violate people's boundaries.

This shows that the path to generating healthy nations will involve learning how to create and hold healthy boundaries. Fortunately, boundary-setting is a skill that anyone and any group can practice and improve at over time.

What would it be like to have a satisfying resolution after, for example, an accidental homicide? And what would it be like to never have resolution, and for negligent homicides to just keep happening endlessly? Find out in *Chapter 5: Encouraging Healing vs Discouraging Healing*.

Chapter 5: Encouraging Healing vs Discouraging Healing

A human nation is a living organism. Just like a tree or lion or ant colony, human nations can become injured. Any disrespect between two people is a type of cultural injury and not just a personal concern. Nancy Basket, a woman of Cherokee descent, says, "If there is trouble in a family, the whole nation suffers."[1] Martin Luther King Jr echoed this when he wrote, "Injustice anywhere is a threat to justice everywhere."[2]

Like all living organisms, human nations that are injured try to heal themselves. Healthy human nations heal their wounds of disrespectful behavior by deeply addressing the trouble and bringing back a baseline of mutual respect. This is the essence of cultural healing.

Unhealthy nations are essentially unable to heal. Returning to that baseline of mutual respect that humans find so fundamentally satisfying would radically threaten the status quo. Rulers and other authorities in positions of power would lose their ability to dominate and exploit everyone else. Thus unhealthy cultural patterns of deep disrespect continue.

Both healthy and unhealthy nations can suffer wounds of disrespect, even including some people unintentionally killing each other. The following stories show how healthy and unhealthy nations respond to these unintended killings very differently. Only healthy nations are able to return to that baseline of mutual respect.

How a Healthy Nation Heals After an Accidental Homicide

In his book *The World Until Yesterday: What can we learn from traditional societies?* Jared Diamond shares a story of accidental homicide and collective accountability he learned from a Papua New Guinea man named Gideon.[3]

Day 1: A young schoolboy named Billy was returning from school in an unmarked mini-bus. Billy exited the bus, went behind it, and then dashed across the road to meet his waiting Uncle Genjimp. Because he darted out from behind the bus, he was invisible to oncoming traffic until he was in the middle of the road. Malo was driving home with a few coworkers and hit the brakes but too late, and Billy died soon after. Malo and Billy were different ethnicities, with Malo being a local and Billy coming from a lowlander group which had migrated from far away.

How could the New Guineans find peace and justice without relying on government court systems? Indeed, how could they have a more satisfying response than government courts would provide?

Day 2: Billy's father and two friends came to Gideon, the office manager at the company which had hired Malo as a driver. At first, Gideon was worried about retaliation. However, Billy's father said, "We understand that this was an accident, and that you didn't do it intentionally. We don't want to make any problems. We just want your help with the funeral. We ask of you a little money and food, in order to feed our relatives at the ceremony."

Gideon offered an apology and vague commitment. After the father left, Gideon went to the store to buy sugar, tinned meat, rice and coffee.

Day 3: Gideon hosted a staff meeting which included a man named Yaghean who had experience with "compensation" negotiations. Another translation for compensation is "sorry money."

Gideon wanted to go directly to the family to formally apologize and defuse any threat of retaliation from Billy's extended family. Yaghean warned against this: "If you yourself, Gideon, go there too soon, I'm concerned that the extended family and the whole lowlander community may still have hot tempers. We should instead go through the proper compensation process. We'll send an emissary, and that will be me. I'll talk to the councilor for the ward that includes the lowlander settlement, and he in turn will talk to the lowlander community. Both he and I know how the compensation process should proceed. Only after the process has been completed can you and your staff have a say-sorry ceremony with the family."

Day 4: Yaghean had a meeting with a counselor and Billy's immediate family and extended clan. He learned that the family does not want violence, though some men felt strongly and were still stirred up. Afterwards, Yaghean told Gideon to purchase more food and bring the equivalent of $300.

Day 5: Gideon, Yaghean, and all the office staff except Malo traveled by car to Billy's village for a compensation ceremony. Billy's uncle opened with words of gratitude to visitors for coming, and he said how sad the child's death was. Then Gideon and the rest of the office staff spoke.

Later, Gideon said how it felt: "It felt awful, just awful, to have to give that talk. I was crying. At that time, I, too, had young children. I told the family that I was trying to imagine their level of grief. I said that I was trying to grasp it by supposing the accident to have happened instead to my own son. Their grief must have been unimaginable. I told them that the food and the money that I was giving them were nothing, mere rubbish, compared to the life of their child."

Gideon described the next speaker: "Next came the talk of Billy's father, Peti. His words were very simple. He was in tears. He acknowledged that Billy's death was an accident, and not due to negligence on our part. He thanked us for being there, and said that his people wouldn't make any problems for us. Then he talked about Billy, held up a photograph of his son, and said, 'We miss him.' Billy's mother sat quietly behind the father as he spoke. A few others of Billy's uncles stood up and reiterated, 'You people won't have any problems with us, we are satisfied with your response and with the compensation.' Everybody–my colleagues and I, and Billy's whole family–was crying."

Gideon and the staff handed over food to "say sorry" with the words, "This food is to help you in this hard time." After speaking, they shared a simple meal and shook hands all around. When asked if there was any hugging, Gideon said, "No, the ceremony was structured, and it was very formal."

Jared Diamond asked Gideon, what if Malo had been driving alone and there had been no company involvement?

Giden said negotiations would have been handled by Malo's uncles and village elders. Compensation would be paid by Malo's whole village, including his family, fellow clanspeople, and villages of other clans. Malo would have to ask them all for help to raise funds. He would then owe them all something in return later on, including to his uncles for their help negotiating. Otherwise, the compensation process would have proceeded similarly.

It's hard for me to imagine a more satisfying resolution. It was impossible to bring Billy back, but Billy's family heard accountability from the entire corporate community in which Malo worked. They also received gifts and shared grief with Malo's people. They had a clear acknowledgement of what happened. I believe the shared grief and crying made it clear to each person that everyone recognized the incident as a tragedy and something to be strongly avoided in the future.

What would it be like to live in an unhealthy nation where one person can accidentally kill another, or even many people, and there is no deep resolution and all signs indicate that the negligent killings will continue?

How Unhealthy Nations Commonly Respond to Negligent Homicide by Corporate Authorities

Personal Level: A Miner Dies Due to Negligence by the Mining Company

Until August 2023, Christopher Finley was an employee at Mine Number 39 owned by Twin State Mining Inc in West Virginia. He was a section foreman with 15 years' experience. On August 18, 2023 he was tasked with installing a dewatering pump discharge line when he was found lying in 8-10 inches of water and mud on the mine floor. After some investigation, the US federal Mine Safety and Health Administration (MSHA) noticed numerous safety issues. Investigators noted that Finley was working with an electrical pump which had multiple serious safety violations. They found that the equipment's GFCI safety mechanism did not work, so if the wiring came into contact with water and short circuited, the worker would not be protected. Furthermore, the pump was energized at the time of death, the pump wiring contained a number of faulty splices, some splices were in contact with water, and the standing water was dirty with contaminants that increased its electrical connectivity.

Furthermore, the mine operator was not complying with the approved water ventilation plan which requires the company to prevent the accumulation of water. The report noted, "Investigators measured water and mud up to 22 inches in depth within the accident area. The mud was extremely thick and created difficulty while walking through it."

Neither investigators nor medical officials could definitively say an electric shock caused Finley's death, but medical officials clearly stated Finley drowned. Finley had been seen in good health 2 minutes before being found face down in the water. In other words, it seems very likely to me that Finley died because the mining company, Twin State Mining, gave him faulty electrical equipment to install in an area that was very wet because the company had not followed the agreed-upon ventilation plan.[4]

Let's zoom out. Was this an isolated tragic incident of accidental death? Or is it part of a broader pattern where the mining company consistently cuts corners with safety to maximize profit?

A Pattern at the Corporate Level: Twin State Mining's Serial Negligence

The MSHA defines a "Significant and Substantial" (S&S) mine safety violation as "one that is reasonably likely to result in a serious injury or illness."[5]

The MSHA released a report indicating Twin State Mining's safety record at Mine 39 met criteria for a "Pattern of Violations." During the 12-month period from November 1, 2022 – October 31, 2023, regulators cited Mine 39 operators for 87 S&S violations. The report noted how this was unsafe even by mining standards: "The S&S rate per 100 inspection hours was 9.11; the national average rate for underground coal mines was 2.90."[6]

In other words, Twin State Mining corporate leaders were very well aware of rampant unsafe working conditions and had been warned with dozens of violation citations by regulators.

The federal MSHA considers a "pattern of violations" citation one of its strongest enforcement actions with this consequence: "If a mine receives notice of a POV and subsequently commits additional S&S violations, MSHA is authorized to withdraw miners from the affected area except those necessary to correct the violation."

So, did the government make even this meager order to pressure the mine owners to correct the safety hazards?

The MSHA report noted:

> Although the mine met the initial screening criteria, under the POV process, the mine was reviewed for mitigating circumstances, which can result in postponing or not issuing of a POV notice. MSHA determined that postponement was warranted, pending the agency's continued evaluation of Mine No. 39's operations and issued a postponement notice to Twin State Mining Inc.

In other words, even after Finley died likely due to multiple safety violations by the mining company, and the mining company had been found to have dozens of significant safety violations in a single-year time span at this mine alone, and even though the government acknowledged it fit the criteria for their toughest-but-still-not-very-tough citation, regulators decided to indefinitely postpone the citation without giving any reason.

Nowhere in any MSHA reports do they acknowledge a culture of cost-cutting that sacrifices safety for corporate profits, nor do they acknowledge the executives' role in creating such a culture. Clearly the government did not hold the Twin State Mining company executives or owners accountable for their behavior.

Let's zoom out again and ask: is this just a corrupt relationship between the US government and Twin State Mining, or is it part of a broader pattern of low accountability within the United States mining industry?

The Same Pattern at the National Level: Federal Regulators Consistently Fail to Hold Mine Owners Accountable

A joint investigation by Mine Safety and Health News and National Public Radio investigated 20 years of mining company safety violation records up to 2014. They found a large number of companies simply had chosen not to pay the fines while continuing to operate. Their findings included:

- $70 million in unpaid penalties was still owed by 2,700 mining company owners.

- The top nine delinquent mine owners had more than $1 million in unpaid fines.

- Delinquent mine companies had injury rates 50 percent greater than mine companies that pay their fines on time.

- Delinquent mines reported almost 4,000 injuries during the years they failed to pay up, including accidents resulting in 58 permanent disabilities and 25 deaths. These do not include the many injuries and deaths at mines where owners paid on time.

- Delinquent mines continued to operate illegally without paying fines for 130,000 violations.

While the investigation found that most coal mining companies paid their fines, they noted that there were unpaid fines related to 40,000 S&S safety violations likely to lead to serious injury or illness. 15,000 violations "were the kind found in fatal accidents, major disasters or mining deaths."[7]

Another tactic to avoid paying fines is to contest them. In February 2010, a US House Committee met to investigate the backlog of contested fines and found that between 2008-2009, the MSHA cited mining corporations for over 372,000 mining safety violations with over $335 million in fees. However, about 82,000 violations and $210 million in fines remained unpaid due to being contested by the companies.[8]

Note the worst case scenarios for mine owners who get cited: slightly reduced corporate profit due to government fines or lost mining time due to a "pattern of violations" citation, but only if they are then later found to have subsequent S&S violations. There is no personal risk to the mine owners' or executives' comfort or wealth. Clearly these threats were not enough to prevent what assistant secretary for mine safety and health Chris Williamson called a "troubling increase in fatalities" in 2023.[9]

It seems the trouble is systemic. That is, lack of serious accountability is a normal, default mode of operation for the mine company owners and executives and government regulators in the United States, allowing the mine owners to take advantage of workers by skimping on safety to maximize profit.

Let's zoom out one more time. Is this pattern of consistent low-accountability for mining company owners unique to the United States? Or does it exist in other unhealthy nations around the world?

The Same Pattern Across Unhealthy Nations: Chinese and Russians Also Do Not Hold Authorities Accountable for Selfish Behavior

Coal Mine Deaths in China

On February 22, 2023 a coal mine in Alxa Left Banner of Inner Mongolia, a province of northern China, collapsed resulting in 9 deaths, 6 injuries, and 44 people still missing almost 6 weeks later. The company which operated the mine, Xinjing Coal Mining Co, had received over 20 safety warnings and penalties.

The mine chief executive, Chen Fenggan, claimed he faced no liability. He refused to pay out any compensation to the families of the deceased because the miners were all subcontractors, not employees hired directly from the mine. The subcontracting company denied responsibility as well. According to China's Labor Law, subcontractors should not represent more than 10% of workers, but at this mine, every worker was a subcontractor. The workers had been earning as little as $291/month and had no insurance of any kind through their employer.[10]

As of early April 2023, no government actions have been taken against Chen Fenggan.

Was this an isolated incident? Or part of a broader pattern?

Government records show in the previous year, China had 168 mining incidents resulting in an injury, about one every 2 days.

Examples from government records include:

On January 17, 2022, a worker died in Ordos, Inner Mongolia after a mechanical accident due to negligence in maintaining equipment.

On March 12, 2022, a worker was crushed to death after a mining vehicle failed. The mining company operating in Hunan Province had illegally entered and operated in a closed well.

On April 10, 2022, three workers died from suffocation in a Shanxi Province mine.

Coal Mine Deaths in Russia

In 2021, 51 coal miners and rescuers died due to a methane explosion at the Listvyazhnaya mine in Russia. Investigators found that government safety inspectors had issued a safety certificate without actually inspecting the facility like they were supposed to.[11]

Inna Piyalkina, whose husband died in the 2021 explosion, noted that this was not an isolated incident, but part of a pattern: "There was an explosion at this mine 18 years ago and 13 people died. The whole village went mad. Just imagine how they're going to bury 46 (miners)." Before the explosion, her husband repeatedly said methane levels were too high, sensors were constantly beeping, and "it wouldn't end well." He was right.

Clearly, Russians have not been able to hold mine owners accountable in a way that actually allows miners to work safely. In other words, they have not been able to keep the mine owners from cutting corners on safety to increase profit.

I could not find any sign in any of these cases from Russia, China, or the United States that the company owners were held personally liable for the deaths their selfishness caused.

Russians, Chinese, and Americans all seem to have similar troubles. When these negligent deaths occur, they are unable to resolve the trouble and get to a baseline where executives treat workers with respect.

This is a common problem in nations where a few people impose law on the rest, and the vast majority of individuals are forbidden from holding others accountable for inappropriate behavior.

What if We Embraced the Responsibilities of Living in a Healthy Nation?

In the story from the Nootka in Chapter 3, when the priest threatened the clown, the entire community instantly responded to protect the clown. They stood in solidarity with each other from the start, not allowing anyone to threaten anyone else.

Many Americans think of their country as the "land of the free, home of the brave." But if America is so free and the people are so brave, why do we continue to tolerate this abusive behavior by corporate owners and government "regulators?"

What would it be like if, every time there was a negligent mining death, the entire country stood in solidarity with the mining family, demanding that corporate and government authorities either fully end negligent deaths or lose their jobs?

What if the whole country demanded that mining company owners either embrace safe practices or they lose ownership of their company? If coal company owners could lose their ownership due to negligence, America would ensure that only respectful company owners operated coal mines.

This solidarity wouldn't just be helpful with coal mines.

When whistleblowers release evidence of government corruption, what if Americans stood in solidarity, making sure it was the corrupt officials who lost their job rather than the whistleblowers?

When governments make vague catch-all laws and then enforce them selectively, what if Americans said this was inappropriate, and insisted on having clear laws that were universally enforced?

Like so many other healthy nations, the Nootka show that humans can have this kind of solidarity, and they show how beautifully people can live when they do.

Many people notice a few inappropriate parts of their unhealthy nation. Yet, over time, most people living in unhealthy nations seem to hardly notice the degree to which they are being so deeply manipulated. Next, *Chapter 6: Blind Belief 1 - When People Ignore Reality to Maintain Safety and Comfort* seeks to answer the question: how can people learn to ignore such obvious truths?

Chapter 6: Blind Belief 1 - When People Ignore Reality to Maintain Safety and Comfort

Remember that old story "The Emperor's New Clothes"?

A con man tricks an emperor into believing that he is dressed in beautiful, expensive clothing when, in fact, he is wearing nothing at all. Afraid to be called a fool by this very confident man, the emperor pretends that he really is wearing beautiful clothing, and his close officials go along with it. The emperor then goes out among the public stark naked, and the masses of people pretend to admire his fine clothing. Everybody maintains this pretense until a child blurts out that the emperor is stark naked.

The emperor's "new clothes." Why don't the adults feel comfortable acknowledging the obvious truth?

It is no accident in this story that a child speaks the truth. Children may play games of make-believe, but they know they are pretending. They know it's not real. I believe all humans have a sacred urge to align with the truth. Somehow, the adults in this fairy tale had learned to pretend as a way of life, but the young child had not. It took a child to break the spell and speak the truth.

When I was a child, I found this story confusing. Why would anyone purposely ignore an obvious truth?

Eventually, I understood better.

Part of our inherent divine nature as humans is not to tolerate abuse of ourselves or others, and yet every authoritarian nation either ignores abusive, exploitative behavior or makes poor excuses for it. Living in such a nation requires that people ignore some aspects of reality just to get by. Those who learn to avoid reality are repeatedly rewarded, while those who insist on acknowledging the truth are reliably punished.

In unhealthy nations, there is a tension between people's drive to see and speak the truth, and people's drive to fit in with their culture and survive. Healthy nations do not tolerate abuse, and so people can acknowledge reality freely without threatening anybody. In authoritarian nations, people often learn to "go along to get along" even when it means pretending the emperor isn't naked. People develop *blind beliefs* where they believe things not because they've observed reality and made reasonable conclusions, but because the beliefs help them remain safe and feel comfortable in their abusive nation.

Unlike in a fairy tale, this creates far worse trouble than an old man marching around naked.

Let us begin with religion.

Religious Blind Beliefs

Rulers commonly encourage or forbid certain beliefs to encourage submission to authority. For example, starting in 380 CE, Roman law decreed that all people were forced to convert to Christianity. Roman law labeled nonbelievers "demented and insane" and said, "they shall be smitten first by divine vengeance and secondly by the retribution of Our own initiative, which We shall assume in accordance with the divine judgment."[1]

While Christians might have feared punishment by the Christian God, for those who didn't believe in that god, the government retribution was the greater threat. This illustrates how authorities may claim that God supports their abusive behavior ("retribution… in accordance with divine judgment"). Religious submission to God, in practice, means submission to human rulers.

Judaism, Christianity, and Islam all preach submission to divine and human authority. The Christian Bible preaches submission in 1-Peter 2:13: "Submit yourselves for the Lord's sake to every authority instituted among men: whether to the king, as the supreme authority, or to governors… Live as free men, but do not use your freedom as a cover-up for evil…"

How could people be free if they must submit to the whims of a king? Clearly the Christian Bible trains people to believe they are free when in fact they are not free, a deep manipulation indeed.

The word "Islam" itself means "peace through submission"[2] as if true peace is even possible when some people are forced to submit to others. The Quran specifically gives this command: "O believers! Obey Allah and obey the Messenger and those in authority among you."[3]

This requirement for religious submission shows vividly in the history of Islam. After the founding of Islam, Muslims formed the Umayyad Caliphate and expanded rapidly through warfare throughout Africa and west Asia. They sometimes allowed more freedom of conquered people than the rulers they defeated. For example, the Muslims specifically allowed Jews and Christians to maintain their religious practices, whereas under Byzantine rule, all religious dissenters had been persecuted. However, the Muslims were unwilling to tolerate the polytheistic belief systems among the Berbers of North Africa, requiring them to convert to Islam or be killed.[4]

Why this difference? I believe the Muslim rulers were willing to tolerate any religion that preached submission to authority, while forbidding any religions that did not.

The Jewish Torah also preaches submission to human authority: "you shall come to the Levitic kohanim and to the judge… and they will tell you the words of judgment… According to the law they instruct you and… the judgment they say to you, you shall do…"[5]

God supposedly ordained that disobedient people would be killed and the rest scared into submission: "And the man who acts intentionally, not obeying the kohen who stands there to serve the Lord… that man shall die… And all the people shall listen and fear, and they shall no longer act wantonly."

Islam, Judaism, and Christianity all claim that their holy books represent the literal word of God. In each, God supposedly demands that we obey our rulers. Is it any wonder so many rulers throughout history have forced these kinds of religions on their subjects?

Abusive authorities manipulated people's religious and cultural beliefs in order to force and maintain submission. Acknowledging this truth could get someone in very deep trouble. Instead, people were forced to believe this abusive manipulation was the natural result of their God's direct instructions. This creates a deep internal conflict. It is our divine nature to not tolerate abuse of ourselves and others, and yet many humans have been forced to accept such abuse as God's intention. When people remain conquered and their belief systems are forcibly manipulated for centuries or millennia, deep confusion results.

Unfortunately, such confusion is not restricted to religious beliefs.

Secular Blind Beliefs: The Drapetomania Diagnosis

Different rulers have found different ways of establishing abusive, exploitative relationships in their nation. Each ruler or ruling class develops its own ideology that excuses or ignores the abuse. To outsiders, these ideologies seem ludicrous, but people trapped in the nation have to believe them to maintain their careers and safe and comfortable lives.

One such bizarre ideology existed in the southern United States in the 1850s. By this time, the region had had an extremely abusive form of slavery for centuries. Black men, women and children were underfed, worked to exhaustion and heavily physically abused. Family members were sold apart from each other on the owner's whim.

In 1851, a licensed physician named Samuel Cartwright published a paper in The New Orleans Medical and Surgical Journal where he proved he had learned to ignore this clear torture and abuse. Presenting his professional paper at the Medical Association of Louisiana, Cartwright acknowledged what seemed obviously true under the reigning ideology: that slavery was clearly good for slaves, and approved by God. Since he was willing to ignore the abuse, he concluded that runaway slaves had a mental illness which he officially labeled Drapetomania. This new medical diagnosis established that merely running away from such profoundly terrible conditions was enough to be diagnosed with a "disease of the mind."[6]

Just as religions can authorize rulers to dominate and abuse their subjects, secular blind beliefs backed by medical and other authorities can justify any abuse.

American slaveowners, for example, commonly raped enslaved women and then financially profited by owning the resulting children. Women's sexual attractiveness was a clear selling point on the auction block where they were routinely groped, had their skirts raised, and were asked degrading questions.

As one observer noted after an enslaved woman was asked such questions at a public auction, "tears rolled down her cheeks, and her refusal to answer those most disgusting questions met with blood-curling oaths."

Yet slaveowners propagated belief in the Jezebel Libel, which stated that black women were licentious, always sexually willing, and forever dishonored from birth. Black women simultaneously were believed to always want sex and to deserve their suffering due to their supposed inherent dishonor.

These fabricated stories of mental illnesses, unconditional sexual willingness, and inherent dishonor covered up the truth that doctors were forbidden to acknowledge. As one author summarized, "One of the functions of this slave-breeding machine was to chew up the black family, systematically, in every generation. Why might elite whites want a machine with which to destroy the black family? Most immediately, because the family was the strongest unit of social cohesion and resistance to slavery. But longer term, because destroying family webs systematically in every generation was the best way to guarantee the perpetual existence of an abject underclass whose labor and upkeep would remain as cheap as possible."[7]

Like with the naked emperor, these realities were ignored by medical professionals and others who had to pretend not to see in order to maintain their comfortable careers and social lives. Doctors who trained to treat mental illness were not allowed to diagnose, let alone treat, the actual causes of mental distress among enslaved people.

After chattel slavery ended, southern doctors stopped pretending that Drapetomania was a valid diagnosis. Scientists have since dismissed it as an example of scientific racism[8], but I believe the root cause runs deeper. Unlike healthy nations that don't pick winners and losers, unhealthy nations require people to maintain blind beliefs to keep their career and social standing.

Other examples illustrate this pattern too.

Political Blind Beliefs: Activists Considered Mentally Ill in China and the Soviet Union

A common assumption in abusive, unhealthy nations is that the nation is obviously right and good, and anyone who wants to significantly change it must be mentally ill. That was the assumption at the heart of the Drapetomania diagnosis: the doctors and their slave-owning bosses assumed slavery was obviously good even for the slaves, and therefore, any slave who wanted to escape must obviously be mentally ill.

This assumption of cultural goodness and assumption of mental illness in dissidents was also clearly evident in the Soviet Union and China in the 1900s.

Diagnoses of sluggish schizophrenia and paranoid psychosis were both widely used in the Soviet Union. Sluggish schizophrenia could present with relatively mild symptoms, and patients could function almost normally. However, these patients showed "obvious" signs of mental illness when they worked to address problems of corruption, lies, pollution, and incompetence in their government.

Thus, according to the Moscow School of Psychiatry, symptoms of sluggish schizophrenia included "struggle for the truth," "perseverance" and "reform delusions."[9] A survey of official psychiatric reports also found symptoms of "litigation mania," "overvalued (or excessive) religiosity," "persistent ideas of reform that tend to be convincing to others and tend to cause recurrent illegal actions," "serious illegal acts [such as] the writing of complaints," "slander and dissemination of false information," and "an interest in poorly understood and bizarre foreign fashions."[10] All these supposed symptoms of mental illness simply describe activists trying to address the problems in their unhealthy nation.

According to an official review of 19 cases in the Soviet Union, such people might undergo a transformation where they dedicate themselves entirely to their ideas, commonly called a "struggle for justice." With evident relief, the reviewer noted that "environmental change, the strict regime of a psychiatric ward, the impossibility of a continuation of their pathological litigious activity, [and] sedative and neuroleptic medication all served to normalize their behavior rather quickly."

The leading group of psychiatrists who developed this schizophrenia concept likely did so on the orders of the Soviet secret police and the reigning political party.[11] Top soviet leader premier Nikita Kruschev acknowledged government support for labeling activists as mentally ill when he said, "A crime is a deviation from the generally recognized standards of behavior frequently caused by mental disorder. Can there be diseases, nervous disorders among certain people in Communist society? Evidently yes... To those who might start calling for opposition to Communism on this basis, we can say that... clearly the mental state of such people is not normal."[12]

This is what the made-up story of the "Emperor's New Clothes" looks like in real life. This top political leader was saying that anyone who disagreed with him and the nation that he ruled had mental health issues and should be imprisoned and drugged. And extremely few, if any, psychiatrists were willing to acknowledge the truth.

When Amnesty International investigated political activists accused of mental illness, it found that they could be detained "pending recovery," that is, until they stopped showing symptoms of mental illness and became obedient again.[13]

Yury Belov was sentenced to 5 years' imprisonment in 1967 for writing a samizdat essay called "Report from the Darkness." "Samizdat" refers to censored or illegal literature. During his imprisonment, he continued his activism and he was charged with "anti-Soviet agitation" within the prison. Researchers learned that Belov was transferred to a hospital-prison where the head doctor told him "that they would treat him until he changes his opinions." Others were imprisoned for protesting about pollution or even advocating for a two-party political system. Many prisoners never had any role in their own criminal proceedings.[14,15]

Chinese officials likewise adopted this attitude towards protesters and activists. Hinting at Chinese citizens' tremendous courage, police noticed a puzzling "absence of instinct for self-preservation" when people spoke officially banned views, held peaceful protests, or pursued litigation against corrupt officials. Many activists who simply sought to address official corruption, pollution, and other troubles would be persecuted as mentally ill. One survey of forensic cases in the early 1970s at the psychiatric hospital at the Shanghai Municipal Mental Health Center found that over 70% of psychiatric cases were actually political.[16]

As explored throughout this book, authorities and those who adopt their nation's authoritarian ideology will commonly assume that their abusive nation is right, and dissenters must be bad, wrong or ill. Thus a textbook published by the Chinese Ministry for Public Security in 1983 noted that mentally ill people showing counterrevolutionary symptoms commonly also showed symptoms of "delusions of grandeur" or "delusions of persecution." I suspect they were diagnosed with "delusions of grandeur" for believing they could make a difference, and "delusions of persecution" for noticing their actual persecution.

The government textbook described one extremely sad case of a person who believed wholeheartedly in political orthodoxy, but didn't keep up with the times when the required beliefs changed: "A mentally ill person, for example, owing to his divorcement from reality, applied the former political orthodoxy to China's present-day context: the patient insisted that the Cultural Revolution had been entirely necessary and extremely timely, and he even went around publicly arguing his case with others." This government textbook called a man mentally ill because he believed in the previous dogma, not the current one.

Chen Lining was a Communist Party member who upset other party members when he criticized "revisionist" policies of the president, creating various articles and posters to publish his views. He was incarcerated seven times in mental hospitals between 1962 and 1966 and secretly placed under arrest by police. He described his treatment later: "During my political persecution at the Hunan Provincial Mental Hospital, I was subjected to numerous bouts of drug interrogation, given electro-convulsive therapy more than 40 times and insulin-coma shock therapy altogether 29 times, and was fed large quantities of chlorpromazine. They treated me like an experimental object and it was all a disguised form of physical torture. It was extremely painful, and by the end, I was left trembling and sweating all over and my memory had started to go."

A psychiatrist's note about Chen Lining in December 1963 illustrates his plight: "The patient's mental illness has recurred; his counterrevolutionary statements are none other than a pathological mental symptom of his longstanding reactionary views. Diagnosis: schizophrenia." In 1964, another psychiatrist noted, "Patient's mental condition: thinking clear and alert, interacts well with others, answers questions appropriately… But lacks self-knowledge and is unclear as to why he was placed under criminal investigation in the first place. Initial diagnosis: schizophrenia (paranoid type.)"

Like the American doctors who ignored the abuses of slavery, the Soviet and Chinese psychiatrists ignored the motivation of social activists trying to address corruption in their nation. Why didn't these Soviet or Chinese psychiatrists or American doctors simply notice the situation in front of them and acknowledge reality?

21st Century Blind Beliefs: Punishing Drug Addicts in Russia

A 2018 report on Russia's medical treatment of drug addicts shows the same pattern, and the author described the root trouble. Russia's official policy towards drug addicts is "social intolerance," and it legitimizes punishing drug addicts rather than helping them heal. Doctors who focus on drug treatment are legally and officially required to honor patients' trust, make independent judgments, and honor their patient's human rights. However, doctors are also expected to embrace the government's punitive ideology that sees drug addiction as "a serious evil… fraught with social and economic danger to mankind."[17]

Doctors who embrace this ideology treat patients abusively, reporting them to the police rather than helping them end their substance abuse. These doctors are known for avoiding treatment regimes that actually reduce addiction such as opioid substitution therapy, focusing instead on punitive measures like electroshock therapy. Doctors who do not embrace this ideology risk losing their medical license and career, with all the other social and financial hardships that would entail for them and their family.

The researchers acknowledged that these Russian doctors face *dual loyalty* which they define as "simultaneous obligations, express or implied, to a patient and to a third party, often the state." This results in physicians who "have voluntarily or under pressure stripped themselves of their professional independence and effectively extinguished any notion of human rights in patient care." This sounds very similar to physicians' behavior in the US slave states, Soviet Union, or China.

What would happen to a Russian physician who suddenly took a stand on behalf of their patients and sought to give them the best care available, regardless of the law's demands? I suspect they would face similar consequences to an American physician from the slave states who suddenly acknowledged that the slaves were mentally sound, and it was the slaveowners who were severely disturbed. Soviet and Chinese psychiatrists faced a similar trouble: who of them would want to face the wrath of the state simply for acknowledging the truth of their clients' experience? These professionals faced a continuous choice: do I acknowledge reality and act in service of my patients at potentially great personal risk, or do I protect my career and social standing? Keeping their careers required giving up that deep responsibility for the wellbeing of their patients. This is the essence of dual loyalty.

These nations all illustrate what I call *blind belief*. A healthy person observes reality, forms their beliefs, and then chooses how to act. With blind belief, a person chooses to obey authority and protect their own comfort and safety, then lets their beliefs form to justify this obedience. As Upton Sinclair said, "It is difficult to get a man to understand something, when his salary depends upon his not understanding it."[18] This illustrates how early American doctors could believe runaway slaves had mental illnesses, or Russian doctors avoid treatments that actually cure drug-addicted patients and instead bring in the police and their punitive approach.

Whenever I see a bizarre pattern like blind beliefs play out in other nations, I ask, "where is there a comparable pattern in my own nation, and possibly within me?"

21st Century Blind Beliefs: Pushing the Covid Vaccines in America

I believe the blind belief pattern occurred with the covid vaccines.

Covid started having noticeable impacts in the United States in March 2020. Authorities soon imposed lockdowns, making it impossible to travel except for work or necessary errands. Many people lost their jobs.[19] Government medical authorities in the United States, Great Britain, and many other countries began to tout soon-to-be-released vaccines as the way to end the pandemic-related lockdowns and return to normal economic life.[20]

When the vaccines came out, authorities pushed them hard, claiming there was no alternative. I had never studied vaccines much, though I had only ever heard good things about them since my childhood. I had studied corruption in finance, politics, the military, and other aspects of the economy, but I had never read much about the medical industry. I started to learn a little about vaccines, but mostly I focused on a simple question: *could I trust the people who seemed to be pushing the vaccines so hard*? Could I trust the regulators, media and drug company executives, political leaders, and others to tell me the truth and make sure the vaccines worked as promised, or were too many of them untrustworthy?

I started feeling skeptical even before the vaccines came out. Despite it being an airborne virus, I never heard any government or corporate medical official propose improved ventilation in buildings to help people gather safely indoors. High-nutrition diets can improve immune function, but I never heard a government medical official propose helping people eat better with a regular monthly stipend. Many other potentially helpful non-vaccine measures were ignored.

Censorship of Vaccine Alternatives

Once the vaccines came out, most popular media outlets solely covered the vaccines and blocked information about any other potential treatments. When I and many others hesitated to take the vaccines, officials shamed us and accused us of acting selfishly and prolonging the pandemic.[21]

Meanwhile, some independent-minded doctors reported having success with alternative approaches to prevent or treat covid[22], but social media and news corporations actively censored these alternatives under severe government pressure.[23,24]

Why would the government and media corporations censor information about alternative treatments? Were the vaccines not as good as promised? Or were the vaccines actually great, but authorities didn't trust people to figure that out and choose the best treatment? I couldn't easily tell. But just the fact that censorship was occurring was already enough to increase my skepticism. Trustworthy people present the truth as they see it, perhaps while sharing their own perspective, and let each person decide for themselves. Dishonest people manipulate the truth to trick people into making certain decisions. I was already feeling revulsion at the dishonest behavior, and I had hardly learned anything yet about the vaccines!

Doctors' Careers Threatened if they Didn't Promote Vaccines

Even more insidiously, state medical boards around the country required physicians to unquestioningly promote the vaccines. Vaccines typically require 10-15 years to research, test in multiple ways, and get regulatory approval before finally reaching the public. But the covid vaccines went through the entire development, testing, and approval process in under a year.[25]

This bulldozer approach was striking. When medical authorities expected doctors to unquestioningly give out vaccines, and punished them if they disagreed, it was as if highly trained doctors could not possibly have any valuable medical judgment of their own. It was also tragic because frontline doctors would be best positioned to notice vaccine troubles that a severely shortened development, testing and approval process might have missed. What if the vaccines didn't work as advertised and caused harms not noticed in the drug trials? Were the doctors just supposed to ignore it?

Threatening doctors was one way the government imposed blind beliefs. Medical authorities insisted that doctors recommend vaccines without question, and any who disobeyed authorities and used their independent medical judgment could have their license revoked, threatening their entire medical career.[26] The government even threatened approximately 100,000,000 people to get vaccinated or lose their jobs.[27]

Most doctors dutifully promoted the vaccines. A few bravely did their own research, such as physician Meryl Nass who offered her covid patients ivermectin and other treatments instead. Authorities suspended her medical license, and it remains suspended as I write in 2024.[28]

The more I studied the vaccines, the more skeptical I became. I found research showing that unvaccinated people cleared the virus about as fast as the vaccinated.[29] The US Center for Disease Control and Prevention called it a myth that covid vaccines could alter people's DNA, but researchers found that it did in fact alter people's DNA.[30,31]

A study following thousands of patients found that the effectiveness of the vaccines wore off after 90 days, leaving vaccinated patients *more likely* to develop covid than the unvaccinated.[32] Multiple studies from the Cleveland Clinic also found that vaccinated people were more likely to get Covid-19 than unvaccinated people.[33,34] This implied to me that the covid vaccines might negatively affect some people's immune systems, either temporarily or perhaps permanently. Why else would vaccinated people be more likely to get sick than the unvaccinated?

The problems didn't end there. Further medical research showed that the mRNA vaccines could cause myocarditis (inflammation of the heart), cancer, and even "long covid," a condition where people suffer auto-immune symptoms, neurological symptoms, exhaustion or other troubles for many months or years after the initial viral infection should have cleared.[35,36] The mRNA vaccines were designed to contain a spike protein very similar to a protein on the real virus in order to cause the body to replicate the protein internally and stimulate an immune response[37], and thus the vaccine and virus can lead to some similar symptoms.

Clear Corruption Among Medical and Corporate Authorities

Stories of fraud during the vaccine trials started to come out. I learned fraud was not unusual in clinical trials, as one investigation of the Food and Drug Administration found that it audited only 1% of clinical trial sites. Jill Fisher, professor of social medicine at the University of North Carolina School of Medicine, said, "There's just a complete lack of oversight of contract research organisations and independent clinical research facilities."[38]

A lack of integrity seemed endemic even among high-ranking officials. Anthony Fauci was the most visible government medical official leading the response to covid, with some calling him "America's doctor."[39] Early in the pandemic, he recognized that masks could reduce covid's spread, but there was a mask shortage and he wanted to conserve them for use by hospitals and health centers. Instead of simply telling this to Americans and asking them to find other ways to protect themselves until more masks could be manufactured, he lied and said people should avoid masking. A few months later, he acknowledged that he had lied, and people should mask. Furthermore, Fauci said that he did not regret that he lied.[40]

Fauci thus openly declared that he was comfortable lying to the public. In a time of great uncertainty, at the start of an epidemic when very few people knew much, if anything, about the virus, Fauci was many people's primary source of medical information. When he declared that he was willing to lie, he left Americans without trustworthy leadership that could unify the country with a clear understanding of the challenge, and how each person could help while taking care of themselves.

For as long as Fauci remained in office, every time I heard him speak, I wondered whether he was telling the truth, or if he was trying to manipulate the public again. I'm sure he told the truth sometimes; I just couldn't tell when those times were. This is simply the trouble with people who don't have integrity: one never knows if they're telling the truth.

The longer I waited to vaccinate, the more severe shaming I received. People I'd known for years accused me of not caring about the community and thinking only of myself. I spoke with several doctors about my concerns, offering to share my research. Not one of them would even look at it.

Meanwhile, the companies which produced the most popular covid mRNA vaccines profited astronomically. Pfizer and Moderna together made over *$56 billion* in 2022 alone.[41,42] Government medical regulators benefited too, as many people involved in covid vaccine approval were soon hired by the drug companies. This "revolving door" practice has a long history where companies reward government regulators after they leave their government job.[43] Government regulators who earned money from vaccine-related royalties or consulting with drug companies likely also profited well.[44,45]

The obvious lack of integrity among medical authorities made it difficult to even trust the published, peer-reviewed medical research that supported the vaccines. After all, if doctors were required to promote the vaccines, and if social media companies censored information about vaccine alternatives, did medical journals also reject any research findings that might discourage vaccine use? Did scientists worry that their careers would be threatened if they reported findings that discouraged vaccine use? With these concerns, even the fact that so much research supported vaccine usage wasn't convincing.

I still felt like I hardly knew anything about the vaccines, but what I learned about the American political response to the epidemic was damning:

- *Corruption Among Top Authorities*: the top national medical authorities were clearly and openly dishonest

- *Censorship*: the media was censoring information about alternative treatments

- *Corporate Profit Motive*: the drug companies had a huge profit motive to push the vaccines

- *Corporate Corruption*: there was a history of fraud with drug trials and minimal auditing

- *Regulatory Corruption*: many regulators also had profit motives to push the vaccines due to royalties, speaking engagements with drug companies, revolving-door practices, and more

- *Doctors Required to Obey Authorities*: doctors had their careers threatened if they spoke out against the vaccines

- *Contradictory Medical Research*: much medical research contradicted official statements about how the vaccines worked, and suggested that the vaccines didn't work as advertised

- *Shaming People who Hesitated*: Anyone who expressed hesitation about either the science or authorities' integrity was labeled anti-vax, anti-science, and anti-community

All this caused me to feel extremely skeptical of the vaccines, and just as skeptical of the medical and political system pushing them so hard.

In many ways, the US covid response has been a catastrophe. An epidemic arrived in the United States, and instead of serving the people, corrupt authorities served themselves. It occurred because a few individuals were willing to become fabulously rich at the cost of others' health, and because most journalists, doctors, regulators, and others prioritized protecting their careers and comforts rather than taking responsibility for the wellbeing of their people. Ultimately, this catastrophe happened because, when all these people were behaving inappropriately, too many of their fellow citizens passively accepted it.

What if We Embraced the Responsibilities of Living in a Healthy Nation?

In the story from the Cherokee in Chapter 2, when some people had to leave for a new town, everyone went to build the new town together so that no one had to face a big challenge alone. In the story from the Nootka, when the priest threatened the clown, the entire community instantly responded to protect the clown. Their solidarity was so strong that they never allowed a threat to the clown, even for a moment.

What would it be like if Americans had this solidarity, standing together for a culture of mutual respect?

Could Americans have stood in solidarity with the doctors, not allowing authorities to threaten doctors' careers if they used their own professional judgment to treat covid?

Could Americans have forbidden the government from threatening 100,000,000 people's jobs if they didn't take the vaccines, kicking any official out of office before the end of their term if they acted so abusively?

Could Americans have insisted on having leaders with integrity, kicking out any officials who, with their lies, undermined the medical system and Americans' trust in it?

Like Soviet and Chinese psychiatrists, and Russian narcologists, American doctors faced a choice. Physicians could act with independence and integrity, risking their careers by considering alternative covid treatments, or they could protect their careers and comfortable lives by pushing the vaccines as authorities commanded.

Each doctor is responsible for the decisions they made, regardless of the pressure they faced. Also, if Americans had stood in solidarity with the doctors and people whose jobs were threatened, it would have been much easier for the doctors and everyone to respond to the pandemic using their own best judgment.

Many concerned people focus on changing out one political party for another, but to have a society where everyone is treated respectfully requires creating a nation where *everyone stands for a culture of mutual respect, and nobody rules over anybody else.*

Watching a Blind Belief Form in Real Time

One goal I have for this book is for readers to observe large-scale manipulation playing out in front of them as it happens. What would it be like to watch an unhealthy nation impose a blind belief, making it suddenly dangerous to acknowledge a clear truth in public?

I'm observing this right now with the Israeli-Palestine protests on college campuses throughout the United States. Israel is clearly committing genocide against Palestinians as I write, and many brave college students and others are protesting US government support of Israel. These protests threaten both Israel's genocide and the United States government's ability to pretend that it cares about human rights and freedom, supposedly the motivating force behind much US foreign policy.

Wealthy business owners are now going on mainstream television threatening to permanently ban any protesters from future employment. For example, Kevin O'Leary said that every protester was being surveilled with high-definition cameras, and he would ensure AI algorithms captured every person's identity. He then would ensure people's protest activity would be available on their background checks that any employer could access, and protesters would thus be banned for life from many potential employment opportunities. O'Leary said, "I know who you are." From now on, protesters "won't know why they didn't get that job," and he said this would last "forever."[46]

O'Leary and other business leaders are not just threatening people for protesting. They're also clearly trying to define what beliefs are considered appropriate in their nation by scaring those who disagree into remaining silent. Anybody who recognizes Israel's genocide for what it is has now been put on notice that if they speak up, they risk their livelihood for the rest of their lives. And it is not an idle threat. Many jurisdictions in the United States, including North Carolina where I live, have recently outlawed wearing masks in public as an explicit response to Palestine-related protests. This makes it easier for cameras to see protesters' faces.[47]

This sort of threat, overt or covert, is common in abusive nations. Disagreeing with authorities, and especially seeking to stop their abusive behavior, is quite dangerous. This pattern of creating and enforcing blind beliefs will simply keep playing out until we're able to free ourselves from authoritarian nations.

Different Ideologies Require Avoiding Different Truths

In a deep way, humans want to be members of their nation in good standing. I believe that in healthy nations, people can remain in good standing simply by treating each other and the Earth decently.

In unhealthy nations, authorities decide what beliefs or actions a person has to embrace to remain in good standing. When authorities require people to believe false or hurtful things just to avoid trouble, keep one's career, or stay out of prison, people are faced with a difficult choice. Many choose, consciously or subconsciously, to believe false things or avoid having an opinion.

Different rulers have different insecurities, that is, different truths they're afraid for others to acknowledge because it threatens their legitimacy. Thus authorities ignore those truths and expect others to ignore them too.

Because different abusive ideologies require people to ignore different aspects of reality, people will commonly speak condescendingly about each others' obvious blindness. In the 20th century, for example, many Americans wondered how Soviet citizens could prefer living in a communist dictatorship where they obviously had no control of their government. Meanwhile, many Soviets wondered how Americans could think they were free when so few people owned so much of the country and most Americans were just grateful for a job serving the rich and their corporations.

Sadly, the reverse also happens: some Soviets recognized their nation's blind spots and not the Americans', just like some Americans saw America's blindspots but not the Soviets'. Brave activists in both these countries have faced great challenges.

This pattern of blind beliefs represents a severe weakness in unhealthy nations. If a ruling class collectively believes in their own invincibility, their servants may mindlessly agree, and the society will march off to wars they're likely to lose. If the authorities don't care much about the health of the soil and just want maximum production, farmers will come under intense pressure to maximize output at the expense of the soil. Dustbowls, soil depletion and other environmental degradation are the predictable results.

Because most people are forbidden from holding authorities accountable, authorities can sometimes avoid reality for a long time. Unlike social activists, the authorities themselves often develop the real delusions of grandeur. American journalist Ron Suskind interviewed an aide to US president George Bush and described what he heard in 2004:

> The aide said that guys like me were "in what we call the reality based community," which he defined as people who "believe that solutions emerge from your judicious study of discernable reality. That's not the way the world really works anymore. We're an empire now, and when we act, we create our own reality."[48]

In societies that do not hold leaders accountable for incompetent or selfish behavior, the leaders can learn to ignore reality too, at least for a while.

If these authoritarian nations were normal and healthy for humans, we wouldn't have to ignore so much reality just to get by. The fact that unhealthy nations require various forms of blind belief shows that they are an aberration, not "just how humans are."

Why Didn't More People Acknowledge That the Emperor Had No Clothes?

Humans are generally adaptive, especially when survival is at stake. When an individual is trapped in an abusive relationship for long enough, they can learn to ignore the abuse. Many people learn to ignore the abuses at the heart of their unhealthy nation.

Unfortunately, ignoring abuse and pretending to believe nonsense are pervasive. For example, in courtrooms around the world, a quick way to lose at trial is not to show proper submission to the judge's authority. In many jurisdictions, the law requires participants to address the judge as "Your Honor" regardless whether they believe the judge is actually honorable. In this way, people pretend to show the judge respect when they're actually showing submissiveness, a common confusion in unhealthy nations.[49]

As another example, many people misunderstand the story of The Emperor's New Clothes. One writer warns readers about "the instinct to conform and agree with the majority" and tells readers that the "folly of behaving like sheep leads to the crowd living a collective lie."[50]

However, the story has nothing to do with an instinct to conform or agree with the majority. The story is about how afraid the people were to believe something that the emperor didn't want them to believe, or speak a truth that their ruler didn't want to hear. If I were in that crowd, I wouldn't be worried about the opinion of the majority because the majority couldn't send me to prison for saying the emperor is naked. But the emperor could definitely send me to prison, and that is a real problem that most people are highly motivated to avoid.

Likewise, those Soviet and Chinese police officers didn't arrest activists for having mental health issues because of the opinions of the majority of the other officers. They did this because police chiefs could have fired them and even put them in prison if they disobeyed. Russian narcologists could lose their job if they don't follow official medical guidance. Cartwright might have lost his job and worse if he said that the *slaveowners* had mental health issues, not their slaves. American doctors who spoke up about the real risks and negative effects of the covid vaccines risked losing their jobs and potentially their careers as licensed medical doctors.

In the story of the Emperor's New Clothes, the child spoke up, but not because they were unafraid of their peers. The child spoke up because children are born expecting to live in a healthy nation in which people tell the truth and are not punished for it. The child in the story hadn't yet learned that people can be punished for speaking certain truths, with each unhealthy nation having its own particular set of forbidden truths at any given time.

Sometimes, observers describe people of healthy nations as childlike. Sioux man Ohiyesa even described one of his own chiefs this way in his book *Soul of the Indian*.[51] This story of the outspoken child shows why being childlike in many ways can be a good thing. Children in healthy nations never learn to ignore certain uncomfortable truths. When they reach adulthood, they feel just as free as ever to speak the truth as they see it.

In this case, calling adults of healthy nations childlike is not a comment on their emotional maturity. Because they do not have to pretend to believe falsehoods to survive, both adults and children retain the same innocent willingness to see and acknowledge the truth, no matter how uncomfortable it may be.

Healthy Nations Have No Need to Manipulate Beliefs

I believe that people in healthy nations can feel free to acknowledge reality because doing so does not threaten anyone's safety, comfort, or social standing.

As a result, healthy nations strongly embrace personal integrity, including truth-telling. For any human relationship to be meaningful, there has to be trust, and trust requires people to speak and act with integrity. Many people, including myself, have found that people of healthy nations have very high integrity.

I certainly experienced this among the Ashaninka. In Chapter 1, I described the large bag of gifts I brought and how I left it in an unlocked hut for weeks.

Many of these people had literally no money. I heard that others were just beginning to exchange goods for money, selling cacao to Peruvian river traders for the equivalent of a few dollars per month. I estimated that my $200-$300 worth of items in that bag was roughly a year's income for the financially richest people.

When Mike and I returned to that hut about 2 weeks later, my bag was exactly as I had left it. Mike was right: these were people of integrity.

Such high integrity is common in healthy nations. Ohiyesa visited the Sac and Fox people in the region many know as Iowa in the USA. He was leaving when someone handed him his pocket book which he'd dropped. It contained railway tickets and a considerable amount of money. Ohiyesa said to the missionary with him, "Better let these Indians alone! If I had lost my money in the streets of your Christian city, I should probably have never seen it again."[52]

Ohiyesa described how he faced problems in American cities he'd never faced at home: "I was cautioned against trusting strangers, and told that I must look out for pickpockets. Evidently there were some disadvantages connected with this mighty civilization, for we Indians seldom found it necessary to guard our possessions."[53]

S. M. Barrett worked with Apache chief Geronimo and found him to have strong integrity, saying, "When he once gives his word, nothing will turn him from fulfilling his promise." They were collaborating on Geronimo's biography, and Geronimo became very sick as cold weather arrived. Barrett assumed Geronimo would miss the appointment, but he arrived exhausted, saying in a hoarse whisper "I promised to come. I am here."[54] Researchers Stanley Vestal and George Grinnell likewise found the Cheyenne and Sioux to have high integrity.[55]

This also shows up in how adults mentor their children. When Nez Perce chief Joseph mentored an American boy, his recommendation was clear and simple: "Be brave and tell the truth."[56]

The young boy Wikis' uncle made a similar recommendation as he mentored his nephew, as related in the book *When Buffalo Ran*: "In your life in the camp remember this too; you must always be truthful and honest with all your people. Never say anything that is not true; never tell a lie, even for a joke–to make people laugh."[57]

Unhealthy nations go the opposite direction: the Soviet, Russian, Chinese, and American nations have all encouraged cowardice, dishonesty, and reality-avoidance even as they gave lip-service to bravery and truth. However, bravery and truth-telling are who we are as humans, and I believe that in healthy nations without rulers, people can freely live with bravery and integrity.

In my research, I have found some examples of people of healthy nations lying. For example, European trader Peter Grant commented on the Chippewa, saying, "though naturally honest in their dealings with one another, they often find many occasions to cheat their traders with impunity."[58] Likewise, warriors have acted deceitfully before stealing their enemies' horses or food.

This shows the real value of integrity: it draws a line between the people I value and want a deep relationship with, and those I don't. If I want a deep relationship with a collaborator, friend, family member, or romantic partner, I must speak the truth, keep my promises, and act in service, and I must expect the same from them.

If I want any chance of a good relationship with a stranger, I need to behave with integrity with them from the start. Keeping promises may even be important with enemies, because any possibility of a truce depends on mutual trust, and mutual trust depends on integrity.

This clarifies the common question, "when is it ok to lie?" People have asked, what if I were a German in the 1940s smuggling Jews to freedom, and the Nazi police asked me if I was hiding anybody? Would I tell the police the truth even if they would capture and torture the Jews? Of course I would lie to the Nazi police. They are not on my side and threaten everything I love. And I would practice complete honesty with my family and the people I helped. In this way, we could have deep trust and meaningful relationships built on a foundation of integrity.

For a person to have integrity, they cannot lie to themselves. As shown in the story of the emperor's pretend clothes, there is one type of human who has not been fully trained to lie to themselves: kids!

Children have a lot to teach adults who have lived in unhealthy nations for much longer. To see what children – and all of us – are capable of, I invite you to *Chapter 7: When Children Learn to Take Responsibility*.

Chapter 7: When Children Learn to Take Responsibility

Growing up, I was told that anarchy is a state of chaos, supposedly the natural negative consequence when no government exists to impose law and order to keep humans safe and prevent mayhem.[1]

Eventually I discovered that this is merely another commonly propagated myth about healthy nations. Anarchy actually means "without rulers" (an- meaning "without" and -archy "government" or "rule"[2,3]). In other words, anarchy describes how humans live when everyone stands for a culture of mutual respect, and nobody rules over anybody else. In anarchic societies, people do not live in chaotic mayhem; they collaborate to agree on standards of acceptable behavior and then hold each other accountable to those agreed standards. Everyone accepts responsibility for upholding the agreed norms.

Agreeing on our own rules and taking responsibility for ourselves and each other is so basic to human nature that it doesn't have to wait until adulthood – and it shouldn't. Most children instinctively want to do this.

A friend whom I'll call Jordan works with kids in a variety of camps and schools, helping them learn how to create their own agreements and take deep responsibility for themselves. His stories showed me how well humans can get along without authorities imposing law, and how adults can raise children to treat each other decently by training them for responsibility instead of obedience.

Children Make Shared Agreements

Twice a year, Jordan co-hosts Teen Camp during a weeklong earth skills gathering. Hundreds of people of all ages come to connect with other people and learn traditional skills like friction-fire making and animal tracking in the woods. Teen Camp is a dedicated outdoor space where teenagers can practice intentionally having their own culture.[4]

One night, Jordan was at Teen Camp and noticed the teens kept almost cussing, and each time they stopped themselves and looked at him pensively. Other times they would cuss and then give him a nervous look. He said, "maybe you have an expectation that we're not allowed to [cuss] here, but let's all make that decision together." Jordan introduced a consensus process that allowed everybody's voices to be heard. They sat in a circle and talked. Some kids were amazed at the possibility they might be able to curse freely, with one saying, "oh, we can curse? Of course I want to be able to curse!" Then they thought about it, and another kid said, "you know, it's kind of annoying when somebody just replaces half their words with curses." Other kids said, "yeah, I don't like that either," and the first kid responded, "Yeah. I do curse kind of too much sometimes."

As he related this story to me, Jordan said, "in a way, [it's] not even about the agreement between us, so much as creating this opportunity for reflection. How do we want the world to look? How do we want our culture to look? Do I want to live in a culture where I use cuss words instead of thinking about what I'm trying to say? Do I want to challenge myself in this way?"

The teenagers came to a nuanced agreement. They decided it was ok to cuss, but they would try not to do it excessively. They all agreed to be accountable if someone else felt like they were cussing excessively.

And they did hold each other accountable. Jordan heard a teen say a sentence that was half-full of curse words, and another teen gave them a snarky look and said, "come on!" The cursing teen said, "Oh right." Other times, a conversation would slowly involve more and more cursing until both teenagers noticed it and agreed to curse less.

Right after the teens agreed on cursing, one of the new teens pulled out a phone and asked if the others wanted to listen to music. Some of the teens really enjoyed not having distracting phones. They looked at Jordan nervously, unsure who could make decisions about phone use. Jordan said, "we just learned consensus process. Do you all want to make a decision about… whether we can use our phone at camp?" Jordan trusted that they would make a good decision.

Jordan set a different rule for this conversation. In the conversation about cussing, the adult staff were not allowed to say how they felt, but in this conversation about phone use, staff could speak their preferences too. The whole group of teens and staff would seek consensus together.

Once again, conversation went around the circle. One teen said, "I like being able to use my phone." Another teen said, "I'm actually trying to do a technology detox while I'm here, because I use it so much at home." Another said, "I actually don't have a phone and I don't like them. And I notice how it changes the dynamic when I'm with people who are using them." The teens had a very nuanced conversation about the impact of phones and what kind of culture they wanted to have at the gathering. Eventually, everyone agreed they would not use their phones at all at Teen Camp. They agreed they wouldn't play music, call, or text.

Amazingly, the teens never even needed to hold each other accountable. By the end of the conversation, not a single one wanted to use their phones. The kid who initially wanted to use her phone said, "I realized that this is a habit." Not only did she not use her cell phone at Teen Camp, she avoided using it throughout the gathering.

Jordan described how older teens helpfully influenced the conversation. The older teens were the elders of the culture, and they knew how connected people could feel without digital distractions because they had been coming to Teen Camp for years. These older teens described how great Teen Camp could be without phone use.

This mimics multi-generational cultures, where elders pass on wisdom to children and young adults. Jordan said a lot of his parenting friends are passing wisdom on to him, just like the 17-year-olds passed on wisdom about cell phone use to 15-year-olds at Teen Camp.

10-11-Year-Olds Decide on Cabin Agreements

Jordan described a Quaker camp where the staff would set core rules about things like safety, and then welcome children to agree to their own additional rules called Cabin Agreements. On the first day at camp, Jordan and another staff member would sit down with a half dozen 10-11-year-olds and decide on these Agreements, such as when bedtime would be or what people could do during nap time.

Jordan said, "I had never been there before so I had no idea what to expect… it's entirely up to them." The staff taught a consensus process to the campers. The staff were experienced, as they also used a consensus process with each other to make decisions.

All these kids went to public school and had never encountered consensus processes, so Jordan taught them. He showed them hand-gestures meaning "I agree" or how to raise their hand to add themselves to the list of people who wished to speak. Jordan kept a list of people who wished to speak, and people could give a different signal if they wanted to remove themselves from that list if someone else made their point. When someone finished speaking, he would call on the next speaker.

This was blind consensus, so each time there was a vote, the kids would close their eyes and give a thumbs-up for "yes" or thumbs-down for "no." If anyone gave a thumbs-down, they continued to discuss it. One child said, "I don't think there should be a lights out." Another said, "I actually like it. It's important to me to get sleep." The first responded, "Oh yeah. I just want there to not be rules because I'm so used to rules." At first some kids excitedly pushed for a late lights-out time like 11 pm but then they remembered they would need to get up at 7 am and they realized the consequences. Then someone said lights-out should probably be at 10 pm, and it was ok to read with a flashlight under a blanket for 30 minutes. No one could be on another kid's bed past 9:30 pm. They had come up with a tiered system, where they could be together until a certain time, then in their own bed, then under their blanket reading if they wanted, and then all lights were out.

The conversation about nap time went similarly. They decided that during nap time they could be on each others' beds together but would remain silent. The children came to these agreements and then committed to upholding them. Sometimes during the week a child would speak during nap time, and another child would look at them and remind them of the agreement. In other cases, a staff member would say, "hey, do you remember that you agreed? We had this conversation and you agreed to this." Immediately the child responded with "Oh yeah, I made that decision," and the child did as they agreed. This was very different from other camps where the staff made all the agreements and pushed them on the kids. Jordan noticed that when the kids made their own agreements, they were much more willing to follow them.

The kids made their own agreements about things like cussing and sleeping, while the staff imposed other agreements related to safety. For example, kids were not allowed to hit each other or jump off the top bunks, and that was not up for discussion. But he said, "They were 10 and 11 [years old]. They were the youngest in that camp. They'd never been there before, no idea what to expect… they got to decide how they would handle [certain things]. And having that responsibility was big for them."

I asked Jordan what would happen if a staff member broke an agreement that staff and the kids had set together. He said, "There are certain things that are so clear. Like, knife safety [or] any safety thing. If we start breaking the safety agreements, [the kids say], 'hey, you're not allowed to do that. You can't use your knife like that.' Or, 'you're not allowed to climb that high in that tree.' … My strategy is [to climb down and say], you're right. We all agreed that we wouldn't do that here. And I don't do that here. I don't climb above my head height in a tree while I'm at school. Because you don't. That's what we said we would do."

So when Jordan broke one of the agreements the staff had made with the kids, and the kids held him accountable, Jordan honored this by acknowledging he'd broken an agreement and returning to the behavior they'd all agreed upon. In other words, he returned to being in integrity with his agreement, which taught the child that they had done well by seeking to hold others accountable for their mistakes or broken promises, including adult authority figures.

Jordan reflected on lessons he has learned from working with young kids and teenagers:

> The conclusion that I have come to through working with kids over a period of time has been… There's this transition… that adults should manage for kids throughout their childhood, from being given a culture and given expectations, which is essentially what a culture is. It's like a set of expectations. You're given the set of expectations and then the transition throughout your childhood is the slow passing off of that responsibility to the child until they become an adult.

As an adult, it's entirely their responsibility to hold that set of expectations. In an ideal world, nobody's enforcing that on them because they have taken on complete responsibility for that set of expectations.

…the process… also involves these risks, moments where you're giving them that responsibility, not necessarily knowing whether they're ready for it. And what I see over and over again is that they rise to the occasion. You have to choose when to do that wisely, you don't want to hand a five-year-old responsibility of… setting all of the expectations in a culture. But usually when it feels a little bit scary to give them that responsibility, that's the right time to give them that responsibility.

When it feels a lot scary or just like it would be absurd, it's not time. But when it feels a little bit scary, that's the time to give them that responsibility. You can wait a little bit longer, but they're not going to grow as quickly. They're not going to become responsible as quickly. Any time you give them a responsibility that they didn't believe that they were ready for, or they didn't believe that you would think they were ready for, they rise to it.

Children Embrace Consent and Recognize Their Actions Have Consequences

Jordan has worked for a few nature schools and camps for children and teenagers. He described how nature connection practices help children learn to take responsibility for the consequences of their behavior, honor their own and others' boundaries, and build deep awareness of the nonhumans around them.

Learning Consent and Healthy Boundary-Setting

Children at these camps learn to set their boundaries and honor each others' boundaries. The kids can wrestle, but they discuss it ahead of time. Each child is taught how to speak up if they don't feel good or don't want to continue. They learn how to get consent by asking if someone else wants to wrestle instead of just tackling them. If someone says stop, then the wrestling must stop.

Consent requires both people to participate: a person must be willing to stay "stop" if they don't like the activity, and the other person must be willing to respect that. Kids learn both sides. Sometimes they used verbal consent, and other times non-verbal. For example, the kids might form a ring, and anyone inside the ring consented to wrestling, although they could say "stop" at any time.

Jordan noted, "[we allow] everybody to choose when they want to interact with that. [It's] this process of learning your own boundaries in community, in a group."

Learning That Actions Have Consequences

Jordan has noticed a big cultural shift when kids are allowed or encouraged to take risks. He said, "It's a huge part of nature school that they're engaged in inherently risky behavior." Jordan carefully assesses potential injuries from the kids' activities. He will prevent permanent damage from occurring. Jordan will make sure they don't lose an arm, but if they risk temporary injury like a broken arm, then he allows it.

Jordan described the benefits of allowing children to take risks: "when you are engaged in inherently risky behavior, you experience natural consequences for your behavior, and you learn how to mitigate risk in your life in general."

Through natural consequences, rather than lots of adult rules, children learned how to mitigate their own risks. If they ran down a hill too fast, a sprained ankle taught them to be more careful. Kids also learned the social consequences of carelessness, including "when you're playing with another kid and you hurt them and they get mad at you, and don't want to be your friend anymore. You're experiencing a natural consequence to your behavior, instead of it exclusively being enforced upon you. They're learning that every action has a consequence. And that consequence can be positive and it can be negative."

Jordan found that if a group of kids was misbehaving, he could improve their behavior by putting them in a risky situation. He described one group of kids who were consistently violent with each other and very disrespectful. The staff then decided to give all of these violent kids knives.

He described the response:

> Behavior immediately improves because when you put real risk in their hands, they manage their own risk much more intensively… When there's a perception of safety, kids create risks. They need risk, they know that they need it instinctively. So when there's a perception of safety, they create risks. They're not as effective at managing the level of risk they create as they are at managing an inherent risk. When there's an inherent risk, they can effectively manage the risk. Decide how to engage, keep yourself safe. Safe, but at the edge of safety.

> When they create the risk they often create a level of risk that they can't manage. So if you put them in a risky situation or if you allow them to be in a risky situation, they're going to be safer than if you put them in a safe situation and force them essentially to create the risk.

Children also act differently depending on whether they believe adults are watching them. A watchful adult can save a child from their mistake, but when children are alone, they know they face consequences alone. Jordan noted, "if they think that you're tracking their risk, they'll engage in much riskier behavior than if they think that they have to track their risk. And that's a huge thing in nature connection is you are constantly trying to keep track of them without them knowing that you keep track of them." Jordan got very good at using his peripheral vision to watch the kids without them knowing he was watching so that he could know if he needed to step in.

He has even seen this behavior in very young children. Playing with a two-year-old named Nick, Jordan noticed that "When I hang out with Nick, my attention is on Nick. He'll start climbing all sorts of shit. And even if I just turn and talk to somebody else, he gets off of it." When they walk together, Nick walks on the edge of the stream knowing Jordan will be there if he falls. However, when Jordan walks away, Nick starts to manage his own risk and walks five feet away from the creek.

Jordan described how experiences at nature schools also teach kids to notice and care about their impact on the world around them.

He once taught an advanced scout training program for kids. Participants had already been through scout trainings for two summers where they learned how to make camouflage, make ghillie suits, hide in the woods, and more. In this camp, they discussed how to track other people and evade being tracked. Bird language was a key part of the program, as birds respond sensitively to their environment, and anyone who watches birds can learn from what the birds observe, including where people are hiding.

The kids all went out to hide, and Jordan walked down a trail and noticed a towhee bird excitedly chirping weep! weep! weep! while the bird looked into a bush. Jordan realized there was a kid in the bush, and he said, "I can't see you, but I know that you're there."

A boy named Ben came out and said, "That's not fair. You can't see me! That doesn't count." Jordan said, "I know you're there because that bird is telling me that you're there."

Later the kids assembled and debriefed the game. Immediately Ben asked, "what do I do about it?" He was essentially asking how he could reduce his impact on the environment.

Jordan noted, "The answer to that is very complicated. But the fact that he was asking that question is part of what nature does for kids, for anyone. This awareness of your impact on your environment and your awareness of how your energy influences your environment and how to mitigate that."

Children Learn That it is Worth Paying Attention to Everything

Jordan once ran the youngest group at a nature school. The staff decided they would make it a scout program, focusing entirely on tracking, bird language, and sneaking. He said, "we're going to take these five to seven year olds and just make them sneaky little masters."

The kids learned to scout walk, and they scout-walked to camp each day. During this 20 minute walk, they moved silently in a single file. They communicated with hand signals. Somebody would cup their hand to their ear to communicate "I heard a sound over there." Everybody would stop and direct their attention. The adults taught and modeled that everything was worth paying attention to. They stopped every time they heard a bird alarming.

Each day they practiced scout walking. When someone heard a sound, they would put their hand to their ear and direct people's attention. Everyone looked and perhaps a cardinal would pop out of a bush. They would observe it for ten minutes. They constantly practiced this silent observing.

One day, they decided they would sneak up on the oldest group of kids. They snuck through bushes and a boy made the signal to stop. He directed everyone's attention to a wren bird making a gentle alarm. It wasn't a loud BRP BRP, more of a soft ch ch. The wren was alarming as it watched these sneaking humans. The humans were far enough away from the oldest group that they could whisper. Jordan asked, "which way do you think we should go?" The boy said, "we shouldn't go that way, because that bird is going to make a bunch of noise and tell the other group where we are."

This kid was six years old and it was his first time at camp. Jordan noted, "it was just amazing... [the kid has] an awareness of bird language that most adults I know who are trying to learn bird language don't have." He noticed, "it was so quick that this kid became aware of his impact on the environment and was willing to change his behavior in order to reduce his impact."

They followed a different path and kept encountering more alarming birds, chipmunks, or other animals. Each time, a kid would suggest a path that minimized their impact and gave the other animals their space.

The older kids were playing a loud game of freeze tag and not paying attention at all. The little kids snuck up within 10 feet of them! Jordan said, "it was just amazing. It was so fun. And [one adult] was like, wow, these kids figure this out so quick."

The kids learned how much loud humans impact their environment. At the end of the day, Jordan's group was the first at the meetup spot. They had practiced noticing their impact on the birds. Jordan said, "Let's sit here and see if you can tell when [the group of older campers is] coming, before they get here." Half the kids stopped paying attention pretty soon, but half were willing to wait five minutes. They noticed a crow flying out of the woods, then two blue jays, and then many birds flying away across the field. One kid said, "I think they're coming." A minute later, the older kids came out of the woods chatting and laughing and having fun.

Jordan supports kids in laughing and having fun. He never discourages this. However, he noted how deeply nature connection influences him: "[it's] one of those things where nature is showing so clearly, depending on how you are acting, [how] you can change your impact and you can change your awareness of your environment… that lesson applies to nature. And if it's learned deeply enough, it generalizes to other experiences… I know for myself that those experiences change how I treat other people."

These stories show that young children can care about their impact on the environment, make agreements, and hold each other accountable. They can have disagreements and work through them. They can learn healthy boundary-setting and how to honor humans' and nonhumans' boundaries. They can learn to manage risk and become resilient when injuries happen.

These stories also show how adults can generate this kind of culture. Jordan modeled the behavior he wanted to see in the kids. When a kid caught him breaking an agreement, Jordan acknowledged his mistake and returned to the agreed-upon behavior. He didn't make arbitrary exceptions for himself, which would have taught "might makes right." In some ways, because he was staff, he did have special privileges. But when he agreed to something, kids could hold him to it. Jordan modeled the kind of culture he wanted to have, and the kids responded beautifully.

These children's stories remind me that looking out for each other and taking responsibility for honoring shared agreements is part of who we really are as humans. That's why most kids take to it so readily.

Adults and children both have so much to learn from each other. Unhealthy nations train people to have a lot of bad habits and misunderstandings. Children can show adults what humans are like before they've been so deeply trained. And thoughtful adults can train children in a good way.

The previous chapter on blind beliefs explored misunderstandings that lasted for years or decades. Would you believe that some blind beliefs have lasted for thousands of years? Next, *Chapter 8: Blind Belief 2 - Multi-Millennia Misunderstandings* reveals just how deeply some incorrect assumptions are embedded in unhealthy nations, and how a few insidious falsehoods have helped these nations persist over countless generations.

Chapter 8: Blind Belief 2 - Multi-Millennia Misunderstandings

The deepest question in any nation is this: is it legitimate for a few people to rule over everyone else? I don't think so! And since it is not legitimate, how are rulers able to consistently keep their illegitimate hold on power?

In Chapter 6, the old story of "The Emperor's New Clothes" illustrated how, when people decide to submit to their ruler, they can adapt to whatever lies necessary to protect their personal safety. *Blind beliefs* occur when authorities require people to believe falsehoods in order to avoid prison and maintain a comfortable life. Instead of simply observing reality and deciding for oneself what to believe, people can subconsciously learn to obey authority, and then take on beliefs fabricated by authorities in order to justify their obedience.

Some blind beliefs only last for a few years or decades, such as when some American doctors during the 1850s were motivated by their nation to believe that escaping slaves had mental illnesses. Eventually, that particular blind belief fell out of favor.

Is it possible for authorities to impose false beliefs or misunderstandings that last for thousands of years?

Absolutely, yes. *Blind beliefs can last for millennia.* In fact, there is at least one blind belief that has lasted approximately two millennia, and another one that is even older.

Many religious authorities throughout history have controlled people's religious beliefs. Authorities in *every* unhealthy nation must manipulate people's beliefs to maintain the rulers' perceived legitimacy.

While this clearly benefits the rulers, it also fosters long-lasting cultural misunderstandings. I have found some ancient stories in the Christian, Jewish, and Muslim traditions that I believe are widely misunderstood. For millennia, these misunderstandings have helped legitimize authorities' rule around the world.

I offer two examples of multi-millennia misunderstandings and my interpretation of what I believe actually occurred:

1. *Jesus Christ*

Multi-millennia misunderstanding: Jesus died for our sins.

Reinterpretation: *Jesus Christ was a revolutionary seeking to generate a healthy nation without rulers and with deep sharing.* Authorities encourage selfishness and legitimize their own rule, while Jesus encouraged deep generosity and challenged authorities' legitimacy. The Jews wanted a savior, not because they had sinned, but because they wanted someone to save them from oppressive Roman rule. For millennia, Christian religious authorities have trained Christians to misinterpret and ignore Jesus Christ's revolutionary work.

2. *The Jews' Expulsion from the Garden of Eden*

Multi-millennia misunderstanding: Humans were forced out of the Garden of Eden because we are flawed and violated the will of God.

Reinterpretation: The story of the Jews' expulsion from the Garden of Eden represents their *transition from a healthy nation without rulers into an unhealthy nation with abusive rulers*, a kind of transition that has occurred countless times throughout history for healthy nations around the world, up to the present day. Religious authorities train followers not to know that healthy nations without rulers exist, and so authorities have trained their flock not to recognize the true meaning and implications of the Jews' expulsion from the Garden of Eden.

Reinterpreting Jesus Christ as a Revolutionary

I grew up in a Christian family, so the first story of abusive government I learned was the Roman killing of Jesus Christ. I learned in church that Jesus was the only son of God sent by the Heavenly Father to save the Jews and anyone else who would believe in Him. My parents and religious teachers all encouraged me to be as Christ-like as possible. I learned that after Jesus did a lot of kind things and healed a lot of people, the Romans arrested him and crucified him, meaning they nailed him to a post and left him to die and rot outside.

Growing up, it was never clear to me why the Romans would do this. It seemed mean and unnecessary. Eventually I realized there was more to the story.

The Romans had conquered Jerusalem and the surrounding region about 63 years before Jesus was born. They imposed heavy taxes, unwanted imperialism, a client king that obeyed Roman authorities, and generally treated the people abusively. Many Jews worked to free themselves from the Romans, longing for a country where Jews could be safe. Eventually this led to a series of wars between the Romans and the rebellious Jews, starting with the First Jewish Revolt in 66 CE, about 30 years after Jesus' death.[1]

The Christian Bible makes it clear that the Jews were looking for a revolutionary leader, and were hopeful that Jesus could be that leader. The Bible claims Jesus was "born King of the Jews"[2] who would "put down the mighty from their seats."[3] People were clearly suffering in poverty under the wealthy Romans and they wanted a leader who "has filled the hungry with good things, and the rich he has sent away empty."[4]

Jesus was baptized and went into the wilderness where he faced his fears and temptations and recognized his divine path. Afterwards, Jesus explicitly called for liberty of the oppressed and freeing of captives[5], noting that "The time is fulfilled, and the kingdom of God is at hand."[6]

He even chose at least one Zealot among his disciples. Among other things, Zealots were known for not paying taxes to the Roman state[7] and assassinating tax collectors.[8]

After time alone in the wilderness, where Jesus learned to avoid temptations and follow a sacred path without distraction, he began his ministry. His ministry included healing people, feeding people, and ignoring the law whenever it got in the way of healing or feeding people. Jesus healed people when they needed it, even illegally on the Sabbath (a weekly holy day). He illegally fed people with extra food on the Sabbath, and when authorities questioned him he said, "The Sabbath was made for man, and not man for the Sabbath."[9]

Jesus also publicly questioned the authorities' rules. He said that to enter the Kingdom of God, it was not enough to follow the law, but one must give up all possessions.[10] He violently and publicly attacked the moneylenders who predated upon the poor, a radical act which, if it happened today, would be called terrorism.[11]

Multiple times, Jesus recognized he would soon be killed by authorities, but he continued to preach and do good works.[12,13]

Jesus Christ was eventually arrested and accused of "perverting the nation, and forbidding to give tribute to Caesar, saying that he himself is Christ a King."[14] In other words, he was accused of questioning authorities' legitimacy, encouraging illegal tax avoidance, and claiming he was the rightful leader of the Jews.

The prosecutors' witnesses at the trial could not agree on the facts. But when Jesus himself would not deny these accusations, his accusers responded, "What further witnesses do we need? You have heard his blasphemy. What is your decision?"[15]

In other words, Jesus was killed for taking a stand for his people against Roman authority.

So I began to understand why the Romans killed Jesus, but why the cruel crucifixion?

For years, this was the only crucifixion I'd ever heard of, and I assumed it was unique to Jesus and the two people killed with him. But it turns out crucifixion was simply the common Roman punishment for people convicted of treason, including revolutionaries who sought to free their people from Roman rule.

The Romans crucified two other people with Jesus. Romans called them "bandits," but they weren't just outlaws: like Jesus, they were revolutionaries. Calling them bandits was a way of labeling them outlaws without acknowledging that they were fighting for their people's freedom.[16]

Crucifixions purposely took place in very public areas, such as roadsides or hilltops. After nailing people to a cross and letting them die, the Romans would commonly leave the body hanging for a long time to decompose in the weather as birds pecked away at the flesh. These gruesome scenes publicly conveyed a clear message: "We will act with extreme brutality towards anyone that defies our authority. Obey us." In other words, the Romans were attempting to scare the population into submission.

I call this a *dominance display*, where authorities choose to act abusively in order to remind people of their overwhelming power and scare them into compliance. Many Jews were taking responsibility to free their people from oppressive rule, and Romans tried to scare them into giving up this responsibility and to obey authorities instead.

Finally, I understood a very important reason why so few people truly follow Jesus' footsteps: it takes a lot of courage and a deep sense of responsibility for the wellbeing of one's people. And this courageous responsibility – this deep love – is exactly what the Romans sought to scare people away from.

What Sort of Nation Was Jesus Trying to Generate?

Jesus did not merely resent oppressive government authority and fight to free his people. This alone would have been enough to set him apart for his deep courage and love. But, for me, what sets him apart from many other revolutionaries were two things: 1) his willingness to give up all his possessions so he could walk a divine path without temptation[17], and 2) his willingness to reject being a king, which he clearly did during his time in the wilderness before beginning his ministry.[18]

Many revolutions in history have had frustrating results: one king is deposed but another takes their place, and the lives of most people don't change that much. Instead, I believe Jesus was inviting his followers to regenerate a truly healthy nation, because he was working towards two of the defining features of healthy nations: 1) emphasizing deep sharing rather than hoarding and 2) having strong leaders but no rulers.

This started to become clear when I read about Christian missionaries speaking with people of healthy nations who had recently been overrun by the United States in the 1800s. These people consistently recognized that, when they had lived in a traditional way as healthy nations, they had lived just as Jesus preached.

Ohiyesa grew up in the traditional Sioux nation, and as an adult he trained to be an American doctor and Christian missionary. When he spoke of Jesus Christ with the men of the Sioux, Cheyennes, Crees, Ojibway, and other healthy nations, he said they listened very carefully. He described how one "battle-scarred old warrior" said one time, "Why, we have followed this law you speak of for untold ages! We owned nothing, because everything is from Him. Food was free, land free as sunshine and rain. Who has changed all this? The white man; and yet he says he is a believer in God! He does not seem to inherit any of the traits of his Father, nor does he follow the example set by his brother Christ."[19]

Another old man said, "I have come to the conclusion that this Jesus was an Indian. He was opposed to material acquirement and to great possessions. He was inclined to peace. He was as unpractical as any Indian and set no price upon his labor of love. These are not the principles upon which the white man has founded his civilization. It is strange that he could not rise to these simple principles which were commonly observed among our people."

The Dakota man Gall had a similar awareness when he was baptized in 1892: "What this man Jesus says we must do unto others, I already know. Be kind to your neighbor, feed him, be better to him than to yourself, he says. All are brothers, he says. But that's an old story to me. Of course! Aren't we all Dakotas?"[20]

In other words, Jesus Christ was simply inviting people to a way of life which is fundamental and common in healthy nations: a way of life based on deep sharing, mutual respect, reciprocity, and walking a spiritual path. While many Christians relate to Jesus Christs' wisdom, grace, courage, selflessness, and generosity as an unattainable ideal, to men of healthy nations, Jesus Christ merely seemed like a normal man urging his followers to live as people of healthy nations had lived since the beginning of time!

But Jesus didn't just share a little, he gave away everything and urged others to do this too. Isn't that exceptional?

As it turns out, no. Such deep sharing is a normal practice in healthy nations, and I believe it is part of what makes them healthy.

The Tzutujil Mayans were able to live in a more-or-less traditional way up to about 1990, when the Guatemalan military, heavily supported by the US government and corporations, assaulted and killed many people. Before this, Martín Prechtel, who was a shaman there, described their many layers of leadership. A woman and man would share each position. To get to higher leadership levels, people had to give away more and more, until the last few levels required the participant to give away absolutely everything unto total poverty.[21]

Prechtel described how the Tzutujil Mayans loved to acquire possessions so that they could give everything away, much to the frustration of the Christian missionaries who taught that the way to build security was to build wealth. In order to reach the upper levels of leadership, people had to give away everything and return to total poverty.[22] Shamans were continuously given huge amounts of food by the people they helped, and it was their role to pass that food along to those who needed it. It was a nation based on sharing.

Sioux man Ohiyesa described the Sioux's perspective: "It was our belief that the love of possessions is a weakness to be overcome. Its appeal is to the material part, and if allowed its way it will in time disturb the spiritual balance of the man. Therefore the child must early learn the beauty of generosity. He is taught to give what he prizes most…"[23]

No wonder these men of healthy nations thought Jesus sounded like one of them.

This willingness to share deeply doesn't imply weakness or poor boundary-setting. Just as Jesus was willing to attack predatory money-lenders, people of healthy nations have been willing to defend themselves.

Some Sioux leaders recognized the true character of the American nation which threatened to overrun them in the 1800s. At one council where they debated whether to go to war, Sioux man Sitting Bull said:

> Yet hear me, friends! We have now to deal with another people, small and feeble when our forefathers first met with them, but now great and overbearing. Strangely enough, they have a mind to till the soil, and the love of possessions is a disease in them. These people have made many rules that the rich may break, but the poor may not! They have a religion in which the poor worship, but the rich will not! They even take tithes of the poor and weak to support the rich and those who rule. They claim this mother of ours, the Earth, for their own use, and fence their neighbors away from her, and deface her with their buildings and their refuse. They compel her to produce out of season, and when sterile she is made to take medicine in order to produce again. All this is sacrilege.
>
> This nation is like a spring freshet; it overruns its banks and destroys all who are in its path. We cannot dwell side by side… My brothers, shall we submit? or shall we say to them: First kill me, before you can take possession of my fatherland![24]

The Sioux, Tzutujil Mayans, and others also have a strong relationship with the nonhuman world, something Jesus did not speak of much, at least according to the Bible. Still, these healthy-nation practices of deep sharing, reciprocity, standing up for what's right, servant-leadership rather than coercive-leadership, and so on – that's who we are as humans. I do not see any sign that Jesus learned from ancient healthy nations. It seems like he simply recognized the value of healthy-nation practices in a way few of his neighbors did.

As Sitting Bull said, "love of possessions is a disease," and it is a disease that unhealthy nations propagate, along with abuse of the poor by the rich, defacing the Earth, and other sacrilege. Sadly, these are not unique to the United States. They are simply common patterns in any nation where one person or a few people rule over many others.

For 2,000 years, religious authorities have tried to hide what Jesus was really working towards because they don't want people to know that truly healthy nations exist, and that authorities use many different techniques to keep us from standing for a nation without anybody ruling over anybody else. Authorities may allow Jesus to inspire people, but not in ways that threaten rulers' authority.

Did Humans Really Leave the Garden of Eden?

The Garden of Eden is part of the cultural memory of Christians, Jews, and Muslims.

The Christian Bible and Jewish Torah describe how humans lived in the Garden of Eden immediately after God created all life. They did not have shame of their bodies[25] and they paid close attention to the animals and plants.[26]

Then something terrible happened. According to the Torah and Bible, God forced humans out of the Garden of Eden.[27] The Bible and Torah say God cursed the Earth and made people face great sorrows.[28] Many terrible things began to happen that hadn't happened before, and life became much harder. This transition out of the Garden of Eden marks the beginning of recorded history in the Christian Bible and the Jewish Torah.

The Torah and Bible claim that God expelled humans from the Garden of Eden because they ate forbidden fruit.[29] I believe this ancient Jewish story of humans' expulsion from the Garden of Eden is an allegory for ancient Jews' transition from a healthy to an unhealthy nation. Humans in the Garden of Eden lived in a "state of nature," that is, closely connected with the Earth and in nations that maintained an internal baseline of mutual respect.

After the "expulsion," humans lived in abusive societies where people's lives were primarily shaped by abusive authorities, and all the usual troubles followed: body shame, sexism, extra hard work to pay taxes to the ruling class, and much more. Of course, unhealthy nations train people to ignore their rulers' abuses, so these ancient stories don't acknowledge that the transition occurred because rulers took over and started exploiting the rest.

The reason I believe this is simple: this story keeps happening, over and over up to the present day. Abusive nations force people to disconnect from nature and pay attention to their abusive nation and its laws and money just to survive.

So what would it be like to live in the Garden of Eden, living in a healthy nation amidst incredible natural abundance? And what would it be like to have that abundance deliberately destroyed, so that the survivors could not protect themselves from an onrushing abusive nation?

The story of the United States' deliberate destruction of the wild buffalo in the 1800s provides an example.

Crow woman Pretty Shield told interviewer Frank Linderman, "The happiest days of my life were spent following the buffalo herds over our beautiful country. My mother and father and Goes-ahead, my man, were all kind, and we were so happy. Then, when my children came I believed I had everything that was good on this world. There were always so many, many buffalo, plenty of good fat meat for everybody."[30]

These buffalo which roamed the Great Plains of North America were incredibly numerous. In 1541, Spanish explorer Francisco Vasquez de Coronado noted, "And I found such a quantity of cows (bison)… that it is impossible to number them."[31] Alexander Henry was an experienced fur trader and hunter who wrote on January 14, 1801: "At daybreak I was awakened by the bellowing of buffaloes. I got up, and was astonished when I climbed into the [southwest] bastion. On my right the plains were black, and appeared as if in motion, [south to north]. Opposite the fort the ice was covered [with buffalo]; and on my left, to the utmost extent of the reach below us, the river was covered with buffalo moving northward… I had seen almost incredible numbers of buffalo in the fall, but nothing in comparison to what I now beheld. The ground was covered at every point of the compass, as far as the eye could reach, and every animal was in motion."[32]

Some observers knew they were witnessing an abundance so great that others might not believe it was true. In 1811, HM Brackenridge noted, "I am conscious that with many, I run the risk of being thought to indulge in romance, in consequence of this account: but with those who are informed of the astonishing number of the buffaloe, it will not be considered incredible… On the hills in every direction they appeared by thousands. Late in the evening we saw an immense herd in motion along the sides of the hill, at full speed: their appearance had something in it, which, without incurring ridicule, I might call sublime – the sound of their footsteps, even at the distance of two miles, resembled the rumbling of distant thunder."

This abundance represented a challenge for the rulers of the United States who wanted to control the area of the Sioux, Crow and others. The buffalo allowed them to live solely by receiving the gifts of the Earth, free of any abusive-nation economy. Many of these groups were very capable of defending themselves and they successfully resisted American military attack for decades. The US military's respect for healthy nations' military capability lives on in the names of military equipment like the UH-72 Lakota utility helicopter, AH-64 Apache attack helicopter, C-12 Huron transport aircraft and more.[33]

Unable to quickly dominate them militarily, the United States chose to starve these people into submission by destroying the natural abundance. The government encouraged people to wantonly kill the buffalo. Some people hunted the buffalo just to sell a small part of their body like the tongue or hide. Others shot buffalo from trains as they rode past great herds, wasting the entire animal.[34]

US secretary of the interior Columbus Delano testified before Congress in 1874 and said, "The buffalo are disappearing rapidly, but not faster than I desire. I regard the destruction of such game as Indians subsist upon as facilitating the policy of the Government, of destroying their hunting habits, coercing them on reservations, and compelling them to begin to adopt the habits of civilization."[35] Between 1800 and 1900, with the help of the transcontinental railroads, Americans reduced the buffalo population from 30-100 million to less than 1,000.[36]

This had devastating consequences and made continued military resistance extremely difficult. Ohiyesa described how Sitting Bull led his people in maintaining their free life for as long as they could. They were never finally defeated in battle, but voluntarily entered a government reservation when they could no longer sustain themselves from the land.[37]

What was it like to depend on such incredible wild abundance and then suddenly face starvation after the Americans destroyed it? Frank Linderman asked Pretty Shield what happened after the buffalo disappeared:

> "Sickness came, strange sickness that nobody knew about, when there was no meat," she said, covering her face with both hands as though to shut out the sight of suffering. "My daughter stepped into a horse's track that was deep in the dried clay, and hurt her ankle. I could not heal her; nobody could. The white doctor told me that the same sickness that makes people cough themselves to death was in my daughter's ankle. I did not believe it, and yet she died, leaving six little children. Then my other daughter died, and left hers. These things would not have happened if we Crows had been living as we were intended to live. But how could we live in the old way when everything was gone?"[38]

> "Ahh, my heart fell down when I began to see dead buffalo scattered all over our beautiful country, killed and skinned, and left to rot by white men, many, many hundreds of buffalo. The first I saw of this was in the Judith basin. The whole country there smelled of rotting meat. Even the flowers could not put down the bad smell. Our hearts were like stones. And yet nobody believed, even then, that the white man could kill all the buffalo. Since the beginning of things there had always been so many! Even the Lacota, bad as their hearts were for us, would not do such a thing as this; nor the Cheyenne, nor the Arapahoe, nor the Pecunnie; and yet the white man did this, even when he did not want the meat."

> "We believed for a long time that the buffalo would again come to us; but they did not. We grew hungry and sick and afraid, all in one. Not believing their own eyes our hunters rode very far looking for buffalo, so far away that even if they had found a herd we could not have reached it in half a moon. 'Nothing; we found nothing,' they told us; and then, hungry, they stared at the empty plains, as though dreaming. After this their hearts were no good any more."

Pretty Shield described how the US government then imposed land ownership and fenced off the land:

> "And then white men began to fence the plains so that we could not travel; and anyhow there was now little good in traveling, nothing to travel for. We began to stay in one place, and to grow lazy and sicker all the time. Our men had fought hard against our enemies, holding them back from our beautiful country by their bravery; but now, with everything else going wrong, we began to be whipped by weak foolishness. Our men, our leaders, began to drink the white man's whisky, letting it do their thinking. Because we were used to listening to our chiefs in the buffalo days, the days of war and excitement, we listened to them now; and we got whipped. Our wise-ones became fools, and drank the white man's whisky. But what else was there for us to do? We knew no other way than to listen to our chiefs and head men. Our old men used to be different; even our children were different when the buffalo were here."[39]

Plenty-coups was a Crow chief. When Linderman asked him about the loss of the buffalo, he only said, "When the buffalo went away the hearts of my people fell to the ground, and they could not lift them up again. After this nothing happened. There was little singing anywhere. Besides, you know that part of my life as well as I do. You saw what happened to us when the buffalo went away."[40]

Pretty Shield acknowledged how difficult it was to learn to live with the abusive American nation: "I do not hate anybody, not even the white man. I have never let myself hate the white man, because I knew that this would only make things worse for me. But he changed everything for us, did many bad deeds before we got used to him."[41]

These stories of the Sioux and Crow illustrate how Americans systematically forced free, independent people into a state of dependency by deliberately destroying their primary food source. After this, the survivors faced the same essential plight as all Americans and all people of unhealthy nations in general: they had to find a way to make a living by serving people with money or power, or starve. Unhealthy nations spread and are maintained by trapping people into unequal, abusive relationships where a few people exploit the many.

This story shows a major technique of social control: making people dependent on the unhealthy nation itself rather than simply living from the Earth. Suddenly the Crow and the Sioux had to care about the American economy: were there enough jobs available? Were employers racist against them? Did employers and government leaders keep their promises? Were government leaders causing the economy to serve the rich, or were they causing it to serve everyone? Was inflation causing the value of their money to diminish? The Crow and Sioux and many other nations in central North America were now subject to all the usual ways that money-dependent people can get scammed by those in power.

Reading these stories really highlighted for me how the dependence on money isn't normal or natural. This dependence was engineered in the past and continuously maintained now as a way of maintaining exploitative relationships.

And it doesn't have to be this way.

Seeing This Abusive Pattern in Deep History

Prior to the Europeans' arrival in large numbers after 1492, many people in North America lived in close relationship with the Earth. Lakota man Black Elk described this clearly when he said, "Once we were happy in our own country and we were seldom hungry, for then the two-leggeds and the four-leggeds lived together like relatives, and there was plenty for them and for us. But the wasichus [white people] came, and they have made little islands for us and other little islands for the four-leggeds, and always these islands are becoming smaller."[42]

Black Elk shows his attitude of reverence for the Earth when he described, "the story of all life that is holy and is good to tell, and of us two-leggeds sharing in it with the four-leggeds and the wings of the air and all green things; for these are children of one mother and their father is one Spirit."[43]

Ancient Jews used to live in a state of nature they remember as the Garden of Eden. Just like the Jewish people were forced out of the "Garden of Eden" thousands of years ago, Americans forced the Sioux, Crow, and others out of the "Garden of Eden" and into an abusive nation. Fortunately, many living descendents of the Crow and Sioux maintain their ancient traditions and knowledge and continue to stand in solidarity with the Earth as brave environmental activists. Unlike people whose ancestors have been trapped in abusive nations for millennia, they have not forgotten their old ways.

Their experiences taught me what the story of the Garden of Eden was really about. "Living in the Garden of Eden" means living in close connection with the Earth in nations where everyone stands for a culture of mutual respect, and nobody rules over anybody else. I believe this is why so many people of healthy nations talk about the time before encountering unhealthy European nations as a time of freedom.

Ohiyesa decided to go to an American school when he was 15 years old on his father's urging, but he almost chose instead to return to "my freedom and wild life."[44] Sioux man Red Cloud noted, "We were as free as the winds and like the eagle, heard no man's commands. We fought our enemies and feasted our friends."[45] Apache man Geronimo described the times before entering the reservation as "the days of freedom."[46]

The Earth is the Garden of Eden. We're living in paradise right now because the Earth itself is paradise! Humans never left; many of our ancestors simply forgot they lived in paradise when they were forced into abusive nations. When people are forced to deal with abusive authorities' laws, money, speech control, and other pressures, it becomes very hard to connect deeply with the Earth. Hopi man Wayne Sekaquaptewa once told a New York Times reporter, "You can talk to the wisest man out here, a man who can tell you all there is to know about the clouds and plants and the animals, and what use is that to you when you have to be at your nine-to-five job in twenty minutes?"[47]

These stories hint at the terrible transition my ancestors must have experienced as they became trapped in an abusive nation at some point in the deep past. It also taught me that the history of the United States' expansion represents an epochal shift in the history of humans in North America. Previously, most people lived in healthy nations, but afterwards the vast majority now live in abusive nations. Mexico and Canada have obviously been part of this too. This cultural disease continues to spread around the world today.

All of these stories show the power of religious and secular authorities to distort history to maintain their control. In an abusive relationship, the abuser will often try to trick the victim into believing that the abusive relationship is actually healthy, or the abuse is normal and "just how relationships are."

Abusive authorities likewise trick people into believing that abusive nations are normal or universal. That's why the expulsion from the Garden of Eden marks the beginning of history in the Jewish Torah and Christian Bible: ancient religious authorities didn't want people to know about the respectful nations that people lived in before they became trapped in an authoritarian society.

The false, authoritarian belief is that "Authoritarian nations are the only kind that has ever existed. They are normal and 'just how humans are' or 'part of human nature'." This belief gets propagated in non-religious schools too. In my secular schooling, my ancient history classes started with studies of ancient China and Egypt, both authoritarian nations. They focused exclusively on monarchies, empires, dictatorships, and authoritarian democracies. Even in the rare times my teachers mentioned healthy nations like the traditional Cherokee or Pueblos, we only learned about their superficial differences, like clothing or eating habits. I never once was taught that they were non-abusive nations, with strong leaders and no rulers.

These perspectives on Jesus Christ and the Garden of Eden show how unhealthy, abusive nations can maintain distorted beliefs that literally last for millennia. I do not think that authorities of every Christian, Jewish, and Muslim nation have coordinated a common campaign to spread lies. Instead, I believe all these authorities have benefited from propagating similar misunderstandings that support the legitimacy of their rule.

If every society in history has had rulers, then that's human nature, and there's not much to be done about it. But if these authoritarian nations are an aberration, and not "just how humans are," then that changes everything.

It is not legitimate for a few people to rule over many. There is a better way.

One remarkable aspect of that "better way" is explored next in *Part 3 - Gift Economy vs Profit Economy*. For those of us in unhealthy nations, the idea that a whole society could reward generosity rather than selfishness might seem like a fairy tale.

And yet this is exactly how some healthy nations live today. Others used to live this way until, like Pretty Shield and the Crows, the people were forced to either join an unhealthy nation or die. Even today, many groups and sub-cultures practice a relationship-driven, gift-based economy that rewards generosity instead of an individually focused, profit-based economy that rewards selfishness.

Hard to imagine? Come see for yourself in the next chapter, *Chapter 9: Gift Economies*.

Part 3 - Gift Economy vs Profit Economy

Growing up, I heard that "money is the root of all evil." But I've seen money used for good things, so the trouble must run deeper.

What does an economy reward? Does the economy reward selfishness? Or does it reward generosity?

Chapter 9: Gift Economies

Often when activists describe their desire for a culture without rich and poor, and without anybody taking advantage of anybody else, I hear this dismissed as utopian, pie-in-the-sky, or an impossible and unreasonable ideal.

The Encyclopedia Britannica demonstrates this when it defines "utopia" as "an ideal commonwealth whose inhabitants exist under seemingly perfect conditions. Hence utopian and utopianism are words used to denote visionary reform that tends to be impossibly idealistic."[1]

I have good news: the Encyclopedia Britannica is wrong. Utopias are real. Some exist now, and many more existed in the past. I believe living in a utopia is simply the experience of living in a healthy nation – where everyone stands for a culture of mutual respect, and nobody rules over anybody else.

I'm not the only one to consider it a utopia to live in a healthy nation. Describing their way of life before Europeans arrived and imposed their laws, a collection of Mohawk writers noted, "It was, in fact, a kind of Utopia, a place where no one went hungry, a place where the people were happy and healthy."[2]

Many people seem to think of utopias as places where people never suffer, but I think this is misleading. Terrible things like wars, famines, plagues, and other troubles can still occur. What makes a healthy nation a utopia is that people can trust their neighbors to take care of each other and act in service of the group in difficult moments rather than take advantage of each other. It's not that there are no big challenges; it's that nobody in the group needs to face the challenges alone.

One key aspect of living in a utopia is that group sharing is the norm, rather than individual profiting. These nations have variations of a *gift economy*. Gift economies ensure everyone is taken care of, moving resources to where they're most needed or where they serve the greatest good. In contrast, unhealthy nations operate with variations on a *profit economy*. Profit economies benefit individuals or sub-groups, moving resources to people who already have them. In profit economies, the more resources a person has, the more extra resources they're able to get. Thus profit economies reward selfishness, whereas gift economies reward generosity.

Gift Economies Generate and Share Abundance

I experienced a gift economy among the Ashaninka where sharing was the norm. Plenty of other people living in other healthy nations, past and present, show that this is not particularly unusual.

Nancy Basket summarized the traditional Cherokee culture of sharing this way: "If we all had a lot, then everybody had a lot. If there wasn't a whole lot, then no one had a whole lot."[3]

Ohiyesa wrote, "During the summer, when Nature is at her best, and provides abundantly for the savage, it seems to me that no life is happier than his! Food is free – lodging free – everything free! All were alike rich in the summer, and, again, all were alike poor in the winter and early spring."[4]

For centuries, "savages" was an English term for all people of healthy nations around the world. When he referred to savages, Ohiyesa was simply describing a common pattern in nations that shared deeply as a normal way of life. (To learn why people of healthy nations were called savages, see Chapter 22)

In some ways, this deep sharing is comparable to how many nuclear families live in unhealthy nations, sharing food, heat, transportation, and shelter. The parents and children all become poorer or richer together as the family's income goes up or down. Parents don't typically hand the children a bill after every meal.

What is it like when an entire society embraces a gift economy where things are shared as needed, and what cultural practices help maintain such an economy so that people can continually generate and share abundance?

Gift Economies and Indian Givers

One of my earliest childhood memories involves giving somebody a gift and noticing that they didn't use it. When I tried to take it back, I was called an "indian giver." I was told that to be a generous gift-giver, I was supposed to release all interest in what happens to my gift after I give it. I was told that the gift becomes someone else's property and therefore is no longer any of my business.

Not wanting the scorn I associated with being called an indian giver, that's how I learned to give gifts – first it belonged to me, and now it belongs to someone else. It took decades for me to learn that this attitude towards sharing is rooted in private property ownership and is essential to maintaining authoritarian nations. I was amazed to learn that my early childhood self had the healthier attitude to gift-giving!

All of life is simply divine beings giving their gifts. This is the recognition behind the first core spiritual practice of cultivating the practical, aware gratitude for the gifts of life. Chestnut trees give tasty chestnuts, stinging nettle plants heal joint pain, stars provide guidance, and the soil accepts us back and recycles us after we die. All these beings give divine gifts that make life possible and beautiful. No one makes them do this. Humans play their role by giving their own sacred gifts too – the second core spiritual practice.

In gift economies, people simply figure out where gifts are most needed or valued, and everyone helps circulate gifts until they get to that highest use. This is where the derogatory phrase "indian giver" comes from: people of North American healthy nations (known as indians) often gave gifts to European colonists, noticed they weren't being used, and thus asked for them back so the gifts could be given elsewhere. European colonists, who were used to private property ownership where giving a gift gave another person the right to do whatever they want with it, thus saw "indian giving" as a violation of their private property rights.[5]

Nancy Basket described how the Cherokee would commonly ensure gifts got where they were needed, and how European colonists misunderstood this: "We would know each other well enough to see what they might need. And if we would give somebody a gift and they didn't use it, we would be embarrassed. And we would either take it back or something else because it wasn't being used. She didn't need it. And people called us Indian givers for that."[6]

"Indian giver" became a negative label, describing someone who gave a gift and now selfishly wants it back. In reality, an "indian giver" is behaving thoughtfully, paying attention to whether the gift is needed. If the gift goes unused, the so-called indian giver exerts extra effort to retrieve the unused gift and pass it along to someone else who needs it more.

Due to this fundamental difference between caring for others and caring primarily for oneself, the contrast between these two economies is striking. Gift-economy practices can seem offensive to people in profit economies, and profit-economy practices can seem offensive to people in gift economies.

A person in a gift economy may feel upset if a person accepts a gift, doesn't use it, and then refuses to pass it on to someone else. A person from a profit economy may feel upset if they receive a gift only to find that the giver wants it back. Both sides may feel offended, and it reflects a fundamentally different perspective on sharing (and trusting others to share) versus hoarding (and not trusting others to share). Do gifts keep moving until they arrive where they are most needed? Or do people hoard possessions whether they need them or not?

Potawatomi woman Robin Kimmerer noted the consequences when she wrote, "If all the world is a commodity, how poor we grow. When all the world is a gift in motion, how wealthy we become."[7]

This healthy-nation attitude to gift-giving stems from the deep recognition that all of life is simply the giving of divine gifts. Every spider, bear, bush, and cloud is giving its sacred gifts and somehow contributing to the web of life. Who would want to stop all that giving? Gift economies aim to circulate gifts rather than hoard them, and this kind of human economy fits in well with the larger nonhuman economy of all life.

Gift economies also have many practical benefits. They move resources from the haves to the have-nots, minimizing inequality. Gift economies ensure neighbors take care of each other. People might suffer poverty together occasionally, but nobody suffers poverty alone while others have abundance. Gift economies help people take care of each other whenever the group faces a big challenge.

Private Property Rights vs Sacred Responsibilities

Robin Kimmerer described the gift-economy and profit-economy views of gifts. In an economy focused on private profit, people commonly think of a gift as free because they don't pay for it. But in a gift economy, *a gift is not free*. Instead, Kimmerer said, "The essence of the gift is that it creates a set of relationships. The currency of a gift economy is, at its root, reciprocity." Nations that view private property as a collection of rights miss out on this essence of a gift as a collection of responsibilities.

If I am in a nation where hoarding is the norm, I could easily feel the need to hoard too. If I don't hoard when I have extra, how will I ensure I have enough during lean times? In profit-economies, many people carefully guard their possessions as well as the private property rights those possessions entail. In profit economies, individuals can easily fear poverty, and for many, the clearest way to avoid it is to acquire wealth through profitable work and hoard the savings. This is one way profit economies motivate selfish behavior.

Profit economies also motivate people to care about their private property rights. If someone else can influence how I use my possessions, how can I be sure I'll be able to use them when I'm in need?

This illustrates why, in profit economies, gifts and property ownership are associated with a set of rights, and many property owners jealously guard those rights. On the other hand, in gift economies, *gifts are associated with a set of responsibilities*.

One responsibility is to ensure the gift goes to the highest good. For example, a group can honor food by ensuring it goes to the hungriest person. A hungry person honors an apple much more than someone who throws it in the compost because their belly is already full.

Anyone who receives a gift also has a responsibility to the giver, and this stems from that third core spiritual practice, living in reciprocity. I get to give back to the people and nonhumans who give to me.

One aspect of this responsibility is to honor the gift, and one way to honor the gift is to make sure it goes to where it's most needed. Another way to honor the gift is to only take what is needed so that nothing is wasted. If I am collecting vines to make a basket, I make the basket only as big as I need, and I only collect the amount of vines required to make the basket.

Another aspect of responsibility is to serve the giver. If I take an apple from a tree, I am responsible for taking care of the apple tree. I might do this by watering or pruning it. If I kill a deer, I am responsible for taking care of the deer's family. I might do this by protecting the deers' habitat, protecting deer from disrespectful poachers, or educating others about respectful hunting. If I take water from a stream, I'm responsible for helping take care of the stream. I could honor the stream by protecting it from pollution or erosion.

When I take the apple, deer meat, and stream water, I enter into a relationship with those beings. In spiritual terms, I get to take care of the beings who take care of me, otherwise someday they may stop giving their gifts. In ecological terms, I need to protect the beings whom I choose to depend upon, or else someday the food and water may no longer be there.

These spiritual attitudes underlying the gift economy are not about creating poverty by ignoring one's own needs. These attitudes generate abundance by training people to act in ways that allow everyone in the nation to meet their needs indefinitely, generation after generation.

When Europeans arrived on the North American east coast several centuries ago, they did not find forests full of tangled brush. They found forests they described as "open, park-like woods," which would have made it easy for deer to get around. Various North American groups had been using carefully controlled forest fires to tend the forest and grasslands for centuries.[8]

One of the most common trees in eastern North America was the American Chestnut. The chestnut was once so abundant and its late-spring white flowers so thick in the forest canopy, people said it looked like the mountains were covered in snow in June.[9] Many people of North American healthy nations had tended the forest to encourage supportive habitats for animals and fruit and nut trees.[10]

The same fruit and nut trees that fed humans also fed animals like deer, bear, and bison which humans could hunt. This deep spiritual practice of living in reciprocity with the Earth meant that humans generated abundance that spanned countless generations. Humans honored the nonhumans who gave so many gifts in part by protecting and enriching those nonhumans' habitats, which caused them to give even more gifts.

In ecological terms, when humans increased deer habitat, the deer population grew, increasing the number of deer that humans could hunt without overhunting. This was also true for the bear, bison, fish, and other beings humans depended upon. The human gift economy interacted with the larger non-human gift economy to generate tremendous abundance for all beings.

This shows how taking care of ourselves and taking care of the Earth are the same thing. When humans don't survive by working for bosses to make money, and instead serve the nonhumans they depend upon, they protect themselves from lean times by building natural abundance and sharing it rather than hoarding.

The opposite of selfishness doesn't have to mean selflessly ignoring one's own needs. The opposite of selfishness can also mean ensuring that everybody's needs get met, humans and nonhumans alike. "Ensuring that everyone's needs get met" is also a good definition of solidarity.

When the Potawatomi, Cherokee, and other healthy nation people lived in their traditional gift economies, this was the practical and spiritual result: they generated incredible abundance. And this explains why they strongly encouraged sharing and heavily discouraged selfishness, even going so far as banishing or killing people who repeatedly insisted on behaving selfishly and showed no willingness to change, as explored in Chapter 4. Tolerating selfishness would have threatened the entire human and nonhuman gift economy. When allowed to fester, selfishness destroys abundance.

The different perspectives underlying gift economies and profit economies explain why so many European colonial traders were called selfish and greedy by the healthy-nation people they encountered. James Adair, a trader in southeast North America in the 1700s, noticed this and wrote, "they say we are covetous, because we do not give our poor relations such a share of our possessions as would keep them from want. There are but few of themselves we can blame on account of these crimes, for they are very kind and liberal to every one of their own tribe, even to the last morsel of food they enjoy."[11]

Even after my time with the Ashaninka, I still struggle to imagine living in a nation that protects everyone and generates such abundance. When sharing is the norm, everyone can routinely feel safe, as neighbors commonly support each other through difficult times. And this feeling of shared abundance and security motivates deep generosity.

On the flip side, many people in my unhealthy nation seem to have little interest in me unless they can profit. This creates an ongoing background experience of insecurity, no matter how much I have.

Kimmerer described this dichotomy. When she visits a store and sees food at low prices, she feels an urge to buy as much as she can. But when she imagined walking through a grocery store in which all the items were free, meaning she could leave with as much cheese and vegetables as she could carry, Kimmerer suddenly only felt like taking what she needed. When the food was being given, she said, "I felt self-restraint. I didn't want to take too much." In fact, this inspired an urge in her toward reciprocity: "I began thinking of what small presents I might bring to the vendors tomorrow."[12]

When a gift economy forms and everybody trusts everybody else to share, magic happens. Okanagan Jeannette Armstrong described this magic when people make decisions taking both the land and human relationships into account. I believe she was also describing life in a gift economy when she said, "Something happens inside where the material things don't have a lot of meaning, where material wealth and the securing of it or being fearful and being frightened about not having 'things' to sustain you, disappears." She called it *"the most secure feeling in the world."*[13]

This deep security enables people to find a freedom that is chronically elusive in unhealthy nations. Ohiyesa described how "Our great men not only divided their last kettle of food with a neighbor, but if great grief should come to them, such as the death of child or wife, they would voluntarily give away their few possessions and begin life over again in token of their sorrow." Unhealthy nations that encourage fearful hoarding make it difficult to respond to a personal tragedy through deliberately giving up everything and rebuilding a new life of abundance.[14]

I believe that this freedom that comes from "the most secure feeling in the world" is the result of living in a gift economy rooted in the three core spiritual practices: cultivating a practical, aware gratitude for all the gifts I receive, giving my own gifts fully, and living in reciprocity.

This also clarifies how humans can be part of nature and why so many unhealthy-nation activities are called unnatural. For example, coal mines, clear-cut forests, and toxic chemicals are all generally considered unnatural. Human behavior is only unnatural when people act selfishly without taking the needs of the Earth into account. When fishers scour the ocean floor for every last fish, developers pave new roads, or cities pile up trash in landfills, these are only unnatural because the people aren't acting with the needs of the land in mind. Selfish behavior is unnatural.

Acting with generosity towards the Earth and building up abundance is what it means for humans to be part of nature. This explains why Western Shoshone man Corbin Harney said, "native people are not separate from the environment. We are the environment!"[15]

What makes people of healthy nations part of the environment? They are part of the environment because they take nonhumans' needs – the needs of animals, plants, insects, water, soil, air, and more – into account in everything they do. Caring for all life and caring for my life is the same because I am a part of all life.

This illustrates how anyone of any nation can choose to be part of their environment or part of nature: *take the nonhumans' needs into account in everything you do.*

Stories of Sharing

Stories of deep sharing permeate the writings of European colonists as well as people of healthy nations describing their way of life.

Jesuit Christian missionaries noted that the Huron would never let someone go without food or shelter. When someone's house burned down in the Huron village Ossossane, their neighbors came together to build them a new one. They did not have markets for trading or bartering, but instead embraced hospitality, gift-giving, and ceremonial exchanges. Visitors to a village were given food and shelter for as long as they wished to stay.[16]

The Huron would publicly announce whenever someone donated a large amount towards a feast, funeral, or ceremony, and this raised the donor's status. People thus enjoyed accumulating goods so that they could give away as much as possible, and thus earn their neighbors' gratitude. Feasts were common as people sought to build up their stash of food only to give it away.[17]

The Sioux commonly modeled deep giving for their children. They would host feasts to celebrate every accomplishment. Ohiyesa wrote, "[Crazy Horse] was carefully brought up according to the tribal customs. At that period the Sioux prided themselves on the training and development of their sons and daughters, and not a step in that development was overlooked as an excuse to bring the child before the public by giving a feast in its honor. At such times the parents often gave so generously to the needy that they almost impoverished themselves, thus setting an example to the child of self-denial for the general good. His first step alone, the first word spoken, first game killed, the attainment of manhood or womanhood, each was the occasion of a feast and dance in his honor, at which the poor always benefited to the full extent of the parents' ability."[18]

When a couple was courting, their parents would celebrate this with feasts and gifts for those who had little.[19]

Ohiyesa described how parents intentionally raised children to give: "It was our belief that the love of possessions is a weakness to be overcome. Its appeal is to the material part, and if allowed its way it will in time disturb the spiritual balance of the man. Therefore the child must early learn the beauty of generosity. He is taught to give what he prizes most, and that he may taste the happiness of giving, he is made at an early age the family almoner. If a child is inclined to be grasping, or to cling to any of his little possessions, legends are related to him, telling of the contempt and disgrace falling upon the ungenerous and mean man."[20]

Crazy Horse's mother demonstrated such mentoring. When Crazy Horse was four or five years old, the band faced a severe winter, and hunters struggled to get food. His diligent father finally killed two antelopes, and the little boy promptly got on his pony and rode around inviting all the old people to come get meat.

Neither his mother nor his father had authorized this! Soon a long line formed, and by the end the mother only had enough meat for two meals. The next day, hungry young Crazy Horse asked for food, and his mother told him the old people had taken it. She said, "Remember, my son, they went home singing praises in your name, not my name or your father's. You must be brave. You must live up to your reputation." Instead of punishing her son, Crazy Horse's mother invited him to remember he had done a good thing and bravely face the consequences even if he had to suffer a little for it.[21]

The Sioux intentionally trained their children to be brave, and one reason was that brave children would be willing to share instead of acting selfishly out of fear. This brave generosity was commonly publicly acknowledged and rewarded even in adulthood. For example, each year in June, Black Elk's village held a sun dance, and they would select a warrior who had recently shown special bravery. After playing a role in the ceremony, Black Elk described what came next: "he had to give gifts to those who had least of everything, and the braver he was, the more he gave away..." They raised the status of a specially brave warrior by giving him a special ceremonial role, and then allowed him to raise his status further by giving away many things to people in need. Abundance begets abundance.[22]

I believe that helping to redistribute resources is a core leadership role in healthy nations. Martín Prechtel described how the Tzutujil Mayans had a "self-impoverished theocracy" where people "loved to get more than someone else, just so they could dress fancily and give it all away to be big." Prechtel wrote how the Tzutujil Mayans became leaders: "To get anywhere in traditional Mayan society, you had to work really hard to get wealth, get appointed to office without campaigning, and then give it all away." Each time a leader rose to a new level in their hierarchy, he or she gave away all their things so that they were equally as impoverished as everyone else.[23]

Shamans also played this role. Whenever a shaman helped someone heal from an illness, they would give the shaman a great deal of food. The shaman would feed his family from these gifts and then give the rest away to whomever needed it most.[24]

I witnessed a similar pattern while traveling in Peru. I was skeptical of every so-called shaman I encountered – except one. This shaman of a local healthy nation accepted donations for holding ayahuasca ceremonies and letting visitors stay on his land. Based on the normal amount of donations, I noticed he must be living pretty well. Then I learned from an assistant that every few weeks, he took a cab into town and distributed the money to whomever needed it. When I discovered that he helped spread abundance rather than hoard it, I was willing to trust him in a way I hadn't trusted many self-anointed Peruvian shamans.

Jesus Christ Wanted to Create a Healthy Nation that Generated Abundance for Everyone

Christians worship Jesus Christ as the sole son of God, and one of his defining qualities was his willingness to give up all his possessions so he could walk a spiritual path without distraction. A rich man once came to him and asked for guidance. Jesus asked if he'd followed the basic rules, including avoiding murder, theft, and lying. The rich man said he had, and what else was there? Jesus told him to give up all his possessions. The rich man declined, and Jesus exclaimed to his disciples, "How hardly shall they that have riches enter into the kingdom of God!" Jesus' disciples felt astonished. Jesus said, "It is easier for a camel to go through the eye of a needle, than for a rich man to enter into the kingdom of God."

His disciples could hardly believe this. Almost everyone in that nation was either rich or trying to get rich. They were so used to their nation that encouraged profiting and hoarding that they asked themselves, "Who then can be saved?" I believe Jesus' own disciples worried he was putting impossible demands on people which would keep almost everyone out of Heaven, when he was actually asking for a level of sharing that would be normal in a healthy nation![25]

Different religious and secular leaders have used different words and imagery to try to express the same core spiritual truths. I believe "living in a utopia," "living in a healthy nation," and "living in the kingdom of God" are all the same thing. All of these describe the profound satisfaction that comes from giving one's love fully in gratitude for all the gifts one receives from humans and nonhumans, while living in a nation based on sharing rather than profiting.

Creation and Creator are one, so receiving the gifts of life with deep gratitude is the same as receiving the gifts of God – the first core spiritual practice.

The second core spiritual practice is to give one's love fully without reservation, participating in Creation by giving one's own sacred gifts. How many people learn to withhold their love out of fear of losing their comforts, privileges, and possessions? How many more people would willingly stand up to abusive authorities or speak out against foolish racism or sexism if they were not afraid of losing their comforts and safety?

Unhealthy nations punish people in countless ways for behaving appropriately, and this is the result: many people learn to cling to their possessions and somehow withhold their love. Since a person's love is their own manifestation of divinity (since we're all divine beings), a person withholding their love is actually withholding their own divine nature and thus disconnected from divinity.

When Jesus Christ said that a person who trusted in riches would struggle to enter the Kingdom of God, I believe this is what he was talking about. Anyone who wishes to connect deeply with Creation and Creator must choose to give their love fully rather than selfishly cling to possessions and comforts. Fearfully clinging to one's possessions prevents a person from fully giving their love. Sadly, unhealthy nations and their profit economies encourage people to selfishly protect their possessions rather than give their love freely.

Like so many deep lessons, this practice of giving up one's possessions has nuance. Jesus Christ kept the clothes he wore. Harriet Tubman kept her gun which protected her and the runaway slaves, as explored in Chapter 16. If Jesus Christ had gone without clothes or Tubman had gone without her gun, they could not have done as much good work. When I read Ohiyesa's words that "the love of possessions is a weakness," it teaches me to act in service of what most matters to me without letting fearful attachment to my possessions get in the way. It teaches me not to let the comforts and safety of my privilege get in the way of doing meaningful work in the world.

When American Black Panthers were discussing how to reach their political goals, Don Cox suggested the basic approach: "Use what you got to get what you need."[26] When a person selfishly clings to their possessions and avoids acting in deep service, or a person only acts in service in ways that don't put their possessions at risk, the world becomes a darker place. When a person uses possessions to do important work in the world, with their focus clearly on achieving some greater good, the world becomes brighter.

Generous sharing is who we are as humans, but unhealthy nations make this difficult. Instead of routinely experiencing the "most secure feeling in the world" which comes from living in a gift economy, the majority of people in unhealthy nations focus on advancing themselves, or at least surviving, in a profit economy.

How do profit economies reward selfishness, directing and consuming people's lives? The next chapter, *Chapter 10: Profit Economies*, reveals what happens when rulers and their selfishness take hold.

Chapter 10: Profit Economies

A gift economy may seem like an impossible fantasy to many people living in unhealthy nations – not because it actually is impossible but because they have never fully experienced it. Gift economies did and still do exist. My time with the Ashaninka is just one example.

Gift economies ensure that *resources go where they're most needed*, and I believe that living in a gift economy is simply what it means to live in a utopia.

In contrast, a dystopia is any nation with a profit economy. Unlike gift economies, profit economies motivate individuals to try to get more than they give, training people to profit from their neighbors. Profit economies *move resources to people who already have them*. In these economies, the more resources a person has, the more additional resources they are able to get.

For those of us living in unhealthy nations, it may seem as if profit economies are "just the way life is," as if we have no other choice. This is not true.

Those of us working in profit economies may also assume that people without a "profit motive" would be unmotivated to work or contribute to society. This is also not true.

Beyond these misunderstandings lies a deeper problem: profit economies actively maintain the inequality and exploitation at the heart of unhealthy nations.

Healthy nations are keenly aware of this. They know that, in any nation, anybody may choose to behave selfishly. Anyone may fearfully prioritize their own needs over the wellbeing of the group and behave in ways that threaten the wellbeing of the entire community. That is why many healthy nations specifically train children to understand what would happen if they act selfishly as a routine way of life. Robin Kimmerer illustrated this in her description of the Windigo, a widely known monster among the Anishinaabe.

Traditionally, children would hear stories of the Windigo around a fire so they would know the trouble it brought. Kimmerer said, "The Windigo is a human being who has become a cannibal monster. Its bite will transform victims into cannibals too… Windigo is the name for that within us which cares more for its own survival than for anything else." Steve Pitt described the Windigo as a person who becomes so selfish that they can never be satisfied.[1]

One person's selfish behavior can easily inspire selfishness in others. I believe this is what the Anishinaabe mean when they say that the Windigo monster can bite others and turn them into cannibals too.

Anybody who likes to share knows how hard it is to share with selfish people. Gift economies are amazing, but they only work when everybody participates by sharing. When a few people start to selfishly hoard, the group faces a challenge: do they somehow stop the selfish hoarding, either by convincing the hoarders to share or by banishing them? Or do they tolerate selfish hoarding within the nation, allowing some people's selfishness to encourage selfishness in others and threatening the entire gift economy?

Unfortunately, rulers consistently behave very selfishly, exploiting the people they rule in countless ways. Rulers take great wealth for themselves by forcing their nation to adopt some form of profit economy where people are required to tolerate or engage in exploitative behavior to survive. Instead of embracing gift economies that reward generous sharing, unhealthy nations embrace profit economies that reward selfish taking.

Tragically, even successfully making huge amounts of money does not reduce fear-based selfishness. Often the opposite occurs: people just keep taking more and more for themselves long after they have enough.

The deep security that comes from neighbors reliably sharing with each other in a healthy nation cannot be bought in an unhealthy nation. Employees can be hired or enslaved, and riches can be stockpiled, but true security is always out of reach – after all, what happens when the employees can't be paid or the slaves run away? As each person responds to this dynamic by trying to make as much money as they can, everybody suffers, with impoverished people and nonhumans suffering the most.

A key aspect of a profit economy is that people are trained to get more than they give. This is the definition of the word profit: a gain that exceeds the cost. A profit economy that encourages each person to take more than they give will never generate deep security for anyone, not even for the rich.

Yet in unhealthy nations, just about everyone at every wealth level – rich, poor, and in between – wants to be richer. The idea that getting as wealthy as possible will bring relief from the continual anxiety of living in an unhealthy nation is a lie.

And it is a deeply disturbing lie, because when unhealthy nations train people to seek safety by profiting from their neighbors, they are training people for the opposite of what would really bring safety, which is creating an economy where giving is the norm. Training people to profit from their neighbors trains them to perpetuate the unhealthy nation, even without any further pressure from rulers. This keeps people trapped and continuously motivated to get more and more.

Thus, once established, profit economies are self-sustaining. Trapped in a profit economy, the majority of people end up playing some active role in keeping other people trapped. Like so many other aspects of unhealthy nations, once this pattern is established, it tends to self-perpetuate – until enough people see the lie and choose a better way.

I call this dynamic *systemic selfishness*, where rulers impose profit economies that train everyone for selfishness. The entire economic system is geared to encourage selfishness, training everybody to be as selfish as the ruler. Each individual can choose for themselves whether to act with generosity, but the overall effect is to make selfishness a common quality. In practice, communism, capitalism, socialism, libertarianism, and other widely-studied economic forms are all variations of a profit economy, organized to allow rulers to exploit the rest and to reward selfish behavior.

Hidden behind the lie of profit economies is a tragic truth: while gift economies generate true abundance, profit economies don't generate profit. Individuals within a profit economy may profit, but when all the costs are factored in – including anxiety, despair, pollution, abuse, and all kinds of human and nonhuman suffering – profit economies destroy far more wealth than they produce. The overall gain does not exceed the cost.

Profit economies are simply exploitative scams that just about everyone, in one way or another, is forced to participate in and perpetuate.

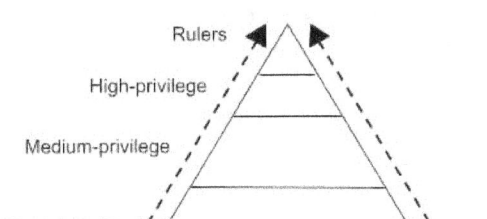 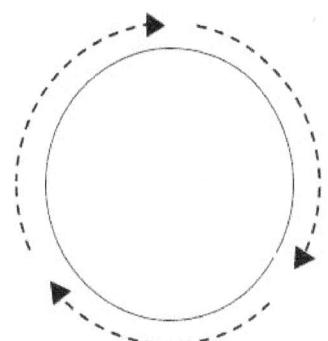

How does the economy move resources?

Two Kinds of Profit Economy: Market Economies and Command Economies

I remember studying economics in college, and I often felt frustrated at the endless unnecessary complexities and definitions. But like with chemistry, math, art, or any other subject, economics can be simple and straightforward when it is boiled down to its essence. Anyone can understand the essence of economics and recognize the basic ways that people can take advantage of each other while pretending not to. That is what this chapter is about: getting to the essence of economics in unhealthy nations.

There are basically two kinds of profit economy: market and command. Most unhealthy nations have some mix of these.

Command economies are simple: an authority figure gives an order, and a trapped person obeys the order or gets severely punished. Militaries, chattel slave plantations, and prisons are examples of command economies. Workers don't choose their bosses, and if workers choose not to work, they receive direct, severe abuse.

In market economies, workers can often choose their boss and even their type of job. Anybody has the choice not to work. Unless they are independently wealthy, people who don't work for money face poverty, social isolation, shame, and worse. Whereas the fear of physical punishment motivates workers in command economies, the fear of poverty motivates compliance in market economies.

Of course, anyone who disobeys authorities may be sent to prison, and thus fear of severe physical punishment motivates obedience in any type of economy.

Market Economies – Desperation Management – Obey or Face Poverty

In command economies, workers are severely punished for leaving their designated working and living spaces. In market economies, workers have more flexibility to move and choose their work. To maintain a compliant workforce despite this flexibility, authorities maintain people in a state of financial desperation so that working an unsatisfying job for an uncaring boss will seem like the best available option.

Stories of Dependency

Stories of people working in unsatisfying jobs are not difficult to find. When journalists went to a small village in Indonesia, they found a man named Nurhadi who contributed to clear-cutting forests by selling charcoal made from cut trees. One villager noted, "Nobody gets rich from charcoal furnaces. We do this to have food on our plate…" Nurhadi didn't like cutting down forests, and he told a government official, "If you can provide farming land or other opportunities, I'd quit tomorrow."

Other men described how dangerous it was cutting down trees, but they saw little alternative. One man said, "This is a high risk job, but my children need to eat."[2]

Financial desperation commonly leads people to accept unpleasant or unsafe work. One sex worker named Deedee acknowledged this when she said, "If I can't get a job I still gotta feed myself. That's the constant scenario that's always going in your mind. Where am I going to eat? Where am I going to sleep? How am I going to get some clothes? You cannot even think anywhere past that because it takes all of that to just live when you don't have a job, you don't have insurance…"[3]

When someone has to beg uncaring people for the chance to serve them just to survive, this is humiliating and can cause people to lose self-esteem. Deedee said, "It's just all those factors that drive you to have unprotected sex, to not value yourself, to not feel good about yourself to where you want to protect yourself from getting [AIDS]." This shows low-privilege entitlement, discussed in Chapter 30, where people develop low self-worth and start to believe that their terrible situation reflects something inherently wrong in them.

Anyone could seek to end or transform a society where rich people or government leaders can create or destroy jobs and livelihoods at will. Instead, when people are financially desperate and see no alternative, they may adopt the ideologies of their abusers. Thus workers may demand a chance to serve a master just to survive. One petition by Russian workers to their government in 1906 acknowledged the master-worker dynamic: "Owing to unemployment, numberless workers' families are now without bread. The workers do not want charity, or doles. We demand work. The masters refuse to give us work."[4] In protests in Bangladesh in 2014, workers marched with signs saying "Chakri Pai!" ('we demand work!').[5] In the United States in 1930, both white and black Americans marched with signs saying "We Demand Work or Wages."[6]

These examples show people demanding a chance to serve their masters instead of seeking freedom from masters. This is ridiculous! Also, it is simply normal when people accept the selfishness and abuse at the heart of their nation as legitimate.

Desperation Motivates People to Consent to Abuse

In response to rampant sexual assault, some people teach seminars on how to have consensual sex. They teach that sex is consensual when both people intentionally, consciously choose to have sex. For sex to be consensual, both people must say "yes," and neither person says "no."

This is beautiful, and I strongly support these teachers. However, this understanding of consent isn't really clear in nations that keep people in financial desperation. Ultimately, the point of keeping people financially desperate is to make them consent to their own abuse. I call this *coerced consent*, where people say "yes" and willingly accept exploitation because it's the best option they have.

In some cases, the beneficiaries are also the ones who keep people desperate. For example, Chapter 27 reviews how West Virginia coal mining companies would threaten a family with eviction if the husband became injured and couldn't work, and the only way to avoid eviction was for the wife to submit to rape by mining bosses and guards. Many miners' wives thus allowed themselves to be raped to support their family. In one sense, the women consented to the rape: they knowingly left their homes and intentionally walked to the rape rooms. Obviously, the women loathed this, and they went to the rape rooms because it was the only option they saw for keeping their family safe. They consented to their own abuse because the coal company kept them in desperate straits.

Sometimes consent is even less clear. Many sex workers have sex with undesirable people to get money to survive. Putting aside people who are sex-trafficked and coerced into prostitution, let us consider people who choose prostitution as the best available option for financial survival. Some sex workers may enjoy the sex sometimes, but often they do not. When sex workers intentionally, consciously choose to seek out clients for paid sex even when they don't really want to, is it actually consensual?

In this case, the sex workers' clients are usually not the ones who keep the sex worker in desperation. Once a person becomes desperate, they are open to abuse by anyone who will help them survive. It helps me to imagine all the richest corporate owners sitting around a table, deciding to keep workers in desperation. None of the owners can predict which worker will serve which owner, but together the owners know that they'll have plenty of willing workers if all of them are kept in desperate straits.

This same pattern isn't unique to sex workers; it is pervasive in unhealthy nations. Do people consent to having an unsatisfying job for uncaring bosses? When job applicants get a job offer and say "yes," and then intentionally go to work each day, are they consenting? Or are they tolerating an exploitative situation because it's the best option they see to survive? What does consent even mean in the context of abusive nations? This is why, in the 1800s, getting a job and earning wages just to survive was called "wage slavery." Unlike chattel slavery where a person cannot choose their abusive owner, in wage slavery, people can choose their abusive boss, assuming they're lucky enough to find a boss willing to hire them.

If it seems extreme to call these both slavery, consider military theorist Carl von Clausewitz's definition of war. He said, "War… is an act of violence intended to compel our opponent to fulfill our will."[7] In wage slavery, chattel slavery, military slavery, and prison slavery, authorities use various kinds of violence, including physical punishments and the threat of poverty, to compel laborers to follow orders. Unhealthy nations simply represent unfinished wars, where the victors continue to impose violence on the losers, sometimes for millennia.

Ultimately, when authorities successfully keep a large number of people desperate, they are trying to make people consent to their own abuse. Workers walk to jobs they loathe, women walk to rooms knowing they'll be raped, prisoners work for pennies per hour, kids walk to boring school to avoid punishment and get a good job someday. Some people watch TV, play with phones, drink alcohol, and seek other distractions to ignore how deeply dissatisfying such a nation feels. Others count how many minutes remain in their shift, how many days remain until retirement, or how much money they're making.

All this is why, when the seminar teachers discuss consensual sex, they also describe how important it is for each partner to verify that the other person truly desires sex so that it's fun for both people. This desire is what's missing when people consent to something that they don't actually want.

When workers and employers both pretend that workers willingly consent to their job, they can also maintain the pretense that they live in freedom. Soviet East German minister for state security Erich Milke once said, "The [German Democratic Republic] is a state that guarantees its citizens freedom, democracy, and basic human rights."[8] On Human Rights Day, Canadian prime minister Justin Trudeau noted that, "defending human rights and democracy has always been, and will continue to be, a priority for Canada… Today, on Human Rights Day, we reaffirm our commitment to building a world where everyone is treated with dignity."[9]

When people learn to ignore the abuse in their nation, and ignore the coerced consent which is pervasive in their economy, it is easy to believe that they are actually free. Authorities willingly reinforce this misconception.

How Do Authorities Manage People's Financial Desperation?

Authorities use a vast number of techniques to make people feel financially desperate no matter how much money they have. Workers may fear not having enough money during retirement, or may not be able to afford health care, especially if access to health care is tied to a job as it often is in the United States. Inflation continuously saps the value of previous savings, meaning the money instantly becomes less valuable starting the moment it's earned.

Banks and landlords regulate the prices of houses and rental units, calculating the proportion of people's monthly income that they can afford to pay in mortgage or rent. This debt-to-income ratio means house prices and rental prices always increase at least as much as people's wages, keeping workers from "getting ahead."

Advertisers trick people into wanting unnecessary and expensive things. Authorities may make the drawbacks of poverty arbitrarily terrible, including putting poor people in prison, forcing poor people to eat less nutritious food, taking away the children of poor people who struggle to provide a safe, clean home, and more. Property taxes force people to pay money to keep even the houses they own free and clear. One of my great-grandmothers lost a home she owned without debt in the midst of the US Great Depression. She was already very poor in the midst of a depression, but at least she owned her own home. Then when she couldn't pay property taxes, she didn't even have that.

These techniques also work to make relatively high-paid people feel insecure and desperate to work. Multiple surveys have found that about half of Americans making greater than $100,000 per year reported living paycheck-to-paycheck. One quarter of people making $175,000 per year described themselves as "very poor," "poor," or "getting by but things are tight," even though they made more money than 94% of Americans.[10,11]

Prison labor also keeps wages low and workers desperate. Bernard Callegari is an ex-inmate union organizer in New York. He described what it's like seeking work after leaving prison: "People who've been incarcerated have been conditioned to work for 35 or 45 cents an hour–and you're taught to believe that you don't even deserve that. So if you've just been working for 45 cents an hour, you are made to feel as though, Who are you to say you don't want to work for $15? On top of that, you've got your parole requirements, and that means you almost don't care about the pay because if you don't get a job, and you don't keep your job, you're going to be in violation and potentially sent back to jail…"[12]

Callegari heard one employer note that ex-convicts are some of the best workers. He described a school-to-prison-to-work pipeline and "how it manufactures a lack of self-worth, that it creates this workforce of people who will work for anything, and even put themselves in danger at work, just because they're glad to have a job at all." Thus abuse in prison may continue to generate financial desperation and coerced consent long after people leave prison behind.

Shaming poor people is a major factor motivating them to do unsatisfying work. I have found many people who assume that poor people must not contribute much to society, associating someone's income with their worth or how much good they do in the world. People may be shamed for relying on government support programs, or they'll be called lazy if they don't take unsafe or unsatisfying jobs even when they could. Shaming the poor and unemployed motivates people to accept unsatisfying work.

The poor are often treated abusively, motivating them to work to avoid abuse. Authorities may allow crime and drugs in the poor parts of town, allow the police to mistreat poor people in a variety of ways, underfund schools in the poor districts, and allow factory pollution to be worse in poor areas. They may mistreat the homeless, endlessly moving them around, arresting them, or forcing them into prisons. This motivates poor people to work harder to make more money to escape abusive poverty, and trains the middle classes to keep working hard to avoid this shame and misery.

All these techniques contribute to trapping people in financial desperation, but authorities can get much more devious. Of course they can; once a nation tolerates selfishness, human creativity allows selfishness to manifest in infinite ways. So, how can devious authorities manage an entire economy to maintain workers in financial desperation?

The Financial Whipsaw – Managing an Economy to Maintain Financial Desperation

The wealthy have a conundrum: they want to make a lot of money, and so they want to increase production and consumption. The trouble is, as the economy grows, workers might start to be in demand. If workers have multiple job options, they can start to bargain for increased pay, better hours, respectful treatment by their boss, and more.

So, how can the wealthy balance this desire to get rich while minimizing workers' relative power so that they'll take whatever jobs the rich give them?

One major mechanism is the *financial whipsaw*, where financial leaders intentionally create temporary economic recessions in order to increase unemployment. With fewer jobs, workers feel less able to bargain for better wages or safer conditions, and the power relationship between the rich and the workers remains intact. The goal is for the economy to recover even while workers remain desperate. Once workers start to have bargaining power and increase their wages, the financial whipsaw is activated, causing the economy to slow and workers to become desperate, repeating the cycle again.

The purpose of the financial whipsaw is to *maximize overall economic production while minimizing workers' wages and bargaining power*.

The financial whipsaw helps maintain artificial scarcity, a core mechanism for keeping people desperate to work in the midst of abundance. That is, regardless of how much material wealth a nation generates, authorities seek to keep the masses of people from receiving that abundance so they will be continuously willing to work unsatisfying jobs in service of their bosses.

Occasionally corporate owners acknowledge this openly. Australian ceo Tim Gurner owned approximately US $598 million in 2023, and yet he complained publicly about how workers were insufficiently grateful to work for him:

> I think the problem that we've had is that… people decided they didn't really want to work so much anymore through COVID and that has had a massive issue on productivity…

> We need to see unemployment rise. Unemployment has to jump 40-50% in my view. We need to see pain in the economy. We need to remind people that they work for the employer, not the other way around…

> We've got to kill that attitude, and that has to come through hurting the economy, which [is] what the whole... world is trying to do. The governments around the world are trying to increase unemployment to get that to some sort of normality.
>
> And we're seeing it. I think every employer now is seeing it. I mean there is definitely massive layoffs going off. People might not be talking about it but people are definitely laying people off and we're starting to see less arrogance in the employment market...[13]

Setting interest rates is one mechanism by which governments and central banks manage the economy and unemployment. Central banks can set interest rates that affect the cost of borrowing money in an economy. When interest rates are low, borrowing money becomes cheap which stimulates borrowing and economic activity. When interest rates rise, borrowing money becomes expensive because the interest payment on the loan is higher, and economic activity slows down.

Many central banks claim to have at least two legal mandates: maintaining "price stability" and "maximum sustainable employment."[14] High inflation reduces the value of everybody's savings and income, so on the surface this policy seems fine.

However, there is a trick. Prices can rise for many reasons. Let us consider an imaginary table company that buys wood, rents a manufacturing building, hires employees to turn that wood into tables, and then sells the tables. Let us imagine that the business executives are able to sell their tables at a price where their revenue is about 10% higher than all their expenses, so they make a 10% profit.

The company's owners could feel pressure to raise their table prices for a lot of reasons outside employers' or employees' control. The cost of wood could go up, or the cost of electricity to run the machines. Rent or maintenance costs could increase. If these business costs increased, the business would either need to accept lower profits if it keeps table prices the same, or increase table prices to keep profits at 10%.

Employees' wages are another business cost. If employees are able to get a higher wage, then the business owners would likewise need to either accept lower profits or raise the cost of the tables they sell.

Finally, the owners could just raise the prices of the tables they sell even if their costs don't change, making their profit level 15%, 20%, or as high as they feel like raising prices. If business owners face less competition, they may start raising prices because customers have nowhere else to go to buy similar products. The extra profit goes straight to the business owners.

This simple example shows that prices in an economy can rise for a lot of reasons. However, when central banks talk about maintaining price stability and preventing excessive inflation, they focus on minimizing a single driver of price increases: wage growth. Central banks essentially focus on keeping prices stable by minimizing wages.

This is evident in a key metric central banks use to decide when to raise interest rates, called *NAIRU*. Australia's central bank defines NAIRU this way: "Historically, a key challenge for policymakers is to *achieve a low rate of unemployment without fuelling excessive increases in wages growth* and inflation. Economists call the lowest rate of unemployment that achieves this the 'non-accelerating inflation rate of unemployment,' or NAIRU."[15] (emphasis added) The central bank clearly states their goal of keeping unemployment low while minimizing wage growth, and NAIRU plays a key part in their strategy.

In practice, what does it mean for workers when unemployment is low? The unemployment rate is the percentage of unemployed people compared to everyone who has or wants a job. Imagine if 20 people want a job, 19 have work and 1 is unemployed and seeking work. The unemployment rate is 5%. So, a low unemployment rate means there are lots of jobs and only a few people without a job – exactly the situation where workers have leverage and can bargain with employers for higher wages and better working conditions. In other words, when unemployment is low, workers are not desperate and feel more able to leave unsatisfying jobs or ask for a raise.

Thus, by focusing on the "NAIRU," central bank officials are actually focusing on exactly that level of employment where workers begin to have bargaining power. By preventing unemployment levels from falling below the NAIRU level, they prevent workers as a whole from ever being able to bargain with their bosses.

In practice, for these central banks, "maximum sustainable employment" is the highest employment level that does not result in wage growth. Central banks keep economic production as high as possible without improving workers' bargaining power.

So, what happens when the economy gets to that low employment level, and workers start to bid up wages? Then central bank officials claim they are concerned with inflation, and they begin to raise interest rates which causes a recession, which causes businesses to fire workers. When unemployment increases, workers become more desperate to find a job or avoid losing their job, and many workers will thus accept longer hours or worse pay.

Sometimes central bank officials use euphemisms or technical jargon to debate how much economic pain to cause and when, and often describe rising unemployment as a necessary unavoidable consequence of their actions rather than the goal, even though rising unemployment is a necessary consequence of raising interest rates.

For example, at a US Federal Reserve meeting in 1996, Janet Yellen noted, "The primary problem that confronts us is that labor markets are already tight… If widespread pressures of this type emerge, it seems likely that firms eventually will be forced to bid up wages to retain workers and then pass through higher unit labor costs to prices…" A "tight labor market" is one with low unemployment where employees can bargain for higher wages. Clearly Yellen is focused on the wage component of business costs.[16]

Central bank officials consistently link wage growth and inflation as if wage growth were the primary driver of inflation, as in this comment by Jerome Powell: "If you look at the data over the last quarter, what you see is stronger than expected growth, a tighter than expected labor market and higher than expected inflation…"[17]

Of course, central bankers do not wish to raise interest rates and slow the economy if other factors cause price increases.

Central bankers are clear that they do not want to slow the economy if issues besides wage increases are causing prices to rise. A 2023 statement by US central bank official Neel Kashkari makes this clear, where he said that if inflation was due to war, government spending, supply chain disruptions, or other factors, "we don't need to overreact." In other words, the Federal Reserve does not want to slow the economy by raising interest rates for any of these other reasons. However, he said, "now wage growth is at a level that it actually is too high to be consistent with our 2 percent inflation target." This explains why the Federal Reserve strongly increased interest rates in 2022.[18]

Central bankers thus have worked to only cause recessions and deliberately increase unemployment when it reaches this NAIRU level because that is when workers have bargaining power and can get higher wages. The following graph shows interest rates and unemployment rates in the US from the 1970s to the 2020s. The blue line, labeled "Noncyclical Rate of Unemployment" is similar to NAIRU level. The red line measures unemployment, and the green line shows the interest rate set by the Federal Reserve. Clearly whenever unemployment gets near the NAIRU level – that is, when employees might start to have bargaining power – officials begin to raise interest rates as they did in the late 1970s, late 1980s, mid 1990s, late 1990s, mid 2000s, late 2010s, and 2022. In each case except the mid-1990s, unemployment increased substantially after the US central bank increased interest rates. The rate rise in 2022 is already showing signs of increasing the unemployment level.

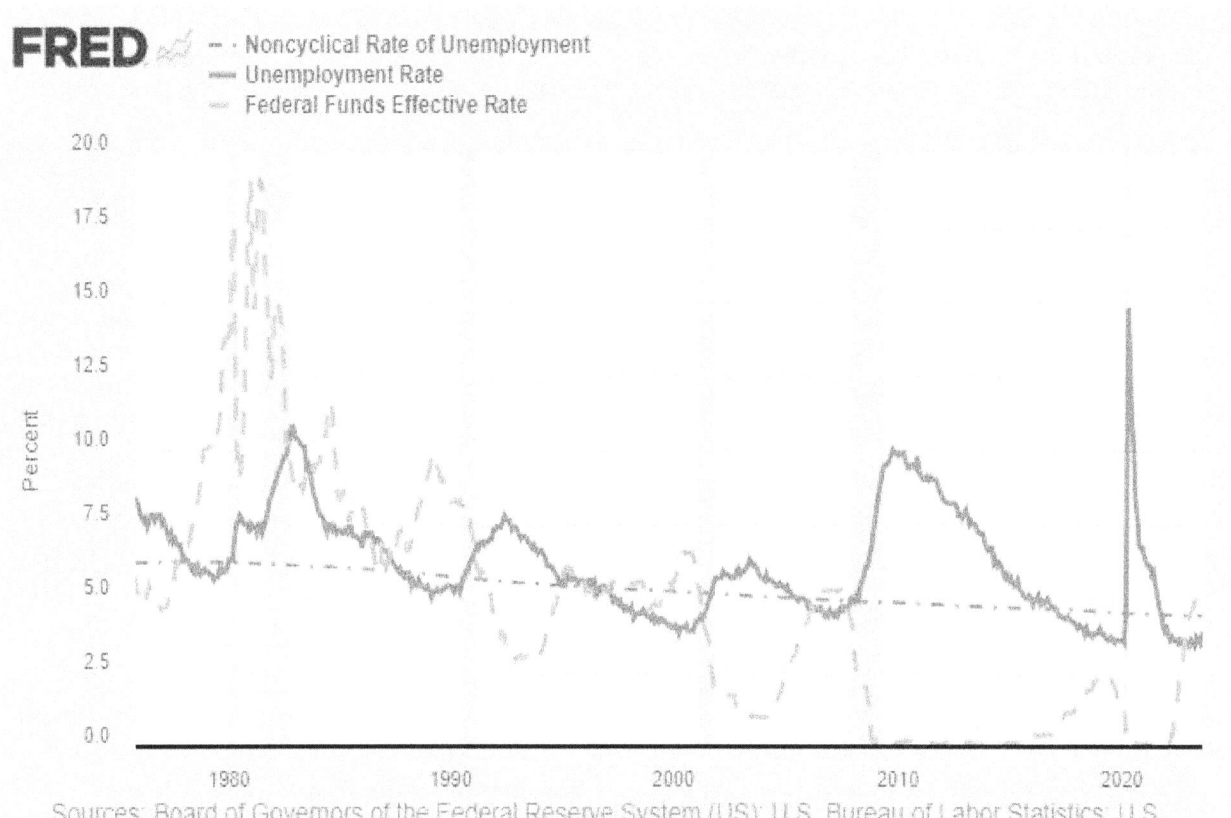

Comparison of non-cyclical rate of employment (equivalent to NAIRU, blue, dot-dash line), unemployment rate (red, solid line), and federal funds effective rate (the interest rate, green, dashed line). Whenever unemployment gets near the NAIRU level (when the red line approaches the blue line) – that is, when employees might start to have bargaining power – officials begin to raise interest rates (green line). In each case except the mid-1990s, unemployment increased substantially after the US central bank increased interest rates.[19]

This graph shows how US central bank officials focus on wage growth as the primary driver of inflation whether or not it actually is. In reality, prices often increase for another reason: price gouging. Analyst Servaas Storm calculated that between 2020 (2nd quarter) and 2022 (4th quarter), US private industry made more than $500 billion every three months in additional profits solely from raising prices without an associated increase in costs.[20] This truth – that corporate price gouging caused a substantial amount of inflation – was ignored by the central bank but acknowledged by corporate executives in public conversations with their investors.

In 2022, Hershey ceo Michele Buck noted, "Pricing will be an important lever for us this year and is expected to drive most of our growth."[21] In other words, Hershey did not just raise prices to keep the same profit level; they were able to increase prices as a source of profit growth. The cfo of Kelogg's, Amit Banati, made a similar remark: "Most of our – if not all – of our net sales growth for 2022 would be driven by price/mix."[22]

Thus US central bank officials, like many central banks around the world, go through the motions of maintaining price stability, while their actual goal is to minimize wages as corporate profits push prices higher.

This illustrates how rulers can manage an entire economy to maintain workers in a place of financial desperation, too scared of poverty to seek a better job or a raise.

Authorities' willingness to temporarily slow the economy also illustrates why selfishness rather than greed is the problem in profit economies. A person who is greedy will keep taking more for themselves no matter what. When authorities cause temporary economic recessions, they are slightly reducing their own wealth to maintain their power over workers. The long-term control of workers is more important than short-term profit, because without the social control – due to keeping workers financially desperate and many other techniques – they cannot profit. When people allow selfishness in their nation, this kind of deep manipulation is one of many terrible results.

One Purpose of Desperation Management: Compelling Poor People to Fight

Keeping people financially desperate does not just compel them to take unsatisfying or poor paying jobs. It also compels people to risk their lives in the police or military when they wouldn't otherwise.

One friend of mine, whom I'll call Jon, was arrested in New York City in 2013. He spoke with one of the arresting police officers and learned why she joined the police force. She told him she grew up in a poor family in the projects. She knew a lot of people who were dying or going to jail or using drugs. She told him that joining the police was a way to escape this life.[23]

William Scott of Peterborough, New Hampshire was a lieutenant who fought against the British in the American revolutionary war. He noted why he fought: "I was a Shoemaker, & got my living by my Labor. When this Rebellion came on, I saw some of my Neighbors got into Commission, who were no better than myself. I was very ambitious…" Scott recognized that if higher-ranking officers died, he could rise through the ranks, saying, "These Sir! were the only Motives of my entering into the Service; for as to the Dispute between Great Britain & the Colonies, I know nothing of it."[24]

The US military and politicians are very aware that financial desperation motivates many soldiers to join the military. This was evident in a story from 2010, when Navy seaman Don Burdette won millions of dollars in a lottery. He was in the middle of a 4-year contract, but the Navy released him, and all the military branches have processes for releasing soldiers who somehow strike it rich. Coast Guard spokesman lieutenant Paul Rhynard said this makes good sense, as the military no longer has any leverage, noting, "He's not worried about whether he loses his job or not."[25]

US politicians take care to maintain financial desperation to maintain military recruitment numbers. In 2022, US president Biden considered forgiving college debt and many Republicans opposed this, questioning whether it would affect military recruitment levels. One letter by 19 Republicans noted, "By forgiving such a wide swath of loans for borrowers, you are removing any leverage the Department of Defense maintained as one of the fastest and easiest ways to pay for higher education… As the services try to adopt unique approaches to tackle their recruiting challenges, including historic bonuses, it feels like their legs are being cut out from underneath them…" One politician noted, "I'm very concerned that the deeply flawed and unfair policy of blanket student loan forgiveness will also weaken our most powerful recruiting tool at the precise moment we are experiencing a crisis in military recruiting."[26]

This illustrates a common theme: *the best way to control people is to keep abusing them*. College costs are already high, and college debt is already a major burden in the United States because it cannot be discharged in bankruptcy. However, it can be very difficult to earn above-median income without a university degree, so many Americans accept the high college prices and debt anyway, another factor causing many people to feel desperate to get a job. US military and political authorities use this abusive situation to motivate financially desperate people to join the military to risk their lives in wars that profit those same devious authorities.

Rulers have been motivating poor people to fight their wars in one way or another for millennia. Sometimes they impose a draft, punishing those who don't fight. Other times, religious authorities like the Catholic Church may offer divine "forgiveness" in exchange for fighting.[27] This chapter shows how rulers trap people in poverty to motivate them to die for the rich. This scam has been going on for millennia. It's time to end it!

Market Economies Without Financial Desperation

Keeping people trapped in financial desperation does not just give masters economic control. It gives them political control. When a person is financially desperate and afraid to lose their job, they are less likely to become politically active because their employer might fire them. If other employers find out and blacklist them, they might not just lose their job but lose their career.

Thus in market economies, keeping people financially desperate is a way of controlling and minimizing people's political activity.

The best evidence for this comes from asking: what happens when a government decides to maintain continuous full employment or guarantee people a job? If workers never feared losing their job, or knew they could always find another job, they might be more willing to become politically active.

In 1943, Michal Kalecki noticed that governments could easily increase employment without increasing inflation. The government could simply hire unemployed people to do productive work, but this would remove a major source of leverage that business owners have over employees, or governments have over citizens: the ability to fire people from their job.

At the beginning of the 1930s, the German government maintained enough unemployment to keep workers desperate for a job, but this changed when the Nazi government decided to maximize economic production. Soon unemployment dropped to zero, and they had a severe scarcity of workers.

When workers didn't fear job loss, the government and corporate leaders needed another way to scare people away from political activism. Kalecki described the transition: "Finally, 'discipline in the factories' and 'political stability' under full employment are maintained by the 'new order', which ranges from suppression of the trade unions to the concentration camp. Political pressure replaces the economic pressure of unemployment."[28]

The Germans put dissidents in concentration camps. They abolished non-approved trade unions. In general, directly or indirectly, they punished people severely for political activism. This minimized the amount of political activism even though workers were not afraid of losing their jobs.

The USSR faced a similar trouble when it guaranteed full employment in its Constitution approved in 1936: "Citizens of the U.S.S.R. have the right to work, that is, are guaranteed the right to employment and payment for their work in accordance With its quantity and quality."[29] And while the Soviet Constitution seems to have been widely ignored, on this point it was upheld: workers were guaranteed work.

The Soviet government wanted high production but it also wanted to scare workers into political compliance. While the Soviet Constitution also guaranteed freedom of speech in Article 125, this was severely limited by Soviet laws against anti-Soviet propaganda and agitation. Under Stalin's reign, article 58-10 of the Penal Code of Soviet Russia forbade any anti-Soviet "agitation or propaganda." Earlier iterations of the law focused on attempts to overthrow the state, but by the late 1920s, the law forbade speech or publication of any message that "weakened" the state, or represented criticism of its political or economic gains.[30]

Aleksandr Solzhenitsyn described how pervasive Soviet speech control was: "Who among us has not experienced its all-encompassing embrace? In all truth, there is no step, thought, action, or lack of action under the heavens which could not be punished by the heavy hand of Article 58."[31] Those convicted were sentenced to many years of hard labor and possibly other punishments, including to their family. As one example, artist Kondrashev-Ivanov attended a literary gathering where he listened to a reading of a "counter-revolutionary" novel. He and everyone else who listened with him were sentenced to 25 years of corrective labor.[32] People were arrested for making politically incorrect jokes, songs, and poems, as well as writing to foreign organizations with supposedly "libelous" reports about life in the Soviet Union.[33]

These examples from Nazi Germany and the Soviet Union make clear the political purpose of unemployment and keeping people financially desperate: keeping workers financially desperate is about maintaining control. When authorities decide to operate a market economy with full employment, they must find other ways of maintaining political control.

Command Economies – Obey or Else

Authorities' underlying attitude in market economies is "find a way to serve us, or enjoy your poverty." Workers don't legally have to have a job, but they face desperate poverty if they don't find a way to serve some master somewhere. However, the worst punishment for disobedience is usually being fired. In command economies, the attitude is simpler: "Obey my order, or I will punish you." Workers in these situations generally do not choose their boss and are physically punished if they do not follow orders.

For example, in US chattel slavery before the US Civil War, if a slave did not pick enough cotton in a day, the boss would whip them severely to motivate higher performance the next day.[34] When Columbus returned to the Caribbean and enslaved the Arawaks, he required them to provide a certain amount of gold or cotton every 3 months. Those who did not meet the quota would have an ear or nose cut off.[35]

Militaries are command economies as well. When there is a draft, people are forced to join. Even when people volunteer, militaries commonly do not let soldiers leave at will, especially for the first several years after joining. Soldiers commonly don't choose their commanding officer and are imprisoned if they disobey orders.

Command economies and market economies can exist within the same unhealthy nation. Each chattel slave plantation, military base, or prison might operate as a command economy where the master orders enslaved people to work and punishes those who don't. However, people living outside these facilities may work in a market economy and use their money to buy goods produced from within the command economies. Some people in command economies are paid, such as soldiers. Others may not be paid or are only paid in some situations, like chattel slaves.

Every unhealthy nation has at least some people trapped in command economies. This allows authorities to extract labor even from unwilling workers and scare the rest into being glad for what they have.

Financial Desperation and Nature Disconnection

This perspective on profit economies shows why so few people in unhealthy nations are deeply connected with nature. In healthy nations, people depend on that close connection with nature to survive. In unhealthy nations, a person's survival depends on maintaining their position in a profit economy. Whether a person is avoiding poverty or some other punishment, a deep connection with nature simply isn't needed and may take energy and time that many workers have in short supply. Authorities also have good reason to keep people from developing a deep connection with nature: if a person could rely on the gifts of the Earth to survive, they wouldn't be so dependent on having a job in a profit economy.

In market economies, people depend on earning money to buy food and shelter. In command economies, authorities provide food and shelter. If people learned how to acquire their own food and shelter directly from the Earth, they wouldn't depend on the human profit economy to provide these things, and dropping out might seem more feasible.

The Root Cultural Disease and its Individual Manifestations

The root disease in unhealthy nations occurs when a few people rule over everybody else, imposing law and choosing how the law is enforced. They forbid people from standing for a culture of mutual respect.

This cultural disease manifests in individual people in a large variety of ways, including selfishness, entitlement, ignorance, low self-esteem, cowardice, despair, isolation, legal or illegal drug abuse, nature disconnection, self-distraction, chronic muscular tension, limited breathing, racism, sexism, and more. These are simply common individual symptoms of that root cultural disease where a few people rule over everybody else. Different people may adopt different hurtful qualities in different ways if they are not careful. All these personal manifestations of unhealthy nations will be explored throughout this book.

Unhealthy nations reward individuals for acting selfishly, and they punish people who don't. This cultural disease shapes the behavior of individuals and thus the cultural disease becomes an individual disease. Profit economies, and especially market economies, train people for deep selfishness. When a person is expected to profit to survive, and sharing (called "charity") becomes an afterthought at most, selfishness becomes the norm. Rulers take so much more than they need, and their selfishness spreads throughout the nation until it simply becomes the default attitude among many people.

Top rulers and political authorities do not need to secretly "pull the strings" to make terrible things happen. Once a nation becomes unhealthy because rulers take over and begin imposing laws, they only need to maintain a culture that consistently rewards and encourages deep selfishness and deep spiritual wounding. Thus, rulers create economies that create systemic selfishness, comparable to systemic racism or systemic sexism which will be explored in later chapters.

For example, rulers do not generally "order" many husbands to abuse their wives, or many bosses to overwork their workers, or many farmers to overdraw groundwater. Rulers simply create and maintain the cultural conditions – such as by imposing economies that reward selfishness – that encourage deep selfishness and spiritual wounding. When people cannot free themselves from rulers, many will embrace selfish or self-centered attitudes in response.

Any individual may choose to embrace generosity instead of selfishness, and many people may do this on a small scale such as adults feeding their children for free, or joining volunteer service organizations. However, embracing deep sharing within an unhealthy nation is very hard. To sustain deep sharing in any culture requires more than one person acting alone; it takes a village. And when the village is already unhealthy, everyone is already engaging in various forms of selfish behavior to secure their own safety and comfort.

Jesus Christ's story shows how rare and difficult it is to embrace deep sharing once selfishness has taken hold. When he said giving up one's possessions was a prerequisite for entering the Kingdom of God, his disciples asked, "Who then can be saved?"

Already two thousand years ago, selfishness had already become so normalized in western Asia and southern Europe that even Jesus' own disciples could not imagine a nation based on deep sharing.[36]

Romans could not free themselves from abusive rulers. When the nation could not heal that root trouble, the cultural disease manifested in individuals in all the usual ways. This chapter explored one of these symptoms, where nations with rulers impose profit economies and thus encourage a deep selfishness in everybody.

Any individual and any group may still choose to share and give generously, and this book will explore many examples of individuals and subcultures embracing deep sharing within an unhealthy nation. Any group of people can create a healthy subculture where deep sharing is the norm. However, beyond what individuals or subcultures can do, I believe that the only way to make deep sharing the normal, default behavior throughout a sovereign nation is to transform it so that *everybody stands for a culture of mutual respect, and nobody rules over anybody else*.

Rulers protecting their wealth and imposing profit economies are the ultimate driver of selfishness in an unhealthy nation, and if this selfishness is not evicted, the unhealthy nation will continue to reward the selfish and make the most generous people suffer.

When I first discovered the financial whipsaw and how economy administrators can keep workers financially desperate, I was amazed and so grateful to the person who showed it to me. Now, I find this uninteresting. Rulers always act selfishly so they can exploit the workers, and it just looks a little different in the United States compared with Russia or Egypt or India. I'm tired of studying how selfish people act selfishly – which is basically what it means to study economics and finance in unhealthy nations. Now that I learned about this pattern of managed desperation, I don't feel like studying it anymore. I just know that having rulers is the core problem, and fixing that will fix so many other problems too.

Is it any surprise that healthy nations with their gift economies and unhealthy nations with their profit economies are entirely incompatible? To continue to function, each type of economy must emphasize either gifting or profiting as the normal, default behavior.

Authoritarian leaders can only make bold proclamations of freedom and dignity by ignoring the coerced consent at the heart of market economies. Their words are hollow, and I'm tired of reading about self-centered, self-important rich people who speak meaningless platitudes while exploiting their neighbors. That's why I want to co-create a nation that forbids exploitation – where nobody rules over anybody else.

What are some other differences between profit and gift economies? How can debt be abusive and divisive in a profit economy, but beautiful and unifying in a gift economy? Find out next in *Chapter 11: Cascading Generosity vs Cascading Selfishness*.

Chapter 11: Cascading Generosity vs Cascading Selfishness

Both gift economies and profit economies are stable, meaning that societies which embrace one or the other can last a long time.

However, the two economies do not mix well. At the root, it is because generosity and selfishness are opposites. The whole point of giving a gift is to give something more valuable than I receive. With gifts, a person may give without even receiving anything at all, whereas the whole point of a profitable transaction is to receive something more valuable than I give.

Clearly, if one person keeps giving and another keeps profiting, eventually the giver will wind up broke and the giving will end. This is why nations of giving take so much care to avoid selfishness, either helping selfish people feel comfortable sharing, or banishing them from the group. Anyone who selfishly focuses on getting more than they give – that is, anyone who profits from their neighbors – threatens a gift economy because once a person begins to act selfishly, others may decide to protect themselves by acting selfishly too.

Sioux man Ohiyesa noted this when he wrote, "Big-heartedness, generosity, courage, and self-denial are the qualifications of a public servant, and the average Indian was keen to follow this ideal. As everyone knows, these characteristic traits become a weakness when he enters a life founded upon commerce and gain."[1]

Gift economies thus generate *cascading generosity*, where gift-giving ripples and reverberates throughout a nation, generating abundance as gifts go where they're most needed. Individual exchanges may not be reciprocal, as each giver gives more than they receive, but relationships are reciprocal over time as different people give and receive as opportunities arise.

In contrast, profit economies generate cascading selfishness, as rulers exploit managers who exploit workers who exploit each other and the Earth. In command economies, the workers labor to avoid abuse while the masters make as much profit as they can. In market economies, everyone is incentivized to make as much money as possible.

Depending on Generosity vs Depending on Selfishness

Gift economies and profit economies are stable for another reason: people can come to depend upon the generosity or selfishness that underlies each kind of economy.

One aspect of a gift economy is that recipients honor the gift by only taking as much as they need so that nothing is wasted. Nobody needs very much, and so nobody winds up having very much. And yet, Okanagan woman Jeannette Armstrong described how abundant life can feel in such a nation, calling it "the most secure feeling in the world."[2] I believe that reciprocal generosity is the foundation for that deep security – both between people, and between people and the Earth.

When an entire community enriches the Earth, the Earth can be a growing source of abundance. And when a gift economy moves resources where they're needed, no one needs to fear the twin challenge of having nothing and having no help in dealing with it.

Even catastrophes are only as bad as they truly need to be. For example, when a Huron house burned down in Ossossane, the house and some items were lost but there wasn't much suffering beyond that because neighbors shared their food and helped build a new home.[3] A culture of sharing makes it safe to not have very much, and it makes it safe to not hoard to protect oneself from every potential future risk.

Gift economies also make it safe to work only as much as needed. Nobody's livelihood depends on anybody else's suffering or wastefulness. This was obvious in the words of one Arikara man to a Canadian trader named Pierre-Antoine Tabeau: "Why do you wish to make all this powder and these balls since you do not hunt? Of what use are all these knives to you? Is not one enough with which to cut the meat? It is only your wicked heart that prevents you from giving them to us. Do you not see that the village has none? I will give you a robe myself, when you want it, but you already have more robes than are necessary to cover you." The trader noted, "their minds not grasping our ideas of interest and acquisition beyond what is necessary, it is a principle with them that he who has divides with him who has not."[4]

The trader kept things he didn't need so that he could sell them, and he likewise benefited when people bought more of his products than they really needed. Reflecting on the Arikaras' culture of sharing, he wondered how he could "hope for success in a nation, imbued with these principles and always destitute of everything." He could not recognize that these people only had as much as they needed to live a satisfactory life. They did not stockpile things they didn't need just to sell them.

This shows why people of healthy nations could react so strongly to selfishness: if selfishness took hold, and people without much personal wealth needed to act selfishly to survive, it would make a materially simple life that seemed abundant and secure suddenly seem very insecure. Thus I believe that people in healthy nations depend on that cascading generosity. This is not the dependency of a mooch. It is a way of life that only works when everyone participates fully by sharing.

This illustrates a major difference in gift-giving in healthy and unhealthy nations. In healthy nations, people can rely on each others' generosity to help them stay resilient and safe in difficult times. In unhealthy nations, gifts often do not have such a big impact on the recipient: toys, books, extra clothes, and other items given at birthday or religious holidays may be thoughtful, but generally do not have the same impact as reliably sharing food during a hungry time, or building someone a new house after their old one burned down. The urge to share is strong in all humans, but in unhealthy nations, gift-giving and charity rarely generate a deep trust that people can rely on their neighbors for help, no matter what.

Sadly, people in profit economies can likewise become dependent on how their economy works, but in this case they depend on exploitation. For example, prison guards and wardens require inmates to exist so they can have jobs. What would happen if laws and courts suddenly changed so that people only went to jail if they were truly unsafe to society, and no one were prosecuted for victimless crimes? What if the government suddenly vastly reduced inequality so that fewer people were driven to crime out of desperation, and prison sentences were reduced so that people only stayed in prison as long as it took them to show sincere personal growth and remorse? Huge numbers of prison staff would be out of a job if the legal system were actually humane.

Similar examples abound. Oil company workers require oil extraction and plastics and fossil fuel-use to survive. Weapons companies depend upon war. Chemical companies depend upon regulators and customers ignoring toxicity issues. Real estate agents depend upon private land ownership. Banks depend upon people in financial desperation to take out loans. Anyone with money depends upon the entire economy to provide goods and services which can be purchased. Anyone who loans out money depends upon the police and courts and prisons to scare borrowers into paying back their loans no matter what.

People even exploit themselves. How many people sacrifice their own integrity to keep their job? How many people use loud tools knowing their hearing will suffer, or bend over all day knowing their backs will ache, or sit at a desk all day wondering when life will start to matter?

When rulers selfishly exploit people, exploited people are then pressured to act selfishly to survive. This is the cascading selfishness at the heart of profit economies.

Sioux man Red Cloud understood the dynamic of cascading exploitation. When the Sioux debated whether to continue resistance to the United States military, he described how submission would mean embracing cascading selfishness and joining in that profit economy's exploitation:

> Friends, it has been our misfortune to welcome the white man. We have been deceived. He brought with him some shining things that pleased our eyes; he brought weapons more effective than our own: above all, he brought the spirit water [heavy alcohol] that makes one forget for a time old age, weakness, and sorrow. But I wish to say to you that if you would possess these things for yourselves, you must begin anew and put away the wisdom of your fathers. You must lay up food, and forget the hungry. When your house is built, your storeroom filled, then look around for a neighbor whom you can take at a disadvantage, and seize all that he has! Give away only what you do not want; or rather, do not part with any of your possessions unless in exchange for another's.
>
> My countrymen, shall the glittering trinkets of this rich man, his deceitful drink that overcomes the mind, shall these things tempt us to give up our homes, our hunting grounds, and the honorable teaching of our old men? Shall we permit ourselves to be driven to and fro–to be herded like the cattle of the white man?[5]

Red Cloud foresaw that participating in a profit economy would encourage cascading selfishness. Sadly, he was correct.

Forced and Unforced Debt

Debt further reinforces both the generosity of gift economies and the selfishness of profit economies. But of course, the two economies have very different kinds of debt.

At its heart, a debt exists when one person owes another person something. The similarities between the different types of debt end there.

I recognize two kinds of debt in profit economies: command debts and market debts. In both cases, somebody is forced into owing someone else money.

Just like people cannot choose their bosses in command economies, people cannot choose whether to have command debts. Masters force command debts upon their servants. Taxes are a common kind of command-debt. Citizens or businesses have a debt of taxes, not because they chose the debt, but because the government decided they owe taxes. Governments force tax debts on the citizens and businesses, and they pay off this debt by paying their taxes.

For example, when Columbus arrived in the Caribbean and required Arawaks to pay a certain amount of gold or cotton every three months, this was a command debt which they did not choose. When the Spanish conquistador Hernán Cortés ruled Tepetlaoztoc in southern North America in the 1500s, he required annual payments of gold, textiles and food and threatened severe punishment if he didn't get them.[6] In 19th century Tibet, serfs owed their lords a certain amount of work each year.[7] These were command debts, as the residents never asked to be taxed.

Command debts generally do not involve any exchange. A person pays the tax or tribute, not to gain anything, but to avoid punishment.

In contrast, market debts are loans, where a person borrows something and promises to pay back a greater amount later. For example, a person may borrow money to buy a car they need for their job, or borrow money to buy a house. Thus to buy something like a car, a person who cannot afford it has to pay for both the cost of the car and the cost of the loan.

Market debts are one way rich people fleece poor and middle-class people by making them pay to borrow rich people's money.

Market debts aren't forced on anybody in the same way command debts are. Instead, market debts are forced on people through maintaining them in a state of financial need, and often financial desperation. People caught in this trap may intentionally accept debt and even pay a huge amount of interest if they have no alternative.

During the era of Tibetan serfdom, Buddhist lords and monks imposed extremely heavy taxes on serfs. These command debts included taxes on the unemployed, taxes for traveling to work, taxes on going to or leaving prison, and taxes for each person's birth, death, and marriage. There were taxes on singing, drumming, keeping animals, public dancing, or planting trees. All these taxes and more kept people in financial desperation, and of course the rich were happy to "help" them out with loans at 20% to 50% interest. Debts could be passed down from one generation to the next. And those who did not pay faced enslavement or torture.

Market debts can be used to exploit people of any income level. I knew a man in 2010 who earned approximately three times the national average income. He should have lived comfortably. Unfortunately, shortly before home prices fell in 2006, he had taken his banker's advice to buy the largest home he could afford. When I knew him, his house was worth 70% what he'd paid. This seemingly well-off man and his wife ate cheap noodles most nights so they could afford to keep paying their mortgage, ensuring his family suffered instead of the bankers.

Market debts can give the appearance that everyone involved is free to go into debt or not. Just like workers in a market economy can choose their boss and choose not to work, people willingly seek out market debts. However, due to the rich maintaining the poor in a state of financial desperation, the truth is that many market debts are simply a case of coerced consent, as people's choices are managed by the rulers and other authorities who administer the unhealthy nation.

This is why so many revolutions throughout history have had a shared goal: destroying the debt records.[8] For example, after the Chinese took over Tibet, Anna Strong got to witness a meeting where ex-serfs confronted their ex-lord Lhalu. After the ex-serfs had finished stating their accusations, a loud shout went out to "Burn the debts! Burn the debts!" Several boxes of debt paperwork were brought out as well as many torture implements from Lhalu's prison, and they finally found release as the paperwork erupted in a huge bonfire.[9]

In contrast to these forced, exploitative debts, unforced debts arise anytime someone receives a gift. Just like forced debts are the basis of profit economies, I believe unforced debts are the basis of gift economies. No one makes the sun shine or rivers flow, but they do and the sun gives gifts of warmth and light and rivers give water for cleaning and drinking. Trees transform sunlight, soil and air into food and shelter for many critters, including humans. Cats minimize the number of rodents around farms. Mushrooms break down dead trees into rich soil. No one forces these beings to give their gifts – they just do.

As Robin Kimmerer noted, these gifts establish a relationship: "The currency of a gift economy is, at its root, reciprocity."[10] This is what an unforced debt is: when a person feels deep gratitude for a gift they receive and desires to somehow return the favor. This deep gratitude for others' gifts is the first core spiritual practice, and living in reciprocity is the third core spiritual practice.

Sometimes a grateful recipient can give back to the giver. Someone may write a thank-you note for a gift they receive, or a new gardener may share her first produce with an expert gardener who mentored her.

Other times, the recipient can only pay it forward. For example, children may never be able to repay all the gifts of money, play, mentoring and other resources they received from their parents, but they can give their love to their own children. I can never repay the gifts I've received from all the mentors in my life, but I do my best to pay it forward, including in the form of this book.

Unlike forced debts, unforced indebtedness feels good. It feels good to be indebted to someone who gave me things when I needed them just because they cared enough to help me. I still remember an older friend Mark in high school who helped me train to make the basketball team. I still remember Patricia who let me worktrade on her homestead in 2014, giving me a welcoming home and smooth transition out of my old career as I looked for a better way to live in the world. It feels good to remember those gifts, and it feels good to feel indebted to them.

There's something beautiful about unforced debts. They never get canceled, they don't expire, and they are never repaid. Anyone who's ever experienced a healthy relationship knows what it's like when two people just keep endlessly giving to each other. A wife cooks dinner one night so it's ready for the husband as he arrives home from work late. The husband watches the kids to make sure the wife has time for her weekly women's group. The wife holds her husband as he grieves the death of his father. The husband supports his wife as she goes to school to get a degree.

The more these two serve each other, the greater their indebtedness grows. Whereas forced debts can be divisive or stressful, unforced debts bind people together. When spouses or friends remember their indebtedness and gratitude, this can help the relationship persist through stresses that might otherwise drive them apart. In healthy nations, these same patterns play out across entire villages and nations.

People are usually happy to pay off forced debts and forget about them, but who would ever want to forget mutual unforced indebtedness, that affection that forms when two people each feel grateful for the other's presence?

Unforced debts – that is, gifts and the resulting gratitude – are the bonds that make people actually want to be together. When there is no ruler, no money, and no property, why would anybody stay in relationship with anybody else? It is gift-giving that actually forms deep bonds between people. And of course, giving one's sacred gifts, or giving one's deepest love, is the second core spiritual practice.

These three core spiritual practices are who we are as humans: receiving gifts with gratitude, giving our own gifts, and living in reciprocity. I believe healthy nations encourage and train people to be their deepest selves and live this way all the time.

Unfortunately, forced debts are only one way people can take advantage of each other in unhealthy nations. Another way occurs when someone takes the profit for themselves but makes others pay the cost, a situation called an *externality*.

Externalities: Who Pays for the Costs of My Behavior?

One of the most reliable ways for a person or group to profit in a business is to not fully account for all of the costs.

Consider a coal power plant that produces huge amounts of toxic smoke while making electricity. That smoke is harmful to many people and nonhumans, and many people will end up spending money to deal with the health effects. If we were to calculate the *full cost* of producing coal-based electricity, it would have to include those health effects, but the power plant owner does not pay all of them.

Without enforced regulation, business owners commonly only pay the money they actually need to lay out to make their plant run. Instead of paying the cost of cleaning up after themselves, owners often find it cheaper to spread the pollution around so much that no one can pinpoint quite where it came from.[11] This is one reason so many smokestacks are so high: it dilutes the pollution so people can't tell the source of their sickness.

This cost-shifting is called an externality. In this example with coal plants, the business owner profits from coal-based electricity but does not pay the cost created by the smoke they produce. Instead, other people pay the cost of the pollution. The cost has become external to the business, borne by society and the nonhumans.

This dynamic exists everywhere in unhealthy nations. Nuclear power plant operators do not pay the multi-millennia cost of storing nuclear waste safely. Plastic producers do not pay the cost of fully recycling the plastic, and only producing plastic which can be recycled. Large animal farms do not pay the cost of remediating the pollution as the animals' poop is washed into rivers.

This happens on a personal level too. When I walk on a sidewalk near a road, it is common for someone to leave their house and start their car as I walk past, pushing smoke into my face without giving it a second thought. Many smokers throw their cigarette butt on the ground, and many people leave lights on all night without considering the impact on birds, insects, and others whose lives depend on darkness.

These are all externalities where a person, business, or government does something that creates a cost, but someone else pays the price. They are common in economies that reward selfishness and forbid people from holding each other accountable for inappropriate behavior. If parents have kids who are getting sick from a nearby factory's smoke, and they are not allowed to hold the factory owner accountable somehow, then all they can do is protect their family by making more money so they can live in a less-polluted area. This does not address the problem, and it also doesn't work for families that cannot make more money.

This shows another way that selfishness cascades through a nation. When people cannot hold each other accountable for behaving selfishly (such as by forcing polluting factories to pay the costs of the pollution), this motivates individual selfishness as people try to protect themselves the best they can.

When healthy nations welcome anyone to hold anyone else accountable for inappropriate behavior, they ensure that everyone faces the consequences of their own actions. No one is allowed to shift costs onto anyone else. It also helps address potentially big problems early on, before remediation becomes astronomically expensive – or impossible.

When everyone accepts responsibility for holding others accountable, thoughtfulness cascades through a nation instead, as each person considers the impacts of their actions on others, including nonhumans. People consider the impact of harvesting trees on the forest, or who would benefit most from a gift. These examples are explored in detail in Chapter 9 and Chapter 34.

This shows the importance of holding people accountable when they misbehave. When a person is allowed to misbehave, thinking only of themselves, selfishness ripples out into the nation as others respond to only protect themselves. Accountability is closely tied to either selfishness or thoughtfulness. Low-accountability nations encourage selfishness, whereas high-accountability nations motivate consideration of others.

Once again, these two kinds of economy, one based on gifts and the other based on profits, are incompatible. The obvious way to stop the cascading selfishness is to hold everyone accountable for inappropriate behavior. Of course, this is forbidden in unhealthy nations where selfish rulers try to avoid accountability at all costs. This is why the path to creating a nation that fully embraces a gift economy is the same path explored throughout this book: ensuring that everybody stands for a culture of mutual respect, and nobody rules over anybody else.

Mutual Aid Societies: Starting a Different Cascade

I don't believe in spiritual good and evil. I do believe in generosity and selfishness. Whenever I notice someone behaving in a way that others call evil, and I really investigate, I notice the person is actually behaving selfishly.

Profit economies pressure people into acting selfishly. Fortunately, many people have still found ways to act generously instead.

I know various homeowners who have their own debts and who could easily rent out rooms to tenants for a lot of money. Instead, they charge a small fraction of market rent, just enough to cover the tenant's costs such as utilities.

In other cases, people form mutual aid societies where they pool funds to help each other through difficult times. For example, I personally know a man recovering from alcohol addiction who received a zero-percent car loan from a group of friends so he could travel and hold a reliable job.

Formal mutual aid societies have flourished throughout history in unhealthy nations as people help each other survive in spite of exploitative rulers. One charter from a town in Flanders, Belgium in 1188 reads, "All those who belong to the friendship of the town have promised and confirmed by faith and oath that they will aid each other as brethren, in whatever is useful and honest." This included defending each other from theft in all its forms, protecting each other from "anyone [who] takes anything from any one of them, or makes one pay contributions." Hundreds of European mutual aid society charters in the middle ages contained similar commitments.[12]

Like a full gift economy, mutual aid societies stem from sacred urges towards solidarity and caring for one's friends and neighbors. Unfortunately, rulers may see this solidarity as a threat to their ability to continue exploiting the public.

Guilbert de Nogent was born to French noble parents and he clearly showed this negative attitude when he described these mutual aid societies: "The Commune is an oath of mutual aid… A new and detestable word. Through it the serfs… are freed from all serfdom; through it, they can only be condemned to a legally determined fine for breaches of the law; through it, they cease to be liable to payments which the serfs always used to pay." In other words, mutual aid societies fulfilled their function: members were able to protect each other from predation.

Workers' unions are one form of mutual aid society, as the union helps the workers collectively bargain for safe workplaces, livable wages, and tolerable work schedules. Many unions, such as the National Union of Healthcare Workers, establish hardship funds that help striking workers pay for essential items while they're not earning any money. In this way, workers with resources help those without as they collectively bargain for better working conditions for everyone.[13]

Immigrants and oppressed people throughout history have supported each other through difficult times. The Charitable Irish Society was founded in 1737 in Boston, Massachusetts with the goals of helping the poor, elderly, disabled people, and the sick. They also helped shield each other from anti-Irish discrimination.[14] Many similar mutual aid societies have arisen around the world. Some organize all neighbors in a region, while others organize everyone of a certain religion or ethnicity to help each other out. Some focus on specific themes like literacy and education, especially where public schools teach children poorly due to lack of resources or discrimination.

I recognize mutual aid societies as healthy subcultures within unhealthy nations. Mutual aid societies are an example of anarchy in action as people take care of each other without any ruler or authorities giving orders. They are also powerful evidence that even though rulers behave selfishly and pressure others to behave selfishly too, any individual or any group can choose to start a cascade of generosity that ripples and reverberates far and wide.

Abundance Begets Abundance, Abuse Begets Abuse

There are so many ways that either generosity or selfishness can cascade through a nation, reinforcing either a gift economy or profit economy.

The best way to keep a gift economy alive is for everyone to keep giving. When each person offers their special skills, their joy and laughter, their leadership in difficult moments, food in hungry times, or anything else, gratitude just keeps building. The only threat to this gift economy is that someone might start acting selfishly, and so people go to great lengths to ensure everyone feels comfortable sharing.

In contrast, the best way to trap people in abusive relationships is to treat them abusively. The more a master abuses the slave, the harder it is for the slave to escape. As later chapters will explore, this is why slaveowners don't just beat slaves for disobedience, they also often torture or humiliate them at random just to establish that they can, and sell apart family members to disrupt solidarity. Selfish slaveowners use divisive practices like making some slaves oversee others, creating division where there might otherwise be unity. Prison wardens make prisoners' lives extra miserable and then dangle expensive food and hygiene products in commissaries to motivate them to work even for pennies per hour.

The greater people's financial desperation and the lower their self-esteem, the more they will tolerate disrespectful bosses and unsatisfying work. This explains why authorities work to maintain financial desperation, hatred, racism, privilege, sexism, and more: the more abusively rulers act, the more securely they can trap millions of people in exploitative relationships. All these divisive techniques are covered in this book.

Just as selfishness is the biggest threat to gift economies, generosity is the biggest threat to profit economies. This explains why Guilbert de Nogent considered "commune" a "detestable word" because "through it the serfs... are freed from all serfdom." People with great wealth only have it because many people are trapped in states of dependency and desperation. If enough people acted generously towards one another, the dependency and desperation would end.

This is the reality of unhealthy nations and profit economies, where some people's attempt to seek freedom threatens other people's wealth and comfort.

Thus abundance begets abundance, and abuse begets abuse. While there is sadly much abuse in the world, there is also good news: each one of us gets to choose which pattern we want to send cascading through the lives of the people we touch.

Despite this freedom to choose on an individual level, much of our lives are shaped by the broader nation in which we live. How do unhealthy nations trap and control so many people so effectively for so long?

The next section of the book, *Part 4 - What Defines a Person's World?*, pulls back the curtain to show how authorities insidiously manipulate the lives of many people. It also offers a heroic tale of one woman who ignored this manipulation, instead charting her own path in service of those she loved.

Part 4 - What Defines a Person's World?

The more I studied unhealthy nations, the more I began to see just how much these nations impact every aspect of people's lives. The rulers and authorities who control the nation directly and indirectly shape the lives of the people in ways I had never imagined.

Chapter 12: The Family and the Burglar

I believe that sometime in the distant past, every single human lived in a healthy nation. Most of us now live in abusive unhealthy nations, and that means at some point in the past, our ancestors went through some kind of traumatic transition.

These traumatic transitions have happened countless times around the world, and in some ways each transition was unique. Yet, despite the differences, these transitions also tragically show some common patterns.

What might it have been like to experience a transition from the comfort and deep security of life in a healthy nation to the disruptive and fearful realities of an unhealthy nation? Without actually experiencing it, it is impossible to fully know. But to get an inkling, it helps to think of this on the scale of a single nuclear family. What kind of intrusion might cause a loving family to transition into an abusive nation?

Let's suppose something terrible happened.

Imagine you were enjoying dinner with your loving family one night. In this story, you're a child with three siblings and a mother and father, all gathered around a table sharing a meal and telling stories after a long day. Halfway through the meal, a burglar suddenly enters the house, points a gun at the group, and demands everyone's money.

The family is now in an emergency situation, and if you're fortunate, it ends in one of a few ways: the family escapes, the burglar leaves, the family overpowers the burglar, or the family persuades the burglar to stop threatening them and become friends.

But what if none of those things happen? Suppose your family gives the burglar their money, and the burglar decides to stay, demanding that your family continue to give the burglar more money every week. Otherwise he will hurt you, your siblings, and your parents.

The burglar moves in and demands a weekly payment. After a week of this, your dad confronts him, but he is severely beaten and your family backs down. A few weeks later, your sister resists an order and the burglar cuts off the child's ear to scare everyone into submission. And every so often, he beats a family member just to prove that he's serious. [Authoritarian symptom: dominance display, covered in *Chapter 41: The Deepest Lessons From Thousands of Years of Spiritual Leaders*]

The burglar then insists that he, your parents, and all the kids are part of the same family. He punishes anyone who disagrees. Of course the family knows this is not true, and the burglar is an imposter, but no one can speak the truth in front of the burglar. [symptom: Blind Belief, covered in *Chapter 6: Blind Belief 1 - When People Ignore Reality to Maintain Safety and Comfort*]

A one-time horrible invasion has now become an even worse ongoing catastrophe. Your family's culture becomes unhealthy as it adapts to the new conditions, an environment where the abuser and victims live together and the abuser forces the victims to pretend that everything is ok. After the burglar moved in, in a sense, everyone became one culture. Now the greatest threat is within the culture itself, not outside the culture. And pretending as if all is well is required for survival.

At this stage, no one believes that the burglar is actually part of the family. No one accepts the burglar's rule as legitimate. But since no one can escape, make the burglar leave, or defend themselves, you all are stuck pretending whenever he's around.

Your parents are allowed to leave to go to work, but they're forbidden to discuss their home situation, or else the burglar will hurt their children. Your parents are forced to work to their limit, according to the burglar's calculations of how much money they can make if they work absolutely as hard as possible. The burglar then requires them to give him 95% of that amount, leaving them only enough to sustain themselves while they work for him.[symptom: desperation management, covered in *Chapter 10: Profit Economies*]

Schooling also changes. Previously you and your siblings studied things you really cared about and you were excited for each day. Now, your two oldest siblings drop out of school to make money to pay the burglar. You and the other youngest sibling go to school, no longer to follow your curiosity and passion, but to train for jobs so you can make more money for the burglar. The burglar requires everyone to prioritize obedience over doing what they know in their heart is right. [symptom: coercive schooling, covered in *Chapter 42: Training Children to Give or Withhold Love, Part 1*]

One day the burglar decides to make his job easier, so he appoints the second oldest boy to the position of overseer. As long as the child remains obedient, he is never hit, gets better food, does not work for money, and can come and go as he pleases. In exchange, the burglar makes this overseer child responsible for the family's behavior and financial output.

The boy doesn't want to cross his family at first, but he feels afraid of the burglar and recognizes that the family isn't standing in solidarity anymore and he worries no one would help him if the burglar got angry at him for refusing. And if he doesn't take the special role, he thinks that surely someone else will, so it might as well be him.

This child recognizes deep down that he is betraying his family and siding with the burglar, but he sees no alternative, so he does everything he can to keep his special privileges and tries not to reflect on his own behavior. As he learns to ignore that inner voice telling him that what he's doing is wrong, this overseer child quickly becomes even more vicious than the burglar, demanding that the parents and other children work even when the burglar is absent. He informs the burglar of any gossip or potential threats. And along with the burglar, this overseer child threatens any family member who conspires to fight or escape.

After a while, the overseer kid decides to make his job easier by offering extra food to anyone who snitches. Pretty soon, the parents and other children lose trust in each other, not sure who can be trusted to keep a secret. After all, the whole family is no longer united, and if one child can be bribed to snitch on other family members, who else might be next? [symptom: lift-and-turn privilege, covered in *Chapter 26: Privilege 1 - Lift-and-Turn*]

The burglar continuously tells the family, "This is how things are, how they always have been, and how they always will be. God decided this is how life is, and you deserve your suffering."[symptom: justifying exploitative rulers, covered in *Chapter 33 - It All Starts with Justifying or Ignoring Exploitative Rulers*]

The burglar starts to claim that God says the boys are better than the girls and therefore they deserve special social standing. As always, anyone who disagrees is severely punished.

Soon the boys start to receive more food than the girls for similar work. The boys find that they can give their sisters orders and the girls are punished if they decline or if they try to make their own demands. Whenever the burglar hears about conflicts between the children, he makes sure that the boys win more often than the girls. [symptom: systemic sexism, covered in *Chapter 24: Sexual Discrimination vs Sexual Equality*]

After learning not to notice that their privileges were due entirely to the burglar, eventually the boys start to agree that they're better than the girls because why else would God put them in this superior position? One sister wonders what's wrong with the boys, and the other, with a very hurt heart, eventually decides they must be right. [symptom: entitlement, covered in *Chapter 30: Privilege 4 - Entitlement*]

This ongoing catastrophe has now reached a new stage. Some individuals have begun to adopt the ideology of their abuser by believing some people are better or more deserving than others. Some family members still want to stand in solidarity, but others such as the overseer child now fully embrace a selfish attitude and start to actively support the burglar against their own people. It has become harder to identify the true threat. Without being able to speak openly about the nature of the trouble, it becomes very difficult to agree on what's really going on and what to do about it.[symptom: adopting authoritarian ideologies, covered in *Chapter 21: Training People To Adopt Authoritarian Ideologies*]

Rather than the tight knit family you once were, you have become a collection of not-very-trusting individuals who happen to live together.

What might happen if your family finally gives up hope of escape and accepts your ruler's legitimacy? One older sibling who insists on remembering the good times is called "naive" and "childlike." Parents and children might start ratting each other out as each person tries to secure a safer and more comfortable life in spite of the burglar. The better-off family members turn their attention primarily towards getting their personal needs met and staying safe while the worse-off seek ways to support each other. Some of the family members pretend to help each other while they're really buttering up the burglar, causing even more resentment among the others. [symptom: going through the motions, covered in *Chapter 29: Privilege 3 - Going Through the Motions*]

All the urges the family had felt earlier still exist – for camaraderie, trust, joy, celebration, integrity, sharing food, connection, and so on. And perhaps you can still enjoy moments of these at times. Still, without real trust and solidarity, it becomes difficult to deeply enjoy life and each others' company. Your family is experiencing a continual catastrophe, but once everyone has given up hope of change and learned to accept the burglar's rule as legitimate, your family has essentially chosen to ignore the catastrophe. When anyone learns to ignore the most meaningful issue they face, life itself begins to seem less meaningful.[symptom: heart-closure, covered in *Chapter 17: Heart-Opening vs Heart-Closing*]

Over time, maybe your family members develop hobbies or seek out new, more appealing paid work. Maybe you play with friends sometimes or tell each other stories. But each person's relationship with the abusive burglar becomes the overarching, controlling pressure in their lives.

Your whole world begins to be shaped by the need to avoid punishment and secure food, shelter, and some comfort in your abusive nation. Each family member's "world" is shaped by the abusive authority because dealing with the burglar's rewards and threats takes most of everyone's attention.[symptom: world-shaping, covered in *Chapter 14: Same Planet, Different Worlds*]

Is this just a make-believe story? Or does this kind of deep manipulation really happen, keeping people trapped in various abusive nations all around the world?

To see these patterns play out in real life, let's look at an example in the next chapter, *Chapter 13: An Endless Nightmare Descends on a Healthy Nation*.

Chapter 13: An Endless Nightmare Descends on a Healthy Nation

I studied many different ancient wars growing up, but they all seemed similar. Two kings would send their armies to fight each other, and after the war, the winning king took some land, gold, or slaves from the loser, or he might take over the loser's land entirely. War was brutal for the fighters, but when it just seemed like kingdoms endlessly fighting, the outcomes didn't matter much to me.

Eventually I realized that not all military conquests involved two kings vying for more power and wealth. Some wars involved authoritarian nations seeking to conquer healthy ones. In some cases, the healthy nations were able to defend themselves or escape for decades or centuries. In other cases they were not.

What would it be like to live in a healthy nation, like the Ashaninkas described in Chapter 1, and suddenly encounter an abusive nation's military that forces everyone to obey abusive authorities?

Christopher Columbus and the Arawaks

Christopher Columbus sailed from Spain and landed on Hispaniola, an island between North and South America that today is home to Haiti and the Dominican Republic. There he encountered the Arawaks.

On October 13, 1492, Columbus described in his journal how he and his crew were greeted: "At daybreak great multitudes of [Arawak] men came to the shore, all young and of fine shapes, and very handsome."[1] In one letter, he noted that, "They all go around as naked as their mothers bore them; and also the women."[2] In a later report to the Spanish royalty, Columbus described how his hosts, without exception, willingly shared what they had. He was so amazed, he said, "no one who has not witnessed them would believe it."[3]

Many of Columbus's journal entries illustrate the Arawaks' routine generosity:

> They became so much our friends that it was a marvel... They traded and gave everything they had, with good will... [October 12].

> I sent the ship's boat ashore for water, and they very willingly showed my people where the water was, and they themselves carried the full barrels to the boat, and took great delight in pleasing us... [October 16].

> They are the best people in the world and above all the gentlest... [December 16]

> They are very gentle and without knowledge of what is evil; nor do they murder or steal [November 12].

> Your Highnesses may believe that in all the world there can be no better or gentler people... for neither better people nor land can there be... All the people show the most singular loving behavior and they speak pleasantly... [December 24].

> I assure Your Highnesses that I believe that in all the world there is no better people nor better country. They love their neighbors as themselves, and they have the sweetest talk in the world, and are gentle and always laughing [December 25].[4]

Bartolome De Las Casas, an early arrival in the Spanish colonies, wrote about the Arawaks' freedom to have relationships that last only as long as they are satisfying. For example, they had no marriage laws: "Men and women alike choose their mates and leave them as they please, without offense, jealousy or anger. They multiply in great abundance; pregnant women work to the last minute and give birth almost painlessly; up the next day, they bathe in the river and are as clean and healthy as before giving birth… Indian men and women look upon total nakedness with as much casualness as we look upon a man's head or at his hands."[5]

Unfortunately, despite receiving so much generosity, Columbus remained deeply selfish. In his ship's log, Columbus noted: "They would make fine servants… With fifty men we could subjugate them all and make them do whatever we want."

The Spanish government had financed the trip, promising Columbus 10% of any profits, governorship over any lands he found, and a fancy title: admiral of the ocean sea. His mission was to bring back gold and spices. Columbus saw that the locals wore bits of gold as body decorations. He asked where he could get this gold, and he believed they told him where he could find "a king who possessed great cups full of gold."[6,7]

During his first voyage, Columbus kidnapped between 10 and 25 people to help him find gold and to bring them back to Spain as slaves. Only a few arrived in Europe alive. He left thirty-nine crew members in a fort they created called Navidad (Spanish for "Christmas") with a mission of looking for gold.[8,9]

Back in Spain, Columbus requested that king Ferdinand and queen Isabella pay for another trip. The king and queen could afford this because in Spain, 2% of the people owned 95% of the land, and the royalty were among the richest Spaniards and controlled the government's spending. In exchange for their financing, Columbus promised to bring "as much gold as they need … and as many slaves as they ask." The Christian explorer noted, "Thus the eternal God, our Lord, gives victory to those who follow His way over apparent impossibilities."

With a mission to bring back slaves and gold, Columbus returned to the Arawaks in 1493 with 17 ships containing 1200-1500 men, guns, cannons, cavalry, attack dogs, and crossbows. Columbus and his group demanded food, spun cotton, sex with the women, and gold. When someone resisted an order, the invaders cut off an ear or nose, attempting early on to scare people into obeying Spanish authorities.[10,11]

Columbus' ships went around the Caribbean islands capturing and enslaving people. As time went on they found more abandoned towns as people sought to avoid them. They found resistance many times. Columbus learned that all the sailors at Fort Navidad had been killed by the local people after the sailors had roamed the area capturing women and children for labor and sex.[12]

Bartolome De Las Casas described the differences in the Arawaks' and Spaniards' war-making ability. The Arawaks had inferior weapons which he called "ridiculous weapons in reality," and he described how "[Columbus] chose 200 foot soldiers and 20 cavalry, with many crossbows and small cannon, lances, and swords, and a still more terrible weapon… this was 20 hunting dogs, who were turned loose and immediately tore the Indians apart."[13]

Columbus' son Ferdinand would later write about the battle's outcome. Soldiers killed dozens of Arawaks with point-blank volleys, ordered the dogs to tear open bellies and limbs, and chased down anyone who tried to escape. Ferdinand wrote, "with God's aid [they] soon gained a complete victory, killing many Indians and capturing others who were also killed."

Columbus could not find fields of gold like he'd hoped, but he needed to pay off the investors in his trip. He went on a large slave raid, capturing 1500 people. The 500 highest-value slaves he sent to Spain, although only 200 arrived alive. The next highest-value he kept as slaves to work for the colonists, and the rest he released. One eyewitness described that even mothers with infants were so terrified that they "left their infants anywhere on the ground and started to flee like desperate people." Some ran seven or eight days' journey away from the colony, even across huge mountains and rivers.

Columbus described how pleased he was in a letter to the Spanish royalty: "In the name of the Holy Trinity, we can send from here all the slaves and brazil-wood which could be sold." He started strategizing about various slave markets and how many slaves they might need. He was not concerned with the death rate because he'd seen high death rates with other newly-enslaved people: "Although they die now, they will not always die. The Negroes and Canary Islanders died at first."

Columbus set up a tribute system. Every Arawak above the age of 13 owed tribute to the Catholic authorities every season. Some paid in gold, others in cotton, depending on the region. Each person received a token they would wear which proved they had paid. Anyone without such a token would be punished by having a hand cut off.[14] Sexual violence was also widespread.[15]

The Spaniards began hunting Arawaks and other local people for sport and used their bodies as dog food. De Las Casas described their savagery. The Spaniards "thought nothing of knifing Indians by tens and twenties and of cutting slices off them to test the sharpness of their blades." Las Casas described an incident where "two of these so-called Christians" encountered two boys, each carrying a parrot. They took the parrots and beheaded the boys.[16]

Because the Spaniards demanded impossible levels of tribute, they eventually switched over to the encomienda system, which later became the model for the Spanish in other parts of the Americas. Entire local villages became granted to individuals or groups of colonists. Locals would mine their gold, grow their food, and more.

Resistance continued at various times, mostly without success. Pedro de Cordoba wrote a letter to king Ferdinand in 1517 describing many people's response: "As a result of the sufferings and hard labor they endured, the Indians choose and have chosen suicide. Occasionally a hundred have committed mass suicide. Trie women, exhausted by labor, have shunned conception and childbirth…" Many women avoided conception, deliberately aborted, or killed their baby after birth "so as not to leave them in such oppressive slavery."[17]

Estimates of the pre-1493 Arawak population vary widely. De Las Casas arrived in 1508 and estimated that 60,000 remained out of an initial population of 3 million, writing, "Who in future generations will believe this? I myself writing it as a knowledgeable eyewitness can hardly believe it…"[18] By the 1540s, De Las Casas estimated 200 Arawaks remained after decades of foreign disease and extreme violence.[19] The encomienda system persisted for a very long time, and colonists imported slaves to replenish the supply of laborers.

As I write in 2024, this region has never since had a sovereign human nation without a few rich exploiting many poor.

All People Once Lived in Healthy Nations

In the distant past, every human being lived in a healthy nation. That means all of us born into unhealthy nations have ancestors who went through this kind of transition.

The Arawaks' story was a catastrophe for the people affected, but it was not so different from how Europeans treated millions of other people around the world in the past few centuries. Similar stories of extreme violence are also part of the history of imperial China, Japan, the Ottomans, and other non-European nations going back millennia.

As I kept studying conquests, I noticed that this same kind of story keeps playing out, again and again, whenever a few people consolidate their rule over many others, especially those who aren't used to being ruled.

Revolutions may happen when enough people become upset with their rulers. However, even after a victory, people usually have been unable to return to their original freedom and live without rulers. Superficial revolutions such as the American Revolution or Mexican Revolution may occur, where one group of powerful people replaces another group as leaders within a still-abusive society. But most revolutions have failed to bring people back to a society with a baseline of mutual respect.

Thus, for most humans, we and our ancestors have been stuck in authoritarian nations of one kind or another for centuries or even millennia.

What is it like to grow up in an unhealthy nation where authorities can manipulate the lives of their subjects to maintain their rule? And how different would it be to grow up in a healthy nation?

These are not abstract questions. The next chapter, *Chapter 14: Same Planet, Different Worlds*, paints a picture of how different day-to-day life can be in nations controlled by rulers compared to nations with strong leaders and no rulers. The differences run deep.

Chapter 14: Same Planet, Different Worlds

What happens if an unhealthy nation never heals, and the abuse just continues year after year, decade after decade, century after century? In what ways might rulers manipulate the lives of the people to maintain their control, in obvious and subtle ways?

For people of healthy nations, each person's "world" is shaped primarily by the Earth as well as a human nation that is strongly connected to the Earth. In unhealthy nations, each person's "world" is shaped primarily by a nation that is heavily manipulated by its rulers.

That means that, although everybody lives on the same planet, different people can live in very different worlds.

What defines a person's world? Many perspectives could be helpful. When I started exploring my own world, I asked these questions:

1. *Depending on uncaring people's cooperation*: Do I require an uncaring person's involvement in order for me to eat?

2. *Energetic boundaries*: What energetic boundaries do I have? By "energetic boundaries," I mean "What things in my life define what is ok and not ok?" or "What feedback tells me to do more of something or do less of it?"

3. *Is the Earth or the nation most important?* Do cultural stories and practices direct my attention to the Earth as of primary importance, or to the nation and authority figures as primary? When the nation and Earth become out of sync, does the nation adjust, or is the Earth expected to adjust?

In healthy nations, humans' lives are shaped primarily by energetic boundaries of the Earth itself. People depend directly upon nonhumans and caring people to eat. And cultural stories and practices direct people's attention to the Earth as primary. Such a person's world is thus defined primarily by the Earth, supported by their nation's deep connection to the Earth.

In unhealthy nations, humans' primary boundaries are defined by the human nation. Nearly everyone depends on uncaring people to eat. Pressures such as imposed laws and the need to make money direct and dominate most people's attention and energy most of the time.

Cultural stories and practices also direct people's attention to the nation and away from the Earth. Often the Earth is ignored, exploited, or considered a nuisance rather than the essential source of all life. Instead, the unhealthy nation itself is treated as most important, and so each individual lives in a world defined primarily by the abusive nation.

This means that people of unhealthy nations live in *controllable worlds*. If law or money availability shape my world, and if rulers can easily change these, then they can easily manipulate my world. In this situation, such a person's life is essentially administered by other people, with their personal degree of flexibility and autonomy dependent on their particular nation and the individual's culturally-provided privilege level.

Despite these narratives, pressures, and dependencies, I can still choose how to act within the physical limits I face. That is why it is so important to see these patterns of deep manipulation clearly – seeing the patterns of manipulation and recognizing what matters to me helps me truly find solid ground.

To illustrate the unhealthy-nation patterns, I'll start by answering these 3 world-shaping questions for myself, a person in an unhealthy nation. I will share a few stories of others from unhealthy nations, too. And for each of these world-defining questions, stories of people in healthy nations will illustrate how they might answer them differently.

1. Do I Require an Uncaring Person's Cooperation in Order for Me to Eat?

I get my food mostly from grocery stores, farmer's markets, and a little bit from foraging and gardening. I require money to buy food from stores and markets, and I choose to work for people or corporations so that they'll give me money. My boss at work may say she cares about me, and in some sense I believe that is true, but she wouldn't pay me if I didn't work for her as she directed. Likewise, the cashier at the grocery store may say pleasant words, but they would not let me leave the store with food I did not pay for, no matter how hungry I was.

Thus, to get food, I must work a job so a boss will pay me money so I can give it to the grocery store cashier. The cashier and grocery store owner must approve of me to sell to me, and my boss at work must approve of me to keep paying me. In this way, I depend on people who don't actually care about me. If they do not cooperate, I do not eat.

While I am fortunate to have a stable job, income, and steady access to food, others in my unhealthy nation are less fortunate. For example, Malcolm X illustrated this dependency on uncaring people in heart-wrenching detail in his autobiography. His American mother, a single woman raising several children, was a very light-skinned woman that most Americans still considered "black." She was very capable and diligent in her work, but due to local racist attitudes she could only get a job if people thought she was white, and her bosses at various jobs would fire her once they discovered that she wasn't an acceptable race. Then she would not be able to feed her children. She depended on uncaring people to feed her family, and she struggled greatly when they did not cooperate.[1]

People forced to live in prisons are another example: if the jailors did not bring food, they would starve to death. And the jailors only do their job because someone pays them. How many jailors would continue doing their job if they stopped being paid?

The very richest are another example: farmers do not grow and sell food to the rich because the farmers personally care about the rich; they do it for the money. If the rich did not have vast amounts of money, plus the advantages of cooperative law enforcement, the rich would not eat so well. The rich, like most people in unhealthy nations, depend on the involvement of uncaring people too. The rich are simply in a better position than the poor to ensure that uncaring people treat them well.

This need for uncaring people's involvement goes far deeper. For example, if certain government officials disapprove of me, they can freeze my bank account and prevent me from legally working for money. Or the government can disincentivize food from being sold in my region, or even forbid it. For example, the British government forced food to be shipped out of Ireland during the Irish Potato Famine[2] and forced food to be exported from India during times of famine there.[3] Likewise, the Soviet Union forbade food from being available in various food-producing regions during a famine in the 1930s. Both the British and the Soviet rulers caused millions of deaths by manipulating the availability of their own subjects' food.

Healthy Nation Stories - When People Depend on the Earth and Caring People to Eat

What's life like when a person depends only on the Earth and other caring people to eat?

During my time with the Ashaninka, I never went without food, paid anyone for food, or had to leave to find a store. I brought basic staples to share, but even when I didn't have my own food nearby, I was just fed. Growing, harvesting, catching, preparing, and eating food were group activities woven into everyday life.

One day, I saw three women sitting on mats on the ground around a big pot. I guessed that two women were in their 40s or 50s, and one woman was in her 70s or 80s. This older woman was very petite and thin, and her skin was very wrinkled. Earlier in life, I'd have assumed she was frail and physically weak. As I was about to see, that would be a foolish assumption.

These women had boiled white yuca root along with a purple root vegetable, both grown in their gardens. They were making a drink called peorentsi. Referred to as masato in Spanish, it is a fermented, mildly alcoholic beverage. As I watched, the women passed around a wooden paddle, taking turns stirring and mixing the boiled mash. This was not a small pot; I estimate it was about 10 gallons and over half full. The mash started with large regions of white and purple which then became pink as the ladies kept mixing and mixing. Each woman would strain to move the paddle through the thick mush, but I never heard them breathe heavily because each woman passed the paddle to the next before she got too tired. They seemed relaxed, and I did not hear them speak much.

This sort of fermentation requires either yeast or bacteria to consume sugars in the vegetables and produce alcohol. As I watched these women, I learned a new source of useful bacteria for fermentation. The paddle wasn't the only thing mixing the two colors. The lips and chin of each woman quickly became pink, because the women who weren't paddling would dip their hands into the pot, pull out some mash, chew it, and then spit it back into the pot! This imbued the mash and liquid with the microbes in their saliva which would feast on the starchy sugars and produce the alcohol. These women didn't just share their joyful company and labor, they shared their bacteria!

Ohiyesa described how the Sioux people he lived with in childhood would gather maple tree sap each spring and boil it down to make syrup. Before the sap began to run, all the participants would make little pans out of basswood and birch to catch the sap dripping from the maple trees. They hollowed out a huge maple tree log to hold all the sap in preparation for boiling in big metal pots. They would move to a bark sugar house they used each year near a large grove of maples on the edge of the Minnesota River, and begin gathering wood for the long fires ahead.[4]

Ohiyesa described how "the women began to test the trees–moving leisurely among them, axe in hand, and striking a single quick blow, to see if the sap would appear." When the women found a likely tree, they would drive a hardwood chip into the hole they'd made with their ax and leave a birch pan underneath to catch the sap.

Next they made a long fire in the sugar house and hung a row of kettles over the blaze. The women carefully transferred sap from the pans to larger containers to the hollowed log and eventually to the pots to boil down. Ohiyesa described the excitement, and how each boy who participated had a special way to contribute: "The hearts of the boys beat high with pleasant anticipations when they heard the welcome hissing sound of the boiling sap! Each boy claimed one kettle for his [special] charge. It was his duty to see that the fire was kept under it, to watch lest it boil over…" Ohiyesa's grandmother found many ways of preserving the finished syrup so it would last all year, including protecting it from the children.

Ohiyesa described another way the boys contributed when rabbits and squirrels gnawed holes in the birch-bark pans: "…we little boys for once became useful, in shooting them with our bows and arrows. We hunted all over the sugar camp, until the little creatures were fairly driven out of the neighborhood. Occasionally one of my older brothers brought home a rabbit or two, and then we had a feast."

In 1967, Mongolian hunter-shepherd Bilgee took a young Chinese student named Chen to watch a pack of wolves hunt a huge herd of gazelles. The herd was grazing on a nearby hill, and over the course of several hours in dense snow, Bilgee and Chen watched as the wolfpack slowly encircled the unaware gazelles. When a wolf ran away, young Chen worried the wolves were giving up, and they'd waited for nothing. Belgee said, "The pack won't pass up an opportunity like this. The leader must have felt there are too many gazelles, so he sent a runner to bring more troops… They're getting ready for a major battle… patience is the key to a good hunt."[5]

Six or seven new wolves silently joined the enclosure on three sides, leaving the fourth side open. As both the humans and wolves watched the gazelles eat, Bilgee quietly described a favorite wolf solo hunting strategy. He described how a wolf would watch a gazelle during the day and all night long. Even asleep, the gazelle is too alert to be caught, and normally a gazelle could easily outrun any wolf. However, at sunrise the gazelle awakens with a full bladder, and the wolf attacks before the gazelle can urinate. Because the gazelle cannot urinate while running, the bladder eventually ruptures during the chase, allowing the wolf to go in for the kill.

Bilgee and Chen were watching the wolves play out a similar strategy as a pack. Eventually the gazelles' bellies became full, and some were so stuffed their legs were splayed out in all four directions. Bilgee looked through his old telescope and said, "They're so full they can't run. Watch closely. It's time for the wolves to strike."

The lead wolf and two others suddenly dashed to the open edge, completing the encirclement and trapping the gazelles. This was the signal for all the rest of the wolves to charge after hours of patient waiting. They made no shouts or howls, but launched a vicious coordinated attack in utter silence. A few gazelles escaped, but most were totally trapped. The wolves had a great feast, but they weren't the only ones.

The wolves killed much more than they could eat. After watching the wolves, Bilgee and Chen went back to their village and returned the next day with many wagons and neighbors to collect the leftovers. All the people ate well, depending only on the wild abundance and their caring neighbor Bilgee who brought in a huge bounty of meat.

2. What are My Energetic Boundaries?

To better understand my world, it helped me to ask, "What are my personal energetic boundaries?" In other words, what are the sources of feedback that tell me to do more or less of something?

The first energetic boundary I noticed was the law. The need to avoid legal punishment, with its huge costs and possible prison time, is a major boundary. Property lines limit my ability to explore the land. Legal obligations like completing tax paperwork or appearing in court control my time. The law forbids me from interrupting others while they behave inappropriately, such as when loggers clear cut forests or police abuse protesters. If I had a child, the law could threaten to take them away from me for certain kinds of noncompliance.

The next energetic boundary I noticed was money, which determines my quality of life. When I have a lot, I can have nice clothes, a clean home in a safe area, nutritious food, and health care. With enough savings, I can tell a boss "no" when he asks too much of me, knowing that if I get fired, I'll be ok. If I don't have much money, my quality of life drops, desperation increases, and I'm more willing to tolerate disrespectful bosses, lower quality food, etc.

Thus the need to make money dominates my life. I trained intensively in school to someday get a reliable good-paying job. After college I went into full time work that consumed most of my waking hours and energy. So long as I stayed fully employed, all other hobbies and relationships had to fit in around the job schedule. Furthermore, I may feel compelled to do work I find meaningless, as I continuously need money to survive. I may tolerate meaningless work if it helps me pay my bills.

Law and money affect my boundaries in countless ways large and small. For example, I do not have pets if the landlord forbids it. I do not talk politics at work for fear of losing my job if the boss disagrees. I do not intervene with the police when I see them acting abusively towards protesters.

This means that the opinions of my friends and neighbors are less relevant than the opinions of the uncaring people who shape my world. So long as I have enough money and avoid legal trouble, I could waste water during a drought, or have great feasts while the job market is poor and many neighbors go hungry. The opinions of uncaring people such as my boss at work, store clerks, the landlord, the police and bureaucrats have a bigger impact on me than the opinions of my neighbors and friends. So long as I please the people who don't care much about me, life can be ok even if my neighbors become upset with me.

In the story of the clown from *Daughters of Copper Woman* (see Chapter 3), she described the value of "the mirror in the eyes of the people you loved." I realized that unhealthy nations shape my world so I don't need to care much about the eyes of the people I love. So long as I please authorities and their uncaring servants, I can survive, regardless of how my friends and neighbors feel about me.

Healthy Nations Honor Boundaries Set by the Earth

It's true that humans hunt deer, and deer eat from humans' gardens. Humans hunt wolves, and wolves hunt the sheep in humans' herds. All animals eat plants or eat animals that eat plants. And despite how much animals and plants kill each other, it's also true that we're all in this together; that there's a big sacred dance of life we're all part of, and it requires a certain balance in order to continue. If this balance falters, the dance will change, or perhaps even end, and so humans must honor the role each animal and plant community plays and ensure they can keep playing it.

This is the sacred predator-prey relationship: I become dependent on anything I eat, and so I take responsibility for ensuring the health of an animal or plant's community even as I take from it.

When Chinese student Chen went to live with Mongolian hunter-shepherds, he learned from Bilgee how they relate to the wolves. The wolves sometimes ate humans' sheep, but they also ate the gazelles. Without the wolves, the gazelles would multiply and rapidly consume all the grass which the sheep needed for grazing. Bilgee said, "Gazelles are a scourge on the grassland… they… eat all the time." Bilgee said he sometimes hunted wolves, but not often, saying, "If we killed them off, the grassland would perish, and then how would we survive?"[6]

Bilgee even said his people don't use wolf pelts as bedding, even though they are far superior to sheep pelts, saying, "We respect the wolves too much… Tengger [God] is the father, the grassland is the mother, and the wolves kill only animals that harm the grassland. How could Tengger not bestow its favors on wolves?"

When a person's boundaries are honored in childhood, and they also grow up around people with strong boundaries, they learn to honor other people's boundaries in adulthood. In other words, when a person grows up in a culture where respect is the norm, then such a person is used to behaving respectfully in adulthood. Thus each person's sense of right and wrong becomes its own boundary that other people in a healthy nation honor under normal circumstances.

Jean Liedloff watched an example of this. Yequana man Tududu spent a morning lashing sticks together with vines to make a pen for his young son. Liedloff noticed he seemed pleased afterwards, and he excitedly put his son into the pen. The little boy had just taken his first step a week earlier. He moved to one side of the pen, turned around, and then realized he was trapped. Liedloff described how "in an instant he was screaming a message of utter horror, a sound rarely heard from children of his society. It was unequivocal. The playpen was wrong, unsuitable for human babies…"[7]

Instead of imposing his will, Tududu recognized he'd made a mistake and released his son, who promptly ran to his mother.

Tududu honored his son's boundaries not just by taking him out of the cage, but by recognizing that the cage itself was a mistake. His son's response demonstrated that it had no place in his nation. He recognized that his experiment had not worked, and he destroyed the cage.

These stories showed me what it's like in healthy nations where people learn to honor all boundaries, including those of children and nonhumans.

3. Does My Nation Draw My Attention Primarily to the Earth or to the Nation?

I notice that my nation constantly tries to direct my attention to the nation, rather than the Earth.

- *Metrics of success*: National metrics of success include gross domestic product, employment figures, and stock market levels. Humans' and nonhumans' health do not factor in.

- *Schools*: the vast majority of my time in grade school was spent studying human inventions: math, writing, literature, and science. I learned from books rather than studying the Earth and nonhumans directly. History classes focused almost exclusively on the history of the unhealthy nation I was born into. Teachers also taught about other unhealthy nations, such as the ancient Roman and Egyption empires and later the European empires, but almost never about healthy nations. Even classes such as biology presented various life processes as mechanisms to be mentally understood separate from the rest of my life, not webs of relationships in which I could play an integral part.

- *Perception*: For years I walked around with earbuds in my ears, hearing human-made music as a continual background sound rather than noticing all the sounds from the wind, the trees, the birds, and unexpected human noises happening around me.

- *Religion*: In childhood, my church and family directed my attention to a book called the Holy Bible and told me I should study it if I wanted to understand God and learn valuable life lessons. Religious gatherings were consistently held inside human-built structures called churches. I learned to pray by thinking thoughts in my head, directed toward an abstract entity called God. No one suggested that I could connect with the Divine outside in the natural world. No one suggested that non-humans, such as squirrels or dandelions, might have profound spiritual and practical life lessons for me.

- *Life environment*: my time in school, at work, and during my commute has been spent almost entirely inside human-built structures, not outside. My time has been structured by authority figures based on clocks and calendars rather than natural rhythms like the position of the sun or season of the year or simply what feels satisfying to me. My clothes and houses have been manufactured by other people from materials which I can't easily make, such as plastics, acrylic, stainless steel, asphalt, and so on. I rely on licensed professionals to maintain my house for me and keep it legally habitable.

The point of this exercise is this: my life is overwhelmingly shaped by my nation, from religion and sources of mentorship to my perception of space and time. It would be easy to go my entire life without really considering my relationship with the Earth and the non-human world in any concrete way. My nation constantly tries to draw my attention to the abusive nation itself instead of to the Earth and nonhumans.

The law and need for money are dominant influences, but these examples show that unhealthy nations shape people's lives in many more ways besides. How each person responds to these incentives and threats and narratives is, of course, up to them.

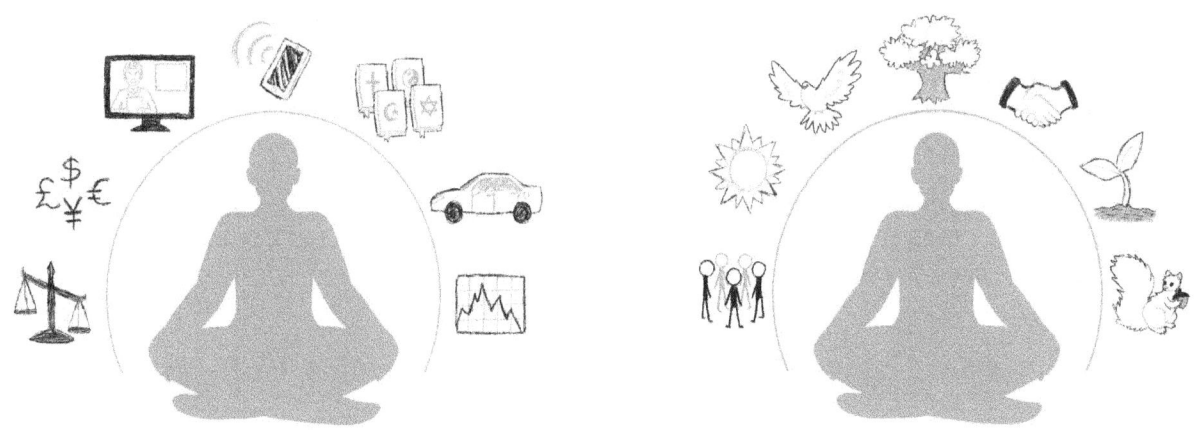

Do teachers and leaders draw my attention primarily to the nation or to the Earth?

Healthy Nations Draw People's Attention Primarily to the Earth

Does my nation draw my attention to the Earth or to the nation as the primary aspect of my environment? Is the nation or the Earth the primary source of deep lessons, sustenance, adventure and boundaries?

Bilgee showed the power of making nonhumans one's primary teachers. Bilgee said, "In war, wolves are smarter than men. We Mongols learned from them how to hunt, how to encircle, even how to fight a war." Bilgee directed Chen to watch the wolves as they prepared an attack on gazelles. Watching the wolves, young Chen realized how the Mongols had been able to conquer much of northern Asia many centuries earlier: they had learned from the wolves. Instead of directing Chen to study human teachers of war, Bilgee directed his attention to wolves as his primary teacher.[8]

Ohiyesa described the birth of a baby Sioux girl named Winona, and how she was immediately directed to pay attention to nonhumans. She was wrapped in soft white doeskin, lined with cattails, and laced into a beautifully embroidered buckskin bag attached to an oaken cradle. Her grandmother told this luxuriously wrapped newborn, "You must come with me. We shall go among the father and mother trees, and hear them speak with their thousand tongues, that you may know their language forever. I will hang the cradle of the woman-child upon Utuhu, the oak; and she shall hear the love-sighs of the pine maiden!" Immediately after birth, young Winona was being trained to pay attention to the Earth.[9]

I heard a story that illustrated how capable children can become when their attention is directed lovingly towards the Earth. A friend described meeting a woman who grew up in a healthy nation in California. Sadly, I did not learn the nation's name. However, this woman told my friend that when she was a little girl, she believed all humans were born knowing the names of all the plants around them. She estimates that by the time she was 5 or 6 years old, she knew the names of two hundred plants.

It wasn't until she went to public school, and met children brought up as most little Americans are, that she learned the truth: humans aren't born knowing the names of the plants. Her mother had simply carried her on her back as she walked through the woods and fields and as she tended the garden, and everywhere she walked she would point out to her young daughter the names of the plants. In this way, the daughter became so familiar with the plants that she thought she was born knowing their names!

When healthy nations focus on the Earth as the most important, they are not devaluing their nation or putting themselves down. It's not that *either* the Earth *or* the nation is valued. When a healthy nation draws people's attention primarily to the Earth, they learn how to live with the Earth in a good way, ensuring there is space for humans and nonhumans alike. They also consider their nation important. It's just that, if the nation and Earth get out of sync, they understand that the nation needs to adjust to living with the Earth rather than try to make the Earth adjust to the nation.

"Trying to make the Earth adjust to the nation" is a good summary of how unhealthy nations relate to the Earth. It explains why there is so much destruction, pollution, soil degradation, biodiversity loss, species extinction, and so many other troubles.

Unhealthy Nations Control our World While Disconnecting Us from the Real World

In abusive relationships, the master instills fear so that all other considerations become secondary to staving off punishment and getting one's needs met. The master sets the energetic boundaries with rules and rewards. The master decides who eats well and who does not. And the master directs everyone's attention away from intimate connection with the Earth and each other, so that humans live in a world defined primarily by the nation which the master controls.

This same dynamic can occur in abusive families of two or more people, on slave plantations of 200 people, and vast civilizations of millions of people. There might be a single master such as a king, or a group of masters such as oligarchs. Unhealthy nations are massive, multi-generational abusive relationships.

Because people's worlds are defined by the human nation, and authorities can control the nation, authorities can control and define people's worlds, often in very subtle ways. If my nation is my world, and rulers control my nation, that means rulers can control my world. This is true of everyone in unhealthy nations, whether they know it or not. People of unhealthy nations live in controlled worlds.

Of course, the Earth is always present, and anyone can direct their own energy and attention as they wish. Unhealthy nations condition people to think it's normal to live in a controllable world where one's life is primarily defined by one's nation. But each person can acknowledge the pressures they face from the unhealthy nation while choosing for themselves where to direct their energy and time.

If authorities can and do control the nation, and the nation controls people's worlds, then authorities can change anybody's world at will. What is it like to experience one's world being radically altered by authorities who don't care about people's wellbeing?

You can see for yourself in the next chapter, *Chapter 15: Unhealthy Nations Shape the Worlds of Millions of People*.

Chapter 15: Unhealthy Nations Shape the Worlds of Millions of People

The ruler or ruling class in unhealthy nations assert their power by manipulating the lives of many people, and this is the core disease that creates and maintains unhealthy nations.

In contrast, I have never found a single healthy nation, past or present, that has rulers of any kind. Nations without racism, sexism, dishonest leaders, and pollution don't have rulers. Nations with these problems do have rulers in every case I have found. This is why I believe that the presence or absence of rulers is what makes a society healthy or unhealthy.

Rulers and other authorities actively shape the lives of huge numbers of people. But this manipulation is so pervasive that many aspects of living in an unhealthy nation can seem "normal," as if nothing is being imposed. Instead, in unhealthy nations, many things can seem permanent, like the law, money, who is in charge, official ideas of what God supposedly wants, who is rich and who is poor. They're "just how life is."

But in truth, an individual or small group of people with power are creating and maintaining all these things, deciding "just how life is" for everybody else. This allows rulers to exploit the rest and maintain control.

I didn't realize how much people's lives were administered in unhealthy nations until I discovered stories of authorities selfishly manipulating the lives of thousands or even millions of people on a whim.

This chapter explores a sampling of these stories, showing what it's like to have rulers administer a person's world, and how radically that world can alter when authorities decide to make an adjustment.

What would it be like to wake up and discover that all of one's money was no longer legal tender?

What would it be like to start out life as a servant and end up as a chattel slave or poor "free" person because some rich people wanted to diminish solidarity among the lower class?

What would it be like for the government to deliberately make food completely unavailable in huge regions and then accuse hungry people of undermining the country?

What would it be like for a government to threaten to turn off the water whenever a community protests corporate destruction of the land?

The following stories provide a glimpse of just how deeply authorities can shape the worlds of the people they rule. Studying these patterns in other nations helps me see them more easily in my own.

Money: Demonetization in India in 2016

When I think about all the ways I depend on money, the list is quite long! Parents may use money to clothe and feed themselves and their children, to drive their children to school, or to pay for healthcare. People may use money to pay rent, mortgage, or property taxes. Transportation (vehicles, bikes, etc) and communication (computers, cell phones) and their ongoing maintenance all require money. All manner of comforts like travel, entertainment, socializing in restaurants, and more require money. Money may be needed to pay debts such as auto loans, credit cards, and business loans.

If any of these expenses aren't paid, the punishment is severe. A person may lose their vehicle or job, go without healthcare for themselves or their children, or suffer other serious consequences.

How would you respond if all of your financial needs and obligations continued to exist – you still needed money to buy food, pay rent, and so on – but the government suddenly decided to make your money no longer usable?

Millions of people faced this very situation in India, beginning at 8:00pm on November 8, 2016. On this date, Indian prime minister Narendra Modi gave a surprise speech announcing a policy called Notebandi, meaning demonetization. The speech provided only 4 hours' notice that beginning at midnight, 86% of all cash was no longer legally usable for making purchases in an economy where 9 out of 10 transactions occur in cash.[1,2]

Although the Indian government planned to replace a fraction of the currency with other bank notes, these were not widely available at the time of the announcement.

The Indian Finance Ministry stated that the policy's purpose was "To curb corruption, counterfeiting, the use of high denomination notes for terrorist activities, and especially the accumulation of 'black money' generated by income that has not been declared to the tax authorities."[3]

Many Indians questioned this, as government income tax data showed that more than 90% of illicit funds were held in real estate, jewelry, and stocks, not in cash. Thus, limiting cash use would have little impact on corruption.[4]

Almost a year later, the Reserve Bank of India acknowledged there was practically no impact on the availability of "black money," justifying people's skepticism. However, the policy went into effect regardless of how much sense it made to the people whose worlds were about to suddenly change.[5]

Whether or not fighting corruption was truly the prime minister's intention, his policy went live with almost no notice, and instantly upended the lives of millions of people who relied solely on cash outside the banking system to survive.

This illustrates a core problem in unhealthy nations: it is often difficult to tell the difference between a dishonest official and an incompetent one. The same is true of both corporate and government officials, or anybody who isn't held accountable for their behavior.

As a result of this radical decision, banks closed until November 10, and ATMs stayed closed until November 11.[6] When ATMs reopened, countless lines formed with hundreds of people waiting hour after hour to access their money. Many were disappointed.

Millions of people who had to work every day without fail to make ends meet faced a difficult choice: do I go to work to earn money, or do I stand in endless lines at the ATM to access what little savings I have to pay my immediate bills?

The lines were so long that some senior citizens fell to the ground and died of exhaustion. Private hospitals stopped accepting the old currency, making health care suddenly unavailable for many people.[7]

This rush to the ATMs meant that by end-December, only 35-40% of ATMs nationwide had any cash available at all.[8] To keep more than about $68-equivalent in cash, people could deposit the old currency into their bank accounts.[9] This was understandably difficult in a country where fewer than 35% of people above 15 years old had ever used a bank account. More than 90% had never used any kind of non-cash payment tool at all, such as a credit card.[10]

In a country of 1.3 billion people, this single surprise change suddenly had a massive impact on more than 1 billion people.

Farmers struggled to hire laborers, and thus many farmers' crops died in the field. Laborers couldn't get work, as the cash wasn't available to pay them. Shop owners couldn't sell their merchandise. One journalist interviewed a farmer named Uday Hazra and said he "spoke of a stifling feeling of cashlessness."[11]

Many people committed suicide, including collective family suicides. Farmer Deshraj Singh had taken out a loan against his land to support his daughter's marriage. When he couldn't access money to repay his loan, he risked losing his land and his ability to support his family. He killed himself.[12]

As stress increased, domestic violence increased as well, with one man pushing his wife out of a 10th story apartment because she did not return from the ATM with cash.[13] Financial predators took advantage of people's desperation, trapping even more people in debt.[14]

Indians' troubles continued for years, with many suicides and general hardship. One single government decision radically transformed the lives of hundreds of millions of people. Many faced destitution, loss of their property and livelihood, and uncertainty about how they would take care of their families.

The people responsible for this decision faced none of these troubles.

The legal and monetary systems that shape people's lives are designed and run by people. In unhealthy nations, humans can manipulate each others' lives by adjusting these systems. The administrators' uncaring attitude was made clear in an Indian Ministry of Finance economic report which noted that "short-term costs have taken the form of inconvenience and hardship, especially those in the informal and cash-intensive sectors of the economy who have lost income and employment. These costs are transitory, and may be minimised in recorded GDP…"[15]

Suicide and lost homes are hardly transitory. The administrators simply make clear that they don't care about "hardship… in the informal… sectors of the economy." This is just what selfishness can look like in a nation that rewards selfishness instead of generosity.

Many people complained about the policy and its execution, but the root problem – which no one ever seemed to point out – is that so many people are trapped in a social system that gives a few people power over the rest. In this particular case, millions of people were trapped in exploitative relationships where they were unable to effectively prevent a new, highly destructive monetary policy from being forced upon them.

Law: Institution of Chattel Slavery in British Colonial Virginia

In the early 1600s, after the British defeated the local healthy nations in war in British colonial Virginia, a few wealthy colonists controlled vast tracts of land, with some individuals owning 20,000-30,000 acres and at least one small group owning a tract of 80,000 acres.[16,17]

The trouble was that the land was considered worthless without laborers to work it (after all, one could hardly expect rich people to do the labor themselves). The wealthy landowners encouraged the immigration of servants from Europe and Africa, both voluntary and involuntary, to work the land so the rich could generate income. The landowners implemented a system of indentured servitude, where they would pay for a migrant's journey to North America in exchange for seven years of labor. The government sweetened the pot, giving landowners 50 acres of land for every migrant they could bring to work on it.[18]

British colonial Virginia in the early 1600s had no judicial ruling or statutory law forcing all black people into enslavement. Many Africans were forced to Virginia as slaves, but those who migrated there willingly could expect similar treatment as other migrants. Black Christian men, for example, could testify in court, and after finishing their period of indentured service, they were no longer bound. Some black people, such as Anthony Johnson, later become landowners and slaveowners themselves.[19]

As part of the same class, black and white indentured servants were exploited similarly by a few rich people who owned far more than they could ever need. While poor white and black people's situations weren't always identical, they were close enough that many white and black people would help each other escape their servitude. This solidarity between white and black people threatened to reduce the rich people's wealth.

This presented a problem for the wealthy white planters, and over time they devised a 3-part solution. In order to create a large, reliable workforce and discourage solidarity between poor white and black people, the rich landowners over time selfishly developed these goals:

1. Lift the privilege level of white people and lower the privilege level of black people so that they would fight each other and not unite against the rich landowners who exploited them both.

2. Discourage friendship and intimacy between black and white people.

3. Create a consistent narrative that justified these new divisive social patterns.

How did the rich white planters achieve each of these goals?

1. Lift the Social Status of Whites and Lower the Social Status of Blacks

While some racial discrimination had existed in Virginia for a long time, originally it was justified by a belief in the superiority of Christians, where most Europeans were presumably Christian and most others were presumably not.

Starting in 1640, Virginia law began to discriminate against black people and discriminate favorably towards white people solely by their skin color without reference to religion.

When black and white indentured servants were caught escaping together, Virginia courts treated them differently. When the black man John Punch was caught escaping with white people, the whites were given three additional years of labor while Punch was condemned to labor for life. When a black man named Emanuel was caught escaping with six white accomplices, all were given a whipping. The whites were given an extra year of labor. As Emanuel was already required to work for life for his master, he was "burnt in the cheek with the letter R. and to work in shackle for one year or more as his master shall see cause."[20]

Later in 1670, when the law made the punishment for escape even harsher, it still included different penalties for fugitive white people compared to fugitive black people. Escaping white servants were only whipped after their second escape. Black servants, by this time already required to work for life, were given whippings after their first failed escape.[21]

The wealthy colonists found other ways to impose racial differences. Prior to 1640, all colonists were allowed to arm themselves. In 1640, the Virginia General Assembly passed a law prohibiting black people from owning weapons unless they owned land. The law also required masters to give guns and ammunition to healthy members of their households with the exception of black people.[22]

This racial disparity became even greater in 1706, when the governing council required that white people be issued a gun upon completion of their period of service, encouraging them to embrace a policing role over black people, many of whom by then could never legally hope to be free or own a firearm.[23]

The law began to explicitly state which race should have power and which should not, inviting poor white people to see the rich white people as allies. In the mid 1600s, black people were prohibited from owning or even supervising white people, although black people were allowed to purchase other black people as slaves. For example, a white servant named Hannah Warrick avoided punishment after running away because her overseer was black.[24]

Black people were forbidden from congregating or leaving their plantation without a pass from their master, and they were forbidden from having any weapon, including a "club, staffe, [or] gunn." A black person who raised their hand against any white person could automatically receive 30 lashes, but white people could legally kill black people for "lying out and resisting."[25]

Because enslaved black people were slaves for life, they could not be threatened with an extension of their term. Thus a law in 1669 gave slaveowners and overseers the legal power to kill enslaved black people. This homicide was not considered murder, because murder supposedly requires malice, and the General Assembly reasoned that nobody would destroy their human property with malice.[26]

Terrorizing black people into submission was lawmakers' clear, explicit goal. A 1705 law allowed slaveowners to request a county court to dismember a habitual runaway, which could involve castration or cutting off a foot. Hoping to discourage runaways, the General Assembly stated that this law would have the effect of "terrifying others from the like practices."[27]

To make black people a permanent underclass, the government decided to make children born of enslaved mothers also slaves for life. In 1655, an enslaved woman named Elizabeth Key successfully sued her owner for her freedom, and her legal claim to freedom was partly justified by having a white father. The government cut off this avenue of escape with a new law in 1662 that decreed that children were "bond or free only according to the condition of the mother."[28]

Free black people were also targeted with discriminatory laws to keep them in poverty. After the slave code law was passed in 1705, black people were forbidden to hold any civil, military, or religious role, effectively denying them any role of official leadership or authority in the colony.[29]

Further, the government imposed a tax on free black women as field laborers which white families did not have to pay, leading to financial devastation even for unenslaved black people.[30]

Similar to how an executive administers a corporation, rulers administer their societies, and sometimes they make rules with unforeseen loopholes. For example, once black people were enslaved for life, why would slaveowners report their slaves' crimes? For decades, slaveowners often hid their slaves' criminal behavior because they would receive no compensation if he or she went to jail. The Assembly rectified this in 1705, such that the government would compensate the slaveowner for any imprisoned slave. Governor Gooch wrote that this would serve as an "encouragement to People to discover the Villainies of their slaves."[31]

These examples illustrate both the increased social status of whites and decreased status of blacks. Black people were punished more heavily and given life sentences when they broke the law. Blacks were forbidden from owning firearms or even defending themselves but whites were actively armed after finishing their temporary service and allowed to kill disobedient blacks. Free black and white people were taxed differently, and white people could become overseers while black people could not.

In these ways, the social status of whites was intentionally raised, the status of blacks intentionally lowered, and the two groups were made to oppose each other. The poor blacks wanted to alter or escape the system, and the poor whites were encouraged to enforce the authority of the owners.

This is simply the kind of thing that happens when people have rulers. They behave selfishly, manipulating the lives of everyone else in countless ways to maintain their control. Rulers will keep behaving selfishly, each ruler or ruling class in their own way, until we can create a nation where nobody rules over anybody else.

Unfortunately, these colonial authorities weren't done yet.

2. Discourage Friendship, Intimacy, and Collaboration Between Black and White People

The Virginia colonial government discouraged any intimacy or collaboration between white and black people. Lawmakers understood that black people trapped in lifelong slavery could not be threatened with additional work time. A 1661 law discouraged white people from escaping with black people by requiring that the white worker face additional time for their own escape plus time for the black person's escape. This extra penalty made collaboration even riskier for white people.[32]

Sex between black and white people was officially heavily punished, although the government did not protect enslaved people from their predatory slaveowners. Because of black men's slave status, rich landowners who controlled the government acknowledged that sex between black men and white women was "implicitly most dangerous to the social order... [and] threatening to patriarchal authority, property, and the security of labor."[33]

Of course, it was difficult to catch people having sex. Thus in 1691, authorities passed a law punishing white women who gave birth to biracial children. A free white woman who birthed a mixed-race child was heavily fined, and if she could not pay, then she owed five years' labor. If she was already a servant, she owed five additional years after her contract expired and her child was bound to the church until they became 30 years old. Biracial marriage was also outlawed in 1691.[34]

Furthermore, white people were forbidden from sympathizing with black people, and even the law wouldn't protect them. This is clear in many stories from the time after Virginia stopped being a colony and became a US state, supposedly subject to the US Constitution. Anyone who possessed literature that showed enslaved black people in a sympathetic light could go to jail for years, or worse.[35,36] Clearly this was in violation of the first amendment of the US Constitution which protected freedom of speech and freedom of the press, but authorities ignored that law. When chattel slavery ended after the US Civil War, the wealthy ex-slaveowners launched a paramilitary terror campaign called the Ku Klux Klan (discussed in Chapter 22) which raped, killed, mutilated, and otherwise terrorized huge numbers of black people – as well as any white people who sympathized with them or supported them. Terrorizing poor white people who dared to sympathize with poor black people was a major mechanism for imposing severe anti-black racism over centuries.

Thus, the government and the wealthy land owners who controlled it strongly discouraged any kind of intimacy or collaboration between poor white and black people.

3. Settle on a Consistent Narrative that Justifies the Exploitative Social Relationships

In the early 1600s, wealthy colonists justified the enslavement of some Africans by stating that Christians are superior people, and so people from non-Christian regions supposedly should be slaves of Christians. It made sense to use this narrative, as the superiority of Christians was also used to justify the imperialist wars and economic exploitation that Europeans had brought against people in Africa, North America, and South America for many years.

But there was a catch: what if black people became baptized as Christian and sued for their freedom? The legal status of enslaved Christians was unclear. In the mid-1600s, an enslaved Christian man named Manuel petitioned the General Assembly for his freedom, stating that his legal owner William Whittacre had wrongly purchased him in 1644. Manuel's Latin name indicates he may have previously lived in a Hispanic nation where he had become Christian.[37]

Whittacre traced Manuel's ownership back to two previous owners, and he believed Manuel had been marked "as a Slave for Ever." However, the General Assembly ruled that Manuel "was to serve as other Christian servants do." They fined Whittacre 25 pounds Sterling. Whittacre unsuccessfully contested the ruling, and Manuel was freed in 1665, 21 years after the purchase.

This doubt about a Christian's status represented a tremendous liability for slave owners. Much of the value of their wealth resided in the people they owned, and they demanded certainty about the legal status of their property, Christian or not. In 1667, the General Assembly relieved slave owners of this concern with a law stating that baptism would no longer affect a person's status as slave. This act allowed Christ-following, proselytizing masters to safely christen their bonded laborers. Thus property rights were maintained while enslaved people were conditioned with Christian ideas. Over the mid 1600s, the Assembly passed various laws justifying different groups' status as free, servant or slave based on their region of origin or region of their ancestors' origin.[38]

The legislators and their funders were trying to craft a good cover story that allowed them to use Christian superiority to justify enslavement. However, they realized their cover story needed further adjustment. After a 1682 law, anyone "whose parentage and native country are not christian at the time of their first purchase" could be enslaved for life, such as Africans or North Americans "taken in warre." These changes would prevent both "great losse and damage" to slave owners and "great discouragement" to people "bringing in such slaves for the future."[39]

Thus, slave owners need not worry whether a particular person was Christian. Only the supposed Christian status of their ancestors in their home territory was relevant. The slaveowners had successfully used laws about Christianity to radically alter the privilege levels of white and black people, as well as slaves native to North or Central America.

The law treated black people abominably, whereas poor white people could avoid trouble so long as they obeyed the law. In contrast, the rich broke the law at will. For example, the law clearly outlawed sex between black and white people, but many accounts of US antebellum slavery noted that slaveowners routinely raped black women[40], recognizing that babies stemming from this rape increased their financial wealth. The rich slaveowners had created a society where the law treated poor black people unfairly and poor white people more-or-less fairly. Law enforcement treated rich white people unfairly but in their favor, letting them get away with illegal behavior.

The purpose of adjusting all these laws was to trap both poor white and poor black people in an exploitative social system and to motivate the poor white people to support it. This deliberate, large-scale social manipulation allowed a few rich white people to keep their wealth and privilege for centuries with poor white people's support.

It helped me to recognize that while both black and white people got screwed over, and black people got screwed over much more than whites, it was the poor white people who got scammed. I don't think black chattel slaves were ever under any illusion that rich whites were on their side, but poor white people were tricked into thinking they were allied with the rich. The rich propagated all manner of false ideas about white solidarity, white supremacy, and other nonsense that they clearly didn't mean. The rich white people didn't care about white supremacy. They cared about their own supremacy, and they tricked similarly-colored poor people into supporting their selfish policies.

Racism, "white supremacy" and other nonsense are simply scams that an unfortunate number of white people fall for. The moment a poor white person stops supporting the rich whites' selfish policies, or when they start organizing a union to seek higher wages, they will be punished too, and they find out how little the rich whites care about their skin color. Propaganda about "white supremacy" simply trains poor whites to support abusive authorities instead of standing in solidarity with other abused people to change things for real.

The sooner people stop falling for these scams, the better!

Rulers and other authorities manipulate huge numbers of people in their own society and lie about it. The results are rather gruesome.
This is a normal pattern in any society where people allow themselves to be ruled.

Food: The Holodomor, aka Terror Famine in the Soviet Union

The Soviet Union offers another example to illustrate how those in power deeply manipulate the lives of everyone else in their unhealthy nation. In 1933, a terrible famine had descended upon Soviet Ukraine. Visitors to cities like Kiev, Stalino, and Kharkiv witnessed hundreds of thousands of people standing in bread lines, often lining up at 2AM for shops that opened at 7AM. People would wait in line all day, and sometimes for two days, desperately afraid of losing their place in line. Pregnant women and maimed veterans stood in line like the rest. Some women would wail, and visitors remarked that a vast bread line would sound like a profoundly suffering animal.[41]

One person called the children "living skeletons." Another person felt upset about the starved corpses outside his door. Police rounded up starving children so they could die in the barracks instead of the streets. The children often found the streets easier, with one child begging, "Let me die in peace, I don't want to die in the death barracks." Some peasants who were not allowed to leave hung themselves on trees visible from the trains. Visitors saw mothers holding up their children to trains, which one man described as "horrible infants with enormous wobbling heads, sticklike limbs, and swollen, pointed bellies."[42]

This starvation was the direct result of the Soviet policy of collectivization.

Collectivization began in January 1930 when the Soviet government faced huge opposition from capitalist countries that had already begun spreading anti-Soviet and anti-communist propaganda. These capitalist countries' rulers sought to scare their own workers away from seeking to end capitalist exploitation in their own nations. One example was the so-called "Red Scare" in the United States.[43] (To explore how authorities can encourage unclear thinking and assumptions, see *Chapter 39: Even More Propaganda Techniques*.)

The Soviet leadership felt great pressure to industrialize their economy. Other countries were mass-producing food with larger and larger mechanized farms while the Soviet Union still relied heavily on small-scale family farms and did not have a large mechanized industrial farming sector. In any future war, the Soviet leadership knew they would need a large army and surplus food to feed that army. Thus they believed that they needed a more productive mechanized farming sector.[44]

The plan was to take away small farmers' private land, pushing some farmers into government-run industrialized collective farms and others into factory work. Crops would be state-owned, and the government could decide how much surplus to take and how much to compensate workers. (To see how unhealthy nations control land, see *Chapter 34: Who Controls the Land?*.)

The trouble was that many farmers were content on their private farms. These private land-owning farmers were called kulaks. There was no clear definition of "kulak," and in practice local administrators would decide who was a kulak and who wasn't. However, a kulak could be anyone who owned land, several horses or cattle and was able to hire workers. Because of widespread poverty, this wealth was enough to make kulaks influential in local villages, often rivaling Soviet administrators for power.[45] Soviet leader Josef Stalin set out to remove their political power and confiscate their land. In December 1929 Stalin announced that kulaks would be "liquidated as a class."[46]

Government-generated stories and posters depicted kulaks as a threat, inspiring hate and anger towards kulaks which then justified their upcoming policy. For example, one anti-kulak poster said, "We Will Annihilate Kulaks as a Class!" and it contained a picture of a farmer under a tractor's wheels, another farmer as an ape hoarding grain, and another sucking milk directly from the cow's teat, implying it was the kulaks' selfish hoarding that caused food shortages. The state portrayed these people as subhuman animals and treated them as such.

"We Will Annihilate Kulaks as a Class!" – a government poster intended to spread hatred towards farm owners to justify taking their land for state-run farms.[47]

Soviet leadership authorized the police to screen the Soviet Union's entire peasant population. In each locality, a group of three people called a "troika" decided the fate of the peasants without appeal. The Soviet Union had laws and courts, but these were now ignored. Farmers were given a simple choice: sign over their farm or be sent to a prison slave camp. The government recruited 25,000 workers as police and told them the peasant farmers were responsible for food shortages. The police foolishly believed what they were told and promised to "make soap out of the kulak."[48] (to explore how rulers can train people to hate each other and see harmless people as threats, see *Chapter 22: Imposing And Maintaining Hatred*)

From January-April 1930, over 113,000 people were removed to Soviet prisons in Siberia, Kazakhstan, or other distant locales with little or no warning where they worked as slave laborers building canals or factories.[49]

The government expected a 5% death rate in the prisons, but it was 10%-15% in practice, prompting one prisoner to note, "it is one thing to destroy the kulak in an economic sense; to destroy their children in a physical sense is nothing short of barbaric." So many children died in the Soviet gulag prisons that one person reported, "their corpses are taken to the cemetery in threes and fours without coffins."

While the collectivization had begun, it didn't go smoothly. Rather than engage in careful planning, local bureaucrats competed with each other to carry out their orders the fastest. By March 1930, about 70% of farms had been collectivized. However, this rapid, massive assault generated huge resistance. The Soviet police registered almost 1,000,000 acts of resistance in Ukraine in 1930.[50]

The Soviet leadership recognized that collectivization had not fully succeeded and in late 1930 it disbanded the collectives. Stalin and the Soviet Politburo, the Soviet Union's top governing body, reconsidered their approach and tried again in 1931. They purged the lower levels of the Ukrainian Soviet communist party, ensuring loyalty at all levels of government. The government raised taxes on independent farmers until they were forced into the collectives, which began to form again.

Collectives were given power to coerce neighboring private farmers. With just an internal vote, they could choose to force nearby farmers to give the collective their seed grain. Seed grain is the part of the crop that farmers keep so they have something to plant next year. Thus this policy of allowing collectivized farms to take private farms' seed grain threatened private farms' existence. Farmers without seed grain could not raise crops and could not survive off their own labor. (To explore how rulers can train one group of people to oppress and misunderstand another group, see *Chapter 27: Privilege 2 - Social Class and Promise Keeping*.)

Collectivization came on more slowly in 1931 than the previous year, happening family by family rather than whole villages all at once, making it harder to resist collectively. Deportations to the Gulag system of work camps continued. A few letters sent back home that managed to escape the censors included messages like, "No matter what, don't come. We are dying here. Better to hide, better to die there, but no matter what, don't come here."

One party activist noted that yielding to collectivization meant choosing, "to face starvation at home rather than banishment to the unknown." By the end of 1931, Ukraine again reached 70% collectivization, and this time it stayed that way.

This year's harvest went poorly for many reasons. The best farmers had been deported, hungry peasants had killed or sold livestock which limited animal power, and fewer tractors had been produced than anticipated. Peasants who had lost land felt little motivation to work hard.[51]

Stalin believed the peasants must be hoarding grain as so little had been produced. In December 1931, he ordered that all collective farms which had not met their quota must give up seed grain. He expected that this would pressure holdouts to stop hoarding, but the truth was that farmers simply had nothing. By this time, many peasants were hungry. They had no land and no ability to resist expropriations. In early 1932 they lacked seed grain to plant that fall's harvest.[52]

At this point, the collectivization policy had clearly disappointed the Soviet leadership. However, rather than acknowledge their own mistakes, Soviet and Ukrainian leaders lied to each other and themselves, pretending that starving workers must be purposely going hungry in order to undermine the state.

For example, the Ukrainian party leader Stanisław Kosior reported to the Soviet leadership in August 1931 that grain targets were unrealistic given the low yields. A member of the Soviet Politburo responded that the real problem was concealment and theft by the peasants. Though Kosior knew better, he enforced the Politburo's belief on the rest of the Ukrainian communist party. (To explore how people can go through the motions of serving their people when they're really serving themselves, see *Chapter 29: Privilege 3 - Going Through the Motions*.)

The danger of mass starvation was clear to all; the question was who to blame, and what to do in response. Soviet party members and secret police filed endless reports of death by starvation. Many became numb to the slow massacre, with one letter stating, "Collective farm members go into the fields and disappear. After a few days their corpses are found and, entirely without emotion, as though this were normal, buried in graves…" On June 18, 1931 Stalin privately admitted that there was a famine in Soviet Ukraine. The previous day, the Soviet Ukrainian leadership had requested food aid but Stalin declined, stating that "it is imperative to export without fail immediately."

Stalin continued to refuse to admit his mistakes – one of the many drawbacks of rulers, as opposed to leaders who are accountable to their people. He worried that starving peasants might tarnish the reputation of his collectivization program with their "whining."[53] In one letter, Stalin accused peasants of using hunger as a weapon against him. Another Soviet leader supported Stalin's biases, claiming the Ukrainian party was using talk of "innocent victims" as a "rotten cover-up." They speculated that sabotage was the real cause of hunger, or local party members were saboteurs, or Polish intelligence agents were to blame. The leaders were willing to hold anyone but themselves accountable for their mistakes.[54] (To explore issues of accountability in unhealthy nations, see *Chapter 4: Shared Accountability vs Abusive Law Enforcement*)

However, fears of Polish interference were unfounded. Polish spies and diplomats did witness the famine. They knew that "cannibalism has become a habit of sorts" and wrote that "entire villages have died out completely." But the Polish government did not cause the famine, did not help the victims in Ukraine, and did not publicize to the world what their diplomats found.

Thousands of Ukrainians had fled to Poland, including some whole villages. During the famine, these immigrants spread awareness of the terrible conditions in the Soviet Union. Some of the peasants even begged Poland to invade. However, after the Soviet Union and Poland signed a non-aggression pact in 1932, this hope was dashed.[55,56]

Stalin decided collectivization only needed the correct legal basis. Among other rules, he decided that all crops would be state property, and anyone who so much as picked up a potato peel for themselves would be shot. Simple possession of food became evidence of this crime. This law came into force in August 1932.[57]

The nightmare would only get worse from there.

In the book *Catch-22*, Joseph Heller illustrates how people can be put into impossible situations by contradictory bureaucratic rules. Because Soviet leadership was unwilling to face reality, the Ukrainians found themselves in just such an impossibility: they could only eat if they produced enough grain, but they could not do so for a large number of reasons outside their control. However, not producing enough grain was considered proof that peasants were stealing or sabotaging the government, and their punishment was death or imprisonment. (To explore how rulers can impose unjust or nonsensical laws, see *Chapter 3: Shared Agreements vs Imposed Laws*.)

The anti-kulak propaganda continued, with young people in official youth organizations of Soviet schools being trained that their "main task" was "the struggle against theft and the hiding of grain as well as kulak sabotage." Immersed in their unhealthy nation and unwilling to seek out the truth for themselves, many young government leaders really believed that rural peasants were a big threat to the country and enthusiastically participated in anti-peasant campaigns. The government both encouraged and rewarded ignorance and lazy thinking in the anti-peasant police and party members. (To explore how rulers train people to misunderstand each other, see *Chapter 37: Culture Jamming*.)

Watchtowers went up in fields to keep peasants from taking any food for themselves. Thousands of police went from hut to hut seizing all the food they could find. One peasant said, "They looked everywhere and took everything, down to the last little grain." They even took supper from the stove which they ate themselves. They often humiliated the peasants, urinating in barrels of pickles, making hungry peasants fight each other, or forcing them to kneel in the mud and pray. Many women who lived alone were raped before their food was taken. (To explore how police can be trained to serve authorities who behave illegally rather than protect their own people from threats, see *Chapter 32: A Study in Privilege and World-Shaping - the Police*.)

Surprisingly or not, this starvation, rape, theft, and unrealistic quotas meant that collective farms only met 1/3 of their annual target.

Stalin's disconnection from reality worsened. Though he'd already acknowledged the famine in Ukraine, he now considered it a "fairy tale," a malicious rumor spread by subversives. He believed that resistance to socialism increased as it became more successful, and so greater resistance indicated greater success.

Any problem in the Soviet Union could thus be defined as the result of enemy action. Hungry peasants were supposedly signs of capitalist countries' efforts to smear the Soviet Union. These were not merely Stalin's beliefs; they were enforced by top party leaders as they traveled through Ukraine and other regions of mass starvation in 1932.[58] (To explore how people in unhealthy nations struggle to protect themselves from predation by authorities, see *Chapter 38: Endless Predation When the Root Disease Goes Unhealed*.)

In unhealthy nations that do not hold their leaders accountable for inappropriate behavior, there is little to stop rulers or a ruling class from believing whatever they like, and acting as if their beliefs are true. It would be funny if it weren't so tragic. Sometimes it seems like the foolishness never ends – and of course, it won't end so long as a nation has rulers.

It was easier for Stalin to believe this nonsense as he never bothered to witness the carnage. Local party leaders in the midst of mass government-enforced starvation had difficulty maintaining this false narrative in their own minds, but they did their best and succeeded remarkably. Local party leaders could have simply acknowledged the truth of the helpless desperation all around them. Instead, knowing they might be deported to the gulag prison slave camps, they protected their own safety and comfort by pretending to themselves that the peasants must be saboteurs who were so opposed to socialism that they let their families starve. In the cities, young Ukrainian communists were told that starving peasants "risked their lives to spoil our optimism." (To explore how people can pretend to believe obvious falsehoods, see *Chapter 6: Blind Belief 1 - When People Ignore Reality to Maintain Safety and Comfort*.)

In the fall of 1932, military units accompanied police and party officials on their farm raids. Stalin's goal was to deliver the "shattering blow" to the totally imaginary resistance to his policies.[59]

In late 1932 and 1933, seven policies combined to produce mass death. Peasants were required to give up all grain and return any advances they had received. But because they received no documentation for giving up grain, they were subject to repeated hassling. Peasants who could not meet the grain quota were assessed a meat penalty and still owed the grain. The family cow or pig which might be their last protection from starvation was confiscated.

Soviet authorities introduced a black list of villages which were immediately required to give up fifteen times the normal amount of grain. Hoards of party activists and police descended, and since the quota could never be met, these enforcers took everything they could. Further, these villages were forbidden from trading or receiving deliveries of any kind from the rest of the country. Nobody was allowed to leave. Village leaders were arrested. All stores were closed.

They were essentially blockaded by their own government. With their food stolen and totally cut off from supplies, black-listed villages became death zones. One researcher compiled a list of black-listed villages which filled 180 pages. Many villages were black-listed to target particular minorities or ethnicities which might resist Soviet rule.[60] (To explore how rulers can impose systemic racism or ethnic discrimination, see *Chapter 20: Imposing And Maintaining Racism vs Generating Unity*)

Even the Ukrainian officials who worked so hard to ignore reality and obey Stalin were not safe. The Ukrainian chief of security claimed that the famine was a plot of Ukrainian nationalists. Anyone who did not support the requisitions was thus supposedly a traitor to the state. He had many local communist officials sent to the gulag.[61]

Stalin sealed the border of Ukraine in 1933 and forbade peasants from traveling to cities. The sale of long-distance train tickets was forbidden to peasants. Stalin justified this by claiming that peasants were not begging for bread, but rather engaged in a "counterrevolutionary plot," acting as living propaganda in support of capitalist efforts to discredit collectivization. By the end of February 1933, 190,000 runaway peasants had been arrested and returned to their villages to starve.[62]

The result was total devastation. Party activists were too afraid of being purged to stop it. One party official described what he witnessed: "I saw women and children with distended bellies, turning blue, still breathing but with vacant, lifeless eyes." He avoided insanity or suicide because, "As before, I believed because I wanted to believe." Party leaders knew they could either oppress the peasants or suffer the same fate.[63]

The mass death proceeded with government support, with whatever emotional and mental gymnastics were required. Estimates were that by spring 1933, 10,000 people per day were starving to death.[64]

Approximately 300,000 Ukrainian peasants were sent to the gulag prisons for missing grain quotas or other reasons. The Soviet leadership imposed similar policies in other regions. In total, nearly two million kulaks were imprisoned.

The government imposed endless suffering. Children collapsed in class and were buried, and this stopped being remarkable. Marriages struggled as some wives prostituted themselves to party leaders for flour, sometimes with their husband consenting.[65]

In a time of total catastrophe, the state turned the screws tighter, sabotaging solidarity even within nuclear families. Members of the Young Communists helped requisition food for the government. Children in the Pioneers were placed on the watchtowers to ensure adults in the fields did not steal food. These children were trained to be "the eyes and ears of the party inside the family." 500,000 pre-teen and young teenage boys and girls stood in watchtowers in the summer of 1933. Schools taught all the children to report on their parents. (To explore how authorities can give some individuals higher privilege and pressure them to turn against their own people, see *Chapter 26: Privilege 1 - Lift-and-Turn*.)

In the face of this apocalypse and humiliation, families reacted in many different ways. Most Ukrainians did not engage in cannibalism, and anybody caught could be spontaneously beaten or killed by their neighbors. Still, police records showed that in Soviet Ukraine, "families kill their weakest members, usually children, and use the meat for eating." Not all cannibalism was selfish though. Some Ukrainian children told their siblings, "Mother says that we should eat her if she dies."[66]

The government did not keep good records, but estimates just for Ukraine range from 2,400,000 to 3,900,000 deaths. Millions more died at the same time in neighboring Russia and Kazakhstan, also part of the Soviet Union.

Life in an unhealthy nation may seem predictable, with little major change from day to day. But this story from the Soviet Union shows how artificial this predictability actually is. Rulers' decisions can and do affect everybody in unhealthy nations. Often this is only obvious in moments of change. These people lived in a "controllable world," their life shaped substantially by their nation and administered by the government – a predictable world that they may well have thought would go on forever. But they were unable to protect themselves from the deep incompetence, selfishness, and make-believe of their own government leaders.

Water: A Shuar Community Loses Access to the River and Gains Dependence on the Government

In 2015 I traveled from Quito, Ecuador into the Amazon where a new friend invited me to stay with his family for a month. After arriving, I learned that they were a nationality called Shuar, and his father was a chief in his community.

When I arrived, I noticed a strange contrast. In some ways, the family seemed very well off. They owned 250 acres of lush land that bordered a major river. Lots of fruit trees provided plenty of food, and we could fish at the river occasionally. The household consisted of a mother and her 12 children. The husband and father had a second family elsewhere.

In other ways, they did not seem so well off. The single mother of 12 children seemed to be raising them mostly by herself. The family had friends, but they had to travel some distance to come together. The mother needed money for kids' clothes, school equipment, and transportation to school, and she struggled to earn enough money for this. The family had a small amount of electricity in their kitchen cabin.

The father only came to visit once during my visit, but when he did he explained his village's transition from living in their traditional manner. He told the story very simply. He said the river downhill from us was at the center of his people's lives. They fished there, drank from it, bathed in it, and more.

This came to a sudden end when a corporation set up a factory a few hundred kilometers upstream. He didn't name the factory, but he named the consequences: the factory owners began polluting the nearby water, and the water became unsuitable for drinking and bathing. He said they still fished in it, but the sudden loss of drinking water was very difficult.

The Ecuadorian government offered to pipe water to the homes of the Shuar, integrating them into the central plumbing system. The chief told me that the community accepted this as they saw no alternative.

Ever since then, whenever a corporation or government agency wished to do something that this community resented, the chief would protest and a government official would threaten to cut off their water unless they complied. And inevitably they would comply because now they depended on the government for water.[67]

These stories show how rulers and others in power severely shape the worlds of millions of people. They might seem far away or long ago, and people who are safe and comfortable now may like to think that they are safe from such disasters.

Every single one of us in unhealthy nations is subject to this level of manipulation continuously, whether it involves law, money, food, water, false beliefs, hate, racism, or anything else. This is simply what happens when a few people rule over everyone else and shape their lives in countless ways.

As long as people do not hold their leaders accountable, stories of epic selfishness and incompetence among rulers will continue. The way to end this catastrophe is to generate a nation where nobody rules over anybody else.

No one person trapped in an unhealthy nation can heal it alone. It takes a village to heal a village. But each person can take responsibility for facing the truth and doing their best. This book will explore collective responsibility later. Now, in *Chapter 16: Courageous Solidarity in Action*, I want to introduce you to one of my favorite heroes – a person whose stories of love and bravery bring joy to my heart and tears to my eyes.

Chapter 16: Courageous Solidarity in Action

When I think of courageous solidarity, one person's name stands out.

Born into chattel slavery in 19th-century United States, she survived one of the most terrifying unhealthy nations I've ever studied. Not only did she find a way to escape, she bravely returned over a dozen times to help others escape too, risking her life every time.[1]

For all this enormous risk and hard work, this courageous woman received no pay and no material gain of any kind.

She worked to free people by herself or with others' help as changing conditions allowed. In between, she got jobs, saved up money, and planned for future trips, becoming what some present-day governments would call a "self-radicalized, lone-wolf terrorist."

Not only was this fierce freedom fighter never caught, she kept on guiding others to freedom until she joined the Union army during the US Civil War, helping in the fight against the slave owners' army.

Given that she was committed to stealing human "property" in order to free them, and that property was very expensive, she is one of history's great thieves. She faced potential violence and death during each trip, and when people's lives hung in the balance, her self-control spoke to her total bravery. Estimates vary, but she personally freed about 70 people and assisted another 70 in escaping a life of brutal bondage.[2] Then she worked with the Union army to free millions more.

Whenever I feel down, I reread the following stories about my top hero: Harriet Tubman.

Tubman's Childhood

Harriet Tubman was born into an unhealthy nation where some people could own other people as property. Someone owned her mother, so they automatically owned Tubman too.

Tubman's childhood was difficult in ways that were common for enslaved people. As a young child, an overseer flew into a rage and threw a heavy weight at Tubman, breaking her skull and causing pressure on her brain that affected her throughout her life.[3] This pressure also led to fits of somnolency, a tendency towards sleepiness. For this terrible abuse, the overseer faced no accountability.[4]

Later, Tubman's master sold her two older sisters. She watched helplessly as they were dragged off crying in a chain gang, to no one knew where, leaving behind their intensely grieving mother and father.

Tubman's master rented her out to neighbors where she tended a child all night after doing housework all day. When she was given chores she didn't know how to do, she sometimes performed them poorly. Her temporary mistress yelled at her savagely and whipped her anew each time she failed at her chores. Only when the mistress's friend arrived and taught young Harriet Tubman how to do the chores did she finally please the mistress.

At the end of the day, Tubman was expected to tend the child. Her sleepiness due to her brain injury made this especially difficult, but if the child's mother found Tubman asleep, she would lash Tubman again with the whip. All this practice at forced wakefulness would serve her well later, but Tubman could not satisfy the mistress. The mistress finally returned Tubman to her master saying, "She wasn't worth a sixpence."

Tubman grew up with a strong faith in God. She didn't just pray occasionally. Whenever there was a need, she would tell God of it and trusted him to make things right. Tubman became very sick, and her master decided to sell her away from her home and family. Tubman said, "as I lay so sick on my bed, from Christmas till March, I was always praying for poor ole master. 'Pears like I didn't do nothing but pray for ole master. 'Oh, Lord, convert ole master;' 'Oh, dear Lord, change dat man's heart, and make him a Christian.' And all the time he was bringing men to look at me, and dey stood there saying what dey would give, and what dey would take, and all I could say was, 'Oh, Lord, convert ole master.' Den I heard dat as soon as I was able to move I was to be sent with my brudders, in the chain-gang to de far South. Then I changed my prayer, and I said, 'Lord, if you ain't never going to change dat man's heart, kill him, Lord, and take him out of de way, so he won't do no more mischief.'"

Tubman's Escape

In 1849, Harriet Tubman learned that her master planned to sell her and two of her brothers within a day or two. She was about 27 years old.[5] She convinced her brothers to escape with her, but couldn't have such a frank conversation with the family and friends she would leave behind. The overseers didn't like seeing slaves talk to each other, so she communicated through familiar hymns, singing, "When dat ar ole chariot comes, I'm gwine to lebe you, I'm boun' for de promised land, Frien's, I'm gwine to lebe you… I'll meet you in de mornin', When you reach de promised land; On de oder side of Jordan, For I'm boun' for de promised land." Tubman did not tell her mother of her departure, as she knew her mother's crying would have alerted their overseers.

Harriet Tubman and her brothers left, but the land was foreign to them and the hoped-for freedom was very far away. The brothers' fear of the slavecatchers loomed large and they turned back, choosing the horrors they knew over the consequences they'd face if they were caught.

Their sister, however, continued on alone.

Slavecatchers were offered a bounty for her capture[6], and she never knew how close they were. Tubman described her mindset: "I had reasoned dis out in my mind; there was one of two things I had a right to, liberty, or death; if I could not have one, I would have de oder; for no man should take me alive; I should fight for my liberty as long as my strength lasted, and when de time came for me to go, de Lord would let dem take me."

Without money or friends, she traveled through unknown regions. Moving by night and hiding by day, she trusted her intuition and faith to know whom to ask for food or shelter, or when to sleep alone on the cold ground under the stars.

Finally she crossed over to freedom. Tubman described her first thoughts: "I had crossed de line of which I had so long been dreaming. I was free; but dere was no one to welcome me to de land of freedom, I was a stranger in a strange land, and my home after all was down in de old cabin quarter, wid de ole folks, and my brudders and sisters. But to dis solemn resolution I came; I was free, and dey should be free also; I would make a home for dem in de North, and de Lord helping me, I would bring dem all dere. Oh, how I prayed den, lying all alone on de cold, damp ground; 'Oh, dear Lord,' I said, 'I haint got no friend but you. Come to my help, Lord, for I'm in trouble!'"

Tubman Becomes the Moses of her People

Tubman spent the following years working diligently and saving her money for one single purpose: to rescue her people from slavery. Whenever she saved enough, she would disappear from her northern home, returning at great personal risk to help others escape too.

The passage was very difficult, with escapees crossing rivers, scaling mountains, passing through forests and deliberately avoiding the easy-to-patrol trails and roads. Sometimes the escapees would lay flat in potato fields while slavecatchers walked just a few feet away.

One thing I admire about Tubman is that she knew exactly what she wanted, and she wouldn't let anything get in the way of her goal of freeing her people. She brought the opiate paregoric to give babies so that they wouldn't cry and betray the whole group. She brought along a pistol, not only to protect herself from slavecatchers and their dogs, but also to keep the group together. The way was so difficult that men would sometimes give up, their feet sore and bleeding, claiming they could not take another step. They would say they were ready to die, or if their strength returned, go back to their old home. Looking to protect the whole group, Tubman would pull out her revolver, point it at the head of the exhausted man, and say, "Dead niggers tell no tales; you go on or die!" Thus she ensured nobody could betray the group, even accidentally, and everyone escaped safely.

Her faith and bravery were beyond words. Once on a train, she overheard passengers reading a posted flier with a bounty for her capture. She couldn't read or write, but she knew that spelled trouble. She sent her escape party onwards without her and instead did what her captors might least expect: she went back south, to the very village where she was most likely to meet her old master and be recognized. Covering her face with a sun-bonnet and walking in the bent and slow way of an old woman, she stopped at a market and bought two live chickens. Then she turned the corner and saw her old master approaching her! Thinking fast, she pulled the strings tying the birds' legs together so they started to screech and flutter. Her old master passed so close that their clothes touched, but he remained totally unaware as she bent over to deal with the loud birds.

Tubman built trust relationships with white and black people who helped slaves escape, relying on them to point her to other trusted supporters along the way north to freedom. These trust relationships put the helpers in extreme danger. One previously enslaved black man named Sam Green helped Tubman and her escapees. In 1857, suspected of helping escaping slaves, Green's home was searched. Authorities found no direct evidence that he helped runaways. Disregarding the US Constitution's guarantees of freedom of speech and of the press, Green was sentenced to 10 years in prison simply for having a copy of "Uncle Tom's Cabin," a book that dared expose the realities of slavery.

Traveling by boat, train, or foot, sometimes in combination and sometimes separately, helped by friends in disguises, Tubman led the runaways north. At one point, an escaping group found itself with a final long bridge to cross over a river near Wilmington, Delaware. Contacts warned Tubman that bounties for her and her party had led to extra patrols. Police were stationed on the bridge. Tubman split up the party, putting each person in a different safe house while she devised a plan. Tubman worked with Sam Green to arrange for two wagons of bricklayers to cross the bridge, a common sight. They crossed the bridge, singing and carousing unremarkably during the daytime, then coming back as they went. When the same wagons crossed again that night, the drivers singing and carousing again, they carried the escaping group past the guards to freedom.

In one journey northward, just as daylight broke, Tubman knocked on the door of a black man that she knew helped runaway slaves. The escape party huddled in the middle of the street in the pouring rain. Tubman knocked using a special signal several times but got no response. Finally a white man appeared, asking her identity. Tubman asked about her friend, and discovered he was forced out of town for "harboring niggers."

Immediately recognizing that they were in big trouble, Tubman hid the group where the authorities were least likely to look: a nearby swamp. She led the way to a little island in the swamp where smelly tall grass grew, and everybody waded out to it. Tubman carried two well-drugged babies in a basket. Cold, wet, and hungry, Tubman dared not seek out supplies because she knew the whole town was probably on alert.

Yet Tubman's praying did not falter.

After dusk a lone Quaker man walked along the path next to the swamp. Seeming to talk to himself, he said out loud where he kept a wagon, horse, and harness, and then walked away. Tubman found the wagon well stocked with food. Tubman found a known Quaker friend in the next town who could provide aid and was able to return the wagon to its owner. She never found out how the first Quaker knew they were in the swamp.

Because of her faith, such a blessing did not seem so mysterious. Whenever people noted her courage, daring, or unexpected good fortune, she would say, "Don't I tell you, Missus, 'twan't me, 'twas de Lord! Jes' so long as he wanted to use me, he would take keer of me, an' when he didn't want me no longer, I was ready to go; I always tole him, I'm gwine to hole stiddy on to you, an' you've got to see me trou."

On one of her many trips South, Tubman met a young woman named Tilly, whose fiance from another plantation had escaped with Tubman earlier. Desperate to join her freed partner, Tilly begged Tubman to help her. Together, they traveled north, arriving at the Chesapeake Bay too late to catch their boat. After waiting another day and night, they discovered that the boat they had expected was disabled and another took its place. Black people required paperwork to travel, and Tilly and Tubman had none. However, Tubman's network of friends influenced the boat's clerk to write a note stating that the two women should be allowed passage without question.

When Tubman and Tilly arrived at the boat, the helpful clerk was absent. Attempting to board the boat without paperwork was extremely risky, but they decided to go anyway, trusting in Providence. A group of white men commented, saying, "Too many likely looking Niggers traveling North, about these days," and "Wonder if these wenches have got a pass," and "Where you going, you two?" Tilly clung to Tubman, trembling while Tubman put on a bold face as she walked past the men, her note in her hand.

Tubman went to get her ticket and the unknown clerk eyed her suspiciously, telling her to wait. Tubman and Tilly waited at the front of the boat alone. With no other help available, Tubman kneeled on a seat, looked at the water and started praying. "Oh, Lord! You've been wid me in six troubles, don't desert me in the seventh!" Tilly begged Tubman to go get the tickets again, but Tubman kept repeating, "Oh, Lord! You've been wid me in six troubles, don't desert me in the seventh." Tilly exclaimed, "Oh, Moses! the man is coming. What shall we do?" Tubman exclaimed, "Oh, Lord, you've been wid me in six troubles!"

The clerk touched Tubman on the shoulder. Tilly believed the end had come, but the man just said, "You can come now and get your tickets." Tubman never knew why this man's suspicion dissipated, saying simply it was "de Lord." When Tubman prayed she expected deliverance unless God chose otherwise, in which case she was willing to accept His decision.

Rejecting the Authorities' World

When authorities shape a person's world, one goal is to train the person to follow others' directions or prioritize making money rather than listen to their own heart. People who succumb to this training value others' direction over their own sense of right and wrong.

Tubman showed me how a person can reject the world given by authorities, listening instead to the voice in their heart. She looked at reality with eyes wide open instead of getting lost in scripture, the news, pointless political conversations, or career advancement. She recognized what mattered to her, and she chose her own path in service.

Courage, Solidarity and Faith

For many years I strongly preferred rational action and I looked down on faith. I sometimes heard people pray and trust in divinity without taking concrete steps to help themselves, and this seemed foolish to me. But these stories of Harriet Tubman showed me the power of faith. All any of us can do is our best. I believe that Tubman committed to doing the most meaningful work she could imagine in solidarity with the people she loved. She kept her heart open, continuing to give her deepest love no matter the challenge. To give the gift of freeing her people from slavery, Tubman prepared diligently and did her best at each step, with boundless courage, hard work, and ingenuity. What else was left, except to have faith that the universe would provide until it was time for her work to end?

Humans are born with their hearts wide open. What does that mean, and how can a nation systematically work to close people's hearts? *Part 5 - Heart-Opening vs Heart-Closing* exposes the great scam of unhealthy-nation narratives that promote heart closure, and how to defend against this by remembering who we really are.

Part 5 - Heart-Opening vs Heart-Closing

Every baby is born with their heart wide open, giving their deepest love. How can a nation train people to close their hearts and withhold love?

Chapter 17: Heart-Opening vs Heart-Closing

In the early 1600s, French Christian missionaries traveled to North America and stayed with a nation called the Huron. They were very puzzled by what they found.

The missionaries clearly saw that the Huron had leaders, and the people followed rules, and yet there were no police, no prisons, and no capital punishment, all of which they considered essential to French society. How could thousands of people possibly get along with each other without the threat of punishment?[1]

The Huron leaders seemed strange too. They didn't selfishly enrich themselves at the expense of their neighbors as did every European monarch. And they did not remain leaders until their death. In fact, they only remained leaders as long as people valued their leadership.

Even more shocking to the French missionaries, who had come to "save" these uncivilized people, was the Huron's unwillingness to beat their children. Unlike the prevailing European view of children as neutral beings who needed to be pressured and restrained to grow up well, the Huron recognized that children had rights and needs like people of any age, and they refused to resort to corporal punishment to control their behavior.[2]

What could account for such deep differences between these two kinds of nation?

Are People Basically Social or Basically Selfish?

I believe the French missionaries had a fundamental misunderstanding about humans, which is common in authoritarian nations. It comes down to a simple question: Are people basically social, or are they basically selfish?

If people are basically social, and we are *caring people who want to contribute to a meaningful nation*, then a person behaving inappropriately is *a good person making a mistake*. Such a person needs guidance, and probably wants guidance, to help them live well with others.

On the other hand, if people are basically selfish, and we're all just looking after ourselves and need the threat of punishment to force us to get along, then we need a punitive legal system with a strong threat of punishment. With this view, people behaving inappropriately are simply *bad people being themselves*.

The highest political leaders in every unhealthy authoritarian nation I have found propagate this belief in inherent human selfishness. In capitalist terms, we're inherently selfish. In religious terms, we're inherently bad, conditionally good, or separated from God. This belief in our inherent badness or selfishness justifies and legitimizes a punitive legal system that imposes law on supposedly inherently antisocial people.

Fortunately, the truth is that humans are fundamentally social. Just as each person has their sacred gifts – their own life purpose, or special ways of giving to the world – each person also has *universal sacred urges*. These are urges that every single person has for things like integrity, sharing, gratitude, self-defense, dignity, connection, solidarity, joy, authenticity, trust, meaning, aligning one's life with the deepest truth, and personal growth. Each person manifests these sacred urges in unique ways, but the sacred urges are universal in all people.

I realized that every person has these universal sacred urges when I noticed that people in healthy nations exhibit them as a normal way of life. Someone might occasionally behave inappropriately, but this becomes an opportunity for mentoring, holding them accountable, or another response to return to a way of life where everyone embraces these qualities. That means these urges also exist in people in unhealthy nations – but in unhealthy nations, many people are trained not to act on them.

There is something special about these sacred urges: they are deeper than feelings, in the sense that humans expect each other to act on these urges even when it doesn't feel good. If I accidentally break a friend's tool without having asked to borrow it, it might not feel good to own up, but having integrity and taking accountability for my mistake is the right thing to do. The deeper satisfaction of following sacred urges outweighs any transient discomfort of embarrassment or shame. In fact, following sacred urges often displaces shame, particularly the shame of not doing what we know in our heart is right.

Likewise, if people only stood in solidarity when it felt good, solidarity would not be worth much! It's our willingness to stand in solidarity or act with integrity even when it feels difficult that gives relationships strength. It's also what allows people to deeply trust each other.

These universal sacred urges are who we are as humans. They're part of how we manifest divinity into the world, each in our own way. But if these sacred urges really are part of who we all are as humans, how come deep integrity, connection, joy, and other of these universal sacred urges seem so uncommon?

Open Heart vs Closed Heart

Divinity speaks to us and moves us through our heart. A person with a wide open heart manifests divinity into the world as they give their sacred gifts (ie live their life purpose), honor their sacred urges towards values like integrity and joy, and express their feelings. Since divinity and love are the same, a person with a wide open heart is giving their deepest love.

A person with a closed heart is somehow holding back. The closed heart blocks that divine wisdom so it doesn't manifest into the world, and instead the person acts selfishly. Different people may close their hearts in different ways in different circumstances.

How can we know that all of us, even the most selfish and cruel, have divinity speaking to us through our heart? The more wealth a person has, the more they have to close their heart to maintain their wealth even while their neighbors suffer in poverty. At the wealthiest levels, kings and billionaires are often said to have "hearts of stone" or be "cold-hearted," as their hearts are so completely closed.

People with open hearts recognize everybody as basically good, although some people are making mistakes. Don Cox's mother illustrated this open heart. Cox said, "Mama was a saint. She taught me that there were no bad people in the world, only those who made mistakes or stumbled along the path of righteousness. That naïve simplicity touched me to the marrow…"[3]

I don't know any one definition of an open heart. But I notice open-hearted people generally seem to have these beliefs or attitudes:

Open-hearted	Closed-hearted
Life is basically good	Life is basically bad
People are basically good, and people behaving inappropriately are making	People are basically bad or selfish or conditionally good, and people misbehaving are being

mistakes	themselves
The world is alive; everything is divine	The world is dead; nothing is divine
I am a divine being, part of divine creation	I am separated from God / there is no God
The world welcomes my deepest love	I must hold back my love to protect myself; my deepest love is not welcome
People can take care of each other and stand for a culture of mutual respect	People need authorities to keep society safe and functioning smoothly
Everybody matters	Nobody matters or only I matter
Everything matters	Nothing matters
I can find trustworthy people who accept me for who I am	People are not trustworthy; it's not safe to be myself
Life is an adventure	Life is a drag
I am worthy of respect	I deserve my lot in life

Does "Having an Open Heart" mean "Believing That Everyone is Kind?"

Obviously in unhealthy nations many people act with extreme cruelty to each other, sometimes even to their own neighbors and family members. Having an open heart and recognizing divinity in oneself and others does not mean being blind to this truth.

A great example of open-heartedness comes from Martin Luther King Jr, a black American. He had many reasons to feel angry towards white people. His and his family's lives had been threatened many times. Their house had been firebombed. Two days before he was assassinated, his flight to Memphis was delayed due to a bomb threat. Yet, one day before he was assassinated by white people, what did he call them?

King acknowledged white people's threat on his life this way: "And then I got to Memphis. And some began to say the threats, or talk about the threats that were out. What would happen to me from some of our sick white brothers? Well, I don't know what will happen now… I just want to do God's will…"[4]

I believe King had a wide open heart: he recognized his own and others' divinity, while recognizing that some others were really sick. He stood in solidarity with people who wanted to walk a good path, and he invited everyone to walk that good path with him, including white people. King even stood with the Vietnamese who suffered so much in the US-Vietnam war.

So, having an open heart does not mean thinking everyone is kind. An open heart simply allows my consciousness to be aware of mine and others' divinity, and allows me to fully and courageously manifest my divine gifts in service of what I care about most. This chapter explores a deep question: when a person acts hurtfully towards their neighbors, are they a good person making a mistake or a bad person being themselves? King calls certain white brothers "sick," which to me means he recognized that they were good people with a sickness, not bad people being themselves.

Recognizing that some people are sick does not necessarily mean tolerating that sickness. I believe Harriet Tubman kept an open heart even when her prayers about her master changed over from wishing that the Lord would "change dat man's heart, and make him a Christian" to saying "Lord, if you ain't never going to change dat man's heart, kill him, Lord, and take him out of de way, so he won't do no more mischief."[5]

Tubman escaped the plantation and never killed the master, so far as I know. But her prayer for her master's death does not mean she closed her heart. It seems analogous to the Cherokee response when someone committed too-gruesome of a crime: if a person is set on behaving hurtfully, then exiling or killing them may be the only way to preserve the nation's baseline of respect. This does not mean closing one's heart to their divinity. *The inappropriate behavior itself is the bad thing, not the person.*

Keeping an open heart simply allows a person to act in service of what they most deeply care about. They feel the love in their heart so strongly that to act in any other way would feel too painful to even consider.

I remember attending a seminar on institutional racism towards black people and Latin American immigrants in the United States. It discussed how brutal the immigration and prison systems can be, the history of the Civil Rights movement, and the history and suppression of the Black Panthers, an American revolutionary movement from the 1960s-1980s focused on the liberation of black people. At the end, the host invited the attendees to share one lesson they learned from the seminar, and one concrete action they would carry out after leaving.

We were all arrayed in a big semicircle, and the vast majority of us were white people, mostly in our 20s, 30s, and 40s. Over and over I heard white people say things like, "I'm going to go home and write a post on the internet" or "I am going to go home and journal about this." Finally it was the turn of a Latina woman in the corner. When she spoke, fire leapt from her eyes and there was a steely resolve in her voice that was utterly lacking in anybody else's: "I will never let those immigration agents take my daughter. I will do whatever it takes."

That woman had spoken a few times about her daughter that day. In every word she spoke, her priority came through loud and clear: protecting her daughter.

Like King and the "sick white brothers," I am sure this woman would have preferred the immigration agents to open their hearts and stop acting with such cruelty. But since the agents kept their heart closed, this woman decided she would do whatever it takes in service of what she most cared about: her daughter. I believe she had an open heart and acted in service of the person she loved most in very difficult circumstances.

Living Life as a Gift in Each Moment

I grew up believing that spiritual leaders walked spiritual paths, and everyone else walked "normal" paths. I didn't understand that we're all spiritual beings walking a spiritual path, with some of us holding back much more than others. This is obviously true because each of us is a divine being surrounded by other divine beings in the form of people, trees, squirrels, streams, and everything else, and every action or inaction has a rippling effect on all the beings around us. Every action can build others up and enrich their lives, or diminish things.

Reading stories from healthy nations helped me recognize what it would be like to live each moment as a divine offering. In other words, I found stories of whole nations of people living each day with a wide open heart.

Martín Prechtel described how Tzutujil Mayans would court each other so well that they fed the Gods with beauty:

> The Tzutujil people approach living in general with a sense of courtly behavior. This meant knowing how to approach a spirit of another's soul without scaring it away, and still present one's true natural self unaltered. There were boys and novice shamans who were very good at touching the hearts of ladies and of spirits. They had inborn abilities and a fierce affection for what they were courting. Still others were successful because they loved the age-old courting process itself on whose back the whole ceremonial Tzutujil culture survived. The panache, fine stories, beguiling songs, offerings, and love-drunk attention to what they loved, either woman or spirit, were all part of this. The people knew that young men and women and shamans were feeding the Gods with beauty when, through their excellent speeches, heroic gifts, and serenades, admiration was created for what each loved.[6]

In 1980, Peter Nabokov went to watch Pueblo people celebrate the 300-year anniversary of a successful revolution against Spanish rule, after which they were able to return to living without rulers. Long distance running was essential to their earlier coordinated uprising and a big part of their 300-year celebration. He interviewed a Pueblo runner named Talawema who had run American marathons, such as the Boston marathon, achieving very competitive times.

Talawema said, "Running was something the elders used to preach to us. Anytime you go somewhere on foot, you should try to run. It is a big part of our life. Even when you are old, as long as you can race or trot, at whatever pace, it makes you feel younger."[7]

When Nabokov asked him to compare American marathons and Pueblo running, his answer illustrated what it's like to run-as-a-gift to bring people together: "There's no comparison. There you're running for yourself. Here it's all tribal. We're running for the people. The other Pueblos are feeling the same thing. It is a matter of getting there and what we're carrying in terms of the message of peace and harmony and uniting as a people. Not to the extent that there might be another revolt, that's pretty much out of the question, but to find each other again. Time is not important to us, it's how we do it."[8]

Before training to be a shaman with the Tzutujil Maya in present-day Guatemala, Martín Prechtel grew up in the American southwest. He said, "As young children on the reservation I remember the deep need to run. For all the young Indian people, both girls and boys, running was as great a characteristic of the Indigenous life of Pueblo, Navajo, and Apache people still living in their original beloved homelands of the arid highlands of New Mexico as was their sense of comic joy or the generous ceremonial house-to-house feasting throughout their villages, for which they are still famous…"[9]

These children related to school as an "imposed irrelevancy," as they learned at home everything they needed to live well with the Earth. Thus their American teachers characterized them as "arrogant, troublesome, and incapable of learning," when the truth was that school failed to teach them what they wanted to know. The school's running coaches embraced a common domineering attitude, where someone needed to win and someone needed to lose. They struggled with these kids though: while most of the boys over 13 years old had marathon times better than adult Olympians, they didn't feel like competing. They just wanted to run, preferably over wild land.

The kids loved to run hard, but not to race. They also didn't like to run alone. They liked running as a group. If a runner passed a relative or friend, they would run with them, no matter how much they had to slow down. The coaches had world-class Olympic-level athletes among these students, and their frustration was intense as the kids simply didn't care about their run times. If one person in a running group was slow, the others would wait or run in circles so they could catch up. They would run hard, but togetherness was important too.

Prechtel described the attitude: "Living and running were holy things you were supposed to get good at, not things to use to conquer, win, and get attention for. Running was not meant for taking but for giving gifts to the Holy in Nature. Running was an offering, a feeding of life."

Occasionally white people were invited to Pueblo foot races which were run by young men. There was no finish line, and runners would stop running when they felt like it. Visitors would ask, "How do they know who wins? How do they know when to stop running? Why do they run at all?"

Prechtel acknowledged how the sun and moon and other beings are kept strong by the boys who run. The sun each year runs its own race to help the animals thrive. When the sun tires, the world and all animals begin to flag and die, and the running boys keep the Sun strong and moving. Likewise the Moon runs and keeps the waters moving and the plants growing which everybody depends upon. There are no finish lines for the moon and sun; they must keep moving or the world dies.

Boys might compete to outdo each other in beauty, strength, and dedication, but without a finish line they simply ran until the gods had revived enough to run themselves.

Prechtel wrote, "everything in Nature ran according to its own nature; the running of grass was in its growing, the running of rivers their flowing, granite bubbled up, cooled, compressed and crumbled, birds lived, flew, sang and died, everything did what it needed to do, each simultaneously running its own race, each by living according to its own nature together, never leaving any other part of the universe behind. The world's Holy things raced constantly together, not to win anything over the next, but to keep the entire surging diverse motion of the living world from grinding to a halt, which is why there is no end to that race; no finish line. That would be oblivion to all."

When the boys eventually stopped running, they would return home and eat the food they knew their running had kept alive.

Growing up, I sometimes saw exercise as a chore or work, something to do and get out of the way so I could get back to a relaxed comfort. Even when I ran voluntarily, I often wore earphones so loud music would distract me from my tiredness, thoughts, and other life stresses.

These stories from the Pueblos, Apache, and Navajo helped me learn how to live life as a gift, even the supposedly-mundane or "normal" parts of life. When the young runners offered themselves as a gift, they brightened the world and they also strengthened themselves so they could show up in a good way should emergencies arise. I learned this when I studied the Bedonkohe Apache, led by Geronimo. Even after the Apaches acquired horses, the war parties often preferred to move on foot. Geronimo would lead warriors in guerilla strikes in Mexico, then split up his men and have them reconvene 3 days later. One of Geronimo's Apache warriors recalled that they traveled up to 75 miles and 14 hours per day, carrying three days' worth of food with them. When difficult situations required these warriors to face great challenges to feed or protect their people, they were ready.[10]

When I first read of these running capabilities, they seemed too outlandish to be true. But once I learned that the runners had practiced giving their deepest love by serving the divinity of life through their running since childhood, it made sense. Running becomes a relaxing joy in service of divinity, a gift of love, not a chore to grind through or avoid. Is it any wonder that the Apaches produced far more capable runners than their local hyper-competitive American high school running coaches?

Training Heart-Closure in Adulthood

People of healthy nations invite each other to live with a wide open heart, continuously giving their deepest love through their sacred gifts, universal sacred urges, and clear feelings. This explains why the French Christian missionaries encountered a Huron nation of thousands of people without abusive rulers, police, or prisons. The Huron needed systems of conflict resolution and accountability, but they had no need for punitive law. They all basically wanted to get along, and had figured out a satisfactory way to do that.

In unhealthy, authoritarian nations, people are commonly pressured to close their hearts in various ways. In other words, they're repeatedly trained not to act on their sacred urges, not to give their deepest gifts, and to ignore their feelings or ignore reality in various circumstances.

Studying highly abusive situations helped me start to see how authorities require people to withhold their love. Allen Sydney was enslaved in Mississippi, and described a moment when many slaves were working the field, and one worked too slow. The enslaved black gang driver tried to "whip him up" to pace, but the worker fought back. The white overseer rode up on horseback and shouted "take him down!" shooting the man dead in front of everybody. Sydney said, "None of the other slaves said a word or turned their heads. They kept on hoeing as if nothing had happened."[11]

I believe the other slaves saw this as extremely inappropriate, but the threat of further overwhelming violence in that moment caused them to block their own sacred urges towards solidarity and self-defense. When describing overseers' torture of slaves, ex-slave Henry Gowens said it "cramp[ed] down [the] minds" of victims and witnesses.

Stories from Nazi concentration camps show the same pattern. Bruce Bettelheim described how guards constantly beat, shot, and stabbed prisoners. Prisoners were made to stare into bright lights or kneel for hours. Prisoners weren't allowed to help each other; even worse, they were forced to hit each other, curse their God, and accuse each other of vile actions. Husbands were forced to accuse their wives of prostitution, and this would continue for many hours. People who tried to act on their sacred urges – that is, people who tried to help each other, maintain their integrity, or fight back – were killed.[12]

While each person can choose whether to keep their heart open or not, these extreme examples showed me how abusive authorities can pressure people into withholding their love.

Single and Triple Inhibition

When a person becomes trapped in an abusive situation, they feel urges and feelings which say, essentially, "This is not ok. I either need to escape or stop the abuse." But what happens when a person is continuously trapped in abusive relationships for years? There are basically three ways to respond.

One possible response is for the abuse victim to openly defy authorities. This may lead to quick imprisonment, torture, impoverishment, or death if they're caught. We'll skip this option for now as we explore how people cope with long-term abusive relationships.

A second option is what I call *single inhibition* where a person recognizes authorities as illegitimate and sees their own feelings, perceptions and sacred urges as legitimate. In other words, the person thinks "This abuse is not ok. I'll do what I need to stay safe but I will keep doing my best for myself and the people around me."

One enslaved man named Joe illustrated this. One day a new master bought him from his old master. The very next morning, the new master rode up to Joe on a big horse, interrupted his breakfast, and demanded Joe accept a whipping. He just wanted to prove he was the master and establish that Joe was the submissive slave.

Joe recognized in his situation there wasn't much he could do, so he took the whipping. But he knew in his heart that this whipping was not ok, and he resolved to escape as soon as he could. A little while later, Harriet Tubman helped him escape.[13]

I believe that Joe clearly recognized in his heart that slavery wasn't ok. He felt an urge to stand up for himself, but he blocked this urge. He remained aware of his urge towards dignity and considered it legitimate, but he didn't act on it in that moment because disobedience was so heavily punished.

Joe showed single inhibition. Joe inhibited his own urge towards dignity when he submitted to the whipping, even though he recognized the beating as illegitimate and his urge towards dignity as legitimate.

There is a another possible response, what I call triple inhibition. This occurs when a person ignores a feeling, urge, or perception that feels too unsafe or painful to acknowledge. As one example, they may associate fear or shame with a particular feeling or urge, and learn to ignore or reject it. This allows a person to diminish the pain of what they're experiencing.

A person can learn to hold back an urge or feeling with three separate blocks: 1) the initial feeling or urge is blocked, 2) awareness of the feeling or urge is blocked from consciousness, and 3) awareness of the block is also blocked from consciousness. Or, a person can ignore some observation, and then ignore that they're ignoring it. In other words, the entire feeling, urge, or perception becomes blocked and subconscious. These blocks may be stored in the mind or in the body, but one way or another, people can learn to ignore or block part of their own experience and ignore that they're doing this.

What does this look like in practice?

Before Harriet Jacobs escaped from slavery, she saw a young black slave woman dying soon after giving birth to a nearly white baby. In agony, the young mother cried out, "O Lord, come and take me!" Her white mistress stood nearby mocking her, saying "You suffer, do you? I am glad of it. You deserve it all, and more too."

The young woman's own mother said, "The baby is dead, thank God; and I hope my poor child will soon be in heaven, too."

The mistress said, "Heaven! There is no such place for the like of her and her bastard."

The older mother and her daughter consoled each other as the daughter was dying. When the suffering became too intense, the mistress left the room, still with a scornful smile. Jacobs described how this older black woman, who'd just watched her grandchild die, now watched her only child die "while she thanked God for taking her away from the greater bitterness of life."[14]

What could cause this white woman to speak with such cruelty towards the helpless older black woman and and young black woman and not offer any help?

The newborn baby was very light skinned and born to a dark-skinned woman, indicating that a white man, likely the slaveowner and husband of the white woman in this story, had raped the young black mother. The black woman had no choice in the matter, and the white man did.

I believe the rapist slaveowner's wife, the mistress in this story, was deeply disturbed by his behavior. Deep down, I believe she did not want her husband to rape the black women but felt helpless to do anything about it. Consider her deep anger and bitterness in the story: where did that energy come from? She did not just calmly go about her business while the young woman and infant died; she actively stood by and exclaimed how glad she was at their suffering. She even explicitly mentioned the "bastard." She had tremendous energy, but why would she have so much anger-energy towards helpless victims? On the surface, it makes no sense.

White women at the time had no legal say in the household which was run by their husbands. Mary Boykin Chesnutt was a plantation mistress from South Carolina. She wrote in her diary in 1861, "[O]urs is a monstrous system and [full of] wrong and iniquity… Like the patriarchs of old our men live all in one house with their wives & their concubines, & the Mulattoes one sees in every family exactly resemble the white children–& every lady tells you who is the father of all the Mulatto children in every body's household, but those in her own, she seems to think drop from the clouds or pretends so to think."[15]

I believe that commonly, when a higher privilege person gets upset with a lower privilege person like this, they are actually upset about something else but deep in their hearts, are afraid to confront the truth of the situation. If I am willing to ignore the terrible truth, then I'll believe whatever is most convenient. If I am not going to do the most meaningful thing, I will do whatever is most comfortable, safe, or easy. The white woman's meaningful response – the response which would have best addressed her unhappiness that her husband was raping black women – would be to confront her rapist husband, ideally with the support of others.

Unfortunately, if the white woman had taken a stand with the black women, she might have faced terrible retribution from her husband and been stigmatized by others in her social circle, since white slaveowning men commonly raped black women and the white wives commonly pretended it wasn't happening. She might have been socially cast out, not just losing her family and friends but possibly her wealth. In other words, to stand in solidarity with the black women might have cost this white woman tremendously, even though deep in the white woman's heart I believe she hated what her husband was doing.

This white woman demonstrated triple inhibition when she blocked awareness of her original urges and feelings (ie, she blocked the urge to stop the rape), blocked self-awareness of these urges and feelings, and then blocked awareness that she was blocking her awareness. Likely she learned to do this from a very young age, trained by her parents so she could grow up to be a proper slaveowning wife, one who could pretend that evil things weren't constantly happening all around her.

I believe that in her heart, she still sensed that rape was deeply wrong, and her anger-energy was very real in her body. Unfortunately, after all her fear, ignoring-the-deepest-truth, shame, pretending, and other self-repression, what remained was a bitter anger that she safely directed at the black people who were least responsible for the situation and were least able to protect themselves. I believe she really did feel anger towards her husband. When she felt she couldn't express anger safely towards him, the energy came out as anger and bitterness at the enslaved women. All this happened subconsciously because she'd been practicing – like so many other people in unhealthy nations – the practice of triple inhibition since early childhood, learning to hold herself back. In other words, she had been practicing withholding her love.

This is how blind belief plays out in individuals. When people learn to avoid the obvious painful truth, they will accept a more comfortable lie. This woman's husband was raping helpless women, but it was a manifestation of chattel slavery that she'd learned never to question, likely from early childhood.

Thus, nothing the rich white woman said or did addressed her deepest concerns. Instead she exacerbated others' suffering while remaining safe in her privileged social position. She had learned to hold back her love to avoid the punishment she may have faced if she intervened against her husband's rape. She coped with this physically comfortable but spiritually difficult life by accepting abusive chattel slavery as legitimate, and learning to hold back her own feelings and sacred urges and ignore certain aspects of reality.

I find the English language a little confusing on matters of the heart. A "broken heart" and "closed heart" are very different. The older black woman in this story had a broken heart. She felt extreme sadness watching her daughter and grandchild die, and felt so upset about slavery that she even saw their death as a relief. In other words, having a broken heart is actually a healthy response to a very challenging situation.

The spiritually wounded white woman in this story had a closed heart. She blocked some of her own sacred urges, perceptions, and feelings, ignored the truth of her abusive life situation, and directed her anger in unhelpful ways.

Appropriate and Inappropriate Feelings

An open-hearted person approaches life with deep gratitude, recognizes divinity in themselves and others, and gives their deepest love or their sacred gifts in service of whom or what most matters to them.

In addition to this attitude of gratitude and giving one's sacred gifts, an open-hearted person acts on those universal sacred urges for things like integrity, solidarity, joy, and so on. I believe there's one more piece that helps a person really have an open heart and channel divinity: expressing how they really feel.

My feelings are how I relate to my circumstances. If a friend dies, I feel grief. If I leave an unsatisfying career behind to seek more meaningful work, I may feel excited and scared.

At a really basic level, my feelings help me know what's good and what to do more of, and what's not good and what to avoid. It doesn't feel good to speak hurtfully to a friend, so I avoid that. It feels good to eat tasty nourishing food, so I strive to eat that way.

I believe that in a healthy nation, just like healthy friendships or romantic relationships, people welcome each others' authentic feelings. If a friend is feeling dissatisfied with some aspect of our relationship for example, I can only help address it if I know about his or her dissatisfaction. If a dissatisfied friend holds back their feelings and pretends things are ok when they're not, and if I don't notice, it's impossible for me to help address the trouble.

In unhealthy nations, where it's not always safe to express one's honest feelings, people can learn to hold back those feelings, even from themselves. That's what triple inhibition is: where a person learns not to feel their own feelings or urges or even be aware of them, and they're unaware that they are holding themselves back. Or, people may learn to ignore some other aspect of their experience, dimming their own awareness.

The result is that people can have inappropriate feelings. Feelings are a person's response to the world around them, but when people learn to ignore or reject part of their experience, they can have feelings that do not seem to make sense in the situation to any objective observer. The feelings reflect the person's distorted experience of the situation, not the situation as it's really happening.

I believe that the white mistress who spoke so cruelly to the enslaved women held back her authentic feelings. As Mary Boykin Chesnutt said at the time, it was common for such high-privilege women to pretend this cruelty wasn't happening. I believe this woman was angry about her husband raping defenseless women. This was an appropriate feeling that responded to what was really happening. It was her authentic relationship with her circumstances. If she had expressed the feeling of anger-towards-her-husband, she would have at least responded to her actual concern.

Instead, she held back this anger at her husband, and the energy found another way out through vindictive rage and scorn at helpless victims. These are examples of inappropriate feelings: they don't really address the whole situation. When she acted on her rage and scorn, she did not really address the problem – her rapist husband. When a person has triple inhibition about a particular feeling, urge, or perception and they hold it back, this is one common result: some other feeling comes out which may feel safer to express, but doesn't address the real trouble.

The Many Manifestations of a Closed Heart

Open heartedness and closed heartedness aren't black-and-white, all-or-nothing. Different people may hold back different feelings in different circumstances, or make different hurtful assumptions or associations, or give their love with more or less courage. Some people close their hearts much tighter than others.

Likewise, heart closure shows up in many ways, as there are many ways to withhold one's love, or "hold back" or "shut down" part of oneself.

Every one of us is a divine being who can make a difference in the world. But after holding themselves back often enough, many people can internalize the belief that life is not divine, and that they cannot make much difference. The Gumbaynggirr people in Australia have worked hard to stop old-growth logging. Some local Australians support those efforts, but others seem indifferent, saying, "What's the point of protesting? You won't win."[16]

In unhealthy nations, people become used to holding themselves back as children, and this continues into adulthood as people can hold back a meaningful response to authorities' inappropriate behavior, or to being given meaningless work, or other unsatisfying situations. For example, it's easy to feel like a cog in a gigantic machine. The basic attitude is, "if I can't make a difference in the world, I might as well take care of myself." I knew a man who'd trained as a carpenter and then spent years living off-grid, learning to use unpowered hand tools to build structures, preserve food by hand, and generally minimize his expenses, his income, and his impact on the land. We lived together for a couple years, both learning to live very minimally, and then we moved apart.

We met up a year later, and he had returned to full-time employment building houses. He told me of his goal to save a large amount of money, and acknowledged that he was building homes on rural land that had recently been a vibrant forest, then clear-cut and razed to a field of orange clay. He looked at me sheepishly, shrugged his shoulders, and said, "someone's going to do it."

Even high-ranking people can feel this small. In 1920, Russian admiral A. V. Kolchak described how he related to the political implications of his military work. He said his perspective "was that of a serving officer" who did not concern himself with politics. He said, "I considered the monarch an existing fact, neither criticizing nor considering the issue of changing it. As a military man I considered my duty to fulfill my oath and that was the whole of my relationship to the monarchy."[17]

Where and when to use violence is one of the most important political decisions any society makes. This man was a top decision maker and leader in the Russian armed forces, and he essentially chose not to consider the political implications of his decisions. He was willing to accept the monarch's orders and do as he was told. This top admiral accepted being a cog in a machine.

Adolf Eichmann was a top Nazi German official who coordinated the mass killing of millions of Jews and other people. The Israelis kidnapped him after World War II and put him on trial. Listening to the trial proceedings, Hannah Arendt noticed that Eichmann seemed "neither perverted nor sadistic," but was rather a "terrifyingly normal" man with "manifest shallowness."[18]

Arendt called this *the banality of evil*, where people could cause massive suffering not because they are inherently evil, but because they are shallow and clueless, people who are "joiners" or just trying to get along. Eichmann didn't stand for anything on his own; I believe he had learned to ignore his own sense of what deeply matters, likely beginning in early childhood. He sought out meaning externally, and the Nazis offered meaningful work, comfort, dignity, and camaraderie. I believe this is why Eichmann said that when he learned about the fall of the Nazi government, "I sensed I would have to live a leaderless and difficult individual life, I would receive no directives from anybody, no orders and commands would any longer be issued to me, no pertinent ordinances would be there to consult–in brief, a life never known before lay ahead of me."[19]

From his words, I believe Eichmann may not have even wanted to kill all those people. When he received Hitler's order to complete the "physical extermination of the Jews," he said he had "never thought of such a thing, such a solution through violence. I lost everything, all joy in my work, all initiative, all interest; I was, so to speak, blown out."

I don't believe Eichmann said this to avoid punishment at his trial. I believe he meant it. His boss ordered him to do something he didn't feel like doing. The work felt really bad, and he lost his joy and interest, but he learned to focus on the work and not think much about the consequences of his actions. These emotional contortions are common – how many workers find their job basically unsatisfying or uninteresting, but ignore their feelings so they can keep making money or avoid punishment?

Arendt described how Eichmann seemed more like a clown than a monster. He said in one moment that he would never take an oath, and then a little later made a solemn oath. He repeatedly assured the court that the worst thing a man could do was escape his responsibilities and plead for mercy, and then a little while later he sent in a handwritten note requesting mercy. Eichmann didn't stand for anything, even his own convictions.

In other words, Eichmann learned how to be a cog in a machine. He learned how to close his heart to his own divine knowing of right and wrong, his sacred urges towards meaningful work, integrity, alignment-with-truth, and so on. Millions of people suffered as a result.

Going Through Life Giving One's Deepest Love

Each of us is a divine being who can make a difference in the world. Each of us has sacred gifts to give and sacred urges towards authenticity, solidarity, integrity, joy, and more. When a person has an open heart, it simply means recognizing their own divinity, recognizing the divinity of all life, and giving their deepest love in service of what most matters to them.

Authoritarian nations encourage people not to believe in themselves and somehow hold back their love. This way people will follow their rulers' or boss's orders, or allow inappropriate behavior all around them, instead of doing what they know in their heart is right. Some people seem capable but self-centered or unaware, and others seem very unconfident or they dream small. There are many ways a closed heart manifests in the world.

I don't believe anybody is inherently evil. Where many people see evil, I see selfishness or self-centeredness which results when a person closes their heart as authoritarian nations deeply encourage and train us to do.

Nobody can control the future, but each of us can control how we show up in the world. Each person can decide whether they will acknowledge hard truths or choose comfortable make-believe. Each person can actively seek to discover their sacred gifts or life purpose and give it fully, or keep the seemingly comfortable life they've built for themselves.

Eichmann taught me something very helpful. There's a time and place for comfort in life, but never at the expense of meaningful work and personal integrity. Eichmann chose a comfortable career but found it very unsatisfying, losing "all joy… all initiative, all interest."

When I study great spiritual leaders like Harriet Tubman, Jesus Christ, and Martin Luther King Jr, I notice that their paths are often not very comfortable. Yet they seemed deeply satisfied with their work. They prioritized walking a meaningful path and welcomed comforts along the way. Once they embarked on their most meaningful path, they continued doing their best in service of those they loved no matter the challenge in front of them. To me, this is what it means to move through life with an open heart, giving one's deepest love.

I grew up learning that Jesus Christ was special because he was the only son of God, and no normal human could give love as deeply as him, though everyone should try. Eventually I realized the truth: what made Jesus so special was that he *gave his love fully even in an unhealthy nation that didn't always welcome it*. Jesus Christ seemed so remarkable only because he was surrounded by people who had learned to hold back – a normal thing in an unhealthy nation that trained people to close their hearts.

Jesus saw that he could do tremendous good for the people around him, and he did not hold back, even though the authorities threatened him and eventually killed him. This is why I see Harriet Tubman and Martin Luther King Jr as spiritual leaders similar to Jesus: Tubman and King both gave their love fully, even risking their lives, in service of the people they loved.

Anyone can give their love fully. All of us are divine beings. Calling Jesus the son of God doesn't make him special, because all of us are children of Creator, or divinity, or Allah, or whatever word people use. Any of us can give our love fully at any time, even in unhealthy nations that don't always welcome our love.

All babies are born with an open heart, but in unhealthy nations, few adults live with a fully open heart. So, how are unhealthy nations so effective at training people to close their hearts in various ways as they grow up? Investigate one of the most common techniques in *Chapter 18: The Great Scam of Heart-Closing Cultural Narratives*.

Chapter 18: The Great Scam of Heart-Closing Cultural Narratives

Prior to the Civil War, the US imposed a terrible system of slavery on millions of people while pretending it was good for them. Under this ideology, anyone who tried to escape slavery must have a mental illness and should be treated that way, because why else would someone escape a society that is supposedly good for them?

Likewise, the Soviet and Chinese police in the 20th century maintained the fiction that political activists must have mental health disorders. Since their societies were obviously so great, anyone who disagreed must be disturbed and criminally insane, requiring imprisonment.

These are examples of *The Great Scam of Heart-Closing Cultural Narratives*.

Heart-closing cultural narratives take many forms. Some narratives train people to believe their unhealthy nation is good, and thus anyone who protests or escapes must be crazy. Other heart-closing narratives train people to believe they were born disconnected from God, or that humans are inherently bad or selfish.

Some heart-closing narratives are religious, and some are secular, but they all share similar goals: to justify a culture of exploitation where a few people rule over many others. They cause a deep insecurity in people so that they are highly unlikely to stand together against authorities.

How can a religion commonly practiced by millions of people instill a sense of shame or inherent badness in its followers? And what other hurtful, disconnecting attitudes might these religions teach?

Examples of Religious Heart-Closing Narratives

The three core spiritual practices of healthy nations recognize and promote the best in people: deep gratitude, recognition that each person has their own gifts to give, and living in reciprocity. These practices train children to be the best version of themselves and live in solidarity with others. They promote connection and a sense of each person's inherent worth.

In stark contrast, unhealthy-nation religions commonly emphasize disconnection, domination, submission, and an internalized personal sense of badness or, at best, conditional goodness. As a result, they train people for shame, distrust of oneself and others, isolation, disconnection from divinity and nature, selfishness, self-loathing, and other negative qualities.

For centuries after its publication in 1486 CE, the Malleus Maleficarum was the Catholic Church's standard handbook on witchcraft and hunting witches.[1] It described how evil could easily permeate a person who was careless or showed too much will:

> Now the motive of the will is something perceived through the senses or the intellect, both of which are subject to the power of the devil... This evil, which is of the devil, creeps in by all the sensual approaches; he places himself in figures, he adapts himself to colors, he attaches himself to sounds, he lurks in angry and wrongful conversation, he abides in smells, he impregnates with flavours and fills with certain exhalations all the channels of the understanding...[2]

It would certainly take tremendous willpower to take a stand against abusive religious authorities; is it any wonder they called this "motive of the will" evil?

The Malleus was written centuries ago, but even present-day doctrines continue to instill hurtful attitudes. Catholic doctrine still states that all humans supposedly have Original Sin: "By his sin Adam, as the first man, lost the original holiness and justice he had received from God, not only for himself but for all human beings. Adam and Eve transmitted to their descendants human nature wounded by their own first sin and hence deprived of original holiness and justice; this deprivation is called 'original sin.'"

The Catholic doctrine goes on to describe human nature as "subject to ignorance, suffering, and the dominion of death; and inclined to sin-an inclination to evil." Baptism supposedly erases original sin, but humans remain "weakened and inclined to evil."[3,4]

Not only do Catholics preach that humans are born disconnected from God and inclined to evil, they go on to teach that humans' sins "put the world as a whole in the sinful condition" where humans engage in "dour combat with the powers of evil."[5]

This message of deep disconnection and alienation permeates many Christian teachings, with one Bible study resource claiming that "life is full of sorrow. Jesus came to give us hope. His message is that this place is not our home and we don't belong here. In our sorrow we all long for a better place and by drawing closer to God, our sorrow will become less intense. We all have sinned. Shame and guilt keep us down in the pits."[6]

Christian authorities even twisted the meaning of Jesus Christ's death in a way that encouraged Christians to feel shameful or inherently flawed. Many Bible verses misconstrue the meaning of Christ's death, claiming he died to atone for peoples' sins.[7,8,9] But Jews didn't want a savior because they had sinned; they wanted a savior to save them from their oppressive rulers. And Christ did not want to die; he wanted to free his people from oppression and kept working even knowing that the authorities would kill him for it. When authorities claim Christ died to atone for peoples' sins, they simultaneously train followers to ignore the oppressive authorities they live under as well as encourage people to believe they are inherently sinful or bad. This is a major way Christian authorities train Christians not to understand their own primary spiritual leader, Jesus Christ.

And Christianity is not the only religion that instills hurtful attitudes. The Islamic Quran likewise causes people to doubt their own sense of right and wrong. The Quran repeatedly states Allah's omniscience: "Allah is All-Forgiving, Most Merciful.[10]... Surely Allah is Almighty, All-Wise.[11]... And Allah is All-Hearing, All-Knowing.[12]" The Quran paints Allah as omniscient, and how should a person respond if they have a feeling, urge, or thought that does not align with their religious text? It is clear: "Perhaps you dislike something which is good for you and like something which is bad for you. Allah knows and you do not know."[13]

Only religious leaders and their books supposedly have full access to truth, while followers are encouraged to doubt their own inner source of divine wisdom.

Visitors to Tibet prior to the Chinese takeover in the 1950s found Tibetan Buddhists teaching that the world is full of evil. Every bend of the road, stream crossing, or village entrance had to have a row of flags to exorcize evil spirits. Lakes, wells, and streams teamed with demons who brought floods and hail storms upon anyone who violated their religious leaders' rules.[14]

Evil could exist almost anywhere, from doorways to cracks in stones. Events as important as birth and death and as inconsequential as spilled milk required special care to fend off evil. Unfortunately, individual prayer was not effective; true spiritual defense required the assistance of a Buddhist priest for a customary fee, paid in money or labor or both. This ideology scared people from the wilderness, seeing nonhumans as full of evil spirits rather than teachers and siblings offering gifts. It further trained people to live in fear and kept them in poverty.

Dale DeBakcsy taught at a Buddhist school in the United States for 9 years and claimed, "I have no doubt that Buddhist religious belief, as it was practiced at the school, did a great deal of harm." The leaders trained children that they must deserve any suffering or inadequacy, as any trouble in this life implied that one had behaved wickedly in a past life, and any present suffering was simply karma at work.

One young girl had trouble memorizing information for tests and went to the monks for help. The monks told her that she was having trouble now because in a past life she'd been a murderous dictator who burned books, and thus in this life she is doomed to be forever learning challenged. The girl was deeply hurt, believing her soul was polluted and fatally flawed and that there was nothing she could do to learn like her peers.[15]

This attitude towards Karma has been used to excuse extreme exploitation by rich monks and lamas. The fourteenth dalai lama implied that serfs clearly deserve their suffering when he said, "A poor Tibetan was less inclined to envy or resent his Tibetan landlord because he knew that each of them was reaping the seed he had sown in his previous life."[16]

These stories from authoritarian religions make clear why a Christian missionary could hear this from a chief of the Sac and Fox nation: "The white man had showed neither respect for nature nor reverence toward God, but, he thought, tried to buy God with the by-products of nature. He tried to buy his way into heaven, but he did not even know where heaven is."[17] I believe this man recognized that Creation itself is divine, and we are living in paradise (or heaven) right now. In contrast, for millennia, white people and others living in unhealthy nations have been trained to think that they are not living in heaven, and instead God is somewhere off in the sky. The same is true for authoritarian religions around the world that try to disconnect people from nature and from the divine voice in each of our hearts.

Examples of Secular Heart-Closing Narratives

Sadly, even non-religious authorities can propagate heart-closing narratives, the secular equivalents of the Catholics' Original Sin.

Capitalism Teaches That People are Selfish, and Selfishness is Good

Growing up, I was taught that capitalism is supposedly a great economic system because people are basically rational and selfish, and markets channel everyone's selfishness to produce goods and services that benefit society. This perspective doesn't just teach that people are basically selfish, it also teaches that selfishness is supposedly good for everyone because it motivates people to work and generate wealth for the economy.

This attitude that humans are basically selfish and incapable of sharing was famously illustrated in Garrett Hardin's paper "The Tragedy of the Commons" published in the prestigious journal Science in 1968. World Bank researchers called it "the dominant paradigm within which social scientists assess natural resource issues," and one anthropologist noted that the paper "has been embraced as a sacred text by scholars and professionals."[18]

Hardin reasoned that in a pasture shared by many herdsmen, each individual would try to keep as many animals as possible. This would be personally smart as each individual maximizes their wealth, but it would destroy the pasture for everybody. He wrote, "The rational herdsman [will conclude] that the only sensible course for him to pursue is to add another animal to his herd," as he would get the profit while other herdsmen would suffer. He wrote, "Freedom in a commons brings ruin to us all."[19]

This famous paper helped justify many people's belief that humans are inherently selfish. However, the paper was wrong because, as one observer noted, "Hardin simply ignored what actually happens in a real commons: self regulation by the communities involved."[20]

Hardin essentially assumed that communities could not set their own rules and hold each other accountable, so he assumed that each person would keep selfishly seeking more and more until the pastures were exhausted. In truth, when there are no authorities forcing laws on people, they self-regulate, making up their own rules to prevent selfishness from taking hold.

In practice, when many people share a pasture, they tend it so everyone can benefit, and cheaters are quickly noticed and dealt with. Nobel Prize-winning economist Elinor Ostrom studied commons management in small-scale communities and found that "all communities have some form of monitoring to guard against cheating or using more than a fair share of the resource."

When Depression is Seen as Pathological Rather Than as a Healthy Response to an Unsatisfying Life

It can be difficult to maintain one's mental health in an unhealthy nation. Depression, despair, anxiety, and other troubles are common. And they exist for many good reasons: many people live in financial desperation, don't trust their political leaders, face discrimination, are spiritually wounded from early childhood, and have other troubles common in unhealthy nations. Humans who are born expecting a culture of integrity, solidarity, and connection with the Earth instead grow up in a culture of exploitation, domination, disrespect, division, and abuse.

But clearly, if anyone suffers mental health disorders, it cannot be the deeply abusive nation that's to blame. It "must" be a personal problem.

For over a century, medical institutions in western European-descended countries have recognized mental health patients as somehow inherently deficient. Wilhelm Reich described how people suffering depression were diagnosed with a "hereditary taint," which meant they were "bad." He noted, "Mental patients and criminals were looked upon as biologically tainted, severely deformed creatures, for whom there was no help and no excuse…Everything was hereditary, i.e., biologically determined, and that was the end of it."[21]

I personally experienced the present-day equivalent of this in 2013. Is depression always unhealthy and a sign of a genetically predisposed condition? Or can depression be a healthy response to an unhealthy situation, a feeling that motivates a person to deeply change their life for the better?

I offer my own personal story where I grappled with these questions and a doctor who insisted I had a genetic problem that only drugs could cure.

> Everything was going as planned, and yet I was deeply unhappy. It was summer 2013. A few years earlier, some friends had invited me to their very lucrative cybersecurity startup and made me an executive in charge of technology investments, a dream job since I loved both technology and

investing. It paid over six figures with the very likely promise of millions of dollars in stock payouts later if I applied myself. I had recently become engaged to a beautiful woman I'll call Dorothy, whom I loved very much and who loved me too. I had a very safe financial cushion, good friends, good health, and family living nearby.

And I was really unhappy.

For years I had been studying economics, politics, and finance obsessively. I wanted to know what was really going on around me, to see through the bullshit and lies and find truth. By 2013, I had studied the financial frauds leading up to the 2008 financial crash, and I learned how the government I served through my company and with my taxes had bailed out the criminal bankers while screwing over masses of homeowners, all while pretending that was their only viable option.

I learned how the military industrial complex, for which I worked, was busy wasting massive amounts of money on low-functioning machines like the F35 and wars like in Afghanistan, causing huge amounts of suffering in people in foreign countries for reasons informed Americans could only speculate on.

I studied how the intelligence agencies fomented coups abroad and funded vicious death squads in central America while agency leaders testified in Congress about supporting democracy overseas.

I learned how, while the US government said it fought abroad in part to protect women's rights, it used radioactive ammunition in places like Iraq, causing many women to become infertile or give birth to extremely deformed children, and these radioactive munitions will continue to poison these regions for centuries to come.

I had only ever worked for the United States' military industrial complex since my first internship in college, and by 2013, I believed it caused tremendous harm both to Americans and foreigners and wasted tremendous amounts of money and opportunity. The lies about supporting democracy and human rights abroad which were used to justify all this only made it worse.

I don't like being lied to, I really don't like living a lie, and I could not stand being part of this any more. I had set my sights on becoming rich, but the big banks and financial regulators seemed deeply corrupt and I did not trust the financial system. I further recognized the great risks of environmental destruction, and it seemed clear that the only viable way to generate a healthy life in the face of looming resource scarcity and an increasingly poisoned environment was to go "back to the land" and seek nature's abundance in community with other people instead of financial abundance on my own. Part of me also wanted to fight against the injustice rather than just run away, but I found these urges even harder to acknowledge.

Unfortunately, I struggled to discuss this with my friends and family. My fiance and I spoke of my concerns often, but she did not feel as strongly as I did, and I started to wonder whether we were a good match. In short, I felt very alone, very dissatisfied with the life I had built, and very very stuck.

In late May 2013, Dorothy and I went to a conference where I encountered people who had been part of the back-to-the-land movement of the 1970s. For the first time, I met people who had lived in intentional communities. I met people who had transformed their own lives in response to what they cared about rather than just griping or ignoring our society's problems.

I was inspired, and I knew I wanted to transform too. I did not know how or when, but I knew I would make that transformation soon, and within a few months both my fiance and I wondered if our relationship would survive my desire for radical change. It was a stressful time.

I admitted to my doctor one day that I had been feeling depressed. I shared a few of my political concerns, something I'd done in previous visits as well – concerns about unsafe commercial food and fear about environmental troubles. I acknowledged I did not feel as mentally sharp as I used to, and my memory had become less clear. I'd known my doctor for many years and we had a close relationship, but she still surprised me with a deeply personal story before making her medical recommendation.

My doctor told me how, when her family had lived on an Air Force base in Germany in the late 1980s and early 1990s, she began to question the US' war in Iraq. She told me that she had asked herself, "Are we really there to bring democracy? Or are we there to get oil? And is that ok?" Her husband led a US Air Force squadron of fighter pilots, so he was actively engaged in this war she was concerned about. She also described how stressed she felt at the time, at one point standing up from a table during lunch with her friends, cursing at them, and storming off. From her story I sensed she was in a situation similar to mine: very concerned about the government's behavior, but isolated, with no one to talk to about it and unsure how to respond to her concerns.

As I sat transfixed, she described to me how she had worked very hard to become a doctor of internal medicine. She told me how she and her husband had started a family with children, but their relationship became stressed. They discussed divorce, moved, and later in the early-mid 90s, they considered divorce again. My doctor told me she saw two options: as she put it, she could stay with the man of her dreams, maintain a stable family for her children, and maintain the career she had worked so hard to build. Or she could risk all of it. She chose to keep all these things she'd worked so hard for, and one thing had helped her do it: antidepressant drugs.

My doctor told me that her depression stemmed from a genetic predisposition, meaning depression ran in the family. She said she could have thrown away everything she'd worked so hard for, but instead she took the drugs, and she told me they had saved her life.

Then my doctor looked me in the eye and told me she saw me in a similar situation. I had a great career with great prospects, a beautiful fiance who adored me, friends, and more. And she saw that I might throw it away, just as she almost threw away everything she'd built. She told me she saw in me the same depression that she'd struggled with, and she knew how to handle it: take the same antidepressant drugs.

In her strong medical-professional opinion, there was no good alternative anyway, as the depression was genetic; it was simply part of me and would not go away otherwise. I told her I would think about it.

I did think about it. A few weeks later I visited her again, and she asked me again if I would take the antidepressants, and I told her I was really thinking about it. She was very happy and enthusiastically encouraged me to take the drugs.

Still, I had a sense that something was off. Over time, a question finally dawned on me: what if my depression was a healthy response to an unhealthy situation? In other words, what if the depression-feeling wasn't the problem, rather the dissatisfying life situation was the problem, and the depression was just a symptom?

A few weeks passed before my next visit. Little did I know I was about to have one of the most influential conversations of my whole life.

My doctor told me how important it was that I begin antidepressants. She told me firmly that she knew depression was genetically predetermined. She told me that I must have a genetic predisposition to depression, and the only appropriate response is to take the drugs. As a doctor, she could cite study after study supporting her view, and she had a big stack of the studies printed out in front of her. From every perspective imaginable, there was only one good option: take the antidepressants.

These were powerful perspectives, and I could tell how much my doctor cared about me. I thanked her for telling her story. I told her that I had an idea I wanted to share.

What if the reason I feel depressed is because I care about something and I don't know what to do about it? And maybe that was true for you a long time ago too. What if my depression isn't the problem? What if the problem is that I'm really unhappy with my life, and I feel unable to discuss my concerns with people around me, and I feel stuck and unable to respond effectively? If that's true, then the best thing to do to confront the depression is to go live at one of those intentional communities with people who are open to living unconventionally while I seek out a new vision for my life. And if that doesn't help, I could consider taking the antidepressants then.

I will never forget my doctor's response: "I just think you need to take these drugs."

Her answer was clear. After months of visits and conversations, I would have to make my decision myself, because she wouldn't help me confront the concerns I felt so strongly about.

A few weeks later, Dorothy and I began visiting intentional communities in our region, and we continued visiting throughout autumn 2013. In early February 2014, I gave my employer three weeks' notice. I went home feeling elated. I left to live full-time at one intentional community the 4th week of February 2014, a time I have celebrated every year since.

Countless People are Suffering Unnecessarily

I managed to avoid taking antidepressants, something I still feel great relief about. But many people do not find the perspective that I found. Instead of recognizing that their life is unhealthy and their depression-feeling is a healthy reflection of this, many people accept the official medical perspective that their life is fine and their feelings of depression are unhealthy.

The broader nation labeled a healthy feeling as unhealthy with all the authority of the medical-industrial complex: huge expensive hospitals, very official doctors, wealthy corporations with fawning media and respected government regulators all combined to create an edifice of official foolishness. This shows how an unhealthy nation can generate stories that confuse people and cause them to behave in counterproductive ways. In this case, the nation urges depressed people to treat the symptom (depression) rather than the cause (a dissatisfying life).

For a small percentage of people with depression, it may be that short-term use of certain medicines can help, depending on the circumstances and medication. But given the widespread use of antidepressants to shut down so many people's healthy reactions to unhealthy conditions, I believe these drugs are yet another way that unhealthy nations maintain their exploitative dynamics. A person's dissatisfaction is what motivates them to change their life and maybe even change their nation. These drugs keep people from noticing their dissatisfaction.

Another insidious aspect of widespread use of these drugs, rooted in this hurtful belief about depression, is that taking them encourages people to align with the authorities.

My doctor's story is a great example: I believe she used antidepressants to suppress feelings and political concerns she did not know how to deal with, and thus preserved her professional and personal life. Would the drugs have had the same effect on me, helping me feel less strongly so I could tolerate the life I found so intolerable?

What if my story with my doctor had occurred 20 years earlier when I was seven years old instead of 27? At seven years old, I had not chosen to study the world and create a life path on my own terms, nor had I learned to think about feelings separate from their cause. I wouldn't have had the legal and financial independence to refuse my doctor's suggestion when she pushed so hard.

Many children suffer in this situation as I write. One mother named Debbie described how her son Brandon began floundering in the first grade, developing hives and depression and stress. Every night he asked his father "Is tomorrow school, too?" And he cried at the response.[22]

His teacher, another school authority, a doctor, and a psychiatrist all determined that Brandon had attention deficit disorder and required medication. If he were not medicated, he would be sent home. Debbie said, "I cried as I watched my parenting choices stripped away." He took drugs for a year but the hives and tears continued until she finally began homeschooling him. She said, "It was his salvation. No more pills, tears, or hives. He is thriving. He never cries now and does his work eagerly."

All the authorities assumed the school was fine, and the child who had a problem with it must be ill or deficient. Finally Debbie accepted that her child was fine and it was the school that was not fine.

Jon Young tells a similar story of a misunderstood child diagnosed with attention deficit disorder. This student was able to monitor sounds in all four directions, hearing bird calls all around him simultaneously at Young's nature connection classes. He was the first to find the hawk, first to find the hidden instructor, the first to find a particular pattern in the trees which Young pointed out.

Inside the classroom, the child had trouble sitting still, but outside the child was extremely perceptive. His learning style and his gifts simply weren't suited to sitting in a chair and listening to an adult talk. Jon Young asked, "is that a disorder or a gift?... I think that having the gift to pay attention to many things at once is not necessarily a disorder."[23]

Inappropriate beliefs about what constitutes healthy and unhealthy behavior can be insidious. I recall speaking with an elementary school teacher, whom I'll call Dana. She described her students as gullible because they trusted the adults around them. But what is the difference between "gullible" and "trusting?" "Gullible" means to trust foolishly, to trust when someone should know better. But all human children are born expecting to be raised in a healthy nation where integrity is the norm, and where adults can be trusted.

I asked her: what if the kids are trusting in a healthy way, and we adults are the ones with a problem? What if our nation is sick and allows people to maintain low integrity? And then we expect kids to learn to adjust to this while dismissing their trustfulness as gullibility? Again, this shows the same pattern: Dana assumed the nation is healthy, and then spoke dismissively of the children as they struggled to adapt to it.

Obviously it is important to help children develop appropriate skepticism so they can live in their unhealthy nation. The question is whether the children have a deficiency (gullibility) or whether the children are healthy (trusting) and the nation is diseased.

When authorities assume that school is appropriate, then of course any child that can't do well "must" have a disorder or deficiency.

Seeing the Great Scam Helps Me Avoid It

All these examples of religious and secular stories are examples of The Great Scam of Heart-Closing Cultural Narratives. They train people to believe that people are inherently bad or conditionally good, or disconnected from god, or that people deserve their lot in life. They train people to believe that the world is bad, or people are untrustworthy and inclined to evil, and that any of a person's feelings or urges that go against societies' expectations are bad and wrong and must be repressed.

What the Catholics call "dour combat with the forces of evil" is really people struggling to withhold their love as they were taught growing up. Instead of giving their love sexually, many learn to hold it back or feel shame. Instead of speaking truth to authority, or joining a union to strike for better pay, or standing in solidarity with the Earth to stop logging, many people learn to hold back.

There is good news: all these stories are scams. Every human is divine and the only thing potentially separating a person from divinity is their own closed heart through which Creator speaks to each of us. Humans all have the same urges towards integrity, solidarity, authenticity, gratitude, and more, although many of us sadly have trained to embrace other patterns instead.

Heart-closing narratives train people for selfishness, shame, distrust, low self-worth, or self-doubt. Sometimes I still fall into these old traps. When this happens, I have found one technique that helps me open my heart again: laughter.

Anytime I return to old habits of doubting my self-worth or feeling disconnected and alone, I just remember: that's bullshit! These self-diminishing feelings are just remnants in my body from when I believed these ridiculous scam stories for so many years. And I just start laughing; in fact I'm laughing as I write this section right now because I know I'm never going to let myself fall for any such scam ever again.

It is possible for a person to close their heart for so long that they forget how to open their heart and listen to its divine voice. It can be especially challenging if a person started closing their heart in early childhood before they formed lasting memories. But people can remember how to open their hearts and practice living in a good way again, as explored in *Chapter 19: Creating a Culture of Remembering*.

Chapter 19: Creating a Culture of Remembering

In his book *Secrets of the Talking Jaguar*, Martín Prechtel described the Tzutujil Mayans as a culture of remembering. He described the book itself as "keeping the interconnectedness of life alive by remembering."[1] People continually remembered the kind things their neighbors had done for them, remembered their elders, and remembered their Gods. They practiced remembering the divinity of all life and their divine place in it.[2]

Prechtel said, "Our forgetfulness of where we came from killed life and the Gods." When they forgot to remember their stories and their place in divinity, often under pressure from Christian missionaries and the Guatemalan military, Prechtel said they ceased to be Mayan and became Guatemalan citizens.[3,4]

All of us now living in unhealthy nations have ancestors who once lived in beautiful healthy nations of deep remembering. Sometime in the past few millennia, we were ripped out and forced into authoritarian nations. Since then, many of us have forgotten our divine place in creation, and how to live without rulers and imposed laws. Many of us have forgotten how to resolve conflicts, hold each other accountable for inappropriate behavior, take the Earth's needs into account in our day-to-day lives, or come to each others' aid when someone is in need or in danger.

What would it be like to try to regenerate a culture of remembering, even if just for a few weeks? Even if they couldn't remember as deeply as a fully intact nation like the Mayans, if a group of people only had a few weeks, how much could they remember about how to live well with each other and the Earth?

A friend whom I'll call Leia described her experience with Rainbow gatherings exactly this way. They are envisioned as "a returning and a remembering of a different way of life."[5]

There are many ways to remember how to live in a healthy nation. What follows is one example.

Emphasis on Sharing and Connection

Ranging from dozens to a few thousand participants, Rainbow gatherings are held around the world and last about a month. They are commonly held on public land or land that the owner makes freely available.

Leia described the major emphasis on sharing. In her first Rainbow in Tasmania, the gathering had about 75-200 people. She described the beautiful rhythm she found where, starting in the morning, she would wake up and check if anyone needed help making breakfast. If not, she would see if anyone needed help collecting firewood. If not, perhaps the water lines needed fixing. If nothing needed doing, perhaps she would hang out with friends under a tree. She said, "one of the philosophies of Rainbow is [if] you see something that needs doing, you do it."

Everyone is autonomous, and there is no hierarchy ordering people around. This works better at some gatherings than others, as people who are new or poorly integrated or unused to being part of a community sometimes let others do the work. But at this Tasmania gathering, everyone embraced this community ethic.

She described how valuable it is to live without land ownership, and how this helped bring people together. People could set up their own fires if they wanted, but people didn't have to stay in their own little campsite and brew their own coffee. They could go to the community kitchen and help make a big fire to feed their neighbors, contributing to something bigger than themselves.

Much of life was filled with taking care of basic needs, and even this became special. Leia would go down to a pristine river with seven other women and wash clothes together in the water. Leia described how that "was a big remembering moment for me, like remembering how my ancestors used to do that, and how… washing [and other] monotonous tasks could be so community building. And so wonderful because it includes song, it includes nature time, it includes connection with sisters, as opposed to going to a laundromat and throwing your clothes into a machine, which is really disconnective, and actually becomes a chore instead of a joyful act that can fulfill your life. I feel like that is the crux of it, that the monotonous daily tasks are joyful when you're not just doing it for yourself, but you're doing it for the greater community… cooking for 200 people is a feat, you know, and so there's often 10 people in there chopping veggies, half naked, telling stories. There are people in the kitchen making music, so making it a really fun experience."

This generosity showed up in the children too. Leia described "feral children that run around, and they are somebody's children, but they're also everybody's children… seeing it for the first time with new eyes was so overwhelming, it was so beautiful to be in this place of 200 adults and everyone is expected to pick up firewood. You're expected to be an auntie to these children…"

Leia was inspired by a 5-year-old girl who went into the woods to collect blackberries and proceeded to hand one to each person in the kitchen. It was beautiful to see this attitude that "these are the people that are feeding me tonight so I'm going to feed them… that was really really radical for me." Leia described how infectious, expansive, and inclusive it is being part of this kind of group sharing, not just living in the confines of her own home or being the only provider for her family or herself.

This sharing manifested in so many ways. Leia described many freezing nights in a Rainbow gathering in the Himalayan mountains in northern India. Instead of each person shivering alone in their sleeping bag, they'd huddle together to stay warm in groups while singing songs.

This sharing also manifested in the form of mutual self defense.

Mutual Aid, Safety and Accountability

Rainbow gatherings have a safety team called shanti sena. They're the emergency response group, and normally they meet every other day to check in with each other and ensure they know what's going on. Anybody can volunteer to join. If anyone feels genuinely unsafe at any time, they can yell "shanti sena!" and people will come running. Even people not part of shanti sena may come running, because someone being in danger is so important to address.

Leia described how in many Rainbow gatherings, especially outside the US, people agree not to bring alcohol. But at this Tasmania gathering, one man with an alcohol disorder came, and he drank heavily and caused issues with other people. People tried to speak with him gently, but it didn't help.

One evening he accosted a woman, and someone called shanti sena. Many people came. A few men tackled him to the ground and formed a circle around him. Unable to stop his offensive behavior, eventually they tied him to a tree.

Several people attended to the woman to help her feel safe again. She received a lot of care from her neighbors. He hadn't succeeded in what he'd tried to do, but it was clearly inappropriate. Now they had to decide, "how do we respond to this?" They had no one imposing law on them; they had to decide for themselves. Leia illustrated that open-hearted attitude, saying, "this brother… needs help. You know, he's not… a bad person, he is a troubled person with a lot of love in his heart."

Even so, they couldn't tolerate his inappropriate behavior. Would they kick him out? If not, how could they safely invite him to stay and help him integrate better? If they just evicted him, he might just continue behaving inappropriately elsewhere. They realized that this might be the best place for him because they could give him loving support in growing beyond his hurtful behavior.

They ended up speaking to him in a respectful and compassionate way. They sang songs, and they also responded with firmness. They took away his alcohol, saying, "there is no space for your alcoholism." They appointed a community watch person, a buddy who would check in on him and his neighbors regularly to make sure everything was ok.

They tried to have several clear conversations about appropriate behavior once he became sober. He had a background of abuse and alcoholism and wasn't used to being shown compassion. Nor was he used to being asked to acknowledge his faults. Alcohol addiction can be difficult to heal, but the group would not tolerate threatening behavior. These were difficult conversations, and they didn't always seem successful.

Unfortunately, he later got more alcohol and caused another disturbance. At this point, the shanti sena team escorted him out of the gathering, again with love and compassion. No one claimed he was bad. It was his behavior that was inappropriate, and they invited him to return when he could participate in a more appropriate way.

Leia described this as a "really radical and really beautiful way of dealing with this kind of thing." Instead of a constant focus on punishing, it allowed space for personal growth, possibility, and compassion. At the same time, it held community protection and care as a core requirement. She noted how they were "dancing with the awkwardness of it. We're not going to get everything right. We're just a group of people trying our best."

This showed me how a nation can have healthy boundaries that block bad behaviors rather than blocking people. Rainbow gatherings welcome anyone who is willing to behave respectfully. When this man behaved inappropriately, the shanti sena team made it clear that his behavior was a problem and they invited him to change. When he wouldn't change, the shanti sena team evicted the bad behavior from the gathering, telling the man he could return when he could behave respectfully.

Sharing Agreements

Leia described the importance of having shared agreements, and the best gatherings are the ones with the strongest agreements and clearest accountability. No alcohol is allowed. The main kitchen is always vegetarian, and people can cook what they wish in their private campsite. People use the shit-pit in very specific ways, and people know how to treat the water and where to bathe. With clear agreements, people understand how to get along.

Continuity really helps. When people meet again, year after year, and experience which poop systems work and which do not, over time they wind up with working systems that protect the water and people's health. Some Rainbow gathering participants come from healthy nations who are already deeply connected with the Earth, and they can offer working systems based on generations of experience. And when a new trouble arises and no one has an immediate solution, people simply do their best and adjust as they go along.

Accounting for the Needs of the Earth

Rainbow gatherings also work to take the Earth's needs into account. Treating the water respectfully is a consistent theme. Leia noted, "there are very strong agreements… There are very specific ways in which you use a shit-pit. There are very specific ways in which you treat the waterways, like what you don't put into the water, and where to bathe. There are people [who] come up with very specific guidelines, and it's not one person. As a community, people come up with guidelines that feel good for the whole, and everybody adheres to them."

Respectful foraging is another consistent theme. Foraging means to harvest wild plants or mushrooms that live around the gathering space, and when they are available, they can provide a lot of free food for participants. However, it would also be easy for a Rainbow gathering to wipe out local populations of some plants, and experienced foragers teach people to notice their impact and avoid over-harvesting that might permanently reduce local plant populations.

Resolving Conflict

Sometimes people object to an agreement, such as the ban on alcohol. People who depend on alcohol may set up a camp outside the regular Rainbow space, and as long as they don't cause disturbances, the gathering often tolerates it.

When disagreements arise, they have a clear system: people will form breakout circles to discuss the issue. One gathering in India was supposed to be vegan, but some local mamas would come around selling cheese, and some people bought some and ate it at their private camp. This offended others who insisted that the whole gathering should be vegan.

They agreed to hold a circle. Anyone who cared should come, and those who didn't care shouldn't come. As Leia said, "If you're not there, your voice doesn't matter… If you want your voice heard, come." Ultimately a half dozen people came and agreed that the main, public meal would remain vegan, and people could eat as they wished in their private camp.

Leia noted that this is a common pattern: someone will try to impose norms on everyone else, and others will push back. They have shared agreements about shared resources like group meals or public spaces or waterways, and in purely private matters people are commonly free to make their own choices. There's a high tolerance for behavior that doesn't cause harm or disruption, even if it seems strange.

When circles reach a certain size, people would use the talking stick system. Whoever has the stick may talk and no one interrupts. When a person finishes, they pass the stick and the next person speaks. This continues around the circle until there is consensus. Sometimes it takes a long time. Other times a person will decide to accept the group's decision even if they don't agree, helping the group come to a decision that works well enough even if everyone isn't totally satisfied.

Sharing Resources

In a month-long gathering, there isn't time to grow food or raise animals. Rainbow participants would commonly buy food from town, but this raised a question: how can people contribute if some participants have much more money than others? What if some people were intentionally poor, and others are poor due to systemic racism or other factors?

Thus the Magic Hat system was born. After each meal, the Magic Hat gets passed around, and "you can put money in or you can put your love in." Nobody knows who gives money or who doesn't, but there's always enough. Leia has never been to a Rainbow that ran out of food. Sometimes she hasn't given any money, but she's given a lot of time to help support the gathering. With this Magic Hat, people give in the ways they are able to, without shame.

She's never been in a Rainbow that ran out of money. Sometimes they ate rice and lentils three dinners in a row, but then people would see the need and pitch in, or new people would arrive with funds. Sometimes newcomers wouldn't know that the Magic Hat was the source of their food, so somebody would get up and gently remind everybody that this sharing is part of how they generate abundance. Someone might say, "We only have rice and lentils, so if anybody has more resources to share, please do." It always works out.

The money and most of the food have to come from somewhere outside the gathering. This is one of many ways that Rainbow gatherings are unsustainable over a longer term. But given those limitations, people find a way to share resources such that everyone contributes and everyone's needs are met.

They would form missions of around five people to go to town and fill sacks with vegetables and bulk foods like rice or lentils. The return trip might be multiple miles long, up and down mountain trails. It wouldn't do to have this same little group then have to transport the food back by themselves.

The community came up with a solution. At Rainbows, people commonly put away their watches and electronics, so it's easy to be present with each other without distraction. They also rely on their environment to help keep time. For example, they might say, "Let's meet when the sun reaches the top of that mountain." Before leaving, the food mission group would agree to return by a certain time. At this time, a runner in camp would look down at the rendezvous point. Once the food mission had returned, the runner would give a call.

Leia described how people formed a human line a mile and a half long, passing the bags from person to person, moving the food slowly into camp together. She said, "It was so epic. It blew my mind." She described how special it was without electronics, and how that facilitated connection and further encouraged people to participate.

Some of Leia's best Rainbow memories came from doing mundane tasks together. After a few weeks, the gathering could use up all the nearby firewood. One time a person found a big thick dead tree high in a mountain and 10 people went to get it. They decided to bring it down on their shoulders, walking with small steps for about an hour. Leia described how the big tree didn't feel too heavy until one person stepped out, and suddenly everyone could feel the extra weight and someone else would step in. They finally got to the bottom and had a huge feeling of accomplishment and elation. Leia said, "all my favorite Rainbow experiences are from doing a very mundane task with an epic amount of support."

Gathering firewood together.

Sharing Wisdom

Because there are no authorities giving directions, Rainbows really emphasize personal initiative. If you see a need, you fill it. After dinner people would make announcements to let others know what needs they saw or upcoming opportunities to help out.

As new people came into camp, they needed an introduction, and so some people volunteered to specially greet newcomers. First-time participants would get a special introduction so that everybody knew the agreements and could integrate well.

People commonly host workshops, sharing knowledge on things like forest ecology, identifying edible plants and insects, macrame, friction fires, self defense, astrology, activist projects and stories, and more. Leia described getting a neuroscience lecture from a neuroscientist in a cave in the Himalayas. Nobody needed credentials to share what they knew.

Silly things happen too. Leia described one man who stood up in a circle and said that people should listen to women more, and he began ranting about it. Another man interrupted and pointed out how much he was talking, doing just what he was complaining about. Pretty soon three men were arguing about how they should listen more to women. Eventually someone suggested calling a circle to invite women to speak.

Bringing These Patterns Outside of Rainbow Gatherings

Leia noted how transformative these Rainbow gatherings could be, saying they were "just cracking my heart open again and again and again." After her first one, she said, "it felt like my whole world was turned upside down…[it] was beautiful but also really jarring… How do I go back to anything different?"

She described how Rainbow changed her deeply. She described herself as community-centric, continuously building support networks and friendships where people really support each other. She gardens collaboratively with her friends. The tools and resources needed to garden for a family may be too much, but it doesn't take much more to feed five families than one, so she enjoys finding ways to pool resources. She noted, "if you work together with a number of different people, you can create a lot more bounty. You also create the gifts of connections and community and sustainability."

She and her fiance invited help with their Rainbow-themed wedding, welcoming dozens of friends to pitch in with a variety of roles. Some people created decorations, others helped scout the wedding site in a national forest, and others helped cook the food or make music. I worked with a few friends to create the wedding cake and walk it safely to the site. Children helped dish out food or put up decorations. Leia had no need to hire a wedding coordinator. Instead, she worked with a few friends to lay out the general structure and plan and let people volunteer and self-organize. It was beautiful as I looked around and noticed where dozens of people had added their own personal touch to help make the wedding special.

Leia said Rainbow gatherings have helped her become more patient and resolve conflicts better. She noted, "I've got a lot of faith in the magical. Those stories live in my body and I know what's possible when you create a beautiful experience that everybody can completely participate in… trusting in the bounty, that the abundance is always there, and that if you let yourself fall, you'll always be caught."

The Value of Remembering, Even for a Little While or in Limited Circumstances

In *Braiding Sweetgrass*, botany professor and Potawatomi woman Robin Kimmerer described trying to teach university students about plants. At first she taught students in a big lecture hall with diagrams and slides and stories, and she regularly encountered a "sea of blank looks [which] suggested that most of them found this as interesting as, literally, watching grass grow."[6]

When Kimmerer asked which students had ever grown plants, only the most engaged students raised their hands, while the disengaged students did not. Eventually, she was able to engage many of the disinterested students by taking them out of the lecture hall and into the living world so they could experience plant life with all their senses. Once students could see for themselves how flowers transform into fruits, and how some plants get along and others stay away from each other, and why, their interest in the class began to bloom. They listened to the plants, touched them, and moved among them. Once students had directly experienced the plants and explored them in a personal, connecting way, they were more interested in the details Kimmerer wanted to share in her classroom. Nothing she could have said or done in the classroom alone would have had the same impact.

These students did not get to live in a fully interdependent way with plants, and likewise, even the most beautiful Rainbow gatherings are a far cry from living in a fully sovereign, fully healthy nation. But just as the students' brief experiences helped them see the value in Kimmerer's plant teachings and stories, Rainbow gatherings help people get an experience of living without rulers, helping participants recognize and remember how it's possible for humans to live well with each other. And it helps participants remember how good that feels.

For many people in authoritarian nations, freedom is an abstract concept with which they have little direct experience. Rainbow and other similar gatherings help people get a taste of what freedom would actually be like, so that we can remember.

When I talk about healthy nations with people who have spent time in radical intentional communities, they nod their head knowingly. They get it because they have experienced aspects of life without rulers, even if in a limited way. Many people in these communities have worked with others to set agreements and hold each other accountable, learned to resolve conflicts, learned to pay attention to the Earth, and more. These are not abstract concepts to them. However, most people I speak with have had no such experience. For them, healthy nations may sound beautiful, but the stories don't seem to resonate in the same way. And some people consider healthy nations an idealized fantasy, not an achievable human experience. They just seem too foreign.

Words have their place, and I strongly desire for this book full of words to make a difference. But both Kimmerer's and Leia's stories show that there is nothing like experiencing the real thing so that important ideas don't seem like mere theories or wishful thinking.

Rainbow gatherings commonly take place in forests with clean water and space for outdoor latrines, so there are some aspects that city dwellers cannot easily reproduce in an urban setting. But any group of people, in any location, can generate a healthy subculture at any time. Rainbow isn't magical because some event planners set up rules that participants have to follow, and thus everyone gets along. They are magical because participants follow many of the healthy-nation patterns explored in this book: people agree on how to live together and hold each other accountable when someone violates an agreement. People can trust each other to show up and help if someone is mistreated. People share with each other as a normal, daily way of life while also respecting individual autonomy. People really think about how to interact with their environment in a good way. In short, people take responsibility for themselves and the health of their culture. They make their culture what they want it to be given the limits they have.

Any group of people who set their minds to it can do this anywhere at any time. Mutual aid societies, book clubs, unions, businesses, sports teams, revolutionary movements, governments, intentional communities, and any other group all have their culture, and it can be whatever participants want it to be.

Leia's stories showed me how easily people can remember how to live with each other again when we bring certain attitudes and keep to certain agreements. We can make up our own systems of accountability and conflict resolution and collective self-defense. We can remember how to share knowledge and resources. We can turn off our distracting electronics and be present with each other. We can live with integrity and enjoy doing simple, life-serving work together.

Her stories also showed me another truth which might sound silly at first: if we don't keep remembering, we might forget.

For example, I sometimes fall into the habit of treating property lines as if they were real. But when I see a family of deer meander across a property line, they remind me that property lines are entirely made up. Fences are real, and the police who might be called if a person gets caught trespassing are real, but the invisible property lines themselves exist only in people's heads. The deer thus inspire me to cross property lines without permission, just for the sake of practicing it and feeling in my body what it would be like to live free on the Earth, without property lines. I always feel rejuvenated afterwards.

Experiences like these Rainbow gatherings similarly help people remember in their bodies what it's like to live in a healthy nation, even if they're not fully autonomous and integrated healthy nations. People get to practice setting their own agreements, resolving conflicts, sharing, collaborating, singing, boundary setting, foraging, accountability, mentoring, and more. Even a little practice and personal experience can activate that body-memory that helps people build healthy subcultures everywhere they go.

Humans are born with a wide open heart, and they are not born despising each other. Yet racism, sexism, and other discrimination persist around the world. Next, *Part 6 - Unhealthy Nations Impose Division* explores why.

Part 6 - Unhealthy Nations Impose Division

All unhealthy nations discriminate in a variety of ways. If all humans are divine, and no one is born with racist, sexist, or hateful attitudes, how come these attitudes are so widespread and persistent?

Chapter 20: Imposing and Maintaining Racism vs Generating Unity

Growing up, I learned there was power in numbers. Then I started looking around and noticed that wasn't always true.

In French St. Domingue in the Caribbean in 1789, there were 32,000 white colonists, 24,000 mixed race and unenslaved black people, and 500,000 black slaves.[1] In Brazil, for more than 250 years starting in the early 1500s, over half the population was enslaved in some form.[2] In 2020, Forbes magazine counted 2,095 billionaires globally, while nearly half the world population, totaling over 3 billion people, earned less than $6.85 per day.[3,4]

Clearly, without solidarity, there is little power in numbers. The single greatest threat to authorities' rule is that abused people might unite and overthrow their abusive rulers. Rulers and other authorities are acutely aware that in order to maintain their power and control, they must prevent or at least minimize solidarity by keeping people divided.

To keep people divided, authorities commonly impose systemic discrimination, where different groups of people are treated very differently by the government and corporate leaders. It is a simple and effective divide-and-conquer strategy.

I grew up in a nation where the government maintains a story that it treats everyone equally, so I didn't learn until adulthood that racism and other discrimination is actually imposed by authorities.

My first introduction to the idea that authorities might deliberately impose divisive racism came from reading the Attica Manifesto. In 1971, the prisoners took over Attica Prison in New York and delivered their manifesto, listing their grievances and demands that they wanted met before relinquishing control of the prison. Many were predictable to anyone who has studied prisons: they wanted enough toilet paper to properly clean themselves and they wanted clean water for washing instead of the dirty water the guards brought. They wanted work that paid at least the legal minimum wage that would allow them to support themselves and their families outside of prison. There were many other demands that could be summarized simply: they wanted to be treated respectfully.[5]

However, I was amazed to read two parts. The inmates clearly said their manifesto reflected the will of all the races in the prison who were united, and then they made many demands not to be discriminated against based on race, including a demand to end discrimination in parole quotas for black and brown people and a demand to provide ethnic counselors to black and brown inmates. Besides their racial unity, the other part that amazed me was their demand for "an immediate end to the agitation of race relations by the prison administration of this state."

I had certainly heard of racism, but when I noticed that all races of prisoners were united in demanding that prison authorities stop deliberately agitating race relations, it changed my thinking. It showed me that racism doesn't "just happen." Racism has a source, and that source is abusive authorities seeking to divide people.

Systemic Solidarity Prevention: The Three Core Drivers of Deep Division

I believe racism and other kinds of discrimination arise from three underlying drivers:

1. *Systemic discrimination*: Rulers and lower authorities artificially impose differences between races by purposely treating different groups of people in different ways in terms of the law, pay, exposure to toxic pollution, how they are commonly represented in news and entertainment, access to food, school funding, and many other conditions.

2. *Adopting an authoritarian attitude*: Many people learn to adopt racist attitudes that are imposed or encouraged by authorities in order to maintain or advance their own privilege, comfort, and safety in their abusive unhealthy nation.

3. *Child abuse*: Some kinds of child abuse predispose people to embrace authoritarian attitudes.

This chapter explores how authorities impose systemic racism based on race, caste, region, and ethnicity, while other chapters reveal how authorities impose systemic sexism, hatred, and selfishness. The same three drivers of deep division create all these troubles.

Racism, like every other form of discrimination, does not just happen randomly. Rulers are the driving, animating force behind racism, using various techniques to initially impose and then maintain racist differences in their nation. To survive in a racist society, many people learn to adopt racist attitudes encouraged by authorities, further promoting and maintaining race-based discrimination. Of course, each person is still responsible for their beliefs and actions.

Every unhealthy authoritarian nation I have studied practices systemic discrimination in some form. Some hide it while others proudly acknowledge it. Where authorities pretend to stand for equality while imposing discrimination, I call it *covert discrimination*. *Overt discrimination* occurs in societies that acknowledge and legitimize treating some people much worse than others.

Overt Systemic Discrimination

Overt systemic discrimination is simple to observe, but in some unhealthy nations it is less common than it used to be.

The Kafala system in many west Asian nations is a legal system allowing employers to import cheap foreign workers with almost no labor protections. As of late 2022, it was active in Saudi Arabia, Bahrain, Lebanon, Oman, Jordan, Qatar, Kuwait, and the United Arab Emirates. In most countries, an employer sponsors the migrant, paying for their travel and housing.

The system gives employers overwhelming control over the migrants. The employer may terminate the migrant's travel visa at will. Migrants in most countries have fewer legal rights to unionize than citizens. Migrants require their employer's permission to change jobs or leave the country. Employers commonly confiscate passports, visas, and phones and confine domestic workers to the sponsor's home. Employers may impose fees or withhold wages, forcing the migrant into debt bondage and giving the employer further legal leverage over the worker. Crowded housing, low wages, sexual assault, and other abuses are common. Workers are often afraid to report crimes as they could face retribution from their sponsoring employer or even be charged with crimes themselves. Thus the Kafala system represents overt discrimination towards migrants, many of whom are from Africa or south Asia.[6]

For many centuries until the 1950s, Tibet had a system of serfdom with many different categories of serf. Some were tied to the land while others had no access to land. Some were able to own livestock while others owned nothing. But all of them were completely subject to the will of their masters. They had to get their lord's permission for even a short trip away or to marry. Serfs could be sold away at will, separating families. Even higher-privileged serfs with land "rights" might be degraded to slavery status at the will of the lord, or a slave's status might be raised to become an overseer or steward. However, if a higher privilege serf or slave gained any wealth, the lord could confiscate it at will. This was another very explicit, overt form of discrimination between serfs and lords.[7]

For centuries, India maintained a rigid caste system said to be created by the Hindu God Brahma. Almost everyone belonged to a caste and sub-caste, called a jati, which matched their parents' sub-caste, and their sub-caste determined their job. Thus everyone knew their occupation from birth. The law required people to marry within their sub-caste. The Brahmin, or highest caste, were the priests and teachers, followed by the Kshatriyas who were warriors and political leaders, Vaishyas who were traders, farmers, and merchants, and Shudras who were laborers.

Unfortunately, the lowest rank of people were the Dalits, who were entirely outside the classification system. Mirroring the Catholic belief in Original Sin (that people are born disconnected from God), the Dalits were believed to be born outside the divine classification system, and thus were also called "untouchables." They were given the dirtiest jobs, such as cleaning latrines and removing garbage.[8] One Dalit woman, 14-year-old Mukta Salve, was able to learn to write and described the abuses Dalits faced. Women gave birth in squalid conditions, education was forbidden, and higher-caste people could kill them at will for minor transgressions. She wrote, "The Brahmins have degraded us so low; they consider people like us even lower than cows and buffaloes."[9]

These systems of overt discrimination are fairly straightforward to understand, as the law explicitly gives one group power over another. However, some nations maintain a pretense of treating everyone equally while still imposing discrimination. I call this *covert discrimination*. How does this work?

Covert Systemic Discrimination

In overt discrimination, legal officials including police treat one group differently than another and openly acknowledge this.

In covert discrimination, legal officials still treat one group differently than another, but they claim to treat everyone equally.

This can take many devious forms, but some kinds can be quantified by researchers. These include giving different groups different lengths of prison sentence for the same crime, or having police officers patrol and harass people in certain areas but not others.

The United Kingdom, United States, and China all show these patterns of covert discrimination.

In a study in China published in 2020, researchers reviewed 10,000 drug cases in Yunnan province and noticed that minorities commonly received a prison sentence 1.5-7.5 months longer than the majority Han ethnicity. This held even after researchers controlled for the type of crime, amount of drugs, defendant's criminal history, and many other factors.[10]

In a study in the United Kingdom published in 2022, researchers found that after a drug offense, a Chinese person was 1.7 times more likely than a white British person to get a custodial sentence. Black Caribbean males were 1.6 times more likely, and an "other white" person was 1.5 times more likely than a white British person to go to prison. Researchers noted that, "Legally relevant factors however, do not fully explain disparities in sentencing."[11] Racist policing is common as well. Almost 90% of tribunal judges are white, while 93-94% of police officers, court judges, and prison officers are white. They used a stop-and-search policy, and in 2016-2017, they stopped black people at a rate eight times that of white people. Black people form about 3% of the population but 37% of prisoners.[12]

Similar patterns exist in the United States. A US government report found that between 2017-2021, black men received sentences about 13% longer than white males, and Hispanic males received sentences about 11% longer. Hispanic women were given sentences about 28% longer than white women, while women of "other" race received sentences 10% shorter than white women. White people were more likely to receive probation than time in prison compared to others.[13]

In a report published in 2018, researchers found that black men represent 13% of the male population but approximately 35% of those imprisoned in the United States. Black women represent 13% of the female population but 44% of imprisoned women. Researchers believe that one in every three black men born today will be imprisoned in their lifetime, while only one in six Latino men or one in 17 white men will be incarcerated. One out of every 18 black women born in 2001 will be imprisoned at some point, much worse odds than the one in 111 white women who will be incarcerated.

Discriminatory policing is a major cause. For example, one study in Seattle found that black people represented about half of those delivering crack cocaine but almost 80% of those arrested. About 40% of those delivering crack cocaine were white, yet whites counted for only 9% of arrests.[14]

These and many other studies illustrate covert discrimination, where a government pretends to apply law equally but actually treats some people much worse than others.

Racist Attitudes Justify Oppression

Whether openly or secretly, authorities purposely and systematically create the reality of racist, ethnic, ideological or class discrimination. One group of people live in squalor while another lives in comfort. One is better educated while another is less educated. One group seems more law-abiding according to statistics while the other group is supposedly more prone to criminality.

Authorities then propagate stories that excuse or ignore this systemic discrimination, and people can choose to accept these stories or not. Unfortunately, in authoritarian nations, the vast majority of people seem to accept the stories and attitudes propagated by authorities, and thus adopt discriminatory attitudes as well.

Every person is responsible for their beliefs and how they treat others. When I consider where racism comes from and what might end it, it helps me to realize why so many people adopt racist attitudes. Racist attitudes help people fit into their abusive nation. Racism excuses or justifies the life that they are born into. Authorities make racist differences seem like "just how things are" with racist policies and then encourage people to adopt racist attitudes that justify these differences.

Consider a white male French colonist born into a slaveowning family in Haiti in 1750. He was likely born into a very racist family and had racist friends, teachers and political leaders. He lived a comfortable life growing up, while all the enslaved black people around him lived in misery. This young white person may have expected to grow into a wealthy slaveowner in adulthood, a path for which his parents groomed him. This young man faced a choice: he could easily keep his life of comfort and wealth and social connections – all he had to do was keep his racist attitudes. Or, he could reject his racist attitudes and risk losing everything.

Multiply that reality by hundreds of millions of people whose social position has depended on keeping racist attitudes, and it is not surprising that this pattern plays out at all levels of society, in many unhealthy nations, over many centuries.

For example, if a legal system is racist, a prison guard faces a similar choice. They can keep their comfortable, safe career so long as they ignore their society's racism or consider it legitimate. Alternatively, they could acknowledge that all of us are divine beings and systemic racism is not ok, and decide to only guard prisoners who they believe truly should be in prison. Of course, this person would be risking their prison guard career as well as friendships and other social connections.

Sometimes the punishment for standing against discrimination is explicitly written into the law. For example, any American in the pre-Civil War south who spoke out against slavery could be imprisoned or killed. Merely having a copy of an anti-slavery book was enough to get one man a 10-year prison sentence.[15]

In other societies, discriminatory attitudes are enforced in other ways. The US maintained a strong anti-communist stance in the 1900s, shaming people and threatening their careers if they supported communist political efforts.[16]

Likewise, the Soviet Union maintained a strong anti-capitalist stance, strongly shaming people and threatening them with imprisonment or other punishments if they ran a small business or advocated for capitalism.[17,18]

None of this excuses any individual's racist attitudes or behavior, but it shows where racism comes from. Discriminatory attitudes don't just spontaneously arise in everybody. Racist government isn't a reflection of a racist society. Government leaders (or the people who give them directions) are the ultimate drivers of racism and then many people learn racist attitudes as they grow up and adapt to their unhealthy nation.

In other words, rulers are the ultimate source of racism. Racism helps justify the exploitation of some people by others, so it's in the rulers' interest to spread it. In one form or another, this kind of discrimination is just a common condition in authoritarian nations where a few people rule over everyone else.

In a healthy nation with strong leaders and no rulers, respect for everybody in the nation (the opposite of discrimination) is the norm. Not only that, people in healthy nations cannot be bullied into adopting racist attitudes as easily as those in unhealthy nations, because mutual aid is a normal part of their gift-economy culture. People who are less anxious about their ongoing safety and comfort because they normally share things like food and self-defense are a lot harder to turn against each other.

In unhealthy nations based on profit economies, authorities have much more leverage to control and artificially divide people. This fact does not excuse anyone from taking on racist attitudes, but it does help explain it. People are being duped.

Thus racism is not just mean or incorrect. Racism is a scam! Racism is a scam that racist people fall for. It justifies people exploiting each other, and justifies each person's place in an exploitative society. But it is the rulers who exploit everyone. In the United States, white people on average may be more comfortable than black people on average, but many poor white people are homeless, live in poverty, or have unsatisfying jobs or disrespectful bosses. Even somewhat comfortable white people are subject to pollution, inflation, isolation, and many other troubles. If it weren't for racism, poor black people and poor white people might team up to stand against their oppressive rulers. When too many people believe in the racism scam, it prevents solidarity and meaningful change.

This perspective shows me how to address systemic discrimination, whether by class, region, race, sex, religion, or ethnicity. I still support engaging with racist people and helping them recognize the scam they're falling for, but I don't believe that speaking with random people will address the main driver of racism. The driver of racism is the rulers themselves. The way to finally end racism is to generate a way of life where everyone stands for what's right, and nobody rules over anybody else.

Authorities train people to believe that without rulers there would be chaos in the streets and no hope of a decent life. Healthy nations show, again and again, that people have no need for rulers. Healthy nations maintain mutual respect, individual autonomy, shared agreements without imposed laws, strong leaders but no rulers, and shared responsibility for the wellbeing of the group – this is not just possible; it's who we really are as humans.

Racists are not born. They are made. And racism will remain until nobody rules over anybody else.

Generating Unity

What's it like living in a healthy nation that encourages unity without hurtful ideologies and without ignoring abuse? What do healthy nations actually do to generate solidarity and help people get along in a deep way?

I was pleasantly surprised when I noticed that nature connection practices helped me connect with people in a deeper way than I ever had before. After practicing for years, it's clear to me that if a whole group of people embraced these practices, they could be closely connected indeed.

There are many ways to connect deeply with the living world, and this takes time and discipline. Here, I share more about my own path.

The *Kamana* program produced by Jon Young introduces students to a very special nature connection practice called the sit spot. I picked a place outdoors within a few minutes' walk from my home where I could view wildlife. My first sit spot was next to a stream winding through a big forest, but during times when I've moved around a lot, I've also used my backyard or a nearby park.

The goal is to go to the sit spot daily and explore and notice what's going on. What plants grow at what times of the year? What birds live there, and how do they interact with each other and the plants? What animals live there or pass through? I learned to pay attention with all my senses, my eyes, ears, taste, smell, touch, temperature, and more. And I learned to feel curious about the experiences of the beings around me.

I asked myself questions about what I saw. Why would a bird constantly look up as it eats? I learned that they are continuously aware in case predators arrive, so birds constantly eat, look around, eat, and look again. Do some species of tree like growing together and others don't? For example, I learned that black walnuts produce a compound which only some plants find toxic, and thus black walnuts like growing with trees like sugar maple and box elder but avoid trees like white pines.

I continually practiced feeling into the experiences of other beings. For example, I studied hawks and songbirds, and I imagined being a songbird and how terrifying it would be to have a sharp-shinned hawk swoop out of the sky and snatch me in an instant. If I were a songbird, I would probably eat carefully too!

Eventually, I learned that plants and animals could help me notice parts of the landscape I couldn't observe directly. The movement of a bird might indicate a hidden possum moving through low brush. Or, some birds and other animals like deer can see ultraviolet light that is invisible to humans. I might not be able to see rodent poop directly, but birds can see the ultraviolet light reflected off the poop. If I notice birds responding to it, I can learn about the rodents' presence with the birds' help.

The first core spiritual practice – cultivating a practical, aware gratitude – is a big part of this sit spot training. I learned that birds and plants and other beings could teach me about my environment, or they could show me when I'm feeling anxious or stressed. They could help me become more aware about my environment or myself if only I became more aware of them. This awareness is a gift that they give. I learned to feel into the birds and plants and streams around me so that they were extensions of me. Their awareness became an extension of my awareness, and the only limit was how carefully I could pay attention, and how well I could interpret the behaviors I observed.

This is training in deep empathy, and I noticed it also helped me with people. For example, growing up, I learned that women can get extra sensitive during their period. For years I found this annoying and learned to leave women alone during this time. But as with my nature connection practices, I started asking, "how is this a gift?" or "what does this have to teach me?" And I noticed that some women friends would reject food during their period that they normally ate, and when I asked, they said the food was rancid. I would try it and I couldn't taste any rancidity at first. Over time, I learned to taste my food more and more, and I began to notice the occasional rancidity, especially in store-bought food. I realized that the sensitive women had noticed something I couldn't notice. Like the birds, women could show me something about my environment that I couldn't notice directly. When a woman said some food was rancid, even if I couldn't detect it, I began to trust her, and I rejected the food too. Over time this helped me notice rancidity I couldn't notice before.

The more I practiced, the more this deep empathy helped me see. For example, when black people complain about police brutality, it shows me where my society isn't as healthy or fair as it seems in my experience. When children complain about being forced to sit through boring classes at school, they show me where adults can behave hurtfully without knowing it. I started treating everyone around me like an extension of me, whether men or women or children or nonhumans. I paid attention to what other people observed or how they behaved and let it show me things I couldn't see by myself. I don't blindly trust everyone, but I take care to notice what lessons I can learn from others.

Noticing all the different ways a person makes the world a better place is one way to receive their gifts. After everyone else went home, which coworker stayed late to get the project done on time? Which activists show up to meetings early so we can start on time? Who maintains a sense of humor in stressful moments, or gives solid constructive feedback instead of lashing out angrily when someone makes a mistake? I just practice noticing and either giving thanks or offering constructive feedback when that seems appropriate.

Receiving nonhumans' gifts is similar. I notice all the ways each tree, stream or deer makes the world a better place. I also notice when they're annoying, like the deer who recently ate my garden, but even that deer had a lesson for me. They taught me where my security was lacking.

I've had women tell me "you're not a woman, so you can't know what it's like." In a sense, that's true. I'm a man, so I can't know what a woman's experience is like. But by the same logic, I cannot know other men's experiences either. I'm not a black man, so I can't know what a black man's experience is like. I'm neither rich nor impoverished, so I can't know what the rich or poor men's experiences are like. I wasn't born into a healthy nation, so I can't know what that experience is like. And I can't know the experiences of birds or trees.

Ultimately, I can only know my own experience, but this doesn't have to limit me when I practice deep empathy. With enough practice asking questions and paying attention, I can see others' perspectives even if their experiences are really different than mine. I might not always agree with someone else's perspectives, but I can at least understand them and understand their behavior. And when I get it wrong, that just becomes another chance to grow my observation skills and learn.

I believe these nature connection practices are a key part of generating unity in a nation. Once I started really noticing the perspectives of insects and bears and plants, I found it easier to understand people's perspectives. I believe when everybody is raised with these nature connection practices, empathy can be common, and this helps healthy nations find and maintain a deep unity. They also help me make fewer foolish assumptions. Assumptions are simply unexamined beliefs. When I continuously pay attention to what I observe, I notice what I know and what I don't know. There's little room for unexamined beliefs.

The Haudenosaunee showed me the kind of unity that comes from these nature connection practices. They have a very special Thanksgiving Address where they methodically go through different forms of life and give thanks to each. They thank the medicine herbs for removing sickness and the fish for purifying water. They give thanks to the trees for providing shelter and food. They give thanks to all the divine beings who give so much to create the web of life that we're all part of.[19]

The Haudenosaunee open every gathering with the Thanksgiving Address, calling it the Words Before All Else. While each rendition is unique, the version I learned ends in this way:[20]

> Now we have arrived in a very special place where dwells the Great Spirit that moves through all things. As one mind we turn our thoughts to the Creator with Thanksgiving and Greetings.
>
> We have now become like one being, with one body, one heart, one mind. We send our Prayers and special Thanksgiving Greetings to all the unborn Children of all the Future Generations. We send our thoughts to the many different Beings we may have missed during our Thanksgiving. With one mind we send our Thanksgiving and Greetings to all of the Nations of the World.
>
> Now our minds are one.

Healthy nations generate unity in many ways. In this example, I believe the Haudenosaunee become a people of one heart by collectively recognizing divinity in all things, recognizing their sacred place in divinity, and giving thanks together. This is the opposite of divisive racism! This Thanksgiving Address helps me remember to feel gratitude and feel connected with life. It softens my heart, and it does much more too. It shows me how a nation's leaders can encourage unity and awareness rather than division and ignorance.

Even the little nuances of the Address taught me a great deal. Robin Kimmerer learned from the elders of the Onandaga, a member nation of the Haudenosaunee Confederacy, that it would be a mistake to see this Thanksgiving Address as a prayer.[21] When I prayed growing up, I closed my eyes, bowed my head in a submissive posture, and drew my attention inward to pray to my idea of God. As I practiced this Thanksgiving Address, I learned to give thanks with all my senses awake and open to the living world around me. I held my head high. This showed me that spirituality and submission don't have to go together. I believe that a submissive posture during prayer or thanksgiving is an artifact of authoritarian religious teachings that encourage people to be submissive.

This Thanksgiving Address showed me something else. The Haudenosaunee people collectively give thanks for the divine gifts of the nonhumans. This showed me that God is not off in the sky; Creator is alive in Creation. I believe that's what it means to recognize the Great Spirit That Moves Through All Beings, a perspective I've found in many healthy nations. In Christianity, this is called the Holy Spirit. And since Creator is alive in Creation, when people stand in solidarity with the Earth, they're standing in solidarity with Creator.

Being in solidarity with life means being in solidarity with God. Being One with the Earth and being One with God are the same thing. The same three core spiritual practices that generate solidarity among people in healthy nations also generate solidarity between people and all life, and with divinity itself.

Racism and other kinds of discrimination do not have to exist. Humans are capable of incredible unity when they base their way of life on the three core spiritual practices.

If healthy nations reflect who we are as humans, how come so many people adopt racist, sexist, or other discriminatory attitudes, not just once but again and again over thousands of years? The next chapter, *Chapter 21: Training People To Adopt Authoritarian Ideologies*, looks at some extreme examples to shed light on this vexing question.

Chapter 21: Training People to Adopt Authoritarian Ideologies

At some point in the distant past, every human alive lived in a healthy nation with strong leaders and no rulers, respectful treatment of children, roles of dignity and influence for both women and men, and a mutually enriching relationship with the Earth. Nobody tolerated disrespect towards anybody else in the group.

If that's true, what was the psychological process by which people of once-healthy nations transformed into participants in unhealthy nations? Why do so many people not only tolerate their unhealthy nation, but actively support their authorities and imposed laws rather than continually seeking to escape, build a revolution, or somehow transform their nation? How come so many people adopt racist, sexist, or other hurtful attitudes?

As David Mantell noted: "It is difficult to live in a permanent state of rebellion, and rebellions rarely occur when people do not have standards of comparison or do not see the chance of changing their circumstances."[1]

In other words, when a person suffers endless abuse, where they either humiliatingly serve their captors or face torture or death, many will ultimately submit internally, closing their hearts, "shutting down" or "holding back" parts of themselves, and accepting the legitimacy of their abusers. This is especially a risk when victims see no alternative and no hope of change. Ultimately, people may learn to not even notice the abuse.

Examples of these psychological transformations have occurred in extremely abusive situations like the Nazi concentration camps or Catholic boarding schools. Stories from these places show how similar psychological transformations – where people learn to adopt the ideologies of their abusers and to normalize abuse – happen in unhealthy nations continually, even in less dramatic settings, causing people to maintain the authoritarian nation through time.

Watching People Accept the Authorities' Legitimacy in a Concentration Camp

Stories from the Holocaust shed light on how people can respond to endlessly abusive situations, both in prisons and in an abusive nation in general.

Bruce Bettelheim was sent to a Nazi German concentration camp in the 1930s, and over time he witnessed prisoners' responses to abusive treatment first hand. Not every prisoner adopted the authorities' ideologies, but the ones who did showed many of the same behaviors as most citizens who live in the supposedly "free" world outside of prisons. These prisoners' responses to their abusive prison shed light on how many people respond to the abuses in their unhealthy nation.

Bettelheim described how abusively the Nazi guards treated the prisoners. Prisoners were arbitrarily beaten, shot, or stabbed. They were made to stand or kneel for hours to exhaust them. They were made to soil themselves, and their latrine use was severely regulated.

Even more degrading, they were made to abuse each other. Bettelheim described how they were forbidden from treating each others' wounds. Bettelheim wrote, "They were forced to curse their God, to accuse themselves of vile actions and their wives of prostitution. This continued for many hours. The purpose of the tortures was to break the resistance of the prisoners, and to assure the guards that they were superior."[2]

This illustrates how abusers train triple inhibition. Abusers forbid victims from taking any external action in response to their abuse, so victims learn to hold back their spontaneous responses. Victims can then block their own awareness of their urge to resist, and then learn to ignore the fact that they are blocking their awareness.

In this case, people were trained to ignore their own sacred urges for integrity, authenticity, solidarity, and so on. They could honor these urges and be tortured or killed, or they could block their own urges. This is what it meant to "break the resistance of the prisoners." Bettelheim interviewed people about their experience and heard "vague statements which sounded like devious rationalizations, invented for justifying that they had endured treatment injurious to their self-respect without trying to fight back." He could not interview anyone who had taken a dignified stand for themselves and their people. They were dead.

These and similar abuses went on for years. Prisoners were trained to tolerate their own abuse and the abuse of others. Some were forced to abuse their neighbors or else suffer severe tortures. Many described how hard it was to continue to hold onto their values and sense of self throughout this ordeal. Bettelheim described his major goal as "to safeguard his ego [so] that, if he should regain liberty he would be approximately the same person as he was when deprived of liberty." When he interviewed other prisoners, they commonly acknowledged, "The main problem is to remain alive and unchanged." They had to behave inappropriately to stay alive, but this was hard to reconcile with their dignity and sense of right and wrong.

In other words, their challenge was to maintain single inhibition. Their challenge was to remember that their own sense of right was correct, and their abusers' ideology was wrong, even if they had to continuously act contrary to their values or face death.

What behaviors did Bettelheim see among those who, through triple inhibition, embraced the authorities' legitimacy and blocked their own sacred urges and self-awareness? He described behaviors which are also common in many people who live outside of prisons in unhealthy nations.

Consider these observations of Bettelheim's, and how they also apply widely to people born into unhealthy nations:

Directing one's efforts to living well in an abusive nation:

- *Bettelheim observed in prison camps:* "All the emotional efforts of the new prisoners seemed to be directed toward returning to the outer world as the same persons who had left it. Old prisoners seemed mainly concerned with the problem of how to live well within the camp."

- *In unhealthy nations:* How many Americans, Russians, Germans, or others seek to live in a nation with a baseline of mutual respect, and how many seem "mainly concerned with the problem of how to live well within" their authoritarian nation, focusing instead on their career, travels, superficial politics, televised sports, and other distractions as opposed to seeking transformative change?

Fear of freedom or doubting it exists:

- *Bettelheim observed in prison camps:* "When they reached this stage [of giving up on leaving prison] the prisoners were afraid of returning to the outer world. Moreover, they then hardly believed they would ever return to it…"

- *In unhealthy nations:* How many people believe that it is impossible to live in a nation without a few ruling over many, without racism, without sexism, with leaders of integrity? And how many call this a childish or utopian fantasy, or try to avoid thinking about it? How many even fear living in a nation where they have deep responsibility for themselves and their neighbors, and how many actively prefer for authorities to have this responsibility?

- *Bettelheim observed in prison camps:* "How long it took a prisoner to cease to consider life outside the camp as real depended to a great extent on the strength of his emotional ties to his family and friends."

- *In unhealthy nations:* How many people believe that "life outside the [unhealthy nation] is real?" In other words, how many people believe that there are humans alive right now living in nations of mutual respect? In general, the people most likely to believe that healthy nations exist are the ones who are only a few generations removed from living in their traditional way, without rulers.

Cannot imagine true freedom:

- *Bettelheim observed in prison camps:* "Some of the old prisoners admitted that they no longer could visualize themselves living outside the camp, making free decisions, taking care of themselves and their families."

- *In unhealthy nations:* How many people can visualize what it's like to live in a nation without authorities imposing law, or living in a nation without money and bosses, and real solidarity?

Aspiring to be like the abusive authorities:

- *Bettelheim observed in prison camps:* "A prisoner had reached the final stage of adjustment to the camp situation when he changed his personality so as to accept as his own the values of the Gestapo [the German police]." Bettelheim described how some older prisoners began speaking like the Gestapo, sewed items on their clothes in mimicry of Gestapo uniforms, and became even more cruel towards newer prisoners than the guards. People bragged about how well they stood at attention during the twice-daily prisoner counts.

- *In unhealthy nations:* How many people are proud of their obedience to abusive authorities? How many people learn to act, dress, and speak like the rich?

Escapism and despondency:

- *Bettelheim observed in prison camps:* "The prisoners developed types of behavior characteristic of infancy or early youth... such as ambivalence to one's family, despondency, finding satisfaction in daydreaming rather than in action."

- *In unhealthy nations:* These are some of the coping behaviors many children learn when trapped in school. How many people spend much of their time daydreaming or with a voice in their head that seems to run continuously?

- *Bettelheim observed in prison camps:* "His fellow prisoners, who had been normal persons, now behaved like pathological liars, were unable to restrain themselves and to make objective evaluations."

- *In unhealthy nations:* How many people commonly lie or make excuses for lying rather than act with deep integrity? How many people seem unable to make objective evaluations in politics and instead seem divorced from reality?

Even if most people in an unhealthy nation are "free" and not suffering in harsh prison camps, they still show many of the same behaviors as people trapped in oppressive prisons. These are simply common patterns in nations where some people rule over everyone else.

Before being imprisoned in Nazi German concentration camps, these people had already been living in an unhealthy nation. The extreme additional abuse they received in prison led many of them to further give up responsibility and withhold love when they were threatened with torture or death. This illustrates what many people in unhealthy nations experience: when many of us grow up learning to withhold our love and pretending things are ok when they're not, and see no alternative in adulthood, many fully accept authorities' legitimacy. Certainly not everyone falls prey to this, but most do accept that it is legitimate for some people to impose law on others, and they learn to somehow hold back their love. People may not like this or that ruler, but most people accept life under rulers as legitimate and normal.

When I was a child, I only considered people enslaved if they were legally owned by another person. But Sioux man Sitting Bull saw all the authoritarian patterns in the American unhealthy nation and noted: "The life of white men is slavery. They are prisoners in their towns or farms. The life my people want is freedom."[3]

Sitting Bull described white men, but his observation applies to any unhealthy, authoritarian nation. Unhealthy nations are massive, multi-generational, abusive relationships, and while some people are more comfortable than others, no one is free. This explains why the emotional patterns that Bettelheim observed in prisons are so common throughout unhealthy nations.

Abusing Children so They Will Accept Authorities' Legitimacy

When authorities want to integrate people of healthy nations into an unhealthy nation, one technique is to kidnap their children and abuse them with a simple goal: to get the children to adopt the ideologies of the abusers, and reject their own traditional practices and wisdom.

Some people speculate that humans somehow biologically evolved to live in authoritarian nations, as if this were a natural way of living as a human. However, people only consider their unhealthy nation normal if they've been raised in disrespectful ways so that *disrespect itself seems normal*. I believe anyone raised in a fully respectful way would never accept their authoritarian nation and its exploitation as normal.

The truth is that when people of healthy nations have their children kidnapped and trained in authoritarian boarding schools, those children commonly develop the same kinds of deep emotional and spiritual wounds that are so common among people whose ancestors have lived in unhealthy nations for generations.

The Lakota's experience in Christian boarding schools such as Holy Rosary illustrate this. Priests and nuns would "beat the Indian out of you" or hit the children's hands with a ruler 10 times "to remind you of the Ten Commandments." Wallace Black Elk noted, "Sometimes they would break that ruler."[4]

Initially the boarding schools allowed some home visits but they soon put an end to that when the children refused to return to school. School authorities blamed the "savage potency" of traditional ways, but I think kids don't like abusive or meaningless learning environments.

Beatings and whippings were common, although humiliation was more often used for girls. A girl's first lesson upon entering school was that she was dirty. Lillian Giago once spilled a bowl of sugar on the floor and the nun forced her onto her hands and knees to lick it up. They were taught to be perfect, which meant white, Christian, and not Lakota.

These children were shamed and heavily punished for speaking their language or embracing any other aspect of their healthy nation, and this often had the desired effect. Many children showed clear signs of adopting the ideology of their abusers. The priests and nuns were cruel, but Albert White Hat, who attended the Holy Rosary Mission, said that other "indians" were the strictest disciplinarians. He said, "Indian kids at school were ridiculing me for being an Indian… Every time I spoke Lakota, I was a 'buck Indian' and they were making fun of me… we were trained to be ashamed of who we were." White Hat noted, "I was so angry that I was born an Indian that I didn't want to live." He concluded that this widespread shame was a major cause of alcoholism on his people's land reservation.

They had grown up with a simple diet of meat, fruit and vegetables but suddenly were made to eat white bread, coffee, sugar, and other processed foods. Luther Standing Bear called this "doubtless the most injurious." Half the children in his class died within 3 years.

One Lakota man asked why his granddaughter Mary Rough had been whipped at a government school, and the school official responded, "What the hell are you going to do about it? We've got a right to give her a whipping." In 1929, construction engineer H.J. Russell described the Indian School in Leupp, Arizona: "I have seen Indian boys chained to their beds at night for punishment. I have seen them thrown in cellars under the building, which the superintendent called a jail. I have seen their shoes taken away from them and they then forced to walk through the snow to the barn to help milk. I have seen them whipped with a hemp rope, also a water hose."

Comparing the United States with the Soviet Union, one Senate investigator who found a student jail in Wahpeton, North Dakota, wondered "if Dakota is not the Siberia of the Indian Service." Boys were humiliated in other ways. Traditionally, when a man's head was shaved, it meant either he'd been exposed as a coward, or he was grieving after losing a loved one. Yet at Carlisle Indian Industrial School, all the boys' heads were shaven, similar to the military's policy for soldiers. And both boys and girls faced years of sexual assault by Catholic Christian staff.[5,6]

This illustrates how children of healthy nations can be repeatedly abused for years, training them to adopt the authoritarian ideologies of an unhealthy nation. They were trained to associate shame and anger with the Lakota nation and trained to forget their traditionally respectful way of life. Many even learned to police each other. Sadly, the Lakota children's stories were far from unique.

When the Nootka's children were kidnapped by Christian conquerors and sent to boarding schools, their mothers noticed terrible things when they returned. The girls had learned to feel intense shame and believed that once a month they became filthy. The Nootka storyteller said, "instead of going to the waiting house to meditate, pray, and celebrate the fullness of the moon and their own bodies, they were taught they were sick, and must bandage themselves and act as if they were sick."[7]

Likewise boys were taught that women were filthy and sinful and had no valuable opinions and only existed to serve men. Within a generation, the priests assumed they had defeated the matriarchy. When the Christian conquerors finally let the children return home, the Nootka mothers "saw the fighting and the drunkenness where once there was love and respect. They saw men beating their wives and children. They saw mothers beating their children and even abandoning them. They saw girls who should have been clan mothers become prostitutes in the cities the invaders built."

I believe these consequences were not accidental, but the rulers' actual goals. Authoritarian nations are inherently exploitative, where a few rule over the many, and so they set up schools where teachers and religious leaders actively trained these children to tolerate and even perpetuate abuse. Drunkenness, domestic abuse, shame, isolation, and other consequences of these boarding schools mirror common patterns throughout unhealthy nations generally. Solidarity requires solid relationships between solid people. What better way for authorities to preempt solidarity than to encourage infighting, domestic abuse, alcoholism, and self-loathing instead?

These stories show how entire generations of children were trained to close their hearts and exhibit triple inhibition. They were trained to recognize authorities and their hurtful narratives as legitimate and their own sacred urges, perceptions, and feelings as illegitimate and hold back their love as they were taught to reject their healthy nation.

That these massive, tragic changes could happen within a single generation shows that humans did not biologically evolve to live with exploitative rulers. Having authorities impose laws on us runs counter to all of our instincts, and only spiritual and intellectual confusion leads many of us as adults to accept our unhealthy nation as normal and ok.

Fortunately, the Lakota were able to maintain much of their healthy nation through this terrible boarding school period, and as I write in 2024, they remain a source of wisdom and environmental activism. The Nootka also preserved aspects of their nation despite the onslaught. I believe this has been difficult for people of all healthy nations who tried to maintain what they could of their old ways. One Nootka storyteller hints at the difficulty. The invaders did not notice that some women kept and protected the wisdom of the matriarchy at great personal risk, "meeting in secret, often in the churches of the invader. Pretending to believe what the priests taught. Being very careful of what they said, guarding jealously that which they knew."

For a while, I wondered why these schools were consistently so physically violent and shaming while mine was not. Was it a matter of racist discrimination, similar to how schools of higher-privilege people are better funded than schools of lower-privilege people?

I believe the truth is more devious. The Nootka, Lakota, and other healthy-nation children had basically respectful upbringings from birth, and thus were not predisposed to authoritarian ideologies. It took a massive amount of violence and shaming over years to instill deep spiritual and emotional wounds in children that didn't already have such wounds. This wounding is essential to making people think of their unhealthy nation as "normal." I believe anyone raised in a fully respectful way would never accept their authoritarian nation and its exploitation as normal.

My own early school experiences did not require so much violence and shaming because I was already born in an unhealthy nation and well on my way to thinking of it as normal and "just the way life is." I had already begun to "hold back" or "shut down" parts of myself and not notice it, the process of triple inhibition and heart closure. I never learned about my healthy-nation ancestors, because their memory had likely already been forgotten for many generations within my family.

Once people have these deep spiritual and emotional wounds, they're quite likely to pass them on to their children starting from birth. It takes a great deal of personal growth to avoid this.

When children develop deep spiritual or emotional wounds beginning in early childhood, authoritarian schools don't need to be nearly so violent to train children to accept the legitimacy of their authoritarian nation.

The Spiritual Transformation Required to Adopt Authoritarian Ideologies

What started out as a psychological defense became a deep spiritual wound as the abuse continued. These stories illustrate what it's like for people to close their hearts. These abusive institutions trained people to withhold their love.

They illustrate the transformation from *single inhibition* at the start which eventually became *triple inhibition* over time.

With single inhibition, a person recognizes that their circumstances are unsatisfying, and they still recognize their own feelings and urges as legitimate. For example, in the concentration camps, all the prisoners at the start recognized the prison was illegitimate and their own sense of right and wrong was legitimate.

Bettelheim observed many prisoners ultimately internally submit, accepting the authoritarian camp as legitimate and their own sense of right and wrong as illegitimate. People in these circumstances can learn to block their own feelings and urges, block awareness of the feelings and urges, and block awareness of the block so that any feeling or urge contrary to authority gets fully suppressed from consciousness (triple inhibition). The more urges, perceptions, and feelings a person learns to suppress in this way, the more fully they internally submit.

The basic reason this happens is simple: it hurts to have an open heart and want to give one's love while being punished repeatedly for giving that love. It hurts to be proud of one's people and be repeatedly punished for this, as the children at the disastrous Indian boarding schools experienced.

It also hurts tremendously to close one's heart. After all, who would not want to give their deepest love fully in every moment? But the tragic truth is that authorities can make it hurt even more to keep one's heart open, and when people see no hope of change, many can ultimately close their hearts in various ways to reduce the pain so they can tolerate the unending disaster they're experiencing.

While these gruesome stories from prisons and Indian boarding schools vividly illustrate these patterns, all people in authoritarian societies are subject to similar pressures in various ways.

This is clearly intentional, as authorities have used abuse throughout history to train people for obedience. Although any particular priest or teacher might not fully understand the implications of their behavior, rulers and other authorities know they need to abuse people to train them to obey their masters, which effectively trains people to close their hearts. One captain who transported slaves from Africa to the Americas was asked, "Are you very severe with [the slaves]?" He said, "We have to be pretty strict at first – for a week or so – to make them feel that we are masters. Then we lighten up for the rest of the voyage."[8]

This same process plays out all throughout unhealthy nations. Whenever people start to question authorities' legitimacy, authorities can become very strict indeed. Once people give up resistance and accept authorities' legitimacy, the authorities can lighten up, and everything can seem "normal." This explains the common pattern in unhealthy nations where authorities exploit people for years, leading to waves of popular protests, followed by intense police crackdown, and then years of further exploitation to be followed eventually by more protests, more crackdown, and then more years of exploitation.

This is simply an unending cycle in unhealthy nations, and it will continue until we can generate a nation where nobody rules over anybody else.

When People Legitimize Abuse

I honor the Nootka's, Lakota's, and other people's terrible experiences by asking, "what are the deepest lessons I can learn?" And so I ask, "Where do I or many other people learn not to notice abuse or subconsciously accept abuse as legitimate?" Countless examples illustrate this deep pattern.

One obvious example of legitimizing abuse involves electoral politics: people argue over which parties or leaders should rule them and impose law instead of seeking a nation with rules that work for everyone. The people who vote for the losing political candidates are supposed to just accept having laws imposed on them that they don't like.

When the Soviet Union drafted a new Constitution in 1936 and released it for public comment, many citizens clearly supported their abusive authorities, with one writing that "using free speech, meetings, and so forth to oppose the Soviet state constitutes a betrayal of the country and should carry heavy punishment." In some regions, large percentages of people commented that priests and members of certain "alien classes" should not be allowed to vote at all.[9]

This blindness to abuse shows clearly in the attitude of many men towards female prostitutes. Many people accuse such women of "selling their bodies," which is incorrect. They are actually renting their bodies in exchange for money, the same as anybody who serves a boss or customer in exchange for money. The men (and any women who have this perspective) only fail to notice that they and the women prostitutes are in similarly abusive situations where they must do unsatisfying work to live.

One example shows this vividly. In Great Britain in 1914, women faced massively increasing unemployment, with textile employment falling over 40%, clothing manufacturing by over 20%, and layoffs of women in many other industries.[10] When trains full of soldiers arrived in London, they were quickly surrounded by large crowds of both professional and amateur prostitutes. One medical officer described how "…the scenes were disgraceful. One saw 100s of men… they could hardly get through the streets… on account of the women crowding about them."[11]

This officer described the scenes with these women's behavior as disgraceful. Other officials referred to the women as "evil" people living "an immoral life."[12]

And yet I believe the women were simply responding to life in an authoritarian nation where they depended on money to live, depended on a job to make money, and suddenly had no job prospects. The male soldiers were in no better position, having been forcibly drafted into a military where many would soon die gruesome deaths in service of their political and corporate masters' imperial ambitions. These male soldiers could have recognized that both they and the women were living in a very abusive nation and sought meaningful change together. If change seemed impossible, they could have at least treated each other with dignity. Instead these men ignored the women's desperation and pretended that the prostitutes were acting solely on supposedly-immoral sexual urges. They had adopted the ideology of their abusers.

People can learn not to see abuse and desperation even when it happens right in front of them. These soldiers' hearts were closed to the women's divinity and their own. They embraced the hurtful attitude that these women were disgraceful or evil, rather than good people making desperate choices.

Professionals and academics can likewise adopt abusers' ideologies. Anthropologists may believe that emperors benefit people they conquer by imposing law enforcement, as if the previously-free people hadn't been able to resolve conflicts on their own and needed an abusive emperor to save them.[13]

Even government surveillance agencies can pretend not to be abusive. In 2023, the US National Security Agency released a directive noting that its surveillance targets "should be treated with dignity and respect."[14]

American general George Patton showed a remarkable ability to maintain his anti-Jewish beliefs in the face of Jews' obvious abuse during World War II. In 1945, Patton was put in charge of US Displaced Persons operations in Europe, meaning he dealt with many victims trapped in Nazi concentration camps. Despite clear evidence of the Nazis' abuse, he wrote in his journal, "[Some people] believe that the Displaced Person is a human being, which he is not, and this applies particularly to the Jews who are lower than animals…[with] no sense of human relationships."[15]

Patton noted how the trapped Jews would defecate on floors and live in filth, but apparently ignored how they were forced into this position by Nazi prison guards when he wrote in his journal, "We entered [a makeshift prison] synagogue, which was packed with the greatest stinking mass of humanity I have ever seen. Of course, I have seen them since the beginning and marveled that beings alleged to be made in the form of God can look the way they do or act the way they act." Because Patton ignored the Jews' abuse, their filth and squalor seemed despicable. Patton's attitude only makes sense if the Jews had chosen their squalor rather than having it forced upon them. This shows his deep blindness to the abuse.

Many people have debated what it means to be a good man. Do bravery and integrity make a man, or is it his ability to boss people around? Father Membre, a French Christian missionary, was traveling through North America in the 1700s. After visiting healthy nations where nobody ruled over anybody else, he visited the Natchez which did have rulers. He illustrated this authoritarian understanding of manhood when he wrote, "[they were] all different from our Canada Indians in their houses, dress, manners, inclinations and customs… Their chiefs possess all the authority… They have their valets and officers who follow them and serve them everywhere. They distribute their favors and presents at will. In a word we generally found men there."[16] Clearly this French Christian missionary believed "real men" boss other people around.

Starting in the 1980s, many US police officers adopted "broken windows policing," where they aggressively prosecuted minor crimes in the hopes that overall crime rates would drop. In practice, they focused on crimes of poor people that affected nobody or a few others rather than the crimes of the rich that affected millions.[17]

Anybody who believes one sex or race is worse or specially deserving of punishment likewise has adopted authoritarian ideologies.

Anyone who believes "humans are basically bad" or "humans are basically corrupt or selfish" or "all human societies are oppressive" has adopted an authoritarian ideology.

In an Organization of American States report on violence against women, researchers noted that officials at all levels of judicial systems throughout North and South America discriminated against women, and yet they insisted that effective judicial systems are the key to reducing violence towards women. If all authoritarian nations have discriminatory judicial systems that commonly allow male violence towards women, why would academics think judicial systems can make things better?[18]

In healthy nations where everybody accepts responsibility for the wellbeing of their nation, and the entire group agrees on norms of appropriate behavior, I don't observe this discrimination. When academics adopt authoritarian ideologies that only authorities can keep people safe, their solutions boil down to asking the authorities to please follow and enforce their own laws. This leads to predictable results.

If trusting in judicial authorities leads to predictably poor results, why would academics consistently advocate for trusting judicial authorities? The answer is clear: the alternative is for people to protect each other outside the law. This is illegal, and so is advocating for it.

When the only viable solution to a problem is illegal, is it any wonder that many people in positions of privilege and comfort focus only on solutions which are guaranteed to fail?

Authoritarian Views of Freedom

Authoritarian nations encourage a few misconceptions of freedom.

Authoritarian nations train people to feel deep shame or guilt for not behaving as expected, and so people can find a sense of freedom by believing that nothing matters. The attitude is "I can do whatever I feel like because nothing matters." This helps release any sense of guilt or shame, but such a person also denies their own divine nature and sacred gifts.

A deeper freedom comes from realizing that each of us is a divine being. A person is internally free if they recognize what they care about and then act in service whenever they can. A person is externally free if they can routinely give their deepest love to their people without risk of punishment.

Another authoritarian view of freedom is that the path towards freedom involves making more money or gaining a higher level of privilege. This is true in a sense: obviously a person trapped in a prison is less free than someone on the outside. Someone with little money has fewer options than someone with great wealth. But none of these people, at any level of privilege, are free. They are all trapped in authoritarian nations where rulers retain the option of acting abusively.

For example, black people in the United States were certainly better off after chattel slavery ended and they could no longer be legally owned by private individuals. Their privilege level was certainly higher. However, they were still far from free.

One limited definition of "slavery" is any situation where one person legally owns another as property. I find another definition more illuminating. I recognize "slavery" as any form of coerced labor. In chattel slavery, the slaveowner could legally order slaves to do as they wished and punish them for disobedience. This was very similar to another abusive institution: the military draft.

In 1917, the US government instituted a draft, leading to military slavery. Drafted men were legally required to join the military and were heavily punished if they did not. Soldiers were then legally required to do as they were told, and were severely punished if they did not.

At that time, black men could be drafted into the military just like white men and legally forced to risk their lives in service of American imperialist ambitions. Many black men resented this deeply. In one of the earliest written uses of the term "mother fucker," black American Sydney Wilson wrote to his draft board stating, "You low-down Mother Fuckers can put a gun in our hands, but who is able to take it out?" In another letter he wrote that black people would do "what little fighting we is going to do in this country and not France… once we gets through with you all, you wont be quite so anshous to draft the nigroes in any more."

Unsurprisingly, Wilson was arrested and sentenced to 10 years of hard labor for not behaving submissively to military authorities.[19,20] This black man was thus about as free as the poor white soldiers who were also forced to risk death in service of their rich masters. This shows how people may be able to increase their privilege level, but no one is free so long as they live under rulers who retain the option of behaving abusively.

Parents, teachers, and financial planners commonly teach that having more money gives one more freedom, another authoritarian perspective. One financial planner described the goal of financial independence: "You gain choices and flexibility, which is really the point of being rich… you have enough money that if you hate your job, you can leave it."[21] Indeed, having a higher-paying job or more reliable income does offer a person more choices, or the ability to leave abusive bosses or unsafe neighborhoods. But having flexibility and being free are different!

These perspectives show the authoritarian views of freedom: that freedom is the ability to avoid abusive bosses, or behave however one feels like. By this view, freedom means having no responsibilities or obligations to anybody. This is the freedom of kings who can do absolutely whatever they want without caring how anybody else feels about it. But what about the freedom to stand together and take care of each other in a deep way? No one in unhealthy nations is allowed this freedom.

I always support people in gaining choices and flexibility in their life, and I'm glad when low-privilege people can raise their privilege level and avoid abuse. However, I imagine unhealthy nations like a big bus. Some seats are luxurious, others are comfortable, and a lot of seats are really uncomfortable. Different people may have different seats, but they're all stuck in the same abusive-nation bus. Authoritarian views of freedom train people to focus on getting a more comfortable seat rather than exit or transform the bus.

This authoritarian view of freedom only exists in unhealthy nations. Healthy nations all recognize a deep responsibility for reciprocity as one of the core spiritual practices. Indeed, the three core spiritual practices are a recipe for freedom: 1) recognize what gifts I feel profoundly grateful for, 2) consider what sacred gifts I have to give and give them, 3) give in service of the people and nonhumans who give so much to me. This freedom stems from a person seeking the most meaningful life imaginable and acting in service of what they love. It's the freedom to be oneself and give one's deepest love. In nations that welcome people to live this way, I believe they find a deeply satisfying freedom.

Where Do Hurtful Ideologies Come From?

The core cultural disease in unhealthy nations is that a few people rule over and exploit a much larger number. Examples in this chapter all illustrate the corresponding personal disease, where individuals accept abuse and abusive authorities as legitimate and adopt some sort of abuse-tolerating ideology.

For a long time, I wondered where things like racism or sexism come from. I believe that these divisive cultural patterns have three major drivers:

1. *Systemic discrimination*: Rulers impose systemic discrimination. Then they encourage people to adopt hurtful attitudes, rewarding those who do and punishing those who don't.

2. *Adopting an authoritarian attitude*: This chapter has explored how many people trapped in abusive nations learn to adopt authoritarian attitudes in order to excuse and justify the role they have in the nation they were born into.

3. *Child abuse*: Some kinds of child abuse predispose people to more readily adopt very hurtful attitudes.

This same three-part pattern also helps explain where things like selfishness, sexism and hatred come from. This perspective does not excuse anybody's hurtful attitudes. But it clarifies that systemic racism, selfishness, sexism, and hatred do not spontaneously arise because a lot of people have these hurtful attitudes. In other words, a racist citizenry isn't the source or cause of systemic racism. Divisive rulers, acting through the government and major corporations or aristocrats, are the driver or ultimate cause of systemic racism.

When enough people adopt these hurtful attitudes, it makes social change very difficult. If a particular dynasty or ruling class loses power, and people are used to profit-focused economies and used to giving up responsibility for the health of their nation, they may just look for a new person to rule them instead of forming a society without rulers. People who don't know what freedom is like might not even seize it when the opportunity presents itself.

I believe the deepest transformation will come when enough people recognize that no authorities' rule is ever legitimate. It is not legitimate for a few to impose law on the many. Each of us has a responsibility to take care of each other and the Earth. Each of us is a divine being with sacred gifts – a life purpose – to give. When enough people hold back their sacred gifts or diminish their awareness in order to avoid poverty or abuse, the world becomes a darker place. As more people give their deepest love in spite of the rulers' efforts, the world brightens more and more.

The next chapter, *Chapter 22: Imposing And Maintaining Hatred*, digs even deeper into why and how people in unhealthy nations can learn to stray so far from being their true selves.

Chapter 22: Imposing and Maintaining Hatred

I didn't understand anger and hatred until I studied abuse. It turns out they're pretty simple.

Anger arises when someone behaves disrespectfully or inappropriately towards me or someone I care about. The anger-energy is the motivating force that drives me to address the disrespect so it doesn't happen anymore.

For example, when I was about 10, my younger sister was playing in the snow with her female friends. Some older boys came and messed up their snowmen and teased them, and my sister came home crying. I felt angry. I silently put on my heavy coat while my mother consoled my sister, and I found the four boys hanging out where my sister had been.

I told them very clearly that what they'd done wasn't ok. I didn't want them bothering my sister or her friends any more. We didn't fight, but they could tell I was serious. They never harassed my sister or her friends again.

This is a good example of channeling anger in an appropriate way. It could have been violent, but it didn't have to be. I used my anger-energy to address the disrespect so it stopped happening.

My anger was appropriate for two reasons. First, it resulted from disrespectful behavior towards me or someone I cared about, in this case my sister. I verified this by hearing my sister tell her story. Secondly, my anger was directed towards the people who behaved disrespectfully, the group of boys.

Both the cause of the anger and the anger's target were appropriate – I was angry because of a real problem, the boys' hurtful behavior, and the target of my anger was the group of boys who had caused trouble.

Hatred arises when disrespect is repeated again and again and there isn't any prospect of stopping it peacefully. The disrespectful person becomes a major threat. No discussions work and no truce is possible. A person who feels hatred has some recognition that the only way to successfully deal with the abuse is to either escape or fight the abusive person or group.

What Might Cause Appropriate Hatred?

In his book *The Hate Factory*, WG Stone described the United States' most violent prison riot at the New Mexico State Penitentiary in 1980. He summarized it as an "overdue response to years of abuse, mental and physical. All that overdue rage, though, made people go crazier than anyone expected."[1] After years where prisoners were arbitrarily beaten at the whims of the guards, placed in solitary confinement, publicly shamed and ridiculed, forced to live in filthy conditions, given terrible food, forced to work for wealthy corporations for pennies per hour, charged extremely high prices for less terrible food and basic hygiene products, encouraged to snitch on their friends, humiliated in countless ways, and forced to pretend to respect the bullying guards, eventually an extremely violent riot broke out.[2,3]

I consider this an example of appropriate hatred. I'm not commenting on whether the prisoners channeled the hatred appropriately with their behavior. I do believe the hatred itself was appropriate for the same two reasons my anger was appropriate: their hatred sprang from their real, verified experience of disrespect, and the targets of their hatred were some of the people who acted disrespectfully, the prison guards.

If everyone were able to channel their anger-energy and hate-energy towards the people most responsible for it, unhealthy authoritarian nations would not last very long.

It is normal and healthy to feel and act on appropriate hatred. Unfortunately, authorities have many devious ways to block and manipulate people's appropriate anger and hatred.

Unhealthy Nations Create Synthetic, Inappropriate Hatred to Distract People from Appropriate Hatred

A common manipulative strategy in unhealthy nations is for authorities to create *synthetic hatred*. Synthetic hatred occurs when authorities of various types deliberately cause one group to hate another. For example, media corporations may print false new stories or censor truthful ones to encourage people to feel hatred. Authorities may spread false or hurtful rumors, claiming that some helpless group is behaving aggressively. People are commonly punished in confusing ways for not hating, making it difficult for thoughtful people to dispel falsehoods and stand up for the victimized group. There are many techniques, but the ultimate goal is this: to make one group of people feel hatred toward another group of people, even when no one has personally experienced behavior from the target group that justifies hatred.

Authorities may deliberately encourage synthetic hatred for many reasons, and this chapter covers three: scapegoating, making people fear and hate non-abusive nations, and motivating people to support a war they would otherwise not support. This hatred is basically inappropriate because, while the feeling of hatred is real, it does not stem from a person's own perception of disrespect. The hatred is also inappropriate because it is generally not directed towards an actual problem the person faces.

Examples of Scapegoating – Encouraging Hatred Towards Non-Threatening People to Avoid Solidarity and Accountability

Creating Synthetic Hatred to Avoid Accountability: The Stab-in-the-Back Myth in World War I Germany

Nations that hold their leaders accountable for their mistakes or selfishness are able to learn from those mistakes. Nations where rulers are able to avoid accountability often wind up blaming innocent people for the rulers' mistakes. Instead of resolving the problems of incompetent, selfish, or cowardly leadership, this blame-shifting only creates new misunderstandings and problems without addressing the old ones.

Germany in World War I provided a vivid example. By 1918, the German government faced severe trouble. World War I was so destructive that, after it ended, it was known as the Great War or the War to End All Wars. Germany lost decisively and suffered massive economic depression in the following years. Many Germans found the loss confusing because the enemy armies had never crossed German pre-war territorial boundaries, and German media kept reporting that Germany was winning almost until it lost.[4] So why did the war end in German defeat?

The German leadership certainly understood that, militarily, they had been defeated. German military leadership began urging an armistice.[5] However among the public, there was no resolution to the key questions: Why did Germany lose when, to many Germans, it seemed to be winning? Who was responsible for the defeat and economic hardship, and how could Germany hold those people accountable so the mistakes wouldn't happen again?

German leadership did not want to be held accountable for their failures, so I believe they found a way to shift blame elsewhere. The view in the military was "that the parties of the Left have to take on the odium of this peace. The storm of anger will then turn against them. There are hopes then of later vaulting back into the saddle and ruling again in the old way."[6] German Jews and socialists especially wound up taking the blame. This stab-in-the-back theory was called Dolchstoss, claiming that Jews and socialists had supposedly undermined the German war effort and caused Germany's defeat.

German political and military leadership went to great lengths to avoid accountability. General Ludendorff urged the king to give socialists many ministry positions so that they would be associated with the loss.[7] The king abdicated two days before the armistice was signed on November 11, 1918, and chancellor Graf Hertling also resigned beforehand. The new socialist Weimar government thus signed the war-ending armistice instead of the military and political leaders who had directed and lost the war. This later supported widespread rumors that the undefeated military had been betrayed by the socialists.

The Dolchstoss theory claimed that Jews had undermined the German war effort, but this was contradicted by many German Jews' active support for the war. Early in the war, German Jew Gertrud Kantorowicz wrote, "the war itself is pure greatness… my being relates to Germany as a life's breath relates to the body out of which it arises." Gertrud's cousin was Jewish-German historian Ernst Kantorowicz, who earned the Iron Cross for his fighting in the Western Front. Jewish-German philosopher Martin Buber wrote, "Never has the concept of the Volk [People] been such a reality to me than during these last weeks." When Russia entered the war against Germany, Jewish politician Ludwig Haas said it had committed "the greatest crime in world history." Many Germans saw the war as an opportunity for national renewal, and plenty of Jewish Germans were caught up in this fervor.[8]

Unfortunately, the war and authorities' management of it brought tremendous economic hardship. One narrative which took hold near war's end promoted the idea that Germany's victory was likely in proportion to how hard the population worked. If everybody worked hard, then victory would be likely and if people did not work hard, defeat was likely.[9]

Food became scarce and a black market formed. Large price increases at the start of the war had already sapped people's savings. Many family breadwinners had been drafted and killed. Employers were unwilling or unable to negotiate so workers could earn living wages.[10] Near the end of the war, 200,000 laborers stopped work in Berlin, calling for more and better food as well as peace and democratic reforms. In the following days, thousands more men and women left their factories to go on strike all across Germany's major industrial centers. Workers even called for a role in peace negotiations. Some prominent strike leaders were German Jews, including Hugo Haase who described the strike as "one of the greatest events in working-class history."[11]

These striking workers weren't anti-German; they simply wanted food, living wages, and peace. However, German authorities feared a communist upheaval as had happened in Russia. They broke the strikes, arresting large numbers of workers and sending them to fight at the front, a subtle but effective death penalty.

Plenty of prominent Jews opposed the strikes and continued to support the war efforts. Jewish owners of large factories, such as the AEG and Ludwig Loewe weapons factories in Berlin, opposed the strike movement. The Jewish newspaper Allgemeine Zeitung des Judentums described the strikes as "unfortunate disturbances" and urged "the naive masses to come to their senses," saying their behavior "only played into the hands of our enemies." Jew Georg Bernhard exclaimed that every shell that workers didn't produce "represents a weakening of the military's clout," saying the workers were "stabbing the frontline army in the back."[12,13]

Thus, the 'stab-in-the-back' narrative was already taking hold. The question was: who should be held responsible? Would Germany hold its top leaders and decision-makers responsible, such as the military generals, monarch, top government administrators, and rich business owners who had managed the war and economy?

The rulers wouldn't allow themselves to be held accountable, and instead the Jewish Germans and socialists became convenient scapegoats. Even before the war's end, socialists and Jews began to be publicly blamed for the war's loss. By the early 1920s, hatred towards Jews was strong. In 1922, Jewish German wealthy businessman and foreign minister Walther Rathenau was called a "Gottverfluchte Judensau" (translation: a Goddamned Jewish pig) and assassinated despite having fully supported the war.

Over the 1920s, a narrative spread that the German armies hadn't been defeated. Few Germans knew that their military leaders had told the king clearly that the war was lost as their allies dropped out of the war and the troops started mutinying.[14] Instead, the German army must have voluntarily quit fighting; they must have been tricked with the help of treasonous Germans. Who were these supposedly treasonous Germans that caused the loss of World War I? As the Nazis rose to power, they blamed socialists, liberals, and Jews.[15]

Thus Jews and socialists were made to seem like an existential threat to all Germany. This allowed the military and political leadership to avoid accountability for its mismanaged imperialist war, as well as foment popular opposition to socialist efforts to shift the tax burden towards the rich.[16]

When German Nazis took over the German government, they continued to play up this supposed Jewish threat, generating hatred for the Jews and punishing anyone who voiced opposition. This blaming and dehumanizing resulted ultimately in the mass-killing of millions of Jewish people in German-occupied territories in the 1930s and 1940s. Socialists also were heavily persecuted, as were many others.

The German authorities manipulated the population to create synthetic anger and hatred towards scapegoats so that the authorities could avoid accountability for their mistakes. The German people didn't know how to collectively hold its leadership accountable for their mismanaged war. The German rulers essentially tricked the population into "kicking down," directing their rage at groups that couldn't protect themselves instead of the culpable political and military authorities who could.

The first time I heard this story, I was amazed that Germans avoided holding the real culprits responsible for mismanaging the war. Then I learned that in unhealthy nations, rulers always work hard to avoid accountability, and they usually succeed. And this was just one example among many!

Creating Synthetic Hatred to Prevent Solidarity: Rich White Americans Use the KKK to Train Poor White Americans to see Poor Black Americans as the Biggest Threat

In 1865, wealthy white slaveowners of the American South experienced what was to them a massive catastrophe. After losing the Civil War, their slaves were suddenly legally free.

These ex-slaveowners and their ancestors had spent centuries crafting their slave society to grow and maintain their wealth and control, as detailed in Chapter 15. When white and black indentured servants showed more solidarity than they wanted in the early 1600s, the wealthy planters put an end to that by raising the status of the whites to wage-laborers and lowering the status of blacks to permanent chattel slavery. They further encouraged division by outlawing sexual intermingling and hiring poor whites to become part of the slave security apparatus as slavecatchers and overseers.

Slaveowners also benefited because slavery reduced white workers' wages. After all, it was hard for a white laborer to ask for a raise when slaves could do the same work for merely the cost of feeding, housing, and security. And much of the security was funded by taxpayers rather than slaveowners, as the government maintained the courts, prisons and slave patrols. The slave owners had given themselves quite a deal.

Not only did enslaved people often develop appropriate hatred of their captors, I believe the slaveowners also developed appropriate hatred of their slaves. The biggest threat to the slave was the slaveowner and his whips, brands, chains, and other torture devices, not to mention the slaveowners' ability to rape at will or sell families apart. The biggest threat to the slaveowner was actually the slave him or herself. Slaveowners lived in constant fear of slave uprisings like the one in Haiti that ended in 1804. Any slave's sense of dignity or urge towards self-defense or solidarity was a threat to the slaveowner.

Thus, the slaveowners created a society where they lived next to their biggest threats as well – the slaves they abused so deeply. Suddenly, in 1865, those slaves were legally free. This opened up many questions. Would ex-slaves seek revenge, or somehow treat the slaveowners the way they'd been treated? If poor whites and blacks were now the same status, would they join in solidarity and take a stand to redistribute some of the aristocrats' unneeded wealth and land? Would wages start to rise now that they couldn't count on low-cost slave labor? What would happen to rich ex-slaveowners when black people started becoming judges and politicians? White aristocrats had built their whole identity on a sense of divinely-ordained racial superiority evidenced by their vast wealth, and they considered it unthinkable that blacks might expect dignified treatment or even give orders. These concerns were compounded by the south's utter post-war economic devastation. Poverty, joblessness, and discontent spread among blacks, whites, and others.

In response to their concerns, the wealthy planters fomented a campaign of hatred coupled with paramilitary terrorism, called the Ku Klux Klan. I believe the campaign had at least these two goals:

- *Oppression of black people*: Keep black people oppressed and effectively permanently second-class citizens.

- *Make poor whites side with rich whites*: Train poor white people to align with the rich white people instead of the poor black people.

Rather than recognizing rich white people as the greatest danger, poor whites were trained to see black people as the greatest threat. This discouraged any potential solidarity among poor black and white people.

Within a year of the war's end, white people began riding on horses at night, scaring newly-freed black people and any whites who supported them. Violence quickly escalated, and within a few years, these night raiders killed, mutilated, robbed, raped, and intimidated vast numbers of people.

Because many sheriffs and politicians were themselves secretly part of the Klan, there is no accurate count of the crimes, but a few investigations hint at their scale. A US Congressional hearing found that Klansmen committed more than 400 murders across Georgia, Alabama, and Florida between 1868 and 1871, not accounting for its activity in 9 other states. One estimate for a six month period in South Carolina in 1871 counted 35 killings, 262 floggings, 2 rapes, and 101 victims injured, mutilated, or evicted from their homes.[17] Anyone who considered voting for the party sympathetic to blacks, the Republicans, was at risk of violent attack regardless of their skin color.

The KKK and sympathetic southern newspapers spread propaganda painting black people as a great threat, and the United States as an inherently white country. Klan members described fears of "negro domination" and called black people "depraved."[18] Klan-sympathetic newspapers consistently stoked unfounded fears of a massive negro crime wave.[19]

The founding ideology, described in the pamphlet *Ideals of the Ku Klux Klan*, notes that "All Christian Civilization depends upon the preservation and upbuilding of the White Race, and it is the mission of the Ku Klux Klan to proclaim this doctrine…" It espoused an either-or attitude, saying either whites or blacks will dominate. The pamphlet insisted that whites and blacks could not live side by side as equals: "The supremacy of the White Race must be maintained, or be overwhelmed by the rising tide of color."[20]

Indicating that God himself supports white supremacy, and anything else is an affront to the divine order, the KKK pamphlet stated, "Distinction among the races is not accidental, but designed… and indicates the wisdom of the divine mind." Recognizing blacks as normal citizens not only supposedly threatened white people and Christians, it supposedly threatened the Constitutional order itself. The pamphlet noted that any effort to take control away from whites or share control with any other color was "an invasion of our Constitutional prerogatives and a violation of divinely established laws."

The newly-freed black people were thus cast as a massive and permanent threat to white people, Christians, and Americans, not merely a threat to rulers and ex-slaveowners. Of course, many white poor people also may have had appropriate fears of ex-slaves, as many ex-slaves surely remembered their overseers, slave catchers, cruel judges, and others who persecuted them brutally until 1865.

The KKK did not merely engage in random mob violence and hate-mongering. It showed clear signs of being coordinated by wealthy and politically connected individuals. Klan members showed great precision and coordination in attacks using expensive horses that few could afford. Klan members would go on raids in distant regions so that locals wouldn't recognize anyone whose disguise might slip. When someone was identified, Klansmen provided false testimony and murdered witnesses. Within courtrooms, written records of testimony were mysteriously altered to nullify indictments. Klansmen sat on juries or worked as police officers, making it difficult to build or prosecute cases.

Newspapers owned by wealthy businessmen initially denied the existence of the Klan, but then openly excused its violence. The Daily Sentinel claimed negro violence was so bad that, "nothing but lynch law will do." The Greensboro Patriot complained when whipping became outlawed, calling it "the one great incentive" to negro morality and encouraged the practice anyway.[21]

Republican judges were consistently insulted and shamed in the newspapers, such as the Daily Standard which called them "a disgrace to the bench, a mockery of dignity and decency, a laughing stock for the legal profession and a curse and blight to the people…"[22] The Daily Sentinel predicted that Klan violence would only subside once "Dark Savages and white ignoramusses wearing the oath of office" are removed from political power.[23]

When the Republican judge Albion Tourgée indicted dozens of Klansmen for felonies and murders beginning in 1872, he found that many defendants were from wealthy and politically connected families. The state legislature, dominated by the KKK-sympathetic Conservative party, took only three weeks to pass a new law voiding the older law under which the indictments were made. They then passed another law granting amnesty for crimes committed on behalf of secret organizations. In other words, the state government rescued wealthy criminals who murdered and intimidated law-abiding ex-slaves and white supporters.[24]

Tragically, this campaign of hate and terrorism worked. Many white people adopted racist attitudes towards black people who were the least responsible for the problems in their society. The ex-slaveowners regained political control when the post-Civil War Reconstruction Era ended. I suspect many of their descendants remain among the most wealthy and influential people in the South as I write in 2024.

I studied the KKK in school, but I never understood why people would act with such extreme violence, manipulative propaganda, and hateful feelings. I had to learn that abusers and victims can become trapped in relationships of mutual threat and mutual hatred, and this means that once the victims are free they can seem like a threat to the abusers regardless of whether they really are a threat or not. Black and white solidarity – and solidarity among any groups – poses an existential threat to authorities who benefit from division. Once these realities became clear, I understood why a relatively small number of extremely influential people would intentionally coordinate a massive campaign of synthetic hatred and terrorism.

Synthetic Hatred Designed to Dehumanize Others Motivates People to Support Wars They Wouldn't Otherwise Care About

Rulers who want to go to war face a common conundrum. How can they motivate a whole country to support a war when the vast majority of people have no personal reason to want a fight?

Some military authorities have promised soldiers a cut of the spoils, so at least they had selfish reasons for fighting. But most soldiers don't benefit much from their country's wars.

Governments do not honestly let their people know the country's true strategic security situation. If they did, citizens would be able to decide which wars needed to be fought for self-defense and which were unnecessary. Such well-informed citizens would not support wars that only benefited their rulers' ambitions. So, once rulers decide to attack some other country, how can they motivate people to fight despite the economic hardship, wartime censorship, risk of mass injury or death, and other common negatives of authoritarian warfare?

There are many effective techniques for tricking people. One major technique is to cultivate dehumanizing synthetic hatred towards the "enemy." A constant stream of propaganda makes some foreign country's rulers seem like dictators, their people seem inferior or subhuman, their way of life seem backwards, and their sexual urges immoral. Above all, the targeted foreigners are presented as a major looming threat, because a sense of unending threat is what initially generates fear and later leads to hatred.

The Soviet Union and Nazi Germany in World War II offer good examples. Both generated massive amounts of dehumanizing, hate-inducing propaganda to motivate their soldiers and civilians to support their war efforts. True atrocity stories were circulated widely, while stories of their own side's atrocities were hidden. Other stories were false or cherry-picked. Deception of their own people was the necessary cost of creating and maintaining enough synthetic hatred to effectively pursue the war effort.

Nazi German leader Adolf Hitler gave orders to act with extreme brutality towards Soviet civilians and soldiers, including granting immunity from prosecution for killing certain categories of people upon encounter. The Soviets were presented as an existential threat to Germans and connected with Judaism. As the Nazis had been fomenting hatred towards Jews for years, this further increased the supposed threat from the Soviets. One report by German general Hoepner stated that the war was an unavoidable "struggle for existence of the German Volk" against "Jewish-Bolshevism" and enemies should be treated "with unheard-of harshness." Soldiers should keep "an iron, pitiless will" and show "no mercy for the bearers of today's Russian-Bolshevist system."[25]

Many soldiers adopted these hateful attitudes. Albert Neuhaus, a traveling salesman before joining the military, wrote to his wife that the Soviets didn't know what hit them, "And they certainly deserve it, this riff-raff have earned nothing better." One German machine gunner wrote in his journal about the "the dirty brown heap of destruction," referring to the Soviet soldiers in his line of fire.

Soviet leader Josef Stalin in a public statement said the people's task "consists of annihilating to the last man all Germans." In 1942, poet Ilya Ehrenburg turned out regular works saying things like, "Let us kill! If you haven't killed a German in the course of the day, your day has been wasted." The enemy was commonly presented as dogs, snakes, and other reptiles. One publication called Germans "executioners, bloodsuckers, cannibals, killers, thieves, dogs." A poem described Germans as a fascist snake, saying, "We should pull out its teeth/pull out its insides/smash its spine." Stories of Germans raping Soviet women circulated widely, along with other atrocity stories towards women and children, and Germans were presented as depraved beasts.

These German and Soviet synthetic hate campaigns both presented their opponents as subhuman, amoral, existential threats. While it's true that the Germans attacked first and did indeed plan to enslave or kill many eastern Europeans, this was completely outside the direct experience of most Soviets who never personally interacted with any German people. After all, the eastern-most Soviet province lay several thousand miles from the farthest German advance. The synthetic hate campaign was essential to keeping Soviets motivated to accept mass mobilization and conscription, as well as all the economic hardships for a war that for many was happening thousands of miles away.

The need for this hatred campaign becomes clear when we compare the Soviet Union's anti-German effort with the Lakota's, Apache's, and other healthy nations' responses to the English and later Americans who steadily pushed westward from their eastern North American colonies. The Americans wound up killing and enslaving many people of healthy nations, meaning that the Americans in the 1700s and 1800s posed the same threat to the North American healthy nations as the Germans posed to the Soviets in the 1940s. But the nature of the American threat was simply outside the experience of most people of healthy nations.

For example, by the mid-1800s, the English and Americans had been massacring, enslaving, and displacing native North Americans for two centuries, but the American threat didn't become urgent for the Lakota until the United States started imposing on them directly. In contrast, the Soviets forced all the people of northern Asia to mobilize for war regardless whether they personally had any reason to feel fear, and thus they used a propaganda campaign to instill motivational fear and hatred in people who wouldn't feel these feelings otherwise. This allowed the Soviets to galvanize people across northern Asia to defend against the Germans, whereas healthy nations across North America defended themselves against the Europeans and Americans one at a time or in small local alliances which, in the end, were not powerful enough to protect themselves for more than a few decades or a century after recognizing the threat.

For healthy nations to have effectively protected themselves, they would have needed to clearly recognize the American threat much earlier. Like the Soviets who responded immediately after the Germans attacked, and immediately began moving resources and building new armies, the healthy nations across North America would have been much more able to protect themselves if they could have collectively recognized the threat posed by the Europeans as early as the 1500s. Sadly, they simply did not have this level of communication and coordination across the continent.

This illustrates the functional value of synthetic hate campaigns in mobilizing many people for war. Synthetic hatred – that is, hatred motivated by authorities whether or not it has any basis in reality – motivates people to fight in a war they wouldn't otherwise support.

Generating Hate Towards Peace Activists and Truth Tellers Trains the Public to Perceive Honest, Courageous Patriots as Traitors

These war-related hate campaigns face a common trouble: they're often based on lies. Even worse, their whole purpose is to motivate people to support a war they often wouldn't support if they knew the whole truth. Peace activists commonly try to counter these hate campaigns by communicating the truth.

Truth is a real problem for authorities waging campaigns of synthetic hate. This is why authorities will commonly attack the peace activists, calling them traitors and a threat to their nation which is supposedly under attack. When one of the top Nazi German leaders, Hermann Goering, was interviewed after World War II, he acknowledged this common pattern:

> Why, of course, the people don't want war. Why would some poor slob on a farm want to risk his life in a war when the best that he can get out of it is to come back to his farm in one piece. Naturally, the common people don't want war; neither in Russia nor in England nor in America, nor for that matter in Germany. That is understood. But, after all, it is the leaders of the country who determine the policy and it is always a simple matter to drag the people along, whether it is a democracy or a fascist dictatorship or a Parliament or a Communist dictatorship.[26]

The interviewer thought he saw a problem with this logic, and said, "There is one difference. In a democracy the people have some say in the matter through their elected representatives, and in the United States only Congress can declare wars."

Goering explained that the game is the same everywhere:

> Oh, that is all well and good, but, voice or no voice, the people can always be brought to the bidding of the leaders. That is easy. All you have to do is tell them they are being attacked and denounce the pacifists for lack of patriotism and exposing the country to danger. It works the same way in any country.

In other words, Goering noted that authorities commonly pretend there are two threats: the foreigners whom authorities want to conquer, and the peace activists who try to stop the unnecessary war.

This same trick keeps playing out over and over. Authorities pretend that patriotic truth-telling social activists are the threat when, in reality, the authorities are the threat. It's a scam! And it's ridiculous that it keeps succeeding. The fact that this same scam keeps working repeatedly in unhealthy nations around the world shows that somehow, we are not learning the lessons we need to learn.

As I write in 2024, I heard this same scam playing out earlier today in Germany. People who want to reduce aggression towards Russia are called Putin trolls, the present-day American and European equivalent of calling someone a traitor. The implication is that any American or European peace activist must secretly be controlled by Russian president Putin, someone that propaganda has been labeling a dictator for a decade.[27,28] This is profoundly manipulative, making it very difficult for people to have calm, thoughtful conversations about matters of war and peace. This manipulation is common in nations where rulers manipulate people into wanting war that they would not support otherwise.

Authorities will keep playing this same trick, and it will keep working as long as people tolerate having rulers. The way to finally end this scam – where peace activists, truth-tellers, and other true patriots are treated as traitors – is to create a nation where nobody rules over anybody else.

Seeing Hate Campaigns Motivate Extreme Violence in Real Time

This same synthetic hate-creation pattern plays out commonly when authoritarian rulers decide to go to war. Currently, as I write in 2024, the Israelis are generating hatred towards Palestinians to justify slaughtering civilians in massive numbers[29], with the majority being women and children.[30]

Over decades of occupation, Israel turned the Gaza region into an open-air prison where Israelis controlled the amount of food entering the territory, even calculating the amount of calories Gazans require to maintain them near starvation levels.[31,32] For decades the Israelis have subjected the Palestinians in Gaza to mass surveillance, incarceration, and displacement, keeping them in extreme poverty.[33] Like American slaveowners who saw slaves as a threat, I believe the Israeli government sees Palestinian self-defense as a threat.

When Palestinians fought and killed Israelis and took hostages in October 2023, the Israeli government began a massive campaign of fear and hatred towards the Palestinians to motivate Israelis to support a brutally disproportionate war against them. While the Palestinians did take hostages and cause some deaths, the Israeli newspaper Haaretz gathered testimony from soldiers and Israeli officers indicating that many of the Israeli deaths had been due to deliberate Israeli military decisions to fire on their own soldiers and civilians rather than risk them being taken captive, a policy known in the Israeli military as the "Hannibal Directive."[34] Nevertheless, all deaths were blamed on the Palestinians. The Israeli prime minister called Palestinians' October 7 assault "an attack whose savagery I can say we have not seen since the Holocaust," clearly tying this Palestinian attack to a mass-slaughter of millions of Jews, among others. The implication was that all Jews or all Israelis faced an existential risk.[35]

On October 9, 2023, Israel's defense minister Yoav Gallant said, "We are fighting human animals and we are acting accordingly."[36] The New York Times spread stories of Palestinian atrocities which were later debunked, including that they beheaded babies or ripped a fetus out of a woman.[37] Israeli censorship keeps its citizens from fully understanding Palestinians' perspectives or their military's real behavior.[38] All these create the impression of Palestinians as an existential threat, even as they are occupied by the Israeli military. Tragically, many Israelis believe this narrative and support a massacre of hundreds of thousands of Palestinians who struggle to defend themselves.[39]

It is common in hate campaigns for authorities to punish anyone who sympathizes with the targeted group. In one instance, a 12-year-old Israeli-Arab school girl expressed concern in class that Palestinian children are dying of hunger, and she said that she wanted them to be able to return home. Immediately after class, other students angrily accused her of supporting Palestinians and said, "your village should be burned down." She was suspended from school as false rumors continued to spread about her statements. Not only did teachers and school staff allow other students to threaten the girl and spread false rumors, but Israel's Ministry of Education itself accused the girl of "incitement against IDF [Israeli] soldiers." When authorities want to spread fear and hatred, this sort of biased response by officials has a powerful effect, as people can easily become afraid to acknowledge sympathy with the targeted group. Authorities thus discourage dissent and alternative points of view from spreading.[40]

Authorities Generate Synthetic Hate Towards Healthy Nations to Prevent People from Learning that Life Without Rulers is Possible

When two people are in an abusive relationship, the abuser will commonly try to confuse the victim about the nature of the abuse. The abuser may claim that no abuse is happening, or the victim deserves it, or "this is just how things are" and no other kind of relationship is possible. They will do just about anything to encourage passive acceptance and prevent the abuse victim from clearly seeing their situation, which might lead them to escape or fight back.

This pattern plays out on the much larger scale of entire unhealthy nations, where authorities try to convince people that authoritarian nations are the only kinds that exist. If people learned that they could live without rulers, and if they saw healthy nations living nearby, they might start to get ideas about overthrowing their own rulers and healing their nation. Thus, authorities train people to believe that human nations must have rulers, and no other social configuration is possible. Rulers try to make people forget what actual freedom is like.

There's a trouble though: healthy nations do exist! One technique authorities have used to deal with this trouble is to encourage people to fear or hate healthy nations.

Authorities Train People to See Healthy Nations as Threatening

Christians, Muslims, and Jews have been systematically taught to hate pagans for millennia, making it potentially the longest-running synthetic hate campaign in human history. Whether this has been one large hate campaign or a hundred smaller ones that work the same is hard to say. Every new political regime or religious authority in the Abrahamic traditions (Jews, Muslims, Christians) has had the same motivation for generating fear and synthetic hatred towards healthy nations, and all have effectively trained their population to hate them. Of course, not every polytheistic nation has been healthy, but every healthy nation represents a threat to authorities' legitimacy in unhealthy nations. This multi-millennia-long hate campaign against pagans is, among other things, a scam to scare people so they never learn that actually-free societies exist, or what freedom is really like. After all, the mere existence of healthy nations shows that people can live without rulers.

The spiritual perspectives described in this book are essentially pagan. That is, healthy nations see every being as divine and worthy of being worshiped. As described in Chapter 2, this simply means that each being is worthy of respect. But religious authorities for millennia have trained their followers not only to find no beauty in this perspective, but to deeply fear it.

What were religious authorities so afraid of that they decided they must, for thousands of years, train others to fear pagans? And why the enormous focus on one God and only one God?

Pagans in ancient Rome were quite open-minded. Different pagans may emphasize different Gods, but for them the choice of God wasn't exclusive because divinity manifested in the world in many ways. Christianity was the opposite. Christians believed in only one God to the exclusion of all others who were false idols.[41] As Roman emperor Theodosius made Christianity the official religion of the Roman Empire and banned all others in 380 CE, a "with us or against us" mentality set in when Theodosius called nonbelievers "demented and insane," and deserving of both divine and legal punishment.[42] Thus, millennia of religious close-mindedness stems in part from abusive authority figures demanding people believe a certain way or face severe punishment.

During the middle ages, both Christians and Muslims referred to pagans as uncivilized. Christian Spanish conquerors of North and South America called the locals "indian barbarians." The English referred to the people they encountered as savages, uncivilized, and worse.

Leading up to the English colonists' massacre of the Pequot people in the 1630s, they recognized the so-called Indians as savages in league with Satan himself. Colonists called them the Antichrist.[43] Once cast as an existential threat, it became easier to treat the Pequot as subhuman. After a period of brutal war, the Christians sought to destroy what remained of their nation. The survivors were sold as slaves, many to the West Indies thousands of miles away. Those who remained and avoided execution were forbidden from returning to their homeland, speaking their language or even acknowledging themselves as Pequot. Fortunately, some Pequot descendents survive to this day.[44]

Political and religious authorities had successfully motivated the Christian colonists to willingly attack and subjugate people of healthy nations rather than be inspired by their ability to live without abusive rulers. Poor Christians had also been trained to conquer others' land mostly for the benefit of the rich, as Christians continued to spread their unequal nations of a few rich and many poor.

Throughout history, authoritarian leaders train people to see "civilized" people as good, peaceful, and moderate, and "uncivilized" people as bad, threatening, and extreme. They maintain this illusion even while the civilized go around the world conquering and enslaving the uncivilized and forcibly converting them to authoritarian religions.

Spanish conqueror Juan Ginés de Sepúlveda described "that with perfect right the Spaniards rule over these barbarians of the New World and the adjacent islands, who in wisdom, intelligence, virtue, and humanitas are as inferior to the Spaniards as infants to adults and women to men. There is as much difference between them as there is between cruel, wild peoples and the most merciful of peoples, between the most monstrously intemperate peoples and those who are temperate and moderate in their pleasures, that is to say, between apes and men."[45] Clearly some people were merciful and temperate while others were cruel and monstrous. Sepúlveda just had it backwards!

Spanish historian Gonzalo Fernandez de Oviedo y Valdes justified the Spanish invasion of South America based in part on the healthy nations' free sexual behavior, calling it depraved that people might not keep to one sexual partner their whole lives. Echoing centuries of anti-pagan propaganda, he wrote, "they have no knowledge of the all-powerful God and worship the devil in diverse forms and idols…"

Signs of this Hate Campaign Against Healthy Nations can Easily be Found Today

Throughout this book, I cite some anthropologists who have observed people of healthy nations and called them "savages," such as Bronislaw Malinowski who titled his book *The Sexual Life of Savages*. This racism has infected a huge amount of media coverage and anthropological research about healthy nations, causing widespread misunderstandings. Unfortunately, many of these ancient misunderstandings persist today.

The present-day American Heritage dictionary defines "civilized" as "1. Having a highly developed society and culture; 2. Showing evidence of moral and intellectual advancement; humane, ethical, and reasonable; 3. Marked by refinement in taste and manners; cultured."[46]

In contrast, "savage" is defined as "1. not domesticated…wild… not civilized, barbaric… vicious or merciless, brutal…unforgiving…extreme."[47] Barbarian means, "A member of a people considered uncivilized or culturally inferior…crude, uncivilized, or brutal person"[48]

In other words, civilized people are supposedly good and kind, and uncivilized are bad and threatening. These beliefs made European and American colonists feel like they were good people who were surrounded by constant threats, a core technique for generating synthetic hatred.

The earliest American dictionary, created by Noah Webster in 1828, clearly illustrates the manipulative propaganda in its definition of the term "savage":

> SAVAGE, n. 1. A human being in his native state of rudeness; one who is untaught, uncivilized or without cultivation of mind or manners. The savages of America, when uncorrupted by the vices of civilized men, are remarkable for their hospitality to strangers, and for their truth, fidelity and gratitude to their friends, but implacably cruel and revengeful towards their enemies...
>
> 2. A man of extreme, unfeeling, brutal cruelty ; a barbarian.[49]

This term "savage" was the label applied to all people of healthy nations that Americans encountered, a label also used by the Spanish, English, and other conquerors. Yet Webster's definition was obviously contradictory: how can people be in a "state of rudeness... without cultivation of mind or manners" and also show remarkable hospitality to strangers? How can they demonstrate truth, fidelity, and gratitude to their friends while being "extreme" and "unfeeling?"

The truth is actually stated in the definition itself: Americans believed savages were "remarkable for their hospitality to strangers... but implacably cruel and revengeful towards their enemies." Obviously, this implies that so-called savages were, in general, kind to anybody who was kind to them while also defending themselves from threats. How is this unreasonable? Unfortunately, when authorities want to create synthetic hatred, reason and truth are quickly discarded.

Authorities trained conquering Christians to believe that conquering was good and moral and even an act of self-defense. Because Christians had learned not to see the abuse in their own culture, and they ignored their own abusive behavior towards so-called savages, Christians learned to see healthy nations' self-defense as "cruel and revengeful."

I call this technique *ignoring the first strike*, where authorities train people to ignore the abuser's initial attack and view the self-defense as if it were the first, inappropriate act of violence.

This early dictionary definition of savage illustrates many of the patterns highlighted in this book. People of healthy nations have often been kind and welcoming to outsiders who approach in a respectful way, just as the Arawaks initially welcomed Columbus, and how the Ashaninka welcomed me. But carefully orchestrated propaganda has, for centuries, highlighted or fabricated so-called savages' atrocities while ignoring the Europeans' provocative behavior, making the people of healthy nations seem like an endless threat and generating the synthetic fear and synthetic hatred necessary to motivate Christians to fight them.

The power of this anti-healthy-nation propaganda became vivid to me when I spoke with a Christian man who was about 18 years old. I described some perspectives on healthy nations over dinner. He said he found them interesting but had read about how Native Americans had scalped Christians, and he didn't like that.

He was completely unaware that English colonial governments began a program in the early 1600s where they would pay citizens to kill natives, essentially at random. The murdered people's scalps were turned into the government as proof of the murder. English and later Americans could kill to make extra money, or perhaps make it their livelihood if they could gather enough scalps from unsuspecting people. For decades, the governments didn't care if the murdered people were men, women, or children. Later, authorities officially encouraged scalp-hunters to kill more men, but it was often hard to distinguish a person's age and sex by their scalp.[50]

This was a centuries-long program of state-sponsored terrorism aimed at severely disturbing all the people of healthy nations who might stand in the way of English and later American expansion. The program continued late into the 1800s in the United States.

As a single example, *The Daily Republican* newspaper in Winona, Minnesota printed the following on September 24, 1863: "The State reward for dead Indians has been increased to $200 for every red-skin sent to Purgatory. This sum is more than the dead bodies of all the Indians east of the Red River are worth."[51]

The settlers gave a name to the bloody bodies they left behind: redskins. This was the name of the professional football team in Washington DC when I grew up nearby in the 1990s. How is it possible that English and American governments could openly, publicly pay citizens to murder and scalp random foreigners for money for centuries, and present-day Christian Americans think that only those foreigners scalped? This showed me the power of propaganda in unhealthy, authoritarian nations. Propaganda trains people to ignore their own nation's abuses and see themselves and their rulers as good, while the unconquered are cast as bad and threatening.

This anti-pagan campaign continues today. Another Christian friend once expressed great concern for me when I called myself pagan. However, the anti-healthy nation propaganda in North America is now much less intense than it was 150 years ago.

After the Lakota were militarily overrun in the 1890s, it became extremely difficult for Americans to run away to live in an intact healthy nation. Almost the entire North American continent had been militarily conquered by unhealthy nations. Thus the anti-pagan propaganda campaign was no longer needed. Now people of healthy nations – commonly called indigenous or native people – are often simply ignored. When people of healthy nations make the news, they are often presented as wise environmentalists tragically destined to be ignored in a hopelessly selfish world.

Modern propaganda continues, just as it has for millennia, to hide the basic truth: people of healthy nations know what it's like to stand for a culture of mutual respect, and live without anybody ruling over anybody else. Their mere existence is proof that we don't have to live with rulers.

Triple Inhibition Explains Why These Hate-Redirection Techniques Work So Well

When people feel angry, but they've learned subconsciously not to stand up to authority figures, where does their anger go?

It helped me to remember that abusive societies are constantly generating anger and hatred because these are normal responses to disrespect. Uncaring bosses and landlords, unfair police officers and judges, rude customers, and others constantly generate stress and anger for many people. It's clear to anyone who looks that the rich are living in extreme luxury while many live in abject poverty, and corrupt politicians maintain this disparity. And yet rulers commonly manage to manipulate people's anger and hatred, directing it at oppressed ethnicities, anti-war activists, foreigners, people of healthy nations, and others.

Why does this work so well? When children are raised to practice triple inhibition, many learn not to express their anger at authorities, but instead block their feeling and also block their awareness that they are blocking the feeling. When enough adults have practiced this, and when enough anger builds up, they can be ripe for authorities to point out exactly who deserves their scorn and wrath. People who have learned not to direct anger towards the true cause will be ready to direct their rage almost anywhere else.

And of course, those who don't hate as their rulers expect may be punished in many ways. Not everyone hates as authorities demand, but when enough people do, they can make it very hard to hold their abusive rulers accountable.

Sources of Abusers' Hate

For a while I wondered why hate is so common throughout history. When I finally recognized authoritarian societies as abusive, and how abusers could perceive their victims as a threat, it became clear.

Hate may show up in abusers for several reasons:

- *Appropriate hatred for the victim*: Appropriate hatred is a common response to being trapped with a threat. Abusers often relate to their victims as threats, and with good reason. If the victims ever had a chance to defend themselves, the abusers might be in trouble. The Haitian slave revolution in 1804 and the New Mexico State Penitentiary riot in 1980 were extremely violent for similar reasons: people who'd suffered endless indignity and abuse had a tremendous rage built up. I believe abusers know this at some deep level and recognize the risks they'd face if victims ever had a chance to act on their anger. Even though abusers trap themselves with the victims, abusers can still learn to hate them as a threat.

- *Inappropriate hatred of the victim*: When a person practices triple inhibition, they may feel anger, frustration, fear, or other feelings towards abusive authorities but learn to hold the feelings back. The energy behind these feelings has to go somewhere though, and often an abusive person will take out their anger on victims. People who receive abuse may abuse lower-privileged people in this way. This is what occurred in the story Harriet Jacobs told of the young black mother dying in birth while the white woman said cruel things, as told in Chapter 17. I believe the white woman felt appropriate anger towards her husband, the slave-rapist, but she'd learned not to express anger towards its real target. Instead she directed inappropriate hatred to a safe outlet: the victims themselves.

- *Hatred of oneself*: Every human has those universal sacred urges towards integrity, solidarity, alignment with truth, and so on. Once a person has committed to acting inappropriately, they have to learn to hold back these urges. Later, this book will explore how children can learn to do this from early childhood, so that in adulthood this self-suppression happens spontaneously and subconsciously.

Ultimately, these sacred urges may themselves actually seem like a threat. Consider a king who faces no serious opposition in his kingdom. He is able to imprison or scare away any activists who seek change. The biggest threat to his continued rule may well be his own deep sense that he's behaving extremely inappropriately, and this sense never goes away. Thus people can learn to hate these divine parts of themselves that threaten their own privileged social position. To me, this explains why kings are said to have hearts of stone: they close their hearts extremely tight because the person perceives the divine urges themselves as a threat to their choice to remain an authoritarian ruler or a billionaire.

This explains one reason authoritarian nations generate so much abuse: abusive rulers can feel threatened by the people they exploit, and thus hate them and hate themselves.

Authoritarian Nations Generate Hatred, Low Awareness, and Heart-Closure

All authoritarian nations generate hatred, to differing degrees in different people, because they all involve abusive relationships where a few people exploit the many and people of higher privilege exploit people of lower privilege. This abuse is obviously not ok, but many people have to behave abusively just to keep their careers, jobs, homes, etc. I believe many such people treat victims with dehumanizing hatred just to cope with having to behave so abusively just to maintain their social standing.

In other words, many people have to practice closing their hearts, or "shutting down" or "holding back" some part of themselves, in order to keep the life they've built for themselves.

This is obvious when we consider the perspective of poor white slave catchers from the 1700s in the many North and South American countries that had chattel slavery at the time. Their livelihood depended on catching slaves, but they faced a problem. If they recognized an enslaved person as a human being subject to endless abuse who posed no threat at all to them and just wanted to escape, how could they emotionally come to terms with catching them and returning them to a life of slavery in exchange for a little money for next month's rent? Many slave catchers thus learned to treat slaves as inhuman, savage animals (not that animals should be treated poorly). They learned to close their hearts to the people they were about to abuse.

This hatred, ignoring-the-truth, and heart-closing is common even in nations without official slavery. Consider prison guards in the United States. They can believe that prisoners all committed crimes before being arrested, presented their evidence in a fair trial, were found guilty by a jury of their peers, and then sentenced by a stern but fair-minded judge who believed prison was the best way to respond to the person's crime. The prison guard who believed prisoners had gone through such a rigorous process might then believe they were keeping their community safe and helping inmates learn new ways in their "correctional" facilities.

Obviously this is a fairy tale. Prisons will be investigated more in other chapters, but suffice it to say that approximately 98% of federal criminal cases in the US do not involve a trial with the presentation of evidence.[52] Instead, the prosecutors threaten defendants with decades in prison if convicted, and then offer plea bargains in which defendants can admit guilt to lesser charges, even if they are innocent, and go to prison for fewer years.

The vast majority of prisoners never get any trial. How many prisoners are fully innocent, even of the charges they admitted to under duress? 30%? 50%? 80%? And if I'm a prison guard, how could I cope with a job where I had to keep people trapped in cages even though some large percentage clearly should not be there? Prison guards clearly have to learn to ignore reality. And I believe many of them go a step further and cultivate that dehumanizing hatred, that belief that prisoners are bad and deserve their forced labor, humiliation, isolation, and other suffering.

Blind beliefs make hate campaigns even more successful. One reason hate campaigns work so well is that authorities commonly punish people for not hating. Poor whites were punished if they sided with blacks instead of hating them during the time of the American KKK. Soviet and Nazi authorities punished any citizen as a traitor if they didn't hate the other side. The Israeli school girl was punished for sympathizing with the Palestinians. Peace activists are punished for not hating the desired adversary. Hateful ideologies become blind beliefs, and those who don't hate can face severe punishment. When rulers punish the open-minded and open-hearted, for centuries or in some regions for millennia, intolerance and hate can become widespread.

My desire with this book is that future courageous activists who choose to stand up to hate campaigns can at least do so fully aware of the threats they face, and thus be able to plan for them.

The Three Core Drivers of Deep Division also Drive Synthetic Hatred

Widespread hatred can occur due to the same three core drivers that lead to racism, sexism, and other discrimination:

1. *Systemic hatred*: Rulers impose systemic hatred through deliberate hate campaigns. Then they encourage people to adopt hateful attitudes, rewarding those who do and punishing those who don't.

2. *Adopting an authoritarian attitude*: Many people trapped in abusive nations learn to adopt these hateful attitudes that excuse and justify the role they have in the nation they were born into. Those who don't are commonly punished.

3. *Child abuse*: Some kinds of child abuse predispose people to adopting very hurtful attitudes.

Mass hatred does not happen randomly. Mass hatred might be appropriate, if a whole group of people is endlessly abused. Or, mass synthetic hatred might happen if rulers impose systemic hatred with their hate campaigns. Just like a prison guard has little influence over prison policy, most people individually have little influence over government policy, regardless of their beautiful or hurtful attitudes.

None of this excuses any particular person's hurtful attitudes. However, this understanding does show the path towards ending hatred: generating a nation where everybody stands for a culture of mutual respect, and nobody rules over anybody else.

What if We Embraced the Responsibilities of Living in a Healthy Nation?

What would it be like to see the synthetic hatred scam for what it is and stop falling for it?

What would it be like if everyone opposed these synthetic hate campaigns, not just the targets?

What if poor white people stood in solidarity with poor black people and demanded that everyone be treated decently?

What if people who supported a particular war stood up for the peace activists, so that even if people disagreed, they made sure it was safe for everyone to express their concerns?

What if conservatives and liberals stood together to ensure that authorities didn't blame one side or the other for the country's collective problems?

What if everyone took a stand to remove any leader who spread synthetic hate, instead of falling in line or fearfully keeping quiet?

If people want a culture based on mutual respect, this is what it would take.

The Individual's Role in Cultural Healing – Feel the Dissatisfaction

Many people in authoritarian nations learn to play along with the belief that the legal system is essentially fair and the prisoners more or less deserve to be in prison. How difficult would it be to drive past a prison over years and consistently think, "a large number of prisoners shouldn't be there, even assuming prison is an appropriate response to crime in the first place?" I can say from experience that this is hard, especially when I feel helpless. Over time, I found it helpful to keep noticing the truth, and keep feeling dissatisfied, and keep asking, "what am I going to do about it?"

A nation is wounded whenever there's disrespect between people. Cultural healing happens when people are able to address that disrespect in a deep way so it doesn't happen again, and then return to a baseline of mutual respect. I believe the path to cultural healing starts with a person acknowledging their dissatisfaction. I know things aren't ok, and I don't feel good about it. Maybe I feel angry, depressed, isolated, disturbed, or some other feeling. All these feelings can be healthy responses to an unhealthy situation.

I don't always know what to do, but the feeling of dissatisfaction is the motivating energy that drives me to somehow help address the trouble. It drives me to meet other dissatisfied people and so we can share our perspectives and ask together, "what are we going to do about it?"

Ever since I started noticing the terrible patterns exposed in this book, this is the only way I've ever found satisfaction: by acknowledging the difficult truth, deciding what I'm going to do about it, and then doing my best. And it starts with allowing myself to feel dissatisfied instead of ignoring it, and using that energy to make things better.

My Dream is for People to Laugh at the Scam Together

Ultimately, these hate campaigns are big scams. Rulers try to trick poor people to hate somebody they wouldn't otherwise worry about. Soldiers and colonists may think they're serving their God while they're really enriching their rulers. It's a scam that we don't have to fall for.

My dream is that anyone who chooses to watch TV will see the propaganda and think "Ahhh, so that's who I'm supposed to hate now! Hahaha, how silly!" Then people can come together with their neighbors and consider what to do about their situation, their minds freed from the hate-inducing propaganda efforts.

For example, as I write, American authorities are trying to get me to hate Russia, Iran, and China. Sure, they're unhealthy nations too, but I'm not falling for the hate-mongering.

Of course, not all propaganda is false. Sometimes the threat is real, as when the Nazis invaded the Soviet Union and threatened many Soviet citizens. But even this was not clear-cut; many Ukrainian citizens in the 1930s hoped for a Polish or German invasion to save them from the Soviet government.[53] After the Soviet government had starved millions of Ukrainians in the 1930s, it's remarkable that the Nazis managed to treat the Ukrainians even worse.

Thus there may not be an easy path or clear "good guys" and "bad guys." But when a person acknowledges their dissatisfaction, accepts responsibility for seeking the truth, and accepts responsibility for the consequences of their actions, they'll find the best possible outcome. When such people come together, they can support each other as they walk a good path together. And they won't unintentionally support the authorities who are the real driver of so much unhappiness.

Anyone can do good things on their own, but deeper change comes when people work to solve their shared problems together. What sort of process can respectfully give everyone an equal voice, help people understand their troubles, and help everyone agree on how to move forward together? One such practice is explored in *Chapter 23: Addressing Shared Challenges With the Sacred Circle*.

Chapter 23: Addressing Shared Challenges With the Sacred Circle

In winter 2014-2015, a coalition of healthy nations in Ecuador was suddenly threatened by the Ecuadorian government.

This coalition was called "CONAIE," which in English translates as "Confederation of Indigenous Nations of Ecuador." The government had provided a large office building in Quito, the Ecuadorian capital city, which gave them space to host a large staff that coordinated the coalition's political efforts and hosted meetings.

Without warning, the government suddenly announced that it would end the coalition's lease on their building, threatening their ability to organize effectively. The Ecuadorian government had recently sought a loan from China and in return promised access to natural resources including oil and other minerals. This would result in pollution and deforestation, and thus the coalition would surely oppose this deal. I suspected that this decision to evict CONAIE was timed to make resistance even more challenging.[1]

I happened to be volunteering with CONAIE, so I got to witness their response. And I learned a lot.

Within a few days, hundreds of people from various healthy nations all around Ecuador arrived, often in groups of 3-5. After hosting a public protest in the street outside their building, they invited me to join them for a special closed meeting indoors.

Well over one hundred people packed into a conference room. They spoke in Spanish, so I could only vaguely follow along. First, people took turns speaking, without interruption, while others listened respectfully. I never noticed any speakers rambling on or wasting people's time. They seemed to speak their piece and then give up the floor so the next person had a turn.

Next, it was time to agree on a public statement. A woman stood in the middle with a notepad and read her proposed statement, and instantly a man in the crowd started shaking his fist and made what sounded like a strenuous objection, and others nodded or waved in approval.

I expected the lead woman to get defensive or belligerent, but she just calmly wrote something down. She again read out her statement, and someone else had a very strong response, and again I saw no defensiveness. I realized they weren't arguing or attacking each other. They seemed to simply have strong feelings, and they accepted each others' strong feelings.

Over the next 30-40 minutes, she kept hearing people's feedback and reading back from her notes until finally they all decided it was good enough. Soon the meeting adjourned, and people brought out TV cameras.

Within 30 minutes, the coalition's leaders were delivering their statement to an international audience where they described the situation and their response. I was amazed at how efficient and productive the large and potentially contentious meeting had been.

For the first time, I had witnessed something I now call a *sacred circle*. Sacred circles occur when people feel threatened or face a big challenge, and they come together in a circle to address three questions:

1. What is really going on?

2. What are we going to do about it?

3. How are we going to take care of each other along the way?

Sacred Circles Step 1: Acknowledging a Shared Challenge Together

Understanding a problem isn't enough to resolve it, but it is the crucial first step.

In late 1966, black American Don Cox noticed his political consciousness was growing by leaps and bounds. By then, he had a deep understanding that capitalists and workers had opposing interests, and he'd studied racism and colonization. He was about to find a way to put his knowledge to use.

Cox, who shared a large apartment with several others, came home from work one day to find a noisy crowd. At first he just wanted to relax, but eventually he noticed what they were talking about: "everyone in the room was recounting their personal histories of having been fucked over by either some policeman or judge or someone they had been or were still working for."[2,3]

Cox ran upstairs and grabbed some of his guns and a copy of a Black Panther newspaper. These people weren't members of the Black Panthers yet, but that night the whole crowd studied that newspaper line by line. Many people could not read well, so they went only as fast as the slowest person could understand. It was important that everyone was fully informed about what they were reading. They left no one behind.

Cox then gave everyone a short introduction to the use of guns. They decided they would meet regularly to explore their history, and they would begin hunting rabbits to get weapons practice. Soon they began engaging in direct actions to raise their neighbors' awareness and stand up to oppressive police.

This was a sacred circle in action, whether the people involved thought of it that way or not. They came together and acknowledged their shared grievances, then decided what they would do about it: further history studies, weapons practice, and various direct action efforts. They took care of each other by sharing their guns, books, knowledge, and other resources. In the coming years, this solidarity allowed them to stand up to the abuse they faced in their unhealthy nation.

When I find stories of people standing up to oppression, I often notice it starts with a sacred circle.

Sacred Circles Step 2: What are We Going to Do About It?

The first part of a sacred circle involves people agreeing on their shared challenge, often by sharing their grievances if they aren't already clear. In abusive nations, there's plenty of disrespect and that commonly builds up a dissatisfying tension. A person's dignity demands they stand up to disrespect, and tension arises as this urge to take a stand goes unfulfilled. The longer people receive disrespect without standing up to it, the more this tension mounts. I believe there's only one deeply satisfying way to release the tension: acknowledge the challenge and decide to take action. Hence the second question in a sacred circle is "What are we going to do about it?"

A deep sense of relief or satisfaction comes from committing to meaningful action. The tension arises when a person receives disrespect but doesn't stand up for themselves, so relief comes once a person commits to standing up for themselves. Collective excitement builds when a group decides to take a stand together. This relief and excitement was clear in one man's description of a sacred circle that led to the biggest prison riot in US history.

One evening in 1980, eight inmates at the New Mexico State Penitentiary sat around discussing the terrible conditions they faced, with guards putting various racial groups in lockdown on top of the usual beatings, moldy food, rape, and other cruelty they faced.

Finally the conversation took an unusual turn. One participant described the key moment:

> "So what are we gonna do about it?" [one man said]. "We've been talkin' about a riot for so long now– I'm fuckin' tired of waitin'."
>
> [Another man said,] "Okay. What about tonight?"
>
> The eight men sat stunned for a moment, then, nodding agreement, grins spread across their faces.
>
> "Well, all right, that's what I want to hear!"
>
> They poured another round of brew, toasted their decision, and began discussing the details of the takeover.[4]

Some satisfaction can come from sharing frustrations and hearing others' complaints. But a deeper satisfaction – the grins spreading across everybody's faces – came the moment they agreed on meaningful action together.

Sacred Circles Step 3: How Will We Take Care of Each Other Along the Way?

At the age of 17, Geronimo was finally admitted in 1846 to the council of warriors of his nation, the Bedonkohe Apaches. This brought many benefits, but his greatest joy was that he could now marry Alope. They'd been lovers for a long time and were soon married.[5]

Geronimo made them a new home close to his mother's, a teepee made from hides of bears, lions, and other animals. Alope made decorations of beads and drawings on buckskin on the walls of the teepee. They lived happily and had three beautiful children together, who played and worked as their parents had.

In 1858, Geronimo's people were at peace with neighboring tribes and nearby Mexicans. They traveled to one Mexican town to trade, and each day men would go into town while leaving an armed guard to protect the supplies and women and children. One day they returned to find a few women and children who said the camp had been attacked by Mexican troops. The entire guard had been killed, all the ponies and weapons stolen, and many women and children were also killed.

The returning warriors quickly separated and hid until nightfall when they reassembled at a chosen place. One by one, they entered the site of the massacre and placed sentinels to keep watch.

Geronimo discovered that his mother, young wife, and all three children had been killed. He was in shock. Warriors gathered in council and he joined them but did not cast a vote. They did not have the weapons nor sufficient warriors to counterattack, and they were in unfriendly territory.

They decided to leave. Geronimo remained in silence, not eating when the group stopped to eat, not hunting game on the way. There was nothing to say, and Geronimo noted, "I had no purpose left… I had lost all." He soon vowed vengeance on the Mexican troopers who had killed his family.

After they replenished their supplies, the chief Mangus-Colorado called a council. All the warriors agreed to go to war against Mexico. At this sacred circle, they decided to invite other Apache groups to participate, and Geronimo took responsibility to recruit them. He went to the Chiricahua Apaches and then the Nedni Apaches. At each place, they held a council, and Geronimo acknowledged the recent attack and his desire to avenge it. He recruited many volunteers.

After this preparation, they had a shared motivation – responding to the Mexican military's attacks. They also had a clear plan: attack and kill the troops who'd murdered so many of the warriors' families.

They also considered how they would care for each other as they carried out the plan. After all three tribes assembled, they selected a secret mountain rendezvous near the Mexican borders where they would hide their remaining families. They designated several other rendezvous sites in case the hiding place was disturbed, and left an armed guard with them. In this way, they ensured the safety of their families while they avenged their loved ones' deaths. They took care of each other while they stood up to the people who had attacked them.

The warriors of each tribe followed their chief's lead. However, because Geronimo lost more loved ones than anybody else, he was made leader of the combined fighting force. They encountered four companies of Mexican troops, two companies of infantry and two of cavalry. Geronimo sent flanking detachments and led advances and they kept fighting even as all the Apaches' arrows were spent and their spears were broken. After hours of vicious fighting, many Mexicans and Apaches lay dead on the ground. Finally the Apache warriors were the only ones remaining, having fully vanquished the Mexicans. The ferocious Apache war-whoop rang over the gruesome field.

At each stage, the Apaches decided how to address their challenges with sacred circles. When they had been attacked but could not fight, they chose to escape together. When they were ready to fight, they held a sacred circle and agreed to raise forces from other groups. Geronimo led sacred circles at each community he visited, where he discussed their trouble and what he proposed to do about it. And finally, when all three groups finally convened, they considered how they would take care of each other, including the ones who wouldn't fight.

What Makes a Practice Sacred?

I consider anything sacred if it connects caring people with each other or if it connects people with the Earth. And since Creation and Creator are one, and each of us is a divine being living in divine Creation, any practice that connects people with each other or the Earth also connects people with God, that Spirit-That-Moves-Through-All-Things. This is why I consider sacred circles to be sacred: they help caring people connect deeply with each other as they address shared challenges together.

Likewise, the three core spiritual practice are sacred because, when a whole group bases their way of life on them, they can live well with each other and the Earth. The universal sacred urges are sacred because, when a person acts on those urges, they show up in a good way for the people around them and for the Earth.

In contrast, I consider something sacrilegious or evil if it disconnects caring people from each other or disconnects people from the Earth.

Sacred circles are an essential part of cultural healing. Anytime people experience disrespect, this represents a cultural wound. To heal the culture, the group must decide how to respond to stop the inappropriate behavior and return to that baseline of mutual respect. Sacred circles are where people agree on how to heal their culture or respond to any shared challenge.

All these stories show me the power of sacred circles. Sacred circles transform scattered, angry individuals into a group that meaningfully addresses people's shared concerns and takes care of each other along the way. Sacred circles are where people get clear on why they need solidarity and how they'll stand together. Nothing can ever guarantee success, but when people come together with a strong sacred circle, they will achieve the best outcome they possibly could.

One of the benefits of practicing the sacred circle in any community or nation is that it reminds people that everyone in the circle is "on the same level." No one is inherently superior or "above" anyone else. Not only is each voice respected, each person in the circle can see everyone else in the circle – a clear visual and visceral reminder that we are all equal.

This spiritual practice helps create and sustain respectful relationships outside the circle as well, which is the norm in healthy nations. Sadly, in unhealthy nations, one of the most important relationships is often unequal and sometimes abusive. The next chapter, *Chapter 24: Sexual Discrimination vs Sexual Equality*, shows this stark contrast.

Chapter 24: Sexual Discrimination vs Sexual Equality

Scholars have debated for centuries whether it is possible for men and women to be treated with equal respect in society. Some scholars have concluded that sexual equality is impossible.[1] Once I studied healthy nations, I discovered the answer: not only is it possible, sexual equality is common in nations without rulers.

Healthy Nations Seek a Balance Of Feminine and Masculine Leadership

Balance is a common theme among every healthy nation I've studied.

Having both strong men and strong women contributing to the nation brings balance in many helpful ways. In his writings about the Tzutujil Mayan leadership, Martín Prechtel wrote, "It was not that a man or woman was incomplete without the other; it was that the village was imbalanced otherwise."[2]

Male and female partners would serve as chiefs together except in special circumstances. Even Tzutujil Mayan gods came in pairs.

Different healthy nations have found very different ways of achieving this balance. Cherokee woman Rebecca Adamson described how the traditional Cherokee would have a White Council of women who led during peacetime and a Red Council of men who led in war. She said, "The goal was the balance, the harmony, the bringing together of both wisdoms and both energies for the good of the Nation."[3]

In other healthy nations, trusted elder women may be responsible for picking the male leaders or picking candidates for leadership who then go on to get further approvals. The eldest healthy woman in every Huron clan was designated the clan matron, responsible for choosing both a civil chief and a war chief.[4]

Onondaga chief Oren Lyons described how, when a chief position opens up in the Haudenosaunee Confederacy, a clan mother is trusted to choose a male candidate from her clan to begin the approval process. If her clan reaches consensus in support of the candidate, then the process continues; otherwise she must pick somebody else. Once the clan reaches consensus, the candidate then goes through several more rounds of approval, including full acceptance by the council of chiefs. While the chiefs meet to consider the candidate, men without titles stay home to prepare food so the women may attend the meetings and observe closely. In this role, women keep the records and teach the children.[5]

Finally, after all the other approvals, the candidate chief is presented to the people, and they are asked if anyone knows a reason why the man should not be chief. As Lyons said, "the final word is the people. That is democracy in its full form." He described what sort of man the community would typically choose as a leader: "He must simply be a man of good health and courage, a family man, responsible and honest." In both the Huron and Haudenosaunee, trusted elder women must first choose the men who go on to hold leadership positions.

Even when the men lead in healthy nations, I find that they highly value women's input. For example, in February 1757, when male Cherokee leader Attakullakulla went to South Carolina to discuss trade agreements with the governor, he was surprised to see no white women present. Cherokee women commonly advised their council on issues of peace and war, so it was strange not to see any women in the white people's council.

The Cherokee leader asked, "Since the white man as well as the red was born of woman, did not the white man admit women to their councils?" The South Carolina governor was so surprised that he took a few days to respond, saying, "The white men do place confidence in their women and share their councils with them when they know their hearts are good." The Cherokee were not convinced.[6]

In another example where male leaders welcomed women's input, Crow woman Pretty Shield described a time when they were traveling in a group of about 60 households and they had lost track of where their enemies were during the move. They were quite hungry and men went off hunting buffalo before all the lodges were put up.

A woman named Little Face opened a food pouch and discovered a woman mouse with her children. Little Face did not disturb them, but retrieved food from another pouch and went to sleep. In a dream, she heard the mouse exclaim, "My friend! In four days your people will be attacked by the Lakota. Can you make the men believe this, get them to go back to the place that you came from?" The mouse knew there were many more Lakota than Crow, and she was worried for her children.

Little Face told her mother of her dream and began packing immediately. Her mother found Red Bear, leader of the whole community, watching the countryside from a hill top. Red Bear knew she would not signal him unless it was important, so he listened. He said, "I, too, have felt that some trouble was near us," and he quickly responded to bring in the hunters. When he reached them, they had just found a dead cow with a fresh Lakota arrow in it, and they were ready to heed Little Face's warning. They all packed up and left, avoiding trouble.

Little Face continued to feed the mother mouse and her babies, allowing them to stay in her pouch till the young mice ran away. Then the woman mouse told Little Face where she wanted to be let go, and Little Face took her there. Before the mother mouse left, she looked at Little Face and said, "I will always hear you if you call me." After this, Little Face never stepped on mouse holes in the ground. She considered the mice her special medicine who helped her. And the community's leader, Red Bear, would often ask Little Face for her advice in the future.

These stories and many others show healthy nations embracing a balance of male and female input in making important decisions.

Healthy nations welcome feminine initiative in other ways as well.

Stories of Women Spreading Abundance

I found many beautiful stories of women contributing to their healthy nations by redistributing abundance. Jesuit missionaries stayed with the Montagnais-Naskapi and noticed that men left household affairs almost entirely up to the women. Regardless how much food he or she brought in, it never lasted long because she commonly shared the food with everyone. Paul Le Jeune wrote, "I have never seen my host ask a giddy young woman that he had with him what became of the provisions, although they were disappearing very fast."[7]

Huron women likewise pooled their food in common storage so there would be enough for everyone.[8]

Nancy Basket described the traditional role of the Cherokee gigau (GIG-ah-oo), meaning beloved woman. A woman was chosen to be gigau because she was especially kind, fair and wise. Her job was to make sure all the collective food sources were stored well so there would be enough for everybody. Basket described the goal: "The Cherokee, if we all had a lot, then everybody had a lot. If there wasn't a whole lot, then no one had a whole lot." The gigau had another role too. If the council could not agree on whether to go to war, and they were split down the middle, the gigau would cast the deciding vote.[9]

Basket described another way that women redistributed goods. In one ceremony, all the women would honor the oldest woman in town by bringing her gifts. They knew she didn't need all the stuff, but they trusted that she would know where the goods needed to go. This old woman would then distribute the gifts to whomever needed them the most.

When I lived briefly with the Ashaninka, women's willingness to share their wealth seemed magical to me. At every single house I visited, a woman graciously shared food and drink, and she invited me and my fellow travelers to rest. There was never any payment. I had to find other ways to give back.

I like to notice when people around me embody healthy-nation qualities even though they grew up in an unhealthy nation. When I ask myself who helps redistribute the wealth and looks out for people in need, I think first of my friend Kelly.

Kelly is an herbalist, constantly giving away her healing gifts for free. She runs a free foot clinic for homeless people, and she volunteers or receives token pay as an herbalist or first aid medic at various events.

Between her friends and her healing work, she has quite a list of contacts. Whenever someone's in trouble, Kelly sends out emails requesting donations on their behalf. When someone feels isolated, she arranges a party. When someone struggles financially and hits an emergency, she invites people to pitch in funds. She has raised funds for one person to replace their broken vehicle, for a couple to buy laundry machines in preparation for an expected birth, and for another person to buy a kitchen appliance so they could make quality meals for themselves instead of buying pre-made junk food.

In each case, she saw the need and sent out an email requesting donations. The recipient was grateful to all the givers, and the givers were grateful to Kelly for informing them about the opportunity to give! Like women of healthy nations, Kelly moves resources where they're needed. She also generates gratitude and meaningful connection between people who might not have felt it otherwise.

Men also take responsibility for distributing wealth in their healthy nation, as seen in Chapters 9 and 31. And one need not live in a healthy nation, nor be a woman, to actively care for others in meaningful ways. But living in an unhealthy nation makes this much more challenging. Deep sharing is difficult when land is tightly controlled and financial desperation is common.

The natural balance between masculine and feminine energies is lost in unhealthy nations, with women commonly treated as less valuable than men. As with racism or hatred, anyone can adopt sexist attitudes and behave hurtfully, but sexism does not just randomly happen. Systemic sexism initially starts with rulers who impose law, propaganda, and other pressures on people in order to divide and control them. Like other aspects of unhealthy nations, once sexism is established, it is promoted and maintained by the nation in a wide variety of ways.

Sexism has existed in unhealthy nations throughout history and around the world, and in most settings, women commonly get the worst of it.

Sexual Discrimination Against Women

In some authoritarian nations in some eras, women were forbidden from entering contracts and married women were forbidden from holding jobs without their husbands' approval.

In business settings, women have faced many kinds of discrimination. Coverture, an ancient English practice which spread to parts of the United States until the mid 1900s, offers an example. Unmarried women were legally independent, but married women were not. As one scholar described it, "the very being or legal existence of the woman is suspended during the marriage, or at least is incorporated and consolidated into that of the husband: under whose wing, protection, and cover, she performs everything."[10]

English and American men had significant control over their wives. One American judge in 1966 noted how men and women were supposedly joined in legal union, but it was severely imbalanced as it was based on the "old common law fiction that the husband and wife are one. This rule has worked out in reality to mean that, though the husband and wife are one, the one is the husband."[11]

As English husbands could be liable for their wives' misbehavior, they also had the right to restrain or punish them, analogous to how a master might address a servant's misbehavior or a parent might punish a child. The law varied over time, but was contradictory and inconsistently enforced. Under coverture, the law forbade husbands from using violence against their wives "other than lawfully and reasonably pertains to the husband for the rule and correction of his wife." For some misdemeanors he could beat her with whips and sticks, but for other troubles he could only use "moderate punishment."[12]

A husband also had the legal right to have sex with his wife against her will. As recently as the 1970s, raping one's wife was not considered a crime in the United States. The law presumed that the husband had the right to have sex with his wife whenever he wanted, regardless of her consent. The last US state to outlaw a husband raping his wife was North Carolina in 1993.[13]

Legally sanctioned marital rape dates back at least to the 1600s in England, when chief justice Michael Hale proclaimed, "for by their mutual matrimonial consent and contract the wife hath given up herself in this kind unto the husband which she cannot retract."

This old English practice of coverture has much in common with the present-day (2024) practice of male guardianship in Saudi Arabia. From birth on, women always have a male legal guardian, usually a father or husband, and women themselves are essentially permanently legal minors. The male guardian's permission is required for the women to get a passport or to travel. Women face severe trouble finding work without their male guardian's approval. Women have no choice in marriage and may be married at any age. Domestic violence was not outlawed in Saudi Arabia until 2013, and the law continues to be poorly enforced.[14]

Many religious leaders and books cast women in a negative light. Tibetan Buddhist authorities, prior to the 1951 Chinese takeover, stated that working women were bad luck, and "among ten women you'll find nine devils." Women were subject to many religious taboos, including restrictions on what they could study and what work they could do.[15]

An ancient myth from the Indian state of Madhya Pradesh tells of a woman whose vagina would amputate men's penises. In this story, amputation by the mythical toothed vagina required a drastic response, so a local wealthy landlord ordered four men to rape and subdue her. Holding her down, a man thrust flint into her, knocking one of the teeth out. The woman wept with pain, but she was consoled when the landlord arrived and said he would marry her, completing the masculine control of the dangerous woman. Other myths tell of the vagina as a dark and dangerous place, and focus on the need to subdue the woman through death or marriage having first knocked the "teeth" out of her vagina.[16]

Christian authorities have repeatedly proclaimed that women are the devil. In one story, an angel in the Christian Bible pointed to a woman and noted "This is wickedness."[17] Written in 1486, The Malleus Maleficarum was a theological and legal document describing the Catholic understanding of witchcraft. It noted, "When a woman thinks alone, she thinks evil."[18,19]

Bishop Tertullian, who lived in 160-225 CE, described how women were responsible for all the sin in the world: "And do you not know that you are Eve? God's sentence hangs still over all your sex and his punishment weighs down upon you. You are the devil's gateway; you are she who first violated the forbidden tree and broke the law of God…"

Bishop Tertullian blamed women collectively for Original Sin and therefore causing Jesus to need to return and die to save everybody's souls.[20] This bishop was only mirroring the humiliation and punishment God supposedly ordained for all women for eternity after Eve ate forbidden fruit. The Bible says, "To the woman [God] said, I will surely multiply your pain in childbearing; in pain you shall bring forth children. Your desire shall be contrary to your husband, but he shall rule over you." This supposed feminine evil only reinforced the need for men to control women, as God supposedly instructed.[21]

The word "bishop" stems from the Greek word for "overseer," and Christian bishops through the millennia have overseen many things about women, including their sexuality. For centuries, Christian women were only allowed to have sex within an approved Christian marriage and only when they were fertile. If they did not give birth for several years, they had to cease sexual activity. Men and women were only allowed to have sex in a single position, with the woman on her back and the man on top of her. When Christian missionaries visited people of healthy nations, they brought these teachings, and this is why that particular sex position is called "the missionary position."[22,23]

In authoritarian nations in which women are allowed to work for money, they commonly receive less pay than men for the same work. One study reviewed 10 million Chinese job seekers and found that women earned just over 70% of men's pay.[24] In Russia, women earn less than 70% of men's pay for similar work.[25] In the USA as I write, women earn just over 80% of the equivalent man's salary.[26]

In any particular setting, individual men may treat women with decency in unhealthy nations, and many stories from history show this. As with racism, each individual is responsible for their own behavior and nothing here excuses sexism. However, it is important to understand the rarely-acknowledged driver of sexism: authorities seeking to divide people.

The trouble is that sexism is systemic in authoritarian nations, meaning sexist differences are imposed by rulers and sexist beliefs in unhealthy nations are explicitly or implicitly encouraged by them. Many men and women then adopt sexist attitudes that justify the society into which they are born and the roles they are trained to have. Chapter 20 offered examples of covert and overt systemic racism imposed by governments. Sadly, systemic sexism is also imposed by authorities even in nations that pretend to support equal relations. One common mechanism is that legal courtrooms propagate rape myths.

Rape myths are widely believed falsehoods about rape. Common examples include, "it didn't really happen, or the woman lied to cover up infidelity," "no harm was done, or sex between partners can't be rape," "women secretly want to be forced, and they could prevent rape if they chose," and "women who get raped deserve it somehow."[27]

One textbook in India regarding medical law states that working-class women, presumably physically strong, would need to show signs of visible injury as proof of their lack of sexual consent. By this logic, working-class women were strong enough that if they had truly resisted the sex, they would have been injured, and since no injuries were visible, the sex must have been consensual.[28]

Many Indian political leaders excuse rape. Ramsewak Paikra was the minister for law and order in the Indian state of Chhattisgarh, and he noted that rapes "do not happen deliberately… These kinds of incidents happen accidentally."[29] A minister of the nearby state of Madhya Pradesh, Babulal Gaur described rape when he said, "sometimes it's right, sometimes it's wrong."[30] He also noted that rapes happen less frequently in his state because women there dress more modestly and act more piously than women in other states.[31] Women are often blamed for being attacked, as when Vibha Rao, chair of the Chhattisgarh State Women Commission said in 2013, "Women display their bodies and indulge in various obscene activities. Women are unaware of the kind of message [their actions] generate."[32]

In 2018 in Ireland, courts acquitted a man of raping a 17-year-old because she was wearing a "sexy" slip, suggesting she must have consented.

In 2017, a court in Italy acquitted two men of raping a woman since she apparently looked masculine, suggesting she could have defended herself if she truly didn't want the sex.[33]

A report by the Organization of American States noted that countries throughout North and South America have legal systems that discriminate against female victims of sexual assault. The report said that many sexual assault cases are never investigated, and many women choose not to report an attack to the police who may mistreat them. The report noted, "This combination of factors leaves the victims with a sense of insecurity, defenselessness and mistrust in the administration of justice. The impunity that attends these crimes merely perpetuates violence against women as an accepted practice in [North, Central, and South] American societies, in contempt of women's human rights."[34]

I had a personal experience where I discovered how common rape is among women in the United States. I was once part of a leadership training group with four women. I spoke with another female acquaintance in a 1-on-1 conversation about her life and her dreams, and I learned that she avoided thinking about her dreams. When I inquired further, I found out that she'd been sexually assaulted, and it seemed clear these two things were connected for her.

I later shared this story with my leadership team, only to discover that all four women had stories of being sexually assaulted. They talked about it very openly with me on the call. The acquaintance with whom I'd spoken and every woman on that call were well-spoken, educated white women in a nation that, on average, treats white people better than those of other colors. I do not know what the true rate of sexual assault is in any given unhealthy nation, but I certainly believe the rates are higher than most statistics show.

Transition Stories: From Healthy to Unhealthy Nations

This disastrous anti-women sexism is not part of healthy nations. Stories where healthy nations transition into unhealthy nations, often under severe pressure, also show the rise of anti-woman sexism.

When the Colombian government, in collaboration with Christian missionaries, sought to integrate the Bari people into Colombian society, they deliberately lifted men's privilege and lowered women's. Prior to the 1960s, the Bari were so egalitarian that they had no word for "chief." However, the Colombian government appointed seven male chiefs and seven assistant male chiefs, and these became presumed decision-makers for the Bari, as well as the only people legally allowed to own land. Researchers doubted whether the appointed men understood land ownership at first, but it was significant that no Bari women were initially allowed to own land.[35]

Likewise, while the Bari continued to communally gather and share food, only men were helped to go sell that food for money, making them the first individual to control money in the family. Previously, the Bari had no concept of surplus production, often not even preserving their food.

Bari women had been predominantly responsible for healing, gathering herbs and preparing and administering medicines. Anthropologists noted that men had never done this. However, the government and missionaries offered the Bari new drugs in place of their herbal medicines, and they only offered the drugs to men, displacing women as the primary healers. Researchers noted that all these changes created a "foreign and traditionally unheard of antagonism between the sexes."

A similar story played out for the Montagnais-Naskapi after the Jesuits arrived. Jesuits wrote disapprovingly of how much freedom women had in marriage, divorce, and sexual relations. The Jesuits noted that the women were under no obligation to respect, obey, or remain married to their husbands, doing so only by choice. Jesuits noted that women had a large influence on decision-making, such as when to move to new locations. The Jesuits wanted the Montagnais-Naskapi to adopt Christianity and integrate with the French colony as farmers.[36]

In the 1620s-1640s, the Jesuits at first struggled to convince the Montagnais-Naskapi to convert to Christianity, complaining they had "a life of idleness" and they would have "difficulty in embracing one of hard work such as cultivating the soil… the bond, so strong, which holds man and wife under the same yoke, will be very hard to fasten upon the savages." The Jesuits later complained that they preferred "to live in repose and in the idleness of animals to enjoying the fruits of labour." In other words, these people did not work any harder than needed to live a satisfying life. They remained in the Garden of Eden, and the Christian missionaries struggled to evict them.

However, the Jesuits were persistent, and the Montagnais-Naskapi struggled when they began to suffer from attacks by the Haudenosauenee. A French colonial governor offered them protection and land if they converted to Christianity. Once Montagnais-Naskapi men became sole landowners and adopted other French practices, women suffered a rapid drop in status. As the Montagnais-Naskapi adapted to French Christian rules, they also showed common symptoms of authoritarian nations. Husbands began to speak in condescending or humiliating ways towards their wives and controlled the family by being the sole breadwinner.

Women who left their husbands were beaten, starved, or thrown in jail. Even more tragically, women began to police themselves. One older woman locked up younger women at night to prevent them from seeing young men. Women began to reject suitors they would previously have accepted. In 1640 one Jesuit noted the Montagnais-Naskapi women had become "as docile as little lambs."

These stories again show that sexism isn't who we are as people. Women don't have to have lower privilege, and privilege of any kind need not exist. Sexism has been consciously imposed by political and religious authorities. Healthy nations commonly resisted such hurtful changes until governments and missionaries used military violence or, as with the Montagnais-Naskapi, took advantage of difficult times with conditional offers of "help."

Sexual Discrimination Against Men

As it turns out, women are not the only ones who face common misunderstandings about rape. Men also face their own rape myths.

Some of these rape myths are the same as women's myths: that the man must have consented, or secretly liked it, especially if he became erect.

One pervasive myth is simply that male-victim rape doesn't exist. This pattern of ignoring male-victim sexual assaults shows up in many ways.

Academic researchers note that male-victim sexual assault has hardly been studied in comparison to female-victim sexual assault, and resources for male victims are lacking. One researcher noted that "what is known about adult male sexual victimization is dwarfed by the knowledgebase on female victimization. It is estimated that the help and support for male victims is over 20 years behind that of female victims. Furthermore, male victims have fewer resources and greater stigma [than] female sexual assault victims." Researchers estimate that 10-20% of female sexual assault victims report the crime, but researchers estimate a far lower percentage of male victims report it.[37]

This willingness to ignore male-victim sexual assaults shows up in law as well. In many jurisdictions until very recently, the law only recognized an act as rape if a female was the victim. In English law, until 1994 an assault could only be considered rape if a vagina were penetrated, thus the law did not protect men. Before 1994, unwanted penis-anal penetration was called "buggery" and given a much lighter penalty.

In the United States until 2013, the Department of Justice's Uniform Crime Reporting definition of rape was "carnal knowledge of a female forcibly and against her will"; only in 2013 did the legal definition of rape expand to include males as well.[38] The US just barely made this change before China, which amended its legal code in 2015 to note that rape could apply to both sexes, not just women.[39]

Sexual Assault in Prison

I have encountered this pattern of ignoring male-victim sexual assaults many times. When people ask what myths I address in this book, I like to ask this question: "Do you think there are more female-victim sexual assaults or male-victim sexual assaults in the United States?" And of course, I commonly hear that there are many more female victims of sexual assault than male victims.

This is incorrect. Men are sexually assaulted at far higher rates than women in the United States.

In 2008, research in the United States showed that women were sexually assaulted more than men nearly everywhere – homes, businesses, churches, vehicles, and almost everywhere else. The US Department of Justice (DoJ) produced a report, the National Crime Victimization Survey, which counted 203,830 victims of sexual assault. 39,590 of these victims were men, and 164,240 victims were women.

However, this survey was incomplete. It explicitly did not include prisons or military bases.[40]

That same year, the DoJ also estimated the number of sexual assault victims in prisons, jails, and juvenile detention facilities. The survey did not count the number of sexual assault incidents, but rather the prevalence: the number of people assaulted one or more times. The survey showed over 216,600 people who claimed to have been sexually assaulted at least once within the past 12 months.

The number of sexual assault incidents was much higher, as many inmates were assaulted repeatedly. 81% of youth who were victimized by other youth in juvenile detention facilities reported being victimized more than once, and 32% of these youth reported being victimized more than 10 times. 88% of youth who reported sexual assault by staff reported more than one incident, and 27% reported at least 10 incidents. Among adults, one half to two thirds who reported a sexual assault reported more than one incident. Given that there were over 216,600 known victims of sexual assault in prison, with many of them repeatedly victimized, and about 203,830 known incidents of assault outside of prison, there were more sexual assault incidents inside prison than outside in the United States in 2008.[41]

The report does not state how many inmate victims were male or female, but it notes that the "vast majority of prison sexual assault victims are male." Men were 93% of the prison population in 2008, and women just 7%.[42,43]

To make a very rough estimate of male and female overall sexual assault victims in prisons, let us calculate it in proportion to how many men and women were in prison. Thus as a rough estimate, since about 216,600 people were sexually assaulted in correctional facilities and 93% of the population was male, let's estimate .93 x 216,600 = 201,438 male victims of sexual assault in correctional facilities. To estimate the number of female victims of sexual assault, .07 x 216,600 = 15,162.

When I count that each victim of sexual assault in prison was assaulted only once (a gross underestimate), and I add the counts of male and female assaults together inside and outside prison, I get these numbers: in 2008, there were at least 241,028 sexual assaults of men in the United States, and there were at least 179,402 sexual assaults of women. In other words, despite men having higher privilege than women in so many facets of life, men actually suffer far more sexual predation than women in the United States. Nothing indicated that 2008 was an unusual year, and so I believe these approximate levels of sexual assault continue as I write in 2024.

Unsurprisingly, being in prison makes it harder to deal with sexual assault. The DoJ report noted that both the psychological impact and risk of contracting sexual diseases are much worse after being assaulted in prison compared to sexual assaults outside prison.[44]

Anecdotal data suggests that prison sexual assault is common in many authoritarian nations. Reports from 2021 and 2022 hint at similar troubles in Russia. Russian lawyer Snezhana Muntyan defends many victims of sexual assault in Russian prisons and she noted how Russian law officially treats prisoners equally and with dignity, but in practice this is not the case. Ex-prisoners describe large extortion schemes run by the guards but executed by long-time prisoners, called "activists," who do the guards' dirty work under their orders.

One prisoner named Ivan described begging family and friends to send tens of thousands of rubles to avoid being raped. After he secured 50,000 rubles, he was transferred to another facility. In another incident, prisoner activists demanded a prisoner write a report saying everything was fine, and he had no complaints. He refused to lie, so he was beaten for hours and raped by four men several times each. These activists who made the threats and committed the sexual abuse were long-time prisoners with special relationships with the guards, and clearly acted on their orders and with their approval. The activists had special jobs and salaries at the prisons, could move around the prison freely, and could access prisoners' personnel files. Activist prisoners even have a separate menu, while normal prisoners eat "food for furry animals."[45] Other prisoners found that doctors would fabricate diagnoses to enable torturing prisoners in prison hospitals.[46] Many Russian ex-prisoners shared similar stories.

In healthy nations where anyone may hold anyone else accountable for inappropriate behavior, and everybody stands for a culture of mutual respect, this sort of abuse simply does not occur. Such widespread abuse of people by their own neighbors or fellow citizens only happens in unhealthy nations that make it illegal for people to hold each other accountable for their behavior. Healthy nations honor each member's boundaries. By abusing and humiliating people for years, prisons in unhealthy nations train inmates to tolerate having their boundaries violated.

Rulers maintain control by acting abusively. The more cruel the rulers behave, the stronger their control. This was clear with US chattel slavery, where slaveowners benefited by selling slaves away from their families. This cruelty reduced black people's solidarity and helped solidify the slaveowners' rule. Cruelty in prisons fulfills a similar function, where vicious cruelty in prisons scares both imprisoned and unimprisoned citizens into obedience. The more cruel the prisons, the more willingly people will remain compliant to avoid being sent to prisons, and the more they tolerate being exploited outside of prisons. Thus abuse simply begets further abuse.

Hurtful Attitudes Towards Girls and Boys

Sadly, both girls and boys often face hurtful or dismissive sexist attitudes from adults.

The most common hurtful attitude towards girls that I see is some variation of "you're not good enough" or "you're not as productive as boys." In countries where parents commonly kill a child based on their sex, like China, India, Nepal, and South Korea, girls are far more likely to be killed than boys. In China and India alone, approximately 2,000,000 girls are lost each year due to selective abortion or infanticide. Some regions of China have 140 men for every 100 women.[47] And Chinese orphanages are full of girls given up for adoption.[48]

Around the world, polling shows that about one out of every six people believe that women are inferior to men. Even more tragically, approximately equal numbers of women and men believe this. In Russia and India, almost half the respondents believe in women's inferiority. In many countries, including Brazil, the United States, Turkey, and Germany, over one in six respondents believed women are supposedly less capable than men at holding jobs, teaching, gaining an education, or earning money.[49]

These attitudes are hurtful towards girls for a few reasons. They do not value the girl and what she has to give for its own sake. When girls hear themselves compared with boys in negative ways, this can encourage them to constantly compare themselves to others, a sure path to insecurity.

Boys commonly face a very different hurtful attitude which suggests that boys are inherently selfish, uncaring, or abusive. The most common manifestation is the phrase, "boys will be boys," and people who excuse male rapists commonly say this phrase as if sexual assault were part of boys' nature.

Mulayam Singh Yadav was a political leader in India in April 2015 when he responded to concerns about rape by saying, "boys are boys."[50] American researcher Karen Weiss studied rape myths in the United States and found that a common excuse or explanation for rapists is that "boys will be boys."[51]

While rape is clearly hurtful to the victims, this attitude that "boys will be boys" is hurtful to boys and men. The selfishness that drives some men to rape is pathological; it is not men-being-themselves. In unhealthy nations that encourage deep selfishness, rape is simply another common and disastrous result. After all, rape is simply a behavior in which one person is being extremely selfish.

No little boy was born to act so hurtfully. Just like girls, boys were born with their hearts open, giving their deepest love. When adults excuse or explain deeply inappropriate behavior by implicitly claiming that selfishness or hurtfulness is part of boys' nature, this sends an abusive message to boys and men. Unfortunately, because unhealthy nations encourage deep selfishness, these sexist attitudes towards boys are often not even recognized as hurtful.

People commonly live up or down to the expectations set for them. It takes great personal strength to hold oneself to much higher standards than what others expect. When adults teach girls that they are less valuable or less capable than boys, the easier path for girls may well be to live in a way that justifies this hurtful attitude. Likewise, when boys and young men repeatedly hear that "boys will be boys," some will start to internalize the belief that selfish or uncaring behavior is simply part of who-they-are. These hurtful and wrong attitudes can become self-fulfilling prophecies.

By adulthood, many people are used to being held to low standards, so this may no longer seem so hurtful. However, at some point, it is deeply hurtful for every child that is held to low standards and low expectations. Nobody likes being treated as if they are basically less capable or basically selfish. In unhealthy nations where adults are not allowed to hold each other accountable for inappropriate behavior (because this is supposedly the job for police and courts), few people have much practice holding each other to a high standard of behavior, and so I believe many parents struggle to hold their children to high standards in a loving way.

I have seen the excitement and self-assurance in girls' faces when they're told they can do or be whatever they want when they grow up. And I have seen boys grow in confidence and thoughtfulness when their parents lovingly hold them accountable for inappropriate behavior, holding them to a high standard of what it means to be a good man.

All children are very capable, and all children are born giving their deepest love. Believing anything less is deeply hurtful and reinforces the worst aspects of unhealthy nations.

Equal Respect While Acknowledging the Differences

It is not important to me whether women or men suffer more sexual assaults in any particular unhealthy nation. Because men's and women's experiences are so different, I do not find comparison very helpful.

Women's experiences of sexual assault typically occur in their day-to-day lives, outside of prisons. Domestic violence, date rape, and predation by family members or strangers generate a background feeling of unsafety many women have told me they carry routinely as they move through life. And of course, many women who go to prison are horribly abused there.

Few men seem to truly sympathize with women's experience and consider what it would be like to routinely feel unsafe or feel the need to regularly take extra precautions. Similarly, few women seem to understand the disproportionate sexual assaults that men face in certain settings.

This is why I do not ask what group suffers more. In some settings in unhealthy nations, women may receive more sexual assaults, and in other settings men receive more. *The point is that neither men nor women are safe in unhealthy nations.* Sexism is just another divisive scam imposed by rulers, like racism, hate campaigns, privilege, and so on. Sadly, like these other scams, many men and women adopt sexist attitudes that male superiority is somehow natural or justified.

Some feminists justify seeking equal rights for women by saying that women are just as capable as men at certain tasks, or just as smart or just as ambitious.

Often I agree, but I don't find this argument helpful. Women and men are equally capable in many ways, and also we each bring something special. Men and women have strengths that complement each other. This is why people of healthy nations emphasize balance. If women and men were exactly the same, we would be interchangeable and there would be no need for balance.

Thus, saying that women should be treated respectfully because they are just like men misses the point. A nation can give equal respect to men and women while fully acknowledging their differences. I believe this is the basis for a healthy nation: the group welcomes everyone's sacred gifts, everyone's special contributions, everyone's love. A healthy nation maintains a baseline of mutual respect that applies equally to everyone all the time, celebrating people's differences as well as similarities.

Systemic sexism also has a big impact on people's sexual relationships, as authorities commonly make rules about many aspects of human intimacy. The next chapter, *Chapter 25: Sexual Freedom vs Sexual Repression*, illuminates many of these patterns in unhealthy nations. It also shows how healthy nations encourage people to have deeply satisfying relationships throughout their lives.

Chapter 25: Sexual Freedom vs Sexual Repression

I had to overcome a big misconception after I started hearing about matriarchies.

The words "matriarchy" and "patriarchy" sound similar. The suffix "-archy" means to rule, and I figured if men rule in patriarchal societies, women must rule in matriarchal societies. I assumed matriarchies are the same sort of culture, just with a different sex on top.

Fortunately, I was wrong!

In 2006, Cynthia Barnes visited the Mosuo who live inside China's borders. She described what she found as "not so much a kingdom of women as a kingdom of family." Instead of just men's needs or just women's needs being taken into account, everyone's needs were met.

There were no politicians or preachers encouraging "family values," no "broken homes," no social workers worried about single mothers, and no rape. There was no poverty, shame or stigma resulting from parents separating. Both men and women had sexual relationships as they felt the urge, and relationships waned when they ceased to be satisfying.

I don't believe there are "right" and "wrong" ways for people to have consenting relationships. However, healthy nations have norms that encourage each person to find deep satisfaction throughout their lives and feel deep freedom in all their relationships. Different healthy nations do this in different ways.

In unhealthy nations many people go their entire lives without a deeply satisfying intimate relationship. Commonly imposed norms cause many people to feel stuck or trapped in their primary relationship rather than free.

What would it be like to live in a nation that continuously encourages everyone to have satisfying relationships? And how can healthy nations be vastly more satisfying and secure for everybody, women, men and children?

How Can Sexual Freedom Generate a Profoundly Free Society?

Healthy nations around the world have a huge variety of beliefs and social structures that promote satisfying relationships. One such belief common in many healthy nations of South America and around the world is *partible paternity*, the recognition that a child can have multiple fathers. In these nations, including the Kulina, Barí, Matis, Yequana, and others, women can be partially pregnant, and most sexually active women are.[1]

The underlying belief is that a fetus forms in a woman from the accumulation of semen. If a woman stopped having sex, people in these nations believe her pregnancy would pause.

Like any mother, these women feel a responsibility to give their child every advantage they can. Thus women seek out joyful sex from an assortment of men, each of whose contributions she somehow values. She may value one lover for his leadership, another for his sense of humor, and another for his kindness. She may seek out sex with other men for their creativity, strength, wisdom, knowledge, good looks, or hunting prowess.

In such nations, women honor their children by having sex with the most attractive men they can, in the recognition that the essence of each man will be imbued into her child. Of course, fulfilling this responsibility is commonly a pleasurable affair as well.

Indeed, the more men this aspiring mother has sex with, the more stable her child's life will be, as each man then embraces his role as one of several fathers. Children may have 2, 12, or any number of fathers at birth, each man feeling fully invested in the wellbeing of the young one, and none bearing the responsibilities of fatherhood alone.

Social norms like these have profound implications for men's, women's, and children's ability to live freely and find satisfaction in their lives.

Children: children in these nations have many adults supporting them, mentoring them, and modeling for them as they grow up. If one parent dies, they have many others they can rely on. If one father dies, others are available to provide for the family so that the children are never solely dependent on a single father.

Women: Women who want strong men in their lives and the lives of their children do not depend on just a single man. The mother may decide to begin a sexual relationship with a man, and even if one of them breaks off the relationship, she will still be ok and her children will still be ok because she has a lot of other support from other fathers.

She is also more free to leave unsatisfying relationships. If a lover treats her poorly, or if she and a man disagree about some major life choice and want to go separate ways, she doesn't have to consider how hard it would be for herself and her children if she leaves the man. A particular man might be incredibly important to her, but she has so many other sources of support that she's not overly dependent on any one relationship lasting forever.

With so many people supporting each child, women are more free to invest energy outside mothering, including craft work, caring for the home, time out in the wilderness away from the village, cultivating their creative energies in art, music or dance, spending time with other adults and children, or whatever they choose.

And women are free to take on new lovers and leave old lovers as they wish. Women's sexual freedom isn't restricted as it is in legallly-enforced nuclear families. Having sex with a man who isn't a father doesn't jeopardize her relationships with the fathers, and breakups don't jeopardize her safety or her children's safety.

All this makes having a baby and rearing that child a much safer and more comfortable prospect for women.

Men: Men benefit tremendously from this narrative and social structure. As with women, men are free to let relationships ebb and flow, knowing their relationship with their children doesn't depend on staying in an intimate relationship with the mother. The man can continue to provide for the children and mother even as he finds new lovers, and perhaps takes on a second or third family to support. Men share the responsibilities of providing for the family and raising children with other men.

I believe men in these nations also feel a profound freedom few men experience in unhealthy nations: the freedom to risk their lives in service of the people they love, knowing that no one risks starvation or homelessness if the man dies.

What happens if a man is a woman's only husband and his children's only father? What if he's the only provider, with the woman tending the home while the man generates income?

As the only husband and father, even if he loves and is loved by a woman and their children, his life becomes too important to risk, which means he is not as free as he could be. In some unhealthy nations a single mother whose husband dies can find a job and generate income, but since she is also taking care of children, this becomes very difficult at best. Many men find nuclear families a very difficult trap to navigate in part because being the only male adult makes the stakes higher for any risky decision.

In unhealthy nations, a man may have an unsatisfying job and want to start a business that he knows could be risky. Alternatively, he may have some political view he wants to express freely but worries about speaking out and losing his job. Being the only male adult in the family makes the risks of potential failure or loss of income higher stakes than it needs to be.

One friend's story illustrates this masculine trap in unhealthy nations. A friend, whom I'll call Seamus, was one of 11 siblings. In his 20s, Seamus became politically conscious, learning about all manner of political and corporate corruption and he began exploring nontraditional ways of life. He tried to speak with his father about these ideas and alternative life paths, but his father wasn't interested. He said that every ounce of energy had to be focused on keeping his factory job so he could provide for his wife and children.

Seamus believes his father didn't want to risk getting angry at his employer or hopeful for a different life because he just didn't believe he had energy for that. Instead of broadening his awareness and considering other possible life paths which might be more satisfying, he purposely closed himself off from other possibilities so that he could continue to provide for his family. After all, his wife and many children whom he loved depended on him – and only him.

In nations where children have many fathers, I believe this kind of problem is much less likely to occur than in unhealthy nations.

And it turns out that encouraging people to have pleasurable sex more often has a lot of other benefits too.

Sexual Sharing: When the Nation Encourages People to Have Sex With Someone Other Than Their Regular Partner

Human communities can develop very strong bonds indeed when people feel free to take on sexual partners besides their spouse.

The Inuit found that exchanging sexual partners helped strengthen long-distance bonds. Greenlandic-Danish explorer Knud Ramusen was pleasantly surprised to find one village chief gave up space in his bed for Ramusen with the understanding that Ramusen and the chief's wife would likely have sex. In the harsh arctic climate, villages may be very far apart. Bonds formed by sexual sharing helped to ensure that people would come to each others' aid even across great distances.[2]

Sex can strengthen bonds across entire communities, as the Kulina illustrate. In a ritual called *the order to get meat*, women travel in a group at dawn from house to house. At each stop, they sing to the men and "order" them to go hunting. One or more women step forward with a stick and bang on the house; they will have sex with the man that night if he is successful in his hunt. They have only one rule: in this ritual, women are not allowed to select their husband.

With a pretend reluctance, men go off to hunt, but not before holding a meeting together where they agree on a time and place to meet up before returning. Each man hunts alone, and before returning to the village, they all meet at their rendezvous. Here, the men who caught animals share with those who don't so that every man returns to the village with something.

When the men finally enter the village, the women form a large semicircle and sing erotic songs, provocatively asking the men to share their "meat." The men put their catch in a large pile in the center, sometimes with wry smiles and great drama. After dinner, each woman goes to bed with the man she selected. Everybody wins! As one researcher described, the "Kulina engage in this ritual with great humor and perform it regularly."[3]

Sex can also be healing and enlivening for observers. The Huron had a ceremony called Andacwander, most commonly requested by older men and women. When the ceremony served an old woman, all the unmarried young women in a village would meet in the old woman's house, and each young woman would decide with which young man she wished to have sex. Chiefs would notify the chosen young men who would arrive the following night. Couples occupied the entire house end-to-end and remained until dawn. The old woman and chiefs would sing and rattle tortoiseshells through the night. When Andacwander ceremonies were performed for an old man, a young woman would have sex with the older man. This was not a rare ceremony.[4]

Transition Stories

Is an intimate relationship only successful if it lasts "until death do we part," or is it successful if it lasts only as long as both people feel satisfied?

When French Jesuit missionaries lived with the Huron, they felt frustrated because the Huron believed that marriages should last only as long as they are satisfying. One Jesuit described "the ordinary practice of the savages … to change wives at almost every season of the year."[5]

Both men and women were fully autonomous and could leave their partner at will. When Jesuits tried to convince middle aged men to convert to Christianity, they commonly heard men say that their wife would likely leave them, and they would be unable to remarry.

The Jesuits tried to impose their own understanding of marriage and cheating on the Huron, and so they missed many nuances about their relationships. In practice, individuals might commonly have sex outside of marriage or divorce before childbirth, but rarely afterwards.[6]

The Huron raised young men to take deep responsibility for their actions. If a young woman with many lovers became pregnant, each man would claim the child as his own. The young lady would then choose which to take as her husband.

The Jesuits were shocked to find young Huron women vying to see who could take the most sexual partners. One Jesuit, Gabriel Sagard, noted that each village had its "procurer" who helped arrange sexual liaisons. Another report by Samuel de Champlain, who became governor of the colony of New France, described his surprise when he left his cabin and a woman followed him and asked if he would like to have sex.[7]

None of this suited the Jesuits, who complained about the "libertinage to which the girls and women here abandon themselves." The Jesuits repeatedly tried to convert the Huron to Christianity, and the women especially kept refusing because they did not want to bind themselves to a single man for their whole lives. One Jesuit noted that the church "cannot hold the women to the marriages." He said marriage is only a "conditional promise to live together so long as each shall continue to render the service that they mutually expect from each other."

In other words, the Huron liked to have their relationships last only as long as they were satisfying. This way, relationships could be nourishing and enlivening, and never a trap.

Huron men normally lived with their wives and their wives' extended family in a longhouse after marriage. A man who did not stay on good terms with his wife or mother-in-law risked eviction, and men who converted to Christianity early on could face severe rejection not only from the wife's clan but also from his own.

Clearly many Huron, and especially the women, recognized how terrible Christianity could be for them, severely limiting their ability to have satisfying relationships and live without shame. The Jesuits described what happened to one man who remained Christian despite his family repeatedly imploring him to stop:

> They drove him away from their cabins, and refused to give him anything to eat; they reproached him with the death of one of his nieces, who had been baptized. He was left without means of support, and was compelled to do what is usually the work of women. He was mocked at, and spurned from every company; and quarrels were picked with him. If at any time he was invited to a feast, some insolent persons present would call out that he should not have been invited, because he was a Christian, and because he brought misfortune wherever he went; that he might certainly make up his mind to die sooner than he expected; and that he would be clubbed to death as a Sorcerer.[8]

I believe many Huron recognized how much the Christian missionaries sought to limit their sexual and other freedoms, and reacted energetically to protect their nation.

When everyone is free to seek a satisfying relationship, and each person respects others' autonomy, a huge number of potential social systems are possible, including life-long marriage that people enter into on their own terms.

Ohiyesa described how the American government directed him to survey Sioux families but not to recognize more than one wife. However, an old man named White Bull had two wives, and when Ohiyesa told him he must choose one to satisfy the American government requirements, White Bull refused, saying, "these two women are sisters, both of whom have been my wives for over half a century. I know the way of the white man; he takes women unknown to each other and to his law. These two have been faithful to me and I have been faithful to them. Their children are my children and their grandchildren are mine. We are now living together as brother and sisters. All the people know that we have been happy together, and nothing but death can separate us."[9]

That White Bull and his wives felt happy together was not relevant to the unhealthy nation, which was intent on forcing people into highly restrictive family structures.

In his book *The Sexual Life of Savages*, Bronislaw Malinowski witnessed a time when the Trobriands retained some of their sexual openness, though not as much as they had before Christian missionaries arrived. He described how Trobriand villages would have buildings specially made so that young couples could stay there temporarily, for weeks or months or even just an hour. The town Omarakana had five of these buildings, and Kasana'i had four.[10]

However, Malinowski arrived long after the first missionaries who commonly directed shame at anyone who behaved as the missionaries didn't like, preaching and singling people out for seeking satisfying sexual relationships. Ten years before Malinowski's visit, each town had had 15 of these buildings, and the oldest residents remembered when the town had 30. Sometimes fathers even built these buildings for their daughters. This reduction in the number of buildings that supported romantic relationships occurred for a variety of reasons in addition to the missionaries' shaming, including a large decrease in population and different living arrangements as more people moved into missionary compounds.

Psychotherapist Wilhelm Reich believed that withheld sexual energy was the root of human neuroses. He noted that sex-negative morality based on restrictive marriage and families actually generates widespread antisocial behavior, perversions, and neuroses. In contract, in sex-positive nations, he saw no perversions, neuroses, or antisocial sexual behavior. Common perversions and neuroses may not necessarily be the goal of authorities, but a necessary by-product of nations that work so hard to train people to ignore their natural urges and willingly work unsatisfying jobs.[11]

Malinowski saw this difference when he visited the sexually open Trobriands and their sexually repressed neighbors on a nearby island. None of the dozens of Trobriands he met showed any signs of nervousness or neurotic behavior. He said, "Nervous tics, compulsory actions or obsessive ideas were not to be found," and he characterized them as "open, gay, hearty, and accessible."[12]

In contrast, after staying with the sexually repressed people on the nearby island for a few months, Malinowski said, "my first and strongest impression was that this was a community of neurasthenics… [After spending time with the Trobriands,] it was astonishing to find oneself among a community of people distrustful of the newcomer, impatient in work, arrogant in their claims, though easily cowed and extremely nervous when tackled more energetically." Malinowski found the women very reticent, and found numerous people "affected by nervousness."

Cynthia Barnes described the agricultural Mosuo people, and related stories of their sexual openness as well as Chinese officials' attempts to repress their sexuality.[13]

Barnes noted that when a young Mosuo lady reached puberty around 13 or 14, she would receive her own bedroom with two doors, one entering the inner family area and one opening onto the street. In her room, called a flower room, she could have visitors as she wished, and young women had complete autonomy. She could easily have lovers visit. There was never an expectation that sexual partners raise the children, as a woman's brothers and other neighbors helped raise her children. Every man knew that his sister's children were his primary responsibility, and so adults could have many sexual partners without having to worry about who was or wasn't the father.

Indeed, sexually active Mosuo men and women would have shamed anyone for demanding "sexual fidelity." Any request for fidelity would be seen as a restraint, an act of aggression that makes sex an exchange or negotiation. Any sign of jealousy likewise resulted in shame and ridicule, as it was seen as controlling.

One Mosuo person, Yang Erche Namu, described how incredibly freeing it was as a child in this nation: "We children could roam at our own will and visit from house to house and village to village without our mothers ever fearing for our safety. Every adult was responsible for every child, and every child in turn was respectful of every adult."

Namu also described how freeing this society was for young women who wanted to have sexual partners without unnecessary fears: "Sassy and confident, [a Mosuo girl will] grow up cherished in a circle of male and female relatives… When she joins the dances and invites a boy into her flower room, it will be for love, or lust, or whatever people call it when they are operating on hormones and heavy breathing. She will not need that boy – or any other – to have a home, to make a 'family.' She already knows that she will always have both."

All this illustrates why Cynthia Barnes would call the Mosuo a "Kingdom of Family." The nation supports the needs and desires of everyone in the family.

Showing similar disturbances as Europeans, the Chinese have worked hard to disrupt these beautiful Mosuo social norms. In 1956, Chinese government officials began lecturing the Mosuo on the dangers of unrestrained sexuality, urging them to adopt "normal" marriages. One year, the Chinese arrived with a movie showing actors dressed like the Mosuo who had gone mad and were covered with syphilis. The Mosuo burned the movie setup.

However, Chinese officials persevered, with Yang Erche Namu recalling "meetings night after night where they harangued and criticized and interrogated… [The Chinese officials] ambushed men on their way to their lovers' houses, they dragged couples out of their beds and exposed people naked to their own relatives' eyes." The Chinese stopped essential shipments of children's clothes and seed grain, until finally many starving Mosuo people agreed to adopt the Chinese system of restrictive marriage.

There is a saying that "misery loves company," and these stories from the Chinese and Christians show how true that can be. Instead of seeing healthy nations as an example to learn from, many sexually repressed nations have worked to spread their repressive practices to their neighbors. Instead of seeing the beauty in sexual sharing and openness, these close-minded nations pushed their unsatisfying patterns on people who didn't want them.

Two Kinds of Sex Economies: One Based on Morals, the Other Based on Pleasure and Connection

When most people speak of a nation's "economy," they're talking about how a nation moves resources around. Similarly, Wilhelm Reich used the phrase "sex economy" to describe how a nation decides who can have sex and when.

There are essentially two kinds of sex economies. In one, people's sexual activity is regulated primarily through their natural sexual instincts and people's desire for pleasure and connection. In nations that welcome people to give their love fully, this also includes welcoming people to give their sexual love fully.

This doesn't mean anything goes. For example, the Huron disapproved of public displays of sexual intimacy between men and women.[14] Healthy nations can still agree on norms of behavior so that nobody bothers anybody else. But these norms didn't severely limit Huron people's ability to enjoy satisfying intimate relationships.

In another example of a nation placing restrictions that served a good purpose, the Apache man Geronimo said he was not considered ready to marry until he joined the War Council at the age of 17. However, he said, "I had not been under the control of any individual," and indeed he had already been lovers with a woman named Alope for a long time. When his nation acknowledged that he was ready to marry, he excitedly sought her as his wife.[15]

When healthy nations set clear expectations of what it means to be an adult and embrace rites of passage into adulthood, children know how to prepare and what to work towards. Geronimo knew his nation's expectations of him, and I believe this was helpful. In this context, restrictions against premature marriage are not intended to unnecessarily restrict young adults, but rather channel the elders' wisdom about what childhood training a person needs before they are ready to be a parent.

The other basic form of sex economy is based on morals, internalized abstract ideas of right and wrong. In nations with heart-closing narratives, children can learn that certain behaviors, ideas, or feelings are inherently bad, dirty, or evil, including normal healthy sexual feelings and behavior.

Unhealthy nations train people to withhold their love, and this includes training people to withhold their sexual love. Thus rulers commonly control how, when and why people may have sex, and punish those who disobey. In unhealthy nations where rulers impose law on everyone else, restraining and dividing people would be very difficult if each individual felt fully empowered to seek pleasure and connection with anybody they chose.

Thus children are commonly taught that if they obey their elders, they are good, and if not, they are bad. Many children in unhealthy nations learn to associate severe guilt or shame with deep pleasure, making it difficult to have satisfying intimacies in adulthood. Thus many children learn to suppress or inhibit their sexual feelings.

Unhealthy nations train individuals to control themselves by denying their own healthy urges towards pleasure, deep connection, and dignity. Rulers that try to cause division between people likewise encourage division within a person, where a person sees their own healthy urges as bad or dirty. When people act based on internalized abstract ideas of right and wrong and fears of being bad – that is, when people act based on morals – unhealthy self-restraint and pleasure-rejection are the results. People are trained to control their supposedly evil or immoral urges, when they are actually denying their natural human desires for pleasure and connection.

Unfortunately, in sex economies that regulate sex with morals and excessive restrictions, rulers use many techniques to discourage deep sexual pleasure and connection between people.

Repression of Human Sexuality

Driving a Wedge Between Men and Women

Two people can have satisfying sex when each person respects the other and wants the other person to feel pleasure. When one person thinks they're superior or inferior, this diminishes the couples' capacity for deep connection and mutual pleasure.

Unhealthy nations commonly define a family as one man and one woman, or one man and many women. Either way, unhealthy nations embrace systemic sexism by placing the man in a privileged position, and men are commonly trained throughout their lives to think they deserve it.

In the Islamic Quran, Allah says that while women and men have similar rights, men have responsibility above women. For anyone who doubts this, the same verse assures the reader that "Allah is Almighty, All-Wise."[16] The Quran also notes that "Men are the caretakers of women, as men have been provisioned by Allah over women… And righteous women are devoutly obedient…"[17]

Islam clearly sets men in a position of authority over women. The Quran commonly relates to women as the "other," many times speaking only to men. In one verse, Allah says, "Enter into Paradise, you and your wives, with delight."[18]

One Muslim woman named Waajida described how she mentored young Muslim girls. She did not want to exclude men from her work, but found many Muslim men combative and dismissive, labeling her a feminist as if this were a bad thing. She said, "I cannot find the kind of men out there that are willing to sit on a table and respectfully negotiate and discuss and feel the plight of women the way women feel them." She was even called Margaret Thatcher when she suggested women should sit beside men instead of behind them in classrooms, or for both women and men to present at programs rather than just men.[19]

The Christian Bible likewise places men in a superior position over women, training men to think they're superior.

Regarding women's voice, the Bible says, "Let your women keep silence in the churches: for it is not permitted unto them to speak; but they are commanded to be under obedience, as also saith the law."[20]

Regarding equality in marriage, the Bible commands, "Wives, submit to your own husbands, as to the Lord."[21]

Regarding women's role as mentors and leaders, the Bible commands, "I suffer not a woman to teach, nor to usurp authority over the man, but to be in silence."[22] It also notes, "I would have you know, that the head of every man is Christ; and the head of the woman is the man."[23]

In such nations, many men sadly adopt the authoritarian belief in their own superiority. In one instance, a Christian church needed to hire a secretary, and a man was available and needed the work. However, the church would not hire him, as it considered secretarial work too demeaning for a man. The pastor sought out a woman instead.[24]

Threat of Punishment for Sex Without Authorities' Approval

Authoritarian nations commonly regulate what relationships are appropriate or legitimate, and forbid others. Many unhealthy nations then forbid or discourage sex outside approved relationships.

The Quran requires that fornicators (people having unapproved sex) be whipped 100 times each.[25] It also notes, "Do not go near adultery. It is truly a shameful deed and an evil way."[26]

The Christian Bible and Jewish Torah note that a husband who discovers that his wife had sex before marriage must bring the woman outside her father's house and "the men of her city shall stone her with stones that she die: because she hath wrought folly in Israel, to play the whore in her father's house: so shalt thou put evil away from among you."[27]

The Bible likewise punishes adultery, with both people required to be stoned to death. In some cases, men and women in unhealthy nations receive comparable punishments for disallowed sex. In other cases, women are punished much worse, or abusive men not punished at all.[28]

This discouragement from pre-marital sex can show up even in secular settings. I was a young boy when a doctor showed me pictures of men with disgusting venereal diseases. I was told that men with these diseases felt searing pain every time they urinated, and they would have these diseases the rest of their lives. The doctor then said that this was a predictable consequence of having premarital sex.

Nearly every unhealthy nation pressures adults into some form of restrictive marriage, threatening people with many problems if a child is born outside marriage. If a child is born out of wedlock, the mother may be stuck raising the child alone, or the father may lose access to his child. Unmarried parents often must pay higher taxes.

One common form of restriction is to outlaw or shame non-heterosexual sex. Countries like China in the 1980s[29] and Nigeria in the 2020s[30] outlaw homosexual sex. Iran punishes homosexual sex with death.[31]

Discouraging and Denying Pleasure

Rulers in unhealthy nations have found many disturbing ways to discourage people from feeling deep pleasure. These include training people to feel shame about their bodies, shame about their urge to seek pleasure, and even suppressing people's physical capacity for pleasure.

French king Louis IX supported Vincent Beauvais in writing the Speculum Doctrinale, a widely referenced encyclopedia in the Middle Ages. Beauvais shamed pleasure even within a marriage when he wrote, "A man who loves his wife very much is an adulterer. Any love for someone else's wife, or too much love for one's own, is shameful… The upright man should love his wife with his judgment, not his affections."[32]

Christian leaders have equated pleasure and sin for a very long time. Saint Augustine lived from 354-430 CE. He believed procreation was divinely ordained, but it was initially supposed to be like eating or walking, without any lust involved. According to him, sex isn't the problem, lust is the problem. According to Augustine, God supposedly created humans with free will, but then people started acting out of lust, and Original Sin occurred and humanity succumbed to sin forever. Of course, all humans at some level desire pleasure. By equating pleasure and sin, Augustine sought to convince people that humans were inclined to sin.[33]

Saint Augustine himself was mirroring even earlier dismissiveness of the natural human urge for pleasure. Saint Paul, who lived approximately 5 CE-65 CE, said, "For if you live according to the flesh, you will die; but if by the Spirit you put to death the misdeeds of the body, you will live."[34] The Bible itself implicitly condemns the human urge for pleasure when it says, "There is a way that seems right to a man, but in the end it leads to death."[35]

This trend sadly continues in recent years, as shown by the well-known American Christian minister Billy Graham. When someone asked him whether the Bible forbids unmarried people from having sex, Graham responded, "I can't help but wonder if he is only looking for an excuse to live a life of self-indulgence and immorality… Yes, we live in a sex-saturated society–but with God's help we can follow a far better path."[36]

For many centuries starting in ancient Rome, Christian leaders trained men to see orgasm as deviant and a loss of control. This trained men to reject their own urge for deep sexual gratification, and it also trained men to see women as a threat. If a man's orgasm supposedly represents a concerning loss of control, then who gains control? These same teachers taught that women who seduced men sought to control or dominate them. When pleasure itself is seen as a threat, those who inspire pleasure can likewise be framed as threats.[37]

The Malleus Maleficarum, the Catholic Church's medieval handbook on witchcraft, reinforced this masculine fear of women and pleasure when it noted, "All witchcraft comes from carnal lust, which in women is insatiable… Wherefore for the sake of fulfilling their lusts they consort with devils." The Catholic Church associated pleasure and lust with women, witchcraft, and the devil, and trained men to recognize all these as threats.[38]

From the late 300s CE until the 1500s, the Catholic Church imposed its perspectives on millions of people throughout Europe, sometimes in alliance with local kings and sometimes on its own. It threatened endless suffering after death and severe punishment before death to anyone who did not comply. This illustrates how authorities can impose structural sexism and require sexist beliefs simply as a condition of surviving in an unhealthy nation.

This does not excuse any particular man who adopts hurtful attitudes, and many European women and men during this time joined social movements such as the Albigensians and Waldensians which sought alternative religious and social practices.[39]

However, as but one example of the Catholic Church's response, the Church launched the Albigensian Crusade of 1209-1229 CE, when French Catholic armies massacred huge numbers of people, including almost the entire population of the city of Béziers, in an effort to stamp out what Pope Innocent III called heretical beliefs.[40] This illustrates how difficult it can be to uphold norms of appropriate behavior when rulers insist on sexism, racism, or other hurtfulness.

And sadly, it has not just been Christians who discourage deep pleasure. The Buddha laid out the Four Noble Truths. The second is the Noble Truth of the Cause of Suffering, which is "craving that causes rebirth and is bound up with pleasure and lust and finds delight now here, now there. That is, the craving for sensual pleasures." The third is the "Noble Truth of the Cessation of Suffering" which "is the complete fading away and destruction of this very craving, its forsaking, its renunciation, the liberation from it, leaving no place for it." Thus Buddhism equates desire with suffering, and especially the desire for sensual pleasures. Renouncing this desire for sensual pleasures is supposedly the path to ending suffering.[41]

Probably the most direct way to limit a person's capacity for sexual pleasure is to cut off parts of their genitals. Many unhealthy nations also do this.

The United Nations Children's Fund defines female genital mutilation (FGM) as "all procedures involving partial or total removal of the female external genitalia or other injury to the female genital organs for non-medical reasons."[42] Many procedures are used, including partial or total removal of the clitoral glans, clitoral hood, labia minora (inner vulva), or labia majora (outer vulva). Additionally, some procedures narrow the vaginal opening by cutting and moving the vulva and moving it with stitching. Other procedures include piercing, cauterizing, scraping, or otherwise injuring the genital area.[43]

Often these surgeries are performed in informal and unclean settings, so immediate consequences of FGM might include infection, urinary problems, shock, death, and severe pain. Longer term complications may include higher risk of birth complications, pain or decreased pleasure during sex, menstrual, vaginal, or urinary problems, and mental health issues including depression or anxiety.

The World Health Organization estimates that over 230 million women globally have experienced FGM, approximately 5.8% of the global female population, with the vast majority living in north-eastern or north-western Africa. Greater than 85% of women 15-49 have experienced FGM in Sudan, Eritrea, Mali, Egypt, Djibouti, Guinea, Somalia.[44,45,46]

Ethiopian woman Bogaletch Gebre described experiencing FGM when she was twelve years old. She and her mother kept crying, and her mother said, "I wish they would do away with this. I wish they would do away with this." But they had been taught this practice would make them "whole women." It wasn't until many years later that Gebre said, "I began to understand that the real purpose of female genital excision was to excise my mind; my ability to live my life with all my senses intact." This practice is known as "removing the dirt," an extremely derogatory and heart-closing label for women's genitalia.

Gebre experienced infections, chronic pain, and physical and psychological numbing and scarring. Her sisters died from it. She has worked with many others to reduce FGM in Ethiopia, and young men and women are increasingly opposing the practice.[47]

The most common form of male genital mutilation is circumcision, a procedure where the sensitive foreskin of a boy or man's penis is removed. Short term complications may include bleeding, pain, shock, infection, or urine retention. The foreskin plays an important role in protecting the soft glans, so men may feel discomfort if this is continually abraded, have painful erections, visible scarring, desensitization and emotional distress including a sense of loss and resentment. Circumcision may cause the sensitive glans, now without its protective covering, to dry out, toughen, and thicken, which causes further desensitization and limits the pleasure a man and his partner may feel during sex.[48]

65 countries have at least 85% of males circumcised.[49] Almost 40% of men are circumcised globally.[50]

Both Judaism and Islam expect males to undergo circumcision, while they have no corresponding practice for women. Besides citing tradition, some religious authorities claim circumcised penises are more hygienic, as if boys could not simply learn how to wash themselves properly.[51,52]

Circumcision in the United States was initially touted by medical authorities in the 1800s as a way to prevent masturbation, which supposedly caused blindness and other disease. When it turned out that masturbation doesn't cause blindness, and circumcision doesn't prevent masturbation, other theories to justify circumcision arose, such as that it prevents syphilis, paralysis, insanity, and cancer.[53]

While international medical authorities such as the World Health Organization unequivocally claim that female genital mutilation is a "violation of the human rights of girls and women" in part because it "violates a person's rights to health, security and physical integrity,"[54] many medical and religious authorities in dozens of countries violate infant boys' health, security, and physical integrity without his consent.

These examples from religious and secular authorities around the world show how, for millennia, unhealthy nations have discouraged people from seeking pleasure and even associate pleasure with immorality or evil.

What impacts has this deep manipulation had on many people's sex lives?

Common Masculine Sexual Confusion

One common feature in unhealthy nations is that many men wind up deeply confused about women's and men's sexuality.

For example, Christians of ancient Rome commonly taught that a woman could only get pregnant on her back.[55] Many scientists in early 20th-century Europe claimed that gratification supposedly is not part of women's nature, or that the vagina is supposedly inherently insensitive, or that women supposedly do not feel pain when giving birth.[56] The English Catholic lord Acton claimed in 1875 that "The majority of women, happily for them and for society, are not very much troubled with sexual feeling of any kind."[57]

Clearly, in sexually repressed nations, male religious, political, and scientific authorities can become quite confused about women. However, I believe many men can become equally confused about their own sexuality.

Authorities had trained men to fear and reject pleasure for millennia, and this has had profound effects on many men's sexual experiences, as Wilhelm Reich's investigation made clear.

Wilhelm Reich began his psychoanalysis career in Vienna in 1919, a time when many psychoanalysts had deep misunderstandings about healthy male sexuality. A man was considered potent if he could have a satisfactory ejaculation in a woman, and he was considered very potent if he could do this with more than one woman in a night. One psychoanalyst even defined male potency as a man's ability to have sex in a way that causes vaginal inflammation.[58]

For years, Reich observed some form of sexual disturbance in all of his women patients, and he believed that about two-thirds of his men patients suffered from sexual disturbances and were incapable of sexual gratification. Either the men could not become erect, lost their erection too early, or ejaculated prematurely.

Reich did not give much thought to the remaining men who seemed able to have satisfactory sex, even though they were otherwise clearly neurotic. However, by 1943 Reich recognized that every single one of his male patients was sexually disturbed, even including the ones who claimed to have satisfactory sex.

Reich believed that the most disturbed men were the ones who viewed sex as a way to possess, overpower, or conquer as many women as possible, and who boasted of "doing it" over and over in one night. He described these men as erectively potent, but noted that they experienced very little or no pleasure at the moment of ejaculation, and many even experienced the opposite – displeasure or disgust. Reich investigated these men's fantasies and found they had conceited or sadistic attitudes. Reich uncovered in these male patients a desire to prove their potency or be admired for their endurance, and thus the behavior was based on a deep insecurity and selfishness. He found that in none of his male cases did a man show any sign of involuntary behavior or loss of conscious control in sex.

Reich studied Malinowski's research on the Trobriands, a healthy nation near Australia, to understand sexuality better. Malinowski noted, "Altogether the [Trobriands] are certain that white men do not know how to carry out intercourse effectively." He also described how "the brevity and lack of vigour of the European performance were caricatured. Indeed, to the native idea, the white man achieves orgasm far too quickly." White men who visited the Trobriands would ejaculate when they felt like it and then end sexual intercourse, whereas Trobriand men would find gratification together with the women.[59]

Reich thus found that all of his male and female patients showed sexual disturbances, including struggling to feel deep pleasure. In contrast, the Trobriands seemed clearly capable of feeling deep pleasure. Malinowski reported one Trobriand woman saying to her lover, "my whole body melts with pleasure… my body feels so pleasant." Reich remarked that his patients seemed incapable of feeling this level of pleasure, instead often feeling stress, anxiety or some other unpleasant response instead.[60]

Reich discovered what healthy sexuality looks like by studying healthy nations. He found that both partners feel deep pleasure and satisfaction together, often lasting for a long time. This showed him not just how unhealthy his patients were, but how deeply even professional psychoanalysts misunderstood human sexuality.

Countless European religious, scientific, and political leaders had trained people to fear and reject pleasure for centuries, resulting in many people having a variety of sexual disturbances. Sadly, Reich's research showed that, at least in some substantial portion of the population, authorities had succeeded.

Sexual Healing: Learning to Give One's Deepest Love

I believe a person's capacity for joyful, pleasurable sex is tied to how fully a person gives their love without inhibition.

A person who withholds their love in life will struggle to give their love fully and joyfully during sex. Different individuals may struggle in different ways, as people learn to close their hearts in different ways. Some may struggle due to low-self worth, low trust in others, fear of losing self-control, selfishness, insecurity, fear of pleasure, shame, or many other reasons, or a mix.

Heart-closure manifests in many different ways. Some people learn to withhold their love by breathing shallowly. Love is like a fire, and just like a fire needs oxygen to burn bright, a person needs oxygen to fuel everything they do. When adults require children to sit endlessly or otherwise do not make space for children's energy, many children learn to breathe shallowly as a way to suppress their own life energy.

People may learn to block their own internal energy and urges with muscular rigidity, something Reich called "armoring." While psychoanalysts at the time mostly focused on talk therapy, Reich found that simply helping people relax their chronic tension could help them release pent up emotions and feel deeper pleasure in life, even restoring their capacity for pleasurable sex.

This chronic, often subconscious muscular tension represents a person's attempt to control or block their own urges, and it limits a person's ability to surrender to pleasurable sexual feelings. When Reich was able to help people surrender to genital gratification, he said, "the patient's personality underwent such a thorough and rapid change that, initially, I was baffled by it." Moralistic attitudes began to seem alien and peculiar, and moralist demands had no effect on these patients.

Before they released their internal restraints, Reich found that his patients would often work mechanically and show little interest in their work, viewing it as a necessary evil. Once they stopped repressing their sexual energy, they sought out only meaningful work which seemed personally interesting. Office employees, businessmen, and mid-level attorneys who didn't really care about their work suddenly found it to be "an almost intolerable burden." Teachers suddenly rejected the usual ways they were expected to relate to children. Reich noted two major changes after patients could experience full sexual gratification: "(1) a growing immersion in a social activity to which one was fully committed; (2) a sharp protest of the psychic organism against mechanical, stultifying work."[61]

In other words, patients who were able to feel deep pleasure and sexual gratification would only seek meaningful activities and they rejected meaningless work. This helps explain why unhealthy nations so consistently train people to reject their own pleasure and natural instincts. People who don't feel deep pleasure are much more willing to tolerate meaningless or self-serving jobs and unsatisfying lives.

Reich described an incredible learning journey: "At the base of the neurotic mechanism, behind all the dangerous, grotesque, irrational fantasies and impulses, I discovered a simple, self-evident, decent core. I found it without exception in every case where I was able to penetrate to a sufficient depth." Reich consistently found that so much perversion and harmful behavior was due to people withholding their love and fearing their own healthy urges, perceptions, and feelings as evil, immoral, or somehow not ok.

However, all energy has to go somewhere, and when a person could not express their feelings and urges in a healthy way, the energy would build up and manifest in unhealthy ways instead, including self-mutilation, grotesque fantasies, overwork, suicide, child rape, alcoholism, and many other problems, with different people showing different disturbed behaviors. These kinds of problems are tragic but predictable consequences of certain ways of raising children, including raising them with morals based on shame and guilt while teaching them to avoid pleasure and connection. Other aspects of child-rearing can ameliorate or worsen these effects.

I learned about this connection between my capacity for joyful sex and my willingness to give my deepest love in life during a difficult time in 2013-2014. In winter and spring 2013, I was dating a woman I'll call Dorothy, and we had a happy and sometimes loud sex life. When I proposed marriage in June 2013, I told her

I wanted to have neighbor-bothering orgasms with her for the rest of our lives, and she giggled and happily accepted my proposal.

A month earlier, I had begun to seriously consider changing my life path. I was not happy with the career I had built serving the so-called defense industry. I felt personally financially secure, but I grew more and more concerned with many problems in my nation and I felt really unhappy with my role. I was either ignoring most of the problems or, through my job, making them worse. I began to feel depressed, as described in Chapter 18.

Shortly after proposing, I began to feel severely trapped. I felt unable to have constructive conversations about my concerns with friends, family and coworkers. I was living a pretend life at work. I began considering how to significantly change my life path.

Immediately after Dorothy accepted my marriage proposal, we agreed on a wedding date and she began planning the wedding. Over a few months, it became clear to me that I had proposed too soon. I was very unhappy in my life path and wanted a significant change, but she wanted to have the life we had anticipated sharing when I proposed. A few times, I suggested we postpone the wedding to give ourselves time to see if we could walk a satisfying path together, but she did not want to question our relationship and conversations quickly became emotionally difficult and unproductive. I did not know how to help us have this difficult but important conversation. The wedding planning continued.

When the depression sank in, my sexual energy vanished. I felt unsatisfied at work, unclear about my intimate relationship, and unsure where to go in life. I was not very good at expressing my feelings clearly, and so I didn't even acknowledge my diminished sexual energy with Dorothy; I just felt nervous believing she probably wanted to have sex while I had no sexual energy at all. Acknowledging the troubles behind my depression would have required acknowledging my concerns about our compatibility, and that was a conversation we were unable to have.

I finally felt a little better when I committed to a date by which I would leave my job and go live at the intentional community full time. Dorothy and I agreed we would remain together as a couple while I went to the community alone and explored life there. By late fall 2013, I knew I would leave sometime in February 2014. This gave me a path forward and something to plan and save for.

I resigned with three weeks' notice in early February 2014. I felt such a relief and so much happy anticipation. Three weeks later, for the first time as an adult, I had no job and no income and I felt freer than ever before. I was taking a big risk and charting my own course into the unknown. Suddenly, my sexual energy came rushing back, and before I left for the community, Dorothy and I played, laughed and had sex in ways we hadn't in months. I felt grateful for her patience during a time when I was struggling.

This experience showed me how closely my sexual energy is tied with my ability to give my love fully in life. Since 2014 I've found many other skills that make sex fun – breathing well, circulating energy, strong self-awareness, grounding, and more. However, any time my sexual energy drops, I take it as a sign that I'm somehow holding back in life. When I stop holding back, my sexual energy returns.

Where Does Sexism Come From?

Like with selfishness, racism, and mass synthetic hatred, sexism ultimately stems from the three core drivers of division:

1. Rulers impose systemic sexism, where women and men are treated differently by the rich and legal authorities. Then they encourage the population to adopt these attitudes, rewarding those who do and often punishing those who don't.

2. Many people trapped in abusive nations learn to adopt sexist attitudes that excuse and justify the role they have in the nation they were born into.

3. Some kinds of child abuse predispose people to adopting very hurtful attitudes.

As with racism, selfishness, and hate, each person is responsible for the attitudes they adopt, regardless of the pressures they face. Unfortunately, these divisive patterns are simply normal in unhealthy nations where rulers encourage and impose hurtful attitudes so that cultures of selfishness and inequality will seem appropriate to many people.

I am not the first to recognize that individual racist or sexist people are not the problem; the problem is a culture that encourages deep division. In their book *Witches, Midwives, and Nurses*, Barbara Ehrenreich and Deirdre English explored the history of sexist oppression of women healers in Europe and the United States. They wrote:

> Our enemy is not just "men" or their individual male chauvinism: It is the whole class system which enabled male, upper class healers to win out and which forced us into subservience. Institutional sexism is sustained by a class system which supports male power.[62]

I agree with this perspective, and the same is true for institutional racism, hatred, and selfishness. Rulers impose systemic sexism and racism. They impose hate campaigns and economies that reward selfishness. Then rulers reward people for believing in ideologies that excuse these hurtful patterns.

Healthy nations show how beautifully people can live together when everyone stands for a culture of mutual respect. Anyone can work to reduce sexism in their community by opening neighbors' hearts and minds, and I always support this. However, the only way to end widespread sexism is to generate a way of life where everybody stands for a culture of mutual respect, and nobody rules over anybody else.

In this part of the book, the spotlight has been on many forms of discrimination – racism, sexism, and hatred. If only this were a complete list of divisive patterns! Sadly, the troubles do not end there. The next section of the book is *Part 7 - Even Deeper Division Through Privilege and Entitlement*, and it reveals how unhealthy nations prevent solidarity by systematically treating some groups decently while deliberately disempowering others.

Part 7 - Creating Deep Division Through Privilege and Entitlement

How is it possible for two neighbors to have very different perspectives on their nation, where one person thinks it is fair and the other thinks it is very unfair?

Chapter 26: Privilege 1 - Lift-and-Turn

Many obstacles make it difficult for people to stand in solidarity in unhealthy nations, including financial desperation, blind beliefs, laws that forbid anybody but police from enforcing the laws, hate campaigns, and land ownership. Terrible as these are, I believe privilege is an even more challenging obstacle to solidarity.

Systems of hierarchical privilege allow authorities to engage in both overt and subtle forms of deep manipulation that make it very difficult for different groups of people to agree on the abusive nature of their nation, and even harder to work together for meaningful change. Systemic sexism and racism are examples of how privilege can work in unhealthy nations.

For centuries, many people have worked to understand privilege by trying to answer questions like "Why do different people get different prison sentences for the same crime?" or "How come some people can get high-income work whenever they want, while others have to beg for any work to survive?" or "Why do some people like it when prices go up and others like it when prices go down?"

A person's privilege is determined by how uncaring people treat them. My level of privilege is high if I am treated well by people who don't personally care about me. For example, a prince might have many fawning servants who don't actually care about him, but treat him well out of self-preservation.

On the other hand, I have lower privilege if people who do not personally care about me treat me poorly. Perhaps employers will only hire me for menial jobs, or judges assume I'm guilty before evidence is presented.

The benefits of higher privilege can accumulate across generations as parents pass their wealth, social connections, patterns of thinking, education, and so on down to their children. Likewise, the challenges of lower privilege can accumulate, as parents with fewer resources struggle to provide stable households, healthcare, education, and other things for their children.

Stability, healthcare, education, and wealth are all just symptoms of privilege. The heart of privilege is this: *my privilege is determined by how people, who do not personally care about me, treat me.*

Depending on People Who Don't Care About Me

The vast majority of people in unhealthy nations depend on the support of people who don't care about them. Whether it's the boss at work, customers, the landlord, tax collectors and other bureaucrats, police, politicians, or clerks at a grocery store, nearly everyone needs uncaring people's cooperation in order to survive. People can still help each other through mutual aid organizations, but core aspects of life – earning a living, keeping a home, remaining out of jail – commonly depend on the cooperation of someone who doesn't care about them.

For example, as described in Chapter 20, police officers and judges commonly discriminate by race. A black person and white person may commit the same crime and be treated very differently by people who don't care about them. This goes deeper than just the length of the prison sentence: is the judge more likely to assume the white person speaks the truth or the black person? Is the police officer more likely to let the white person or the black person off with a warning?

This pattern extends everywhere. Which grade schools are bureaucrats going to give more money to? Which students do top universities accept? When a boss has a choice between competent workers, which people are they more likely to hire or fire? Who is more likely to get a risky bank loan for a new business venture?

Even if my boss or landlord says kind words, if I'm not productive enough on the boss's schedule, or if I'm unable to pay my landlord the rent due to a personal crisis, I would quickly find out how caring they really are. Many bosses and landlords have to learn to close their hearts to maintain their position and level of privilege, and thus commonly act in uncaring ways when they think their income is at risk.

There are a vast number of ways authorities generate varying levels of privilege by treating different people differently. Let us begin with one of the most destructive, anti-solidarity, privilege-generating mechanisms I've found: *lift-and-turn*.

Subverting Solidarity With Lift-and-Turn

The Nazi German government began moving millions of people into concentration camps in the 1930s, including homosexuals, socialists, union leaders, Roma, Jews, and anyone else the government declared as impure or a threat to the state, or who simply was unlucky.

This was a crisis for prisoners, as authorities would force them to work as prison slaves. Camp authorities treated them brutally, overworking them and killing and raping people in huge numbers. But the prisoners had one big advantage: they had each other. Many spoke the same language and everybody was trapped in the same terrible circumstances. This held out the possibility that they could help each other survive the difficult times, or perhaps even help each other escape.

It did not take long for the Nazi leadership to recognize this prisoner solidarity as a problem. In response, they created the Kapo system, where they treated certain prisoners better and made them overseers of the other prisoners.

In other words, the Nazi authorities lifted certain inmates to a higher privilege and turned them against their fellow prisoners. This is *lift-and-turn*.

Prison guards gave kapos better food, housing, and clothing. Guards did not give kapos harsh punishments or hard labor. Kapos could keep better hygiene, which was important when disease ran rampant.[1]

Heinrich Himmler, leader of the German secret police, described the system bluntly: "We organised our system of control over these sub humans… One prisoner is the overseer of others, if you like, with the responsibility for 30, 40 or even more than 100 other prisoners… He is responsible for meeting the work target, for preventing any sabotage, for seeing they are all clean and that the beds are set up."

Some people rejected the offer to become kapos, and some kapos used their position to help other prisoners as they could. However, many kapos developed a reputation for being even more brutal than the Nazi prison guards. They could engage in physical and sexual violence at will against fellow prisoners and many did.

Once a kapo began acting abusively on behalf of the Nazis, he or she found it very difficult to stop. Just as American slaveowners learned to fear their slaves, kapos learned to fear the prisoners they abused. Heinrich Himmler recognized this when he said, "A kapo gets special privileges. The minute we are not satisfied with him he stops being a kapo and goes back to sleeping with others. He knows only too well that they will kill him on the first night."

This illustrates the solidarity-killing power of lift-and-turn: the Nazi guards didn't care about any of the prisoners, but to exert control they treated some, the kapos, much better than others. The guards raised the privilege of some prisoners and pressured them to abuse their peers.

This made continued solidarity very difficult. All of a sudden, Jewish prisoners could no longer all feel united. The same was true for the Roma and other prisoners, whether Russians, Poles, French, or others. This sowed distrust even among non-kapos. After all, how could a prisoner trust a stranger with secrets if that stranger might later become a kapo?

This strategy was so successful that the Germans expanded this program into the Jewish ghettos, recruiting Jewish Councils, Jewish police, and others to assist the secret police.

This lift-and-turn practice of turning prisoners into overseers also reduced the need for Nazi guards, saving the Nazis substantial costs in prison enforcement and work oversight. Thus lift-and-turn was both financially and politically efficient for the abusive prison authorities who wanted reliable and cheap slave labor.

The kapos complicated a simple 'us-vs-them' narrative. After the war, many Jews disagreed: were the kapos Nazis? Should they be punished, or excluded from collective mourning, or be recognized as victims in their own way? Some Jews attacked or murdered kapos they'd been forced to live with. In Displaced Person camps, some Jews set up Honour Courts to put kapos on trial. Later, Israel put some kapos on trial too. The Nazis' ability to severely disrupt solidarity and turn people against each other continued to disturb victims long after the war.

The Privilege-Responsibility Tradeoff

Nazi prison camp wardens had roughly three levels of privilege within the camp: guards, kapos, and normal prisoners. Guards had the highest privilege, with the most comfort, autonomy, authority, sanitation, and so on. Kapos had medium privilege, and the rest of the prisoners who were kept in dirty conditions, beaten, murdered, and overworked had the least privilege. Each level of privilege was deliberately chosen by camp administrators. In other words, guards, kapos, and normal prisoners were all treated very differently by administrators who didn't personally care about any of them.

Unfortunately, privilege always comes with a cost. To maintain one's privilege in an unhealthy nation, a person always must act obediently and give up responsibility for the wellbeing of other people. Even the guards who had so much autonomy were not allowed to do anything that reduced the camp's slave labor output, or helped enslaved people escape. Kapos could not keep their privilege if they helped other prisoners. And of course, normal prisoners received severe extra punishment if they were caught acting disobediently in any way. No matter how badly the guards treated the prisoners, they could always threaten to abuse them worse in order to scare them into obedience and give up responsibility for each others' wellbeing. In other words, guards could always lower a person's privilege, no matter how low it already was. Many people still tried to help each other even under these terrible circumstances, but they did so at great personal risk.

Uncaring people – the prison administrators – offered different incentives and threats of punishment to different people to create different privilege levels. So long as a person paid the price of acting obediently and giving up their healthy and natural sense of responsibility for the wellbeing of other trapped people, they could keep their relatively higher level of privilege.

This is the privilege-responsibility tradeoff. Everyone of every privilege level in unhealthy nations is living this tradeoff, knowingly or not.

Lift-and-Turn is Common

The stories of Nazis and kapos illustrated the power of lift-and-turn to disrupt and block solidarity. Unfortunately, it is a common technique.

In American pre-Civil War slave plantations, some black slaves were raised to the status of gang driver and required to punish their fellow slaves if they didn't keep pace.[2]

In Soviet Gulag prisons, guards would similarly appoint some prisoners as work-gang foremen.[3]

This pattern is not limited to slave plantations, prisons, and concentration camps. It can play out at any level in a society, both increasing efficiency for authorities and subverting solidarity.

In the Soviet Union, young children joined the Pioneers and were trained to be "the eyes and ears of the party inside the family." Half a million early teenage and preadolescent girls and boys stood in watchtowers over farm fields observing adults in Soviet Ukraine in summer 1933. All children were taught to rat on their parents to authorities.[4]

When the United States conquered the Sioux, they hired some individuals to police the rest. Ohiyesa described how tensions rose on a reservation in the early 1890s during the Ghost Dance movement, and there was talk of a revolt. He described how the Sioux who policed on behalf of the government faced extra risk if this revolt had been carried out: "It is a fact that those Indians who upheld the agent were in quite as much danger from their wilder brethren as were the whites, indeed it was said that the feeling against them was even stronger."[5]

This occurs with present-day police forces as well. In America as I write in 2024, while black people are still severely mistreated in a variety of ways, they're also allowed to be police officers whose job it is to enforce racist policies.

For example, in New York City, police officers have carried out the stop-and-frisk program since 2002. Under this program, police can stop a person on the street at will by claiming probable cause for suspecting them of some crime. The police officer could either let them go or, at the officer's discretion, frisk, search, arrest or give a summons. Records show that in 2023, 60% of people stopped were black though they represent only about 20% of the population.[6]

Black police officers who follow orders end up carrying out racist policies against blacks and other oppressed groups. Though not as drastic as the experience of Jewish people with kapos, this again illustrates the pattern where a group is systematically mistreated, and a few members are lifted up and allowed to participate in that mistreatment in exchange for special privileges.

In 1789, the population of the French colony Saint-Domingue was about 556,000. Of these, 500,000 were chattel slaves and the rest were European colonists and free mixed-race or black people called affranchis. To encourage them to support slavery, the affranchis were allowed to become wealthy and own slaves themselves, even though they were not full citizens.[7]

The French colonial leadership sensed trouble after thousands of slaves rose up in rebellion and isolated fighting occurred between Europeans and affranchis in 1791. The following year, the French assembly strengthened the lift-and-turn system, raising the privilege of the affranchis by granting them full citizenship. They hoped this would cause affranchis to side with the white French against the rebelling slaves. And sadly, their scheme worked.

Lift-and-turn also allows entire societies to maintain a pretense that they rule themselves while the truth is that they're ruled by foreigners. Jesus Christ was a Jew born into the Kingdom of Judea. Judea was led by the Jewish king Herod, but he was appointed by the Romans.[8]

When the US imposed a violent government change on Guatemala in 1954, they replaced socialist Guatemalan Jacobo Arbenz Guzmán with Guatemalan Carlos Armas who promptly undid Guzmán's reforms. The Guatemalans still had a Guatemalan ruler, but he served the Americans instead of his own people.[9]

When the Japanese decided to take over Vietnam from France in March 1945, they appointed the Vietnamese citizen Bao Dai as emperor. Bao Dai promptly declared Vietnamese independence from France while he continued taking orders from Japan.[10]

In every case of lift-and-turn, authorities use threats and bribes to raise some people's privilege in exchange for turning against their own people. How can people maintain solidarity in the face of such deep manipulation?

Soviet Prisoners Maintained Solidarity Despite Lift-and-Turn

If you were a prisoner, what would you do to maintain solidarity with the other prisoners even while guards tried to use lift-and-turn?

Prison guards around the world commonly bribe or threaten prisoners to get them to snitch on each other. In the New Mexico State Penitentiary in the lead-up to the huge 1980 prison riot, guards felt concerned that they understood so little about the inmates. They began a coercive snitch system, where prisoners could receive better jobs, earlier parole, or transfer to reduced security areas. Uncooperative people might get parole requests rejected, stripped naked and sent to solitary confinement until they cooperated, and more.[11]

In other cases, guards may need to pay almost nothing. Aleksandr Solzhenitsyn described how guards would bring a few cigarettes to interviews.[12] How can people maintain solidarity even when some are tempted to behave selfishly?

Chapter 4 offered many beautiful stories where healthy nations use dance, respectful discussion, or ostracizing to help wayward people get along and behave respectfully again. I believe healthy nations rarely need to exile or kill misbehaving people, in part because in healthy nations, I believe these gentler measures usually work. People basically want to get along; we naturally want to give and receive the safety of respect.

The trouble with authoritarian nations is that these gentler accountability patterns may not work when authorities can manipulate a person's privilege. A person's privilege is determined by uncaring people. A prison snitch may thus choose the bribes of the prison guards over solidarity with fellow prisoners, prioritizing their own safety over the safety of others. A snitch acts in solidarity with the abusive guards rather than the other prisoners.

Snitches, also known as informants, further generate an atmosphere of anxiety, fear, isolation, and mistrust. If I'm a prisoner, how can I know what prisoners to trust? If a prisoner was trustworthy last week, are they still trustworthy this week as their parole date approaches? What do the guards know that they have no business knowing? Abusive authorities continuously seek to undermine solidarity of their victims, and snitches choose to help the abusers rather than stand in solidarity with their peers. If gentle conversation doesn't help the snitching prisoner to see the error of their ways, what can be done?

Aleksandr Solzhenitsyn described the sense of resignation and hopelessness that had pervaded his Soviet slave labor camp. He described the common attitude that "you die first, I'll wait a bit; there is no justice, so forget it; that's the way it was, and that's the way it will be." The prisoners could be chained, separated, beaten or shot at any time. They engaged in long hours of slave labor or they were heavily punished, and were fed grubby food. He described the way people learned to survive: "In camp, after all, it is even more difficult to hide, everything is out in the open. And there is only one salvation for a person: to be a zero! A total zero." The prisoners were trained not to stand for anything.

Solzhenitsyn described how prisoners took responsibility for generating the kind of culture they wanted. In just a few weeks, they created a prison culture that prized integrity and solidarity, and disallowed snitches.

Change began when a few groups of people escaped. They were all caught and heavily punished. Even though they failed to escape, they showed what it was like for a group of people to stand up for themselves. The prisoners realized that "they were not spiritual paupers, that they had a nobler conception of what life should be than their jailers, than their betrayers, than the theorists who tried to explain why they must rot in camps." Thievery diminished, and prisoners could leave their shoes beside the bed or the food on the locker and trust it would be there come morning.

Things took a radical shift with the arrival of a group of western Ukrainian soldiers. Prisoner snitches were heavily sabotaging solidarity. Many innocent men and women faced long sentences because cowardly snitches lied to police and camp guards in exchange for minor favors. These prisoner-soldiers "were horrified by the apathy and slavery they saw, and reached for their knives." They consulted together and decided on a new law: they would kill the snitches. Wardens and guards were allowed to live, but the informants must die.

Murders followed as needed, anonymously, confidently, and with careful preparation. They knew the guards' schedules, when people would be asleep, and when an opportunity might present itself. They masked and covered their prisoner-numbers to remain anonymous, prepared their knives, and executed the traitorous snitches before walking quickly away.

Occasionally another prisoner observed the killers, but they would divulge nothing to the guards. They refused to snitch, because they knew they would be next on the killers' list.

There was no centralized way for prisoners to report snitches. One would name an informant to another, and the executioners heard and took care of it. While there could never be documentary confirmation that a man was a snitch, it was clear that, as Solzhenitsyn said, "this improperly constituted, illegal, and invisible court was much more acute in its judgments, much less often mistaken, than any of the tribunals, panels of three, courts-martial, or Special Boards with which we are familiar."

Even when the Ukrainian soldiers were removed from the camp, the other prisoners now knew how to stand up for themselves, and the snitch-killing continued.

After fewer than a dozen murders, the camp was transformed: "A remarkable fresh breeze was blowing! On the surface, we were prisoners living in a camp just as before, but in reality we had become free – free because for the very first time in our lives, we had started saying openly and aloud all that we thought! No one who has not experienced this transition can imagine what it is like!"

The snitching stopped, and the guards were now deaf and blind. They needed their snitches to understand the prisoners, but nobody was snitching.

They even had a hard time recruiting prisoners to lead work gangs. Before, when guards took a prisoner for questioning, they might get information for hours. Now, "they summoned a man, and instead of dragging himself there with his heart missing beats, instead of trotting in with a servile look on his silly face, he preserved his dignity (his teammates were watching) and refused to go!" When the guards snatched him anyway, other prisoners would loudly protest and come to his defense, standing in solidarity. Even when the guards successfully grabbed a prisoner with overwhelming violence, they couldn't change the fact that the prisoners stood in solidarity with each other. The prisoners might not be able to resist the guards, but they knew they could trust each other.

The guards offered endless punishments, including longer sentences, isolation cells, starvation, disease, and cold. On the other hand, the prisoners offered a single thing: a knife, meant for anyone who gave in. Not someday maybe, but tomorrow morning. This gave strength to the weak and helped people say no to the guards. Prisoners would invite each other to read notes they planned to give to the guards to prove there was no denunciation in it.

Prison authorities called it gangsterism and urged prisoners to resist it. The prisoners recognized the guards' weakness when they were afraid to acknowledge the political nature of the prisoners' self-defense. When the guards encouraged snitching by increasing people's workload to total exhaustion, the prisoners endured.

A curse was lifted, and prisoners found a new dignity and integrity. Solzhenitsyn described how they were still trapped from the neck down, but their hearts and minds were free, and they were free with each other in a way which was never possible before.

This story showed me what it's like to take a stand for a culture of mutual respect in the midst of profound abuse. The guards clearly stood for a culture of disrespect, giving prisoners who snitched higher privilege. This is lift-and-turn, where some people were incentivized to become traitors. The prisoners stood for a culture of mutual respect and did not allow each other to accept that extra privilege. Snitching was forbidden, and traitors were treated harshly. Thus the prisoners successfully stopped lift-and-turn from destroying their solidarity.

While the prisoners used violence, they did not use it selfishly. No prisoner killed another for personal gain. The murders were intentionally used to stop the predation and generate a culture of mutual respect.

Ideally, people can resolve differences through constructive dialog. When that's not enough, people face a choice: what are we willing to do or risk to stand for a culture of mutual respect?

Every person is a divine being. However, some attitudes and behaviors are absolutely poisonous and can kill any healthy nation if they're allowed to persist. A person transforms themselves when they cultivate bravery instead of cowardice and an attitude of service instead of selfishness. A culture transforms when people collectively embrace bravery and an attitude of service and then set boundaries to protect themselves from predation. In other words, transformation happens when people stand in solidarity.

The lesson of this story for me isn't that violence and killing are always necessary. Often people can gently but firmly hold each other to high standards of integrity, courage, and service through their words and actions, or by modeling it themselves, and this is ideal. But cowardice and selfishness are toxic, and one way or another, they need to be removed from a culture before it can be healthy.

When a cowardly or selfish person is willing to grow into a deeper bravery and attitude of service, this is great. If they resist this growth, and instead consistently sabotage solidarity, the question remains: how can the group best stand for a culture of mutual respect, and not tolerate anything less? Or will they accept isolation, trivialities, environmental pollution, meaningless work, and lives where they pretend things are ok when they're not? If collective self-defense is the only remaining option, is the group willing to take that stand?

This story also demonstrates a transition from triple inhibition to single inhibition, as first discussed in Chapter 17. The prisoners stopped accepting their abusive authorities' rules as legitimate. Instead, they recognized their own sense of right and wrong as legitimate, and created their own laws. They still did slave labor as they were ordered, but they were clear in their own sense of right and wrong and took a stand for each other as they could (single inhibition).

Rise-and-Turn Happens Spontaneously in Any Nation That Rewards Selfishness

Lift-and-turn is a deliberate strategy used by authorities to sabotage solidarity as well as save on enforcement and oversight costs. An authority figure deliberately lifts a person's privilege by offering unusual bribes and threats, pressuring the person into turning against their own people.

Rise-and-turn describes the same process, but without any deliberate intent. In healthy nations that practice widespread sharing, sharing is the norm. What happens in nations that encourage or reward selfishness? A few seemingly lucky people get rich and then turn against their neighbors, protecting their wealth and corrupting their society.

No higher human power placed the top billionaires into power in the US, or placed the emperors in power in ancient China or Japan. Societies that tolerate and promote selfishness, or a few people exploiting the rest, will always have some people who successfully reach the top levels of wealth and then turn against their own people, securing their wealth and creating poverty all around them.

I believe people of healthy nations recognize this, and it explains why they have had such harsh prohibitions against hoarding wealth. When I study healthy nations, I commonly see that it's ok for a person to use the tools they made or eat from the garden they tended. It's not ok to control land that's not used, or selfishly hoard more resources than the person could possibly need.

I don't believe anybody is inherently evil, but people can do many terrible things when they cultivate selfishness or self-centeredness. I believe that all the terrible cruelties in unhealthy nations ultimately stem from selfishness. Rulers and other authorities act selfishly, creating and sustaining an environment in which others are rewarded for selfishness as well.

This explains why healthy nations recognize selfishness as the severe threat that it is, and they actively seek to maintain a culture of sharing and solidarity that humans find so deeply satisfying.

The lift-and-turn pattern so common in unhealthy nations around the world and through the ages is highly effective at keeping people continually divided. But privilege can be divisive in even more ways, as exposed in *Chapter 27: Privilege 2 - Social Class and Promise Keeping.*

Chapter 27: Privilege 2 - Social Class and Promise Keeping

One special day, Don Cox had an epiphany. The day started like many others. He was a poor black American man in the mid-20th century working at a printing shop. He'd started out as an entry level employee but had recently become production manager. He had no boss in the shop; only the owner could give him orders but he often was not present.

Cox liked the freedom of choosing whom to hire and fire and not having to punch the clock. He felt good when he hired some underprivileged people and fired a racist man. He began seeking raises for all the staff, getting into repeated arguments with the owner who kept rejecting or minimizing the raises. The owner never brought up issues of productivity or how long the workers had been at the company. He only discussed wanting to make a profit, and this was his reason for minimizing wages.

That led to Cox's epiphany. He wrote, "It was through my experience as a boss that one day, as suddenly as you flip a switch, I finally understood that it was the system that was all wrong." As a boss, it was Cox's entire job to sell services at the highest price while keeping workers' salaries as low as possible. The workers wanted a higher salary, but the owner wanted them to have a lower salary so he could pocket the difference. Cox saw from personal experience that there were people directly opposed to what the workers wanted – the owners themselves and the bosses they hired.[1]

The vast majority of people want lower rent, but a few people want much higher rent – the rental owners. The vast majority of people want cheaper food, honest political leadership, or honest news media companies. But there are a few people who profit massively by raising food prices, getting corrupt politicians elected, or using all manner of tricks to bury important news items or to plant false stories.

This is a nation of "haves" and "have-nots." This is what it means to be in an authoritarian nation where a few people rule over others, though the details look different in different economies.

In capitalism, for example, business owners own the assets like a factory, apartment building, or coal mine, and they live off the income from the asset. In contrast, workers have to sell their labor to live.

In a monarchy, the king may own literally everything within the kingdom and divvy out profitable enterprises to aristocrats as he chooses. When the Spanish conquered much of central and south America, they instituted the encomienda system, where the monarch granted land and human workers to rich colonists. Of course, it was the workers who did all the manual labor.

Jesus Christ said, "If a kingdom is divided against itself, that kingdom cannot stand."[2] In 1381, English activist John Ball said, "Nothing will be well in England until we are in the same condition."[3] For thousands of years people have known that a divided nation is really unhealthy. But clearly, every kingdom and every authoritarian nation is divided against itself. The haves and have-nots have opposing interests. The vast majority of people don't want to be exploited, and a few very privileged people want to exploit them.

This is a simple two-class analysis which dates back to the dawn of authoritarian nations. It explains a lot about why people in unhealthy, authoritarian nations struggle to resolve troubles like poverty or government corruption.

However, there are many troubles that this simple two-class model of haves and have-nots cannot explain.

Whose Side is the Middle Class On?

I remember feeling absolutely astonished as I read *Thunder in the Mountains*, a book about the West Virginia coal miners' strike in 1920-1921. Miners had worked for years in very dangerous mines for low wages. They had no union. The mining company controlled much about their lives: it provided doctors, teachers, and preachers, and even employed law officers. It chose what silent movies would play locally. The company told them where and how to live, and fired those who wouldn't conform. Miners had to buy goods at the company store for inflated prices.[4]

These living arrangements were profoundly abusive, but the men weren't the only ones who suffered. What would happen if a miner got injured at their very unsafe job? The injured male miners couldn't work, and few wives made money. The company would offer the injured worker a special company money they could temporarily use at the company store. If the miner returned to work quickly, the debt was written off. If the miner remained injured and unable to work, the company money spent by the worker needed to be repaid in full on day 30. But the miner was unable to work, so how were they supposed to pay off the debt?

To avoid eviction, homelessness and total poverty, the family had a single option: the wives were expected to submit to sexual predation by company men. One woman named Joy has turned an old West Virginia coal company store into a museum so that young people can know their past. Joy has had 10 women visit the museum who called a place on the 3rd floor the "rape room." Women would go to the store to try on shoes, get food for their family, or request another week's rent. Submitting to rape by coal company guards was the price they had to pay because their husbands were still injured.[5]

While approximately 20% of West Virginia coal miners were black people who faced additional discrimination, most of the rest were white and these problems affected all the miners.[6]

Miners and their families were trapped in a terrible situation, subject to extreme abuse by any definition of the word. They began seeking to form a union so they could get a decent pay raise, freedom from the company store, justice, and more.[7]

This was terrible, but none of this is what I found astonishing. I didn't feel astonished that the mining company owners worked closely with the sheriffs, private detectives, and other armed thugs to physically attack the miners, or that West Virginia's governor declared martial law and banned public gatherings and news reports, in direct violation of the first amendment to the US Constitution. I knew that authorities commonly cancel existing laws for their benefit, just when the laws about freedom are needed most. None of that astonished me.[8]

I was astonished to discover that so many comfortable, middle-class people were enthusiastically willing to join the anti-miner militia. Within two weeks after that martial law declaration was made in May 1921, a stunning 800 men volunteered for the anti-miner militia, including engineers, lawyers, automobile salesmen, bookkeepers, real estate men, contractors, merchants, and clerks.[9] A large number of people with dignified, comfortable jobs volunteered to use violence to force the mining families to accept their terrible jobs.

Why were they so willing to do that? Why didn't the middle-class people help the lower-class miners?

The more I looked, the more I saw this same pattern playing out in unhealthy nations around the world and across time as explored throughout this book:

- Chinese and Soviet police arrested political activists and pretended they were mentally ill even though activists worked against corruption that affected the police too.

- Many poor whites sided with the rich whites in the KKK after the US Civil War, even though they themselves had little wealth or power.

- Many male British soldiers spoke ill of female prostitutes during World War I even though the men and women were merely being abused by authorities in different ways.

The simple class analysis of "haves and have-nots" does not explain this muddled middle. Bookkeepers, lawyers, police officers, and salesmen are all workers too, selling their labor to survive just like the miners. Why the quick and enthusiastic willingness to side with rich capitalists and politicians against their fellow workers?

I believe the roots of this disturbing lack of solidarity lie in the answer to a simple question: does my unhealthy nation keep its promises to me?

The Power of Promises to Shape a Person's World

Chapter 26 offered a basic definition of privilege: privilege is how people who don't personally care about me treat me.

Authoritarian leaders in every unhealthy nation make certain promises. While there is much variability across different nations and times, on a really basic level, there are two common promises in every unhealthy nation:

1. If you work hard, you can provide a decent life for you and your family.

2. If you obey the law, you'll avoid legal trouble. If you break the law, you will receive an appropriate punishment.

These promises may not be explicitly written down, but they're commonly understood. These aren't necessarily promises from a particular politician or even the government. People "just know" and expect this from their nation. Politicians may repeat variations of these two promises on a campaign trail. Teachers repeat these beliefs to students in schools. They reflect a deep sense of how a nation ought to be.

It seems intuitively right that if someone works hard and contributes to their nation through a job, they should be able to provide for their family. The law is supposed to define how to live respectfully together, so of course people who obey the law should avoid legal trouble, and law-breakers should face some accountability.

The trouble is that unhealthy nations only keep these promises sometimes, to some people and not to others.

Unhealthy nations keep their promises differently to three basic classes of people:

- *Lower-privilege, promises broken*: lower class people can work hard and remain obedient, and they will still struggle to live a decent, dignified life and provide for their families. They will still struggle with poverty, face arbitrary arrest, have more police presence in their neighborhoods, and more. The nation and life in general seem unfair because the nation generally does not keep its promises to lower-privilege people.

- *Medium-privilege, promises kept*: everything is more or less as it "should" be: people who work hard and obey the law generally live a decent life. People who don't work hard don't do as well. The law punishes law-breakers and generally leaves law-abiding citizens alone. The nation and life in general seem fair because the nation generally keeps its promises.

- *Upper-privilege, promises broken in their favor*: Upper-privilege people may have a comfortable life without working hard. They can break certain laws in certain ways and not get in trouble as long as they avoid exploiting other high-privilege people. These people often believe they deserve their special treatment and privilege, so the nation seems fair or right to them too.

In some nations with clear castes, these are rigid divisions between privilege levels based on skin color, ethnicity, religion, or something else. In other nations, the boundaries between classes are more fuzzy. The higher-level upper class may be able to break most laws at will, while the lower-level upper class can break fewer laws. No single perspective on privilege can explain every dynamic in authoritarian nations, but this perspective explains a lot.

This book has already reviewed examples of these promise-keeping patterns. As reviewed in Chapter 15, in British colonial Virgina, the law forbade rape and it forbade interracial sex. The nation kept its promise to non-slave-owning white people: if they avoided sex with black people, they avoided legal trouble. If they had sex with black people, they got punished. If they raped anybody they got punished, and if they were raped, the perpetrator got punished. The nation kept its promises to them.

But the law did not punish the white slave owners when they raped defenseless black slaves. The law didn't protect the lower class black people from rape because the law explicitly didn't protect enslaved people. And it didn't punish slaveowners for breaking the law against having interracial sex. That legal promise of punishment for disobedience was broken, but the promise was broken in slaveowners' favor. Thus medium-privilege whites had an experience of fairness, while lower-privilege blacks experienced unfairness, and high-privilege whites experienced unfairness in their favor.

These patterns of promise-keeping are pervasive in every unhealthy nation. Every day there are countless examples of low-privilege people being treated inappropriately by law officers, or who work hard and still can barely provide for their family.

- *Russian police*: A study on the Moscow subway found that people who looked non-Slavic were 20x more likely to be stopped by police than people who appeared typically Russian.[10]

- *Chinese police*: Chinese citizens who migrate to large cities and set up vendor stalls are commonly attacked by chengguan government officers who beat people, take their goods, or arbitrarily and illegally arrest them.[11]

- *United States police*: In the United States, Native American women are murdered at 10x the national average rate, and assaulted at higher rates than any other ethnic or racial group. Most assaults are by people of other races. Only the federal police can prosecute crimes by non-natives on natives' land, and typically they fail to do so. The legal system breaks its promises to punish the criminals that prey on low-privilege Native American women and girls.[12]

- Different groups and ethnicities commonly receive different lengths of prison time for committing the same crime. The law punishes some groups heavily while letting others off more lightly, as explored in Chapter 20.

In stark contrast to this, the unhealthy nation's promises to the middle class are generally kept. Working a job generally results in a comfortable life, and laws and law enforcement feel generally fair.

As an example, when I was about 4 years old, I encountered a police officer for the first time. He pulled our family car over on a highway. My father was a military officer, and my mother was training to be a doctor. My parents exchanged worried looks as the officer approached the car, but the officer only let us know that a key had been left in the trunk door. He handed my father the key and wished us safe travels.

As a medium-privilege adult, I've been pulled over a few times for minor traffic violations. Sometimes I leave with a warning; other times the ticket is downgraded from the actual infraction. I rarely encounter police near my home, and many minor traffic violations, like rolling stops at stop signs, go unpunished. Police have always treated me decently and followed the law. I have worked diligently at various jobs to support myself, and the jobs have always paid enough to let me afford a clean home in a safe neighborhood, nutritious food, and extra money to save up. The nation has essentially kept its promises to me.

Upper-privilege people routinely break the law without punishment on a vast scale in every unhealthy nation:

- *Rich people's litter*: Highway signs may say "no littering, fine $500" to protect the environment, yet laws do not effectively stop many large factories from polluting the rivers and air for decades, harming millions of people and nonhumans as reviewed in Chapter 4. Factory and mining pollution are examples of rich people's litter.

- *Protecting predators*: In Portugal, former secretary of state for families Teresa Macedo sent information about a child prostitution ring to police in 1980. They did nothing. Wealthy international businessmen continued to visit the children's school, and even after president and general Ramalho Eanes heard about this ring from five abused boys, he did nothing to stop it.[13]

- *Protecting the greediest*: In 1996, 18-year old Kurt Danysh was inappropriately prescribed Prozac, an antidepressant produced by Eli Lilly. Despite having no history of violence, about two weeks later Danysh shot and killed his father, whom he loved very much. In private conversations, his own attorney repeatedly claimed there was no public evidence that Prozac led to violent behavior. With no hope of winning in court, Danysh accepted a plea bargain of 22.5-60 years in prison.

    In 2004, a whistleblower leaked Eli Lilly research revealing that the company had knowingly concealed data for over a decade showing that Prozac, an SSRI, can cause violence.[14] Neither the Eli Lilly corporation nor its directors were punished for withholding information on their drugs, contributing to possibly thousands of drug-induced murders and unjustified imprisonments while profiting massively.[15]

Authoritarian nations promise fair treatment under the law, but they commonly break their promise to the rich and politically connected – that is, they break the law *in their favor*.

Of course, upper class people are not entirely immune from legal persecution. Higher-level upper class people may exploit lower-level upper class. Factions of upper class people may fight each other in turf wars and use each others' corrupt behavior as an excuse to remove each other from power. An occasional instance of upper-class criminality may get punished to maintain the pretense of the rule of law. Occasionally a politician gets elected that tries to enforce the law fairly. There is a lot of noise, but the underlying signal is clear: wealthy and politically powerful people commonly get away with breaking the law.

The Consequences of Keeping or Breaking Promises

Unhealthy nations keep their basic promises to some people, while breaking those same promises to others. This makes worker solidarity very difficult to achieve.

Obviously not all promises are broken for one group and not all are kept for another, and there can be many subgroups with different privilege levels. But to simplify this discussion, let's consider the consequences when a nation breaks its promises to the lower class while keeping its promises to the middle class. In the following class analysis, I'm going to generalize for the sake of keeping it readable and succinct. There are exceptions and nuances to every pattern, but the overarching patterns are real and help explain deep divisions between low-privilege and medium-privilege people.

Is the Nation Fair? And is it "Good Enough?"

The root experiential difference is that the unhealthy nation seems basically unfair to the lower-privilege group whereas it seems basically fair to the medium-privilege group. The lower-privilege group gets harassed or persecuted by police even when they obey the law, while medium-privilege people only get harassed when they break the law or if they meaningfully oppose authorities' exploitative behavior.

Furthermore, the nation provides a life of basic comfort and security that typically seems "good enough" to middle privilege people. Their jobs might not be especially meaningful and politicians and bosses might be harsh, but as long as the person keeps working, life is "basically ok." Their core physical needs are met.

However, for lower-privilege people, the nation is not "good enough." They work hard for long hours, and may or may not make enough to provide decently for a family. They're more likely to live near pollution, eat less nutritious food, find less dignified work, and have less savings for emergencies. They struggle for a decent income without a union, and corporations commonly discourage unionizing. The nation makes it difficult or impossible for low-privilege people to legally create a comfortable and secure life.

Lower-privilege people experience their nation as unfair and life is, in a basic sense, not good enough or not satisfying. In contrast, medium-privilege people, when they focus only on their own experience, are likely to see the same unhealthy nation as basically fair and good enough.

Authorities shape the world of low-privilege people to allow the rich to exploit them more than medium-privilege people, so life seems unfair and hard work does not guarantee comfort and safety. Authorities shape the world of medium-privilege people so the nation seems basically fair, and hard work and obedience result in a safe and comfortable life.

Privilege and the Need for Stability

Rulers face a difficult challenge. When rulers exploit their nation, this motivates exploited people to seek change. Rulers want stability, but if they're not careful, everyone else will want deep transformation.

A core purpose of privilege is to motivate enough people in an unhealthy nation to also want stability. Upper-privilege people value stability because they get a forgiving legal system and a relatively comfortable life without hard work. Medium-privilege people likewise value stability because life and their nation seem basically fair: hard work is rewarded and laziness punished; obedience is rewarded and disobedience is punished.

Thus medium-privilege people, such as doctors, lawyers, engineers, managers, economists, medium-ranking military officers, and others commonly side with the abusive upper-privilege group, instead of standing in solidarity with the lower-privilege people seeking deep change to end the exploitative nature of their nation. In a nation without deep solidarity, change can seem very threatening. After all, without solidarity, how can a medium-privilege person know they'll still be treated decently after the nation goes through a big change?

How Can People of Varying Privilege Levels Agree on the Abusive Nature of Their Nation?

Low-privilege people commonly know from personal experience how abusive and unfair their nation can be. Medium-privilege people commonly do not. Two or more low-privilege people can relatively easily discuss their nation's abuses even if they each experience different types of abuse. For example, one may have experienced a dishonest judge, and another experienced police violence during a peaceful protest, yet they understand each other.

Chapter 23 reviewed the story where a roomful of black Americans began sharing their frustrations about racist bosses and police, all recognizing something needed to change. Each person had been disrespected, so they were open to each others' stories of mistreatment.

In contrast, many medium-privilege people may go their whole lives without encountering abusive authorities like dishonest police or spiteful landlords, and as a result they may feel no need to protest. Not protesting further ensures they do not encounter abusive authorities.

Many sayings describe the same deep trouble: "everyone thinks they're free until they rattle their chains," "you cannot escape a prison if you don't know you're in one," and "if you don't think there's a problem, you're not going to heal it."[16] Medium-privilege people generally don't notice their chains. They may easily believe in the impartial, law-abiding legal system ("with a few bad apples") that they first heard about in grade school. They may easily believe that they live in a non-abusive nation, and thus do not recognize the abusive patterns that low-privilege people know all too well from experience.

This was vividly clear in a story told by a friend whom I'll call Nathaniel. He was a white man from a medium-privilege background who engaged in political protests in the 1960s. The authorities wanted to strongly discourage these protests, so despite his medium privilege, the police arrested him and treated him abusively, and both the police and judge violated the law.

Nathaniel described his experience to a cousin, a white female lawyer also from a medium-privilege background. She had never protested though, and in her legal work she was only ever treated professionally by police. She did not believe Nathaniel's stories, and still doesn't as I write over 50 years later. Because she hadn't experienced it, she simply wasn't open to the possibility that the police only treat some people respectfully, or selectively follow the law. This shows how divisive it can be when unhealthy nations keep promises to some groups and not others.

Medium-Privilege People are Commonly Less Willing to Take Risks

Of course, medium-privilege people may hear about police who illegally prevent low-privilege people from unionizing, illegally break up a protest, or illegally surveil social activists. However, they commonly feel less urgency for change because their personal safety and comfort are not threatened.

Medium-privilege people are often much less inclined to take personal risks to seek political change than lower-privilege people who have less to lose. Medium-privilege people have more to lose and less to gain, given that they don't face the same abuses.

So, medium-privilege people might not agree in the first place on the abusive nature of their nation. And if they do see aspects of it, many will feel less urgency for change and less willingness to take risks.

But the problems don't stop there.

Medium-Privilege: When an Attitude of Entitlement Makes Sense

Privilege is a set of relationships: "how people who don't care about me treat me." Entitlement is an attitude: "do I believe I deserve how I'm treated?" An entitled person believes the rich and powerful are better than everyone else and the poor are lazy, or offended god, or otherwise deserve their inferior position. In a basic way, an entitled person believes "people get what they deserve, and I deserve my social standing and the life I have in my nation."

This entitled attitude that "people get what they deserve and deserve what they get" actually makes sense in the subjective experiences of many medium-privilege people. If medium-privilege people work hard and avoid legal trouble, they can have a safe and comfortable life. People who don't work hard then struggle as a result, and people who break the law get punished.

What does an entitled person believe about lower-privilege people? They must deserve their poverty or harsh police treatment because in a medium-privilege person's experience, *people get what they deserve*. And this may be more-or-less true for medium-privilege people, but it is not true for everybody.

This belief that everyone gets what they deserve can be reinforced in many ways: adults and teachers teach this to children to motivate obedience, friends and coworkers may reinforce this attitude in each other, and bosses and politicians may reinforce it too.

Medium-Privilege People Can be Deeply Manipulated by Anti-Low-Privilege Propaganda

When low-privilege people protest in the streets or engage in civil disobedience to seek the end of police abuse, unfair wages, or unsafe working conditions, what stories do authorities tell medium-privilege people? Authorities can easily say, "they're just ungrateful, whining, lazy people who want free handouts." The essential entitled attitude assumes that people get what they deserve and deserve what they get. Thus medium-privilege people may easily believe propaganda that low-privilege people are seeking freebies or making groundless complaints against the legal system, a system that seems reasonably fair to most medium-privilege people.

Authorities can easily stoke this sense of entitlement and misperception of what low-privilege people seek by spreading false stories, misrepresenting low-privilege people's demands, and so on.

Propaganda can also encourage lazy thinking in the medium-privilege group. What if the truth is uncomfortable, and I want to believe a pleasant falsehood instead? Maybe I can just avoid thinking about political things at all, or stick to what I "know" is true about government and the legal system being basically good, or maybe the poor really are racially inferior, or God really does put everyone in their place?

Or, maybe hope and love always triumph, and the arc of history bends towards justice all on its own. And all I need to do is keep thinking good thoughts and keep working hard to provide for my family, and that will be good enough.

Authorities want and need medium-privilege people to not stand in solidarity with low-privilege people to end exploitation. Whether medium-privilege people feel hate towards lower-privilege people, believe falsehoods, avoid seeing the abuses, engage in lazy thinking, or whatever other thought process, it all leads to the same outcome that authorities want: most medium-privilege people are either politically inactive or align themselves with the rich.

Medium-Privilege People Tend to Side With the Upper-Privileged Who Create an Apparently Fair and Comfortable Nation

In the two-class analysis of workers and capitalists, it wasn't clear why some workers would side with the capitalists. This promise-keeping analysis makes the reason more clear. Rulers provide medium-privilege people with a life that is basically fair and rewards hard work with general safety and comfort. Any deep political change could easily feel threatening to that safety, comfort, and fairness. After all, if a whole new group of authorities come in, how can people who are comfortable in the current system know how they'll be treated after the change? Thus it makes sense that medium-privilege people commonly side with the upper-privilege class who currently give them a comfortable life.

To See the Truth, Medium-Privilege People Must Make a Massive Mental, Emotional, and Social Leap

No belief exists in isolation. People develop entire worldviews based in part on whether people around them keep their promises. Thus, when a person grows up believing that their nation is basically fair and hard work is rewarded, they may also believe that people get what they deserve, the legal system is basically fair, politicians basically serve the people, and the reigning ideology is true (whether it's capitalism, communism, monarchy, democracy, or whatever).

Humans are born expecting to grow up in a healthy nation. It takes a massive mental, emotional, and social change to see one's nation as essentially unhealthy or corrupt. Ongoing abuse provides the motivation for change in the people experiencing abuse. Lower-privilege people, therefore, are generally more eager for change, and the sooner the better. Medium-privilege people, on the other hand, must make more of a conscious effort to see the abusive reality that they are not fully experiencing – even though they too suffer, to a lesser extent, in their unhealthy nation.

I grew up in a middle-privilege life. I grew up believing in capitalism and democracy. As a teenager I learned to invest so I could make money investing in corporations that supposedly served society. I sincerely believed I could get rich while helping make the world a better place. I believed in representative democracy and felt so grateful to live in the USA rather than some authoritarian country like China or North Korea. I felt excited the first time I voted in a presidential election for Barack Obama in 2008.

It took years of deliberate intensive study for me to finally face up to the hard truths I share in this book. I had to make many uncomfortable mental leaps in order to recognize abusive patterns which I hadn't seen before and had never personally experienced. I had to recognize that my career and my way of life were directly contributing to many of the terrible things I saw in the world. I had to make emotional leaps, in which I suddenly felt much less safe and secure in my nation than I had previously. I had to purposely expose myself to grief and discomfort from which I could have easily hidden.

And I had to make some very big social leaps. In 2014, I left my old life to go live with people likewise willing to question everything they'd learned growing up and find a better way to live. I kept some old friends, but I had to give up much of my previous social life to find other people with whom I felt more aligned. I faced a great deal of opposition, including from some people I loved, who wanted me to stay on my old life path even though I found it deeply unsatisfying.

These difficulties I experienced help me appreciate the difficulty that low-privilege people face in trying to get medium-privilege people to stand up with them for deep political change. One of my big goals with this book is to help low-privilege and medium-privilege people have more constructive conversations about the true nature of their unhealthy authoritarian nation, so we can stand together for meaningful change for everybody.

When Medium-Privilege People Recognize Their Nation's Unfairness Too Late

I graduated from college and started a career in 2008, right as a financial crisis was getting under way in the United States. That fall, huge numbers of people began to lose their jobs. One popular theme in newspapers was the story of a previously high-earning person who suddenly could only find low-wage work. People who had worked jobs of dignity and influence and earned 3-5x the average annual income were suddenly making less than the average income doing jobs they did not like. Many people with multiple post-graduate degrees were unable to find work that utilized their expertise, and they took any job they could get.

Multiple times, I remember reading complaints by these previously high-earning people about how unfair and difficult it was being poor. Things which used to be simple now took a long time. Vehicle breakdowns were now a big deal since they could not afford to just keep a spare car. They could not simply live in whichever neighborhoods they felt like, but had to live far away from where they worked each day.

Their concerns always seemed legitimate, but what stuck out to me was this: the poor had always had these complaints, and these previously well-off individuals had ignored them. They either did not notice the unfairness and hardship or did not care about it until it affected them. In other words, it was not until these medium-privilege individuals suffered a catastrophic loss of privilege that they recognized how difficult and unfair the lives of low-privilege people are.

Another frustrating theme was that these people could no longer enjoy their old social life. They could not splurge at bars, go on the same vacations, go to the same clubs, or buy the same clothes that they and their friends used to. And their old friends, who still had their relatively high privilege, acted like nothing had changed. They were still insulated from the troubles of their nation, spending with abandon and ignoring the plight of the poor. I remember reading that their friends' unresponsiveness was particularly frustrating to these suddenly-low-privilege, suddenly-poor individuals.

Unlike people of healthy nations, these previously medium-privilege, now low-privilege people had not taken responsibility to find out what was really going on and ensure their nation worked satisfactorily for everyone, even when personal disaster struck. Witnessing this catastrophic loss of privilege helped me recognize how privilege can insulate self-centered people from the troubles of their nation.

Sadly, this was not a unique situation where medium-privilege people suffer a dramatic loss of privilege and notice their society's unfairness too late. Medium-privilege people are commonly ignorant of their government's real behavior and have deep faith that people who behave obediently will be treated ok.

When Bruce Bettelheim was trapped in a Nazi German concentration camp in the 1930s, he observed how the prisoners responded to their ongoing torture and humiliation, and he observed that the non-political medium-privilege prisoners…

> …were least able to withstand the initial shock. They found themselves utterly unable to comprehend what happened to them. In their behaviour became apparent the dilemma of the politically uneducated German middle classes when confronted with the phenomenon of [Nazism]… They had no consistent philosophy which would protect their integrity as human beings. They had obeyed the law handed down by the ruling classes without questioning its wisdom. And now the law-enforcing agencies turned against them, who always had been their staunchest supporters. They could not question the wisdom of law and police. Therefore what was wrong was that they were made objects of a persecution which in itself must be right, since it was carried out by the authorities. Thus they were convinced that it must be a 'mistake.'[17]

Bettelheim noted that some people were imprisoned basically at random, which explains why such obedient people wound up in concentration camps. These medium-privilege people had so totally believed in the government and its justice that they could not comprehend that it might act unjustly. More than anyone else, they resented being treated like common criminals. However, "After some time they could not help realising their actual situation. Then they disintegrated."

Bettelheim noticed that these middle-class people, whose whole approach to life was based on obedience and following their government, had no internal anchor when that external foundation proved unreliable. Of all the groups, this group was most likely to commit suicide, cheat on fellow prisoners, or become snitches. He said, "They lost their middle-class sense of propriety and their self-respect; they became shiftless and disintegrated as autonomous persons."

Like all authoritarian governments, the Nazi German government had always treated people however authorities wished, and they treated activists and oppressed groups viciously while treating medium-privilege people with dignity and respect. This lulled them into a false sense of trust in the fairness and righteousness of their unhealthy nation. Those middle-class Germans weren't used to taking any kind of stand, or deciding for themselves what was right and wrong despite pressure from authorities. When faced with the reality of their government's arbitrary cruelty, and without any internal strength to fall back on, many medium-privilege people emotionally disintegrated.

Privilege lets people get away with not taking responsibility for their neighbors. As long as a person is willing to selfishly focus only on their own needs, they can ignore the hurtful patterns of their unhealthy nation. When a person does not accept responsibility for seeking the truth and caring about their neighbors, losing their privilege may be the only thing that shocks them out of their cozy little bubble.

All Accomplishments Result from a Mix of Privilege, Luck, and Effort

It helps me to recognize that all my accomplishments in life are the result of some combination of privilege, luck, and effort, including my effort and the effort of friends and family who have supported me. I develop software for money, and I am quite capable after many years of carefully cultivating my abilities. I worked hard throughout school and college, and took a lot of initiative to get good internships and build business relationships. I can easily look back at my life and see how good decisions led to good results, and how poor decisions led to poor results.

My own efforts account for a lot, but they hardly account for everything. A lot of people with my skill and initiative don't have my comfortable life. My university could have declined admission due to my skin color or religion or sex. Police could have arrested one of my parents when I was young on trumped up drug charges, forcing me to grow up in a very different, less stable household. Instead of telling me that I could pursue whatever career I wanted, teachers could have taught me that I would only be able to get low-wage jobs. They could have told me that's all I deserved.

Actions always have consequences at all privilege levels, and anyone can be proud of obstacles they surpass towards a big goal. Different privilege levels simply mean that some people have fewer opportunities or face many more obstacles than others, and some people are more insulated from the consequences of failure, or get more second tries than others. Acknowledging my privilege doesn't take away from any of my accomplishments or my personal growth along the way. Acknowledging my privilege simply helps me remember that I live in an unfair society, and not everyone has the same opportunities, and that this is something I want to change.

What to Do About Privilege

This chapter focuses on a simplified view of privilege with lower-, middle-, and upper-privilege groups. But the reality is that every unhealthy nation has huge numbers of different groups with different privilege levels, ultimately because the ruler or ruling class simply decides to treat different people differently. For example, India has a caste system with around 25,000 different sub-casts, each with their own privilege levels.[18] Then there are further differences based on gender, region, age, and so on. Other unhealthy nations also have many different privilege levels, though the groups are not as clearly defined.

This chapter also focuses on the promise-keeping aspect of privilege, but privilege shows up in countless ways, whether in school funding, job availability and pay levels, people's ability to protect themselves from pollution, whether mainstream cultural narratives suggest a group is inherently worthy of respect or not, and so on. It becomes difficult for people to agree on the troubles in their society when each little sub-group experiences their society very differently.

I believe that a major benefit to authorities of having so many different privilege levels is to make it difficult for people to know each others' experiences and see each others' perspectives. Additionally, different privilege levels make some people invested in keeping their way of life, and others much more motivated for change. But even the ones who want change might want different changes because they encounter different problems!

For everyone to be treated decently would mean getting rid of privilege entirely. In a nation without privilege, no one would depend on any uncaring people for their food, shelter, or safety. There would not be unequal treatment, since everyone would accept responsibility to ensure that everyone was treated fairly. Thus the path to getting rid of privilege and the path to generating a healthy nation are one and the same. Privilege will only go away when everyone stands for a culture of mutual respect, and a few people no longer rule over everyone else. And the sooner, the better!

Whereas unhealthy nations deliberately and systematically impose divisions and stymie solidarity among people, healthy nations encourage a deep integrity that allows people to trust each other and stand in solidarity, as illustrated in *Chapter 28: The Three Integrities*.

Chapter 28: The Three Integrities

The first core spiritual practice is to cultivate a practical, aware gratitude for the gifts I receive from other humans and nonhumans.

The second core spiritual practice is to give my sacred gifts, or live out my life purpose. It's to give myself fully, or give my deepest love without holding back. These are different ways of saying the same thing.

The third core spiritual practice is living in reciprocity – to give my gifts in service of those who give so much to me.

This attitude of giving one's gifts in service of others is fundamental to human nations. Service is who we are and what we expect of each other as human beings. Because people want to trust each other to act in service, this is its own kind of integrity.

I recognize three kinds of integrity. Honesty and keeping my promises (integrity of word and action) are two kinds of integrity most people recognize. But there's a third, deeper integrity: acting in service, or what I call integrity of service. It means that I act in service of those I love even without any explicit promise. In other words, I "do what's right" or I "do the right thing" even if I haven't explicitly promised to.

Consider these personal examples of integrity of service:

- *mother-child*: A newborn child does not ask for its mother's verbal commitment to care for the child's needs. The infant is simply born expecting this motherly attitude of service. It expects that the mother will care about it and act in service of it without prior agreement. It is not a mental or conscious expectation. Rather, the baby's entire approach to life is based on the expectation that a caring mother will be present. The mother established this expectation by entering into a mother-child relationship.

- *doctor-patient*: When I visit the doctor, I do not ask for a commitment that the doctor will serve my health rather than maximize their own profit. That would be deeply insulting because there's an underlying expectation that, once I've paid, the doctor then will act in service and make my health their priority, or at least tell me honestly when they won't. The doctor established this expectation of service by entering into a doctor-patient relationship.

- *teacher-student*: When I attended school, I did not ask each teacher for a commitment to serve me as a student. Like the newborn with her mother, my unspoken trust in my teachers was the simple expectation that they would have that attitude of service towards me; in other words, that they would do their best to support my personal growth. The teachers established this expectation of service when they entered into a teacher-student relationship.

Acting in service is a matter of integrity because people expect to trust each other to act in a caring way even without explicit verbal or written agreement. This is easy to see: imagine how disrespectful it would be to a doctor if I walk into their office and before saying anything else, ask them to promise to help me heal and not just maximize their own pay. Or imagine a student walks into class on the first day of school and asks the teacher to prioritize teaching well instead of always thinking about protecting their job. Of course, no infant can even ask their mother for such a promise. Once a teacher, mother, doctor, political leader, or anyone else enters into a relationship, humans simply expect this attitude of service.

I certainly saw this vividly during my time with the Ashaninka. They never promised me they wouldn't steal the goods I had brought to the village. Once they accepted me as a guest and we entered into that host-visitor relationship, I could trust them to treat me respectfully.

The Nootka demonstrated this integrity of service too. In their creation story, 13 women and girls set out in a boat deep into the ocean to escape conflict. They knew it was important to share and take care of each other, but the oldest all knew there was far too little food and water available for everyone to survive. When it was time to eat or drink, the oldest twelve all misled the youngest one, claiming that the older ones already had their share of food or water when really they had not. As everybody's clothes turned to rags on the high seas, they were given to the little girl so she could stay warm. When the boat finally washed ashore, the little girl was the only one left alive, and she realized what the others had done so she could live. The older women and girls were not honest with the youngest. But they showed that fundamental integrity of service, putting the little girl's and the group's needs ahead of their own.[1]

The three core spiritual practices of practical aware gratitude, giving my sacred gifts, and living in reciprocity form the basis of our integrity as humans. These three core spiritual practices help me live the most meaningful life imaginable. They help me recognize what deeply matters and they train me to act in service of what matters. That's what integrity of service is – where we act in deep service of what we most love. This is also the spiritual posture of someone living with an open heart.

This integrity of service is foundational for every human. If I'm unsure of what deeply matters to me or I'm not acting in service of what matters, then what am I doing with my life? Why bother being honest or keeping promises if I'm allowing my life to be meaningless or self-centered? If I'm living a meaningless life, I'm already out of integrity.

When a Person is Clear in Their Integrity

I was inspired by the story of the Soviet man Grigory Ivanovich Grigoryev who showed integrity of service to his fellow inmates. That is, he didn't make any explicit promises, but he *did the right thing*, showing integrity of service no matter the temptation – and he had a lot of temptations.

Grigoryev spent much of World War II in a Nazi German prisoner camp. After the war, he got put in the Soviet Gulag prison system for 10 years. Fellow prisoner Aleksandr Solzhenitsyn described how "his forthrightness gleamed from his big quiet eyes, some sort of unwavering forthrightness. This man was never able to bow in spirit." Surrounded by the prison philosophy to look out for oneself and forget integrity, he refused to adopt it. Prison wardens would repeatedly offer bribes to become a snitch. Once he responded candidly, "I find it quite repulsive to talk to you. You will find many willing without me." The warden responded, "You bastard, you'll crawl on all fours." He said, "I would be better off hanging myself on the first branch."[2]

The warden sent him off to a specially grueling work detail for months where he committed further sins: he refused to be a foreman because he refused to falsify work records as was unofficially expected. He refused to steal potatoes while working with food as other prisoners did. He consistently took on hard and unpleasant work to avoid easy work that wounded his conscience.

Amazingly, Solzhenitsyn noticed that Grigoryev's body reflected his strong spirit. Even after years in abusive prisons with awful food and being almost 50 years old, he grew stronger in camp. Rheumatism in his joints disappeared. His health became very strong after a recovery from typhus. In winter he would make holes in cotton sacks for his head and arms and go out in the cold without trouble.

Grigoryev showed what it's like to maintain that integrity of service in the face of great threats. He could have closed his heart to his own sacred urge towards integrity, but he kept his heart open instead. He earned the admiration and gratitude of his fellow prisoners, and even grew healthier in the process.

The Second and Third Forms of Integrity: Promise-Keeping and Honesty

Integrity of action and word (promise-keeping and honesty) are also essential to having a healthy nation. Like any friendship or romantic relationship, people have to be able to trust each other.

If a group of people are going to get along, they have to be able to rely on each other. If someone says they'll do something, they do it, or say ahead of time they won't be able to keep their commitment. This is promise-keeping, or what I call integrity of action.

To get along, people also need to have a shared reality. What is real and what is not real? How do people really feel, what event really happened or didn't really happen? In order to have a shared reality, people need to be honest with each other. Even if people don't get along or don't like each other, at least they can honestly acknowledge this and figure out what to do about it. Honesty is the third form of integrity, integrity of word.

A few perspectives really helped me deal with issues of integrity better.

The first is that a person who lies or breaks a promise is not a bad person. They are a good person making a mistake. In other words, the problem is the inappropriate behavior, not something inherently wrong with the person. The only question is if they are willing to stop making the mistake.

This helped me avoid self-loathing when I noticed myself making a mistake by lying or breaking a promise. Shame can be healthy when it's based on disappointment that I let myself, my friends, or my neighbors down, but shame based on a sense of inherent badness is actually self-loathing and really unhealthy. When I avoid this sense of inherent badness and realize I just have a mistake to correct, the path to personal growth becomes a lot easier!

Another thing that helped is a simple accountability practice called the *return to integrity*. If I lie or break a promise, I'm out of integrity. Returning to integrity involves:

1. *Acknowledge*: honestly acknowledging the mistake

2. *Personal Growth*: acknowledging why I behaved as I did and how I want to grow from it

3. *Commitment*: making a new commitment based on how I need to grow.

When I do this, I know I'm growing from my mistakes. When someone else does this, I know they're doing their best, and they're willing to confront their own hurtful behavior and grow from it.

This accountability practice is also helpful because it provides a *path back to grace*. If someone lies or breaks a promise, how can I know when it's safe to trust them again? If they're willing to return to integrity, I always find it reassuring. At the very least, it means we can have an honest conversation now about their past dishonesty or broken promise.

When a person refuses to acknowledge their mistake, or refuses to grow from it and recommit to integrity, this also is helpful: it makes it clear that I still can't trust them. I don't have to guess, and neither does the other person! We know if we can recover trust or if we cannot.

It Takes Two to Have a Shared Understanding of Reality

In healthy nations, everyone takes seriously the need to acknowledge the truth and avoid falsehoods and misunderstandings. There are two roles any person can play when it comes to acknowledging reality: the giver and the receiver.

Honesty, or integrity of word, is the giver's (the speaker's) obligation. For a group of people to acknowledge reality and deal with their troubles, people must speak the truth.

The receivers (the listeners) have an obligation too so that they do not believe falsehoods: *never make assumptions*. Question every belief, and consider the integrity of every speaker. Assumptions are unexamined beliefs, often due to lazy or biased thinking, or coming to conclusions too quickly.

In his book *The Four Agreements*, Don Miguel Ruiz described four agreements that help a person generate freedom and happiness in their lives, and two of the four involve honesty and avoiding assumptions. This showed me how important it is for everyone to seek the truth, and how truth-seeking isn't just the speaker's job (honesty) but also the listener's job (avoiding assumptions). An old saying goes, "A lie gets halfway around the world before the truth has a chance to get its pants on." However, this is only true in nations where lying and assuming are common.

Anyone in any nation can lie. Many political and media figures in unhealthy nations make an art out of manipulating the truth, but their efforts only succeed when their viewers make assumptions instead of examining their beliefs. When authorities make wild claims about another country, or a vaccine, or some other race, do I embrace the fear or indignation and go along? Or do I do my own research to avoid making assumptions? Is that other country *really* threatening mine? Is the vaccine testing process *actually* rigorous and honest? Are people of another race *truly* more prone to violence, or is there something else going on? Propaganda only works because *people let themselves be tricked*. If a whole nation were able to avoid assumptions because each person intentionally sought the truth for important issues, propaganda simply wouldn't work.

In healthy nations, everyone accepts responsibility for seeking a shared understanding of reality, whether as the speaker by being honest or as the listener by avoiding assumptions.

Integrity forms the Backbone or Structure of a Healthy Nation

The word "integrity" is widely associated with strength or firmness in many fields. One engineering company defines *structural integrity* as "the ability of a structure to withstand its intended load without experiencing failure."[3] When a bridge or building "loses integrity," this means it is close to collapse. Integrity and security are also closely tied; for example, the US Army recognizes that "maintaining the integrity of… communications [is] known as Communications Security."[4] When anything loses integrity, it has been breached and is close to failure or collapse.

Researchers also describe integrity as part of a person's emotional strength. One psychiatrist defines integrity as "maintaining an integrated, whole self – bringing oneself 'wholeheartedly' to a situation."[5] Other researchers have illustrated how a person's integrity allows them to maintain a "solid sense of self and emotional balance."[6] Thus a person without integrity is somehow not integrated or whole, or somehow not solid or balanced.

Whether in engineering, war, individual psychology, or many other settings, integrity is commonly recognized as the essence of something's structure. Anything without integrity is unreliable, prone to collapse, or not solid. The same is true for healthy nations.

Just as a bridge requires structural integrity to remain strong, and military communications require integrity to remain secure, human nations require integrity to remain healthy.

Chapter 4 showed how agreements and integrity allow healthy nations to set boundaries. People can agree to protect each other from attack and uphold norms of appropriate behavior, but will they actually keep their agreements? Integrity allows people to uphold important agreements, and thus I believe integrity forms the structure of any healthy nation. Can I rely on my neighbors to support me if enemies approach? If one neighbor acts disrespectfully, can I rely on the rest of my neighbors to stand in solidarity with me, and ensure that everyone enjoys a baseline of mutual respect?

This all comes down to integrity. Do people consistently speak the truth and keep their promises, even when it might be uncomfortable or dangerous? If not, then I cannot trust my neighbors, and I'm on my own. When people consistently show integrity, then everybody can relax into a deep trust of each other. We know that we can rely on each other no matter what comes, and this is part of what it means to live in a healthy nation.

Unhealthy nations don't train people to have deep integrity. In fact, some kinds of integrity are forbidden. When someone behaves inappropriately, rulers may or may not order the police to take care of it, and everyone else is forbidden from responding. After all, only the police are allowed to enforce the law. No one else is allowed to hold people accountable for inappropriate behavior or uphold the rules of their nation.

In a nation without rulers, how would people protect each other and stand for a culture of mutual respect? I believe it comes down to integrity: people simply make agreements for how they will live together, and they hold each other to a high standard of integrity to ensure everybody upholds those agreements.

Of course, it is not possible to make agreements to cover every scenario and everything that could go wrong. This is where Integrity of Service comes in.

Energetic Boundaries and Integrity of Service

The United States has tens of thousands of pages of laws to carefully require or forbid certain behaviors.[7] In unhealthy nations that encourage selfishness and discourage deep solidarity, governments commonly go into great detail to state what behaviors are allowed and what aren't.

Unfortunately, the laws are still often unclear or leave certain situations unaddressed. Thus the US also has *case law*, which are decisions made by judges after trials. When two people or groups sue each other, or the government prosecutes someone, the judge decides how the law works in a particular scenario. This often becomes a legal precedent that people treat as a law. The US also has tens of thousands of pages of case law.[8]

Thus, anyone who wants to know how to behave legally in the United States must study many tens of thousands of pages of often-confusing and contradictory legal documents. This book offers many examples where governments don't enforce their own laws, or enforce them unfairly, so obviously having such extensive and detailed laws doesn't ensure people can have a healthy nation together.

People of healthy nations make agreements with each other, as Chapter 31 and 40 will explore. But as the United States and many unhealthy nations show, it's impossible to make agreements that cover every nuance of every situation that might arise. This is where *integrity of service* comes in.

When everyone in a nation has integrity of service, people can trust each other to act in service of the group even when their agreements don't cover a particular situation. In other words, people stand together against disrespectful outsiders and help each other through hard times no matter what.

The French missionaries met the Huron and were shocked that they had no courts and prisons because the French could not imagine people serving the group without laws and the threat of punishment (reviewed in Chapter 17). In societies where everybody stands for what's right, I believe this is the norm. Everyone is expected to act in service of the group, even in situations their agreements haven't covered.

Fortunately, integrity of service is who we are as humans. It feels good to stand in solidarity with others in a nation where everyone treats everyone else decently, and healthy nations train their children to embrace this deep form of integrity.

Chapter 4 reviewed how, in order to have healthy boundaries, a nation needs to have agreements and each person needs to uphold them with integrity. But how can a nation maintain healthy boundaries if people cannot make agreements to cover every possible problem that might arise?

When each person has integrity of service and supports the group even in unforeseen situations, everyone can relax into a deep trust knowing that whatever comes, other people in their healthy nation or subculture will not let each other down.

Putting Ideas About Integrity Into Practice

In 2023, I got a reminder of how good it feels when I can relax into deep trust with people around me. These perspectives on integrity helped me get there.

I worked as treasurer for a nonprofit organization that hosted outdoor gatherings with hundreds of participants. The site manager was named Daniel, and it was his job to oversee dozens of helpers who put up tarps, set up equipment, and otherwise readied the land to host everybody.

Near the end of the gathering, Daniel approached me to discuss reimbursements for unpaid staff. These people were reimbursed for using their own vehicles and Daniel said he thought the mileage reimbursement rate was too low. After a long discussion, I agreed, and more than doubled their rate of reimbursement to match the federal standard. Multiple times I heard him say this was satisfactory. He looked me in the eye and thanked me for hearing him out, and said he felt good about our decision. I thanked him for bringing up his concerns with me.

The next day we calculated each person's reimbursements, but as he told me each person's number of miles driven, some numbers sounded strangely high. When I asked him, he acknowledged that he knowingly gave me double the real count of miles for certain drivers whom he still thought should be reimbursed more. He had the real mile count on his sheet as he told me the false numbers.

I confronted him at the gathering in private about this. I said I wanted to trust every word he said, and in order to have that trust, he needed to always speak the truth, especially when we disagree. He claimed he hadn't lied because he "planned to tell [me] the real numbers later." I departed feeling unsatisfied.

Six months later he planned to have the same job again, but I didn't trust him to speak honestly with me or handle money as he said he would. Without the return to integrity path, I might have simply said I wouldn't work with him, or I might have let him retain his job even while I didn't trust him. Neither would have felt good.

Instead I wanted us to either regain trust or recognize that we couldn't. Either way it would be clear. I met with Daniel and another senior staff person to see if we could recover that trust. I said I wanted to work with him, and to do so I had to be able to trust him. I said I wanted to hear him acknowledge that he'd lied to me, tell me what he was thinking or feeling that led him to do that, and commit to always telling the truth in the future. And I would commit to hearing him out. I wasn't looking for a formulaic response, but I did want to feel clear that he regretted what he did, that he valued his integrity, and that he wouldn't lie again.

This process is called *return to integrity* because it allows someone who has stepped out of integrity to recover it. Daniel lied in the past, and he could not change his past dishonesty. But he could be honest now about his past dishonesty, and that would allow us to have a real conversation and potentially allow me to trust him again. But if he couldn't be honest now about his past dishonesty, and acknowledge that lying wasn't ok, then he would remain out of integrity, and I would still be unable to trust him.

Unfortunately, the conversation went in circles for an hour as Daniel kept finding ways to avoid accountability for his lie. He acknowledged deliberately telling me the wrong numbers, but he insisted it wasn't actually dishonest because he planned to tell me the real numbers later. He said someone else had suggested that he give the wrong numbers. He said he was busy, and he didn't regret what he did. He said it was just my experience that he had been dishonest, but it wasn't his experience because he knew he planned to tell me the real numbers later.

I had clarity, although not with the outcome I wanted. I had asked him to return to integrity and he refused. The inappropriate behavior might well continue, and I said I wouldn't work with him as a result. Daniel was my friend and we had many mutual friends, so this was difficult. But I knew the board of directors trusted me to handle the organization's money honestly, and I had to expect that same honesty from everyone I worked with.

I helped recruit a new site manager that all the staff trusted, including myself. At the next gathering, every time I handed the site manager a huge amount of cash, I felt a deep relief. I knew I could trust them to use the money as we'd agreed, or else tell me if they had changed their mind and wanted to use it differently. I felt no anxiety or concern, and I didn't feel a need to secretly double check them. I just knew they behaved with integrity! It felt so good to work with people I totally trusted.

Integrity is Required for Conflict Resolution

Integrity is absolutely essential in part because it is necessary for conflict resolution. Groups of people may kill each other, or steal, or say mean words, and both sides could keep seeking revenge indefinitely. So long as they remain neighbors, the only way to stop this endless cycle of violence is for both groups to make a commitment to peace. For this to work, each group needs to trust that the other will keep their promises. Thus each side must trust each other's integrity.

Crow woman Pretty Shield told a story where integrity was repeatedly necessary to solve a big problem and prevent an even bigger one.

Crow warriors once went to war against the Lakota and returned with one hundred Lakota women. The Crow chief invited each Crow warrior to take a woman, and they all did. When asked how these women were treated, Pretty Shield clarified, "because they were treated well they never tried to get away. They had the same rights as Crow women, and worked no harder." Still, the Lakota men wanted their women back.[9]

A Lakota scout met a Crow scout and said he wished to speak with the Crows in council. The Crow scout said to go to the chief's home, take the medicine-pipe hanging over the door and enter, and he would be safe.

The scout did this, and the Crow chief Silver-tip kept this promise of safety. He fed his guest meat and berries and then asked why he had come. The Lakota scout said the men wanted their women back, and they would trade many things to get them, and asked if the chief would listen.

The Crow chief said he would listen, but he must ask all the warriors for their consent. A crier went through the village inviting the warriors, and they quickly consented to the offer. The chief set a strict requirement: "let no Lakota come here unless he has a woman in our village. One hundred men may come after these women, and no more." The chief did not want a surprise attack if a huge group of Lakota were allowed into the middle of their village.

When the Lakota arrived, two hundred Crow went out to meet them. Only 100 Lakota warriors showed up, as they had promised. And the Crow invited them into their village safely, as they had promised. Some Crow men who had lost fathers or brothers in fighting were angry with the Lakota, but the Crow chief Silver-tip warned these men of punishment if they misbehaved, again keeping his promise to the Lakota.

The Lakota made a huge pile of fine shirts, leggings, moccasins, and other items, and one at a time each warrior took items and horses to trade for a captured woman so she could return home. Eventually the trade was completed, and the Lakota left without violence.

This story required both sides to repeatedly act with integrity. A single broken promise or dishonest word at any point would have prevented the outcome that everyone found satisfying, and may have led to very bloody fighting and many unnecessary deaths. To avoid this, each side had to trust each other, and each side had to have integrity to honor that trust.

This showed me how essential integrity is to good relationships. Whether the culture is a married couple, a pair of villages or a whole nation, people can get into major conflicts. If one or both sides lack integrity, then why bother discussing a peace agreement that won't be kept? Alternatively, even if both sides have acted cruelly, if they have integrity, then there is the possibility of peace as people make agreements and stick to them.

Integrity Especially When it Feels Scary

"Integrity of service," "solidarity," and "taking care of each other" are all closely related. The opposite of all of them is selfishness. Do I serve my neighbors by standing for a culture where everyone treats everyone else decently, and those who don't are held accountable? Or do I withdraw and avoid conflict at all costs?

I have encountered a lot of people who take integrity seriously until they get scared. The board of that nonprofit strongly supported anti-racism and anti-sexism efforts. There had been some troubling instances of racism and sexism among participants in the past, so this was justified. Unfortunately, the leadership was afraid of being called out on social media for being racist or racially-insensitive, and so they ended up causing other troubles instead.

At one gathering a black woman got into a dispute with a white man who led a group in singing some songs by Bob Marley. She said she felt harmed by some lyrics he sang that referred to slavery and freedom. Even after he apologized, both in private and in front of a large group of people, she continued to criticize him, even saying in front of the large group that he clearly had psychosis.

I knew what happens when people start labeling their neighbors with mental diseases (see Chapter 6). Nothing good ever comes from labeling others with dehumanizing mental health diagnoses. I spoke with a board member in a private call about it, and I said, "We need to expect respect for everyone all the time. If we don't, and if we make exceptions, then we're simply opening the space to be controlled by the biggest bully, of whatever color or sex. And that means we have to hold people accountable when they speak inappropriately, whether they're a white man or black woman or anybody else."

Afraid of being accused of racism on social media, the board member's voice wavered as he said, "I agree. But that's really scary." I said, "Yeah, I'm scared too. And we've got to stand for a culture of respect for everybody or else inappropriate behavior will just keep happening, and the only question is who can get away with it."

The scarier the moment, and the higher the stakes, the more important integrity becomes. Two famous political sayings illustrate the power of integrity of service.

In 1758, Claude-Adrien Helvétius published a controversial book in France called "De l'esprit" ("On the Mind"). It was condemned by religious authorities as well as the French Parliament and publicly burned. Voltaire didn't like the book and publicly said so, but he also strongly and publicly opposed the book burning. One historian described Voltaire's attitude as, "I disapprove of what you say, but I will defend to the death your right to say it."[10]

On the other end of the spectrum is a tragic poem based on the writings of German pastor Martin Niemöller. The Nazi government had persecuted many people throughout the 1930s and 1940s, including Jews, Roma, homosexuals, socialists, labor activists, and more. Niemöller described what happened when he wouldn't show that integrity of service:

> First they came for the socialists, but I did not speak out – because I was not a socialist.
>
> Then they came for the trade unionists, and I did not speak out – because I was not a trade unionist.
>
> Then they came for the Jews, and I did not speak out – because I was not a Jew.
>
> Then they came for me – and there was no one left to speak for me.[11]

I admire Niemöller's willingness to later recognize his own mistakes and learn from them. Still, comparing Voltaire and Niemöller, which man worked to create a healthy nation even at the cost of standing up to religious and political authorities, and which man shrunk away in fear when his neighbors most needed him?

Solidarity is a powerful antidote to authoritarian nations, and solidarity really is rooted in integrity of service. Can people in a group trust each other to help when someone's threatened, or is everyone really on their own? When a person is persecuted or mistreated, do their neighbors rally in support, like Voltaire supported Helvétius or the Nootka who protected their clown when she was threatened by a priest? Or do the neighbors retreat into their homes and seek out distractions or excuses to justify their inaction?

Acting in service is fundamental to human nations, but unhealthy nations commonly forbid people from truly acting in service of their neighbors and loved ones. Thus, many people learn to go through the motions of service, pretending to care about their neighbors when they're really prioritizing their own needs, as explored in *Chapter 29: Privilege 3 - Going Through the Motions*.

Chapter 29: Privilege 3 - Going Through the Motions

Corruption and selfishness are the same thing. When a political leader enriches themselves at the expense of the community, people correctly recognize this as corruption, and it is also simply one form of selfishness.

Rulers behave with extreme selfishness, imposing laws and narratives that allow them to exploit vast numbers of people. Unfortunately, selfish rulers encourage selfishness in others, normalizing selfishness as part of abusive nations. In other words, rulers normalize widespread corruption.

At a deep level, rulers require people to prioritize obedience over acting in deep service, and thus rulers require corruption or selfishness to avoid trouble. Anyone who selfishly prioritizes their own needs at the expense of their community's needs has been corrupted. Sadly, the large majority of people in authoritarian nations can become corrupted as a result, subtly prioritizing their own privilege, or their own comfort and safety, over the needs of the people they claim to serve.

When people prioritize their own career, privilege, comfort or safety over acting in deep service, they wind up *going through the motions*, meaning that instead of being driven by a deep desire to serve and the joy of giving their deepest love, they act as if they care, when in fact they are primarily looking out for themselves. Sadly, this selfishness is one of many ways that abusive, authoritarian, unhealthy nations infect people, who then go on to maintain and perpetuate the cultural disease.

Doctors go through the motions of healing, and sometimes they heal patients and sometimes they don't. Lawyers and judges go through the motions of seeking justice, and sometimes they find justice and sometimes they don't. When people have given up responsibility for acting in deep service, and instead prioritize their own needs, healing, justice and other goals become secondary.

When an entire nation goes through the motions, a culture of fakeness results. Let us review examples from religion, law, science, medicine, academia, politics, corporate environmentalism, elections, the media, charities, and the military.

Religion: Missionaries and Scholars Go Through the Motions

Let us imagine two neighboring towns. People in one town have never heard of Jesus Christ. They don't know about the Bible or Gospel, don't treat Sundays differently, aren't familiar with the 10 commandments, and don't follow many of the other Christian-specific religious teachings. However, everyone in this town consistently shares their possessions as Christ suggested so that there are no rich and poor, they have strong leaders that everybody respects and who actually serve the people, and in general, everybody feels satisfied with their relationships to each other and the Earth.

In the nearby town live people who have learned about Jesus. They study the Bible, know about the 10 commandments, go to Church on Sundays, and often discuss Christian teachings. They have marriages but many are unhappy and face marital infidelity. They have rich people taking advantage of the poor and all the needless suffering that results. They have moneylenders who profit off those in need, similar to the moneylenders whom Jesus attacked in the temple. They also have corrupt governments, environmental pollution, soil depletion, and the other common patterns in Christian nations around the world, past and present.

Which of these two towns would Christian missionaries decide to change? Of course, they would visit the non-Christians and try to change them. This has been happening for centuries.

Christ worked to create a culture of strong leaders without rulers, and yet, as this book has explored, Christian missionaries spread abusive nations with a few people ruling over everyone else. Jesus Christ encouraged deep sharing, yet Christian missionaries spread nations that reward selfishness. Christ fought the abusive moneylenders who predated on his people, and yet Christian missionaries help spread nations of abusive moneylenders. Christ loved children, but priests in the Catholic Church have been caught abusing children all around the world (as explored later in Chapter 38).

For centuries, Christian missionaries have sought to spread awareness of Jesus Christ and Christian salvation, and yet they have propagated nations that practice the opposite of what Jesus taught. Missionaries have sought to share Christ's grace and wisdom with people who already had it! Instead, they imposed an authoritarian Christianity upon people who were already living as Jesus preached as discussed in Chapter 8.

In other words, for centuries, Christian missionaries have been going through the motions of spreading Jesus' wisdom and grace while actually trapping free people in abusive relationships and perpetuating unhealthy nations.

I do not think Jesus would be pleased!

Consider the many examples this book explores:

- Jesus rejected being a king, but Christian missionaries have spread slave societies where a few people rule over the rest, whether the rulers are called kings, billionaires, or anything else.

- Missionaries have pressured women into subservient positions (reviewed in Chapters 24 and 25)

- Jesus encouraged deep sharing, but missionaries have propagated nations that reward selfishness (reviewed in Chapter 10)

- Jesus encouraged deep sharing, but missionaries have shamed people for deep sexual sharing (reviewed in chapter 25)

- Missionaries misunderstand nations of deep sharing, considering them rude (seen in Chapter 9).

- Missionaries have forced children into abusive schools (reviewed in Chapter 21).

- Christ taught that we are all God's children, but missionaries propagate hurtful, heart-closing narratives such as Original Sin and disconnection from God. (reviewed in Chapter 18).

For many centuries, Christian missionaries have spread un-Christ-like nations around the planet. Christian missionaries have spread nations that make people miserable if they give away all their possessions and stand up to abusive authorities as Jesus Christ did.

Of course, blind beliefs and privilege have also played a major role. Any Christian who fully adopted Christ's teachings and dared to take a stand against authorities has risked prison or death for millennia, just like Christ was persecuted by the Romans. It's easier and safer to keep one's social standing, such as one's priesthood or missionary role, rather than acknowledge the abusive authorities, give up one's privilege, and face the consequences. Roman emperor Theodosius called those who didn't believe *his version* of Christianity "demented and insane," and threatened them with divine and human punishment. Because Jesus stood up against oppressive authorities, anyone who *actually* followed in Jesus' footsteps and stood up against oppressive authorities has been punished for 2,000 years.

When priests or politicians encourage people to be like Jesus, but label people who actually follow in his footsteps as heretics, terrorists, or mentally ill, it may be easier to believe in hurtful nonsense, pretending in order to survive.

This is the unhealthy-nation trap we're in. And, in order to have a society in which it is safe to stand for mutual respect, this is the trap we get to escape or end so that people can more easily do actual good in the world and not unknowingly propagate misery.

Christians are not the only ones; other religions have spread abusive nations too. But Christians have been among the most successful, and they spread abusive nations which directly contradict the teachings and practices of their revolutionary spiritual leader, Jesus Christ. This is what happens when humans get stuck in abusive nations and learn to ignore or legitimize their abuse: they perpetuate it.

Scholars in many religions go through the motions of seeking to understand God and God's will. For example, ancient Chinese scholars argued over which Chinese ruling dynasties had the "Mandate of Heaven." Did a ruler have God's blessings only if they conquered all of China? Or just a certain area of China? In reality, these religious scholars were not studying divinity. They were debating the rulers' legitimacy.[1]

Religious scholars who assume the legitimacy of their rulers and ruler-imposed religions will only ever find ruler-approved interpretations of divine truth. Much religious scholarship is analogous to a man who drops his keys in a dark parking lot but only searches for them near a lamp because it's the only place where he is willing to look for the keys.

For centuries, many Christians and Muslims faced severe legal or social pressure to believe that the Bible or Quran was the literal word of God, and in many parts of the world, this is still the case. Disbelief could be punished by imprisonment, exile, being ostracized, or death. Thus no allowable interpretation of God's will could contradict the Bible or Quran which were imposed on their nation by their rulers.

Scholars might still learn some valuable lessons by studying their texts, but these lessons will be limited. Huge numbers of people have spent countless hours poring through religious texts rather than studying the nonhuman world which might help observant people notice that they're trapped in unfree, authoritarian nations. Those nonhumans might even offer lessons in how to fight and thus perhaps find freedom, as seen in Chapter 14.

Law: Lawyers, Judges, and Prison Guards Go Through the Motions

Prison guards have a challenging job. Their job is to guard prisoners and not wonder whether the prisoners deserve to be in prison.

Luckily, in the United States, prison guards can rest assured that the law only allows police to intervene when they have probable cause to suspect a crime, or when there's a clear emergency. The law guarantees a jury trial by one's peers where the defendant gets to present all the evidence of their innocence, ensuring that innocent people aren't falsely imprisoned. If a jury believes the defendant really broke the law, a judge sentences the defendant, giving a punishment they believe is best for the defendant while keeping society safe. The prison guard can thus rest assured that all the people he or she guards really did commit crimes and, according to the law, really do deserve to be in prison.

Unfortunately, this is a fairy tale. The truth is rather different. In the United States, approximately 2% of federal criminal trials involve the presentation of evidence and determination of guilt by a jury. The other 98% of cases are short-circuited due to the plea-bargain system.[2]

Plea-bargaining is simple. The government prosecuting attorneys accuse someone of a crime and press charges that carry many years of prison time. Then they offer the defendant a deal: if you legally acknowledge your guilt, regardless whether you are actually guilty or not, we'll lower the severity of the charges and reduce your prison time.

Prosecutors commonly threaten very long prison sentences and then offer a significant reduction in exchange for pleading guilty. One 2012 study found the average prison length for drug charges at trial was 16 years, whereas for plea bargains it was 5 years, 4 months. Charges can easily extend to 30-60 years or longer. Amazingly, the difference between the plea-bargain time and the full prison time is known as a "trial penalty," as if people should be penalized for seeking a trial to prove their innocence.[3]

Former federal prosecutor Mary Pat Brown acknowledged that this put "enormous pressure [on defendants] to plead." US Supreme Court justice Anthony Kennedy confirmed in 2012 that "plea bargaining… is not some adjunct to the criminal justice system; it is the criminal justice system."[4,5]

Even innocent people face tremendous pressure to plead guilty. Defendants may fear racism in the judge or jury. They may fear that the police will speak dishonestly, and the jury will believe the police and not them (police corruption is explored in Chapter 32). They may fear that their court-appointed attorney will be incompetent, unmotivated, or simply overworked. This pressures innocent people to plead guilty, encouraging them to lie to minimize their punishment.

Thus when I drive in my car on a highway and I pass a prison, I think to myself, "I have no idea how many people in there actually committed the crime they supposedly committed." 98% of prisoners never got to present evidence at a trial; they got scared into accepting a deal to minimize the risk of a life in prison. What percentage of prisoners actually violated the law? 20%? 50%? 80%? Nobody knows! How strong was the government's case, and how much corruption in the prosecutor's witnesses or police perjury might have been revealed by a trial? Nobody knows!

The prison guard is thus going through the motions of protecting his or her community from dangerous criminals. The guard has no idea whether most inmates are actually a threat to the general public. The guard has no idea whether they committed a crime, or whether the supposed "crime" should be punishable at all (see an example of laws created solely to persecute people in Chapter 32). Of course, prison guards can believe whatever they want as long as they remain obedient.

Attorneys likewise go through the motions of seeking justice and keeping supposedly dangerous people off the streets. Judges go through the motions of determining appropriate sentences and upholding the rule of law. It's all a farce when there is so little actual justice, and instead the government scares people into accepting a lesser abuse because they are afraid of the much greater abuse of decades in prison.

Science: Researchers Go Through the Motions

Scientists commonly claim to seek deeper understanding of the universe, but for many reasons scientists can become attached to a particular belief and resist new evidence. Physicist Max Planck noted in 1950, "A new scientific truth does not triumph by convincing its opponents and making them see the light, but rather because its opponents eventually die, and a new generation grows up that is familiar with it."[6]

In other words, science advances one funeral at a time. Scientists' funding and social status is not tied to their willingness to acknowledge uncomfortable truths and admit their mistakes. Their status is commonly tied to their ability to make new discoveries and publish papers. Once they've laid out a new theory, published extensively, and even become leaders in their field, it can require a great deal of humility to accept that one's discovery was wrong. This may also threaten a scientist's ability to find work elsewhere. After all, if a potential employer asks about a scientist's career and the scientist acknowledges that their most exciting theories have all been disproven, how likely is that scientist to be hired?

This pattern has actually been demonstrated and quantified in a research study. Focusing on the life sciences in the United States, the study looked for people who were leaders in their field, and researchers investigated what happened when those leading scientists died. It identified leaders by looking at scientists' funding, number of patents, and number of times their papers had been cited.

After most star scientists' deaths, researchers found that their collaborators published far fewer papers than before, and non-collaborators in the same field published far more. Overall, the subfield expanded. Furthermore, these non-collaborators who suddenly published so much more were often new to the field. Study co-author Pierre Azoulay speculates that outsiders may suspect that the star scientist's subfield is closed and seek out other subfields in which to establish themselves. In other words, often one's connection and alignment with the lead scientists in a field is effectively more important than the merit of one's research.

Of course, science may advance very rapidly when there are real consequences for being wrong. For example, political leaders may fund new advancements in weaponry and hold scientists liable for the truth or falsehood of their research. Business leaders may likewise hold researchers accountable when their money is on the line.

Scientific communities have their own processes for holding scientists accountable for doing bad research, but systems like peer-review and auditing only address shoddy research. There are few processes for protecting the careers of scientists who acknowledge honest mistakes or even just proposing reasonable theories that later turn out to be wrong. Thus when no leadership holds scientists accountable, each individual must decide for themselves if they're on the right path. As Azoulay's research and many scientists' experiences show, scientists often prioritize protecting their careers over seeking deeper knowledge when these two different motivations conflict. It is thus no surprise that science commonly advances one death at a time.

Medicine 1: European Physicians Go Through the Motions

When unhealthy nations reward and normalize selfishness, and highly-credentialed people prioritize their own privilege (such as their career and social standing) over the people they claim to serve, bizarre and tragic things happen.

In 1846, Hungarian-born doctor Ignaz Semmelweis became an assistant in the First Obstetrical Clinic of the Vienna General Hospital. His role was to examine patients, assist with difficult deliveries, keep records, and teach students of obstetrics. The hospital had two maternity clinics and he noticed something very strange. In the First Clinic, the death rate of young mothers dying from puerperal fever was 10%, whereas in the Second Clinic only 4% died from this disease.[7]

The clinics admitted pregnant women on alternating days, but Viennese women widely understood that their chances of death at the First Clinic were high and many women begged to be admitted to the Second Clinic. Some women even preferred giving birth in the street rather than risk going to the First Clinic. These patients recognized something Semmelweis soon found out: puerperal fever was less common even among street births than at the First Clinic.

Semmelweis investigated and found that the two clinics followed nearly identical procedures. He carefully eliminated all the differences, including religious practices. The climate was the same in both, and the less dangerous Second Clinic was actually more crowded. The First Clinic was a teaching clinic for medical students, whereas the Second Clinic trained midwives. But they used the same procedures! What could cause this dramatic difference in death rate?

Semmelweis felt disturbed, saying it "made me so miserable that life seemed worthless." Eventually he realized that the medical students were working with cadavers, then directly assisting with births without washing their hands. This was common practice at the time. Semmelweis developed a belief that "cadaverous particles" must be causing the diseases seen in the First Clinic.

In May 1847, Semmelweis instituted mandatory hand-washing with chlorine bleach and saw dramatic results. The mortality rate in April 1847 was 18.3%. In the following months, the mortality rates were – June: 2.2%, July: 1.2%, and August: 1.9%. The next year, there were two months with zero deaths.

Semmelweis had made a profound improvement that saved the lives of many women. However, his theory contradicted widely held scientific and medical beliefs at the time. Instead of diseases spreading via "bad air" or as the result of "unfavorable atmospheric-cosmic-terrestrial influences," Semmelweis dared to propose a new disease vector which suggested that physicians themselves could contribute to the women's deaths. Additionally, many doctors held strong to their status as gentlemen, and of course gentlemen could only have clean hands.

Not only did the medical community reject his theory, physicians at other hospitals refused to even try washing their hands! These doctors were confronted with a choice: they could at least try out an inexpensive, simple, and fast technique already proven to save many lives, which would require humility, or they could protect their social standing and self-image and refuse to even try hand-washing. Refusing and protecting their privilege was a lot easier.

These doctors' privilege didn't depend on the health of the women they treated. They could keep their careers while maintaining their old ways if they wanted, simply out of ideology and personal insecurity. Doctors continued to attend medical conferences, publish medical papers and build new theories of disease all while someone had already found the key to dramatically reducing pregnant women's deaths from causes in their very own hospitals!

Semmelweis moved to other hospitals where he made the same change and saw death rates fall below 1%. He wrote in his book, "Most medical lecture halls continue to resound with lectures on epidemic childbed fever and with discourses against my theories. The medical literature for the last twelve years continues to swell with reports of puerperal epidemics, and in 1854 in Vienna, the birthplace of my theory, 400 maternity patients died from childbed fever. In published medical works, my teachings are either ignored or attacked. The medical faculty at Würzburg awarded a prize to a monograph written in 1859 in which my teachings were rejected."

Decades later, Louis Pasteur showed that microscopic bacteria exist, and doctors began to form theories that justified hand-washing. But this was too late for thousands of dead women and their poor husbands and children. Hundreds of doctors had been going through the motions of studying and healing disease. In this case, their career and privilege were not even under threat; only their self-image was at stake. But the doctors' social status was impervious to the opinions of the people they claimed to help, and so they persevered in causing unneeded deaths.

The large majority of doctors refused to acknowledge a truth they found uncomfortable and refused to even run a simple hand-washing experiment. This illustrates the persistent and, in this case, deadly selfishness that authoritarian nations nurture and encourage, when people learn to focus on their own comfort, safety, and self-image rather than act in service of the people around them.

Medicine 2: Soviet Psychiatrists Go Through the Motions

Chapter 6 explored how Soviet psychiatrists were trained to diagnose political activists with mental diseases. These highly trained physicians intended to diagnose and treat mental health disorders, when in reality they were part of an extremely oppressive regime that punished anyone who sought meaningful change.

A core group of psychiatrists worked with the Soviet KGB, their main security agency, to develop these false, politically motivated diagnoses. But a large number of psychiatrists actually had no self-awareness at all when they then made the diagnoses such as "sluggish schizophrenia" due to activists having "reform delusions" or trying to "struggle for the truth."[8]

Authoritarian societies cast a powerful spell, where people learn to ignore the abuses at the heart of their nation. A few years after the Soviet Union's collapse, Soviet-Ukrainian psychiatrist Ada Korotenko participated in a study on the political abuse of psychiatry. She examined 60 former victims and found that many of her colleagues and even friends had been involved in the abusive use of psychiatry. She interviewed former victims and compared their state of mind with their former diagnoses, and she realized that they had been hospitalized for nonmedical reasons. She even realized that she could have authored the original diagnoses herself. Other former Soviet psychiatrists acknowledged that they saw the same thing in retrospect.

Soviet authorities had carefully set up an hierarchy of mental health institutions to keep psychiatrists in line, and lower-level psychiatrists dared not disagree with higher-level psychiatrists' diagnoses. The hierarchy ranged from scientific organizations, to psychiatric faculties, Moscow and Leningrad psychiatric hospitals, and then down to regional hospitals and outpatient clinics. By controlling who rose through this hierarchy, authorities maintained a medical profession that used mental health diagnoses in politically manipulative ways.[9]

One researcher summarized how it was easier for people to agree with their professional norms than to think for themselves:

> …for many Soviet psychiatrists [the diagnosis that activists had a mental health disorder] seemed a very logical explanation because they could not explain to themselves otherwise why somebody would be willing to give up his career, family, and happiness for an idea or conviction that was so different from what most people believed or forced themselves to believe. In a way, the concept was also very welcome because it excluded the need to put difficult questions to oneself and one's own behavior. And difficult questions could lead to difficult conclusions, which in turn could have caused problems with the authorities for the psychiatrist himself.[10]

This is blind belief in action. When the truth was forbidden, people maintained their career by believing in nonsense. Soviet psychiatrists claimed to be healing mental health disorders, but they were only going through the motions of healing.

Academia: Academics Go Through the Motions

It certainly would be amazing if people could have comfortable careers studying and helping to resolve big problems in their society.

In the United States, a whole academic community has formed that studies the US prison system. They study what policies really help prisoners and reduce crime for society, and what policies make things worse.

These crime-studies academics were part of a broader group of social sciences academics who believed that they could study their society, recommend improvements to policy makers, and then see those improvements enacted to benefit everybody. These academics did their studies and made their recommendations, but they noticed something troubling: policy makers were not implementing their recommendations!

A whole academic field on "research utilization" formed, and they repeatedly found little evidence that their work impacted the making of public policy. In other words, the rulers did as they wished rather than use these academics' research to improve life for everybody.

A 1978 National Research Council report, *Knowledge and Policy: The Uncertain Connection*, noted that many studies had shown how changes in policy could lead to major improvements for society. Researchers had worked to make these studies relevant for policy makers, and yet they timidly noted, "we lack systematic evidence as to whether these steps are having the results their sponsors hope for…" These researchers in the 1970s wanted to make a difference and seemed disappointed that their work wasn't having the desired results.[11]

For decades, academics continued to notice that their work had little impact on policy-making. In 2014, the US National Research Council published a report that cited the 1978 report, and then they noted how, in the intervening 36 years, nothing had changed: "Social science evidence has had *strikingly little influence* on deliberations about sentencing policy over the past quarter century… *Scholars of policy making have long been skeptical* of rational models of the relationship between research and policy." (italics added)

In other words, policy makers commonly ignore these academics' work. This 2014 report on incarceration listed many different prison policies known to be ineffective in controlling crime, including three-strikes, mandatory minimum sentencing, and life without possibility of parole. The authors noted, "Some of these decisions were premised on beliefs or assumptions about deterrence, incapacitation, or both. From a crime control perspective, those beliefs and assumptions were largely mistaken."

When rulers and other authorities decide what to do, then make up a seemingly plausible reason, cover story, or excuse to publicly justify it, this is what it looks like. When a person or institution continues to do whatever they please for decades while citing "beliefs and assumptions [that are] largely mistaken," this has a name: *bullshit*. Obeying their masters, policy makers make up bullshit to justify the policies they have already decided on.

Policy makers and their masters don't need people to agree with their made-up excuses. Indeed, academics are quite free to disagree with policy makers' justifications for the policies they enact. The point of the bullshit – that is, the point of spouting false-but-plausible cover stories that seem to justify the rulers' policies – is to maintain the fiction that the policy makers serve the people, when in reality they serve the rulers who manipulate laws for the benefit of themselves and their supporters, and to the detriment of millions of others.

As long as academics relate to policy makers collectively as if they are acting in good faith, and argue about the truth or falsehood of the individual bullshit justifications for hurtful policies, they're missing the point – that authorities are acting selfishly at the expense of the common good, and they'll say whatever they need to in order to get away with it.

Thus, in 1978, social science academics widely understood that their work had little impact on policy-making. This awareness continued through 2014, when this community of academics who focused on crime continued to recognize that their work had little impact on policy-making. And yet they continued to do their research studies, publish papers, seek tenure at their universities, and go through the motions of improving their society by advising policy makers even while knowing that policy makers were ignoring them.

If these people weren't rewarded with comfortable careers, would they spend their professional lives creating recommendations for policy makers, fully aware they were being ignored?

While these crime-studies academics built their comfortable careers, knowing their work had little practical impact, what changed in the United States between 1978 and 2014?

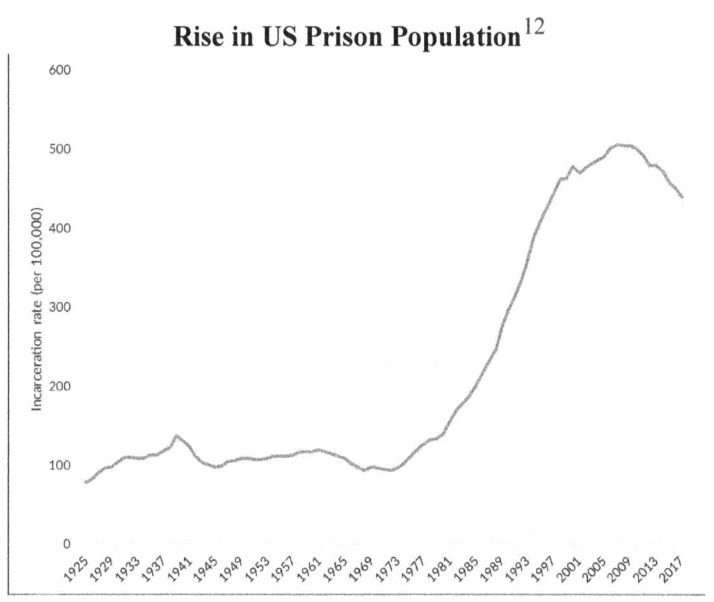

Rise in US Prison Population[12]

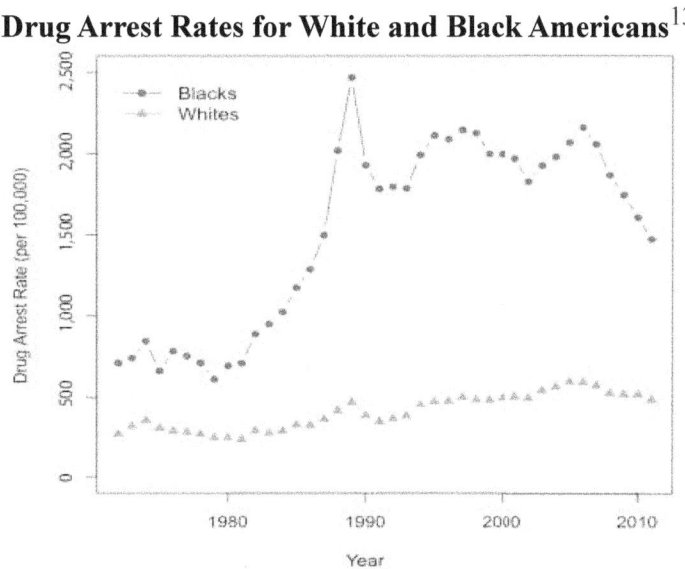

Drug Arrest Rates for White and Black Americans[13]

Drug arrest rates for blacks and whites per 100,000 population, 1972 to 2011.

The US prison population was roughly flat until about 1980. Then it began to massively increase all through the 1980s and 1990s. A major cause of this increase was drug arrests which disproportionately targeted black people.

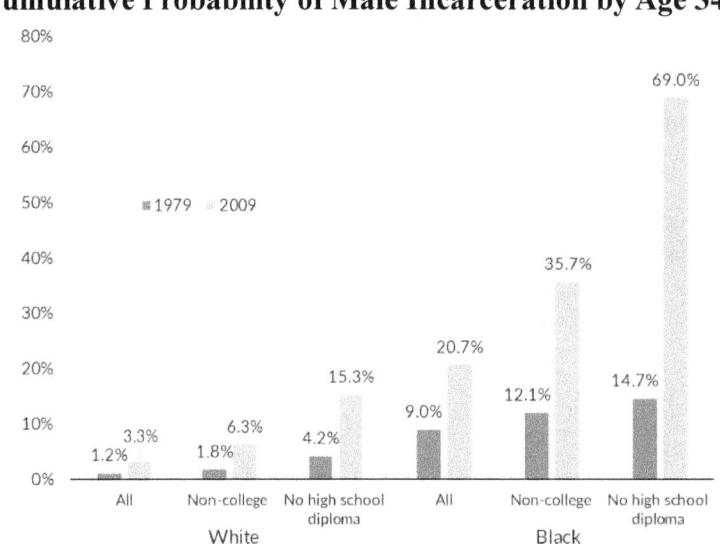

Cumulative Probability of Male Incarceration by Age 34[14]

As the above graph shows, by 2009, more than two out of three black men without a high school diploma had spent time in prison by the age of 34. This was up from 15% in 1979, which was already much higher than the equivalent percentage for white people.

These graphs collectively show that the rulers of the United States launched a system of prison slavery substantially targeted at black people, though every race including Latinos, whites, and others faced higher prison rates too. Recall the 13th amendment to the Constitution that supposedly ended slavery but left a big loophole: "Neither slavery nor involuntary servitude, except as a punishment for crime whereof the party shall have been duly convicted, shall exist within the United States…"[15]

Slavery is alive in the United States as I write in 2024. Consider the defining features of pre-Civil War chattel slavery in the US and how those features exist in modern prison slavery:

- *Arbitrary arrest*:

    - Chattel slavery: People were more-or-less randomly kidnapped and enslaved in Africa or the Americas.

    - Prison slavery: Few people "deserve" to be in prisons, even by the standard of the law, with only 2% of criminal trials involving any presentation of evidence. Furthermore, drug laws were not created to help society, but as a cover story for persecuting black people and anti-war activists, as explored in Chapter 32. Thus arresting people for illicit drug use is essentially an exercise in rulers' arbitrary power as well.

- *Forced separation of families*:

    - Chattel slavery: Families could be sold apart at the whim of the slaveowners.

- ○ Prison slavery: Families are again torn apart as people are arbitrarily imprisoned.

- *Forced labor*:

  - ○ Chattel slavery: chattel-slaves were abused if they didn't work as ordered

  - ○ Prison slavery: prison-slaves are abused if they don't work as ordered, with prisoners subject to time in isolation cells, denial of family visits, and more. They have no legal right to avoid working, commonly for less than $1/hr. Much of this pay is then withheld to cover the costs of their imprisonment. Prisoners who don't work may be unable to buy edible food and hygiene products in the commissary or basic medical care.[16,17]

- *Vast amounts of rape*:

  - ○ Chattel slavery: Slaveowners recognized that raping enslaved women increased their wealth, as the resulting children became their property as well.[18]

  - ○ Prison slavery: So much sexual assault occurs in US prisons that there are more male-victim sexual assaults than female-victim in the United States overall, as reviewed in Chapter 24.

Over the 1980s and 1990s, I believe the US ruling class instituted a system of prison slavery. During this time, academics studying crime continued to do their research, produce their reports, and build their careers. Even while they continuously noticed that their work had little impact on their nation, and politicians kept enacting terrible policies based on false assumptions, academics kept going through the motions of working to make things better. What was more important to them: building their careers, or seeking justice and stopping the new system of prison slavery?

I am not the only person to recognize that academics often go through the motions of doing meaningful work. This understanding is so widespread that it is reflected in the English language itself. According to the Merriam-Webster dictionary, common definitions of the word "academic" include "very learned but inexperienced in practical matters" and "having no practical or useful significance."[19]

Plenty of people have dedicated their lives to improving their society without success. What distinguishes people who go through the motions from people who try and fail? People truly committed to change will notice when their strategies aren't working and try something different. People who are committed primarily to their career or social standing often keep doing the same things over and over, going through the motions of improving their society even when they know they are having little effect.

Media: Journalists Go Through the Motions

When members of the Haudenosaunee traveled to a United Nations meeting in Switzerland in 1977, they encountered very strange behavior from journalists.

These Haudenosaunee representatives wanted to discuss extremely important issues, and they were not alone. At this meeting, they joined with people of other healthy nations, including people of the Lakota in North America, Aymara of South America, and Guaymi of Central America. Together, they discussed the importance of living in ways that respected the Earth and how imperialism and corporate exploitation of the Earth made this very difficult. They discussed apartheid and racism and what could be done about it. They discussed poverty and its impact on people. These were weighty issues that impacted the lives of millions of people and humans' ability to live on the Earth in a good way.

They held press conferences and spoke with journalists, but they were very disappointed, describing, "Many pretty words of welcome, [and] an equal number of insane questions." They asked, "Will they ever understand that this is not a game?"[20]

The reporters wanted to pose with them in pictures and take pictures of their passports. They put tremendous energy into getting just the right angle in their pictures. Everything seemed amusing to the reporters, and indeed, headlines of the next day's news articles showed how seriously journalists had taken the messages of these people of healthy nations: "INDIANS DO SCALP DANCE AT THE U.N.," and "INDIANS COME TO UNEARTH WAR HATCHET!"[21]

The journalists were clearly willing to focus on trivialities rather than substance, and the travelers were amazed at the journalists' shallowness:

> This whole process of media – the distillation of information – is evidence of the insanity. Reporters who learn thousands of facts, write thousands of words, and learn nothing.
>
> The question is not: Why do they do it? We know why they do it – for a salary, for professional recognition.
>
> The question is: Why do they do it to themselves? Why do they care to lead such stupid, confused lives?
>
> Today they cover the Indians; tomorrow the sewage system; the next day the high cost of food. Doesn't anything ever connect for them?

Clearly these journalists had learned to ignore the abuses at the heart of their nation, so they avoided making deep connections. After all, if a person isn't going to take a stand anyway, why bother making deep connections and getting upset? When people learn not to take a stand for what's right, they wind up leading confused lives, focusing on trivialities or amusements, or pretending to care about some weighty problem, only to move on to another issue the next day.

When journalists focus on their salary and professional advancement – that is, when they focus on maintaining the safety and comfort of their privilege – they wind up going through the motions of making their readers well-informed.

Politics: Politicians Go Through the Motions

Even top political leaders can struggle to acknowledge the cruelty their rule requires. When they choose to remain in charge anyway, they may go through the motions of kindness to avoid recognizing the truth of their abusive behavior.

In 265 BCE, Aśoka led an army against the Kalingas, one of the last Indian republics in southern Asia. By his own records, hundreds of thousands of people were killed or enslaved. Aśoka felt so disturbed at this misery that he renounced war, adopted Buddhism, and declared that his kingdom would henceforth be based on the principles of ahimsa, or nonviolence. He had his edict carved into a magnificent granite pillar in his capital, saying that "Here in my kingdom, no living being must be killed or sacrificed." He even replaced sacrificial rituals with vegetarian feasts. Clearly Aśoka went through the motions of embracing nonviolence as he continued to maintain the army, capital punishment, and slavery.[22]

When people go through the motions of service but actually prioritize obedience, comfort and safety, they often work hard while doing the opposite of what they say they want.
This is a normal pattern in any society where people allow themselves to be ruled.

Environmentalism: Well-Funded Non-profits Go Through the Motions

The World Wildlife Fund (WWF) is one of the largest environmental conservation organizations in the world. With revenue of almost half a billion dollars in tax year 2022 alone and over $600 million in assets, it claims that "85% of WWF spending is directed to worldwide conservation." With that much money to spend on protecting the environment, I would think the WWF is doing a lot of good.[23,24]

The WWF does not just survive off individual donations, either. In tax year 2022, it pulled in almost $75 million in government grants, $39 million in corporate grants, and $35 million from foundations. A group called Charity Navigator, which helps people direct their charitable spending to trustworthy organizations, even gave the WWF their highest rating.[25,26]

The WWF's finances are especially impressive. I know a lot of very dedicated environmentalists in other organizations who can barely make ends meet. It does not pay very well to sit in a tree to prevent it being cut down, or stand on a railroad track to prevent another shipment of coal from getting to a power plant, or stand in the way of construction equipment being used to lay more fossil fuel pipelines. Around the world, people doing this kind of real environmental protection are persecuted with made-up legal charges[27], unconstitutional laws designed to suppress their freedom of speech[28], surveillance[29], attacks from thugs hired by rich corporations[30], and other trouble.

What is the World Wildlife Fund's secret to getting paid well for their work while so many environmentalists are practically broke? How can the WWF be heavily funded by governments while other environmentalists are being harassed by governments? How come the WWF gets paid millions of dollars by corporations while other environmentalists get harassed by those same corporations?

It turns out, when an organization is willing to *go through the motions* of protecting the environment, it can make a lot of money!

In fairness, this does have certain benefits: lots of people get to have comfortable careers, feel good about their role in a prestigious organization, and make big decisions involving large amounts of money. Leaders and fundraisers get to have meetings with high-ranking people in wealthy corporations and governments. The only downside is that much of their work, in reality, has the effect of discouraging meaningful environmental activism, meaning that all those millions of dollars are actually making things worse.

After a 2006 United Nations report on the beef industry's very negative environmental impacts, industry leaders decided that, "if the industry ignores the problem, then somebody else will get to define the issue for the industry." Thus many large corporations such as McDonalds, Cargill, and others around the world collaborated with the World Wildlife Fund to operate industry organizations such as the Global Roundtable for Sustainable Beef along with many national roundtable spin-offs, all of which pretend to protect the environment while prioritizing the needs of the beef industry.[31]

For example, the US Roundtable for Sustainable Beef's 154-page "Sustainability Framework" report mostly focuses on improving efficiency or at best reducing pollution from current operations. There is no discussion of how to scale back the beef industry and, even for their less impactful measures, zero effort to impose standards on member corporations or verify their compliance.[32]

The net effect is that the American beef industry increased production more than 13% from 2010-2022 while downplaying its environmental impact, delaying regulations, and assuring policy makers that the industry's voluntary efforts would be good enough. After all, these corporations were partnered with prestigious environmental groups like the World Wildlife Fund which, for many people, made their claims of voluntary change seem credible.[33]

The World Wildlife Fund isn't the only example of supposed environmentalists serving the corporations that do so much harm. The Environmental Defense Fund (EDF) plays a similar greenwashing role, with one EDF employee saying, "Companies want to work with the Environmental Defense Fund because it boosts their reputation as climate leaders. But instead of calling them out for causing harm, EDF lets them pollute and praises them for what little they do in hopes we'll eventually convince them to change. So EDF provides cover for businesses…"

This is what greenwashing looks like, where prestigious environmental groups "collaborate" with polluting, destructive, and dishonest corporations so that the corporations can continue business-as-usual while pretending to care about the environment. Is it any wonder that, just between 2015-2022, McDonalds donated between $4.5-$9 million to the WWF, or that Walmart donated between $3.5-$9 million over a six year period? Other major donors include Tyson Foods, Costco, and Burger King. And their greenwashing and spin has paid off: around the world, most people vastly underestimate the climate impact of the beef industry. The beef industry's methane emissions almost equal the methane emissions from all fossil fuel combustion, and methane is one of the biggest contributors to climate change.[34,35]

When environmentalists go through the motions of protecting the environment while prioritizing the needs of their donors, the rich get richer, a few people get well-paid "green" jobs they can brag about, and millions of people are fooled into thinking that something meaningful is being done, or that the problem isn't really so bad. If it were obvious how little was being done to protect the environment, how many more people would join groups that actually protect the Earth?

Amazingly, when environmentalists go through the motions of protecting the environment, the net effect is worse for the Earth than if they had done nothing at all.

Elections: Voters Go Through the Motions

There was definitely a time when I thought people could create meaningful change through elections. I was taken aback the first time I heard an older activist say, "If elections could make a difference, they wouldn't be allowed."

At the time, this hardly seemed believable. Every election centered on important issues of foreign policy, problems with corruption, or proposals to reform aspects of the country that weren't working so well. My teachers at school considered elections important, just like journalists in newspapers and on TV, politicians themselves, and many ordinary citizens interviewed on television. Furthermore, the United States wasn't the only country with elections; countries around the world from Australia to Russia to Brazil and Mexico have elections that potentially change top government leadership. I felt skeptical that all these countries' populations could be falling for a similar trick. Could elections really just be a giant cover story to give legitimacy to policies that unelected people want enacted?

Finally I figured out the right question to ask. What happens when elections *do* make a difference?

The answer seems pretty clear: as soon as a population is able to elect a leader who serves the people's needs, corporate, military, and intelligence agency leaders conspire to sack the government and replace it with one that serves the rich and restores their power.

All through the 1950s, 1960s, and early 1970s, Australians voted for various government leaders to make the important decisions in their society. Citizens debated what Australia's foreign policy should be, how to use their resources, and how to address crime and inequality. The news was full of serious discussions about important policy decisions. Political candidates had serious debates to see who could sway the public to their side. All this continued into the late 1970s, 1980s, and 1990s, as Australians continued to vote for Australian government leaders who were responsible to their voters every few years.

In 1975, unfortunately, the queen of England didn't like the government's policies, and her vote mattered more. Her representative, governor-general John Kerr, fired the prime minister Gough Whitlam and demanded a new government, entirely overriding the desires of millions of Australian voters.

Most informed Australians can only speculate about why the sacking occurred. Was Whitlam dismissed because he opposed foreign military bases in Australia, including US surveillance bases?[36] Or because he had directly ordered Australia's domestic intelligence agency to sever ties with the US CIA?[37]

News articles continued to assume that Australia really had "national independence" and the British monarch was only a "powerless relic of a former time," but when the queen's representative fired the government at will, she demonstrated that Australians were only going through the motions of self-rule. The fact that the monarch had to fire just one government in the entire 20th century shows how well elections are routinely managed to prevent independent leaders from arising.

This pattern plays out commonly. After Chileans managed to elect Salvador Allende as president in 1970, he increased wages, purchased agricultural land from large estates to give to peasant cooperatives, and nationalized US-owned copper mining companies. Allende initially became president with over 36% of the vote in a three-way race, and three years later he received 44% of the vote, showing that his popular support was rising.[38]

As often happens in unhealthy nations, the rich prioritized their wealth over the wellbeing of their neighbors. As a result, the Chilean military led by Augusto Pinochet launched a coup in September 1973 with US assistance.[39] It was supported by Chilean oligarchs and much of the middle class. Pinochet proceeded to reign for 16 years, torturing tens of thousands of political opponents and undoing Allende's progressive policies.[40]

Chilean voters chose their leaders, election after election, until they chose leaders whom the oligarchs and foreign patrons didn't like, at which point the oligarchs installed someone new.

In authoritarian nations, elections essentially serve to legitimize governments that serve the rich. In unhealthy nations where rulers make the real decisions, voters only go through the motions of self-governance.

Charity: Charities Go Through the Motions

Who wouldn't want to be part of a worthwhile cause, making a difference in society that could benefit everybody? I imagine it feels good to support a movement that surely no one could oppose: fighting cancer.

Many charities have been founded to raise funds to support scientists and researchers in fighting cancer. The National Foundation for Cancer Research is one such group, and on its website they highlight their 51 years of work, with 5,300,000 donors and a total of $415,000,000 raised to help "make game-changing discoveries in cancer treatments, detection, prevention, and ultimately, a cure for all types of cancer."[41]

These are certainly admirable goals. However, I always hesitate to donate because these charities and cancer researchers studiously avoid the truth: causing cancer is extremely profitable for a variety of industries, including fossil fuels, plastics, pesticides, and more. Cancer is quite preventable; America's rulers merely prioritize their wealth over the people's health.

I was recently asked to donate to a cancer-research charity while paying at a grocery store, and I recall looking around at all the cancer-causing agents sold just in the store itself. Pesticides in food are strongly linked with cancer, and the vast majority of food for sale contains these pesticides.[42] The food without cancer-causing pesticides is called "organic" and costs much more money. Food packaging has been found to leach hundreds of different cancer-causing chemicals into the food.[43] As I looked towards the non-food part of the grocery store, I saw home cleaning products in which researchers identified 193 poisonous chemicals which off-gas into the air where they can be breathed by the whole family.[44] Many of these chemicals cause cancer. Other toxic chemicals are coated onto "non-stick" cooking equipment.[45] Some people are making a lot of money causing cancer, and this little survey only covers my grocery store!

Countless charities have supported countless researchers in "fighting for the cure," seeking better ways to prevent, detect, and treat cancer. And yet anybody who pays attention knows how to end cancer: forbid people from producing cancer-causing poisons. To prevent cancer, make it easy rather than extremely difficult and costly to live without being exposed to these poisons.

As long as it remains legal and extremely profitable to make and sell cancer-causing poisons, selfish people will continue to do so and cancer rates will keep steadily rising. And while cancer rates predictably rise, charities and donors will continue to raise funds to meticulously study every aspect of cancer except its actual causes, and scientists will keep recommending ways to reduce cancer that carefully avoid offending the rich. When people learn to ignore the abuses at the heart of their nation, even charities merely go through the motions of fighting terrible diseases.

Military: Military Leaders Go Through the Motions

When I pass by a TV, I commonly see news hosts interview people to discuss the United States' national security. These supposed security experts are often ex-generals or ex-politicians, and they talk about various national security threats in concerned and authoritative voices.

And yet the United States has undermined its own security far more than any adversary over the past 30 years. For decades, so-called national security leaders did nothing to stop it.

The US Army claims that "people are the Army's greatest resource."[46] Given that the military recruits American citizens, anything that dramatically lowered the health of the American public would be a national security threat. An unhealthy population will produce unhealthy soldiers unable to protect the country.

What are the biggest threats to Americans' health?

Researchers have noted an alarming drop in the nutritional quality of fruits and vegetables in recent decades. US researchers studied 12 types of vegetables and found a 30% drop in vitamin C and a 27% drop in calcium from 1975 to 1997.[47] Poor soils produce poor food, and pesticides wipe out the organisms that maintain healthy soils.[48] The United States' own agricultural practices are threatening its food security. The pesticide industry consistently lobbies for reduced pesticide regulation.[49] Where are the national security leaders advocating for organic farming which generates non-toxic, more-nutritious food?

Chapter 37 will explore how toxic chemicals have been dramatically affecting nonhumans' and humans' emotional, physical, and sexual development. In just 2022, the US chemical industry spent over $65 million lobbying against increased chemical regulation.[50] Where are the national security leaders protecting Americans from predatory chemical companies?

Soldiers today grew up with less nutritious food and higher toxin exposure because previous national security leaders decided not to do anything about these threats.

But it gets worse.

The United States won in World War II in part because of its "Arsenal of Democracy." The United States transitioned huge numbers of factories from producing consumer and business goods to producing war material like tanks, bomber planes, and ammunition. American three-star general and president of General Motors Alfred Knudson said, "We won because we smothered the enemy in an avalanche of production, the like of which he had never seen, nor dreamed possible."[51]

However, beginning in the 1990s, the US allowed companies to move many factories to China, a country the US now considers an adversary. The US trade deficit with China was $6 million in 1985, and as the US moved much of its industrial production to China and then imported products built in China, this deficit ballooned to almost $84 billion by 2000 and about $345 billion in 2014.[52] Millions of jobs were shifted to China so that corporate executives could make a little more money due to their lower wages and lower environmental standards.[53]

As I write in 2024, the US military considers China their "pacing challenge," meaning the country most able to potentially protect itself from the US military.[54] US vice presidential candidate JD Vance recently called China the "biggest threat to our country."[55] Suddenly, in the past few years, the government has encouraged corporations to relocate production out of China and into other countries.

Government leaders finally recognized the threat of having the US economy and military dependent on its adversary. Unfortunately, decades of economic mismanagement mean that the US is hardly able to defend itself if it chooses to fight China. One recent military report said that American production capacity "is a shriveled shadow of its former self. Crucial categories of industry for U.S. national defense are no longer built in any of the 50 states…"[56]

Where were the national security leaders while the political and corporate leaders hollowed out America's industrial base? American four-star general Mike Minihan recently predicted a US-China war in 2025.[57] But the US has spent 30 years moving its industrial capacity to China!

In 1961, US president Eisenhower warned that the military-industrial complex could "endanger our liberties or democratic processes."[58] That threat continues today. One study found that over a single five year stretch, 80% of four-star generals and admirals went to work for "defense"-related corporations after retirement where they prioritized these companies' war-profits and their own income over America's actual security.[59]

When top military and national security officials prioritize the personal safety and comfort of their privilege, they only go through the motions of protecting their country from its greatest threats.

Many People Have Gotten Lost on the Trail

People of healthy nations have recognized this fakeness and debated what to do about it. Do they try to integrate? Or keep fighting for independence?

When he was 15 years old, Sioux man Ohiyesa's father urged him to integrate with the American nation and go to school. His grandmother strongly opposed this, saying it went against their spiritual teachings, and many of their children had died in the schools. His father acknowledged the deep trouble they faced: "We have now entered upon this life, and there is no going back. Besides, one would be like a hobbled pony without learning to live like those among whom we must live."[60]

Ohiyesa's grandmother continued to see life in the authoritarian nation as sacrilege. She repeatedly said, "It is not a true life. It is a sham. I cannot bear to see my boy live a made-up life!" Ohiyesa pointed out an important principle she had taught him: "When you see a new trail, or a footprint that you do not know, follow it to the point of knowing." He wanted to follow the trail of integrating into the abusive American nation.

But his grandmother warned him, "All I want to say to you is this: do not get lost on this new trail."

Ohiyesa's grandmother was sadly right, and she was not the only one to recognize how deeply lost people of unhealthy nations are. One group of Haudenosaunee people defined "colonialism" as "the process by which we are systematically confused." They also noted that the word colonialism stems "from the word colony: to be controlled from afar."[61] Being "controlled from afar" is simply what it means to have rulers.

Many people in abusive nations have clearly gotten lost or confused. It's not just the United States; this happens in any authoritarian nation. When people learn to tolerate predatory rulers – that is, when people learn to prioritize their own comfort, safety, career and obedience to authority – they wind up going through the motions, living made-up lives, and generating nations of make-believe.

The Freedom That Comes From Giving Up Privilege

Happily, I also see people finding deep satisfaction from giving up their privilege and instead giving their love fully in service of what most matters to them. Such people also wind up having amazing adventures.

Harriet Tubman offered one example, as reviewed in Chapter 16. She didn't publish articles about how to make slavery more humane; she just freed people trapped in slavery.

A story from Russia shows how people achieve meaningful change when they're willing to risk their privilege. Peter Kropotkin was born in 1842 to an aristocratic family in Russia. He became a scientist and also became involved with political activists seeking to change their government from a monarchy to a republic. In 1874, he was arrested for subversive activity.[62]

After two years in prison, malnutrition, scurvy, rheumatism, and other debilitating illnesses had taken their toll. His brother had been exiled to Siberia, many fellow prisoners had died or lost their sanity, and Kropotkin worried that he too would die soon. Authorities transferred him to a hospital prison in St. Petersburg before his trial.

One afternoon, a guard whispered to him, "Ask to be taken out for a walk." Kropotkin's friends were not waiting for the law to deliver justice. They were going to deliver justice themselves.

Kropotkin was taken out to a prison courtyard about 300 paces long. At the end lay an open gate and sentry box, and Kropotkin could see people and carriages moving on the public street behind it. He began to take regular walks in the prison courtyard. The guard who accompanied Kropotkin allowed him to walk back and forth in a perpendicular line, never in the direction towards the exit. Since the guard was impatient, he often walked a few paces ahead.

Kropotkin used the time in his cell to prepare his escape. In his head, he calculated the exact moment when the guard would walk farthest ahead in the courtyard, and when he would most struggle to give chase. The prison had given Kropotkin a flannel dressing gown which dragged on the ground as he walked, so in between guard visits, he practiced throwing off his gown in two swift movements. When the guard walked past his cell, he was in his sickbed. A moment later he was on his feet practicing taking off his gown and throwing it away, and in the next moment he was wearing his gown again and lay in bed as the guard passed by.

Kropotkin's friends set June 29, 1876 as the date of his escape. They would signal him with a red balloon floating in the sky. Finally the guard took Kropotkin outside. Kropotkin took off his hat, his signal to show he was ready to run to the exit. He scanned the sky, his heart pounding, but there was no balloon! He feared his friends had been captured, and drearily finished his walk and returned to his cell.

However, the truth was more bizarre than that. That morning, his friends had discovered there was not a single red balloon for sale in all of St. Petersburg! They got a red balloon from a child but found that it no longer floated. In desperation, they filled a red ball with hydrogen, but it was too heavy to float high enough. They then attached the red ball to a lady's umbrella and she walked back and forth holding it high outside the prison walls, but not high enough for Kropotkin to see. They just could not give the signal.

This shows the importance of preparing for every contingency. This simple mistake could have easily doomed Kropotkin to life in prison or death.

Fortunately, they improvised a backup plan. Back in his cell, a guard handed Kropotkin a watch that a woman had just brought to the prison for him. Kropotkin examined it and found a tiny scrap of paper inside with a message he decoded.

Two hours later, a guard accompanied Kropotkin out to the courtyard for another walk, perhaps his last before being transferred for trial. He heard a carriage and took off his cap, and on cue a distant violin began a cheerful melody. Kropotkin began walking as he eyed his guard, a powerful man armed with a rifle and bayonet. Beyond the guard, he saw the open gate and freedom.

Kropotkin was ready to run, but then unexpectedly the violinist stopped. After 15 minutes of silence, he saw a row of carriages arrive outside the gate, and the violinist suddenly began a wild tune. In his memoirs, Kropotkin said, "Immediately, the violinist–a good one, I must say-began a wildly exciting mazurka from Kontski, as if to say, 'Straight on now, - this is your time!'"

Kropotkin saw that the guard was several paces back and momentarily facing away. There would never be a moment like this again! He threw his dressing gown to the ground and he began sprinting across the courtyard. His guard and several other people give chase. The guard was so close that his bayonet almost scratched Kropotkin. This was good luck; if the guard had fallen further behind, he might have just stopped and shot the escaping prisoner.

Kropotkin approached the gate where an apparently drunken peasant was engaging the sentry in a furious argument about a disturbing disease. Kropotkin burst past the distracted sentry and leapt into his comrade's carriage who roused the horses to full speed. Kropotkin's friend then passed a fancy overcoat and tophat into his hands. After a sharp turn onto another street, they looked at each other in disbelief as one guard exclaimed, "Catch him! Chase him! Curse you, you imbeciles, I am ruined!"

Back at the sentry gate, a concerned man with a violin approached the guards and asked each person individually what happened, who had escaped, and what they thought would happen next, interrupting their debate about how to catch Kropotkin. The violinist particularly expressed sympathy with the frustrated guard.

Kropotkin was taken to a friendly house where he quickly shaved and changed clothes. Then he switched to another cab and left again as the police were searching houses all through St. Petersburg. Where could he wait before he could get to a safe house?

One friend suggested that they spend the evening at Donon, St. Petersburg's most fashionable restaurant, saying, "No one will think to look for you there!" They got a room dedicated to private parties. One by one, Kropotkin's friends showed up, exhilarated and hungry. They passed the evening drinking, eating, telling stories, and laughing uproariously.

This story showed me what people can accomplish when they are willing to risk their comfort and safety to do meaningful work together.

Each of Us is a Divine Being With Sacred Gifts to Give

If people in authoritarian nations experienced real solidarity, they would know they could trust each other and they would not fear losing their social standing. Without the deep security that comes from knowing one is surrounded by trustworthy and generous neighbors, many people seek what security they can by clinging to their privilege and comforts. Selfish rulers shape nations so that people keep their social status by acting selfishly.

People who act with deep integrity reveal the fakeness of those who don't. Doctor Semyon Gluzman was a Soviet psychiatrist who spoke out against political abuses of psychiatry in the 1970s. He spent years in prison as a result. In a book published in 1989, he acknowledged the need to really seek change, not just talk and pretend. He wrote, "This work must be done: real people, victims of abuse, need protection and help, not academic discussion about humanism and justice."[63]

This is the trap we're in. Authoritarian nations always generate and depend on massive amounts of abuse. Comfortable academics may cope by engaging in meaningless discussions or ignoring large parts of reality. Rulers may spout feel-good philosophies that are obviously contradicted by their actions. Lawyers and judges pretend to seek justice while ignoring the worst injustices.

Authoritarian societies require people to go through the motions to maintain their comfortable lives, ignoring the wretched abuse that always happens when a few people rule over many. It's not just rulers who are corrupt. In unhealthy nations, huge numbers of people become corrupted if they're not careful, acting selfishly instead of acting in deep service.

This shows why revolution is an act of dignity and self-respect. All these doctors, lawyers, judges, military generals, academics, and others who go through the motions prefer to please their bosses and maintain their career instead of walking the most meaningful life imaginable. This is simply what happens when millions of people learn to act submissively to their rulers.

Every one of these people had ancestors in healthy nations who, at one time, lived every moment of every day like it mattered. At some point, perhaps many generations ago, many of us became so disconnected from our healthy-nation ancestors that going through the motions started to seem normal rather than humiliating.

Each of us is a divine being with sacred gifts to give. Every one of us has a way to make the world better that only they can do. When people go through the motions, they prioritize their personal comfort and safety instead of offering their sacred gifts and giving their love fully.

It doesn't have to be this way. Dignity, self-respect, and freedom all lie in the same direction: we've got to end or transform the abusive nations we are stuck in. One way or another, we must stand for a culture of mutual respect where nobody rules over anybody else.

People in unhealthy nations can easily adopt the authoritarian attitude that certain people are better than others and everyone deserves their social position. Whether a person thinks "I am better than other people" or "I am worse than other people," *Chapter 30: Privilege 4 - Entitlement* explores how these attitudes get in the way of deep change.

Chapter 30: Privilege 4 - Entitlement

A person's privilege is revealed by how well or poorly uncaring people choose to treat them. Do police and judges cut them slack, enforce the law as written, or act punitively? If a person works hard with creativity and integrity, do they get a low-paying, low-dignity job, a reliable and decent-paying job, or can they earn many times the average income? If a person is attacked, do police protect them or protect their attackers? Do landlords deny them or seek them as renters? Do government bureaucrats give them breaks or make their life unnecessarily difficult?

A person's privilege is determined by how uncaring people treat them. A person is entitled if they *believe they deserve how they are treated.*

Most people are familiar with *high-privilege entitlement*: the monarch who thinks God made him king, or the business ceo who thinks he achieved great wealth solely by his own work, ignoring all the benefits society gave him that it did not give to others. People with high-privilege entitlement are generally treated better than others and generally believe they deserve it. They are convinced that they are superior, or that they are part of a superior class of people.

If I'm a low-privilege person and I'm physically abused at home, or underpaid at work, or deceived by politicians, or living in squalor, and if I believe I deserve it, I have *low-privilege entitlement*. A person with low-privilege entitlement believes they deserve their abuse and has low self-worth. They either believe they are personally inferior, or they believe they are part of an inferior class of people.

Entitlement is a common manifestation of the core ideology that the authoritarian nation is legitimate and everybody gets what they deserve. The basic authoritarian ideology is that rulers deserve to rule, the engineers and administrators and other credentialed people deserve their comfortable positions, and the workers, prisoners, and people in other lower-class roles deserve their lot.

Rulers clearly benefit from people feeling entitled, as entitled people don't question or threaten the status quo. Entitled people don't question or threaten their rulers' legitimacy.

Entitlement and Spiritual Leaders' Efforts to End It

High-privilege entitlement is easy to notice when it happens in person. After China abolished slavery in Tibet in 1959, the upper class's and lower class's privilege levels were suddenly much more similar. Anna Louise Strong visited the Central Institute of National Minorities in Beijing where ethnic minorities could train for the civil service. Both previous slaves and serfs as well as previous nobles arrived. The institute's director noted: "Those from noble families at first consider that in all ways they are superior. They resent having to carry their own suitcases, make their own beds, look after their own room. This, they think, is the task of slaves; they are insulted because we expect them to do this. Some never accept it but go home; others accept it at last…"[1]

High-privilege entitlement is common in men of authoritarian nations. Islamic activist Waajida found a frustrating pattern. Australian Muslims support her egalitarian portrayal of Islam but are strongly resistant to any change in behavior she suggests. Waajida said Muslims "are not interested in actual change. When I do the kind of work that I do, the Muslim community treats me in two different ways: They love me, because I can speak to non-Muslims… But when I work in terms of real change in the Muslim community, it's 'No, no, no, no good'… They don't want change, everyone's happy. Especially the men who hold the seats. Why wouldn't you be happy on your big throne? They've been taught that men are superior. I don't care what anyone says, they have been taught that, in our mosques they've been taught that. Even the imams when they speak about [equality], they don't believe it… Because if they believed in it, they'd be advocating against domestic violence, they'd be setting up programs…"[2]

High-privilege entitlement – that self-centeredness and belief that they deserve special treatment – is also easy to notice at a distance. Corporate leaders may vote themselves large pay packages while reducing the pay of lower-tier workers. Prison wardens and staff treat prisoners in ways they themselves would never want to be treated. Factory owners pollute the air and water near the facilities while living in cleaner neighborhoods far away. Corporate owners lobby for laws that benefit the rich at the expense of the poor.

Sadly, low-privilege entitlement – where people are treated poorly and believe they deserve it – is also very common.

After the Chinese took over Tibet, some ex-serfs came face to face with previous masters at public meetings. One crippled 57 year old man named Habu came forward to complain. Ex-aristocrat Lhalu had decided to build a new mansion and ordered every serf to bring 900 large rocks and 900 earthen blocks. Lhalu paid a small fee for every hundred, but the workers had to hire carts at personal expense and ended up losing money after being forced to do extra labor for their master. Habu didn't complain about being forced to obey a master or being forced to do heavy labor that took a heavy toll, nor losing personal money.

I believe Habu accepted the legitimacy of the system when he said, "I was your tsaiba [servant], and I owed you labor duty, but my father had died and my household lacked one worker, so I did not owe you as much ula duty as you enforced." In other words, Habu accepted a certain amount of exploitation as legitimate, and complained that the aristocrat had exceeded the agreed level of exploitation.[3]

American teacher James Loewen described how students commonly are not taught the history of classism and oppression of workers in the United States, but instead are taught that the US is a meritocracy. Thus he encountered students from poor families with low self-esteem after hearing questions like, "If you're so smart, why aren't you rich?" He wrote, "Within the white working-class community the girl will probably find few resources-teachers, church parishioners, family members who can tell her of heroes or struggles among people of her background, for, except in pockets of continuing class conflict, the working class usually forgets its own history. More than any other group, white working-class students believe that they deserve their low status. A subculture of shame results."

Loewen and other researchers have called this "the hidden injuries of class," and one experiment demonstrated it clearly. One day, two of Loewen's students drove around their city, and when they stopped at a stop light, they would wait to drive again until the car behind them honked. When they did this in a shiny, nearly new, high-status car, the driver behind them took on average over 13 seconds to honk. When they drove a battered 10-year-old subcompact car, the drivers took less than seven seconds to honk. This experiment captured people of various privilege levels, and students noticed even working class people "deferring to their betters."[4]

When people are not taught the history of class-based, racial, or sexual oppression, it can be easy to develop the low self-worth characteristic of low-privilege entitlement. In her book *The Making of Biblical Womanhood*, Beth Barr described Christian religious leaders who question whether women can preach, or whether women can teach men.

For example, pastor John Piper stated it is not ok and never has been ok for a woman to preach, and Barr acknowledged how few evangelical women know the history of popular Christian women preachers. She described the results: "By forgetting our past, especially women who don't fit into the narrative that some evangelicals tell, we have made it easier to accept the 'truth' of biblical womanhood. We don't remember anything different."[5]

Waajida works to increase women's leadership in Islamic communities and address issues of domestic violence. When asked why more women don't do this sort of work, she said that more women than men were active in their community, but religious leaders consistently give women the less important roles. Highly respected teaching roles only go to men. Waajida described how some Islamic women develop low-privilege entitlement as a result: "Women are told constantly, 'You don't have the knowledge, who are you?' And then we're limited–women only teach women. Women don't teach men. It's like a no-no. But men can teach women of course, and they can teach men. It's like women humble themselves and go,"Who am I to teach, who am I to give lectures?"[6]

In Buddhist Bhutan, a 2012 survey found that 70% of women believe they deserve to be beaten by their partners if they neglect their children, argue, refuse sex, or burn dinner. These women believe they deserve their inferior social standing and deserve their husbands' aggression.

In the United States, one survey found that 20% of women who had experienced sexual abuse gave descriptions that justified or excused the abuse.[7]

In some cases, victims may justify or excuse their abuse with hurtful attitudes towards their attacker. For example, some women victims of sexual abuse may justify it by believing that "boys will be boys," implying that men are supposedly inherently selfish or predatory and thus when a man attacks a woman he is supposedly just "being himself." While men and women have their differences, neither is inherently selfish or predatory. Saying "boys will be boys" when a boy or man sexually assaults somebody simultaneously excuses the attacker's hurtful behavior while implying that boys are supposedly inherently selfish, an attitude which is deeply hurtful to boys and men and holds them to a low standard of behavior.

Hurtful attitudes towards girls and boys, discussed in Chapter 24, illustrate how people's attitudes can adjust to match the systemic sexism in their nation. When rulers impose systemic sexism against women, forbidding them from holding certain jobs or making as much money as men, it is easy for many to believe that girls and women are somehow less capable than men. When abusive authorities do not consistently hold men accountable for rape, and some men commit rape, it can be easy to believe that "boys will be boys," and this is just normal male behavior.

When people are trapped in abusive situations for long enough, it is simply a common coping mechanism to adopt attitudes that excuse, justify, or ignore the abuse.

At some level, almost everyone in unhealthy nations suffers from low-privilege entitlement. Anyone who believes it is legitimate for a few people to rule over everyone else or that it is legitimate for a few to impose laws on everyone else suffers from some degree of low-privilege entitlement.

Raising People's Self Worth and Sense of Dignity by Helping Them Know Their History

These examples illustrate how people's low self-worth is both a result of abuse and a major obstacle to standing together to end that abuse. This is why many spiritual leaders invest a lot of effort into helping increase low-privilege people's self-worth, helping them see they don't deserve their abuse and release that low-privilege entitlement.

Increasing people's sense of dignity and raising their self-worth was clearly part of Malcolm X's spiritual leadership. Randall Robinson, president of the TransAfrica Forum, described the transformation Malcolm X helped bring about:

> [For millions of people,] Malcolm X was a shining model for a new, whole, and proud black personhood.[8]
>
> Before we in the South could see through the mean veil of Southern segregation-there was Malcolm X.
>
> Before we could function beyond the humiliation of Southern bigotry-there was Malcolm X.
>
> Before we could come to know Africa's glorious past-there was Malcolm X.
>
> Before we could find our self-esteem and self-respect-there was Malcolm X.
>
> And we owe him so dearly in ways our young must never be allowed to forget.
>
> Where we have now the very possibility of courage-we owe Malcolm X.
>
> Where we have the wisdom to search for our history before the Atlantic slave trade-we owe Malcolm X.
>
> Where we have the political integrity to simply stand for something because it is right-we owe Malcolm X.

Spiritual leaders commonly build up low-privilege people's self-worth, reminding them that they have much to offer and have a proud ancestry.

To help evangelical Christian women see the possibility of becoming preachers and leaders in their churches, Beth Barr gave countless examples of popular Christian women teachers and preachers going back centuries, including Margery Kempe in the 1400s, Mary J. Small in the 1800s and Ella Eugene Whitfield in the 1900s. Barr described how amazing many of these women were. For example, Baptist minister Samuel W. Bacote described Ella Whitfield: "She can hold an audience indefinitely by the intensity of her earnestness and the clearness and appropriateness of her well-chosen words. The utility of her subjects and the excellence of her delivery have rendered her extremely popular as a public speaker." Similar to how Malcolm X raised many black Americans' self-esteem, Barr worked to raise evangelical women's self-esteem by showing what powerful spiritual leaders women can be.[9]

In addition to sharing the experiences of many present-day Muslim women activists in her book *Fighting Hislam*, author Susan Carland likewise gave a history of influential Muslim women leaders. In the 700s CE, Ibn Kathir disagreed with a decision of 'Umar, the Muslim ruler of the time. She defended her view with verses from the Quran, and he changed his mind, acknowledging, "The woman is right and 'Umar is wrong." She described many Muslim women scholars, teachers, and merchants, and told stories of women interpreting the Quran and challenging the rulings of judges and sexism among foolish men. Carland quoted another Muslim researcher who wrote, "The sheer number of examples from different periods and regions … establish that the answer to some of the 'If men can, why can't women?' questions is 'Men can and women can too'."[10]

Chapter 40 will explore the Zapatistas' revolution in southern North America in 1994. Ana María, a major in the Zapatista army, traveled around the region for years beforehand, spreading awareness and generating support for meaningful change. She described how, in the beginning, mostly men participated in the meetings and few women joined: "We demanded from our comrades in the villages that women also had to organize, represent something, do something, not just men. Because every time we went to the communities there were only men in the meeting, in the study circles we held. We worked hard so that women would rise up and have the opportunity to do something."[11,12]

Women quickly found their voice: "They said: 'If men are going to study or learn things, why can't we? We also want to train [and] learn…' In addition we have comrades who are insurgents and who are showing that yes… we women can, give us the opportunity. That's how many militiawomen joined…" As the Zapatistas celebrated the 10-year anniversary of their revolution, 45% of the fighters in the Zapatista army were women.

James Loewen noticed a big difference when he taught his students about social class and privilege. Once students understood the social mechanisms that kept their families in poverty, they released any shame or guilt they had about being poor. They could forgive their families for being poor when they understood that it wasn't due to any personal deficiency. Loewen described how his students were very interested to learn about the influence of the upper class on all levels of their nation's decision-making, from the federal to the local level. When his students from non-affluent families learn about social classes, he said, "they find the experience liberating."[13]

Ultimately, I want this book to be liberating in the same way. This book illustrates deep patterns of abuse in unhealthy nations to show how they work, and it explores healthy nations to show that we don't have to live with the abuse. There is a better way!

I share so many stories of unhealthy nations because this isn't an academic debate. The abuse in unhealthy nations is real, just as real as the respect within healthy nations. But we don't have to live in an abusive nation – it is just a trap that we happen to be stuck in.

Stories of healthy nations show what it is like to live without abusive rulers, without hate and racism and sexism, and in reciprocity with the Earth. These beautiful stories show that every one of us is a powerful person with a divine nature, and we all have a responsibility to each other and the Earth.

Nobody deserves to be a king or billionaire and rule over others. And nobody deserves to be ruled over or abused. Every one of us has sacred gifts to give in this life, ways each of us makes the world a better place. Every one of us can play a strong part in building a culture of mutual respect.

So long as these abusive nations last, some abused people will continue to accept the legitimacy of their abusive nation and, as they have for centuries, spiritual leaders will try to address the resulting low self-esteem. I only see one way to end this pattern: to transform or end nations of abuse so that people can live without anybody ruling over anybody else.

Releasing Entitlement is Necessary for Deep Change

Low-privilege entitlement generally involves low self-worth and a belief that the person deserves their poor treatment, whereas high-privilege entitlement commonly involves self-centeredness and a belief that they deserve special treatment. Both kinds of entitlement reflect a root trouble, where people accept their abusive nation as legitimate and accept their place within that nation as legitimate.

Attitudes of entitlement are a coping mechanism that help people tolerate living in an abusive nation. Once a person has committed to obeying authority and protecting their own safety and comfort, and given up deep responsibility for themselves and their neighbors, they might as well believe whatever nonsense justifies their behavior. In that sense the attitudes are understandable. Unfortunately, they're also a major obstacle to change.

Chapter 21 shared David Mantell's perspective: "It is difficult to live in a permanent state of rebellion, and rebellions rarely occur when people do not have standards of comparison or do not see the chance of changing their circumstances."[14] Abusive authority figures commonly say or assume that some people deserve their suffering, and others deserve their comforts. Believing otherwise – that we're all divine beings, and it's not right for rulers to impose law, and it's not right for the rich to hoard their wealth while neighbors suffer, and no one deserves special status or misery – is already an internal act of rebellion. Of course, it is also true!

Giving up one's entitlement is a key part of that personal growth from "triple inhibition" or subconsciously holding back one's feelings and urges to "single inhibition," where a person can choose when to express their feelings and when to hold back. Giving up any underlying sense of superiority or shame is a necessary part of standing for meaningful change.

Releasing long-held beliefs about one's superiority or inferiority can be difficult. But even after a person recognizes they're fully worthy of respect, just like everyone else, this only addresses the need for change in oneself. Once a person decides to seek collective change, what should they do?

I don't have any easy answers, but I have found some inspirational stories. To read about people who successfully replaced endless violence in their region with centuries of peace, continue to *Chapter 31: The Story of the Peacemaker*.

Chapter 31: The Story of the Peacemaker

Plenty of humans have gotten trapped in cycles of violence. Even healthy nations that maintain respect internally can wind up in long-term violence with other healthy nations. One Nootka woman said she was taught that if a generation of people were pressured into killing others, the nation needed four generations "to get people's heads fixed afterward."[1]

Unhealthy nations keep millions of people trapped in abusive, exploitative relationships, and rulers use violence, the threat of violence, lies, heart-closing narratives, child abuse, and much more to maintain control. Some of us in unhealthy nations have only been trapped for a generation or two, while others have been trapped for dozens of generations over thousands of years.

Sometimes I almost fall into despair, since it seems like unhealthy nations are so resistant to change. Why bother working for deep change if deep change doesn't seem possible? Why bother walking in the footsteps of Harriet Tubman or Jesus Christ if I'm just going to get murdered or imprisoned, while the abusive society lives on as before?

Plenty of other nations have faced seemingly-endless violence. When the British began colonizing eastern North America, many healthy nations already lived there. One of them was the Haudenosaunee Confederacy, which was composed of five nations at the time: the Mohawk, Oneida, Onondaga, Cayuga, and Seneca. But before those five nations joined in a confederacy, they were at war with each other and suffered much brutal violence for little benefit.

Several centuries before Europeans began heavily colonizing North America, the five warring nations formed the Haudenosaunee Confederacy and have maintained peaceful relations ever since, even expanding to include other member nations. Different researchers and keepers of the Haudenosaunee oral traditions estimate different start dates, but by one common estimate, the Haudenosaunee Confederacy has maintained peaceful relations among themselves for approximately 900 years.

They have still sometimes fought with other nations, and when unhealthy European nations threatened them, they fought to protect themselves. But the Haudenosaunee were able to successfully end their seemingly endless wars and generate a baseline of peace internally that has lasted for almost a millennium.

The story of their transformation from endless war to centuries of peace shows that humans can overcome cycles of terrible violence. Whenever I forget this and need a reminder, I review what the Haudenosaunee call *The Story of the Peacemaker*.

Different Haudenosaunee storytellers offer varying accounts of this ancient story. The following telling is drawn from the *Encyclopedia of the Haudenosaunee*, edited by Barbara Mann of the Seneca nation and Bruce Johansen.

The Story of the Peacemaker

Almost 900 years ago in roughly the region that Americans know as New York State, there was a lot of violence among the five nations. Different accounts offer different explanations for the warfare, but it lasted a long time.[2]

The Huron who lived to the north noticed all the fighting among their southern neighbors, and they feared the fighting might spread to them. Then a woman named End of the Field dreamed that a peacemaker would be born to her daughter, She Walks Ahead, and he would serve his people on a great mission. Later her daughter had her own dream where she learned that her son would bring about a lasting peace among the warring nations.[3]

Soon a healthy boy was born and he grew rapidly. As soon as he could speak, he said repeatedly that it was not good for people to be unkind to each other. He did not have an easy time, as he may have had a stutter and faced derision. But he kept speaking of peace, and Huron clan mothers called assemblies to hear him speak.[4]

Finally the peacemaker decided it was time to travel south to where the nations were at war. He had to cross a large lake, and tradition has it that he crafted a boat of white stone, which may be a reference to a canoe formed of white ice. His grandmother and mother saw him off, although his mother had little faith in his boat. She said, "I love you, my child, but what are you doing in launching a stone boat?" However, past spiritual leaders had used a similar boat, and when the peacemaker's boat carried him safely away, this was taken as a sign of his spiritual power.

After landing on the far side of the lake among the warring nations, the peacemaker was found by hunters who were taking refuge from the fighting. The peacemaker conveyed his message of peace and then set off in search of nearby villages. His next stop was at the Peace House of a Seneca woman named Yegowaneh, known as the peace queen, fire woman, or mother of nations. Yegowaneh regularly fed war chiefs of different sides as they traveled through her land and counseled them to "follow the paths of peace."

Yegowaneh asked the peacemaker why he had come, and he gave a long description of his vision for peace. He described the principles of health, righteousness, and popular sovereignty. By health, he meant physical and mental health as well as peace among women and men. By righteousness, he described the importance of embedding social justice in the rights and duties of each person as well as advocating simple good behavior. By popular sovereignty, he referred to ensuring that the councils reflected the people's sacred will as well as organizing the civil and military capabilities to manifest it.

Yegowaneh approved and asked how the peacemaker would realize these principles. He said he would bring these principles to life under the longhouse, a reference to the ancient structure of clans. Men would be elected to positions of chief, and clan mothers would hold power over these chiefs. Representatives of each of the five nations would make decisions through council instead of war. Yegowaneh supported this plan, making her the first person of influence to support the Peace Plan. In honor of her wisdom, the peacemaker gave her the name Jigonsaseh. She also became known as a peace chief or the peacemaker's speaker to the women.

Jigonsaseh and the peacemaker agreed that she would stop feeding the various war parties that passed through. Instead, she joined the peacemaker and worked diligently, even risking her life to advocate for peace among the fighting groups. They worked together so closely that the peacemaker would not start meetings until she arrived, and they consulted on every significant detail of their work.

Next the peacemaker decided to visit the Onondaga man Hiawatha, a close associate of a famous and vicious war chief called Adodaroh. Hiawatha had been a cannibal, but on the day of the peacemaker's arrival, just before they met, he decided to give up cannibalism. He thought to himself that he wanted "to make amends for all the human beings I have made to suffer." Just at this moment, he encountered the peacemaker.

The two men went hunting together, and the peacemaker repeated his message of peace. Hiawatha came fully aboard and the peacemaker sent him out to other nations to seek an end to the warfare.

Hiawatha, Jigonsaseh, and the peacemaker continued to travel among the warring nations and advocate for peace, but they faced a tough challenge: how could any one nation agree to peace if the other nations hadn't already agreed? They continued to travel and build a consensus so that all the nations could agree on peace together. Their movement grew as more and more people joined them in working for peace.

Unfortunately, the cold-hearted war chief Adodaroh opposed these plans. To discourage Hiawatha, Adodaroh arranged for Hiawatha's daughters and wife to be killed. Hiawatha was consumed with grief, crying continually. He felt no joy, but went off alone and mourned for a long time. During his time alone, he developed a ceremony for helping people deal with grief which used wampum made from rushes and beautiful shells. When the peacemaker met Hiawatha again, they performed what became known as the Condolence Ceremony, with the peacemaker wiping tears from Hiawatha's eyes and releasing the sorrow from his heart.

Adodaroh, alone among the Onondagas, remained opposed to the peace plan. He would block people from coming to council meetings to discuss the plan, and given his reputation, few people were willing to try attending later meetings. Adodaroh was prone to rage, known for assassinating political opponents or their families.

Jigonsaseh, Hiawatha, and the peacemaker continued to seek peace and their movement kept growing. Other people worked for peace in a variety of ways, including running to various villages to announce upcoming meetings to discuss the peace plan. Eventually a majority of people supported it.

Various nations or subgroups hesitated to join, but each one eventually agreed to the peace plan. The last holdout was Adodaroh, the head Onondaga chief, who had been personally responsible for so much suffering. They could not unite all the nations in peace as long as he stood in the way. But what could be done?

The delegates of all the other nations planned to come together with Hiawatha, Jigonsaseh, and the peacemaker. They saw that their challenge with Adodaroh was to "straighten and reconstruct his mind, so that he m[ight] again have the mind of a human being." They developed a plan with several elements.

One element was a compromise proposed by Jigonsaseh, where the Onondaga would become the fire keepers of the nation and have more representatives in the men's council than any other nation. As Adodaroh was already the Onondaga lead chief, he would become the Haudenosaunee's first fire keeper.

Another element was to sing a Peace Hymn. This was a song of thanksgiving to the elders, ancestors, clan mothers, war chiefs, the people, and Peace.

Lastly, they chose to approach Adodaroh all together, to show him that the rest of the people had reached consensus and how far away from that consensus he stood.

Finally the day of the big convention had come. All the delegates were there, as were Hiawatha and the peacemaker. They had their plan ready with their Peace Hymn, unified approach, and an invitation to Adodaroh to be the first fire keeper. They were ready to see Adodaroh and do their best to change his mind so they could have consensus in their final meeting and adopt the Peace Plan together. The group gathered on one side of a lake, knowing Adodaroh was on the other side, and they planned to cross the lake together to meet him. They had everything and everyone they needed except one: Jigonsaseh was missing.

At first she was only a little late, and the peacemaker was only a little worried. But then more time passed, and the peacemaker and Hiawatha worried more. Where was Jigonsaseh?

Knowing what Adodaroh had done to Hiawatha's family, the peacemaker feared that he had done something terrible to Jigonsaseh. The two men worried that they could not complete their work without her. Jigonsaseh's support and approval had been essential to getting all the other delegates aligned with the Peace Plan. She had worked so hard to unite people around the region and ensure the women's needs were met. Without her support, the men feared that their plans for a Confederacy might not succeed.

Time passed and Jigonsaseh still did not show. Where was she? Finally the delegates, Hiawatha and the peacemaker decided they needed to approach Adodaroh soon, even without her. They boarded their boats and set out over the lake. The peacemaker's heart was heavy with concern, both for Jigonsaseh and for the cause of Peace.

As the group crossed the lake in their boats, the peacemaker looked back and saw her. Jigonsaseh had arrived! He quickly turned his boat around and went back for her. The instant his canoe landed, Jigonsaseh "got in and stood up in front." The peacemaker paddled to catch up with Hiawatha and the other delegates. They had one last major challenge to face: changing Adodaroh's mind and heart.

Now Jigonsaseh, Hiawatha, and the peacemaker were all crossing the lake with the delegates, singing their Peace Hymn along the way. At first Adodaroh shouted and taunted them from the far shore. But after they arrived, Hiawatha addressed Adodaroh's confusion and hostility so that his mind straightened and his heart opened and he came to support the peace plan. At long last, Adodaroh was committed to the Peace Plan too.

Adodaroh did become the first fire keeper, and his name became the title for that role in the Council. Likewise, "Jigonsaseh" became the title of the head clan mother or head fire keeper of the women. The year was 1142 CE.

The peacemaker had completed his mission, working with countless others to create peace among several nations that has lasted for nearly nine centuries as I write in 2024 CE.

The Ashaninka taught me that a nation can maintain a deep, respectful internal peace indefinitely. The Haudenosaunee taught me that a confederacy of nations can likewise keep a deep, respectful peace indefinitely. Humans are capable of deep peace and mutual respect, and the Haudenosaunee's story of the peacemaker shows that even people trapped in cycles of epic violence with violent leaders can generate a stable and satisfying peace.

Ingredients for Lasting Peace: Boundaries, Agreements, and Integrity

How were the nations of the Haudenosaunee Confederacy able to make a peace that has lasted so long? If people today wanted to make a lasting peace, what lessons could they learn from the Haudenosaunee's success?

The Mohawks are one member nation in the Haudenosaunee Confederacy, and in the book *Basic Call to Consciousness*, a group of Mohawk writers gave many details about the Confederacy's founding and described the *Great Law of Peace*. The Great Law contains a huge amount of wisdom. Here's what I learned.

First, healthy boundaries are essential, which are brought to life with shared agreements and reliable integrity.

In War, Each Side Violates the Other's Boundaries

Before they founded the Confederacy, the nations were at war with each other, meaning they were not honoring each others' boundaries. That's simply what war is: actions like theft and killing are violations of other people's boundaries.

Healthy nations could be at war because what makes a nation healthy is that it maintains an *internal* baseline of respect. Within each nation's boundaries, they maintained a baseline of respect, but towards other nations who were outside those boundaries, they were at war.

Regardless of why the wars started, over time, each nation probably had good reason to be upset with the others, as each nation was violating the other nations' boundaries. That's the trouble with war. The more people die, the more the survivors may feel angry at the adversaries who have killed so many of the survivors' friends and family. Thus, it is easy for bad feelings and conflict to go on for a long time.

The peacemaker encountered a system of blood feuds, where people commonly avenged their relatives' deaths with more killing. The Mohawk writers said, "blood feuds between clans and villages ravaged the people until no one was safe." Thus, in an effort to protect themselves, people commonly counter-attacked and killed people from the enemy nation, and each new attack then led to a new counter-attack. The peacemaker recognized that this sort of reciprocal violence could go on indefinitely if it were not stopped.[5]

If war is a state where two or more groups of people are violating each others' boundaries, then what is peace?

Peace Happens When People Agree to Respect Each Others' Boundaries

Peace happens when all groups *uphold agreements to respect each others' boundaries*.

Thus, peace isn't just the absence of war. Two groups of people who are strangers to each other might not be at war, but what will happen when they meet? There is no way to know.

Peace is a commitment by two or more groups of people to respect each other's boundaries. When all sides agree to respect each other's boundaries, and then uphold those agreements with integrity, the peace can last indefinitely.

Making peace and starting a new nation are very similar: they both involve creating agreements to ensure that everyone's boundaries are respected. Chapter 4 explored what defines a nation, including agreements for how to set external boundaries (protection from external threats), agreements for internal boundaries (rules and systems of accountability), and how to live well within those boundaries. These agreements require all participants to have integrity, which is why integrity is so crucial to living in a good way.

The simplest peace agreement might state that everyone involved will stop fighting each other. But the member nations of the Haudenosaunee went much further to ensure that their peace remained durable for centuries.

How did they do this?

External Boundaries: The Haudenosaunee Stand in Solidarity if Anyone is Attacked

When a nation establishes an *external boundary*, they protect themselves from disrespect by outsiders. Everyone inside the boundary – that is, everyone in the nation, and their guests – benefits from this protection.

The founding nations agreed to create a new external boundary for the entire Confederacy. If any member nation were attacked, the entire Confederacy would unite to repel the attacker.

In the story of the Nootka, the preacher, and the clown from Chapter 3, when the preacher attacked the clown, every single Nootka person instantly took a stand to protect the clown. That example illustrates solidarity on the scale of a village.

The same solidarity can happen at any scale. The founding nations agreed to have solidarity on the scale of a Confederacy. An attack on any nation was seen as an attack on the group, and all member nations would fight the invaders, even following the attackers into their own land until the Haudenosaunee were confident that the danger was gone.[6]

The Mohawk writers said, "In terms of the internal affairs of the [Haudenosaunee], the first and most important principle was that under the law the people of the nations were one people." As one people, they stood in solidarity to ensure that if anyone were attacked, the entire Confederacy would respond.[7]

Internal Boundaries that Ensure Respect for Everyone and the Land

Internal boundaries are agreements about rules and systems of accountability that maintain a baseline of respect between people. The Haudenosaunee were very careful to set internal boundaries that respected everyone and the land. They did this in many ways, including:

1. studying past conflicts and making changes to avoid them
2. acknowledging the Earth's needs
3. training their children so that they would accept responsibility for upholding the agreements of their nation
4. rejecting private property
5. avoiding conquering other people.

It is impossible to briefly recount all the ways the Haudenosaunee have maintained a healthy nation for centuries. But I believe these five elements have many lessons to teach. Let's look at each.

1. The Haudenosaunee Studied Past Conflicts and Created Agreements to Avoid Repeating Them

The Haudenosaunee founders carefully studied causes of past conflicts and ensured their agreements would prevent such conflicts from happening again.

One cause of conflict was disagreement over hunting territories. Who was allowed to hunt in what areas? The Confederacy agreed to abolish these boundaries internally, and allowed anyone from any member nation to hunt anywhere in the Confederacy's territory.[8]

They agreed that anyone from within the Confederacy could occupy their land peacefully, and no one else could deny this.[9]

They outlawed theft and hoarding so that no one could have a greater share of their society's wealth than anyone else.

Each member nation remained autonomous and handled its own internal affairs.[10]

They reviewed their traditional ways of handling disagreements and "remove[d] those customs of the past that had sparked conflict and fostered disunity."[11]

They also agreed that their Grand Council would "act as judiciary in serious disputes that people cannot resolve among themselves."[12] Thus, the Haudenosaunee created a mechanism for resolving conflicts when people could not do this themselves. However, it was still everyone's responsibility to ensure that the Grand Council did their job well, and to only select leaders who upheld their rules.

Some people think of "peace" as the absence of conflict, but when people do not trust their neighbors, this kind of peace by itself does not feel very safe or satisfying. The Confederacy's founders believed "if absolute justice was established in the world, peace would naturally follow."[13] Thus, they created a society that guaranteed justice, knowing that a durable, satisfying peace would result.

2. Acknowledging the Earth's Needs

The Haudenosaunee's founders ensured that they lived in right relationship with the land, considering the needs of the land and future generations. As a result, they had strict rules around conservation. They only hunted as many animals as were needed. They ensured that their population did not grow so large that they degraded the land. In other words, they practiced what many Americans call "family planning," but they did this at the scale of the whole society to ensure they lived in a way that the Earth could support indefinitely.[14]

As a result, the Mohawk writers said they lived with "almost unimaginable abundance and variety of nuts, berries, roots, and herbs. In addition to these, the rivers teemed with fish and the forest and its meadows abounded with game…"

Whereas one encyclopedia defines a utopia as "impossibly idealistic"[15], the Mohawk writers described how, prior to the arrival of Europeans, "It was, in fact, a kind of Utopia, a place where no one went hungry, a place where the people were happy and healthy."[16]

3. Training Everyone to Uphold Agreements that Maintain Healthy Boundaries

The Haudenosaunee did not just set up a government and let it do the work of proposing and enforcing laws.

I believe a foundational principle of the Haudenosaunee's *Great Law of Peace* is this: *it is every single person's responsibility to uphold the agreements of their nation.* If anyone is threatened, it is *everyone's* responsibility to ensure the threat is dealt with. If anyone breaks a rule, it is *everyone's* responsibility to ensure that the systems of accountability restore justice.

When the Haudenosaunee say that they are "one people," I believe this is partly because everyone knows that they can trust everyone else to uphold the agreements and stand in solidarity with each other. Occasionally some individuals might misbehave, but as a rule, everybody stands for a culture of mutual respect and ensures that individual incidents are resolved to restore justice.

The Mohawk writers said, "[Everyone] was socialized to the ideology that, if an injustice occurs, it is their moral duty to defend the oppressed against their oppressors."[17]

The Haudenosaunee did not just make a strong government to keep them safe. They created a spiritually strong society full of individuals who accepted responsibility for upholding their nation's rules, knowing those rules worked for everybody. The Mohawk writers said that "universal justice is the product of a spiritually strong society, and many of the rules that [the peacemaker] proposed are designed to create a strong society rather than a strong government."[18]

When every person accepts responsibility for upholding the agreements of their nation, the government responds to the will of the people, not the other way around. This wasn't just a mental or theoretical idea, but a core spiritual part of life. The Mohawk writers noted that "In our ways, spiritual consciousness is the highest form of politics."[19]

All the Haudenosaunee's agreements would be worthless without integrity. The Mohawk writers emphasized "spiritual integrity," and said their people represent "integrity, courage, honor, and peace." Integrity is a requirement for peace, because peace requires clear agreements between people, and everyone must have integrity to uphold those agreements.

Every child was raised to embrace this spiritual integrity, not just as a theoretical goal, but as a practical, spiritual way of life. The Mohawk writers said, "The Haudenosaunee raised their children from the cradleboard to be participants in the culture. The ways of the [Haudenosaunee] have always been powerfully spiritual in nature, and it is true that the government, the economy, everything that is Haudenosaunee has deep spiritual roots."[20]

I believe that *spiritual integrity* described by the Mohawk writers is comparable to *integrity of service*, reviewed in Chapter 28.

The Haudenosaunee specifically avoided factions[21], and I believe they could do this because no group of people felt the need to band together to ensure their needs would be met. Instead, everyone in the Confederacy took responsibility for upholding the rules that allowed everyone to live in a good way.

The Mohawk writers acknowledged that maintaining systems of self-governance that coordinate many thousands of people's needs "is a very complex business." However, "the primary rule about the flow of power and authority is clearly that the power and authority of the people lies with the people and is transmitted by them through the 'chiefs.'"[22]

All this explains why Mohawk man Segwalise said, "The national Councils of Chiefs do not govern the people; instead they act as representatives of their clans in a process that coordinates the wishes of the people." Thus, instead of the leadership imposing law, "The confederated Council of Chiefs, or Grand

Council, acts as the coordinating body of the will and determination of the member nations."[23]

4. The Haudenosaunee Reject Private Property and Welcome the Guidance of Their Spiritual Leaders

The peacemaker had clear instructions for the Haudenosaunee's leaders: "When you sit in council for the welfare of the people, think not of yourself, your family, or even your generation. Make all of your decisions on behalf of the seventh generation coming, then you yourself will have peace."[24]

The Haudenosaunee's political leaders are also their spiritual leaders. These leaders do not just say pleasant words. The Mohawk writers said that their leaders conduct many ceremonies that "require the distribution of great wealth. As spiritual and political leaders, they provide a kind of economic conduit. To become a political leader, a person is required to be a spiritual leader; and to become a spiritual leader, a person must be extraordinarily generous in terms of material goods."[25]

The Haudenosaunee strongly emphasize sharing, and do not embrace private property. The Mohawk writers said, "Property is an idea by which people can be excluded from having access to lands or other means of producing a livelihood. That idea would destroy our culture, which requires that every individual live in service to the Spiritual Ways and The People. That idea (property) would produce slavery."[26]

They recognized that a nation that accepted private property ownership would eventually have leaders that exclude people from accessing others' property. These leaders would no longer perform their duties of serving everyone and helping to redistribute goods.

5. The Haudenosaunee Reject Having Rulers, Even When They Could be the Rulers!

The Haudenosaunee knew that terrible things would happen if they won a war and began imposing taxes or religion on their adversaries. Ultimately, this would make their nation unhealthy, where a few people ruled over the rest.

Thus they created rules for themselves around war.

As the Mohawk writers noted, during war, "The opponent had an absolute right to a cessation of the hostilities at any time by simply calling for a truce. At that point the process of negotiation went into action…"[27]

In the Haudenosaunee's *Great Law of Peace*, they agreed that if they won a war against some other nation, they would not seize territory or impose taxes, religion, or any other injustice. The Haudenosaunee's only demand was that their opponents put away their weapons and stop fighting.

Furthermore, any individual or group could approach the Confederacy, learn their Great Law, and agree to abide by it. After this, they would be offered protection by the Great Law and the Confederacy.[28]

In this way, the Haudenosaunee rejected having a nation with rulers, even when they could be the rulers.

Lasting Peace is Impossible in Unhealthy Nations

Unhealthy nations may end any given war, but they cannot create a satisfying peace where everyone feels deeply safe. Creating deep peace requires nations with healthy boundaries, shared agreements, and consistent integrity by everyone.

Unhealthy nations have rulers who selfishly look out for their own interests at the expense of everyone else. This is why unhealthy nations such as the United States have ignored the obvious wisdom promoted by Haudenosaunee leaders. The Haudenosaunee created peace and maintained a baseline of internal respect for everyone. Such a deep peace leaves no room for rulers to exploit their people, and so the rulers of the United States and many other unhealthy nations have rejected the Haudenosaunee's teachings.

While individuals and subcultures can benefit from lessons from the Haudenosaunee, in order to fully embrace these lessons and find deep and lasting peace, we must create a nation where everyone stands for a culture of mutual respect, and nobody rules over anybody else.

Many People Have Studied the Haudenosaunee, but Few People of Unhealthy Nations Have Learned the Most Important Lessons

I am not the first person to seek wisdom from the Haudenosaunee. Both the United States and Soviet Union were heavily influenced by lessons learned from the Haudenosaunee as well as other healthy nations.

How is it possible that the founders of two profoundly unhealthy nations, which have generated so much abusive behavior, could have been influenced by people of healthy nations?

The answer is simple: many people in unhealthy nations learn to ignore the abuses at the heart of their nation. People can really believe that it is supposedly ok for a few people to impose law on everyone else. They can believe that it is normal and ok to have a few rich and a lot of poor. As seen in Chapter 9, people can become so used to economies of selfish profit-seeking that they do not recognize gift economies when they finally encounter one. When people learn to ignore the deepest abuses at the heart of their own nation, they commonly will learn almost any lesson besides the most important one: what makes healthy nations healthy is that *everybody stands for the culture of mutual respect, and nobody rules over anybody else.* They have strong leaders and no rulers.

The Haudenosaunee maintain a nation where the leaders serve the people, not the other way around, and they're not the only ones. The Onondaga are a member nation of the Haudenosaunee, and Onondaga chief Oren Lyons noted that many nations around the world have fundamentally the same relationship with their leaders: "They're there by the will of the people and when they don't perform, the will of the people will remove them."[29]

Many of the United States so-called founding fathers studied and learned from the Haudenosaunee, as well as other healthy nations. By the late 1700s, the Haudenosaunee Confederacy had grown to include six nations, and Ben Franklin referred to them when he said, "It would be a very strange Thing, if six Nations of ignorant Savages should be capable of forming a Scheme for such an Union, and be able to execute it in such a Manner as that it has subsisted Ages, and appears indissoluble; and yet a like Union should be impracticable for ten or a Dozen English Colonies…"[30]

Thomas Jefferson incorrectly thought that neighboring healthy nations had "no law," but he still considered this "preferable" to "too much law, as among civilized Europeans." Jefferson noted, "France and England… [are a] den of robbers… [and] pirates… I would rather wish our country to be ignorant, honest and estimable as our neighboring savages are."

In 1787 at the Constitutional Convention, James Wilson said, "the British government cannot be our model." Charles Pickney agreed, saying in 1788, "from the European world no precedents are to be drawn for people who think they are capable of governing themselves."

John Adams even learned of the separation of powers from healthy nations, a principle embodied in the US Constitution. He wrote, "the three powers are strong in every tribe… the existence of the three divisions of power is marked with a precision that excludes all controversy." Adams also noted that in the Haudenosaunee "the democratical branch, especially, is so determined, that the real sovereignty resided in the body of the people and was exercised in the assembly of king, nobles, and commons together" while he noted that the Mohawks had "complete individual independence."

All these supposedly wise American founding fathers had studied various healthy nations, including the Haudenosaunee. Yet they ignored the key difference between the Haudenosaunee and the British: the Haudenosaunee have *strong leaders and no rulers*. Nobody imposes law on anybody else. I believe the Haudenosaunee spoke to colonists about their "laws" and "governing councils" because these are the English words that most closely match what they have, but as Seneca man Segwalise said, "chiefs do not govern the people; instead they act as representatives of their clans." As Lyons noted, "when [leaders] don't perform, the will of the people will remove them."

The Haudenosaunee are not ignorant savages. They have strong leaders and no rulers. These wealthy European colonists had so deeply internalized the legitimacy and normalcy of people imposing law on each other that they failed to learn the core lesson: so long as a few people impose law on everyone else, there will be injustice. They were also used to their profit economy that rewarded selfishness, and could not see how this would inevitably generate a nation where a few rich people take advantage of many poor. John Adams showed how deeply a person can internalize the legitimacy of rich rulers when he assumed there were kings and nobles in a Haudenosaunee governing council when, in reality, nobody had such coercive authority.

The United States' founding fathers recognized many of the troubles caused by monarchies, so they formed a government structure they hoped would address the root troubles. But since they had so deeply internalized the legitimacy of a few people ruling over others, and economies based on profit rather than sharing, they wound up creating an abusive society with a democratic facade.

The founding of the Soviet Union is similarly tragic.

In the 19th century, many Europeans worked to overthrow monarchies or capitalist governments, and they wondered what sort of society they should generate if they succeeded.

The Soviet Union's founding ideology was based heavily on the writings of Karl Marx and Friedrich Engels. In his book *Origin of the Family, Private Property, and the State*, Engels went into great detail about Haudenosaunee matriarchal families, where both men and women were free to partner with others as they chose. Engels especially described how Haudenosaunee women enjoyed a sexual freedom that few women in Europe had.

Engels also referenced ancient European healthy nations where both men and women had multiple sexual partners and the children were considered the responsibility of all the adults.[31] He wanted to generate a nation that could return to this way of life of deep sharing and sexual openness by "transforming by far the greater portion… of permanent, heritable wealth - the means of production - into social property[. T]he coming social revolution will reduce to a minimum all this anxiety about bequeathing and inheriting. Having arisen from economic causes, will monogamy then disappear when these causes disappear?"[32]

Engels did not just foresee a communist society as a way to end the abusive boss-worker relationship. He wanted to regenerate a healthy nation of deep sharing where people did not need to cling to their possessions and control each other. Instead of spouses locking each other into restrictive monogamy, Engels envisioned a society where adults were once again free to seek out satisfying relationships as they wished, knowing their economic needs would be met by the communally owned property. It was a beautiful vision.

Unfortunately, the Bolsheviks who founded the Soviet Union did not recognize the fundamental difference between the Haudenosaunee and the monarchies and capitalist democracies: the monarchies and capitalists have rulers, whereas the Haudenosaunee have strong leaders and no rulers. In unhealthy nations, authorities forbid people from opposing authorities' selfish behavior. In healthy nations, everyone expects each other to take responsibility to stand for what's right.

The United States' leaders chose capitalist democracy as a response to the troubles of monarchies, and the Soviet Union's communist ideology was a response to the troubles of capitalism. Both the United States' and Soviet Union's founding ideologies and social structure were also based in part on studies of the Haudenosaunee. And yet, because the founders failed to learn that crucial distinction between healthy and unhealthy nations, they generated countries that merely became unhealthy in different ways.

All these stories crystalize two deep lessons I have learned from the Haudenosaunee. First, it is possible for humans to generate centuries-long peaceful relationships even after long periods of intense violence. And second, the way to a durable, satisfying peace is to build a nation where everybody stands for a culture of mutual respect, with strong leaders and no rulers.

Coming up next, *Chapter 32: A Study in Privilege and World-Shaping - the Police* exposes how authorities systematically train police to protect authorities, their supporters, and their institutions to ensure their continued dominance and control over everyone else.

Chapter 32: A Study in Privilege and World-Shaping - the Police

I noticed something strange in the wake of the stock market crash and financial crisis of 2008.

After rich bankers had made billions of dollars by knowingly giving out fraudulent mortgages to goose their stock prices[1], politicians quickly bailed them out while letting homeowners and the public rot with massive job and home losses. Instead of bailing out the victims of the crime, the government bailed out the perpetrators.

Later, many of these same bailed-out banks went on to commit felony perjury by the thousands in the robosigning scandal, where bank staff falsely processed foreclosures on the fraudulent home loans they had previously pushed and cashed in on.[2]

Some protests occurred in 2008, and then Occupy Wall Street occurred in 2011 with huge numbers of people out in the streets seeking legal accountability for criminal bankers, support for suffering homeowners, and other justice.

I noticed that, in response to this ongoing massive protest, riot police commonly went out in force, lining up to protect the criminal bankers and politicians who had broken endless laws.[3] But I never noticed riot police protecting the people from these big criminals.

This didn't just happen in the United States after the 2008 crash. In many countries, riot police protected the authorities and their wealthy supporters, rather than the people. For example, riot police attacked protesters and protected the powerful criminals in Portugal[4], Italy[5], and France.[6]

The riot police had by far the biggest impact of any police activity that decade. Over the years, police officers also arrested drug dealers, investigated murders, and gave out parking tickets, but when police occasionally chose not to do these things, nothing much changed. These were not high-impact police events with the potential to radically alter the shape of society.

But when financial, corporate, and political leaders commit such severe abuses that thousands or even millions of people take to the streets, then there's a reckoning. Will those leaders continue their predatory behavior? Or will the people put a stop to it? When the riot police consistently line up to protect the predatory rich, the politically powerful, and their property, this is the highest-impact police activity. The biggest criminals can't keep exploiting the people if the police don't protect them in moments of crisis.

In authoritarian nations around the world, the police's stated mission is to protect people from criminals, but I consistently saw the police protecting the biggest criminals from the people.

This book explores many examples in which authoritarian militaries conquer free people and threaten them with submission or death. Nobody likes being exploited though, so conquering isn't a one-and-done event. Every time some population gets so angry or so desperately impoverished that they rise up against their rulers, there is a moment of reckoning: will they find freedom, or will they be subjugated again? Every time the riot police line up to protect the rich and scare or brutalize the rest into submission, the rulers re-establish their supremacy. They reconquer the trapped people.

Rulers thus consider it extremely important that the police consistently protect them from the public, regardless of the law. If the police sided with the public even once against the criminal rulers, and if the military likewise stood with the people, the entire exploitative system might end.

How do corrupt corporate and political leaders corrupt the police so that they continue to protect the biggest criminals? And what would it be like for a police officer to conduct his or her own investigation and personally take the deepest responsibility for keeping their community safe?

Corrupt Leadership Corrupts the Police

Chapter 29 explored how corruption and selfishness are essentially the same thing. Anyone is corrupt if they are willing to focus only on their own needs at the expense of the group. People are also corrupt if they passively tolerate inappropriate behavior towards their neighbors while they remain comfortable. This is true for everyone, not just politicians.

Selfish rulers create police cultures that encourage selfishness. Another way of saying this is that corrupt leaders create corrupt police cultures. It is essential for their continued power that corrupt leaders are continually supported by corrupt police who will not stand up for what's right and protect the public. I believe a large number of police officers want to work in an honest work environment protecting their community, but when they have to choose between integrity and keeping their job, the vast majority choose to keep their job and avoid the many negative consequences of not cooperating with authorities.

This is the truth behind American police whistleblower Francesco Serpico's perspective on honesty in policing: he claims that about 10% of officers are honest, 10% are corrupt, and "the other 80% are officers who wish they could be more honest."[7]

In countries around the world, I have observed two common patterns that combine to generate corrupt police forces:

1. *Leaders create or tolerate a culture of low integrity*: Generate a low-integrity work environment by encouraging or tolerating illegal behavior. This gives police officers upper-class privilege, meaning the law breaks its promises in their favor.

2. *Leaders fire officers who show integrity*: Evict police whistleblowers who stand for a culture of integrity and don't just follow orders.

Regardless of the pressures they feel, any individual officer may choose to act with integrity. And clearly, the vast majority routinely choose otherwise.

What exactly does this pressure look like, and how are the officers of deepest integrity weeded out so that the police can be counted on to reliably protect corrupt leaders?

Let us focus on police culture in the United States as a case study.

1. Rewarding illegal behavior

Testilying: Police Perjury is So Pervasive that They Made Up Their Own Word for It

Examples of dishonest police behavior abound. A recent example occurred in Minneapolis in 2020 after the brutal police murder of George Floyd. Floyd died after an officer kneeled on his neck for over eight minutes as Floyd lay handcuffed and helpless on the ground. The autopsy report indicated Floyd died from asphyxia, but the initial police report did not note any police violence towards Floyd, only indicating that he "appeared to be suffering medical distress" when the ambulance was called.[8]

Sadly, this is hardly rare. Several similar cases have been documented as far back as the 1870s. Officer John Russell beat a fully compliant citizen with a whip till he was half-blind, then arrested him for disorderly conduct. At trial, he told an elaborate story of the man's supposedly unlawful behavior, and if it hadn't been for a credible witness, the officer's tale might have been accepted.[9]

If these were isolated incidents of dishonesty in a culture of integrity, this sort of deceit wouldn't have a special name. However, police commit perjury in court so commonly that they invented their own word for it: *testilying*, a combination of "testimony" and "lying."

Some police leaders protest that perjury couldn't be that common. The president of the Boston Police Patrolman's Association in 1995 said, "Every day all over the country, police officers are testifying. Everyone realizes they are testifying under oath. If this was this much a problem, it would have come to light over the years."[10]

He is right. Police perjury has been studied extensively at least since the 1980s. Testilying has been discussed in a wide range of academic research and journalist investigations since at least the 1990s.[11]

A 1982 study of officers in New York City found that, when the law changed to only allow legally-acquired evidence in court, police simply changed their testimony about how the evidence was acquired. The researcher found that lying was "a routine way… to compensate for what [officers view] as limitations the courts have placed on [their] capacity to deal with criminals."

One survey of prosecutors, judges, defense attorneys, and police in Chicago published in 1992 found that participants believed police perjury to be "pervasive." Respondents described "systemic" fabrication of evidence in support of search warrants. Evidence suggested police deceit in about half the cases where officers testified about 4th amendment-related concerns. Respondents also noted that judges and prosecutors often knowingly ignored this deceit.

This perjury pattern extends to federal police as well. One FBI attorney falsified an email used to request a warrant to spy on Donald Trump in the Crossfire Hurricane investigation.[12]

The pervasiveness of lying in court is already clear, both from the police's use of the word "testilying" and from surveys of police, judges, and prosecutors. How does police leadership reward and encourage this behavior?

For starters, police perjury is rarely if ever prosecuted as a crime. One commission investigating New York City police found that leadership was "charging officers with making false official statements in far fewer instances than facts and circumstances seem to warrant."[13]

In other cases, officers received much lesser punishments or lesser accusations such as showing poor judgment or neglecting their duty. In 2012, when some Boston police officers forged court summonses to fraudulently claim overtime pay, the department noted they had failed to "properly record and process evidence." But leaders wouldn't accuse them of dishonesty.[14]

Furthermore, police often receive promotions despite lying, or perhaps because of it. When police leadership pressures officers to reach their quotas, and rewards those who do and punishes those who don't, lying may become a helpful technique. In one of countless examples, after a judge said that little was credible about a police commander's 2016 testimony about an arrest, he was promoted the following spring to deputy chief and led his own group of detectives. Many instances of perjury are only provable because of video surveillance cameras.[15]

This deference to the police extends to the US Supreme Court. During a 10-year stretch from the 1980s-1990s, the Supreme Court heard 30 cases concerning whether police officers had stopped or seized evidence or people illegally. The court found in favor of the officers in 90% of the cases. The Supreme Court repeatedly emphasized that judges should approach officers' testimony and actions with deference as they are experts in their field.[16]

Clearly, routine perjury is a common feature of police departments and courts around the country, dating back at least to the 1800s. Permitting and rewarding perjury is clearly one way of encouraging a police culture of low integrity.

But it doesn't end there. Authorities in unhealthy nations also employ another technique to train the police to protect them and not the public: tolerating or rewarding police participation in scams.

Tolerating or Rewarding Police Participation in Scams

Another way to generate a police culture of low integrity is for police leadership to allow or encourage illegal scams. This exposes people of integrity because they will take a stand to stop the scams, thus allowing leadership to identify and remove them.

In some cases, leadership implicitly encourages illegal behavior through imposing quotas on police officers, and then rewarding those who meet the quotas even when they behave inappropriately. In 2013, two federal judges accused one New York City police officer of false testimony in gun cases. Not only did he keep his job despite committing perjury, he was later promoted. A Bronx police officer gave false testimony in October 2017 and almost sent a woman to prison with a story he apparently fabricated. In November, he received his gold detective shield.[17]

In other cases, police departments practice illegal scams openly and they are widely acknowledged within day-to-day work.

One New York City police officer in the 1970s described how he was supposed to pay to get assignments where he could collect higher bribes. He said, "It's so systematized that the roll-call man actually would know in a dollar figure how many pickups were on your post, and you were supposed to kick in accordingly." By "pickups," the sergeant was referring to weekly payments businesses made to avoid punishment for illegally operating on Sunday. Those who retrieved the illegal payments got a cut, and the police coordinator knew how much each officer should expect to get for themselves and thus how much they could afford to pay for that job.[18]

The numbers racket or policy game is the most consistent source of police corruption in New York, according to many law enforcement experts and the Joint Legislative Committee on Crime. The US Treasury estimated that at one time, it drew in $1.5 billion per year in bets, and about 1% went to paying off government officials, including police. The 600 plainclothes officers tasked with ending this illegal betting wound up as an unofficial regulatory agency instead, taking a cut while protecting the betting organizers. One officer noticed some organizers seemed to pay and were rarely arrested. He said, "It seemed like our real purpose was to beat down the competition of the gamblers who paid, to help them maintain their monopoly."

This officer got in trouble for arresting all the illegal gamblers rather than just the ones who failed to pay. At one point, he was handed an envelope with $300 and made a complaint to the captain. The captain said, "Well, we do one of two things. I'll take you into the Commissioner and he'll drag you in front of a grand jury and by the time this thing is through you'll be found floating in the East River, face down. Or you can just forget the whole thing." This officer chose not to take the illegal money, giving it to a supervisor instead.

There is one misleading element to reading about scams after an insider or investigator makes the details public. A fully explained scam provides the reader with a reassuring clarity. It's still a scam, but at least the reader knows what the scam is and knows how to relate to it. Often, victims don't understand the police scam; they're just left feeling endangered and helpless.

I once knew a woman whom I'll call Bee. She had a long relationship with a man who had some kind of connection with an organized crime group from another part of the country. Eventually they split up unhappily, and she contacted him to try to address an unresolved dispute.

Bee lived in a beautiful mountainous forest along a clear stream. One day, she looked downhill from her home and saw a strange man. She walked towards him without noticing that there was another stranger behind her. The man behind her knocked her unconscious, and she woke up partially laying in the stream. She couldn't see the men anywhere, but she saw the message they had left. One of them had carved the word "cunt" into her chest with a knife.

Bee went to the local police, and the police went through the motions of an investigation. Then they told her to drop the case. They didn't tell her with their words, but rather with their actions: the local police told Bee their list of possible suspects, and she, herself, was listed as the most likely perpetrator! Her children were listed as the other most likely suspects. Bee accepted the unspoken suggestion and dropped the case.

Were the local police just extremely sexist and willing to cover for an unknown hurtful man? Or were they connected with the out-of-state criminal group? Bee never found out. She just tried to put the matter behind her.

2. Evicting Officers of Deep Integrity

To intentionally generate a culture of low integrity, any police officer who stands up for what's right must be punished or fired. This both removes high-integrity individuals and encourages remaining officers to obey their orders to keep their career and perks.

Sheriff's deputy Garrett DeWyse worked in Saginaw County, Michigan in 2016 when he encountered other officers using forfeiture money inappropriately. He stopped one attempt and reported the issue to a county official. The sheriff responded by giving DeWyse undesirable roadkill removal duty even though he later publicly acknowledged DeWyse's claims were correct. DeWyse sued, saying his free speech rights had been violated, but courts sided with the employer and sustained the reprisal. DeWyse lost his career in law enforcement.[19]

In 2021, the newspaper USA Today researched hundreds of cases where police exposed alleged misconduct in their department, and they found a "similar pattern emerged." Most officers who make internal complaints face firing, demotions, and other forms of threat as retaliation.

In 2016, officer Matthew Gutwill was suspended and later demoted after reporting that another officer had lied as a witness at trial. He met with a federal police officer from a corruption unit, and another sergeant assigned to investigate the issue agreed that the testifying police officer had spoken untruthfully.

However, a higher-ranking officer overruled this, worrying that supporting Gutwill would divide the narcotics team. The day after Gutwill spoke to the federal police, he lost his work assignment. Gutwill sued in court, but whistleblower protection laws required him to prove that his behavior "played a substantial or motivating part" in the reprisal, and he could not do this, so he lost the case.

Gutwill said, "I go to work every day embarrassed. I'm embarrassed to be there, and I'm going to leave embarrassed…" He planned to retire within a short time.

Examples of police whistleblower retaliation abound. When Phillip Satterwaite of the Louisville Police Department complained that leadership shut black officers out of leadership roles and asked for data to quantify this, he was told to stop sending emails. He started noticing officers driving by his house, and a supervisor suggested Satterwaite take time off to "get his mental health issues resolved."

Lieutenant Kamil Warraich worked for the Asbury Park Police Department in New Jersey and made many complaints, including that the department targeted minority neighborhoods, allowed officers to use force without reporting it, and used a quota system. Warraich was demoted and placed on leave, then questioned whether he was mentally fit for duty. He was ordered to see a psychologist who "criticized and lectured him for over an hour basically implying that however wrong the Administration is, Plaintiff (Warraich) should just stay in his place and just do his job." The psychologist then evaluated him as unfit for duty.[20]

Recall the basic privilege-responsibility trade-off: anyone may keep whatever life they've built for themselves, including their career, reputation, and so on, so long as they give up deep responsibility for the wellbeing of their culture. Police may keep their careers and privileges so long as they obey their own authorities.

Academic research has explored the "blue code," "blue curtain," and "blue wall of silence" in publications going back to 1970. The blue code discourages any officer from reporting misconduct by their coworkers. In one study in 2000 CE by the US National Institute of Ethics, more than 75% of police recruits agreed that the code of silence "exists and is fairly common across the nation."[21]

Ralph Salerno is a retired New York police sergeant and organized crime expert. He said, "Police officials always talk about the occasional rotten apple in the barrel when corruption comes up. They'd be a lot more honest if they talked about the rotten barrel."[22]

Just as rulers trick people into seeing harmless or even patriotic people as threats (covered in Chapter 22 and Chapter 37), police leaders maintain a police culture where whistleblowers are seen as threats. Seth Stoughton, a former police officer and associate professor of law, noted "Whistleblowers aren't just seen as stabbing other officers in the back, they're almost inevitably seen as a potential physical threat to every officer." Thus officers are trained to see their most courageous and honest coworkers as a danger.[23]

Joe Crystal was a Baltimore police officer who reported an incident of police brutality in 2011. For the next two years, he was harassed and labeled a rat, with someone even placing a rat on his car outside his home. During dangerous moments pursuing suspects, he would call for backup and his call would be ignored. Eventually he left the police and then left the state.

This same dynamic plays out at the federal level. Stephen Friend had been an FBI agent for over 8 years after leaving the military, participating in hundreds of violent crime cases and winning a performance award. When he expressed concerns about inflated Domestic Violent Extremism statistics, unconstitutional surveillance of parents at school board meetings, and a decision to order a SWAT team to arrest a person who had said they would cooperate, Friend lost his top security clearance and his job.[24]

Garret O'Boyle had served in the military in Iraq and Afghanistan before joining the FBI. He stated concerns about Domestic Violent Extremism, unconstitutional surveillance, and a bonus system that rewarded aggressive or illegal policing methods. O'Boyle had been given high performance reviews earlier, but he was suspended without pay and transferred to a new location though he and his wife had a 2-week-old baby and three other children under 10.

O'Boyle testified to Congress, saying, "The FBI will crush you. This government will crush you and your family if you try to expose the truth about things that they are doing that are wrong. And we are all examples of that."[25] He also said, "…they're the law, and they're not going to have someone internally shining a light in the darkness…"[26]

O'Boyle also noted how the police can cause a person severe stress and use that to accuse him or her of mental instability: "I think they realized, we have him in the perfect position to completely flip his life upside down and cause torment to him. Because then they can come back and say, well, look at his mental status… he's clearly unstable."

Many supposedly independent police review offices act like honeypots, as described in Chapter 3. Some civilian review boards, such as the Office of Police Conduct Review in Minneapolis, call themselves "neutral," yet the groups that review internal affairs issues include police officers. In other cases, boards only investigate claims that have been seen by the police department, leaving whistleblowers no way to report misconduct without notifying their supervisors.[27]

Those police that remain after whistleblowers leave face a conundrum. Will they stand for what's right and risk their career and even their safety? Or will they go along and behave inappropriately or at least tolerate inappropriate behavior in others? When Frencesco Serpico described "the other 80% [of] officers who wish they could be more honest," I believe this is what he meant.

Many investigations of police scams reveal stories of a few officers meekly resisting. One New York City officer refused to take any money from the betting racket, and another officer told him he would "just keep it for you. Whenever you want it, I got it. And if you ever change your mind, I'll have it for you."[28]

One police officer described the attitude he heard from a fellow officer:

> One plainclothes man got a bit philosophical about taking [bribes]. He stated he was a poor boy and one of the minority groups and he never had any money and now was his big chance. He said, 'I don't care what they offer me, a thousand, a hundred, two dollars. I'll take it.' And I said, 'Oh, my God, think about it.' And he said, 'If I did, I'd blow my brains out.'

I once spoke with a police officer about how he relates to corruption or incompetence around him. He said he accepted that he could not do anything about it, and just tried to do his work well. He coached young officers likewise to just stay in their lane and focus on themselves.

I believe this is how most people tolerate living in an unhealthy nation – they try not to think about the larger culture or their role in it while doing whatever they need in order to maintain their comfort and safety. These conversations illustrate a police officer cultivating triple inhibition, where he learned to ignore his own healthy feelings and sacred urges that made it clear he was behaving inappropriately. Instead, he accepted the unhealthy nation as legitimate in order to secure his career and safety in that nation.

All these stories in this chapter illustrate the basic two-part pattern. (1) Police leadership creates or tolerates a culture of low integrity, (2) police leadership punishes officers with integrity, thus leaving a police force willing to support corrupt leadership. Whenever the public takes to the streets to protest corrupt political or business leaders, a corrupt police force will be ready to protect the corrupt leadership from the people, rather than protect the people from the corrupt leaders.

I often hear activists wonder why police would side with the corrupt business and political leadership that seems to treat them so poorly. After all, according to most analyses of social class, police are part of the working class, selling their labor and following orders to survive.

When French activists worked to protect a forest in 2014, they were attacked and blocked by French police. One protector said to the police, "You are here to protect the people. You should be on our side. All this, just for people who will never care about your health."[29] Indeed even soldiers are treated abusively by the rulers (as will be explored in Chapter 38). So why would police commonly support uncaring rulers?

Seeing the answer requires looking at privilege. Even though police are financially part of the working class, from a legal perspective, they are actually given upper-class privilege. They have the ability to break the law and get away with it, just like other upper-class people, according to the promise-keeping perspective on social class explored in Chapter 27.

Thus when police officers support corrupt upper-class business and political leaders, they are actually showing class solidarity, collectively protecting the upper class's ability to violate the law and get away with it.

What would it be like if the police really did want to protect their communities from the biggest criminals instead of following orders and protecting their careers?

The Drug War: What If the Police Arrested the Biggest Law-Breakers?

Police officers commonly describe their goal simply: to protect the public from criminals. Let us imagine that an American police officer, whom we'll call John Smith, is fully committed to protecting the public from the biggest criminals. He is willing to question anything. Let us imagine that officer Smith investigates the US "war on drugs" to find out what, if any, threats there are around illegal drug use in the United States. What might his line of questioning reveal?

Why Does the "War on Drugs" Exist?

Officer Smith might start by asking, "why does the war on drugs exist in the first place?" This isn't an ancient war; in the United States it began in 1971 under president Nixon. It began to really have a huge impact in 1981 under president Reagan. Arrests and imprisonment had already begun increasing in 1971, and after leveling out by the late 1970s, drug arrests skyrocketed through the 1980s.[30,31]

Black people have been very disproportionately targeted, as shown in Chapter 29. For example, in 1979 about 15% of black men without a high school diploma had been arrested by the time they were 34 years old. But by 2009, 69% of similarly educated black men had been arrested. In contrast, by 2009, fewer than 15% of white men without a high school diploma had been arrested. Much of this was due to increased drug arrests disproportionately targeting black people.

Was this racial discrimination purely accidental, or the result of some races suddenly committing more crimes than others? Or was there a more nefarious reason for it?

A myth spread that the war on drugs was fought against the "drug kingpins" or large dealers. But the overwhelming majority of arrested people were charged with minor crimes. In 2019, fewer than 14% of drug-related arrests were for drug manufacture or sale, while over 86% of arrests were for possession.[32]

Yet another myth suggests that if black people get arrested more, it must mean they use illicit drugs more. However, research shows that whites use drugs at higher rates compared to black people. A US Department of Health and Human Services 1998 survey estimated that 72% of all illicit drug users were white, at 9.9 million people. It estimated just 15% of illicit drug users were black, at 2.0 million, with the remainder being Latinos and other ethnicities. When police overwhelmingly target black people, it's clearly not because they're the biggest drug users.[33]

Dan Baum researched the politics of drug prohibition and discovered why the United States launched a policy of drug prohibition that has yielded so much misery and so few good results.

He tracked down John Ehrlichman, White House counsel under president Nixon in 1969. When the war on drugs started in 1971, Ehrlichman was the assistant to the president for domestic affairs. Baum asked him some technical policy questions, but Ehrlichman waved them away and bluntly cut to the heart of the war on drugs: "You want to know what this was really all about? The Nixon campaign in 1968, and the Nixon White House after that, had two enemies: the antiwar left and black people. You understand what I'm saying? We knew we couldn't make it illegal to be either against the war or black, but by getting the public to associate the hippies with marijuana and blacks with heroin, and then criminalizing both heavily, we could disrupt those communities. We could arrest their leaders, raid their homes, break up their meetings, and vilify them night after night on the evening news. Did we know we were lying about the drugs? Of course we did."[34]

How were the president and his team able to "arrest their leaders, raid their homes, [and] break up their meetings?" They required the assistance of hundreds of thousands of police officers around the country willing to do and believe what they were told by their supervisors, as well as believe the fear-mongering on the news. Any officer who honestly believed the war on drugs was a matter of public safety was being scammed. Any officer who saw that the war on drugs was simple political oppression had a choice: they could keep their integrity or they could keep their job. Sadly, the vast majority have kept their job.

Is Legal Punishment the Best Way to Help Drug Users Cease Illegal Drug Use? Are There Better Ways?

Our hypothetical police officer Smith might ask, "Well, even if the law is unevenly enforced, does it at least do some good? Is prison the best way to get drug users to stop using drugs?"

The answer is that police's work has little positive effect on drug use rates. A 2018 Pew Research study found that imprisoning people for drug use doesn't lead to reduced drug use, drug overdose, or drug-related arrests.[35] In fact, policing may worsen drug use. Research shows that drug use, both legal and illegal, rises significantly in the year after release from prison. People are much more likely to die of drug overdoses in the first year after prison release than the rest of the unimprisoned population.[36]

Much of the legal drug use is mental health medication as people work to recover from the stresses of imprisonment. I suspect that illicit drugs may be used as mental health self-medication in a similar way. This post-imprisonment increased drug use wouldn't happen if people hadn't been imprisoned in the first place.[37]

So if imprisonment doesn't help reduce drug abuse and overdoses, what would? Director of the National Institute on Drug Abuse doctor Nora Volkow puts the obvious answer in the title of an article: "Addiction Should Be Treated, Not Penalized."[38] Not only are treatment programs more likely to get to the root of the problems that cause drug addiction in the first place, they actually reduce crime. The Treatment Outcome Prospective Study tracked 12,000 people from 1979-1981 as they entered drug treatment programs. Of those who had committed some sort of predatory illegal activity (such as assault or burglary) within a year prior to entering the program, 70% stopped this illegal activity during treatment.[39]

Research consistently shows the same thing, as one study summarizes: "most people who get into and remain in treatment stop using drugs, decrease their criminal activity, and improve their occupational, social, and psychological functioning."[40]

Drug treatment programs reduce drug use, drug overdose, and crime. Arresting drug users doesn't reduce drug use or crime. Thus it's fair to say that policing is not an effective strategy in the so-called war on drugs.

If Drugs Really Are a Problem, Who is the Biggest Culprit?

Let us imagine that even after all these questions, police officer Smith still believes that drugs are a bad influence in his nation and he wants to use his police authority to go after the biggest suppliers and enablers of drug use. What if, rather than simply taking orders from his police chief, he accepts personal responsibility for choosing what to do to end the wide availability of illegal drugs? Which targets might Mr. Smith select?

It turns out, if Mr. Smith were motivated to identify the biggest facilitator of illegal drug sales in the United States, he would go after the US federal government.

This is public knowledge that most of the public ignores. In August 1996, Pulitzer-Prize winner Gary Webb published the *Dark Alliance* series in the San Jose Mercury News. This series detailed how the US Central Intelligence Agency (CIA) facilitated the transfer and distribution of cocaine from South America into the United States throughout the 1980s. The purpose was to fund Colombian revolutionaries seeking to overthrow their socialist government.

In 1981, president Reagan had approved this South American CIA operation but did not budget nearly enough money to sustain the revolutionary movement. The CIA needed to raise its own funds and chose to fan a massive drug epidemic, facilitate drug sales, and take a cut. Some dealers and distributors, such as Juan Meneses and Danilo Blandon, seemed miraculously able to avoid arrest even while many others were busted.[41]

Connected dealers were amazed at the incredibly low wholesale prices, which is unsurprising in retrospect. After all, their distributors were completely unafraid of law enforcement, dramatically reducing their costs. Webb learned much of this by following a 1996 trial in San Diego, CA where Danilo Blandon and others testified. Webb supplemented this with his own investigation.

Webb's investigative work led to an understandable outcry, especially among black communities heavily affected by punitive policing, racism that trapped many in poverty, and the availability of very cheap cocaine. Then-CIA director John Deutch resigned after being confronted in Los Angeles by angry black activists.[42]

Webb's newspaper's top editor came under heavy pressure to disavow Webb's work. A year after Dark Alliance was published, the editor published a statement distancing the newspaper from Webb's series. The editor also relocated Webb to a small bureau 125 miles away from his home and gave him junior assignments. The editor went on to receive a promotion to vice president and won an award from the Society of Professional Journalists for his "superior ethical conduct."

It became difficult for Webb to find work as a journalist, but he continued his investigation into the major story he had helped bring to light. In December 2004, Webb told friends that he was receiving death threats and he noticed strangers around his house. A few days later, he was shot twice in the face. His death was listed as a suicide. Webb's friends said he loved his wife and kids and would never kill himself, casting doubt on how the death was classified.

Clearly, any American police officer who takes responsibility for ending illicit drug use in their community would not go after poor black people, but instead would go after the biggest enabler: the US CIA.

The Moral of the Story

When people debate whether a particular conspiracy theory is true, one argument is that the theory cannot be true because so many people could not possibly coordinate the conspiracy and keep it a secret. But the war on drugs shows how conspiracies can work even while the vast majority of participants are ignorant. For decades, hundreds of thousands of police officers participated in a conspiracy to oppress black people, activists, and probably others. And yet, I suspect the vast majority of officers were unaware. All it took for the conspiracy to succeed was for huge numbers of people to believe what they were told and follow orders.

Gary Webb shows the plight that all of us in unhealthy nations are in, including police officers. Webb could have ignored the very disturbing truth of illegal government activities and kept his career and his life. Instead, he risked his career and safety to give people the chance to know the truth and make things right.

Police are in the same position: they can do what they're told and keep their careers, or they can take responsibility to stop the big criminals, risking their careers and even their lives. As seen in Chapter 29, all workers face this same conundrum in one way or another, and many choose to go through the motions of service. Anyone who accepts their privilege must give up any deep sense of responsibility for the health of their nation. Police can keep their privilege so long as they don't stand for a culture of integrity.

This is the privilege-responsibility tradeoff: anyone who accepts their privilege must give up any deep sense of responsibility for the health of their nation.

This is true in every unhealthy nation. Everyone has to give up responsibility for the health of their nation in order to keep their own privilege, comfort, and safety. That's the privilege-responsibility tradeoff.

Every whistleblower and everyone who sees what happens to whistleblowers knows how dangerous it is to risk one's career and safety alone. As shown in Chapter 4, when activist Tim DeChristopher was arrested, his fellow activists supported him in many ways, including handing out literature to jurors and showing up to witness the court proceedings. They couldn't protect him from prison time, but at least he knew he wasn't alone and unseen. In contrast, many police whistleblowers face retribution alone, without much community support. A person with total integrity will do what they know in their heart to be right no matter what, but when people act in solidarity with each other, it can make acting with integrity less scary and isolating – and more effective.

I have deep respect for many police officers' desire to protect their community from threats. This is a sacred urge, as reviewed in Chapter 47. However, when officers choose not to seek the full truth and purposely ignore the biggest criminals, they end up not protecting their community from threats. When officers simply follow orders, behave selfishly, or try to avoid trouble, they wind up only going through the motions of protecting the people from threats. Instead, these officers protect the biggest threats (rulers and other exploitative authorities) from the people.

Top authorities want obedient police who protect them from the people they exploit, which explains why officers who act with integrity are fired.
This is a normal pattern in any society where people allow themselves to be ruled.

Referring to how police departments consistently punish whistleblowers, former New Jersey police officer DeLacy Davis said, "this is how it was designed to work… We have to change the whole system."[43] I agree. But police reform is not enough, as police dishonesty is simply another common symptom of the root cultural disease where a few people rule over many.

So long as there are rulers, efforts at deep police reform will fail, because corrupt rulers require corrupt police to keep them in power. To get to the heart of the problem requires creating a way of life where everybody stands for a culture of mutual respect, and nobody rules over anybody else.

Unhealthy nations systematically discourage and actively undermine the broad solidarity that real change requires. How is this accomplished so effectively, time and again, around the world, throughout the ages? The next section of the book, *Part 08 - Unhealthy Nations Prevent Deep Cultural Healing*, uncovers some of the key techniques.

Part 08 - Unhealthy Nations Prevent Deep Cultural Healing

I see a lot of troubles in unhealthy nations, such as racism, sexism, pollution, and corruption. I also see a lot of people working hard to address those troubles and heal their nation. How do unhealthy nations disrupt these efforts at deep cultural healing?

Chapter 33: It All Starts with Justifying or Ignoring Exploitative Rulers

Every human nation propagates stories that explain why things are as they are.

Beautiful nations tell heart-opening stories, such as the Nootka whose creation story involved older women and girls sacrificing themselves so the youngest could live (as seen in Chapter 28).

Authoritarian nations tell heart-closing stories, such as the Christian story of a woman secretly feeding a man forbidden fruit and forever disconnecting humanity from God (reviewed in Chapter 18).

Stories of authoritarian nations face an extra restraint, though. Authoritarian nations involve a few rulers exploiting many others, and thus the foundational narratives of unhealthy nations have to excuse or ignore this abusive dynamic.

For some reason, rulers don't like to admit that they behave abusively and generally only have their power as the result of military conquest at some point in the past, possibly centuries earlier. Instead of acknowledging the abuse and deception they use to remain in control, rulers make up cover stories to justify their rule.

The simplest fairy tale is that the monarch rules with God's support. In Europe, this has been called the "divine right of kings." French king Louis XIV had a court preacher named Jacques-Bénigne Bossuet. Bossuet was a Catholic bishop who believed that "God establishes kings as his ministers, and reigns through them over the people," and "the prince must be obeyed on principle, as a matter of religion and of conscience." Those who believed otherwise or disobeyed were thus agents of the devil who opposed God's will.[1]

As I write in 2024, "By the Grace of God" is still part of the full title of the monarchs in Denmark[2], Monaco[3], the United Kingdom[4], and the Netherlands.[5] The Chinese used the term "Mandate of Heaven" to legitimize their emperor.[6]

This narrative excuses a situation where one person rules over many others, and it excuses any abusive decision the ruler makes. And it has a huge advantage over other narratives: it is not falsifiable.

This isn't true for many other cover stories that justify a few people ruling over everyone else. For example, the United States Declaration of Independence notes that "We hold these truths to be self-evident, that all men are created equal, that they are endowed by their Creator with certain unalienable Rights, that among these are Life, Liberty and the pursuit of Happiness." However, at the same time the Declaration was ratified, this nation also embraced a despotic form of chattel slavery which did not treat all men and women equally, nor honor their inalienable rights.

That same Declaration also says that, "That to secure these rights, Governments are instituted among Men, deriving their just powers from the consent of the governed…" Again, the slaves did not consent to being governed. However, even for the supposedly free citizens, recent academic research indicates that the government commonly enacts policies supported by big business, and the government only enacts policies that most people want if big businesses support them too. When business leaders oppose a policy that most people want, research shows that the government essentially ignores most citizens' wishes. In the United States, like all unhealthy nations, the "consent of the governed" is not relevant, despite the nice-sounding words of the Declaration of Independence.[7]

Likewise, the Soviet Union propagated a belief that it was a worker's paradise, part of an ongoing worldwide socialist revolution with the ultimate goal of overthrowing the parasitic capitalist class everywhere. Any workers who pointed out that the government wasn't fulfilling this vision risked being sent to prison.[8]

If God unconditionally supports the king, then this *justifies* anything the king does, no matter how abusive. Instead of justifying the rulers' abuses, the US's narrative of democratic rule and the Soviet Union's narrative of socialist revolution *ignored* the abuses at the heart of their societies.

Rulers do not like having their cover story questioned because it threatens their legitimacy. This is called the Chrysanthemum Taboo in Japan, where the emperor is associated with the chrysanthemum flower, and criticism of the emperor is absolutely forbidden and heavily punished.[9] As explored elsewhere in the book, the Soviet Union heavily punished anyone who promoted capitalism, and the United States has punished people who promote socialism, each of which threatened the ideologies that legitimized those nations' ruling classes.

This explains why rulers can seem so insecure. Rulers are always exploitative and they always want to hide this fact, and so they propagate a made-up story or lie or excuse that justifies their rule. Then they get angry with anyone that questions the story, lie, or excuse. This is simply another silly pattern in unhealthy nations.

Wishful Thinking – the Desire to Believe Things are Not So Bad

People often speak dismissively of others who believe propaganda. I find it helpful to notice a few things.

First, I know vanishingly few people who don't believe at least some amount of propaganda. People who study vaccine-related corruption may really think that America invades other countries to bring them democracy and human rights. People who see through those lies may believe that the environment isn't really in trouble, and climate change is a scam. People who see the troubles in the environment may believe that one political party or another can make a difference in addressing it. People who recognize that none of the political parties can fundamentally make a difference may believe that humans are inherently selfish, and there is no alternative to living in a selfish nation.

All this teaches me humility. Unhealthy nations force people to live amongst so many lies, half-truths, and context-free facts that it is easy to be wrong at least sometimes.

Second, it helps me to remember that most people do not enjoy facing a catastrophe, and especially do not like feeling helpless and alone amidst a catastrophe. For example, it would be bad enough to learn that one's family was in a burning building, but it would be even worse to feel helpless to do anything about it.

Authoritarian nations are in a state of permanent catastrophe, where people are trapped in massive abusive relationships that span decades, centuries, or even millennia. Rulers offer feel-good cover stories that help people pretend that they're not in a catastrophe, and many people willingly believe this nonsense. This happens for several reasons, with different people believing as they do for their own mix of reasons.

- *Blind beliefs*: People may have to believe as they're told in order to survive in their nation, as seen in Chapter 6. When a person's family depends on them, acknowledging the truth does not just risk one's own safety and comfort, but the safety and comfort of one's children and spouse as well.

- *Difficult to live a life out of alignment with one's values*: Even when people recognize the lies, it can be difficult to consciously live in ways that violate one's values. It may be easier to believe nonsense or just not think about the abusive behavior.

- *Hard to acknowledge a catastrophe alone*: Acknowledging the full truth may require a person to recognize the cultural catastrophe they face, and which they may feel helpless to confront. This can be challenging, especially if they have no friends or neighbors they trust to talk with.

- *Hard to remember freedom many generations later*: When a person grows up in a healthy nation and gets forcefully integrated into an unhealthy nation, they know what freedom is like and they know that the authoritarian nation isn't offering it. When a person is only a few generations removed, they may or may not carry on their ancestors' traditions, even at great risk. It becomes harder and harder to hold on to healthy-nation traditions as many people learn to obey authority, do not connect deeply with the nonhuman world, pretend rather than acknowledge the truth, raise their children in authoritarian ways, and consider beautiful old stories to be "naive" or "old wives' tales."

- *Hard to give up a huge interlocking web of beliefs*: Rulers' legitimacy is reinforced by beliefs about religion, government, commerce, humans' inherent nature, history, and more. Acknowledging the truth of their rulers' despotism and illegitimacy may require questioning many of these other beliefs as well.

- *Hard to see the truth when people are conditioned to ignore abuses*: Authoritarian nations train people not to see the abuses at the heart of their own nation, as reviewed in Chapter 21.

- *Many people think it's normal to be ruled*: People who have never encountered healthy nations commonly have no concept of a human society without rulers. Thus they see having rulers as normal, not a state of emergency.

- *Abuse in childhood predisposes people to support abusive rulers and embrace hurtful narratives*: People abused in childhood become much more susceptible to embracing hurtful narratives and supporting authorities' abuses, as detailed in Chapter 42.

Billions of people have lived in a wide array of authoritarian nations and believed many things for many reasons. Some people recognize their rulers' illegitimacy, but many others seem to avoid facing truths that would cause them to question their rulers' legitimacy. Each person who resists the truth does so for their own reasons, but when I read histories, certain repeating patterns of resistance appear.

Here are two examples.

Wishful Thinking as New Unhealthy Nations Pretend to Address the Troubles of the Old Ones

Every authoritarian nation involves a few people exploiting the many. While some rulers are much better administrators than others, every authoritarian nation generates large amounts of misery and dissatisfaction. Thus, when a new ruling class takes power, they commonly propagate a story that helps people finally believe that the old problems are gone, and they can feel relief.

For example, ancient Egyptian kings claimed that they were divine figures whose job it was to maintain divine order on Earth, protecting people from the chaos that would supposedly exist without them.[10]

Living under despotic, selfish monarchs generation after generation can be depressing, so some monarchs decided to adopt a religion that gave people hope. In 380 CE, Roman emperor Theodosius 1 issued the Edict of Thessalonica, making Christianity the official state religion of the Roman Empire.[11]

This began an era, now seventeen centuries and counting, where people in nations which officially worship Jesus as the son of God consistently engage in behavior that Jesus himself very strongly opposed.

Many governments have officially recognized Jesus as the son of God, and held up his teachings as a model for everyone to follow. Who would not want to be part of a nation that preached that people should share food with the poor, that the meek shall inherit the Earth, that good people will be connected with divinity after they die, that the rich definitely should share their wealth… any day now?

However, it was obvious that the emperors and rulers did not follow their own religion. In the late 1700s, English colonists engaged in a revolution and decided to found a democratic government which supposedly allowed people to rule themselves and universally encouraged freedom and justice. After centuries of rule by despotic monarchs, the idea of people voting for their own government was extremely attractive to many people. Finally the government would be accountable to the masses, and hereditary aristocrats would not live in luxury off the backs of overworked peasants!

Of course, the United States remained very unequal, with a few people able to control the government and exploit everybody else. This was also true of the European monarchies that switched over to apparently republican forms of government in the 1800s.

During the 1800s, vast numbers of activists recognized that capitalism was a terrible blight on humanity, encouraging individuals to selfishly accumulate wealth by exploiting their neighbors and the Earth. Huge amounts of socialist and communist literature in the 1800s explored the evils of capitalism and monarchies and speculated about how to create non-abusive societies. Many activists tried and failed to generate a socialist revolution where workers would finally own the means of production – the farms, factories, land, and so on – so that landlords couldn't get rich just by imposing rent, and business owners couldn't get rich just by colluding to keep prices arbitrarily high, and financiers couldn't get rich by loaning money to desperately poor people at interest.

Finally all this activism seemingly culminated in victory in Russia when the monarchy was replaced by revolutionary socialists in 1918 and the Soviet Union was born. Just as the United States had promised to free people from the evils of monarchy, the Soviet Union promised to free people from the evils of capitalism. After millennia of supposedly divine kings and aristocrats, and centuries of selfish capitalists, finally a society was born that elevated workers and would let everybody enjoy freedom and their collective wealth.

Sadly, none of these authoritarian nations kept their promises. Monarchism, democratic capitalism, and socialist worker dictatorships were all cover stories or facades designed to excuse or justify exploitation where a few ruled over the many.

Nonetheless, both the United States and Soviet Union generated huge amounts of enthusiasm and hope. People wanted to believe so badly that a nation could exist where everyone would be treated decently. Since authoritarian nations discourage people from learning that truly healthy nations exist, the United States and Soviet Union each seemed to many people like humanity's great hope.

This led to some ludicrous dynamics.

For example, media and schools in the United States commonly describe the country's mission to spread democracy and human rights in contrast to evil dictatorships, like Nazi Germany under Adolf Hitler. In other words, the US is portrayed as the "good guys" and the other side, in this case Nazi Germany, is portrayed as the "bad guys." However, just as the United States massacred countless people of healthy nations as colonists spread across North America, so too did Germany kill countless people in its imperial activities in Africa. Hitler even used America's continent-spanning genocide as an inspiration for his generals.[12]

Soviet propagandists commonly spoke dismissively of the American capitalist dictatorship, while American propagandists spoke negatively about the Soviet communist dictatorship. Of course, both sides were right: they both were run by rulers and other authorities who manipulated and controlled the rest. They just had different cover stories and social arrangements that excused or covered up their exploitation.

Many people wanted desperately to believe that humans could live without exploitation. When the abuses obviously continued or worsened after the US and USSR were each founded, what was left to believe in? People who had only ever learned about abusive, authoritarian nations and never heard of healthy nations could either acknowledge that the US and USSR were both exploitative, or they could ignore reality and pretend that everything was still ok, and a little exploitation was part of a transition to a better civilization.

Even some foreign communists who witnessed Ukraine's epic government-imposed famine in the 1930s tried to pretend it wasn't really as bad it seemed. It could not mean that the socialist experiment had failed.

Writer Arthur Koestler, living in Kharkiv, Ukraine, believed that the starving rural peasants were "enemies of the people who preferred begging to work." His housemate, physicist Alexander Weissberg, also knew that millions of people were starving. But they both kept the faith. They were surrounded by death in the countryside, yet acknowledging it would mean giving up on their hope that the Soviet Union was better than monarchies and capitalist nations.

In 1933, Koestler left the Soviet Union, and when Weissberg took him to the train station, his last words were, "Whatever happens, hold the banner of the Soviet Union high!"[13]

Unfortunately, this isn't the only kind of wishful thinking that can occur when people don't realize that healthy nations exist.

False Narratives of Progress and the Truths They Ignore

Authorities commonly encourage people to feel hopeful about the future even if present conditions are miserable. Nations that preach that people are disconnected from God may also preach that good people will be reconnected with God after death. Secular narratives of progress also exist. Both the United States and Brazil, for example, propagate narratives that their nation is progressing.

Brazil even emblazons their national slogan on their flag, "Ordem e Progresso" (Order and Progress). One piece of Brazilian government-produced propaganda described a primitive past leading to the arrival of European civilization with positive symbols and happy people, and then progressing further to Brazilian nationhood. The video ended with the statement, "This is a country that advances."[14]

United States propaganda has been similar. Thomas Jefferson described a hypothetical traveler who could move from the supposedly-savage people in the far west towards the east coast. First the traveler would encounter people living in a state of nature, then people living in a pastoral state on the frontier, and "so in his progress he would meet the gradual shades of improving man" in their seaport towns.

American school textbooks commonly encourage this narrative of progress. For example, the textbook *A History of the United States* notes, "Americans - makers of something out of nothing - have delivered a new way of life to far corners of the world."[15]

What would it be like if these nations' narratives reflected reality instead?

Narratives based on reality would point out that before the arrival of the Europeans, most people in North and South America were living freely in healthy nations. These narratives would also have to acknowledge that when the invading European colonists had the opportunity to either stay in their exploitative nation or escape to live with people in healthy nations, many of them chose to escape.

It's no surprise: given the chance to escape their abusive nation, many people throughout history have done so.

When the French and Haudenosaunee Confederacy engaged in a prisoner exchange in 1699, Cadwallader Colden noted how the French prisoners didn't want to return home after experiencing life in a healthy nation: "…notwithstanding the French Commissioners took all the Pains possible to carry Home the French, that were Prisoners with the Five Nations [Haudenosaunee], and they had full Liberty from the Indians, few of them could be persuaded to return."[16]

In other words, French prisoners of war had lived in a non-abusive nation and liked it so much that few could be persuaded to go home. He noticed that this wasn't unique to the French, as "the English had as much Difficulty."

People of healthy nations openly acknowledged that they treated their captives with respect, as that baseline of mutual respect really does apply to anyone within the nation. Sioux man Ohiyesa wrote, "It was a point of honor in the old days to treat a captive with kindness."[17] Pretty Shield, a woman of the Crow nation, described how even captive people were treated with the same decency as everyone else. When asked about captured women, she said, "because they were treated well they never tried to get away. They had the same rights as Crow women, and worked no harder." A captured Lakota woman named Good-trader ended up having a loving family and later refused to return to the Lakota when she had the chance.[18]

Colden noted that in prisoner exchanges, Europeans could rarely be persuaded to leave their healthy-nation captors, but the reverse was clearly not true: "No Arguments, no Intreaties, nor Tears of their Friends and Relations, could persuade many of them to leave their new Indian Friends and Acquaintance; several of them that were by the Caressings of their Relations persuaded to come Home, in a little Time grew tired of our Manner of living, and run away again to the Indians, and ended their Days with them. On the other Hand, Indian Children have been carefully educated among the English, cloathed and taught, yet, I think, there is not one Instance, that any of these, after they had Liberty to go among their own People, and were come to Age, would remain with the English, but returned to their own Nations, and became as fond of the Indian Manner of Life as those that knew nothing of a civilized Manner of Living." Colden found that this uneven prisoner exchange "has been found true on many other Occasions."[19]

This was obviously humiliating for colonial leaders who pretended not to abusively exploit their citizens, but it got worse. In a big prisoner exchange on the Muskingum River in 1764, white people had won out against the local healthy nations in war, but European leaders found the prisoner exchange unsatisfying. People of healthy nations who had been trapped in European prisons ran back to their communities with great joy. Meanwhile, white captives had to be dragged away with their hands and feet tied to keep them from running back to the healthy nation they'd been able to experience.

Benjamin Franklin noted this phenomenon as well. He noticed how children born in healthy nations and then raised in European nations commonly tried to return to their healthy nation. However, Franklin noted, "when white persons of either sex have been taken prisoners young by the Indians, and have lived a while among them, tho' ransomed by their Friends, and treated with all imaginable tenderness… yet [soon] they become disgusted with our manner of life… and take the first good Opportunity of escaping again into the Woods, from whence there is no reclaiming them." Many enslaved people who escaped bondage also ran away to live with healthy nations.

European colonial leaders knew that many of their people greatly preferred life among the so-called savages, and so they often severely punished anyone caught trying to run away. European explorer Hernando De Soto posted guards to keep men and women from defecting to live with local healthy nations. English Pilgrims punished runaways with the death penalty. White people continued to escape to live with healthy nations in North America up until the 1890s, when the last sovereign healthy nations within the political boundaries of the United States finally submitted to military rule.[20]

White women taken captive by healthy nations would later write with envy about how much influence and dignity women in healthy nations had.[21]

Some colonists also recognized that leadership in healthy nations was very different than the oppressive authorities they were accustomed to. Benjamin Franklin noted, "All their government is by Counsel of the Sages. There is no Force; there are no Prisons, no officers to compel Obedience, or inflict Punishment." In 1727 Colden noted, "There is not a Man in the Ministry of the Five Nations, who has gain'd his Office, otherwise than by Merit… Their Authority is only the Esteem of the People, and ceases the Moment that Esteem is lost… Here we see the natural Origin of all Power and Authority among a free People."

These stories show the truth of American, Brazilian, Soviet, and other authoritarian nations' so-called "progress." Authoritarian societies do change over time as various forms of slavery and coercion come and go. However, they have never been an improvement over the free healthy nations that already existed well before unhealthy nations arrived.

Unhealthy nations have always been catastrophes that many people escape when they see the opportunity. This is why authorities try to keep people from knowing that healthy nations exist.

These stories point the way to generating truly healthy nations. People need not feel hopeless just because the United States and Soviet Union and every other authoritarian nation turned out to be manipulative, disrespectful, exploitative, and abusive. We have all the evidence we need to know that humans can do much better. It is not an impossible dream; it is simply a fact that humans can live in beautiful, respectful nations. We just need to figure out how to end the abusive relationships we're trapped in and once again generate a nation where *everybody stands for a culture of mutual respect, and nobody rules over anybody else.*

Prying control away from rulers and their supporters begins with fully acknowledging the rulers' influence on nearly all aspects of life in unhealthy nations. Next, one of the fundamental issues that discourages solidarity between people and the Earth is the focus of *Chapter 34: Who Controls the Land?*

Chapter 34: Who Controls the Land?

I never understood how divisive land ownership is until I learned what life is like without it.

Land ownership is entirely artificial, with countless negative impacts on how humans relate to each other and the Earth. Other animals, plants, sunlight, wind, rain and all aspects of the nonhuman world have no need for pretend property lines and do not recognize them. Humans in healthy nations don't either.

But all unhealthy nations impose systems of land ownership, giving some people exclusive control over certain land, and giving rulers control of the people.

Respectful Harvest – Living as a Gift to the Land

When there is no land ownership, it is much easier to enrich the Earth as a normal, default way of life. Instead of planting trees or gardens as a hobby or a job separate from the rest of a person's life, the Earth's needs can be fully integrated into every decision.

Robin Kimmerer described how Potawatomi people have a long history of making baskets from black ash trees. Traditional tree harvesters recognize each tree as an individual, nonhuman person. A respectful harvest begins with a request. The tree cutter describes their purpose and asks the tree for permission to be harvested and listens carefully for a response, which is sometimes no. Perhaps something in the surroundings, such as a bird's nest or close neighbor explains why the tree declined to be harvested, or perhaps the person just knows. Either way, the respectful harvester keeps asking trees until they hear a yes. Then they offer a prayer and gift of tobacco before cutting down the tree with great care not to damage its trunk or tree neighbors.[1]

Traditional Potawatomi harvesters are very aware of their impact on the black ash, and they became worried when its populations began declining. Basket-making has been a huge part of their culture and livelihood. Could the decline be due to overharvesting?

Kimmerer and an assistant investigated, identifying all the black ashes and their ages in their region in New York State. Ultimately they found that black ash tree populations were dropping in some areas and rising in others, and they found that black ashes were actually thriving wherever there were traditional Potawatomi basket makers. Black ash trees need open space in the canopy to thrive; saplings die in full shade. Basket makers opened up the canopy occasionally as they harvested black ash. Where the basket makers no longer harvested, the canopy remained closed and black ash numbers declined.

Humans thus benefited from the black ash, and the black ash benefited from humans. New generations of black ash thrived wherever people respectfully harvested it. This sort of respectful harvest would be impossible if people were confined only to land that they "owned." A respectful harvester could ask permission to enter another person's land, but if they did not receive permission, that would be the end of their basket making, and black ash populations would decline even further.

Tom Brown Jr, heavily mentored by the Apache man Stalking Wolf, learned how to respectfully harvest a tree to make a bow. Pioneers had usually searched for a straight, tall sapling and harvested it without considering what impact its removal would have on the land. They might harvest several trees, more than they needed, and discard a few. In their ignorance, they might not even recognize what makes a good tree for a bow. Pioneers often chose trees growing in the open, unaware that trees with an easy life and thus consistent growth rings produced poor bows.[2]

Stalking Wolf pointed out that, like people, trees with an easy life lacked strength. The trees that struggled to survive and reach the sun developed tight growth rings, leading to a bow that could generate much more power.

Stalking Wolf said that he and people like him would wander through a forest guided more by their heart than their mind, and he commonly passed many fine saplings. He looked for a grove of saplings in heavy competition for the sun. He then might spend days searching that grove for just the right sapling. He would verify that removing the tree would benefit the surrounding grove. Once he picked such a tree, he would pray to the tree and Creator, explaining how the sapling would be used and how his people would honor the sacrifice. He said how much the sapling would be cherished, and it would be made into an excellent bow that would become an extension of the hunter, not just an inanimate tool. Stalking Wolf recognized that removing the sapling would be good for the grove as well as good for the people whom he served by hunting, and when he received permission from the tree and Creator, he would harvest the tree.

Brown and his friend heard Stalking Wolf talk about deciding who should live and die, and this sounded like playing God. They didn't like that. But Stalking Wolf pointed out that humans have to take other creatures' lives to survive, and that is ok as long as harvesting is done in a respectful way that has a positive impact on the land.

Like the Potawatomi basket-makers, Stalking Wolf studied a large forested area before selecting a tree such that its removal benefited both the forest and the toolmaker. If he had been confined to harvesting a tree on land he owned in a system of land ownership, this respectful harvest would not have been possible, and both humans and the forest would have suffered.

These stories show me how humans can benefit the land as a normal, default way of life even as we take what we need to survive. They show what it's like to live in a reciprocal, mutually beneficial relationship with the land, and how hard it is to live this way when people are restricted to land they personally own or must have human permission to harvest.

Choosing Good Neighbors

As I grew up, my family and many of my neighbors either owned our homes or had long-term leases. Because moving was difficult and expensive, people seemed to feel basically stuck with each other, whether they got along or not. Sometimes neighbors had serious disputes and ill feelings toward each other, and I remember feeling stressed living near people who didn't get along.

This sort of problem – along with so many others – is much less common when there is no land ownership, as people can separate more easily when they don't get along or simply want to live differently. Sioux man Ohiyesa described one method the Nez Perce used to maintain unity: "The Nez Perce tribe of Indians, like other tribes too large to be united under one chief, was composed of several bands, each distinct in sovereignty."[3] Whenever a group got too big for everyone to get along well, they split into groups such that each one had unity.

Pretty Shield described how her community had a quarrel in about 1832 and divided into two groups, the Mountain Crows and River Crows. Pretty Shield was born a Mountain Crow but went to live with an aunt who was a River Crow. She said, "This separation from my mother and my sisters was in fact not a very real one, because all the Crows came together often. These meetings gave me opportunities to see my family, so that I was happy…"[4] I believe the Crows' quarrel did not escalate in part because they could separate easily and come together when they wished, an option that is not easy in nations with land ownership.

Even people who get along well may want to travel or live apart. Ohiyesa described how Sioux bands would unite in summertime for their Sun Dance, writing, "It was midsummer and the red folk were happy. They lacked for nothing… One large circle of buffalo-skin teepees formed the movable village." The group then split into three bands, with one going west, one going south, and the third remaining in place.[5] They could choose to move, choose where to live, and choose neighbors easily because nobody owned land.

Avoiding land ownership also makes it easier to choose neighbors who can be trusted to help in an emergency. One of the earliest memories of Wikis, a boy of a healthy nation in the US Great Plains, was an enemy attack upon his village. A sentinel let out a war cry, and instantly the women gathered the children while the men shouted to each other and went off towards the sentinel to confront the threat. Each person had a clear role in helping the community respond, and each person acted immediately when the alarm went out to protect the village. The coordination and trust required for this kind of collective response is difficult to have in unhealthy nations when each individual lives on their own plot of land and may not trust their neighbors.[6]

This sort of solidarity and collective self-defense becomes much easier when people can easily move to live with people they trust, something that is much easier without artificially imposed land ownership.

Even farmers can live without land ownership. The Huron sustained themselves in part from agriculture, and they moved their villages every 10-20 years. Aware that overfarming could degrade the soil, they were careful to move to another area every few years while the soil was still healthy enough to regenerate. This stands in stark contrast to the US dust bowl that formed in the midwest in the 1930s, where many farmers totally exhausted the soil and left it barren, forcing many farmers to leave their land behind in search of paying work that could sustain them.[7]

The Many Troubles of Land Control

All these stories, as well as my own experience, show how difficult it is for people to live well with each other and the Earth in unhealthy nations dependent on land ownership.

How can a person develop a deep understanding of the region where they live if they're not allowed to walk beyond a few restricted areas? The Kamana nature-connection program guides students to notice their own curiosity and let it guide them as they explore the special area they visit each day. For much of my life I had learned to ignore my curiosity about the nonhuman world. After all, why bother feeling my own curiosity if I have to ignore it for fear of trespassing?

Ohiyesa described how his grandmother taught him to learn important lessons, both in hunting and in life: "When you see a new trail, or a footprint that you do not know, follow it to the point of knowing."[8] When invisible property lines or physical fences constantly block exploration, how are humans supposed to develop deep knowledge of the natural world in which they live? A person may ask landowners' permission, but permission may be denied, or permission may be needed from too many people. A person may trespass, but this brings its own risks and it makes relaxed, open exploration of the land dangerous.

Artificially created land ownership also makes it difficult to take deep responsibility for the land's wellbeing. If a neighbor or official is poisoning the soil, clearcutting trees, or causing some other disturbance, the law forbids me from acting on my deep responsibility to protect the forest. And if I am too afraid to take any action to stop them, eventually it may become easier and less painful to ignore my feelings and look away.

Land ownership makes it hard to let soil rest after a period of intensive farming, because letting the soil rest would reduce the farmer's income and make it difficult to pay taxes, debts, and other costs. Land ownership makes it difficult to live only with trusted neighbors, as buying and selling land can be cumbersome. It makes it difficult for most people to live off the land so that a person doesn't just depend on their job to survive.

Even having a lot of money doesn't make land ownership deeply satisfying. An affluent person may choose to buy a large tract of land, but the larger the parcel, the farther they will live from their neighbors.

Ultimately, land ownership is extremely restrictive and isolating, even for people fortunate enough to own land and a home. I believe this is one reason Sioux man Sitting Bull said, "The life of white men is slavery. They are prisoners in their towns or farms."[9] Sitting Bull said that the life of white people was slavery, many of whom at least owned a homestead or farm. He wasn't even referring to minorities or immigrants, many of whom owned no land at all!

One of the beautiful things about nations without land ownership is that, when no one owns the land, everyone is free to go almost anywhere. Each individual has their own needs for privacy that other people acknowledge, and nonhumans have their own boundaries that people learn to respect. But otherwise, people have freedom to move over the land as they wish.

In nations with land ownership, people are only free to go on public-designated spaces, public roads, and land they personally own. Beyond that, they need permission from others to enter private or government land. Is it any wonder that life could feel more abundant in nations where no one "owns" land?

In unhealthy nations, artificial land ownership and exclusive land access are directly linked to higher levels of privilege. Real estate often makes up a portion of wealthy, higher-privilege people's assets, while the inability to own or access land is often a lifelong limitation of lower-privilege people. Instead they must pay rent money to landlords, share housing with many others, find someplace to squat illegally, or try to live on the streets.

For centuries, land ownership in unhealthy nations has been an important mechanism for maintaining various privilege levels, creating artificial divisions and making solidarity and mutual aid difficult. Thus it is understandable why rulers and other authorities would be motivated to create and enforce many laws protecting so-called "property rights," which are also artificial constructs.

Meanwhile, many healthy nations – including some in existence today – live without land ownership while still accounting for everyone's needs.

Addressing Concerns About Societies Free of Land Ownership

When I discuss nations without land ownership, a few common concerns typically come up.

One is about privacy. How can people ensure their privacy if there is no land ownership? I believe people simply respect each others' personal and home space. When I stayed with the Ashaninka, nobody ever had to ask me to give them more space or privacy. Likewise, I never felt the need to ask for space or privacy. We simply knew how to honor each others' space in satisfying ways.

Another concern involves freeloaders. How can a person avoid freeloaders and benefit from making a building or garden if they don't own the land?

Freeloaders are acting selfishly, and healthy nations quickly notice and strongly discourage selfishness. Freeloaders would threaten the gift economy, as explored in Chapters 4, 9, and 11. They are either encouraged to share generously or leave. This way everyone who chooses to stay can share generously with other generous people.

Additionally, I commonly notice that families can decide whether to share the food from their garden, and even pass their family garden from one generation to the next. When Tzutujil Mayan shaman Chiv expected to die, he asked Martín Prechtel to ensure that the land remained available to those who used it, "because they are the ones who deserve to get what they've been taking care of."[10] Jesuit missionaries noticed that Huron people could clear as much land as they wished and the land remained reserved for family members so long as it was under cultivation. However, any land that went uncultivated became available for others.

Every healthy nation finds its own balance between honoring each person's autonomy and ensuring everyone is taken care of. Whether someone tries to hoard the best farming land, mooches off of others, or some other selfish behavior, any of this could be addressed in the same way healthy nations address other selfish behavior.

Ultimately, once people can establish a baseline of mutual respect, *they will figure out a way to live that works for everyone*. Many nations have found many different ways, but all of them ensure people feel satisfied and nobody mooches or goes without.

A History of Land Enclosure

Black Elk described the Lakotas' first encounter with land ownership this way: "Once we were happy in our own country and we were seldom hungry, for then the two-leggeds and the four-leggeds lived together like relatives, and there was plenty for them and for us. But the wasichus [white people] came, and they have made little islands for us and other little islands for the four-leggeds, and always these islands are becoming smaller."[11]

This process where the islands keep getting smaller is called enclosure. It has been going on for thousands of years, and sadly it is not unique to white people. Before enclosure, no one owned the land, and instead people tended it together for the common good.

After enclosure, individuals or institutions own the land and have more or less exclusive control of it. A few lucky rich people benefit in limited ways, and most everyone else loses out.

Just as there are many ways that people can behave disrespectfully to each other, there are many ways rulers can choose to control land. Below are two examples: oppressive individual land ownership and oppressive collective land ownership.

Enclosing Land With Oppressive Individual Land Ownership

England has had kings for much longer than it has had private land ownership. For many years in the middle ages, English farmers managed land with the open field system. Farmers pooled resources to afford a large team of oxen, and they decided collectively when to graze animals, plant crops, or leave land fallow. During even earlier times with fewer farmers, people could have their own plots of land more easily, but with increased population, sharing access to the land allowed more people to prosper.[12]

Unfortunately, beginning in the 1300s, wealthy individuals with government backing decided to enclose the land, transitioning it to private land ownership. This resulted in many peasant revolts as people fought to maintain a system of shared land stewardship that allowed many people to sustain themselves. The 1381 Peasants' Revolt, Jack Cade's rebellion of 1450, Kett's rebellion of 1549, and the Captain Pouch revolts of 1604-1607 all involved resistance to land enclosure.

New landowners would try to define the boundaries of their land with ditches or fences, and those peasants who resisted were called "levelers" or "diggers," as they secretly filled in the ditches and removed the fences.

When kings James I and Charles I later attempted to drain water which many peasants relied on for fishing and catching birds, peasants resisted by rioting, destroying the dikes, issuing pamphlets, and suing the engineers in court.

This enclosure process also occurred in France, Scotland, and many other unhealthy nations around the world. Simply living on the land has often not been enough to secure ownership when enclosure occurs. For example, in Scotland in the late 1700s, agents of the local lord burned the homes of many people to evict them. Betsy Mackay was sixteen when "the burning party came round and set fire to our house at both ends… The people were told they could go where they liked, provided they did not encumber the land that was by rights their own."

When land transitioned to private ownership systems, a few people became wealthy, a larger portion had a little, and many people had nothing.

Unfortunately, systems of collective land ownership are not much better.

Enclosing Land With Oppressive Collective Land Ownership

Many people recognize the problems of individual land ownership, and a common response is to push for collective land ownership instead. Unfortunately, as long as a few people rule over the rest, collective land ownership can be just as restrictive and exploitative.[13]

Russia had a system of serfdom in place for centuries until 1861. During the time of serfdom, the local landlord would assess tribute from the serfs, and then he would be responsible for paying taxes to the government. After serfdom ended, some peasants owned land directly while many others used land under the control of their village, called the "mir." This came with major drawbacks. The village community collectively owed taxes directly to the government. The mir would assess peasants for taxes and then pay the state. Everyone in the village faced joint unlimited liability for the group's tax obligations, meaning everyone was equally liable for any shortfall whether they'd paid their share or not.

Village governments were thus given police powers and authority over peasants' lives. A peasant could not legally sell their section of the land without permission, nor could they refuse to accept land. The village would allot different parcels to different families, and often farmers would have non-contiguous parcels. A peasant could not leave their village even temporarily without authorities' permission. As one author noted, "in many respects, the peasant exchanged one master, the landlord, for another one, the mir."

The Communist Party of China's Agrarian Reform Law of 1950 revoked all land ownership and distributed land to families on a per-capita basis. Landlords and rich peasants were evicted, injured, and even killed. However, families struggled to pool resources, and the government struggled to mobilize large numbers of people for big projects. Thus they instituted Agricultural Producer Cooperatives where many households together managed land and shared farming expenses.[14]

By 1956, they created another tier of cooperation called "Higher-Level Producer Cooperatives," with each one containing up to 1,000 people. The cooperative managed all aspects of farming, including the land, tools, and animals. Eventually cooperatives or work brigades gained direct control and ownership of much of the land. Families were only left with direct control of a few animals and a little plot next to their home for a garden.

Over the years, the Chinese government instituted many different work point systems to reward farmers for their labor on shared land. The overarching purpose was to increase agricultural production and extract surplus value from farmers while ensuring they received enough food that they could eat and keep working. Work teams might give points for completing tasks, working a set amount of time, or in other ways. But no one knew the value of a work point while they worked. The value of the points was determined after each harvest and the whole team's taxes, production, and social service expenses were deducted.[15]

In another instance of *going through the motions*, Chinese workers insisted on a fair distribution of points and spent vast amounts of time in meetings talking about job allocations, evaluating people's work, and workpoints. Each member paid attention to their relative share of the team's workpoints to ensure they were awarded fairly. However, workers commonly ignored the bigger problem: the government took about half of the team's production before workers began arguing over how to divide the rest.

Because rulers were still exploiting the workers, collective land ownership wound up being as exploitative as private land ownership.

Enclosing Healthy Nations

When people are used to living in intimate relationship with the land, being forced into artificial land ownership is extremely traumatic. Every person's and every group's experience is unique, but they also show some common patterns that suggest what many people's ancestors must have experienced at some point in the deep past as they first encountered land ownership.

Stories from several healthy nations show how they responded to the pressure to own land. Each story illustrates a fragment or phase in the transition from a free life of intimate connection with the Earth to a life limited by land ownership. I present the following stories from several healthy nations to illustrate a tragic arc of starting life without land ownership and winding up impoverished in a nation dominated by land ownership.

Since every healthy nation's experience has been unique, they cannot be accurately summarized with one broad brush. For some healthy nations, everyone was killed, while in others everyone was enslaved. In others, people were allowed to become impoverished and look for jobs. Clearly some of these people were more likely to record their stories than others.

My goal with the following survey is to convey some common patterns in people's experience of enclosure, including how disturbing it has been for people who were used to living free and closely connected with the Earth.

Stories of Enclosure

Before wars began with Americans, Wikis said, "life had been easy for me and for the tribe. We had many skins for robes, lodges and clothing. Food was plenty." Then a great deal of violence began, and often times his people were victorious, at least in the beginning. However, as more fighting happened, he said, "we felt as if some great hand that was all around my tribe and all the other tribes, was closing a little tighter about us all, and that at last it would grasp us and squeeze us to death."[16]

Ohiyesa, Fire Thunder, and Black Elk described what it was like to notice the hand squeezing tight.

Ohiyesa noted that in 1871 he "tasted to the full the joy and plenty of wild existence." There were plenty of buffalo, elk, and other animals in huge herds. Unfortunately, white people found gold in the region, and fighting increased. Ohiyesa asked his grandfather, "the people say the Wasichus are coming… to kill us all… What does it mean?" The grandfather responded, "That they are many."[17]

For a long time, the Sioux successfully defended themselves, both winning and losing battles with the Americans. However, with increasing colonist and military pressure, this became more difficult. Suddenly it became much harder when Americans invented the repeating rifle. During one battle with American colonists, Sioux man Fire Thunder said, "they shot so fast that it was like tearing a blanket." Courageous Sioux warriors kept trying to approach but the horses were too scared. Finally they left their horses behind and approached the colonists on foot, but "it was like green grass withering in a fire." Many warriors died.

When the Americans signed a treaty with Red Cloud on behalf of the Sioux in 1868 which promised them their land, many felt optimism. But the American military pressured many Sioux to enter reservations. Some entered and some stayed in the wilderness, where the military continually chased and attacked those bands who insisted on their freedom.

Black Elk said, "Wherever we went, the soldiers came to kill us, and it was all our own country. It was ours already when the Wasichus made the treaty with Red Cloud [Treaty of 1868]."[18]

In one battle, the American military attacked in a blizzard. The Sioux had run out of rifle ammunition, so the warriors fought with clubs and spears to allow time for the women to escape with the children and what possessions they could carry. Finally Black Elk's band entered the reservation for the last time. The government confiscated their horses and Black Elk noted that, "they said the Great Father [president] in Washington would pay us for [the horses]; but if he ever did I have not heard of it."[19,20]

The Sioux had become low-privilege people to whom the unhealthy nation routinely breaks its promises.

The Cherokee also illustrate one transition from a healthy nation without land ownership to a low-privilege people in an unhealthy, land-owning nation.

War can be expensive. In the 1630s, the British colonies of Connecticut and Massachusetts began to privatize war by offering to pay colonists for heads and later for the scalps of people of healthy nations whom they called "savages," whether men, women or children.

While many people of healthy nations have collected the scalps of dead enemy combatants as trophies, I'm unaware of any healthy nation that has rewarded its warriors for randomly killing non-combatant men, women and children without provocation. This British and later American program of state-sponsored terrorism and civilian murder lasted more than 200 years, affecting many healthy nations.

Besides the terrorist killings of men, women, and children, Cherokee also faced massacres and enslavement by colonial militias. Shortly before what the colonists called the Cherokee War in the early 1760s, the North Carolina governor ordered, "In Case a War must be proclaimed, the three Southern Provinces of Virginia and the Carolinas should exert their whole force, enter into and destroy all the [Cherokee] Towns of those at War with us, and make as many of them as we should take their Wives and Children Slaves…"

Cherokee warriors continuously defended their villages and often won battles and guerilla raids. During the American Revolutionary War in 1776-1783, both the British and Americans still recognized the Cherokee as a formidable military force. However, the Americans were willing to take on both the Cherokee and British at the same time. When the Cherokee avenged attacks on their settlements with attacks on colonial settlements, colonists instituted scorched-Earth campaigns, with one politician stating the Cherokees' behavior "shuts them out from every pretension to mercy." Many militias formed to attack the Cherokee, with one receiving orders to "chastise that nation and reduce them to obedience." Many Cherokee towns were entirely razed to the ground, with survivors either enslaved or fleeing for their lives.

After American independence, the US government began to pressure the Cherokee to adopt many American patterns of government, including land ownership. American agent Return Meigs told the Cherokee that the president wanted "to have every man enjoy his own property, [and] to make estates by industry."[21]

The Cherokee National Council rejected the idea of granting land titles to individuals. The National Council took steps to preserve communal stewardship of the land, but they came under continual pressure to sell, both from Americans and from some Cherokee who had adopted American values.[22]

While traditionally, the Cherokee had women's and men's councils that made decisions during peace and war, the Cherokee nation began changing substantially after 1750 under continual pressure from the French, British, and Americans.[23,24] By the 1800s, a National Council of men made most of the decisions.

Cherokee women made repeated efforts to urge the Council not to adopt private land ownership under US government pressure. In one message during debates in 1817, 13 Cherokee women said, "The Cherokee ladys now being present at the meeting of the Chiefs and warriors in council have thought it their duties as mothers to address their beloved Chiefs and warriors now assembled," and they referred to the leaders of the National Council as "our beloved children." They said, "this act of our children would be like destroying your mothers. Your mother and sisters ask and beg of you not to part with any more of our lands."[25]

The next year, the Council met again to consider the issue of land cessions and private land ownership, and once again many Cherokee women opposed it, saying, "The land was given to us by the Great Spirit above as our common right, to raise our children upon, & to make support for our rising generations." The women recognized how common care for the land bound the nation together, and these Cherokee women "claim[ed] the right of the soil," and unanimously voted "to hold our country in common as hitherto."[26]

Under severe pressure from the Americans, the Cherokee National Council voted over several years to make some land concessions to colonists or individuals but refrained from fully adopting private land ownership. This was sadly not enough for the Americans, who in the 1830s arrested many of the Cherokee and forced them on a five-month march to live in barren Oklahoma. Many Cherokee died on this long walk, known as the Trail of Tears.[27]

Tragically, the Cherokee were not the only healthy nation forced to migrate away from their homeland to make room for colonists.

The Potawatomi called their forced march the Trail of Death. Before their death march, they lived around Lake Michigan. Soldiers came and pointed guns at them and escorted them away from the lakes and forests they knew so intimately. However, colonists repeatedly decided that they wanted the land where the Potawatomi had been sent, so they were forcibly removed to Wisconsin, then again to Kansas, and eventually to Oklahoma, which by this time was controlled by the United States.

Many died along these trails, and much cultural knowledge was lost. Robin Kimmerer's great-grandmother was called Sha-note, meaning "Wind Blowing Through." She was renamed Charlotte, as soldiers and missionaries forbade any name they could not pronounce. As in other healthy nations under siege, Potawatomi children were taken away and forced into abusive boarding schools.[28]

After the Potawatomi arrived in Oklahoma, they faced a momentous decision. They were used to making decisions collectively about the land, but the US government offered each individual their own plot of land and US citizenship. If they became US citizens, they could enjoy government protection of their private property rights. If not, they could lose everything. Kimmerer described how "With heavy hearts, they sat in council all summer, struggling to decide and weighing the options, which were few…" Eventually they accepted the offer.

Thus the Potawatomi accepted US citizenship, and the government indeed gave each new citizen a parcel of land. While they were allowed to have land, they were not safe from other predators. Some could not pay property taxes and lost their parcel to the county. Others were tricked by ranchers who offered whiskey and a little cash. Unallocated parcels were snatched by non-Potawatomi.

During this time, more than two thirds of reserved land was lost. Within a generation after the Potawatomi gave up on holding land in common in exchange for private property, most of their land was gone.

While these are all stories from North America, similar stories can be found from around the world. For example, the Sami of northern Europe struggle to protect their forests from Swedish authorities, as Sami woman Josefina Skerk said: "we should have the right to much more of a say when it comes to what is being done with our traditional territories. But mostly we have no ownership rights to anything. So whether it is private owners or state owners, they do more or less as they please."[29]

Anywhere land-owning nations spread, they generate similarly tragic results where a few people own a lot, a larger group owns a little, and most people own nothing at all.

War, Part 1: Does a Nation Fight for What it Needs, or Fight for More Than it Needs?

Where I live in the United States, I commonly encounter the attitude that violence is "bad" and non-violence is "good." When I hear people debate which side in a war is the "good guys" deserving of sympathy and which side is the "bad guys" deserving of scorn, it commonly boils down to figuring out who physically attacked first, or which side was more violent.

This is a mistake.

Anyone who studies self-defense knows that, once a fight is going to happen, it is important to take initiative and not let the adversary strike first. This same dynamic plays out in war. If one nation is threatening and provoking another, the first nation to act violently might not be the one responsible for the war.

Both healthy nations and unhealthy nations may go to war for a variety of reasons. While I've found many non-violent ways that healthy nations resolve conflicts, they also may fight and displace each other.

However, I commonly find that wars among healthy nations are much more limited, in part because they live in gift economies and take only as much land or other resources as they need.

In contrast, unhealthy nations with profit economies consistently train people to take more than they need, and this is reflected in imperialist wars, military and commercial expansion, economic sanctions, state-sponsored terrorism, and more. When empires compete with each other, they create terrible security situations that can lead to intensely destructive wars, some of which have lasted decades or even a century, and the threat of losing such a war motivates rulers even further to take as much as they can. Why else would a tiny country like Great Britain have a globe-spanning empire in the 19th century over which "the sun never set?"

Unhealthy nations also train people not to notice or take responsibility for the consequences of their actions, which is why there is so much pollution. I don't observe this behavior in healthy nations. Deep selfishness and endless taking only occurs in nations where a few people rule over everyone else and impose a chronic state of poverty and managed desperation on huge numbers of people.

In war, I have noticed that healthy nations fight for what they need, while unhealthy nations fight for more than they need. This explains why, most of the time, I've noticed that healthy nations have been the ones acting defensively in wars with unhealthy nations.

Unfortunately, there are other common misunderstandings about war as well.

War, Part 2: Are Civilians Responsible for Supporting Their Rulers' Wars?

Hate occurs when people are trapped with a powerful threat and see no way to alleviate it except by escaping or fighting (reviewed in Chapter 22). When escape is impossible, the fighting can become "all or nothing" and vicious for both sides, but both sides are not equally to blame. The side that poses the endless threat is responsible for this dynamic.

Imperial expansion has represented exactly this sort of endless threat to all nations throughout the Americas and around the world. For many unhealthy nations, no amount of territory has ever been "enough." In many cases, the only thing that has stopped imperial expansion has been successful, ongoing self-defense.

This imperial expansion has threatened and caused the total extermination of many healthy nations. Besides the continent-spanning massacres, shaming, enslavement, and terrorist scalp campaigns, unhealthy nations have used many techniques, including deliberately spreading diseases like small pox.[30]

This ongoing threat of extermination generates a strong need for people of healthy nations to defend themselves, and as a result they can begin to see the entire onrushing unhealthy nation as diseased. That is, it is not just the soldiers that are a problem; all the colonists are collectively part of the onslaught that kills, enslaves, or displaces other nations.

The reality of exploitation in abusive nations means that civilians play a major indirect role in combat operations. Rulers make civilians grow food to feed soldiers, or manufacture weapons or clothes, or operate bureaucracies that manage the economy. Rulers may pretend that such civilians are not part of a war and should not be attacked. But clearly most civilians in authoritarian nations do obey and support their rulers by paying taxes and producing goods and services that support the economy that sustains the military.

Instead of seeing a nation's military as the sole source of violence, it helped me to *see an authoritarian nation as a system*, where rulers force civilians to make food, weapons, and other material which is then used to support the military. Civilians might not think they are supporting a war if they're "just doing their job" and don't think about what happens to the food or goods they produce. But obviously the military could not fight without workers who manufacture things, nurseries and schools that babysit the workers' children, police that keep the workers in line, or journalists that spread propaganda to keep the workers confused. Civilians are as much a part of the system as military soldiers. The only difference is that their roles in the imperial violence occur in a factory, farm, nursery, office or somewhere other than a battlefield.

When rulers choose to engage in offensive warfare, civilians thus support this too, knowingly or not. Tragically, rulers commonly lie to their civilians with propaganda, motivating them to support a war based on misunderstandings (reviewed in Chapter 39). Civilians may believe an offensive war is actually defensive, or the adversaries deserve their suffering, or some other justification for fighting. Regardless of whether a particular civilian mentally supports a war, anyone who pays taxes and contributes to their authoritarian nation's profit economy physically supports their rulers' wars.

Thus when the Potawatomi, Ojibway, Huron, and others rose up in Pontiac's Rebellion in 1763 to free themselves from oppressive British military control, it is not surprising that Pontiac would say, "It is important for us, my brothers, that we exterminate from our lands this nation which seeks only to destroy us."[31] The British, including the civilians, represented an overwhelming threat as they continually took more than they needed.

This explains why these healthy nations could see the entire British nation as a threat, and not just the military. Pontiac did not just want the soldiers to leave while the civilians stayed behind. He recognized that the whole British nation that invaded his land was sick, and civilians were as much part of it as anybody else. The whole diseased, oppressive British nation had to be pushed out in order for them to survive and live in actual freedom.

War, Part 3: What is the Root Cause of Endless Violence? – Unhealthy Nations Where People Are Trained to Take More Than They Need.

So instead of asking "who are the good guys?" and "who are the bad guys?" I ask what is the root cause of the endless violence around me, and how might I get it to stop?

Because there is so much violence in unhealthy nations, many people seem to think that war is always bad and peace is always good. But that doesn't make sense. If another nation attacks mine, fighting is how I protect myself and my people. Defensive warfare is simply a way to set healthy boundaries when words and other actions don't work.

There has been warfare throughout human history. But the continual overwhelming violence of imperial expansion, colonialism, prisons, and slavery relies on endlessly manipulative propaganda, and it is only a feature of unhealthy nations that consistently take more than they need, even while ensuring that most people chronically have too little.

Thus when I ask what I could do that might generate a meaningful peace, the answer is clear: *end or transform the unhealthy nation where a few people rule over everyone else*. Instead, generate a healthy nation without rich people endlessly trying to get more, so that everyone can embrace a gift economy and feel the deep security and contentment of actually having what they need.

Whenever a group successfully transforms and becomes healthy again, they may still need continual vigilance if they are surrounded by other unhealthy nations. But internally they will have a deep peace grounded in a baseline of mutual respect.

Violence may be necessary to get to that freedom and thus achieve deep peace, as slaveowners rarely let the enslaved achieve freedom without a fight. But as long as authoritarian nations persist, their endless, insatiable, and unnecessary violence will continue.

Land Ownership is Sacrilege

Each healthy nation had its own special experience, but when I put the Sioux', Cherokees', and Potawatomis' stories side by side, it makes many things clear. Nations that control land are not free. They are not workers' paradises, and regardless of what authorities say, they do not protect freedom, democracy, or human rights. Controling land allows rulers to control people.

These stories hint at the common ancestral experiences of everyone trapped in unhealthy nations. Some of our ancestors were enslaved while others were massacred, forced on death marches, or trapped as low-privilege citizens. Each of these moments of transition is a catastrophe, and then the catastrophe simply continues as people deal with life where a few rule over the many, and people are forbidden from standing for a culture of mutual respect. After a few generations, the catastrophe may become normal, or "just how life is."

When debating whether to submit to the Americans, Sitting Bull said, "They claim this mother of ours, the Earth, for their own use, and fence their neighbors away from her, and deface her with their buildings and their refuse… this is sacrilege."[32]

Sitting Bull was right, as were the Cherokee women and so many other people of healthy nations. Land ownership is sacrilege. It separates people from each other, it separates people from the Earth, and it makes it very difficult to have intimate relationships with our nonhuman neighbors.

Capitalists, socialists, and communists endlessly debate how land should be controlled. Should individuals own it or the government? The appropriate answer is: *nobody should own the land*. Healthy nations protect themselves and the land from predation by outsiders. They ensure each individual has privacy and the space they need, and healthy nations may fight to protect their territory from others to ensure they can support themselves from the land. But authoritarian patterns of land ownership – for example, allowing landowners to abuse "their" part of the Earth as they wish, or keep exclusive access to land they're not using while their neighbors are homeless – these patterns do not exist in healthy nations.

Nonhumans can teach us humans so much when we pay attention. Because land ownership makes it very difficult to learn from nonhumans, it keeps us ignorant and overly focused on human affairs. For example, why do so many people obsessively read and write in unhealthy nations? For thousands of years, many religious and academic scholars have spent much of their waking lives with their noses in books. Why would they spend so much time with books when the world offers so much adventure, knowledge, and wisdom outside? Well, what else are people going to do if they're forbidden from moving freely outdoors due to property lines? Books can provide a mental escape when a person's life is severely physically restricted due to punishments for trespassing.

In present times, video games, movies, phones and other computer distractions fill a similar need, offering feelings of adventure, discovery, connection, or at least distraction for people who might otherwise notice that property lines have made their world very small.

The many abusive effects of unhealthy nations run deep. The sooner we can free ourselves from unhealthy nations and this trap of land ownership, the better.

When an unhealthy nation seems to have an iron grip on the land, what can individuals and groups of people do to develop a fun and meaningful connection with the Earth anyway? One growing practice is described in the next chapter, *Chapter 35: Guerilla Gardening - Generating Abundance Without Permission.*

Chapter 35: Guerilla Gardening - Generating Abundance Without Permission

Dandelions inspire me more than any other plant. They are beautiful and nutritious, and they grow in places where I would never expect anything to be able to grow.

Dandelions pop up in cracks in the street and sidewalks. They grow with lots of sun and water or with very little, in fields and parking lots and near abandoned houses. Dandelions bring beauty and food into the world, mostly without human land owners giving them permission.

Dandelions thus set a good example for guerilla gardeners. Guerilla gardeners are people who bring beauty and food into the world without landowners' permission. Like guerilla fighters who don't control land during a war, guerilla gardeners don't own the land where they garden. A guerilla gardener simply decides there ought to be a garden somewhere and creates it on their own initiative. In other words, guerilla gardeners make gardens without permission.

Amy Twigge described the appeal: "It's kind of fun to not ask permission. There's more of a bad ass element to it that way."[1]

One of the most famous guerilla gardeners was Gerrard Winstanley, a leader of the Digger movement in England. He noted the Diggers' goal to "lift up the Creation from the bondage of [Civil] Propriety, which it groans under," because like people of healthy nations, the Diggers recognized that "not one word was spoken in the beginning, that one branch of mankind should rule over another."[2]

After the enclosure movement took hold in England, the country faced many problems. Rulers had claimed that forcing commonly-held land into private ownership was supposed to lead to more responsible use. However, the country still didn't produce enough food, so many people were malnourished. Further, many wealthy people left large amounts of growing land unused in so-called "waste" areas.

The Diggers aimed to rectify this. In April 1649, both women and men Diggers went to St. George's Hill in Surrey, England and planted beans, carrots and parsnips on the Walton manor. Later they added corn, stating their goal as "making the Earth a common Treasury for all, both Rich and Poor, That every one that is born in the Land, may be fed by the Earth his Mother that brought him forth."

There has been guerilla gardening as long as there have been rich people in unhealthy nations trying to control the land. When people are unable to find legal ways to sustain themselves, they get creative, and guerilla gardens offer sustenance for nationless, homeless, and impoverished people around the world. People have grown gardens along train tracks in Mumbai, India, on unused fields in Kenya, and in refugee camps in Syria. Residents of favelas in Brazil co-create and manage their own gardens.[3]

The term *guerilla gardening* likely first came from New York City in 1973, when Liz Christy, an artist who lived next to an abandoned lot, saw that it was filled with garbage like many others. One day she noticed a child climbing into an abandoned refrigerator with the door still attached. She got upset, pulled the child out, and berated the mother. The mother responded, saying if she cared so much about the garbage, why doesn't she do something herself? Christy took that to heart and gathered friends to clear the space. They then planted a garden which became the first of hundreds of community gardens throughout the city. Locals renamed it the Liz Christy Garden after she died of cancer at the age of 39.[4]

Some people have planted guerilla gardens both to feed people and protect the land. In Vancouver, Canada in 1971, a big hotel chain bought beautiful waterfront land near the entrance to Stanley Park. They wanted to build a large complex which would have allowed only wealthy visitors to have a view of the park. In one demonstration, protesters rushed onto the site together at a pre-arranged signal, and they liked it so much they decided to stay. They put up tents, planted trees, flowers, and gardens, and generally had fun. They remained for over a year until a wealthy individual bought the land and donated it so it would remain undeveloped. Today millions of people pass through Devonian Park, mostly unaware of the role guerilla gardeners played in its preservation.

Having fun together while generating abundance without permission.

How to Guerilla Garden

The first requirement of guerilla gardening is initiative. After the mayor of Seattle "chickened out" of a promise to strengthen local neighborhoods, Jim Diers and a group of activists entered his office and released a live chicken to let him know what his constituents thought of him. The mayor ended up appointing Diers as director of the city's new Office of Neighborhoods. Even while he worked in government for 14 years, Diers kept supporting local people in taking initiative, saying, "A lot of it is getting inspired by stories of what people have done. Then find your own way to do it. If it's public property being neglected by the city, go in at night and put in a park. Or, there's property that the city won't even come out and inspect, no one's going to care if you go out and fix it up. A lot of absentee landlords won't even know if a property's been changed… Instead of spending all your time going down to City Hall, just do it."[5]

In his book *Guerilla Gardening: A Manualfesto*, David Tracey noted there are multiple approaches to guerilla gardening. One involves acting in secret, often at night. This kind of gardening is performed quickly and quietly while few people are out to witness it.[6]

Another approach involves working by day, out in the open without any hiding or masks. These gardeners may wear work gloves and clothes and even safety vests if available. As Tracey summarized, "Act as if you belong and everyone will assume you do."

A third approach is for gardeners to make seed balls, also known as seed bombs or seed green-aids. This was popularized by Masanobu Fukuoka in his book *Sowing Seeds in the Desert*. The basic idea is to create a ball of soil, place seeds inside, and put or toss that ball somewhere the gardener wants plants to grow. Just like the sweet edible part of an apple or peach can help the seeds inside grow into trees, the soil in a seed ball offers moisture and nutrition to help the seeds get a strong start in life. Even deserts covered in sand or asphalt can become home for plants again.

Healthy nations are who we are as human beings, and many people with open hearts are constantly working to regenerate aspects of healthy nations. Just as the Potawatomi and Apache and many others live in a way that benefits the land, guerilla gardeners sustain themselves in a way that generates soil fertility and abundance which wouldn't exist without them. Guerilla gardeners show one way that people in unhealthy nations can live in a mutually enriching relationship with the land in spite of private land ownership.

Guerilla gardening is one way individuals or groups can choose how to relate to each other and the Earth in spite of artificially imposed systems of land ownership. Unfortunately, some artificial conditions imposed by unhealthy nations are much harder to see.

Next, *Chapter 36: Sabotaging Efforts at Deep Cultural Healing* reveals several tactics that rulers and other authorities use to undermine social movements.

Chapter 36: Sabotaging Efforts at Deep Cultural Healing

Human nations are living organisms. Like lions, trees, ant colonies, and other organisms, when human nations get wounded, they try to heal.

Any act of disrespect between two people is a cultural wound. Healthy nations respond to disrespect by addressing it and finding a way back to that baseline of mutual respect. This is what it means for people to take responsibility for each other and the nation's wellbeing: instead of ignoring or excusing the disrespect, they address the issue. Cultural healing occurs when people address disrespect so that it stops happening.

In unhealthy nations, not only do rulers behave disrespectfully, they actively block efforts at cultural healing that would bring the nation back to that baseline of mutual respect. Beyond the individual personalities involved, the mere existence of rulers – the fact that a few dominate the many – creates the conditions that incentivize some people to block cultural healing. Full cultural healing becomes impossible until those conditions change.

I have observed many brave people become politically active, only to be attacked or undermined by authorities in ways they did not expect. After observing how authorities around the world use similar techniques over and over to stymie social activists, I dreamed of making a manual of authoritarian tricks so that activists could better anticipate trouble and protect themselves.

This chapter is that manual of tricks – an incomplete survey of techniques that authorities use to sabotage efforts at deep cultural healing.

Techniques for Blocking Cultural Healing

It turns out that when one group of people commits to controlling another group within the same nation, they can get really creative. Some tricks are simple, and some are complex. Some tricks are subtle, and some are quite brutal.

Let us start with the simplest technique.

Arresting Activists

The Nazis worked diligently to scare all of the Germans into submission. Bruce Bettelheim described how a group of activist lawyers objected to various Nazi policies, and so the German police arrested all the leaders.

This led to other group members believing they were safe as long as they stayed out of leadership positions. The Nazis did not want any public opposition, so they responded by arresting lawyers essentially randomly across the group. Nobody was explicitly told why they were arrested, but they all learned it was from their activism work. This scared everyone and allowed the Nazis to leave a few leading lawyers in place when they decided this was helpful to them.[1]

Administrative Attacks

After the Nazis fell and the Soviets imposed a new government on East Germany, the East Germans took a different approach to suppressing activism. Not wanting to be recognized internationally as a state that openly abused its activists, they developed a system called Zersetzung, meaning decomposition or disintegration. This police practice intended to cause activists to mentally, emotionally, and socially disintegrate without any explicit use of force.

Zersetzung took a vast number of forms, and police invested time and substantial effort into refining their techniques. They might cause other government bureaucracies to lose citizens' forms, take longer than usual to respond to citizens' inquiries or requests, or otherwise seriously frustrate the lives of activists. East German police would sabotage people's reputation. They fabricated and circulated love letters or evidence of illegal behavior among an activist's friends and family in order to sabotage relationships, and they often succeeded.[2]

They also surveilled activists to dig up and publicize any private behaviors they might want hidden, such as drug use or criminal records. They might make appointments or order goods in the activist's name. They would even manipulate a person's home, secretly entering and rearranging items like clothes and only removing things no burglar would snatch, such as a single piece of important mail. They might secretly damage a bike or car. Activists would start to doubt their memory and their ability to live a functional life. Police might cause strange noises on a phone line, repeatedly stop and search someone, and make conspicuous visits to the activist's workplace so coworkers would be aware of the police's interest. People's careers were ruined without them even understanding why. Zersetzung was gaslighting on a massive scale.[3,4,5]

When she was 14 years old, East German police interrupted Regina Herrmann's class at school to tell her that they considered her father an enemy of the state, a "capitalist exploiter," because he ran his own hair salon. The police told Herrmann that she could count on being rejected from any university, and she could stop dreaming of being a doctor. In later years, she constantly sensed she was being followed by strange men "like a shadow." Rumors spread that she was a Flittchen, an easy girl. Twice men tried to rape her, and she was often touched inappropriately while working at her father's salon. After the East German government fell, she learned that the police had ordered five citizen-spies to target her in nightclubs and bars.[6]

These sorts of illegal or plausibly legal attacks can take many forms. In 2022, American Matt Taibbi was busily exposing documents which showed how the US government pressured a social media company to censor content. Three weeks after he started, the federal tax authority (IRS) opened a tax investigation of Taibbi, launching it on Christmas Eve, 2022 which was a Saturday. Later on March 9, 2023, the IRS took the very unusual step of sending an agent to Taibbi's home. This happened to be the same day he testified in Congress about the censorship. When congressman Jim Jordan asked the IRS for an explanation, they claimed they had sent letters about his 2018 tax filing, but neither Taibbi nor his accountant ever received them. The IRS also claimed they were concerned about identity fraud. On March 23, just two weeks after Taibbi's congressional testimony and after the IRS encountered congressional questioning into their investigation of Taibbi, the IRS decided Taibbi didn't actually owe any taxes after all and was suddenly entitled to a refund. The investigation was closed.[7]

Reputation Sabotage, Blackmail, and Sexual Shaming

Authorities may also use the law to punish someone regardless of whether they committed any crimes, and Julian Assange's story offers an example. Assange founded Wikileaks, an organization and website that helps whistleblowers around the world expose corruption.

Among these leaks were many examples of US politicians lying to the public or of the military committing war crimes, including the infamous Collateral Murder video leaked by Chelsea Manning, known as Bradley Manning at the time of the leak. The video showed an assault from the perspective of US soldiers sitting in an attack helicopter as they shot about a dozen people in Baghdad, Iraq, with a 30mm cannon. The video showed the American soldiers' birds-eye view and contains their conversation during the massacre. In a press conference after the leaks came out, a lieutenant colonel spokesman publicly stated, "there is no question that coalition forces were clearly engaged in combat operations against a hostile force."[8]

However, the video plainly showed everyone on the ground was very relaxed as they walked down a street together, including the two Reuters news journalists who were killed, Saeed Chmagh and Namir Noor-Eldeen. It also plainly showed that the soldiers knowingly targeted first responders who came to aid the wounded, even getting command approval. Two children who arrived with the first responders were also shot.[9,10]

After helping many whistleblowers reveal leaks that illustrated deep corruption, the US decided to target Assange directly with imprisonment and character assassination. He was accused of sexual assault in Sweden and fleeing to avoid questioning, even though the Swedish authorities allowed Assange to leave the country and the original Swedish prosecutor Eva Finne said, "There is no suspicion of any crime whatsoever."[11]

In Great Britain, Assange feared extradition to Sweden which might then extradite him to the United States where he would face the US government's wrath, so he took refuge in the Ecuadorian embassy where he remained trapped for seven years until a new Ecuadorian president came to power and allowed the British to enter and arrest him.

Assange was held in a high-security prison and his visitors recognized severe signs of psychological torture and declining health while he faced all manner of smears and false accusations. For example, he was accused of leaking secret agents' names unredacted, when in fact, other journalists working for other organizations leaked the uncovered agents' names and Assange warned the State Department directly when he discovered this.[12,13]

After dropping the pretense of Assange's original sexual assault allegations, the US spent five years seeking his extradition for supposedly harming US national security. Assange was trapped in a high-security prison the entire time, eventually plea-bargaining in 2024 and regaining his freedom.[14]

Other authoritarian tricks for blocking cultural healing include blackmail, threats, and even sexual shaming.

Chomden was a citizen of Myanmar living abroad in 2021 when she learned that a video of her having sex with an ex-boyfriend was circulating online. The video was tagged with her name, Facebook profile picture, and the flag of the recently deposed democratic government. The video was spreading among a Telegram group known to support the new Myanmar military government. Chomden had voiced support for the deposed democratic government and opposition to the new military junta from abroad, thinking she was safe.

After the video circulated, many of the Telegram group's 10,000 followers began threatening and shaming her, writing things like, "The whore who is having sex with everyone and recording it in HD… Know your position, slut!" Chomden was blackmailed as well, with strangers claiming to have more private videos. She felt isolated and it took a major toll. She said, "I have to admit that I even thought of killing myself." Researchers found many hundreds of such abusive threats and videos online linked with the military government.[15]

Infiltration and Subversion

A particularly devious technique that authorities use to thwart cultural healing involves developing informants within activist movements, either by having undercover officers infiltrate or by actively corrupting people who are already part of the movement.

Even failed attempts at infiltration can have profoundly negative effects because it can make people unsure whom they can trust, limiting the openness of conversation and activists' ability to collaborate and share resources. Infiltrators may purposely sow discord among activists or between two groups. They may enable surveillance of otherwise secret meetings. Authorities have used infiltration in extremely devious ways, not only to disrupt individual projects, but to permanently deter people from social activism.

Kate Wilson was a British environmental activist who began a romantic relationship with a man named Mark Stone, seemingly a radical environmental activist himself. They shared a taste for country music and a belief that capitalism was destroying the Earth. He attended her grandmother's 90th birthday anniversary and wrote her poetry. He helped her organize a large protest in opposition to the G-8 summit in Scotland. They lived together as lovers for almost two years and remained close friends for years afterwards.[16]

In 2010, Wilson discovered that Mark Stone's legal name was Mark Kennedy. He had a wife and two kids and worked for London's Metropolitan Police Service. For seven years, he had lived a double life until suspicious activists investigated and outed him. Kennedy had been a trusted leader in a movement seeking to raise awareness of climate change and end Britain's dependence on fossil fuels. He had participated in scouting missions to prepare for attempts to occupy and shut down power plants. He had had at least ten sexual partners, none of whom knew the truth until 2010. Wilson described how learning all this "was like a computer virus. It's corrupted all my memories of those times, and it affects all the relationships that I've had since."

Such stories are common. Kennedy's outing led to many other infiltrators being uncovered, including some who had started families with activists and become fathers before suddenly, mysteriously disappearing when the police rotated them to a new assignment. In late 2011 or early 2012, eight British women filed a lawsuit stating they were tricked into having long-term relationships with police who sabotaged their efforts to mitigate animal cruelty, reduce pollution, and more. Prosecutors and police chiefs set up 12 inquiries to investigate police misconduct, but all took place in secret and there has been no sign of change.[17]

The Tsarist Russian secret police provide more examples of police infiltration. Some informants only watched from outside gatherings, while others were trained to pose as members of organizations so they could observe from within. Infiltrators were trained to notice subtle things and take copious notes of even trivial details which police then carefully reviewed.[18]

As a young adult, S.V. Zubatov was active in Russian revolutionary groups, but he later supported the monarchy and in the 1890s rose to the level of chief of one section of the Moscow secret police. He became very skilled at interrogating and winning over radical activists by appealing to their idealism, saying the "monarchist idea, properly understood, can provide everything that the country needs including the unleashing of social forces and all without bloodshed." Zubatov also amazed them with his intimate knowledge of activists' secret activities, friendships, group memberships, and more.

Helpful informants were guaranteed entrance into their university of choice or to get their preferred job, while incorruptible activists could expect to be denied. Police also threatened physical abuse to pressure activists to snitch on their comrades.

Zubatov helped informants get to the innermost circles of activist groups, even permitting infiltrators to engage in extremely illegal activity needed to prove their trustworthiness to other activists.

All this made informants despised as traitors. One activist A.I. Guchkov called infiltrators "swarming worms… feeding on the live organism of the people… who made… from our slow death the justification of their life."

Zubatov was extremely careful with his informants. He taught his subordinate officers never to arrest people immediately after informants told on them, but rather to wait until they had built up a strong case of other evidence. When Zubatov arrested activists, he commonly let a few members of each group remain free to minimize risk to informants as well as to help the police keep tabs on future activist activity. Zubatov would deliberately stage fake arrests or spread false rumors to cause activists to doubt the honest people he couldn't subvert.[19] While the government shut down hundreds of trade unions in the early 1900s, police advocated allowing some unions to continue because allowing official unions made their surveillance work easier.[20]

Infiltration can be extremely difficult to combat. Some infiltrators are revealed from activist investigations. Others are caught when the police make foolish mistakes. For example, in what must have been a strange moment in one East German activist meeting, several infiltrators all introduced themselves with the same made-up name. However, many East German infiltrators were only revealed when the East German government fell in 1989.[21]

When two militaries fight, there is usually a recognizable line of contact or no-man's-land. Soldiers can feel relatively safe on their side of the line, and they know they're in enemy territory when they travel to the other side. In abusive nations, activists try to organize to resist abusive authorities, but they start out already in enemy-controlled territory. Authorities control the society and territory long before any particular activists come together. Thus activists are at a big disadvantage in trying to figure out whom to trust, where to meet in privacy, what obstacles they face, how to safely acquire resources, and so on.

People who benefit from exploiting their neighbors sabotage efforts to stop injustice. This is a common pattern in any nation where people allow themselves to be ruled.

Astroturf Social Movements

In politics, social movements that arise when people spontaneously come together and seek change are called grassroots movements. Corporate lobbyists may try to pressure politicians by creating fake activist groups that pretend to be grassroots and supposedly represent the desires of many voters. These fake social movements are called astroturf groups, named after a brand of fake grass used by soccer and other sports teams.

In school, I learned that astroturf groups were basically a corporate scam designed to trick politicians or voters into voting a particular way on a particular issue. I was taught they were basically front organizations with little actual substance and not very long-lasting. Unfortunately, astroturfing can be much more devious than this.

An astroturf effort from tsarist Russia offers an example. Zubatov was skilled at working with infiltrators, but he realized that this would not be enough to protect the government. With his activist background, Zubatov believed that the monarchy could only survive if the opposition groups were controlled by the police. He decided to secretly found trade unions and labor unions with leaders he controlled. Zubatov gave the unions enough leeway to appear independent while remaining under his direction.[22]

Huge numbers of workers were upset with their corporate bosses and the government that supported them. Wages were very low, the work was dangerous, and the hours were long. Zubatov reasoned that if workers got slightly better pay and better hours, they might continue to support the monarchy. With the support of Moscow's governor-general grand duke Aleksandrovich and chief of police Trepov, Zubatov secretly founded his first union, the Moscow Mechanical Production Workers' Mutual Aid Society in May 1901. Other secretly police-controlled unions soon followed, and many tens of thousands of workers signed up for them.[23]

These secretly government-controlled labor unions were used in all the devious ways one might imagine. Workers were trained to see aristocrats as allies, with 50,000 workers joining a march led by the grand duke Aleksandrovich to celebrate a previous monarch. The labor union leadership was careful to demand minor changes such as moderate wage increases, nothing that would diminish the company owners' or monarch's ability to control the workers. The police chief even held secret wage negotiations with business leaders.[24] Zubatov's handpicked men ran the groups, and they could tell who the real leaders would have been if the police weren't secretly running the show. Zubatov learned which workers showed real initiative, inspired their fellow workers, had anti-monarchy beliefs, and more, and he was able to add their names to lists for further surveillance.

In this way, the fake labor unions were honeypots, attracting labor activists who otherwise might have been able to work away from government surveillance. Even union-sponsored leisure activities occupied workers' time in government-approved, government-surveilled ways.[25]

It got even more devious. Zubatov trained his agents in various theories of socialism, and they would listen to debates. If a group started to agree on one doctrine, the agents would start advocating an opposing theory, preventing activists from ever reaching consensus. Sometimes the agents even convinced each other or themselves of their socialist doctrines. In this way, Zubatov sabotaged activists' sacred circles. The first step of a sacred circle is to acknowledge the full truth of a situation, and the second step is to decide the best response. These infiltrators were trained never to let the group settle on a shared understanding of their trouble or the best response.[26]

This continued for a few years until one of Zubatov's agents lost control of a union and a general strike spread through southern Russia. Zubatov was discredited and fired from his police chief position.[27]

Although Zubatov fell out of grace, the Russian secret police continued trying to control the political opposition. They supported small socialist movements and even sponsored socialist members of the Russian parliament. One of the most successful socialist parliament members was Roman Malinovsky. He was an excellent public speaker, and his speeches were very well planned. First they were written or vetted by the Bolshevik socialist Vladimir Lenin, then they were secretly reviewed by police director S. Beletsky.[28]

Astroturf movements can be extremely challenging to deal with. In one sense Zubatov's unions were fake, in that the leadership was controlled by the police which ensured the unions would never generate substantial change. In another sense the movement was real, as tens of thousands of people participated and honestly wanted worker solidarity and change. Acknowledging that these unions were astroturf groups controlled by authorities does not take away from the honest efforts and desires of many thousands of participants. It simply means the worker activists were tricked, and they did not accomplish nearly as much as they could have if they had avoided the fake unions.

Astroturfing differs from infiltration. With infiltration, sincere activists create a group which then has sincere leaders, and authorities send infiltrators into a legitimate group. In astroturfing, authorities create groups with leadership that they can control from the start. Authorities may also send infiltrators into these groups, but they already control the groups because they control the leadership.

I believe a comparable astroturf movement is active in the United States as I write in 2024. It is called "Black Lives Matter."

I first heard of the Black Lives Matter movement in 2014 after the police shooting of Eric Garner in New York. In the coming years, I noticed more and more media coverage and larger and larger protests as more black Americans were killed by the police, including Michael Brown in 2014, Alton Sterling in 2016, and Breonna Taylor in March 2020. In May 2020, huge protests spread around the country and around the world in response to the police killing of George Floyd.[29] Over the years, I even noticed a few police officers being convicted for the killings.

However, black people had been treated terribly for generations, and there had never been so much sympathetic media coverage and even some low-level police convicted for needlessly killing black people. I started to get suspicious. What was going on? Was long-overdue cultural healing really happening, or something else?

I decided to do some digging and it took me on a wild ride.

Henry Ford was the founder of Ford Motor Company, one of the largest car companies in the US in the early 1900s. He was very wealthy, and one of his legacies is the Ford Foundation. Officially, the Ford Foundation is a philanthropy, and it was the first philanthropic organization in the US to surpass $1 billion in assets which it did in the 1950s. This was four times the size of its nearest rival, the Rockefeller Foundation. It funded arts projects and community development, and in the late 1960s it began funding dozens of civil rights groups like the National Urban League. These organizations were widely recognized as moderate groups seeking economic development for black people, luring some people away from the radical protests and Black Power messages gaining traction.[30]

All this philanthropy may have appeared helpful on the surface, but by the 1960s, the Ford Foundation already had a long history of working with the CIA to subvert social movements. A 1951 classified CIA memo, published in 1999, was directed only to the Ford Foundation. It requested help preparing for psychological warfare operations in Asia, among other projects.[31]

The Ford Foundation was clearly closely connected with America's ruling class. To choose one illustrative example, consider that in 1958, John McCloy became the chairman of the Ford Foundation. During McCloy's career, he worked as president of the World bank, high commissioner for Occupied Germany after World War II, assistant secretary of war, chairman of Chase Manhattan Bank, chairman of the Council on Foreign Relations, and held leadership positions in other major corporations.[32]

It is difficult to imagine an institution more connected to the United States rulers than the Ford Foundation. And, as I write in 2024, what movement has the Ford Foundation been heavily funding for over a decade?

According to their own press release, from 2011-2021, the Ford Foundation funded Black Lives Matter and other racial equity efforts to the tune of $665 million. In late 2020, it announced an additional $180 million.[33]

Black Lives Matter and related racial equity groups are also supported by The Chan Zuckerberg Initiative, funded by Facebook ceo Mark Zuckerberg and his wife Priscilla Chan. They have donated at least $1 million to the cause of Black Liberation, according to the Initiative's tax return.[34] In 2020, Mark Zuckerberg's wealth was estimated at $100 billion.[35]

Pierre Omidyar, cofounder of eBay with an estimated wealth in 2023 of $8.91 billion, donated $100,000 to the Equity and Transformation group and $300,000 to Movement for Black Lives through his Omidyar Network.[36]

Many donations can be difficult to track, as wealthy donors will give to one organization that then donates to others. For example, Omidyar donated to the Democracy Fund, which donated $410,000 in 2020 to the Law for Black Lives organization.[37]

At least one investor financially benefited from their racial equity donations. Omidyar donated almost $2 million to groups seeking to abolish or defund the police while simultaneously investing in private security companies. Examples include Bond, which offers on-demand bodyguards, and Deep Sentinel, which provides AI-enabled security cameras. Both Omidyar and these companies would profit if the police were actually defunded.[38]

As I write, the "impact" page on blacklivesmatter.com proclaims "We are building an institution to fight white supremacy."[39] The "about us" page on m4bl.org (Movement for Black Lives) states "We are anti-capitalist."[40] And yet the movement is heavily funded by some of the wealthiest white capitalists on the planet.

Other signs show how wealthy capitalists and politicians speak words of deep systemic change while actually only allowing superficial change.

Many Democrats in Congress in 2020 made a great show of support after George Floyd died, taking a knee and wearing kente cloth in his honor. President Joseph Biden pushed for Juneteenth to become a federal holiday, celebrating the anniversary of the end of chattel slavery in the US. Many tech companies, like Zoom and Google, rushed to include icons that allow people to carefully choose their skin colors on their devices. Many publishers began capitalizing the words "white" and "black" when referring to people, and the New York Times and Associated Press even changed their style standards to capitalize "black" when referring to people, but not "white."[41,42]

Many companies include some variation of "diversity, equity, and inclusion" projects geared towards helping employees get along and work productively together. Corporate officers that claim to oppose racism commonly discuss microaggressions that hurt an individual's feelings but do not address the massive macroaggressions which generate systems of prison slavery.[43]

With one exception, I am unaware of any notable efforts from these politicians or corporate owners to end any of the major aspects of systemic racism, including police testilying, prison rape, or the plea bargain system, as exposed in earlier chapters.

I have likewise noticed no substantive effort to transform the system of forced financial desperation known as "the economy," which keeps so many black people and others in poverty.

While Black Lives Matter has many sincere members, it is sadly not the only movement within the United States where rich people fund dozens of apparently-different organizations for nefarious purposes. Charles and David Koch were some of the richest Americans with a combined wealth of about $120 billion as of 2019. They were owners of a company heavily involved with fossil fuels, chemical production, and other environmentally damaging operations. To sabotage efforts at addressing climate change, the Koch brothers directly funded a network of 90 shell groups, academic organizations, nonprofit advocacy groups, and think tanks, with indirect funding going to countless others. Each group pretended to speak independently as they cast doubt on legitimate science, attacked people's reputations, and funded fake research while in reality they were 90 heads on the same hydra. Funding for this massive propaganda effort totaled over $168 million from 1986-2018.[44,45]

The Kochs' massive investment in a synthetic anti-climate-change movement is analogous to the Ford Foundation's synthetic anti-racism movement and the Russian secret police's synthetic labor unions. This ability for rich people to fund countless organizations and build huge astroturf movements is simply another manipulative pattern in unhealthy nations.

What if the US Constitution Were Amended to Finally, Fully Outlaw Slavery?

The US Constitution's 13th amendment outlaws slavery "except as a punishment for crime whereof the party shall have been duly convicted." A seeming bright spot from the Black Lives Matter movement has been the introduction in congress of a resolution to amend the US Constitution to outlaw coerced labor in prisons.[46]

However, merely outlawing forced labor in US prisons without making other changes is comparable to outlawing forced labor on 18th century slave plantations without making any other important changes. I wouldn't expect such a law to have much practical effect. That's because when people are trapped in extremely abusive situations and there is no accountability for their abusers, the abusers will find ways to force trapped people to work.

Consider the power that abusive prison authorities have to motivate prisoners to choose to work.

- *Making money essential to reducing inmates' misery*: Prisons offer terrible food for free but better food for money at the commissary. Prisoners who want hygiene products or phone time to stay in touch with their families also need to buy these at the commissary. Prison staff can make inmates' "default" life without money arbitrarily miserable to motivate people to work for money.

- *Prison authorities manipulate income, withholdings, and costs*: US prisons commonly pay inmates less than $1 per hour except in seven states where inmates work for free despite this being far below federal minimum wage. Prisons withhold much of the inmates' pay to cover taxes, room and board, and court costs.[47] Prisons then keep commissary prices high so inmates must work long hours to buy essential goods. All this means that inmates must work very long hours to afford very basic items to reduce their misery in prison.

- *Ability to inflict arbitrary punishments*: Prison staff can inflict arbitrary punishments for arbitrary reasons. They can shorten or lengthen people's time in prison, often by years, a powerful tool to compel obedience. They can punish inmates with isolation, moving them to another region away from their family, drastically reducing rations, withholding medication or giving incorrect medication, forbidding visitation, and knowingly allowing rape by other prisoners, as ex-inmates have described.[48]

The fact that prison authorities have such wide discretion for punishing inmates and so little accountability means they can easily find plausible cover stories for abusing prisoners that refuse to work. It is telling that when the inmates at Attica Prison rioted in 1971, they delivered a manifesto that included demands to hold the prison staff accountable for their illegal or abusive behavior. They also demanded that prisons follow other laws, such as obeying minimum wage laws. Prisons commonly either break laws or get special exemptions that allow staff to predate on prisoners, and when there is already a pattern of law-breaking, it's not clear what changing the law again will do.[49]

As an example of arbitrary power in prisons, consider one of Kamala Harris's actions as California's attorney general, when the US Supreme Court decided that California's prisons were so overcrowded that the state was violating the Constitution. The Supreme Court ordered the state to reduce the prison population, but Harris's office illegally and repeatedly ignored the order or put up obstacles for years, in part because the state needed cheap labor to fight wildfires.[50,51]

When prisons offer reduced sentences or other benefits in exchange for consistent work, how many prisoners decline? So long as prison terms remain incredibly long, prisons remain incredibly miserable, and prison leadership is not held accountable for illegal behavior, prison authorities will find ways to compel obedience so that many prisoners will "volunteer" to work.

As long as prisons remain extremely abusive and prison authorities are not held accountable for their arbitrary power, including the huge amounts of sexual abuse in their facilities, prison staff will find ways to motivate prisoners to work regardless a change to the US Constitution. Even with a change to the US Constitution, without any other change, prison slavery would continue.

Unfortunately, there are even more troubles with merely changing the law. Funding would need to change too.

Prison officials have openly acknowledged that prisoner labor is essential to operating prisons at current funding levels. Prisoners generate more than $11 billion each year in goods and services. However, more than 80% of prison laborers do prison maintenance work, meaning prisoners provide approximately $8.8 billion per year of labor just to keep the prisons running.[52] If Congress were serious about ending forced prison labor, it would need to fund federal and state prisons with an additional $8.8 billion to replace that maintenance work in addition to current funding. It would also need to annually adjust this additional amount for inflation to make this change permanent.

Without substantial extra funding to pay for workers to take the place of inmates, prison leadership will find a way to motivate prisoners to work, as they do today.

If the amendment were passed and prison slavery fully outlawed without any funding changes, the US Supreme Court would face a conundrum. Prisoners would sue, claiming they were still forced to work, and demanding that the system of prison slavery be stopped. But since the prison system depends on prison slavery, the Supreme Court would face a choice: it could either force congress to massively increase prison funding or else shut prisons down. If the abolition amendment passed but prisons received no extra funding, the courts would have to choose between enforcing the law and shutting down prisons, or pretending that involuntary servitude in prisons isn't really happening.

Prisons are essential for maintaining the current social order in the United States, and the Supreme Court has been willing to ignore reality before to justify abusive policies that maintain order. For example, when the government imposed a draft in 1917 and legally required people to join the military, many citizens sued, claiming this was involuntary servitude which had been outlawed by the 13th amendment to the US Constitution.

However, the US Supreme Court held that the US government could force citizens into the military against their will and then require them to obey orders against their will, but this *couldn't* be involuntary servitude, and thus the draft didn't violate the 13th amendment.

The US Supreme Court's primary argument was that *of course* a government must be able to force people into the military. This is simply something governments have to be able to do to stay in power, so the courts have to allow it, regardless of what the law says.[53] The Supreme Court was willing to ignore the clear meaning of the 13th amendment prohibition against involuntary servitude because involuntary servitude is sometimes required to keep the government in power. Abuse is required to maintain order in unhealthy nations, and rulings like this show that when the Supreme Court has to ignore the law and reality to justify maintaining the social order, it will do so.

I support outlawing coerced prison labor, but after seeing the impunity with which officials already break the law and especially the US Constitution, I am skeptical that changing a single law without fixing the funding levels and lack of accountability will lead to meaningful change. Without holding prison officials accountable for abusive and illegal behavior, and without substantially increased funding for prisons, it is unclear how the amendment is supposed to materially change conditions for prisoners who remain trapped, in almost all cases without trial, in hyper-abusive prisons.

What Happens When a Social Movement Threatens Real Change

Studying the Black Panthers helped me recognize how hard it is to seek deep change when corporate owners aren't giving hundreds of millions of dollars in support. For example, for some time the Black Panthers' newspaper was their major source of funds.[54]

However, the Black Panthers faced steeper obstacles than mere funding.

Fred Hampton was chairman of the Illinois chapter of the Black Panthers based in Chicago, and he noticed a lot of people of different skin colors had similar grievances. Poor white people who had migrated to Chicago from the Appalachian mountains had formed a group called the Young Patriots, while Puerto Ricans formed a group called the Young Lords. All of them had similar complaints: poor living conditions, police brutality, poverty, and so on. Unfortunately, Chicago was heavily segregated, so these groups did not mingle easily.[55]

News media smeared the poor white people as "white trash" and "a different breed of hillbillies" who were ignorant, racist, incestuous, and violent. But Fred Hampton saw through that, and he and another Black Panther Bobby Lee went to a meeting where many white Young Patriots were present. At first, the whites were suspicious of the blacks, worried that they were armed terrorists. Some blacks felt concerned about the whites, especially when they noticed the Confederate flag patches on their clothes. But they overcame these concerns and eventually joined with the Puerto Ricans to form the Rainbow Coalition.

These groups acknowledged their superficial differences while celebrating their deep unity. They made multi-colored rainbow pins which showed their different skin colors. Bobby Lee, one Black Panther leader, released tension with humor when he noted that his legal name was Robert E. Lee, a man who had been a top general of the Confederate army that fought in part to preserve slavery in the US south.

Fred Hampton even approved of some members wearing their Confederate flag symbols at meetings. Some white participants added black power symbols and phrases next to their Confederate flag patches to generate conversations about race with other white people. The whites, blacks, and Latinos all ended up getting along because, as Bobby Lee noted, "The Rainbow Coalition was just a code word for class struggle."[56,57]

The Rainbow Coalition of white people, black people, and Latinos grew further to include women's groups, students' groups, and more. They provided health clinics, fed homeless and hungry people, and offered legal advice for anyone who confronted unethical landlords or police brutality.

People of different skin colors, sexes, ethnicities, regions, and all manner of differences were finding connection and common purpose and standing together in solidarity. Fred Hampton was extremely charismatic, and no one could generate this unity alone, but he played a major part in it.

I believe this is why, on December 4, 1969, the Cook County police murdered Fred Hampton. At 4:45 AM they burst into the Black Panthers headquarters, shooting and killing Mark Clark who was on guard. They sprayed bullets all over as they moved through the apartment, heading towards Hampton's room where he and his pregnant fiance were sleeping. Hampton's fiance and another man tried to wake him but couldn't, and police dragged them out of the room. They overheard the police say, "He's still alive." Then they heard two shots, and another officer said, "He's good and dead now." They shot Fred Hampton in the head from point blank range while he was asleep. Hampton had slept through the whole event because a federal police informant in the Black Panthers had drugged him the evening before.[58]

The Black Panthers in the apartment who remained alive were arrested and indicted on charges of armed violence, attempted murder, and various weapons charges. These charges were eventually dropped when investigators found that the police had fired 99 shots while the Black Panthers had fired once.[59]

After this, the Rainbow Coalition went underground and splintered. Some people left Chicago in fear for their lives. The earlier solidarity and public excitement of the Rainbow Coalition was gone.[60]

A huge number of sincere and passionate people have invested countless hours seeking meaningful social change through Black Lives Matter and related movements. It's possible that the Black Lives Matter funders will, like Zubatov, lose control of their investment. But Fred Hampton's story shows where the rulers stand. Hundreds of millions of dollars in racial equity funding by rich white capitalists may pave a tempting road, but it's unlikely they will let that road lead to deep, meaningful change.

Doing the Important Work Anyway

I have a lot of respect for anyone willing to stand for meaningful change. It takes a lot of courage, and it can be stressful, confusing, frustrating, scary, expensive, disappointing, tiring, and generally difficult. And that's why I have an even higher level of admiration for social activists who can face these challenges with a sense of humor.

An activist named Tortuguita showed how it's done. Tortuguita was active in the Stop Cop City effort in Atlanta, Georgia. Despite approximately 70% of residents opposing the plan at a City Council meeting, Atlanta police planned to replace a large forested area with a police training grounds featuring many shooting ranges, a mock city to practice urban warfare, a helicopter pad, and more.[61]

Many activists launched a multi-year effort to protect the forest. They engaged in marches, letter-writing, sabotage, addressing the City Council, filing lawsuits, hosting barbeques and music festivals, public education, and occupying and blockading the forest. Since November 2021, activists have maintained a consistent presence in the forest in spite of tremendous police pressure to desist. They set up their own shared kitchen, outdoor "living room," and library. Activists include doctors, parents with young children, people of all backgrounds and walks of life, and Muscogee people whose ancestors lived in the region before the Europeans arrived.

On December 13, 2022 the police raided their camp and destroyed the kitchen, library, and much of their other infrastructure. Most activists left the forest for safe houses that night, but five stayed behind amidst the devastation. One activist said, "it looked like a tornado had come through there." As they sat around a fire, Tortuguita looked up in the trees and saw a small flag the activists had used and said, "hey check it out, up in the tree." Tortuguita saluted the flag and sang, "…and our flag was still there!", a famous battle cry from the US national anthem. Everyone had a good belly laugh together.

One month later, in January 2023, Tortuguita was shot and killed by police. Many people hold Tortuguita's memory dear as they continue protecting the forest. One activist wrote on an online forum dedicated to Tortuguita's memory, "im so grateful i got to meet tort and experience the joy they had to offer. long live the memory of tort in our hearts long live the forest & long live anarchy."[62]

Unhealthy nations protect those with power while systematically preventing solidarity among the people. How are they able to accomplish this, again and again? Next, *Chapter 37: Culture Jamming* shows how rulers, authorities, and others with power deliberately work to get different groups of people to misunderstand and fear each other.

Chapter 37: Culture Jamming

Culture jamming happens when rulers, authorities, and others with power try to get different groups of people to misunderstand and fear each other. This book has already described many examples, such as the hate campaigns in Chapter 22 that trained one group of people to hate another. Unfortunately, authorities have discovered many other techniques for spreading confusion and resentment.

These techniques are simply tricks that authorities play to divide people so they don't collectively stand up to their rulers. Like many chapters in this book, this is a chapter about scams.

The first divisive trick is pretty simple: authorities straight up lie about a group's perspective so that other people will have false information and therefore feel resentful towards them.

Caricaturing Thoughtful People

The Soviet Union trained many young people to view small-scale farmers as a threat. The official youth organization was taught that their main task was "the struggle against theft and the hiding of grain as well as kulak sabotage." Young people in the cities had experienced an improvement in life by leaving rural areas, and this campaign demonized people living the rural life they had left behind. Sadly, many young city people were thus primed to believe that peasants opposed the state, and they enthusiastically helped impose conditions of mass starvation and other atrocities in the early 1930s.[1]

In Germany in 2024, government policy called for more money to fund the war in Ukraine against Russia and less social spending domestically. The German government and major media organizations label people who question these policies as far-right, racist, or fascist. When farmers blocked one minister from disembarking a ferry in protest of rising diesel prices, a government spokesperson said it "is shameful and violates the rules" of democratic society, and "this transgression is absolutely unacceptable."[2]

However, the supposed "green" government leaders showed no responsiveness to many voters' needs, and so many voters began supporting parties that promised to end war funding. Martin Zühlke said, "When we look at the government's policies, we see a lot of arrogance, ignorance and stupidity packed with ideology…" One farmer complained about a war funding decision, saying, "For a farm like mine, I would lose about 10,000 euros. For our businesses, it's a catastrophe." Calling farmers and other protesters far-right or fascist simply for opposing the government's spending policies made it very difficult to have constructive conversations.

German municipal worker Thomas Strahl noted, "What they are doing today, it's similar to what the Nazis did back then."

Strahl was right. Chapter 22 reviewed the perspective of top Nazi German official Hermann Goering who explained this authoritarian trick: "of course, the people don't want war… That is understood… but, voice or no voice, the people can always be brought to the bidding of the leaders. That is easy. All you have to do is tell them they are being attacked and denounce the pacifists for lack of patriotism and exposing the country to danger. It works the same way in any country."[3]

Goering was right. "It works the same way in any country" because these countries have a few people who rule over the rest. Goering simply acknowledged that rulers commonly read from the same playbook when they manipulate a population to support a war.

As I write, the German government is painting anti-war farmers as fascists, following the pattern Goering described. This is culture jamming that causes people to deeply misunderstand others in their own nation.

Love It or Leave It Campaigns

On March 31, 1964 the Brazilian military took over the country. It began imprisoning and torturing activists and dissenters. Several guerilla groups formed to fight the oppressive military dictatorship. When students in Rio de Janeiro protested high food prices, military police even shot and killed one 18-year-old.

The government propagated the slogan, "Brasil: ame-o ou deixe-o" ("Brazil: love it or leave it"). Brazilians who loved their country but did not like their government were painted as unpatriotic.[4]

Likewise, during the US-Vietnam war, "America: love it or leave it" was a common refrain. Protesters who wanted to end an imperial war with no clear benefit to the United States were cast as people who didn't love their country.[5]

In the 1980s and 1990s, Turkish party Milliyetçi Hareket Partisi (Nationalist Action Party) supported a strong nationalist ideology that expected all citizens to sacrifice to meet the goals of the government. They propagated the slogan, "Ya sev ya terket" ("love or leave the country").[6]

These "love it or leave it" campaigns imply that anyone with grievances against their rulers are unpatriotic and don't love their country. Tragically, activists are actually the ones putting in the most effort and taking the most risk to serve their country. Just as Goering explained how rulers can describe dissenters as unpatriotic, these "love it or leave it" campaigns show another way rulers can spread this divisive misunderstanding and use it to justify oppression.

The result of culture jamming: neighbors see each other as a threat and argue about nonsense while ignoring the real problems.
This is a normal pattern in any society where people allow themselves to be ruled.

Examples of Heart-Closing Narratives That Shame Victims

In addition to simply lying about certain groups so that other people resent or hate them, unhealthy nations sometimes encourage people to shame victims instead of supporting them. This is one of the cruelest and most divisive forms of culture jamming.

Here are some examples.

AIDS in the United States

What would it be like for a pandemic to spread and for religious and political leaders to offer no help for years and instead treat the victims as if they deserved their suffering? Hundreds of thousands of people who suffered from AIDS in the United States found out in the 1980s.

Caused by the HIV virus, AIDS suppresses people's immune systems so that they become susceptible to diseases that would not normally trouble healthy people.

Political leaders behaved dismissively, as seen at a press conference where president Reagan's spokesman Larry Speakes took a question from journalist Lester Kinsolving in 1982. Kinsolving expressed concern about approximately 300,000 people who had been exposed to AIDS, noting that it was already being ridiculed as a "gay plague." Speakes repeatedly insulted him and dismissed the issue. When Kinsolving asked if the president was aware of AIDS, Speakes said, "I don't have it. Do you?" Other journalists in the press pool laughed. Speakes repeatedly badgered Kinsolving, saying, "You didn't answer my question. How do you know?" Kinsolving asked, "Does the president – in other words, the White House – look on this as a great joke?"[7]

Some people within the US Center for Disease Control (CDC) worked to stop the epidemic. CDC epidemiologist doctor Donald Francis created a plan to slow the spread of AIDS in the mid 1980s, but he later described how he found out that his plan was rejected. Doctor John Bennett was the head of the AIDS Task Force at the CDC who said

> In a quiet, but clearly pained voice, [Dr. Bennett] relayed to me what the highest levels of government said about my plan to limit further spread of HIV. 'Don, they rejected the plan. They said, "Look pretty and do as little as you can."'[8]

Many religious leaders blamed the victims' morality for their illness, claiming they must deserve their suffering. Pastor Jerry Falwell stated, "AIDS is the wrath of a just God against homosexuals... AIDS is not just God's punishment for homosexuals. It is God's punishment for the society that tolerates homosexuals."[9]

These hurtful attitudes did not only spread to people without AIDS. Many people with AIDS began to feel shame. Jarvis Hall said, "I was ashamed and embarrassed to tell people I'm HIV positive. Because of the stigma, your best friends would turn on you." Reginald Brown said, "I even internalized it: 'Oh, I'm dirty. Nobody will want me.'" Another person with AIDS said, "That was the thing for me, more than the illness: It was just the shame. And because you were human and did a human thing, that you were less than human now, and people would not see your humanity. We were humiliated and ashamed and waiting to die..."[10]

Some victims were condemned by priests at church, with one woman being told she was a sinner and damned. She told her coworkers about her AIDS and got fired. Other people began taking drugs.[11]

One Christian woman had embraced these hurtful attitudes in the 1980s, and later she realized how she had been tricked: "A half-million Americans died of complications from HIV and I don't recall feeling any compassion at the time. The space in me that should have been occupied with kindness and empathy for people suffering from any deadly disease was instead filled with accusation and disapproval... I distinctly recall formulating judgments: People who died of AIDS got it by having gay sex; gay sex was wrong and against God's plan; therefore, the death was foreseeable and could and should have been avoided by not following lust-filled desires. I am not proud of my behavior."[12]

This is a form of culture jamming, where authorities propagate the belief that victims deserve their suffering, minimizing others' compassion for them and making it difficult to have constructive conversations about the trouble and what to do about it.

Rejecting or Accepting Victims of Sexual Abuse

One of the biggest obstacles to solidarity is the heart-closing belief that victims are supposedly degraded or disgraced by their abuse. Victims can easily feel shame, and for any group to have long-lasting solidarity, it's important for people to help each other release that shame.

A story from the Algerian revolution against France illustrated this in both a tragic and beautiful way. "B" was a 26-year-old Algerian man who became active in the resistance to French rule in 1955. He suddenly had to go underground and was unable to say goodbye to his wife or young child. Two years later, he received a message from his wife asking him to forget her, saying she had brought shame on herself. She demanded that he not think of returning to live with her.[13]

B was worried, but his commanders would not give permission for him to visit her. They did arrange a line of communication, and B learned the terrible truth: after he had disappeared, French colonial police arrested his wife and interrogated her and beat her over several days. After she said nothing about her husband's activities, on the third day multiple police raped her, and one said, "If you ever see that bastard your husband again, don't you forget to tell him what we did to you." After a week she was released.

This woman had shown tremendous bravery in withholding information about her husband and the resistance, but B didn't recognize this at first. He initially felt shock and anger, but he had never felt much affection for her, and he thought, "Oh, it's nothing serious; she wasn't killed. She can start her life over again." Over time he reflected further and realized his wife's power:

> several weeks later it dawned on me that she had been raped because they had been looking for me. In fact she had been raped to punish her for keeping quiet. She could have easily given them at least one militant's name, which would have enabled them to discover and eliminate the network, and perhaps even have me arrested. It was not therefore a simple rape for want of anything better to do or out of sadism, as I had often seen in the douars; it was the rape of a tenacious woman who was prepared to accept anything rather than give up her husband. And that husband was me. That woman had saved my life and had protected the network. It was my fault she had been dishonored. Yet she didn't say: "This is what I endured for you." On the contrary, she said: "Forget me, start a new life, I have been disgraced."

B decided to take his wife back. He did not reject her because she'd been abused and believed in her own disgrace. Other Algerian men also supported their wives who'd been raped, and many men even volunteered to marry women who'd been raped and impregnated by French soldiers.

I disagree with B on one point: his wife wasn't dishonored. When the French soldiers abused her, they only dishonored themselves.

I certainly found this woman's bravery inspiring. I also feel inspired by the men's willingness to accept and support women even after they suffered tremendous abuse. They didn't shame the victims. Both the women and men showed a strong solidarity with each other in very trying times, and this solidarity helped them finally evict the French in 1962.

This belief that victims are supposedly disgraced, dishonored, or shameful is authoritarian heart-closing nonsense and deeply hurtful. A person who was abused yesterday still has love to give today.

Intense Arguments That Ignore the Deeper Trouble

Another way that unhealthy nations engage in culture jamming is by creating controversies and promoting arguments that purposely ignore – and distract from – deeper, more fundamental problems.

The following examples are controversial and many people have already picked a side, making it very hard for those on supposedly opposite sides to discuss these issues respectfully. What makes these touchy arguments a form of culture jamming is that they ignore and obscure important issues, keeping people from discussing, learning about, and addressing the real problems.

Often, selfish behavior by corporate, religious, or political authorities causes problems that ripple through a nation, and people will begin to debate those problems.

Yet instead of discussing the underlying selfish behavior that created these problems, people get locked into one or another repeating, predictable argument that goes nowhere and solves nothing. Such political debates can seem intractable. In my experience, the only way to deal with tough political issues is to take the first step of any sacred circle: acknowledge the entire truth of the situation, including everyone's concerns.

You may recognize the following examples as controversies you've heard plenty about before. And you may already have an opinion, maybe even a strong opinion. But few people have experienced an open, respectful, and thorough discussion of these controversial topics. I'd like to offer a small experience of that now. All I ask is that you keep an open mind.

Liberals and Conservatives – Guns

As I write in 2024, the United States faces a severe problem with gun violence. A *mass murder* is commonly defined as a shooting where four people die besides the shooter, excluding profit-driven criminal activity and state-sponsored terrorism. The US has by far the most mass murders of any country classified by the United Nations as "developed." Within this group, the United States is the only country to have had at least one mass shooting each year from 2003-2023.[14]

Mass murders in the United States have more than doubled from 17 in 2014 to 40 in 2023. Mass shooting incidents, where four or more people besides the shooter were injured or killed, increased from 272 in 2014 to 656 in 2023.[15]

I commonly hear the liberal perspective that mass shootings couldn't happen without guns, and thus the simplest way to reduce mass shootings would be to reduce gun availability. Indeed, both Britain and Australia have enacted laws restricting gun availability and both have seen a resulting drop in gun-related deaths.[16]

However, research shows that gun ownership has also steadily declined in the United States. In 1980, almost 54% of Americans reported living in a household with guns, whereas in 2021 about 35% of Americans reported living in a household with guns. If gun ownership has been falling, what explains the dramatic increase in mass shootings?[17]

I commonly hear the conservative perspective that gun ownership helps citizens protect themselves from a tyrannical government. In this view, people who take responsibility for their family's and community's safety risk losing their safety and even their freedom if they lose their weapons.

If liberals looked at factors besides gun availability that contribute to mass murder, what would they find? And if conservatives looked for examples of tyranny all around them right now, what would they find?

In other words, if conservatives and liberals were to acknowledge the full truth of their situation, what else might they want to talk about? I believe they would discuss:

1. social and economic inequality

2. mind-altering pharmaceutical drugs

Social and Economic Inequality

Research clearly shows that violence is tied to the level of inequality in a society. When US states and Canadian provinces are compared, higher rates of violence are clearly correlated with higher inequality, that is, when fewer rich people have more money, and more poor people have less. Dozens of studies have shown that inequality is a major driver of violence, and unequal societies also tend to have less trust. This makes sense, as the haves increasingly must protect themselves from the have-nots.[18]

This inequality has grown dramatically worse in recent decades. From 1976-2023, income for the poorest 50% of Americans increased about 33%, or $6,000. Meanwhile, the 50-90% range saw income increase about 62%, an increase of about $34,000 per year.

However, the top 1% of earners saw an increase of about 285%, or $1.4 million per year in income. The top 0.01% of American earners saw their income grow by about 672%, an increase of $37 million per year. During this time, the poorest half of Americans saw their total wealth increase by an average of about $7,000. The richest .01% saw their wealth increase by an average of about $560 million.[19]

Inequality strongly correlates with violence, and both inequality and violence in the United States have been increasing dramatically in tandem. However, the usual liberal-vs-conservative arguments regarding guns in the US completely ignore this deeper truth. Typical debates about guns presented in mass media are a form of culture jamming because they trick people into thinking we are addressing an important issue while they keep viewers from noticing the most important problems. Not surprisingly, many people never get around to actually addressing the deeper problems that promote such destructive inequality, and therefore gun violence continues to rise.

Mind-Altering Pharmaceutical Drugs

There is another major factor leading to mass shootings in the United States: the widespread use of mind-altering antidepressant and antipsychotic drugs that are known to cause aggression in some users.

The United States Food and Drug Administration acknowledged the danger posed by antidepressants in 2007, warning caregivers to monitor patients daily for symptoms including suicidality, unusual changes in behavior, anxiety, hostility, aggressiveness, mania, and akathisia.[20]

Akathisia, associated with some classes of antidepressants as well as antipsychotics, can cause a person to feel very restless and unable to stay still. It is particularly challenging, causing many patients to feel continuously nervous and unable to relax.[21]

One patient described their experience: "I ignored the early symptoms because I thought I could handle it… It got worse. It got so much worse. At this point I've been in a living hell for about 6 months with each week worse than the last."[22]

This patient reported that nothing their doctor prescribed helped. They slept an average of two hours per night, regularly not sleeping at all for 2-3 days straight because of a need to constantly move. Sleep deprivation led to hallucinations and blackouts, but they could not stop pacing or rest even briefly. They noted, "the anxiety makes me feel like I'm being buried alive…. I want you to know how bad it can get if you don't stop the medication. I have no idea if what I'm going through is permanent or not, but it may well be. Please don't become me."

Some akathisia patients have acknowledged things like, "I don't feel myself" or "I'm afraid of some of the unusual impulses I have."[23]

Mind-altering drugs can have very different effects on different people. One study followed 1,022 sexually healthy patients who began taking antidepressants, alone or with another drug. Almost 60% of patients reported sexual dysfunction, with some drugs being worse than others.[24] Other research suggests antidepressants can affect people's capacity for romantic feelings or deep attachment with another person.[25]

Even patients without akathisia can behave extremely strangely and in some cases violently. In 2004, David Carmichael was arrested for strangling to death his 11-year-old son in a psychotic episode. During the event, Carmichael believed his son's life was not worth living. Carmichael had recently started taking the antidepressant Paxil. Both Carmichael and his daughter said Carmichael's killing was totally out of character, with his daughter saying, "it just completely changed his behavior. It changed what he viewed the world as when he was on those antidepressants, and then when he went off of them, he was back to the man that he was." Later Carmichael said, "What I find the most difficult is wondering what was going through his mind… What were his last thoughts? That's what I have to live with."[26]

An archive at ssristories.net catalogs evidence of mass shooters who have definite or likely usage of antidepressants and includes more than 5,000 stories. Examples include the Columbine school shooters in 1999.[27]

Executives of the antidepressant drug companies have been aware of these patterns for decades. A lawsuit in 2001 described how, after taking Paxil for only 48 hours, Donald Schell shot and killed his daughter, wife, and granddaughter before killing himself. Though Schell had previously suffered depression, he had shown no signs of this sort of aggression. His surviving family sued the drugmaker SmithKline Beecham (now called GlaxoSmithKline) and won, in part because the company's own internal documents acknowledged that some Paxil users could become agitated or violent. However, the drug package did not include any warning that the drug could cause suicide, aggression, or violence.[28]

Along with inequality and gun violence, antidepressant use has steadily increased in the United States. Though the first chemical antidepressants were available in the 1950s, in 1990 only about 2% of Americans were taking antidepressants.[29] Sales of SSRI antidepressants began in the late 1980s and other new types of antidepressants followed. By 2002, almost 8% of Americans reported using antidepressants within the previous month. And by 2014, antidepressant usage rose to almost 13%.[30,31]

Many people who want to stop taking antidepressants struggle, as withdrawal symptoms can include anxiety, irritability, dizziness, aggression, nausea, and other symptoms potentially including suicide or manic behavior.[32] Because withdrawal can worsen symptoms, sometimes dramatically, even physicians aware of SSRIs' dangers warn users to *seek out medical guidance to stop SSRI usage safely*.

Inequality and antidepressant medications play a large role in the United States' epidemic of mass gun violence. Conversations about gun violence on television commonly focus on gun availability, even though the percentage of households with guns has dropped substantially in the past 50 years while the rate of mass shootings has increased. In contrast, inequality and antidepressant use has substantially increased at the same time as mass shootings.

This illustrates culture jamming, where television news, newspapers, government officials, and others highlight gun availability and stimulate debate about it while ignoring the most important factors causing the violence.

Transgender Issues

Large and complex societies can face large and complex problems that do not lend themselves to a single solution or simple explanation. I believe many people's desires and concerns with the transgender movement reflect such a complex problem.

Does the transgender movement reflect a deep problem in society or is it a long overdue effort to ensure anyone can feel comfortable being themselves? Or both?

Whenever I find myself in a difficult political conversation, it helps me to get back to step one of the sacred circle process: acknowledge the full truth and hear everyone's perspective. What truths and perspectives would a sacred circle about the transgender movement acknowledge?

The Impacts of Human-Made Environmental Poisons

I have probably spent dozens if not hundreds of hours talking about trans issues and the use of pronouns with countless people, and in the context of these discussions, I cannot remember hearing anyone acknowledge that most Americans literally eat, drink, and touch a large variety of poisons on a daily basis that affect childhood emotional and sexual development.

Is this a factor worth looking into regarding the recent surge in transgender issues? If we are fully exploring all the possibilities, I think so.

In 1996, Theo Colborn, Dianne Dumanoski, and John Peterson Myers published a book called *Our Stolen Future: Are We Threatening Our Fertility, Intelligence, and Survival? – A Scientific Detective Story*. It was the first popular book to discuss endocrine disruptors, synthetic chemicals that mimic naturally-occurring human hormones. Even by 1996, researchers had noticed many signs of deformities. Surveys from 61 countries in

North America, South America, Europe, Asia, and Africa had shown an average decrease in human male sperm count of 50% from 1938 to 1990. Increases in testicular cancer and other genital abnormalities were seen in several countries.[33]

Many nonhumans showed sudden population crashes due to chemical poisonings, including dolphins with deformed lungs in Spain[34], female minks who stopped giving birth in Michigan[35], female birds who nested with other females in California and produced thin-walled eggs with low hatching rates[36], and alligators exposed to a pesticide in Florida who developed abnormally small penises.[37]

In another example of chemical poisoning, the US Environmental Protection Agency reproductive toxicologist Earl Gray gave a presentation where he showed an image of a male rat with pink nipples, although male rats of its species are not supposed to have nipples. This male rat's mother was exposed to Vinclozolin during pregnancy and thus his sexual development went awry. Vinclozolin blocked the male rat's androgen receptor, preventing it from processing testosterone. As the authors summarize, "Without these testosterone signals, male development gets derailed and boys don't become boys." They become intersex, trapped in an ambiguous state.

Vinclozolin is a pesticide used to reduce fungus on crops, and has been frequently detected in foods that children eat in the United States. Other chemicals such as once-popular pesticide DDT break down into chemical products known to block androgen receptors similar to Vinclozolin.[38]

Some apparently female-bodied people illustrate what happens when an important hormone is blocked during fetal development. When testosterone is completely blocked, a fetus which should become a male does not develop male genitalia which guide the rest of the boy's development. The child will appear female in every way, and may only discover the truth when she does not menstruate during puberty and goes to a doctor to investigate. Such individuals have the male XY chromosomes and testicles in their abdomen rather than ovaries. They have narrow shoulders, broader hips, and normally developed female breasts, and they act and think of themselves as female. In less extreme cases of hormone disruption during pregnancy, such males may have unusually small penises, undescended testicles, or ambiguous genitals.[39]

Endocrine disruptors affect women in specific ways as well. Exposure to chemicals that mimic estrogen can increase breast cancer risk, and the same effect can occur when other hormones are mimicked as well.[40] From 1940 to 1980, the incidence rate of breast cancer in American women, adjusted for population size, rose approximately 1% per year, and similar increases in breast cancer have occurred in other industrialized countries. Between 1980 and 1987 the number of breast cancer cases in the United States increased by about one-third. Only about 5% of breast cancers stem from a genetic influence, and thus environmental factors account for 95% of these cancers.[41]

This decades-long increase in breast cancer in women matches the increased usage of endocrine-disrupting chemicals present in foods, home products, industrial and business settings, and elsewhere. In 1940, only 5% of American women could expect to get breast cancer. By 2023, 13% of American women could expect to get breast cancer in their life time.[42] For American women between 40 and 55 years of age, breast cancer had become the leading cause of death by the late 1990s.[43]

Often these poisons' effects are delayed. One study found that girls' exposure to DDT early in life led to an early onset of puberty, longer menstrual cycles, and accelerated menopause decades later.[44] Women's average age of menarche (first menstruation) in the United States decreased from 17 in the early 1800s to 13 in the 1950s.[45]

As with so many troubles, privilege plays a role, so that higher-privileged people are better able to escape the pollution. I suspect this explains why, since the 1950s, white American girls have shown breast and pubic hair development one year earlier than previously observed, while black American girls show similar development two years earlier than previously observed. This also shows that, while lower-privilege people are treated worse in unhealthy nations, no one is safe from abuse.

Endocrine disruptors' toxic effects can even span generations. When researchers exposed rats to endocrine disruptors, they noticed reproductive problems in their offspring two or even three generations later. This was true for both male and female rats, and even when intervening generations were not exposed to toxins.[46]

People interact with endocrine disruptors in a vast number of ways. Plastics are endocrine disruptors, and global plastics production has increased from 2 million tons in 1950 to 380 million tons in 2015 and over 459 million tons in 2019.[47]

Many pesticides sprayed on crops are endocrine disruptors, as are chemical weapons such as Agent Orange. From 1962-1971, the US military dumped 19 million gallons of Agent Orange onto 3.6 million acres of Vietnamese forests to kill the trees and make hiding difficult. Returning American soldiers reported an increased rate of cancers and handicaps *in their children*. The Vietnamese certainly suffered worse as they fought off the American occupiers. One major chemical in Agent Orange, 2,4,5-T, was used as an herbicide in the United States. Widely used in lawns, farms, under power lines, and other places, over seven million pounds of 2,4,5-T were dispensed just for non-household uses in the United States in 1974 alone.[48]

Could there be a better example of the power of propaganda than millions of Americans intentionally poisoning soil around their own homes, farms and forests, at their own expense, with the same poison that they used on their adversaries' soil?

Chemical exposure problems are only worsening, with one survey finding endocrine disruptors in the drinking water of almost 90 million Americans. This is likely an underestimate, because I am writing this in 2024, but the national drinking water survey will not be complete till 2026.[49] Rainwater around the world has been found to exceed local government-set limits on allowable PFOS, PFAS, or other endocrine disruptors, meaning that everyone is exposed to these troubles to some extent.[50]

In unhealthy nations that encourage selfishness, a few people have profited tremendously while a vast number have suffered due to chemical poisoning. When *Our Stolen Future* was published in 1996, anyone could have predicted increases in emotional and sexual developmental troubles in populations exposed to endocrine disruptors. However, as I write this almost 30 years later, the dominant political conversations about unusual emotional and sexual development entirely ignore the fact that so many of us are exposed to these poisons on a daily basis – in ever increasing quantities.

I have heard a lot of people speak angrily about trans rights – some people vehemently in favor, and some people strongly against. I have not personally heard anyone speak angrily about the vast amount of pollution that is known to affect people's gender expression and other aspects of their emotional, sexual, physical and mental development.

Both conservatives and liberals seem to see the other side as trying to impose a threatening ideology. I have never had an in-person conversation where someone acknowledged the likelihood or even the possibility that mass toxic chemical exposure is causing developmental problems in humans.

This illustrates one type of culture jamming, where people wind up having highly passionate conversations about some trouble while ignoring the most important factors. Chemical poisons are a major problem, but the deepest problem is that we are trapped in abusive relationships with deeply uncaring people who profit by manufacturing poisons that hurt everybody. Being trapped with such rich and selfish people is simply what it means to live in an unhealthy nation.

In this case, chemical companies generate billions of dollars per year by knowingly manufacturing toxins, and fossil fuel companies generate billions of dollars per year by extracting and transporting many of those toxins' raw materials. Rather than standing against the industries that damage so many people's health, medical authorities, who are supposedly dedicated to protecting people's health, instead focus on supporting people's access to expensive surgeries and other procedures.[51]

Many political and corporate authorities encourage public debates about gender issues, but, coincidentally or not, none of these debates involve discussion of the very profitable toxins that Americans increasingly interact with on a daily basis. Instead of simply acknowledging that everyone is worthy of respect and then investigating the different causes and motivations for gender and identity changes and possible lessons, I believe authorities encourage a focus on identity politics, emphasizing individuality rather than acknowledging collective problems.

Political authorities fan the flames of this debate with divisive and hurtful laws. Multiple US states impose severe penalties for using a person's incorrect gender pronouns, while other states ban trans-related health care.[52,53] However, I am unaware of any political authorities that are addressing the massive and increasing amount of toxins present in Americans' food, water, vehicles, homes, businesses, and elsewhere.

LGBT stands for Lesbian, Gay, Bisexual, Trangender, and other sexual orientations and identities, and wealthy individuals have also played a huge role in shaping the public debate around LGBT issues. LGBT groups have received huge amounts of money from wealthy people, strongly influencing these groups' leadership and messaging about all these issues. Total grant funding for LGBT-related organizations ranged from more than $193 million in 2019 to more than $280 million in 2021. Total funding during 2019-2022 was over $930 million.[54,55,56]

The Ford Foundation donated over $92 million to LGBT-related organizations in this time period. This is the same Ford Foundation that has heavily funded Black Lives Matter-related groups, and also has decades-long connections with the CIA and psychological warfare, as reviewed in Chapter 36. However, the Ford Foundation has only been the second-largest funder of LGBT-related groups. Gilead Sciences, a pharmaceutical company worth almost $100 billion as I write this[57], funded the LGBT movement with over $156 million between 2019 and 2022.

I do not know all the different intentions that these wealthy funders have had for the LGBT movement, but it is clear that vanishingly few Americans talk about the extremely profitable chemical toxins that cause emotional and sexual disturbances in the United States and around the world. While I support people's ability to enjoy any consensual relationship they choose, when the LGBT movement heavily shames anyone who does not immediately support a person's gender identity and other beliefs about themselves, they discourage exploration of all the possible reasons people might be changing their identity or even undergoing surgery.

When I interviewed many people who changed their gender identity, I found a variety of different motivations, described below. I do not believe that chemical exposure is the sole cause that drives people to change their gender identity in the United States. But I do believe that chemical exposure is a significant cause of a variety of emotional and sexual troubles, including related to gender.

Acknowledging this truth would require acknowledging that many humans around the world have been poisoning themselves and their descendents for generations, and the only way to stop this problem is to collectively give up toxic chemicals. This would destroy a vast amount of financial wealth, including stocks and bonds of chemical companies, banks, fossil fuel companies, and others.

Interviews

As I repeatedly listened to different gender-changing people describe their experiences and motivation, I learned that the transgender topic is difficult to discuss in part because there are many different behaviors that are labeled "transgender." People can change their gender identity for many different reasons.

There is clearly a group of people who do not align with the sex-assignment they had at birth, and these people often find gender-affirming surgeries helpful. One meta-analysis of many research trials covering almost 8,000 transgender patients found that less than 1% regretted their decision.[58]

There are also many other reasons people change their gender identity.

Starting in 2015, I began spending significant amounts of time with people who changed their gender identity. I was curious about what would motivate people to change their identity, so I asked several people in 1-on-1 conversations. These were informal chances for me to ask what their gender meant to them, why they changed it, what life was like before and after, and similar questions so that I could hear their perspective.

Several people I interviewed were female-bodied people who felt upset with conventional gender norms. Changing their gender identity seemed like a way to establish a boundary and forbid sexist treatment they didn't like. They wanted to be seen for who they are, not treated in stereotypically sexist ways. I did not notice any unusual mental or emotional trouble, and they were very clear on their sex even as they changed their gender identity. Their concerns about sexist treatment seemed understandable.

Whereas some female-bodied people continue to identify as women and demand that women be treated with respect, these people stopped identifying as women. It seemed like a strategy for taking a stand for themselves, a way of defining their own cultural norms so they could get people around them to treat them respectfully and with an open mind. These people seemed sure of themselves and showed self-confidence.

However, I noticed that another large category of people seemed to have low self-confidence. They didn't seem able to set boundaries, didn't have a clear sense of who they were and struggled to clearly advocate for themselves. Multiple times I have stood in a circle before a meeting or party, and each person would announce their names and pronouns. Many people would confidently announce their pronouns, but people with low self-confidence would say things like, "I'm [name]. they/them… or she/her, or whatever you want."

While some male-bodied they/them-identifying people seemed confident, many male-bodied people who identified as they or she seemed to have very little confidence, or they recognized masculine traits as negative and feminine traits as positive. I never observed these people saying or doing anything that went against their peer-group's beliefs or norms.

I thus found many different reasons a person might change their gender, though they're all called "transgender." Certainly there are other reasons people have identified themselves in unconventional ways that I didn't discover in my interviews. When some people are called transgender after getting gender reassignment surgery or taking hormonal treatments, and others are also called transgender simply because they say they've changed their identity, which can happen for a variety of reasons, it becomes difficult to have a clear discussion about what is happening and why. And without that clear discussion, it is hard to agree on what behaviors are fine and don't indicate a problem. It also becomes hard to figure out which behaviors indicate a problem, such as sexism, and how to address it.

Furthermore, I found many people completely unwilling to consider whether a person's relationship to their gender was healthy. Indeed, one survey found that 44% of Americans aged 25-34 believed it should be a criminal offense to identify a person with pronouns different from what that person chooses for themselves. Only 31% believed it should not be considered criminal.[59] This strong defensiveness makes it difficult to discuss issues of gender openly.

I noticed a few common themes from all my interviews and listening at various gatherings. I commonly heard a recognition that they live in a patriarchal, male-dominated society where women get treated abusively. Restrictive gender roles seemed like a core aspect of patriarchy, and so abolishing socially-constructed gender roles was thus one strategy to end the patriarchy.

A common theme I noticed in all the gender-changing people I encountered is that they didn't seem to have any strong male or female role models. This reality struck me vividly on a camping trip one night. I sat around a fire with two female-bodied people who identified as they/them. Both had identified as women when I met them, and neither had undergone surgery. We had been friends for a few years.

I was shocked when they asked me why I still identified as a man. They couldn't understand why I would want to be a man, and they didn't recognize any redeeming qualities of manhood. They repeatedly asked why I hadn't changed to a neutral gender, and they suggested I change my gender. This was a relaxed, respectful conversation among friends. I could see their perspective – if they had never encountered a good man, they might not know any existed, or could exist. Fortunately, I had encountered good men. I did not change my identity. But I was struck by the possibility that people could go through their lives never encountering a woman or man that clearly modeled a good way to live.

What if We Embraced the Responsibilities of Living in a Healthy Nation?

Culture jamming can make it difficult for people to have clear, respectful conversations and acknowledge the full truth together – the first step in a sacred circle.

If I were in a group of people discussing how to relate to transgender issues, these are the truths I would want to acknowledge:

- *Respect for everyone*: Everyone is worthy of respect. Dismissiveness or condescending attitudes are not helpful. Each person's love and gifts should be welcomed, regardless whether a person aligns with traditional understandings of gender and sex. There were people who did not align clearly as men or women even before the introduction of chemical poisons, and whether or not a person's experience is due to chemical exposure does not affect their worthiness of respect.

    However, respecting someone does not necessarily mean sharing their perspective.

- *Nobody controls anybody else's speech*: How each person identifies others is their own business. A corrupt politician may identify themselves as honest, but I will disagree with that identity and notice their corruption. The Soviet Union identified itself as a workers' paradise, but Americans clearly didn't identify it that way. American pre-Civil War slaveowners identified themselves as divinely-ordained, superior stewards of enslaved people, but how many people today would identify slaveowners this way? How a person identifies people and nonhumans is part of how they relate to the world. Forcing someone to adopt other people's perspectives about themselves is controlling and inappropriate.

- *Acknowledge the pollution*: People around the world, and especially those in industrial economies, are increasingly subject to pollution with deeply disturbing effects, with different people subject to different amounts of different chemicals yielding different problems. None of us and none of our children are safe until we address this.

- *Acknowledge sexism and low self-confidence*: How each person identifies themselves is their own business, and there is nothing inherently wrong or sick with changing one's identity. Also, if some people are changing their identity out of low self-confidence or anger about sexism, then these are also things we need to heal in our nation.

- *Acknowledge exploitation at the heart of the nation*: Like many people around the world, Americans live in an unhealthy nation where wealthy people could lose billions of dollars if toxins were outlawed. Thus we face wealthy predators who use all manner of shaming, confusing propaganda, law changes, persecution, and other techniques to confuse and distract people from addressing the toxic pollution problem that now affects countless humans and nonhumans.

There are many valuable perspectives on transgender issues besides those I present here, and there are motivations for identifying in unconventional ways besides those I found in my interviews. This is certainly not a complete exploration. I simply offer my investigation to show how people could do their own research and come to their own conclusions about difficult political topics rather than fall for the false divisions, simplistic beliefs, and misunderstandings encouraged by authorities.

A Cure for Culture Jamming

Once people have a sacred circle and agree on the truth and the challenges they face, they can move to steps two and three: What are we going to do about it? And how will we take care of each other along the way?

Culture jamming causes different groups of people to misunderstand each other. Whether people are suffering from pollution, sexism, a disease, overt political oppression, or any other trouble, culture jamming makes it difficult for people to discuss their shared troubles clearly and then decide what to do about it.

The stories about sacred circles in Chapter 23 remind me that humans can face severe troubles and still come together to constructively address them. The Apache experienced a massacre. Black Americans experienced centuries of abuse. Ecuadorians faced corporate exploitation backed by an alliance of the Ecuadorian and Chinese governments. Nobody can control the challenges they face, but each of us can choose how to respond. These stories of sacred circles show me that people can respond constructively even to very great challenges.

Sadly, no matter how hard activists and other concerned people try to address individual issues, the root cause of the problem – rulers controlling the people – remains unaddressed. Coming up, *Chapter 38: Endless Predation When the Root Disease Goes Unhealed* lays out the tragic consequences.

Chapter 38: Endless Predation When the Root Disease Goes Unhealed

When people consistently hold each other accountable for inappropriate behavior, the resulting nation has very little inappropriate behavior. When people do not hold each other accountable, and especially do not hold leaders accountable, disturbing behavior flourishes for decades, centuries, or even millennia.

Many Authorities Around the World Sexually Abuse Children

I grew very concerned when I first heard about an ancient religious cult that made it into the news suddenly in 2002 because priests had been sexually molesting children in Boston, Massachusetts. About 900 cases were publicly identified with approximately 11,000 total people making complaints. I stopped worrying when I learned that cult authorities were addressing the issue, with one top official resigning.[1,2] I also knew that this cult had many followers, and I figured that the cult members would surely resolve the issue so that they could have religious leaders who didn't abuse children.

But then I became alarmed as I learned that priests of the same cult were continuing to sexually molest children around the world:[3]

- Researchers in Australia found more than 4,400 incidents of alleged child abuse had been reported to cult authorities between 1950-2010, few of which were ever investigated.

- In Germany, between 1946 and 2014, almost 3,700 underaged people were attacked by at least 1670 priests, with the investigators claiming this was almost definitely an underestimate. Most of the victims were boys.

- In Pennsylvania in the US in 2018, an investigation found the cult had systematically covered up child sexual abuse by over 300 priests, and they counted over 1,000 victims.

- In Ireland, the same cult was found in 2009 to have "obsessively" covered up abuse, with almost 15,000 underage sexual assault victims just between 1970 and 1990.

- Independent researchers estimated that French cult priests had sexually assaulted 216,000 children between 1950 and 2020.

How on Earth could any organization survive with leaders sexually assaulting children on such a massive, global scale and consistently covering up their abuses? This cult is one of the oldest, wealthiest, and most influential institutions in human history. The cult had almost 1.1 billion followers in 2010, about 16% of the entire global population. Why would people remain part of such a group and keep giving these leaders money?[4]

I'm referring, of course, to the Roman Catholic Church.

Ancient Tibet, prior to the Chinese takeover in 1951, showed a similar pattern. Tashi Tsering described the Buddhist culture where child sexual assault was common. He described how monks would compete to see who was toughest and who could sexually assault the most boys. He was able to escape sexual assault for awhile, but then he was raped as well. Tsering tried to talk with other monks and officials about it, and he described their response: "they shrugged and said simply that that was just the way things were."[5]

Unfortunately, this predatory behavior is not limited to only religious authorities. In nations that do not hold leaders accountable for inappropriate behavior, it is common for some proportion of high-privilege people to also engage in child sexual assault.

Secular authorities have also many times been caught sexually assaulting children, although rarely do they face accountability. Suetonius described in disturbing detail how Roman emperor Tiberius sexually assaulted little boys, including putting unweaned babies to his penis as if milking them with a breast.[6]

After his death, famous British media personality Jimmy Savile was found to have sexually assaulted at least 64 people as young as eight years old between the 1960s and 1980s just at the British Broadcasting Corporation alone, excluding his work at other institutions. While he often victimized people at home, investigator Janet Smith found he had assaulted victims in nearly every facility where he worked. When a junior employee complained of sexual assault by Savile, she was told, "keep your mouth shut, he's a VIP." A 16-year-old girl whom Savile assaulted complained to a staff member who responded by calling security to escort her off the premises.[7,8]

Sadly, even top secular officials have been caught either participating in or covering up child sexual assault operations.

In 2002, the Casa Pia orphanage in Portugal was revealed to be the site of a massive, decades-long child sexual assault operation. 32 boys alleged at least 800 crimes, and one staff person pleaded guilty to 600 crimes. A doctor, ambassador, and famous television personality were all involved and prosecuted, but documents indicated that the orphanage had an international reputation, with wealthy predators flying into Portugal to abuse children. None of them faced prosecution.[9]

General Ramalho Eanes had been president of Portugal in 1980 when five boys from the orphanage told him about these abuses, but he did not act on it. Around the same time, former secretary of state for families Teresa Macedo had sent a dossier containing pictures and testimonies about sexual abuse to the police, but her complaint was also ignored. Macedo did receive many calls and letters threatening to "kill me, flay me, and a lot of other things."[10]

In 1988, details began to leak about a child sexual assault ring in Omaha, Nebraska in the United States. Because many cases were connected with the Franklin Community Federal Credit Union, during the following 3 years of investigation, it became known as the Franklin Cover-Up. Many people investigated countless testimonies exposing an extensive network of child sexual abuse across various institutions, including the child foster care system.

Victims testified to the involvement of a US president and vice president, a CIA director, at least one billionaire, a famous TV personality, and many high-ranking corporate, federal, state, and local government officials, as well as people without any known job at all. Many abused children described all manner of satanic rituals and symbols. It is difficult to count the number of sexual assault victims because at least 15 investigators, witnesses, alleged perpetrators, and others died sudden deaths. Many of them died violently.[11,12,13]

In December 1990, doctor Densen-Gerber prepared to travel to Omaha at the request of an investigative committee, but one police officer warned her, "Don't go. Nebraska is death-laced." Black civil rights activist reverend James Bevel visited on a fact-finding commission. He said he had never seen so much terror in people's faces, "not even on the faces of Mississippi Negroes in the 1950s and 1960s," who faced the threat of being lynched by the Ku Klux Klan.

After three years of investigation, authorities found another way to abuse some of the victims. Alisha Owen bravely testified to a grand jury that as a minor she had been sexually abused by a Nebraska district court judge, Omaha city chief of police, the manager of a large credit union, and others. She had observed other children being abused by other famous and powerful people, including the owner of Nebraska's largest newspaper, the Omaha World Herald. She described illegal drug activity by some of Nebraska's most prominent businessmen. Owen's testimony was corroborated by other victims' testimony too.

The jury had a choice. They could acknowledge the disturbing truth and stand up to the authority figures who had engaged in massive amounts of child sexual assault, possibly putting themselves at risk. Or, they could engage in blind belief and ignore the obvious evidence of abusive behavior by their nation's richest and most powerful people. The jurors sadly chose blind belief. While the jury and judge agreed that Alisha Owen had been badly abused, they decided that she was lying about who had abused her and the other victims. In June of 1991, 21-year-old Alisha Owen was convicted of eight counts of felony perjury and was later sentenced to 9 to 27 years in prison.

No authority figures were held accountable, and nothing has occurred since then to suggest that the massive system of organized child abuse ever ended.

When People Cannot Stop Treasonous Rulers

Sometimes rulers face a conundrum. They may have lots of strong selfish reasons for wanting war, and they're all ready to send their soldiers off to fight, but the public is completely unmotivated. Even worse for the rulers, the victim nation that the rulers want to attack is not foolishly picking a fight.

What can the rulers do to get their people to want to attack a non-aggressive country?

One common strategy is for rulers to engage in a secret act of treason, violently attacking their own people while pretending that citizens of the other nation were the perpetrators. This is called a false flag attack, a name which originates from naval ships that would put up an incorrect flag before launching an attack so the victims would blame the wrong country.

False flag attacks are common, but since they threaten a government's legitimacy, it is very difficult to have a clear conversation about them, and any official investigation becomes suspect. Even in democracies where people supposedly elect their leaders, people are commonly unable to protect themselves from these tricks, even when the attacks are poorly executed and it is obvious that the government either perpetrated or covered up the attack somehow.

Amazingly, I believe that Russian and American leaders executed or allowed very similar false flag attacks on their populations within two years of each other, and in each case, the government got the war it wanted.

Let us review the stories.

Russia

In September 1999, Russia experienced four large explosions in apartment buildings in the cities Buinaksk, Volgodonsk and their national capital Moscow. These were mass-casualty events, with about 300 deaths and many more injuries. Vladimir Putin, who was acting prime minister and campaigning for his first term as Russian president, quickly blamed the attacks on Arab terrorists connected with Osama Bin Laden. The Russian federal police chief agreed, blaming the bombings on international terrorists living in Chechnya. Many Russians began to fear terrorism, as images of the destruction and descriptions of the supposed perpetrators were repeatedly displayed on television screens across the country.[14]

Russian Sergei Kovalev said the attacks "were a crucial moment in the unfolding of our current history. After the first shock passed, it turned out that we were living in an entirely different country…"

Unfortunately, a great deal of evidence indicates that the Russian government perpetrated these attacks on its own people. Multiple members of the Duma, Russia's parliament, learned of the attacks in advance. One Duma member, Konstantin Borovoy, learned of the Moscow attacks on September 9 before they happened later that day and warned police, who did nothing to stop them.

In a big "oops" moment, the speaker of the Duma Gennady Seleznev acknowledged the explosion in Volgodonsk on September 13, three days before it occurred on September 16. A transcript quoted him as saying, "According to a report from Rostov-on-Don today, this past night, an apartment house was blown up in the city of Volgodonsk."[15]

In a truly epic "oops" moment, a fifth bombing was planned, but local police arrested the perpetrators before they could set off the explosion. The arrested terrorists turned out to be Russian federal police. The head of Russian federal police Nikolai Patrushev claimed it had been a fake bomb as part of a training exercise. However, tests confirmed the bomb was live and contained hexogen, the same explosive used in the four bombs which had recently successfully exploded.

In spite of all this evidence, Russian acting prime minister Putin presented himself as a brave warrior willing to protect Russia from such terror. Shortly after the attacks the Russian government launched a war against Chechnya, supposedly as revenge. The Russians won the war, the Russian economy grew, Vladimir Putin's support rose, and he became president of Russia for many years.

In summary, the Russians suffered four mass casualty events incompetently carried out and covered up by their own government. Unfortunately, they were not able to protect themselves from the actual perpetrators who then dragged the country into a war based on false pretenses.

The United States

Sadly, the United States suffered a similar fate on September 11, 2001, when it suffered a massive attack for which the perpetrators were not held accountable. While I am unsure exactly what happened on that date, aspects of the official story do not make sense, so I searched for another explanation that did.

On September 11, 2001, like the Russians two years earlier, the United States suffered a huge attack with multiple mass casualty events. Almost 3,000 people died.[16] Four airplanes were hijacked in the air, with two ramming into the iconic World Trade Center skyscrapers in New York City, one crashing in a field in

Pennsylvania, and one smashing into the Pentagon, the US military's primary administrative building outside Washington DC.[17] Another New York City building, World Trade Center-7 (WTC-7), also collapsed even though no airplane hit it.

Like Russian authorities two years earlier, American president George Bush and other national security leaders quickly blamed Arab terrorists linked to Osama Bin Laden, and they then blamed the Afghan government for allowing terrorists to train there. Like the Russians two years earlier, many Americans began to fear terrorism as pictures of the epic destruction blanketed television screens across the country.

President Bush's approval ratings spiked from 55% to 90%. On September 21, he issued an ultimatum to Afghanistan's leaders, demanding that they turn over all terrorists and give the US full access to all supposed training camps.[18] On September 26 the first CIA teams entered Afghanistan to prepare an invasion and on October 7, the US invaded, beginning a war and occupation that would last approximately 20 years.[19,20]

Unfortunately, a great deal of evidence indicates that the US government's official story of the September 11, 2001 attacks is wrong, and that the government at the very least concealed the true perpetrators. An organization called Architects and Engineers for 9/11 Truth (AE911Truth) gathered professional architects and engineers to do independent analyses and experiments as well as review witness testimony to understand the likely cause of the three World Trade Tower collapses.[21]

The US government report on the collapse of WTC-7 suggested that it collapsed due to internal fires.[22] However, the building collapsed evenly and symmetrically downwards, exactly as buildings normally fall under controlled demolition. An internal fire would have caused it to collapse asymmetrically.

Recordings of the WTC-7 building collapse look identical to conventional controlled demolitions. I suggest that skeptical readers search online for compilation videos showing controlled building demolitions and then compare them with the WTC-7 collapse. No uncontrolled internal fires would cause a building to collapse so cleanly and symmetrically in freefall. But controlled demolition would.

Government investigators "found no corroborating evidence" for controlled demolition using explosives[23], ignoring the 118 witnesses who described what seemed like explosions or bombs, including dozens of firefighter and police first responders. Many witnesses testified to a sequence of explosions, and some specifically noted that the explosions moved from top to bottom. For example, on September 11, 2001, Paul Lemos told a reporter, "All of a sudden I looked up and about twenty stories below… the fire… I saw, from the corner, boom, boom, boom, boom, boom, boom, boom, boom, boom… just like twenty straight hits, just went down and then I just saw the whole building just went 'phshew'… and as the bombs were goin' people just started running…"[24]

Additionally, in the skyscrapers WTC-1 and WTC-2, massive steel girders and framing were thrown up to 600 feet from the buildings, lateral motion that is difficult to explain without explosive force. Careful video review indicates signs of explosives emitting debris horizontally outwards at speeds of up to 170 feet per second below the collapse front. A single explosion at the top would not cause lateral explosive ejections all along the height of the building as seen in videos. Also, the near-total pulverization of the concrete into fine dust is not consistent with a building collapse due to fire and gravity, but it is consistent with internal explosions.[25]

Many Americans struggle to accept that their government might mislead them in such a massive effort. However, the 9/11 attacks are reminiscent of a declassified US military plan called Operation Northwoods. It was proposed in 1962 by the Joint Chiefs of Staff, America's top generals, and delivered to the secretary of defense for consideration.

While it was never executed, the proposed operation included plans for the CIA to remotely control civilian airliners, ram them into military and civilian targets, and then blame the Cuban government as a pretext for invading Cuba. If nothing else, even the military's willingness to consider Operation Northwoods shows a willingness to consider fabricating attacks on the American homeland for political purposes. The declassified Operation Northwoods plan is available for anyone to see at the official National Security Archives website run by George Washington University.[26]

Other aspects of the official story seem suspicious too. Although the US attacked Afghanistan and later Iraq, 15 out of 19 hijackers were Saudi Arabian and none were from either Afghanistan or Iraq.[27] Recently declassified FBI evidence shows that a man who worked for the Saudi intelligence service helped plan the attacks and gave logistical support to at least two of the attackers, including help with lodging, travel, translation, and financing. He left the US shortly before the attacks.[28,29]

This Saudi intelligence agent also communicated with the director of Islamic affairs at the Saudi Embassy in Washington, a man who was known by the FBI as a "controlling, guiding, and directing influence on all aspects of Sunni extremist activity in Southern California."

Osama bin Laden himself was from a wealthy Saudi Arabian family with direct support from the Saudi monarchy, and his father had been a Saudi minister. Osama bin Laden had also worked with the Saudi intelligence agency.[30]

Both George W Bush (US president 2001-2009) and his father George HW Bush (US president 1989-1993) had close personal ties with Saudi royalty, with the elder president Bush going on hunting trips with Saudi prince Bandar and collaborating with Saudi royalty in billions of dollars of financial investments.[31] Saudi prince Bandar was the ambassador to the US at the time of the attacks, and recently released evidence shows that he also paid the Saudi intelligence agent's monthly stipend as the agent worked with the hijackers leading up to the attacks.[32]

Why was this information about Saudi involvement in the 9/11 attacks classified for years due to "national security concerns?" Why hasn't the US government shown any interest in holding the Saudi government responsible? Why did the US FBI claim there was no link between Saudi intelligence and the 9/11 attacks for years, only for the FBI to recently declassify information showing the connection?

I don't know all the details of what happened on September 11, 2001, but the official story does not make sense, and so I'm left seeking other explanations that do. Did explosives take down the World Trade Center towers, or was it enough for airplanes to ram the buildings? Did US government officials carry out this project, or did a few top officials knowingly allow the Saudis to carry it out? Or did something else happen entirely? I'm not an expert in explosives, and I'm not an insider in the FBI, Bush family, or Saudi intelligence, so I cannot know the full truth. This is simply the reality of living in an unhealthy nation: when people cannot trust authorities to tell the truth, they're left either trying not to think about it, or seeking other explanations that make sense based on limited information.

Just as the Russians were unable to protect themselves from the perpetrators who caused multiple mass casualty events in 1999, Americans in 2001 were likewise unable to protect themselves by arresting or fighting the actual perpetrators who carried out the 9/11 attacks or allowed them to happen. After suffering terrible attacks, both countries then promptly went off to war based on false pretenses.

These examples also show why the truth is so dangerous in unhealthy nations. What would happen if a Russian commission really investigated the Russian bombings or an American commission really investigated the 9/11 attacks and actually found that top political and business leaders were responsible? Top leaders could lose their wealth and even be imprisoned if the truth were fully acknowledged, so of course they'll do everything they can to prevent people from learning the truth. Activists will be disappeared, bribed, or slandered as unpatriotic. Corporate media will carefully ignore certain questions or topics. Too many people, afraid for their safety and career, will go along with the official narrative without thinking too hard. This is simply what happens when a few people are able to exploit and manipulate many.

It is also simply a common pattern for governments to attack their own people and lie about it to motivate the public to support war or oppression. Whether it's the Soviet army secretly attacking a Soviet town and blaming it on Finland as a pretext to invade Finland in 1939[33], or the Nazis secretly burning the German parliament building and blaming it on the communists as an excuse to take over the government, persecute the communists, and cancel human rights protections[34], this sort of exploitative behavior is normal in nations where a few people rule over everyone else.

Is Anybody Safe from Predation in Unhealthy Nations?

Unhealthy nations seem to be run by the people who have the most weapons and control the most wealth. Are the soldiers and rich at least safe from predation in unhealthy nations?

Sadly, soldiers are not safe. For example, every country which developed nuclear weapons in the 1940s-1970s deliberately tested the effects of nuclear weapon radiation on their own soldiers without their consent.

Not only did the countries deliberately test weapons on their own soldiers, at the time of testing they already knew that radiation caused severe illnesses. Hermann Muller received the Nobel Prize in 1946 for his research in the 1920s showing how nuclear radiation could cause cancer and genetic mutations. After the two US nuclear bombs exploded in Japan in 1945, radiation was widely studied in the local population, and the resulting disease was called Atom Bomb disease.[35]

Authorities around the world knew that nuclear weapon fallout caused terrible diseases in humans by the mid 1940s, but this did not stop them from testing nuclear weapons on their soldiers in the following decades.

Reports from France, USSR, USA and Great Britain all indicate that the governments knowingly exposed their own soldiers and sailors to nuclear weapon radiation without their consent.

British soldier John Hall was one of 22,000 British soldiers required to witness nuclear testing between 1952 and 1967, many of them wearing cotton shirts and shorts. This group had children with 10 times the normal rate of birth defects. John and his wife Marylin's first child miscarried. One child was born with deformed fingers, and another was missing muscle in his legs. After John died of a very rare cancer, Marilyn Hall said, "My husband died because he served his country. We will not go away. We can't – they have poisoned our families for generations to come."[36]

This was common among authoritarian militaries. The French estimate that 150,000 soldiers and civilians suffered from nuclear testing. Alain Peyrot described how "we knew these things," but authorities demanded that soldiers "obey and shut up."[37]

Up to 400,000 US soldiers were exposed to radiation and also sworn to secrecy, forbidding them from even telling their doctors about the likely cause of their illnesses. Many soldiers found that the US military did not follow up to learn about their health and support them in the following years. US gunner's mate Wayne Brooks, who had sailed on the USS De Haven in 1958, said, "They could have watched us all our lives and seen what it did, but they didn't. They dropped us like a hot potato."[38]

The Soviet Union likewise tested nuclear weapons on their own soldiers, including 44,000 troops in a single test in Orenberg in 1954. Soldiers began suffering radiation sickness later that day. They were sworn to secrecy, and documentation of their health issues is scarce. The archives of the local hospital were later destroyed.[39]

So, soldiers are not safe from predation by their rulers.

Are the rich and politically powerful at least safe?

No! No one is safe! J Edgar Hoover was the US director of the FBI and its predecessor organization from 1924-1972. He kept what were known as "secret files," information that allowed him to blackmail hundreds of US senators and congressional representatives over decades. William Sullivan, at one time the third ranking FBI official, said, "The moment [Hoover] would get something on a senator, he'd send one of the errand boys up and advise the senator that 'we're in the course of an investigation, and we by chance happened to come up with this data on your daughter. But we wanted you to know this…' Well, Jesus, what does that tell the senator? From that time on, the senator's right in his pocket." This explains why US president Lyndon Johnson said, "I would rather have [Hoover] inside the tent pissing out than outside the tent pissing in." Is it any wonder Hoover remained head of the US domestic police agency for almost half a century?[40] Not even top political leaders were safe.

Stories abound of the rich and powerful being abused. In November 2017, the Saudi Arabian crown prince Mohammed bin Salman had almost 400 tycoons, ministers, and princes taken to the expensive Ritz-Carlton Hotel and tortured into giving up somewhere between $28 billion and $107 billion. Bin Salman claimed it was a fight against corruption, but one journalist's source said, "This was about consolidating his rule, plain and simple."[41]

Russian president Putin sought to establish control over Russia after oligarchs had looted it extensively in the 1990s. When Mikhail Khodorkovsky opposed Putin's rule by manipulating the media and elections, he was thrown in prison. As one Russian official said, "three days in Butyrke Prison and [Khodorkovsky and his aide Roman Lebedev] will understand who is the master of the forest." Another oligarch, Vladimir Gusinsky, required only a few days in prison, including with prisoners believed to have HIV, before he relinquished his assets.[42]

In healthy nations that maintain a baseline of mutual respect, everyone gets to enjoy that respect. In nations that allow some people to exploit others, everyone is at risk of being exploited.

Who are the Rulers? How Can Most People Know for Sure? And Does it Matter?

I am deliberately vague in this book about who the rulers or authorities are. That's because the vast majority of people simply cannot know who truly rules them.

Identifying the rulers might seem simple enough. In a monarchy, isn't the king or queen in charge? However, in Saudi Arabia, observers note that crown prince Mohammed bin Salman seems to make the decisions rather than the king.[43] And what about the United Kingdom and Australia – is the monarch in charge despite their elections?

Even if a particular person publicly seems to be in charge, how much information or authority does that person actually have? Do they fear international bankers to whom they owe debt or king-makers who could dethrone them? Are there a variety of unaccountable factions vying for power? Are there other high-ranking people secretly undermining the visible leader's plans? How can most people know?

Most people can't really understand these things unless they're insiders, and so most people cannot really know who the decision-makers are.

The people may elect a president, but does that president command the corporate leaders to follow the government line? Or do the corporate leaders, after heavily funding election campaigns, give orders to the president? Do corporate leaders give directions to congressional leaders after funding their campaigns? And if all the politicians, corporate leaders, and media figures maintain the pretense that the president and congress are in charge, how is the public supposed to know who really is in charge? In some unhealthy nations, a king or dictator might publicly acknowledge their power. In other unhealthy nations, it seems like rulers or the ruling class prefer to remain shrouded in secrecy to avoid anyone questioning their actions or legitimacy.

Ultimately, it doesn't matter who the rulers are. What matters is whether a person is trapped in an abusive society or not. I can know a hostile military is approaching even if I don't know who the commander is. I can know I'm in an abusive prison even if I don't know who the warden is. The individual players don't matter as much as the never-ending game. Ultimately, it is the unhealthy nation itself that is the culprit. Individuals can change roles even as the basic exploitative patterns live on.

Many researchers investigate palace intrigues, political factions, and more to study the balance of power at the highest levels of an authoritarian nation. There might be interesting lessons to learn from these intrigues, but they're not fundamentally important to most citizens who are trapped in abusive nations. What's important is that they're subject to rulers, and when various factions compete to decide who gets to rule, for most people it's already a catastrophe.

Child Sexual Abuse Does Not Exist in Healthy Nations

A few years ago, as I was re-reading the book *Daughters of Copper Woman*, I noticed something that astounded me. I was reading the story of the Nootkas' first contact with Spanish conquistadors, which included Catholic priests. The Nootka noticed that they "never saw any of the Keestadore [conquistador] women, they only brought men and young boys who got used as women whether they liked it or not."[44] Even in their first interaction with Europeans centuries ago, they noticed regular child rape that remains so common in unhealthy nations to this day. After a period of uneasy interactions, the Spaniards kidnapped, raped, and murdered two Nootka girls of about 10 years old, leaving their bodies on the beach for their relatives to find. This part did not astound me, as I'd read this sort of story about Catholic, Buddhist, and other authorities many times.

What did surprise me was the Nootkas' response. As I interpret their story, they had never before encountered child sexual assault:

> "…The people had no way of understandin' what had happened. There'd never been anythin' like this in all the time since the beginning of life, and so they could only stare at the proof of horror and feel numb shock. They could see what had been done, but they couldn't understand how, or why. It had been hard enough to believe the Keestadores would force a grown woman to have sex when they didn't want, but the thought of sex with a child was just too horrible for the people to even imagine, so they didn't know what to think.[45]

> The old woman examined both the babies, and it was as if the sure evidence of what she found shook the centrepost of all creation, and threatened the here and now as well as the past and future…"

The Nootka didn't just have less child sexual assault than my unhealthy nation, or stronger laws against it, or better ways of healing trauma, or better self-defense classes for girls and women. I believe they straight-up didn't have *any* child sexual assault. The possibility that a child might be raped had not occurred to them until they encountered an unhealthy nation.

This passage was transformative for me. It showed me that healthy nations and unhealthy nations really are different.

I knew child rape was bad, but why was it so bad that it would "[shake] the centrepost of all creation" and "[threaten] the here and now as well as the past and future?"

Healthy nations see any disrespect as a cultural wound that affects everybody, and I believe that the Nootka recognized that this child rape was a severe disrespect and therefore a severe cultural wound. If this disrespect wasn't fully addressed, everything was at risk, and nothing would be safe.

The Nootka soon allied with neighboring groups and successfully killed all of these conquistadors. They saw how important it was to their nation's survival to protect themselves from predators.

This taught me the importance of maintaining that internal baseline of mutual respect. Once a nation allows disrespect and tolerates predators, there is no end to the trouble.

Non-Predatory Leadership is Unstable in Unhealthy Nations

Of course, not all authority figures engage in predatory behavior. Many leaders, such as Jacobo Árbenz in Guatemala, Salvador Allende in Chile, and Mohammad Mosaddegh of Iran have implemented policies that benefited the poor at the expense of the rich. And all three were taken out in coups by high-ranking military and business officials.

Why is it so hard to get leaders elected who actually seek to serve all the people, including the poor? And why are they so quickly replaced when they do get to power?

Recall that gift economies and profit economies are both stable, as reviewed in Chapter 11. Gift economies can produce generous leaders indefinitely, and profit economies can produce selfish leaders indefinitely. However, mixing both generosity and selfishness is unstable. Like mixing oil and water, they naturally repel each other.

This explains why it would be unstable to have a selfish leader in a healthy nation. In a gift economy that rewards generosity and integrity, the people wouldn't stand for a selfish leader, and the leader would get sacked. Likewise, in an unhealthy nation with a profit economy that systematically rewards selfishness, hoarding, and low integrity, it is unstable to have a generous leader. The selfish rich won't allow a generous leader, so the leader gets sacked.

This clarifies the heart of the troubles that unhealthy, authoritarian nations face. As long as rulers and other authorities successfully prevent deep accountability, predatory behavior will continue. While individual low-level predators, such as some soldiers or priests, may get imprisoned occasionally, top leaders commonly remain unscathed and the exploitation at the heart of unhealthy nations continues.

Rulers and subsidiary authorities represent the greatest threat to the people trapped in any unhealthy nation. Individual rulers or authority figures might act more or less cruel, just like individual prison wardens might be more or less cruel. But just as prisoners cannot influence who becomes prison warden and have little recourse if the warden becomes abusive, people who are trapped in an abusive nation are already in a terrible position when the worst predators rise to power.

These stories of deep predation illustrate what is at stake in seeking the truth. For Russians or Americans to acknowledge that the most powerful individuals in their country were extremely selfish and predatory, and that the government has covered this up for decades, would threaten the government's legitimacy. To take a stand for the truth would mean taking a stand against the rulers who know very well what is at stake. Is it any wonder that so many people prefer to ignore these disturbing truths and seek comfortable blind beliefs instead?

As long as a few people rule over everyone else and forbid deep accountability, and as long as rulers impose profit economies that reward selfishness, hoarding, and low integrity, these sorts of large-scale abuses will predictably continue to happen.

I support individuals joining together to protect one another the best they can. However, the only way to end deep predation is to end or transform the unhealthy authoritarian nation so that nobody rules over anybody else.

Rulers, whoever they may be, don't just prevent accountability to protect their wealth. They are also heavily motivated to protect themselves from being punished by the people they exploit. How can rulers train people to think that terrible things are ok, and go through their day-to-day lives surrounded by exploitation and abuse as if this were normal? To see these propaganda techniques in action, and to learn how people can see through manipulative propaganda and stay sane in a nation of deceit, join me in *Chapter 39: Even More Propaganda Techniques*.

Chapter 39: Even More Propaganda Techniques

Some people have mystical or mind-altering experiences taking LSD or magic mushrooms. I had a mystical, mind-altering experience reading *Manufacturing Consent*, a book by Noam Chomsky and Herman Edwards about propaganda in the United States.

I was sitting alone at my parents' kitchen table, having just finished the first chapter, called "A Propaganda Model." The authors described five major mechanisms that cause privately owned media companies in the US to more or less consistently align with authoritarian corporate and government narratives rather than the most meaningful truths.

News companies' profit motive and reliance on advertising income gives advertisers huge influence over what gets into print and what doesn't. Dependence on government leaders and other important figures for news, as well as the desire to avoid being labeled "communists" also keeps newspaper editors and writers within narrow lanes of acceptable discourse.

The authors also use this model to illustrate how newspapers subtly convey the sense that some far-away victims of some tragedies are worthy of concern and others are unworthy, depending on US imperial interests in the region.

For example, when Polish priest Jerzy Popieluszko was killed by Polish police in 1984, this received vast media attention in the United States because Poland was part of the US's ideological adversary, the Soviet Union. In contrast, when 28 priests, missionaries, and other religious workers were killed in the US client states of El Salvador and Guatemala between 1980 and 1985, these deaths combined received less coverage than Popieluszko's death. It was in US interests at the time to highlight Polish government thuggery because they were an adversary, and it was not in US interests to highlight thuggery in central American client states. The supposedly free US news media played along.[1]

I had sat at the kitchen table every morning in middle school reading the newspaper, trying to figure out what's going on in the world. I mostly ended up confused, and no one I talked with helped much. But sitting in that same spot in my late 20s, as I finished reading and let the implications of the propaganda model sink in, I felt transformed. Suddenly so many things made sense that did not make sense before!

I stood up to stretch, and I walked over to a kitchen counter where I found that day's copy of the Washington Post, one of the United States' most politically important newspapers. I flipped to the editorials section just as I had a thousand times before, but today it was different. I could see the propaganda jump out, like someone had highlighted it with a yellow marker. I could see which foreign governments the editors wanted me to think of as the "good guys" whose elections were basically legitimate despite a few troubles, and which governments were the "bad guys" with illegitimate elections.

I could tell which US government policies were supported by omitting certain consequences they would have, and which were opposed by clearly stating all their negative consequences. I could tell which political institutions and politicians were likewise supported because their hurtful behavior was due to good intentions and occasional mistakes. I could tell which politicians I was meant to oppose, as they were assumed to have bad intentions. The assumptions and half-truths and double standards jumped out like never before.

For years, I studied propaganda voraciously, seeking to understand the truth behind so many lies spouted by various governments and corporations.

Eventually, I stopped studying propaganda because I got bored. As Sioux man Ohiyesa so succinctly said: "while Indians unqualifiedly say what they mean, the whites have a hundred ways of saying what they do not mean."[2]

It turns out, there are endless ways people can lie, manipulate, infer, and conceal. There are white lies, half-truths, and limited hangouts, where authorities publicly reveal part of a damaging truth to avoid revealing the worst parts. People can say words that are entirely true but give the wrong impression. Powerful people can use servants to spout lies so the powerful have plausible deniability. In authoritarian nations that reward selfishness and tolerate low integrity, people have many ways of "saying what they do not mean."

Even though I eventually got tired of studying propaganda, I was glad I had learned to see it vividly all around me. Seeing the manipulation so clearly helped me avoid falling for authorities' tricks.

Many propaganda techniques have already been covered in previous chapters, including spreading hatred, sexism, racism, and scientific misunderstandings. Authorities keep people from learning about healthy nations or even encourage hatred of healthy nations so people will not learn what it's like to live without rulers. Authorities impose blind beliefs, where people are required to believe certain things to maintain their social standing and safety. Authoritarian nations legitimize a few people ruling and imposing law on everyone else. And authorities can sabotage people's reputations, cause people to misunderstand each other with culture jamming, focus on other unhealthy nations' flaws while ignoring their own, label political activists as mentally ill, and rewrite ancient history in religious textbooks.

That is a long list of propaganda techniques. However, as some advertisers like to say, "But wait! There's more!"

What are other common patterns of propaganda that authorities use to distract people with meaninglessness and generate support for inappropriate policies? And most importantly, how can people see through the lies and remain grounded in reality despite being surrounded by nonsense?

Survey of Propaganda Techniques

Rulers and their servants have understood since the earliest unhealthy nations how important it is to shape public opinion so that the majority of people support what the rulers want to do.

American president Abraham Lincoln recognized the importance of public opinion when he said, "…public sentiment is everything. With public sentiment, nothing can fail; without it, nothing can succeed. Consequently he who molds public sentiment, goes deeper than he who enacts statutes or pronounces decisions. He makes statutes and decisions possible or impossible to be executed."[3]

Nazi German minister of public enlightenment and propaganda Joseph Goebbels likewise emphasized that the government does not merely respond to public opinion, but actively shapes it: "It is the absolute right of the State to supervise the formation of public opinion!"[4]

Edward Bernays, who refined many propaganda techniques, noted "The conscious and intelligent manipulation of the organized habits and opinions of the masses is an important element in democratic society. Those who manipulate this unseen mechanism of society constitute an invisible government which is the true ruling power of our country. We are governed, our minds molded, our tastes formed, our ideas suggested, largely by men we have never heard of. This is a logical result of the way in which our democratic society is organized. Vast numbers of human beings must cooperate in this manner if they are to live together as a smoothly functioning society."[5]

Following are some core techniques for managing public opinion.

Encouraging Assumptions and Modeling the Conversation

After swearing off political conversations for a few years, I recently began to talk politics with strangers again. Many conversations have begun similarly to one that I had with a taxi driver named James:

James: Tell me about yourself.

Me: I'm writing a book about politics and how there's so much corruption and what we can do about it.

James: Good! We need that, the Democrats are ruining this country. I'll tell you, you can't trust a word they say. It's amazing we have any jobs left in this country with Brandon [president Joe Biden] in there. Things used to be better, but they're really going downhill now.

Me: You know that both political parties are controlled by the rich corporations and nothing much changes each time the other party comes to power, right?

James: Yeah, that's true.

I paraphrased this conversation because I didn't record it, but this is no exaggeration.

To recap the key points:

- James started by expressing a mainstream narrative that resonated with him – that one political party and especially its leader is the source of our troubles.

- I shared a narrative that explains reality better and contradicted his narrative – that both parties are corrupt and in alignment with rich corporate interests, and nothing meaningfully changes when new politicians get elected.

- James acknowledged that I was right – not because I convinced him, but because he already understood that both parties are equally corrupt. I merely acknowledged a truth he already knew.

I've had many political discussions with strangers start this way.

Eventually, I wondered: if the other person already knew both parties are corrupt, why are they wasting their time picking sides and getting angry at just one party? If I had played along, we could have spent the conversation either deriding Democrats together or, if I sided with Democrats, arguing about which corrupt party was worse. So long as we ignored the truth we both knew – that both parties are controlled by corporate interests – then the conversation would ultimately be pointless. We might as well talk about movies.

This conversation between James and myself mirrors what I see on political TV programs. TV news personalities may pretend to be impartial, or they may support one political faction over another, but I never hear them acknowledge the truth that both parties consistently support corrupt rulers.

News personalities propagate a huge number of assumptions in their programs, on everything from the legal system to corporate regulation to foreign policy and government legitimacy. One researcher noted that "the press is significantly more than a purveyor of information and opinion. It may not be successful much of the time in telling people what to think, but it is stunningly successful in telling its readers what to think about."[6]

Noam Chomsky described one major way this works: "The smart way to keep people passive and obedient is to strictly limit the spectrum of acceptable opinion, but allow very lively debate within that spectrum – even encourage the more critical and dissident views. That gives people the sense that there's free thinking going on, while all the time the presuppositions of the system are being reinforced by the limits put on the range of the debate."[7]

When the press makes assumptions that viewers don't catch, they're training viewers to restrict the range of what to think about and what not to think about. Pointless political conversations and debates, like the one James and I almost had, are the common result.

Feel-Good Cover Stories

In sacred circles, people agree on the truth first and then decide what to do about it.

In authoritarian nations, rulers decide what they want to do, then they decide what to try to get the public to believe so they'll support the rulers' plans.

When someone knows they face an extremely important decision, they will invest tremendous effort into discovering all the relevant facts and answering all the relevant questions. For example, if a military general wants to invade a foreign country, they will intensively study the topography, both sides' logistics, energy and transportation infrastructure, both sides' military capabilities, and more. A military staff may include dozens of full-time professionals whose job it is to do this kind of research to seek the truth, no matter how uncomfortable that truth is.

When people give up responsibility for their decisions and for the wellbeing of their nation and adopt submissive attitudes instead, they commonly choose their beliefs not based on intensive study of reality, but based on what feels good, or at least less bad. In other words, many people choose their beliefs based on what feels comfortable and safe, not based on observation of reality.

I call this pattern *feeling over substance*, where people learn to emphasize subjective perception over objective reality, or what feels good instead of what's real. The obvious sign is that so many people believe things they hear or read in the news without investigating to find the truth for themselves.

Examples abound.

When the Nazis were ready to invade Poland, they faced a conundrum. They wanted to attack Poland, but they didn't have a good excuse because Poland wasn't attacking them, and the Nazis wanted to justify the invasion to their public. On August 31, 1939, Germans disguised as Polish agents sabotaged a German radio tower. This allowed the German government to launch its invasion of Poland the next day on the pretext that it had been attacked, knowing few or none of its citizens would actually investigate to find out the truth.[8]

The United States propagates a belief that the government supports democracy and human rights around the world. When the US government does not like another countries' leadership and launches a coup to forcibly install another government, it will commonly say that the new government is democratic and represents the will of the people. This occurred after the Honduras coup in 2009 which was supported by the United States.

The new Honduran government used state-sponsored death squads, political assassinations, torture, disappearance, and much more to secure its power. Many river and forest protectors and other activists were killed, including Berta Cáceres, a woman of the Lenca healthy nation.[9,10]

Hillary Clinton was US secretary of state at the time. In her biography, she described her approach to the coup: "We strategized on a plan to restore order in Honduras and ensure that free and fair elections could be held quickly and legitimately, which would render the question of [the previous president] moot."[11] In 2016, Clinton's presidential campaign claimed that she had "paved the way for legitimate democratic elections."[12]

However, the Honduras military leader who took over in the coup had received training at the United States' School of the Americas, a notorious training grounds for military and police long associated with torture and repression.[13] After having trained the coup leader, the US continued funding the Honduras military and police, giving $200 million from 2009-2016.[14] Clinton and the US government spoke of democracy and fair elections, but clearly these were feel-good cover stories to justify their desired regime change abroad.

The German government wanted to invade Poland, and the American government wanted to regime-change Honduras, but neither wanted to say so clearly. Both governments generated meaningless cover stories to justify their actions that would feel good to anybody who did not bother to seek out the truth for themselves.

Playing the Victim With Selective Reporting and the Big Lie

As Jesus Christ's persecutors were about to crucify him, he spoke some of the most tragic words I've ever heard: "Father, forgive them, for they do not know what they are doing."[15]

People in authoritarian nations can often have very passionate, deeply held opinions based on a complete misunderstanding of the actual situation. I have encountered many Americans who believe that Russia was completely unprovoked when it invaded Ukraine in early 2022. I have heard several people who consider themselves politically savvy call the Russian president an evil dictator. Early in the war, US news media and government officials consistently used the words "unprovoked" and "unjustified" in describing Russia's attack, reinforcing these beliefs.[16]

The US and NATO military alliance provoked Russia's attack in countless ways, including expanding the NATO military alliance up to Russia's borders, causing a coup in 2014 that installed pro-United States leadership in Ukraine, and much more.[17] In the month before the invasion, this pro-United States Ukrainian leadership showed signs of wanting to build or acquire nuclear weapons.[18,19]

In the weeks before the Russian invasion, Ukraine began a large artillery barrage of the separatist Donbass provinces, launching greater than 1,000 explosive shells per day.[20] Militaries commonly use large artillery attacks to "soften up" their opponents before an assault, like the US Confederate army did against the Union army at Gettysburg in the US Civil War.[21] Thus the Russians may have feared that Ukraine planned to invade the Donbass.

Congressman Adam Schiff explained the US's intentions in arming Ukraine to fight Russia: "The United States aids Ukraine and her people, so that we can fight Russia over there and we don't have to fight Russia here."[22] Republican senator Lindsey Graham noted that Ukraine possesses $10-12 trillion in important minerals and could become a significant "business partner" for the US.[23]

Anyone who questions the official narrative that Russia invaded unprovoked, or who tries to understand the perspectives of all the governments in the war risks being called a "Putin-lover," the present-day American or European equivalent of being accused of treason.[24] This instantly puts people on the defensive; I have commonly seen people switch from trying to point out Russia's perspective to trying to reassure the interviewer that they're not traitors just for acknowledging everybody's point of view in the war.

This claim that Russia invaded Ukraine unprovoked represents what propagandists call a *Big Lie*, where authority figures endlessly repeat a falsehood. Nazi dictator Adolf Hitler explained why this works: "[the public] would not believe that others could have the impudence to distort the truth so infamously." Researchers studying Hitler's propaganda described how the Big Lie works: "if you repeat it frequently enough people will sooner or later believe it."[25]

Advertisers of everything from toothpaste to candy know this is true, and so do rulers and other authorities.

I often hear people talk about Putin's or Russia's supposed intentions, and I ask them "How do you know what their intentions are?" Invariably, the person has only listened to American media. But would anyone trust Russia's news companies to tell the truth about America? If not, why would Americans trust their own media to tell the truth about America's adversaries?

I make no comment on whether it was appropriate or not for Russia to invade Ukraine. I only say that if a person considers it important to have an opinion on the war or any issue, they need to seek out as much of the truth as possible in order to have an informed opinion. If they cannot find enough information to have an informed understanding, they can acknowledge their own ignorance, which is also honorable. Anyone who forms strong opinions based on propaganda may feel very self-righteous and confident while unknowingly becoming pawns in their rulers' games.

Deafening Silence

The greatest propaganda trick is simply for the media and government to ignore uncomfortable truths so that most people never learn about them or they learn to ignore what they know.

Deafening silence can occur with simple censorship. For example, in World War I, every fighting country imposed censorship on the news and mail, regardless of supposed constitutional protections that some countries had.[26] Censorship did not just keep military secrets out of the news; it also withheld any information that might diminish public support for the war. It is bizarre to imagine that the populations of every country likely believed they were winning the whole time regardless of how the war was actually going, with some populations like the Germans suddenly being surprised when they lost the war. Chapter 22 already explored how confused many Germans became after the government had lied throughout World War I.

Other kinds of media manipulation are more subtle. Instead of official censorship, the media can simply choose not to cover certain topics and thus direct people's attention elsewhere.

I was getting worried about the safety of my money in banks in early 2013. I'd been reading about financial scams and bank fraud for years, as well as the corrupt government response to the financial crash in 2008. I tried to share my concerns with a woman I was dating. She listened, but she never got very concerned until she read about the 2013 bank closure in Cyprus, a small European country. The public had no idea there was a financial problem till they woke up one day and could not access their money in ATMs, and banks did not reopen till a large number of people had lost much of their savings. My girlfriend was suddenly very interested in the safety of our money, but only for a few weeks while the stories filled the newspapers. Once the stories of financial disaster trailed off, so did her interest in discussing how to protect ourselves from similar risks. I pointed out the media's role in influencing people's perceptions of risk, but she didn't want to talk about it anymore.

A similar story occurred with another woman I knew in 2020. Huge protests erupted after George Floyd was killed, and she suddenly heard stories of police brutality towards black people and saw examples of police brutality towards protesters of all colors through online media. Over a couple months, we had several phone calls where she described how unsafe she felt with the police, and she wanted to do something but didn't know what. Eventually the protests and visible brutality stopped, and when the news stopped carrying stories of the brutality, she changed too. I no longer heard fear in her voice, and she hasn't brought up police concerns since. She continued her professional career without any changes or engaging in any activism. Her fears rose and fell with the temporary wave of media coverage of police brutality, not with the actual threat of the police, which has remained consistent.

This is the power of propaganda to direct people's attention and manipulate their feelings, including by projecting an air of quiet normality even when things are not ok.

One reason propaganda works so well is that it is humans' nature to live in healthy nations where they share knowledge and support. Healthy nations hold everyone to a high standard of integrity, and so people can commonly trust the words they hear. In unhealthy nations that tolerate so much dishonesty, people must be much more skeptical of what they hear, and this can be exhausting.

The Power of Propaganda – Making Things Seem Ok That Really are Not Ok

Propaganda makes inappropriate behavior or unhealthy situations seem normal. Whether it occurs through TV, movies, music, radio, or any forum; people can be subtly trained in countless ways. Rather than explore examples of propaganda in each medium, let us review what it looks like when people have been trained to believe falsehoods or act in ways deeply contrary to their own interests.

In the Soviet Union, anybody who showed any opposition to the government could be severely punished. One man described a Soviet district-level party conference held in Moscow. At every mention of Stalin's name, people leapt to their feet in applause. At the end of the conference, a tribute to Stalin was expected, so once again everyone stood up and applauded. The observer said the hall contained "stormy applause, rising to an ovation."[27]

This lasted three minutes, then four minutes, then five. People became sore and the older ones panted with exhaustion, but who dared be the first one to stop applauding for Stalin? Even people who admired Stalin could see it was silly. But the district secretary was new to the role and afraid to be the first to stop the applause. The applause continued for eight minutes, then ten. The people in the back could cheat a little, clapping a little slower, but the ones on the podium in full view kept on with their vigorous clapping with make-believe enthusiasm, looking at each other with faint hope.

Finally a strong-willed business owner sat down, and the crowd's enthusiasm quickly evaporated and everyone sat down, grateful that someone had delivered a miracle. Later that night, that businessman was arrested, and during his interrogation a police officer told him: "Don't ever be the first to stop applauding!"

This story seemed ludicrous to me. How could people be so silly? But whenever I see a silly pattern somewhere else, I like to ask myself where I observe similar silliness in my own nation. Sadly, examples are not difficult to find.

Chemical formula instead of breast-feeding: It is hard to imagine something more natural, beautiful, and healthy than a mother breastfeeding her infant. Despite this, I have met women who are afraid to breastfeed their own babies, believing that corporate-produced chemical formula could be superior to mother's milk. I know one brave woman who raised five children in the 1950s, and after feeding her first four purely with chemical formula, she finally decided to breast feed the last one. Women were so commonly shamed for this that she snuck into bathrooms at restaurants to breastfeed in order to avoid other people's negative judgments.

Normalizing food wrapped in poison: Plastic is toxic, and it sheds microplastics continuously into the air, water, soil, skin, and on anything it touches. Researchers have linked microplastics with many health problems, some of which were explored in Chapter 37. And yet food for sale has increasingly been wrapped in plastic, even items like sweet potatoes or apples that can last for weeks or longer in the open air. Chemical industry propaganda has trained many people to associate plastic wrapping with cleanliness and wise storage. Thus many Americans prefer to buy food covered in toxic plastic over food not covered in toxic plastic, believing the food wrapped in toxins is safer and cleaner.[28]

When carrying surveillance devices seems normal: Huge numbers of people carry a phone on them at all times. Phone addiction has become a widespread health problem.[29] However, phones are also incredibly effective surveillance devices which give corporations and governments many insights into each person's location, what they say, with whom they associate, and much more.

Chapter 23 showed how Don Cox and other black people in 1967 spontaneously shared their grievances one night and then started taking concrete steps to address them. They could have those conversations in private because no surveillance devices were present. If those conversations had happened in 2020 instead, likely many people would have had phones with microphones that would record everybody's voices, potentially transmitting that to advertisers and surveillance agencies. Authorities could have listened to the meetings as they happened. Even if people didn't speak each others' names, voice recognition technology could be used to identify all the speakers.

To have such a meeting in private today, all the participants would either need to safely store their phone before entering the room or pause the conversation to ask everyone to take their phones elsewhere. Either choice would make a spontaneous, unplanned outpouring of grievances difficult. Many people have become addicted to their surveillance devices, which they very carefully keep charged and with them at all times. And the vast majority of people I encounter consider this normal.

Such is the power of propaganda.

Successfully Dealing With Narrative Management

A few practices help me deal with propaganda while maintaining my sanity.

Does This Issue Matter Enough to Find Out the Truth?

The core technique for combating propaganda is simple: never ever make assumptions.

Assumptions are simply unexamined beliefs, and so the best way to avoid assumptions is to consistently examine one's beliefs.

Whenever some new issue arises in the media, I ask myself if the issue is important enough for me to find out the truth. If it's not important to me, I ignore it. If I'm honestly worried about something – say, whether or not a vaccine works, or whether or not a journalist has integrity – then I figure out how to research it.

I take responsibility for finding out the truth, not just believing whatever media stories happen to come my way. I commonly read books with footnotes or online articles with linked sources, and I often check over half the references to verify the author's interpretation of their source material. If the truth matters, I try to really figure it out. I can still be wrong, but I'm right much more often than if I just believed what ideologically similar news people say on TV.

And if I can't find a satisfying answer, then I acknowledge my own ignorance. For example, I know I don't trust the covid vaccines and I don't trust the vaccine regulators. But how many other vaccines have been beneficial? I haven't researched this yet so I don't know. If I ever become a father with a child whom doctors will want to vaccinate, I will do that research because then it will matter to me. Until then, I consider other projects to be higher priority. In the meantime, I am comfortable acknowledging my uncertainty.

Getting comfortable acknowledging what I don't know is part of how I avoid assumptions. This takes a lot of humility. I was never rewarded in school for acknowledging my ignorance. I had to learn that it's ok to be ignorant about unimportant matters. It's also ok to say, "I don't know, but I'm looking into it." And it's ok to acknowledge making a mistake.

As one famous saying goes, "It ain't what you don't know that gets you into trouble. It's what you know for sure that just ain't so." I have met many white Americans who take anti-racism work seriously, but many of them also believe Russia and China are evil dictatorships that engage in unpredictable acts of aggression and terror, unlike the US. I believe these same people would likely have been quite racist against black people 200 years ago, because the same American propaganda that paints Russian and Chinese governments as evil today painted black people as subhumans 200 years ago.

Propagandists encourage and rely on all kinds of unexamined thinking, including making assumptions, beliefs in people's inherent badness, fear of appearing ignorant or uninformed, desire to fit in with others, low self-confidence, superficial thinking, choosing beliefs based on what feels good, blindly trusting authorities, and more.

When I describe this book and the propaganda it addresses, I commonly hear people say things like "people are basically stupid" or "humans just aren't that smart." I disagree. Unhealthy nations train people for foolishness, ignorance, and making assumptions, and then punish people who do their own research and stand for the truth. Is it any wonder that foolishness and ignorance are widespread?

Foolishness and shallow thinking are not inherent human qualities. I don't find these patterns in my research and experience with healthy nations. Authorities encourage ignorance or making assumptions so that people will accept living in their authoritarian nation. It's up to each of us to either seek out the truth or acknowledge ignorance in order to avoid falling for propaganda tricks.

As Malcolm X warned: "if you aren't careful, the newspapers will have you hating the people who are being oppressed and loving the people who are doing the oppressing."[30]

This is how I accept responsibility for making good decisions. I either find out the truth with as much certainty as I can, or I accept my ignorance. I can still make mistakes, but either way I'm honest with myself and other people, and I avoid foolish assumptions.

Stop Trusting My Unhealthy-Nation Rulers More Than Rulers of Other Unhealthy Nations

I trust the American, Russian, and Chinese presidents approximately the same – very little. I trust corporate media in all three countries approximately the same, which means I approach all three with the same skepticism. I happen to live in the United States, but I don't engage in any wishful thinking and let myself trust American politicians more than other countries' politicians just because I was born here. That would be just as silly as a Russian person trusting Russian authorities more just because they happened to be born there. No politician or journalist gets my trust by default. This is different than cynism. Cynical people assume everyone is dishonest or self-serving, which is not true. Skeptical people judge each individual on their merits, based on as many verifiable facts as possible.

Practice Noticing What I Observe

The nature connection practices described in Chapter 20 got me into the habit of noticing my own observations. I learned to notice what I know and what I don't know, and this helped me release a lot of assumptions.

This sort of regular practice of deepening awareness is one of the greatest things people can do to avoid being fooled by propaganda.

Avoid Propaganda

I avoid propaganda like the plague.

Deception is toxic. Anyone can make mistakes, but a person is deceptive when they deliberately cause another person to misunderstand something. Individual journalists might not be intentionally deceptive, but if they are willing to do whatever is necessary to keep their job, they will spread whatever misunderstandings the corporate leaders want to propagate.

It's exhausting to try and see through falsehoods, or wonder whether a person who lied before is lying again. Corporate media slips in so many assumptions, I can easily pick one up without noticing. I find it easier to *seek out journalists of integrity* who have proven themselves over time. I still read even their work with skepticism because anyone may make mistakes. Still, it's a relief reading research by people who have integrity and learn from their mistakes.

I believe the root goal of propaganda is to encourage unexamined thinking that supports compliance. With unexamined thinking, people can feel comfortable making foolish assumptions, believing falsehoods, acting scornfully towards innocent people, dismissing the truth as misinformation, unknowingly supporting wars of aggression, adopting racist or sexist attitudes, and much more. I find it exhausting to constantly be on alert for the infinite varieties of manipulation and assumptions. I specifically choose to be around people I admire because I learn and become like the people around me, even subconsciously. I likewise choose to read the research of people whose integrity I respect. Just like I avoid toxins that poison my body, I avoid toxins like propaganda that poison my mind.

Discuss Beliefs and Concerns With Other Trusted People

I feel stressed when I am the only person I know with a certain belief or perspective. It really helps to share my perspectives with trusted friends and hear their perspective too. Even if we don't end up agreeing, sharing my beliefs with others reduces the stress I feel from having beliefs so different from many other people in my nation. I strongly suggest building a friend group where people can share their perspectives with each other and not feel alone in their beliefs or concerns.

This is another benefit of having a sacred circle with trusted people – such a group becomes a forum to discuss what's really happening when public news sources seem untrustworthy or incomplete. It also becomes a forum where people can reassure each other that it's ok to disagree with the mainstream view, building up each others' confidence and willingness to think for themselves.

Notice and Anticipate the Patterns

Whenever an unhealthy nation goes to war, certain patterns seem to consistently play out. For example, as a war looms, people can simply expect that patriotic protesters will be called traitors, the mindlessly obedient will be called patriots, and censorship and hurtful propaganda will increase. Any organization that wants to stop a needless war will benefit from anticipating these patterns and preparing for them.

Support Independent Journalists

An excellent saying in the news media is this: *if you're not the paying customer, you're the product*. So long as advertisers are a news company's primary revenue source, they have strong influence on the company's news coverage. In practice, advertisers don't just pay to put an ad in front of readers. Advertisers pay to control how the news covers events. If advertisers were to withdraw their ads, the company could go out of business.

The readers become the product which newspapers sell to advertisers. Independent journalists ask readers to pay something so they do not have to bow to advertisers. Honest journalists want to serve their readers with the truth as they see it, and they need to be able to support themselves, and a key way for readers to encourage honest journalism is to financially support it.

The third core spiritual practice, living in reciprocity, is how humans generate abundance. When readers and honest independent journalists live in reciprocity, beauty results. Readers receive a deeper awareness from honest journalists, and when readers give money in return, honest journalists receive the gift of being able to provide for themselves and their family while doing good work in the world. In unhealthy nations where authorities make it difficult to learn the truth, readers get as much honest journalism as they're willing to support.

Is it really possible for people who have lived with rulers for centuries to finally free themselves and live in a mutually respectful way again? If so, what rules and practices might they embrace to help them succeed? Next, *Chapter 40: Enough! - The Zapatistas' Successful Revolution* offers an inspiring example and practical guide.

Chapter 40: Enough! - The Zapatistas' Deep Revolution

To many outsiders it seemed like it happened overnight, but the Zapatistas' revolution was motivated by 500 years of pent-up anger, and built on 10 years of careful planning and training.[1]

The rallying cry on January 1, 1994 was Ya Basta! in Spanish, meaning *Enough!* They had struggled against slavery, fought in the revolution against the colonizing Spanish and later against other imperialists. In the end, this was a shallow revolution which replaced one ruling class with another. The Zapatistas wanted a deep revolution, after which they would not live under a ruling class and they could decide for themselves how to live in a respectful way with each other and the Earth.

A century later they still faced rulers who exploited them "without caring that we are dying of hunger and curable diseases, without caring that we have nothing, absolutely nothing, not a decent roof, no land, no work, no health, no food, no education." Despite the facade of elections, they could not choose their leaders or remain independent of foreign corporate exploitation. There was neither peace nor justice for adults or children.[2]

An insurgent major named Moisés said clearly, "We also want peace, but a peace with justice, with dignity…" But they didn't want fake peace: "we do want peace. A peace where there is tranquility, where there is joy… We no longer want… a peace with pain, a peace with sadness, a peace with sorrow, with bitterness, with suffering, sacrifice and even death. We do not want that kind of peace that they have given us out of poverty."[3] They called their war "The Fight Against Forgetting."[4]

The Zapatistas had been low-privilege people and thus the government had routinely broken its promises to them. Moisés complained about the Mexican Army when he said, "They defend that group of rulers and exploiters, of promisers who never keep their promises." And he described their final response: "We are human beings and we are alive and we need to eat like they eat. And if it is necessary that we go out with our weapons, we will go out."[5]

The Zapatistas had been building strength for many years. They created their first guerilla training camp in the jungle in 1983.[6] An earlier uprising led by Zapatista women in March 1993 had also gained them valuable experience.[7] By January 1, 1994, the Zapatistas were ready to rise again.

The Mexican military and the Zapatista military, known as the EZLN, clashed almost immediately in the Zapatistas' home region of Chiapas in the south east. Official fighting continued until a ceasefire was called 11 days later and dialog with the federal government began.[8]

However, this official ceasefire was not the end of the violence. The Mexican Ministry of Defense illegally organized paramilitary forces to attack the Zapatistas. In their "Chiapas 94 Campaign Plan", the Ministry planned to "secretly organize certain sectors of the civilian population… characterized by a high patriotic sense" and "train and support the self-defense forces or other paramilitary organizations."

Neither the Mexican military nor law enforcement stopped the paramilitary fighters from violating all norms of warfare. They fired machine guns into villages, and the leader of the town of Rosario Ibarra had his arm cut off. Women were told their children would be kidnapped if they did not describe the organizations to which they belonged.[9] Others were disappeared, executed, or displaced from their homes. On December 22, 1997, a paramilitary group called Máscara Roja murdered 45 women, men and children suspected of supporting the Zapatistas. Other organized crime groups also participated in the violence, including some with known links to government officials.

Zapatista major Ana María said, "they have begun to arrest and torture the civilian population… The government wants to finish us off, but the Zapatista Army is very large and is everywhere."

Using military force illegally is a common pattern in unhealthy nations. When the rich and powerful need to ignore the law to maintain oppression, they do so. The KKK was another example of illegal paramilitary violence supported by the rich (explored in Chapter 22). "Paramilitary" simply means illegal military forces that governments or rich people secretly support, and the Mexicans predictably used paramilitaries against the Zapatistas.

The Mexican army continued laying siege to some areas despite the ceasefire. Even in 1995, Ana María counted 30 helicopters and "thousands and thousands" of soldiers. Hundreds of tanks and other military vehicles had entered many towns. The rebels acknowledged the need to risk their lives in service of their people with the slogan, "live for the country or die for freedom."[10,11]

In the coming years, violence waxed and waned, with the EZLN issuing red alerts to prepare for defense as needed.[12]

However, the Zapatistas persevered in solidarity with each other and the Earth, led by the Clandestine Revolutionary Indigenous Committee-General Command which oversaw the EZLN. They wanted a nation based on mutual respect, and they maintained this baseline of respect even during war.

No one was forced into military service. Each person was welcome to choose for themselves if they would risk their life in fighting.

Women played key roles from the beginning. Major Ana Maria led the Zapatistas in taking the town of San Cristóbal de las Casas in Chiapas and commander Ramona played a major part in the resulting peace dialog.[13]

They practiced a deep humility, not letting anyone feel like they were special or better than the rest because of their position. When describing their top military leader subcommander Marcos, major Ana María said, "Marcos, like all the members of the [core planning committee], knows nothing and is nothing. Marcos is just another representative…"[14] The top leader was even given the rank "subcommander" to remind everyone that he was subservient to the people.

After enduring many years of the Mexican authorities imposing laws on them, on January 1, 1994, the Zapatistas were ready to establish their own laws, ensuring that everyone would be respected. Among this first set of laws was the Revolutionary Women's Law.

Revolutionary Women's Law

During the founding of the Haudenosaunee Confederacy, a woman named Jigonsaseh played a key role, spreading the message of peace and coordinating with men to ensure the laws and leadership would take the women's needs into account.[15]

Two women, commander Ramona and commander Susana, played a similar role for the Zapatistas. For over four months they traveled to dozens of village assemblies and women's groups to hear women's perspectives and consider what laws would be appropriate. Each village had to vote and give its approval.[16,17]

At a meeting of the Clandestine Revolutionary Indigenous Committee, top leaders finalized the laws which would go into force immediately when the revolution began. Susana stated the women's expectations, including rights to education, family planning, choosing their marriage partner, holding leadership positions, and working and participating in the revolutionary struggle in whatever way they choose. After Susana finished speaking, other women leaders applauded. When the Committee unanimously approved the Revolutionary Women's Law, the women began to sing.[18,19]

There was still some sexism which other leaders helped stamp out. One man at this meeting said to another, "The good thing is that my wife doesn't understand Spanish, otherwise…" A major replied, "You're screwed because we're going to translate it into all the dialects."[20]

Years later, Sylvia Marcos went to find out whether the Zapatistas were upholding the Women's Law, publishing her findings in 2014. The women described their life before 1994 clearly: "The capitalists had us believing this idea… that women are not valuable." Another woman said, "The [women] suffered a lot before '94: humiliation, mistreatment, rape. But none of that ever mattered to the government… and neither to the landowners."[21]

Marcos encountered a deep humility. Instead of people speaking triumphantly, she found them speaking carefully about what they had achieved and what they hadn't, acknowledging their mistakes and how to fix them.

Regarding salaries, one woman noted, "Women have the same rights as men to receive the same salary."

Regarding family planning, a woman said, "We as women have the right to decide how to live in our homes and we have the right to decide with our partner how many children we can have and take care of… Before, the bad government in our villages would promote a lot of bad ideas, saying that women are worthless and that they have no right to speak."

Regarding women's right to participate in their communities and hold leadership positions, one woman said, "Here we are able to say that this is now being achieved…" Another woman said, "As women we have the same rights as men, we have the right to decide which duties we can carry out in the communities as we can now take up positions as [agents], [commissioners], and [promotors] of health, sexual reproduction… and education."

Regarding health care, one woman noted, "we see that some communities do have their health clinics. Where health clinics exist, it is not difficult to find the [women] in good health, and they can also find medical attention for their children there… In terms of feeding ourselves in our zone, our food is not far away from us."

Some women acknowledged disagreements with elders who continued to believe they should choose whom a young woman could marry. Some women thus did not exercise their right to choose for themselves. However, those who wished to choose their marriage partner could.

In some areas, women said progress was not yet fully satisfactory. One woman described how several women were taking charge in areas of education, health care, production, and defense, but "what we have accomplished has not been accomplished 100%."

Women still encountered some sexism where men would occasionally mock women leaders. Sexual assault can still happen, especially while traveling. However, one woman noted that troubles in her region are much less than she encounters farther away, saying, "in those organizations there are many problems of rape and mistreatment, while with us, Zapatistas, it is not that way because we are always explaining the Women's Law."

One woman summarized how they worked towards "something like a re-construction of humanity… another world is what we want… it is the struggle that we are all a part of, men and women, because it is not a struggle of women and it is not a struggle of men. When one speaks of a revolution, they go together, among men and women…"

Other Initial Policies

The Zapatistas put many other policies into force immediately on January 1, 1994.

They passed an agricultural law which preserved rivers, seas, and forests and began reforestation projects. It also canceled all peasants' debts to the government, capitalists, and foreigners. Anyone with more than about 120 acres of quality land would get to keep only that amount, and the rest would be made available to landless peasants to farm.[22] Thus the people who were previously rich would still have enough to take care of themselves, but they would not have more than they needed. All companies were required to provide free health care. Business owners were required to give shares to employees over time.[23]

This land redistribution was a crucial factor in the Zapatistas' success. When Arbenz became president of Guatemala in 1951, 2% of the people owned almost three-quarters of the land. When he worked to pass a law that redistributed just some of that land over the coming years, it was the richest individuals who worked to overthrow him and install a dictator who would protect their wealth in 1954.[24]

Selfishness and generosity do not mix well. So long as a nation maintains a profit economy, the rich will always work to undermine generous leaders. By quickly embracing a gift economy where people were not allowed to hoard unneeded wealth, the Zapatistas ensured that their generous leadership would not be undermined from within their own nation.

Home owners no longer owed property taxes. For people who had rented a home less than 15 years, rent was limited to 10% of income, and those who had rented longer owed no rent at all.[25]

There would now be no taxes due from laborers. A progressive taxation system was put in place for professionals and business owners. For small businesses and professionals, the law noted that people could pay a reduced tax if paying the full amount would affect their ability to do their work. All taxes went to local governing bodies to spend as they wished. The military would only receive funds sufficient to sustain the liberation efforts.[26]

Hoarding important products was outlawed, and considered sabotage and treason. Any business which tried to close down and remove its machinery forfeited that machinery, which would be taken over by the workers.[27]

All people were free to arm themselves and organize their own collective self-defense groups. Anybody could oversee their government to ensure it manifested the popular will.[28]

All prisoners were released except murderers, rapists, and drug trafficking bosses.[29] A new social security system ensured that all abandoned children, wounded veterans, retirees, and elders would be taken care of.[30]

Systems of Leadership and Service

The Zapatistas wanted to maintain a governance system that respected individual and local autonomy, and these systems of autonomous self-governance (anarchy) have changed over time. As of 2024, each village has a *Local Autonomous Government* (LAG) which Moisés described as "the core of all autonomy." Each of these is responsible for their own expenses, elections, and needs, and are subject to the will of the people who live there.[31] Anyone may participate in popular assemblies beginning at the age of 12.[32]

LAGs may send representatives to *Zapatista Collectives of Autonomous Government*. These collectives discuss shared concerns of health, agroecology, justice, commerce, and more. Moisés said clearly, "They are not authorities." Each collective has a director who can summon LAG representatives in an emergency.

The *Assemblies of Collectives of Zapatista Autonomous Governments* coordinate decisions, resource sharing, and defense at the highest levels, but these groups also have no authority and depend upon collectives who depend upon the village governments.[33]

The Zapatistas do not represent a single ethnicity and language. They include Tzeltal, Mam, Chol, Tojolabal, Tzotzil, and Zoque nations, many of which cannot easily speak with each other.[34] However, they use translators to communicate, making their solidarity even more impressive.[35]

People choose their leaders who acknowledge an obligation to unpaid work in service of their people. Any community may remove leaders who they do not find satisfactory. Their practice of "to command by obeying" ensures that leaders do not decide for their community, but act as its delegates and implement decisions made at local levels.[36]

All this ensures that the Zapatistas do not themselves become another unhealthy nation with a few people imposing law on the rest, while still collectively sharing resources and taking care of each other.

The Zapatistas acknowledged that they were experimenting, as Moisés said that "we are just learning and… it will take a while to get going well."[37]

They continue to experiment. One recent effort will remove some land from land ownership entirely. No government, person, or business will own it, but everybody will be responsible to protect it. They call it *land without papers*. Moisés summarized this by saying, "So, in those lands that are going to be defined, if they ask who owns that land or who is the owner, the answer will be: 'nobody's', that is, they are 'common.'" Families will safely keep their own land. For land returned to the commons, residents may farm it but must agree not to grow drugs, sell the land, or allow any business or industry onto it.[38]

The Struggle Continues

Ohki Forest moved to Chiapas in 1986 and got to witness the transformation the Zapatistas created. She noted that the Spanish and later Mexican governments had worked to separate local people from their traditions and memories, and they succeeded to the point that many did not know there had ever been a Spanish conquest.

Still, some had worked to keep their ancient knowledge alive, and subcommander Marcos' frequent public statements helped raise their consciousness further.[39]

One commander said, "Para todos, todo, para nosotros nada" – For everyone, everything; for us, nothing. They offer their gifts for the good of the group. This person acknowledged that being a Zapatista was difficult. They sometimes only have hard tortillas to eat, and sometimes they fall sick due to poor food. They often sleep on hard floors or can't sleep for days and nights. Their lives are often at risk. But this man said why they accept this: "As Zapatistas, we have been declared terrorists for simply wanting to live, for asking for food, for health care, for education. But for us, in the eyes of the true man and true woman, terrorism is greed, racism, hate, and war. For true change, we are ready to die with dignity, in resistance, instead of waiting to die from curable diseases and hunger."

The Zapatistas helped people to face that fear of punishment and choose to take a stand for dignity. They say that they do not just fight for themselves, but for all humanity, in the recognition that every action has countless consequences that ripple out in unseen ways. This recognition of the importance of each moment and each person's potential impact runs so deep that Ohki Forest overheard a Mayan woman tell her daughter, "Don't drop the broom carelessly like that, you can really affect a lot of people!"

The Zapatistas' struggle continues as I write in 2024. The Mexican government changed the Constitution to acknowledge some of the Zapatistas' concerns, but then failed to implement many of their laws.[40] Local landowners continue to coordinate with paramilitaries, police, and the military to fight the Zapatistas, disrupt their water sources, and steal their food.[41]

But the Zapatistas are committed to holding the healthy boundaries they have set. They uphold their external boundaries with fighting, continuing to protect themselves from abuse by outsiders. And they work to uphold their internal boundaries, their laws that ensure that people treat each other and the Earth respectfully.

One fighter noted, "We will always carry resistance and rebellion in our hearts, because we are guardians of Mother Earth, we are not the owners. The Earth is not ours, it belongs to all of us who fight for life. We were born in it, we live in it, we are going to take care of it and we are going to protect it – and if necessary, we will die for it."

Healthy nations are not only possible, they once existed all around the world, and in some areas they still exist today. The Zapatistas show that history isn't a one-way street where unhealthy nations always win out in the end. When enough people give their deepest love together and put the needs of the group over their own comforts, anything is possible.

How can those of us trapped in unhealthy nations embrace who we really are? Next, *Part 9 - Spiritual Healing - Recovering from Our Multi-Millennia Catastrophe* digs deep into emotional and spiritual wounds so that we can fully understand how unhealthy nations continue on generation after generation, and how we can choose a different path instead.

Part 9 - Spiritual Healing: Recovering from Our Multi-Millennia Catastrophe

A lot of people seem unsatisfied with their unhealthy nation. If so many people are unsatisfied, why do unhealthy nations continue to persist, generation after generation, for centuries or even millennia?

Chapter 41: The Deepest Lessons From Thousands of Years of Spiritual Leaders

Throughout history, unhealthy nations have deliberately made it difficult to learn from our greatest spiritual leaders. Instead of recognizing their wisdom and following their lead, rulers and authorities, both religious and secular, have repeatedly blocked, silenced, and often killed the many spiritual guides who have tried to help their people.

Many spiritual leaders have taught many helpful lessons, but there are a few deep lessons that unhealthy nations repeatedly fail to learn. The life stories of Black Elk, Jesus Christ, and Martin Luther King Jr illustrate the deepest lessons from thousands of years of countless spiritual leaders all around the world.

Black Elk

Black Elk was a Lakota man born in 1863. He noted that when he was young, the nonhumans and humans lived happily together, and "there was plenty for them and for us." However, white people had recently found gold in their homeland and more people were constantly arriving in violation of past treaties with the US government.[1]

Black Elk heard voices from an early age but did not understand them, and he forgot about them when they went away. At age nine, he fell unconscious for 12 days, and during this time he had a tremendous vision where great spirits came to him. Some of these spirits appeared as Grandfathers which represented different powers of the world, and he saw many deep and beautiful things.

In one segment, Black Elk said, "Then I was standing on the highest mountain of them all, and round about beneath me was the whole hoop of the world. And while I stood there I saw more than I can tell and I understood more than I saw; for I was seeing in a sacred manner the shapes of all things in the spirit, and the shape of all shapes as they must live together like one being. And I saw that the sacred hoop of my people was one of many hoops that made one circle, wide as daylight and as starlight, and in the center grew one mighty flowering tree to shelter all the children of one mother and one father. And I saw that it was holy." In other parts of his vision he learned how he could help his people live in that sacred way.

Black Elk woke up and knew he'd had a powerful vision but did not know how to share it. For years he had a nagging understanding that he had something beautiful and important to share with his people, but he worried they would not receive it. As he grew into his teen years, the American military became more and more aggressive in their land, and Black Elk fought many battles with other warriors to protect his people. He repeatedly found that he had great spiritual powers, sometimes seeing the future or understanding things which happened at great distances. He kept recognizing he had a great gift, and wanted to share his vision, but he kept holding it back. Some Lakota went on the government reservation and left again, wanting to escape the endless military aggression but repulsed by the American government's broken promises. Times were getting very difficult.

By age 16, he heard the voices more and more, yet he still felt unsure what to do. He felt increased pressure to share his vision, but he did not know how. Crows and coyotes called to him saying, "It is time! It is time!" The daybreak star sang to him, "In a sacred manner you shall walk! Your nation shall behold you!"

Black Elk finally confided in a man named Black Road. Black Road told him he must perform his vision, and if he did not, "something very bad will happen to you."

Black Road, Black Elk's parents, and many others helped prepare a huge enactment of Black Elk's vision. They memorized songs from it, hunted extra to feed people, painted special patterns on their homes and collected many horses and other items from the vision. When it was all ready, the entire community gathered and many of them collectively acted out core parts of the vision, with dozens of people and horses having specific roles. By the end, nobody was passively watching, but everybody was singing the songs, joining the dancing, or somehow part of the event.

Black Elk said, "After the horse dance was over, it seemed that I was above the ground and did not touch it when I walked. I felt very happy, for I could see that my people were all happier. Many crowded around me and said that they or their relatives who had been feeling sick were well again, and these gave me many gifts. Even the horses seemed to be healthier and happier after the dance."

Black Elk's people not only welcomed his spiritual gift, they enacted his vision to manifest its deepest lessons, and this was healing. They welcomed their spiritual leader, and remarkably, no one in Black Elk's nation killed him.

Jesus Christ

Chapter 8 reviewed how Jesus Christ was actually a revolutionary leader trying to free his people from oppression and selfishness. Amazingly, there is even more to learn from his story!

Christ was born to a poor Jewish family in the Roman empire about 2,000 years ago, a time when Jews were oppressed by Romans.

While the Bible hints that Christ was already impressive at a young age, the story of his personal transformation and the beginning of his ministry starts with his baptism in a river by a man named John. Feeling divine inspiration, Jesus went into the wilderness and ate nothing for forty days and faced all the demons in his heart – that is, all the temptations which might sway him from walking his divine path.

Many spiritual leaders have cultivated themselves through extended fasts in the wilderness. This allows them to find in their heart their purpose for being alive, and to confront the temptations to avoid that sacred purpose. In other words, it helps them recognize their sacred gifts.

During this time, Christ recognized his divine path as a minister and confronted all manner of temptations, personified in the Bible as the devil. Christ felt tempted by great wealth or political power, but recognized this was not in service of God, and became strengthened in walking his divine path. Still alone in the wilderness, Christ felt tempted to seek proof of God, for how could a person know anything without proof? And in rejecting this temptation, Christ surrendered to his faith, and this faith became unshakable.[2]

Having recognized his divine path, Christ fully acknowledged and confronted his temptations until each one evaporated and deterred him no more. Even though the Jews were looking for a king to free them from Roman rule[3], Christ chose not to make any demands of God and not to become a king, but rather to *have faith and to act in service*.

Christ began his ministry at the age of about 30 and quickly started attracting large crowds.[4] He healed and fed many people, even breaking the law to do so. Once Christ healed a man's wounded hand on the sabbath while priests watched. Everyone knew this act of healing violated their religious laws, but Jesus acknowledged the law was wrong when he said, "Is it lawful to do good on the sabbath days, or to do evil, to save life, or to kill?"

Christ's willingness to ignore the law in order to do good work threatened religious leaders' authority, so they began plotting with government agents against him.[5]

Christ continued his preaching work while healing and feeding thousands. Huge crowds gathered around the man with so much love and vast wisdom to share. Christ knew that his work increasingly threatened the legitimacy of religious and government authorities, and he knew they would eventually kill him. The Bible says, "And [Jesus] began to teach them, that [he] must suffer many things, and be rejected ... and be killed..."[6]

Christ repeatedly pointed out that his death was approaching even as he continued to do good work. The Bible says that Jesus told his followers: "The son of man [Jesus] is delivered into the hands of men, and they shall kill him..."[7] As Christ approached Jerusalem, he acknowledged his upcoming death again, even suggesting his followers plan for his burial.[8] When Mary anointed Christ with expensive perfume, Judas asked if she should have sold it, and Christ said, "Leave her alone, so that she may keep it for the day of my burial."[9]

Despite seeing his death approaching, Christ's full commitment to his divine path carried him onwards. Growing increasingly angry with the exploitation he saw all around him, he openly attacked predatory moneylenders in the temple, saying, "Is it not written, My house shall be called of all nations the house of prayer? but ye have made it a den of thieves." Again the Bible says, "the scribes and chief priests heard it, and sought how they might destroy him: for they feared him, because all the people was astonished at his doctrine."[10]

Both Christ and the authorities knew what was coming, yet Christ chose to continue his divine work anyway. The authorities behaved predictably. They arrested, mocked, tortured, and killed Jesus Christ. At his trial, witnesses could not agree on important details, but Christ was accused of "subverting our nation. He opposes payment of taxes to Caesar and claims to be Messiah, a king,"[11] The accuser clearly could not imagine a leader who was not a king, assuming Christ must have wanted to be a ruler even though Christ had rejected being a king during his time in the wilderness. Still, Christ did not deny the accusation. His accuser said, "What further need do we have of witnesses? You have heard the blasphemy! What do you think?"[12]

It is clear to me that Jesus Christ was killed because the Romans saw him as a threat to their authority.

But there is more to the story than this.

Dominance Displays

Christ was recognized as a revolutionary and a threat to the Roman state, and so the Romans didn't just kill him, they killed him in a particularly gruesome way. He was nailed through his hands to a wooden post and left to die in a very visible public place. The Romans wanted to deter anyone who admired Christ from following in his footsteps.

This is a *dominance display*, where authorities remind victims that they can act abusively at will. The purpose is to scare victims into compliance. Many Jews were showing their great love for their neighbors by seeking freedom from Roman rule, and the Romans threatened them with extreme violence so they would withhold their love and stop fighting for freedom.

One painting[13] shows how intimidating crucifixion could be, as many political activists' bodies were left to rot on the sides of roads.

Roman authorities left crucified revolutionaries along roads to scare everyone else into submission.

After I understood the Romans' intention behind publicly torturing Christ to death, I began to see other dominance displays in many places throughout history.

I saw slaveowners whipping slaves just to establish that they could. I saw prison guards beating up prisoners who dared stand up for themselves in prison. I saw kings and billionaires publicly disobey their own laws just to show that they can.

Whenever I see an unhealthy cultural pattern from another time and place, I look for where that pattern might be playing out in my own nation. Where are dominance displays commonly occuring in unhealthy nations today?

In healthy nations, when someone behaves inappropriately, people respond in a simple way: they gather in a group, decide what is going on and how to respond, and then work together to address the trouble.

In contrast, when rich people behave inappropriately in socialist Venezuela, and people gather to address it, they see this:

Riot Police in Venezuela[14]

In communist China, they see this:

Riot Police in China[15]

And in the capitalist United States, they see this:

Riot Police in the United States[16]

Riot police are the modern dominance display. Whether they brutalize protesters, arrest protesters to be brutalized in prison, or just stand around looking scary, the underlying intention is clear: to scare people into tolerating inappropriate behavior and obeying abusive authorities. Since standing for a culture of mutual respect and addressing inappropriate behavior is an act of deep love, in spiritual terms, the role of riot police is to scare people into withholding their love.

To understand the deep spiritual implications of dominance displays and Jesus Christ's death, it helps to look at the story of another spiritual leader who shared much in common with Jesus Christ: Martin Luther King Jr.

Martin Luther King Jr

Martin Luther King Jr was a black man born in 1929 in the highly segregated US south. King began his social activism in 1955, the same year he graduated from Boston University School of Theology, began his ministry, and had his first child with his wife Coretta.

King helped organize the Montgomery Bus Boycott which demanded that all bus passengers be treated with equal respect, regardless of skin color. Many of the black participants were attacked and even shot, including a pregnant woman shot in both legs.

King's house was bombed along with several black churches and homes of other leaders. He was arrested for driving 30 mph in a 25mph zone, another act of intimidation.[17,18]

While continuing to preach at church, King kept working towards racial desegregation by supporting the Atlanta lunch counter sit-in movement and a campaign in Birmingham. At one march, people were assaulted with police attack dogs and firehoses.[19] At another event in Chicago, King wrote, "Our marchers were met by a hailstorm of bricks, bottles and firecrackers."[20] The US federal police (FBI) began surveilling him and sent anonymous threats.[21] In September 1958, King was stabbed and nearly died.[22]

Like Jesus Christ, King continued on his divine path despite knowing that his life was at risk. He expanded his focus to include confronting US imperialism. In a famous speech in 1967, he acknowledged the perspective of the Vietnamese who wanted to choose how to live for themselves without American military occupation. He called out the hypocrisy of an American government that talked about freedom but imposed its will on foreigners.[23]

Like Christ, Martin Luther King Jr drew huge crowds. He received five honorary degrees, and in 1963 he was named Time Magazine's "Man of the Year." A year later he received the Nobel Peace Prize and met with the pope.[24]

Like Christ, King began to recognize he would soon be killed, but he continued on with his divine work. He boarded an airplane to fly to Memphis, Tennessee to support a worker's strike, but his plane was delayed due to a bomb threat.[25] Eventually he arrived, and on the night before he died, he gave a speech and said, "And some began to say the threats, or talk about the threats that were out. What would happen to me from some of our sick white brothers? Well, I don't know… it doesn't matter with me now… Longevity has its place. But I'm not concerned about that now. I just want to do God's will."[26]

King knew his time was short, but like Jesus Christ, he would not be deterred from his divine path in service of those he loved. The next day, on April 4, 1968, a sniper murdered Martin Luther King Jr. The government arrested and convicted James Earl Ray for this act, but a great deal of evidence indicated that someone else had actually killed Martin Luther King Jr.

In the following decades, activists were able to gather copious evidence that the US government had killed Martin Luther King Jr, and they presented their case at a civil trial in Memphis, Tennessee in 1999. Because they could not sue government officials directly, King's family sued a private citizen named Loyd Jowers as well as "Other Unknown Co-conspirators." Loyd Jowers had admitted he was involved in King's death, and these "unknown" co-conspirators were the police and intelligence agencies that couldn't be sued directly in court. The purpose of the trial was simply for the King family to publicly share evidence that the federal police and intelligence agencies had coordinated with local police to execute Martin Luther King Jr.[27]

Trial evidence showed that the defendant, Jowers, had said in a recorded meeting that he had helped plan King's death with the Memphis police department. Several witnesses testified that the sniper was on the ground, not in a balcony as the police claimed, and police never gathered these witnesses' testimony. The scope on the supposed murder weapon was not sighted, so as judge Joe Brown said, it "literally could not have hit the broadside of a barn." Also metallurgical tests indicated that the bullet which killed King had a different metallic composition than those in James Earl Ray's supposed murder weapon.

The civil trial court ruled in favor of the Kings, agreeing that the evidence indicated that Jowers and "Unknown Co-conspirators" had indeed killed Martin Luther King Jr.

Authorities Admit One of Their Goals: to "Prevent the Rise of a Messiah"

Both Christ and King were killed by their governments. Unlike Christ, Martin Luther King Jr was not killed in a dominance display. However, something else connects their deaths.

I'm not the first person to compare Martin Luther King Jr and Jesus Christ. The United States federal police, the FBI, actually made the comparison between King and Christ in an official secret memorandum as part of COINTELPRO ("COunter-INTELligence PROgram") which officially ran from 1956-1971:

> Goals
>
> For maximum effectiveness of the Counterintelligence Program, and to prevent wasted effort, long-range goals are being set…
>
> 2. ***Prevent the RISE OF A "MESSIAH"*** *who could unify, and electrify, the militant black nationalist movement. Malcolm X might have been such a "messiah;" he is the martyr of the movement today. Martin Luther King, Stokely Carmichael and Elijah Muhammed all aspire to this position. Elijah Muhammed is less of a threat because of his age. King could be a very real contender for this position should he abandon his supposed "obedience" to "white, liberal doctrines" (nonviolence) and embrace black nationalism. Carmichael has the necessary charisma to be a real threat in this way.*[28] [emphasis added]

In this memo, the director of the police, J Edgar Hoover, strategized how to prevent a Christ-like figure ("messiah") from arising and speculated on possible candidates. The FBI was clear that it was playing the part of the Roman state opposed to the spirit of Christ.

I do not consider the US police to be unusually oppressive. Police forces around the world openly acknowledge a goal of "maintaining order," meaning maintaining control. What could be more disruptive of the social order than someone who leads their people to freedom? After all, the word "messiah" simply means "savior" or "liberator."[29] Thus, I see police forces in authoritarian nations around the world engaging in similar anti-messiah, anti-liberator activity.

This shows that unhealthy nations are the Antichrist in a very literal sense. As the FBI memo clearly demonstrates, unhealthy nations seek to eliminate Christ-like figures or messiahs or prevent them from arising.

The Deepest Lessons From Thousands of Years of Spiritual Leaders

For me, these stories of Black Elk, Jesus Christ, and Martin Luther King Jr collectively clarify the deepest lessons from thousands of years of spiritual leaders.

- *Healthy nations embrace their spiritual leaders*: Black Elk's story, as well as stories from many other healthy nations, shows that healthy human nations embrace their spiritual leaders.

- *Unhealthy nations kill or neutralize their spiritual leaders*: In contrast, unhealthy authoritarian nations kill, imprison, drug, or otherwise neutralize their spiritual leaders, the ones who give their deepest love in service of their people.

- *Authorities scare people into withholding their love*: Authorities use dominance displays to scare potential spiritual leaders into holding back so that they will not seek to end the rulers' abuses. In other words, authorities scare people into withholding their love. This is the spiritual tragedy at the heart of every unhealthy nation.

A spiritual leader is anyone who sees that their people are struggling or somehow not walking a divine path and helps them get back on track. Spiritual leaders may help people remember their divine nature and their rightful place in divine Creation. Spiritual leaders commonly build people's self-worth, self-confidence and willingness to stand up for themselves and others. They may also coordinate efforts to share resources and stand up to abuse. Helping their oppressed people end the abuse is a key way that spiritual leaders give their love.

For people to give their love by seeking to end the authoritarian abuse is strictly forbidden and heavily punished in unhealthy nations. Anyone who wishes to protect their people from threats may join the police or military, but they must follow their rulers' orders or face severe punishment. Nobody is allowed to stand for a culture of mutual respect in unhealthy nations.

This illustrates how laws and law enforcement work by breaking people's integrity. How many people would act in deep service of their people if they weren't scared into submission? Dominance displays train people not to show that integrity of service, focusing on their own comfort and safety instead.

I believe the path to freedom for any group will involve many people giving their love fully, even at great personal risk. Unfortunately, dominance displays are not the biggest obstacle.

It takes a lot of work to scare open-hearted adults into closing their hearts and withholding their love. I believe authorities thus find it helpful to train children from a young age to withhold their love. Additionally, parents with deep spiritual wounds can easily unintentionally pass them on to their children. As a result, many children in unhealthy nations learn to withhold their love from a young age, minimizing the number of adults willing to stand up to end the abusive relationships at the heart of their unhealthy nation.

How do nations train children to give or withhold their love? And how can adults train children to give their love fully instead? Some key patterns are revealed next in *Chapter 42: Training Children to Give or Withhold Love, Part 1*.

Chapter 42: Training Children to Give or Withhold Love, Part 1

Chapter 21 showed how people who are subject to endless abuse can ultimately adopt very hurtful attitudes.

The reason is simple. Although living with an open heart and giving one's love fully feels deeply satisfying, and closing one's heart and withholding love feels terrible, when authorities punish open-hearted, loving behavior for long enough, it can ultimately feel less painful to close one's heart and withhold love in order to numb the pain.

Many patterns of child-rearing in unhealthy nations train children to close their hearts starting at a young age. Of course, there is tremendous variability among people. Different nations in different eras may treat children differently. Different families and teachers within a nation treat their children differently. And each child responds to adults' behavior in their own ways.

Some people, such as Jesus Christ or Harriet Tubman, managed to live with their hearts wide open throughout adulthood. Many people close their hearts in various ways to various degrees, finding ways to give some amount of love some of the time. And tragically, many people close their hearts tight and act hurtfully indeed.

Heart-closure is also not permanent. Some people can learn to open their hearts later in life, whereas others may close their hearts even tighter over time.

With so much variability, there are no abusive child-rearing patterns that apply to everyone. But there are many patterns that apply to large groups of people in each nation, and of course a child is often subject to many kinds of abuse.

Child abuse, intentional or not, is key to allowing unhealthy nations to continue generation after generation. Children raised in a respectful manner typically grow up recognizing their abusive nation as inappropriate, as a few examples in this chapter show. Children raised in a disrespectful manner can become used to disrespect, and their abusive nation can easily seem "just how life is."

Below are some common patterns of child abuse that train children to close their hearts.

Loving Touch and the Consequences of Going Without It

Human babies are born needing loving touch, and studies show that this desire for touch is common among many animals.

Research shows that monkeys reared in isolation have significantly less brain complexity compared with those raised in a colony.[1] A 1922 study found that rats raised without touch were more apprehensive, high-strung, and timid, and had lower survival rates in surgery. Other studies have shown significantly less weight-gain in unstimulated rats compared to those who receive stimulation. Even microscopic nematodes benefit from touch, with those raised in isolation showing smaller body sizes, reduced responses to stimuli, and delayed onset of egg-laying.[2]

Babies are born with a wide open heart, giving their deepest love. "Giving my deepest love" simply means "being myself," and babies are born being themselves without holding back. They are fully present, sensually aware, curious, and playful. They are fully authentic, expressing exactly how they feel.

Babies desire deep connection and pleasure through loving touch. When babies get loving touch, they feel safe and learn that life feels basically pleasurable, that life welcomes them as they are. In other words, life welcomes their love.

Unfortunately, many parents learn not to touch their babies much. Some parents severely deprive their babies of loving touch, or touch them very hurtfully. Studies of monkeys reared without any loving touch, and without any physical violence, show the profoundly negative effects this can have.

In their landmark studies, Harry and Margaret Harlow at the University of Wisconsin raised infant monkeys from birth. Some monkeys were raised in cages so that they could see and hear other monkeys but not touch them. Other monkeys were raised together with some adults. In one experiment, eight-month-old monkeys were then brought together to share the same cage.

The following picture shows the result:

Monkeys Reared in Isolation and Together[3]

Left: *Two eight-month-old monkeys raised in isolation avoid touching and social interaction.*
Right: *Two normally reared monkeys touch and cuddle one another.*

When the two monkeys reared in isolation could finally touch each other, they still chose not to. Monkeys raised with loving touch happily touched each other.

I believe the monkeys raised in isolation essentially learned to close their hearts. They wanted loving touch so badly, but that desire was continuously unmet. To numb the pain of their unmet desire, I think they learned to ignore their desire for connection and touch, and they suppressed that desire so deeply that they continued not to touch other monkeys even when they had the chance.

Desire generates an emotional tension in the body, and under normal circumstances, this is healthy. When a person or any animal desires food, they feel an urge to eat and then feel relaxed as they eat. When someone desires connection, they feel an urge to connect with others and then relax when they can finally have that time with friends or family.

But what would happen if that desire went continually unmet? What would happen if a person wanted something so badly, but was continually unable to find satisfaction? The desire can start to hurt as the tension builds, but the tension and pain just keep increasing as the desire is never satisfied. Eventually, the *unfulfilled desire itself can become scary or unwanted* because it brings so much pain.

I believe this is what happened to these isolation-reared monkeys. They had a perfectly normal desire for touch in early childhood that continually went unmet. Going without touch for so long became painful, and the pain only mounted over time as they were continually denied loving touch.

How did the monkeys respond to the endless, mounting pain of their continually unmet desire for loving touch? The desire itself started to seem like a scary, dangerous, or alien thing that only led to suffering. In other words, the unmet desire itself started to seem like a problem or source of pain, and so they learned to hold back or ignore their desire.

The photo shows the result: the isolation-reared monkeys on the left are choosing to be as far apart from each other as the cage will allow. They were so used to ignoring their own desire that they did not even touch each other when they finally had the chance.

These isolation-reared monkeys are deeply hurt, and I believe that loving touch could be deeply healing for them, and yet they reject that healing touch because of a deep-seated emotional resistance they learned as infants, despite being well nourished and raised in physically safe and clean environments.

This is a tragic response many animals can experience when they have a desire that continually goes unmet, or a threat or other challenge to which they do not know how to effectively respond. *The feeling, urge, or perception itself can start to seem like a problem or source of pain, and the animal can learn to fear, ignore or reject that part of themselves as a way of numbing the pain.*

What does this look like when it happens in humans?

When Humans Learn to Reject Their Own Desire for Pleasure and Connection

In a study called *True Americanism*, David Mantell interviewed 25 male American soldiers who volunteered for special fighting missions in Vietnam. Based on extensive questioning, investigators characterized the large majority of these soldiers' childhood families as "cold," "emotionally isolated," "tense," "overbearing," and almost all could be called "hard," "conformistic," "autocratic," and "intolerant."[4]

When Mantell asked about the soldiers' first sexual experiences, he learned that "the first act of sexual intercourse was emotionally and interpersonally insignificant to nearly all the boys." Only 5 out of 25 had any kind of emotional response. Of these five, two felt satisfied, one felt disappointed, and two of these five men felt disgust at their first sex.

These soldiers described any sort of deepening relationship as a "burden" from which they tried to free themselves. They commonly engaged in superficial and fleeting relationships, or exploited others. Five soldiers were on their second marriage, and none of these men could explain why they had married their first wife. None of these men said they had ever loved their first wife, and several were unsure of their feelings for their second wife.

Many of these men engaged with prostitutes, and they noted a distinct lack of connection and pleasure. One soldier said, "Pleasurable? In a sense it was and in a sense it was disgusting because it was just, you know, you never thought too much of the girls themselves." The soldier explained that it only takes five minutes each time, and it "only takes a couple of times to get used to it and then it doesn't bother you after that."

These men also developed a severe double standard, explicitly stating it was ok for men to be sexually promiscuous but labeling sexually active women as "sluts, whores, easy lay," and "nymphomaniac."[5] Investigators found that "Superficiality and insincerity were the only stable emotional features of their response to women. There were almost no indications of guilt, embarrassment, reflection or self-criticism in their accounts of their activities."[6]

The interviews also showed that these men who didn't feel deep pleasure and connection were very likely to obey their authority figures. When asked about patriotism, these soldiers said things like

- "all people can't serve in high places and somebody has got to be the cog in the wheel…"[7]

- "I'll support my country, right or wrong…"

- "many people have got their thumb in the pie over there. That's definitely the case. But whatever happens, I'll stick by them…"

- "I don't really consider myself too patriotic… I hate politics… Regardless of why we're fighting, it doesn't matter to me why we're fighting or where we're fighting. It's my job as a soldier. I'm professional."

In other words, these soldiers willingly obeyed the orders of corrupt, self-serving leaders. These men weren't standing for anything. Their own sense of right and wrong was muted. Their heart was closed, and so they didn't hear its divine voice. Is it any surprise that so many rulers and their authoritarian religions would discourage pleasure and deep connection and encourage moralistic, deprived or abusive childhoods for thousands of years?

Humans are born attuning to others, and those who receive loving touch learn to attune deeply. People can know each other in a deep way when each is attuned to the other. When two people are attuned, each person's feelings inspire feelings in the other. They can know each other through their eyes and have an energetic exchange that yields a deep connection without words. When children do not get this touch, this attunement can become severely stunted. David Mantell noted, "Either [these soldiers] could not or were not willing to give a genuine response to another person's pain or love."[8]

None of the soldiers came from an impoverished background. They had parents who emphasized morality, religion, and education. After in-depth interviews, Mantell summarized these soldiers' parents as people who were "intent on raising law-abiding, hard-working citizens and executed their responsibility as they understood it."[9]

Many of the soldiers described other kinds of childhood abuse beyond a lack of loving touch. Many also suffered beatings and other physical and verbal abuse.

Some people respond to this with more resilience than others, and some people are able to heal. But overall, the connection is clear: children denied deep connection and loving touch can close their hearts tight and may later struggle to feel connection and pleasure in adulthood. Many become so disconnected from their own feelings and urges that they don't even know what they're missing.

Just like the monkeys who resisted loving touch when they could finally have it, these soldiers resisted deep relationships as a "burden," preferring superficiality instead.

Some soldiers even had radically unhealthy perspectives on love. One American marine named Michael McCusker (not part of the True Americanism study) gave testimony about a group of soldiers pursuing a Vietnamese woman into a village. He said they tracked her down, but instead of arresting her, every man in the squad raped her. He said, "they raped the girl, and then, the last man to make love to her, shot her in the head."

McCusker wasn't the only one to equate rape with making love. McCusker said, "one man said to me later that it was the first time he had ever made love to a woman with his boots on."[10] While I am unaware of McCusker's upbringing, this confusion about rape and love-making shows how deeply unfeeling a person can become.

This unfeeling attitude toward rape is also not a recent phenomenon. 19th-century American soldiers on the frontier had a common saying: "indian women rape easy."[11]

Chapter 25 showed how many religious teachers in authoritarian nations have discouraged men from feeling deep pleasure and encouraged people to either avoid sex or have sex without pleasure. Many men in unhealthy nations have been trained to see women as evil or inferior. These soldiers' stories show one way this works out in practice. *An abusive childhood trains people to live out the unpleasurable, disconnecting patterns that religious authorities have said they wanted for thousands of years.*

These male soldiers demonstrate a disgust with women, a disgust that dates back to ancient times. Almost 2,000 years ago, Christian saint Augustine proclaimed, "There is nothing which degrades the manly spirit more than the attractiveness of females and contact with their bodies."[12] Augustine is widely considered one of the most influential Christian theologians in history.[13,14] This disgust that some men feel towards women and pleasure is a recurring theme in unhealthy nations, and a major cause is child abuse. The ones who close their hearts the most are then primed to take positions of authority in unhealthy nations that elevate the most closed-hearted.

Girls can likewise develop tragic pathologies when deprived of loving touch and abused in other ways in childhood. Harlow noticed that female monkeys who never felt affectionate touch in their first year became "ineffective, inadequate, and brutal mothers." Researchers saw that the mothers' offspring would die if researchers did not step in to feed them. Five of these mother-monkeys, who were raised without affectionate touch, violently attacked their babies when they reached out for maternal contact, hitting, kicking, or crushing their babies. The other two "motherless mother" monkeys were indifferent and one acted as if her offspring did not exist.[15]

People deprived of loving touch during infancy and childhood can develop an aversion to touch, and these people may not experience even affectionate touch as pleasurable. This can be very difficult to overcome in adulthood, especially in an unhealthy nation, and easy to pass on to the next generation.

Research at the University of Colorado investigated three generations of families that abused their children. They consistently found that in abusive families, the parents had been deprived of physical affection as children. Both mothers' and fathers' sex lives were poor. In fact, almost none of the abusive mothers had ever experienced an orgasm.[16]

One researcher in another study noted, "The parent who lacks mothering herself is incapable of mothering her child but expects the child to be capable of loving her; she expects far more than a baby is capable of and she sees its crying as rejection." He interviewed one mother he described as educated and intelligent, asking why she beat her child. Her response shows just how disconnected even a mother can be from her own baby. She said, "When he cried, it meant he didn't love me. So I hit him."[17]

Child Abuse Trains Children for a Very Negative Outlook on Life

These tragic responses to abusive childhoods show that authorities aren't necessarily intentionally lying when they spread hurtful attitudes about people's inherent badness or the evils of pleasure. I believe at least some authorities honestly hold these hurtful attitudes because they are so common among people who were abused as children and learned to close their hearts.

This shows why it is often so ineffective for people to appeal to their rulers' sense of integrity and decency. I suspect that often, it's not that rulers recognize everyone's inherent goodness and deliberately lie to spread stories of inherent badness. I think many authorities really do believe in people's inherent badness, again because this is a common attitude among people abused as children.

The children of the rich[18] and royalty[19] may especially demonstrate these patterns of abuse and heart-closure from a very young age. Ottoman sultan Mustafa I ruled in the early 1600s and cruelly executed many people in his own government. He had spent many years of his early childhood trapped in a windowless room known as *The Cage*. It only makes sense that the most abusive people – the rulers who exploit everyone else – commonly also raise their own children abusively.

While not all abused children respond the same way, a severely abusive childhood does predispose a person to having very hurtful attitudes and deep selfishness in adulthood.

Healthy humans are supposed to find life basically pleasurable. Frustrations or painful injuries may arise, but the basic default attitude is one of joyful pleasure. But when children suffer deeply enough, life can seem basically unpleasurable. Displeasure, suffering, or dissatisfaction can become many people's default attitude or experience.

This attitude that life is basically unpleasurable is present in many authoritarian leaders. As seen earlier in Chapter 6, rich businessman Kevin O'Leary wanted to force lifelong unemployment on anyone who protests in support of Palestinians facing Israeli violence. When asked whether it is fair to punish someone their whole lives for a single act of protest, he said, "Life is hard, then you die." I do not know anything about O'Leary's childhood, but this illustrates that attitude that life is basically unpleasurable or unsatisfying.[20]

This contrasts starkly with a story from the Yequana who emphasize deep pleasure and connection from early childhood. Jean Liedloff noticed that women would walk to the river for water several times a day, bringing a pot and often a little child. They had to walk down steep rocks each time, and it seemed very inefficient when they could just make larger pots and make the trip less often. But Liedloff noticed that the women always went in groups of two or more, and "always a party mood prevailed." They would bathe daily, and "the bath had a Roman quality of luxuriousness. Every move bespoke sensual enjoyment, and the babies were handled like objects so marvelous that their owners felt constrained to put a mock-modest face on their pleasure and pride." These women walked into the stream in a way that "would have done credit to a Miss World coming forward to claim her crown."[21]

As Liedloff reflected on this, she could not imagine a better way for the women to use water-fetching time. They could have been more efficient and traveled fewer times, but they didn't need more efficiency. They enjoyed the time, each woman and baby in their own way. The Yequana mothers raised their babies to feel deep sensual pleasure and connection as a normal part of daily life, and the adults showed none of these disturbing patterns associated with chronic lack of pleasure and connection.

What Effects Do Deep Emotional and Spiritual Wounds Have on People's Behavior and Ability to Get Along?

Countless people have discussed politics with neighbors and come away feeling unsatisfied. It seems like some people have very different outlooks on life, or very different assumptions, or only care about some facts and not others. When two people agree on their values and only disagree on facts, it may be simple enough to investigate and figure out the truth. When people have profoundly different values, it can be really hard to find common ground.

Different childhood experiences train people to have very different values in adulthood. While anyone may heal from their wounds, hurtful childhoods predispose people to embracing very hurtful attitudes and practices.

Humans desire affectionate touch, and when they don't get it for long enough, they develop an emotional tension similar to the monkeys. This tension is perfectly healthy; it's what causes people to want to come together when they are apart. In a healthy person, this tension manifests as an urge to seek loving touch with another person. When two loving people come together and hug, they feel relaxed – because the tension is gone.

In people who have suffered childhood deprivation or other abuse, some learn not to seek out pleasurable connection, but instead relieve the tension with compensatory behaviors like alcoholism, drug abuse, physical violence, and more. After years of deprivation and unhappiness, people can learn not to notice the tension or even recognize what they are missing, minimizing the pain they feel from a continual lack of deep connection with others.[22]

Chronic Lack of Pleasure and Support for Pathological Violence

People who support violence as a default response to problems commonly prefer alcohol and drugs over sexual pleasures. They also tend to become aggressive and violent while drinking alcohol. In contrast, those with a satisfactory sex life and who received a great deal of affection as children tend not to act violently while under alcohol's influence.[23]

Chronic lack of physical pleasure and a person's support for pathological violence are closely related. James Prescott researched this connection and found that people who believed that "Physical punishment and pain help build a strong moral character" and "Violence is necessary to really solve our problems" were also likely to think that prostitution should be punished, nudity is harmful to children, responsible pre-marital sex is bad, and sexual pleasures weaken people's character.

In other words, people who support unnecessary violence and punishment also tend to oppose nudity, sexual pleasure, and unapproved sexual relationships, and all of these attitudes are correlated with child abuse or deprivation.

Pleasure and pathological violence are incompatible, and various nonhuman animal studies show this. Laboratory experiments have shown that extremely violent animals will calm down when the pleasure centers of their brain are stimulated by electrodes. Many experiments have shown that isolation-reared monkeys are prone to pathological violence. These cruel experiments shine light on the cruelty that many humans show to each other in unhealthy nations.[24]

When People Suffer Different Amounts of Child Abuse, Deep Unity Becomes Extremely Difficult

The *True Americanism* study also illustrates how challenging it can be to find deep political unity when different people have vastly different outlooks on life. In addition to studying the 25 male American soldiers who voluntarily fought in Vietnam, Mantell studied 15 American men who consciously worked to stop the war effort, with several even going to prison for taking a stand. Overwhelmingly, their interviews showed a childhood family life that was "warm," "friendly," "gentle," "tolerant," and "nonviolent."[25,26]

The resisters' willingness to take a stand against an inappropriate war was not the only thing that distinguished the war resisters from the war volunteers. As adults, in contrast to the volunteer soldiers who had mostly grown up in "cold" and "hard" homes, these resisters valued sexual relationships based on sharing, sensitivity, and self-restraint. The men who did not exhibit these qualities in early sexual encounters expressed regret and believed that they had lost out on chances for personal growth. Many described having learned deep lessons from women sexual partners, including how to relate to people and enjoy companionship, to "enjoy life," to "treat each person as an individual," to be "compassionate," and to "share." All accepted sexual pleasure as legitimate, and rejected one-sided sexual liaisons because they sought deeper purpose in these sexual encounters.[27,28]

All this illustrates one reason why it's so challenging to find unity in unhealthy nations. Not everyone experiences the same abuses, with some abuses being rare, others common, and some almost universal. But if some people honestly believe that rape and love-making are the same, and others see rape and love-making as very different, how are they supposed to agree on anything?

People's worldviews can be radically different, not just because they have learned different facts, but because their deepest sensory experiences of the world are profoundly different. When pleasure and connection are attractive to some and disgusting to others, is it any surprise that political unity is hard to achieve?

Both Individuals And Whole Nations Can Reject Deep Healing

Babies and children may cope with severe suffering by repressing their desire for pleasure and connection. *Self-repression can feel like safety because it numbs the pain of displeasure and disconnection.* Thus, later in life, things that bring pleasure and connection can threaten the emotional coping mechanisms that feel "safe" and have protected the person from feeling their own suffering since they were a young child.

This also explains why authoritarian nations are so resistant to change even though so many people are so unhappy. This perspective on child abuse made it clear: *abused or deprived people can resist the connection and pleasure that would be so satisfying and healing.* People can close their hearts tight and be afraid to reopen them again, rejecting their own healing. This pattern is reflected at the level of whole abusive nations that reject their own healing, generation after generation.

Reading these studies on child and animal abuse, I finally understood how sexually repressed Christian missionaries could see sexually healthy nations as immoral and ungodly devil-worshippers – and not just upon first encounter, but century after century. It makes sense that people who had learned to associate negative feelings with pleasure would reject as illegitimate and wrong the sexual pleasures of people in healthy nations.

Lessons for Imprisonment

These perspectives on child abuse also illustrate why prisons are antithetical to healthy nations and deep cultural healing. Depriving babies of connection and pleasure commonly leads to adults who show disturbing traits such as sexism, pathological violence, selfishness, and so on. Prisons likewise deprive adults of connection and pleasure; why would they have any other impact on inmates?

Some aspects of prison may be helpful, such as removing someone from a destructive or self-destructive life path so that they can reflect and grow. However, the punitive aspects of prison, including disconnection from friends and family, disconnection from nonhumans, forced labor, submissiveness to abusive guards, minimal pleasure, and minimal sanitation are all degrading and humiliating, and they condition adults similarly to children who are raised in punitive, low-affection environments. Every story I've encountered of personal growth in prisons comes in spite of the punitive, disconnecting aspects of prisons, not because of them.

In fact, the term "hate factory" is a common name for prisons or parts of prisons. The Scottish Peterhead Prison was known as "The Hate Factory" until it closed in 2013.[29] WG Stone's account of the New Mexico State Penitentiary riot in 1980 was made into a book called "The Hate Factory." A friend who stayed in the Iowa State Penitentiary said the highest security building was known as "The Hate Factory." How could anyone think hate factories would fix any of societies' problems? Abusive prisons replicate the worst aspects of abusive childhoods. In the 1971 Attica Manifesto, the prisoners noted how their treatment was like "pouring water on a drowning man, inasmuch as we are treated for our hostilities by our program administrators with their hostility as medication."[30]

Healthy nations have had a range of responses to address inappropriate behavior, as examples from Chapter 4 show. However, none of these responses involve humiliating and abusing misbehaving people. Endlessly humiliating and abusing people in prisons has not addressed inappropriate behavior for thousands of years. Prisons are simply another scam, and it is high time to end them.

Coercive vs Non-Coercive Schooling

Some forms of child abuse are not merely legal, but are legally required. Conventional schooling is legally mandated in many countries around the world, and school is commonly meaningless and boring. How else to train children for meaningless and boring jobs in adulthood?

Of course, many individual teachers try to connect with the children, support their dreams, make school work meaningful, and so on. But teachers don't define the laws, curricula, testing standards, and so many other factors that make coercive schooling what it is. From the perspective of authorities who decide these things, I believe that conditioning children to tolerate boredom and meaningless work is a core purpose of school.

How many adults find themselves looking at a clock near the end of their work shift, wishing it was time to go home? And where did they learn to spend their time looking at a clock, wishing their life away? School!

How many adults pretend to care about their work when they are only doing their job to make a living? And where did they learn to pretend to care about their work, which they're only doing because they feel pressured to do it? School!

How many adults pretend to respect their bosses or political leaders, when they're actually acting submissively to avoid punishment and poverty? Where do children learn to pretend to respect adults who demand obedience, regardless how inappropriately the adults behave? School!

How many adults seem close-minded, where they believe what authorities say or what they were taught as a kid? And where do children learn to believe what the textbook or teacher says, or else they'll get a bad grade? School!

In healthy nations, children are raised to discover and give their sacred gifts, or life purpose. What am I alive to do or be? How can I give my deepest love?

Schools where I live do not help children discover their gifts. I asked one female friend in her early 30s what she would do if she didn't need money, and she said, "If I didn't need money? I'd probably feel anxious and not know what to do with my time." A male friend in his early 30s decided to go to college and get a degree. I asked him why, and he said, "I was feeling kind of lost in life, so I went to college. I didn't like a lot of it. But it was really nice to have structure and direction, someone setting goals and telling me how to get there."

These people struggled to set their own goals, or even felt anxiety just thinking about what they would do with free time. I've heard similar responses many times, and struggled with this myself. This is the essence of spiritually breaking someone or something. Breaking in a horse means to train it to ignore its own direction and accept a rider's direction. Breaking in a dog trains it to accept a human's orders. Breaking people trains them to ignore their own direction and adopt a master's orders instead, such as a boss or anyone who will pay them money.

Healthy Nations Raise Children to Experience Every Day as Meaningful

Like many children, I had a nagging sense that school was nonsense. For one thing, classes seemed very inefficient. I always felt that all the students could potentially become much more capable by any given age. It wasn't until I studied healthy nations that I found out how right I was.

Lakota man Standing Bear described one of his first hunts: "I remember that hunt, for before that time I had only killed a calf. I was thirteen years old and supposed to be a man, so I made up my mind I'd get a yearling. One of them went down a draw and I raced after him on my pony…" Standing Bear killed him with his second arrow. He said, "Hunters cried 'Yuhoo!' once when they killed, but this was my first big bison, and I just kept on yelling 'Yuhoo!' People must have thought I was killing a whole herd…"[31]

Standing Bear was able to hunt and provide for a family by the time he was thirteen, and this was not unusual. Sioux man Ohiyesa decided to go to an American school on his father's advice at the age of 15, and he found it utterly stifling. His teacher handed him a primer with some Biblical and historical lessons, and he called it "the dullest hunting I have ever known!"

Ohiyesa described how frustrating it was to know his full youthful power, and yet be trapped with meaningless school work:

> How well I remember the first time we were called upon to recite! In the same primer class were Eagle-Crane, Kite, and their compatriot from up the river. For a whole week we youthful warriors were held up and harassed with words of three letters. Like raspberry bushes in the path, they tore, bled, and sweated us–those little words rat, cat, and so forth–until not a semblance of our native dignity and self-respect was left. And we were of just the age when the Indian youth is most on his dignity! Imagine the same fellows turned loose against [American general] Custer or [general] Harney with anything like equal numbers and weapons, and those tried generals would feel like boys! We had been bred and trained to those things; but when we found ourselves within four walls and set to pick out words of three letters we were like novices upon snow-shoes–often flat on the ground.[32]

Ohiyesa and these other youths had been trained to hunt and fight to protect their people among many other things. If they hadn't lost a war, they would likely have continued on that path. Instead, they got sucked into an unhealthy nation and forced into schools that fed them seemingly meaningless work "until not a semblance of our native dignity and self-respect was left."

I consistently notice that people of healthy nations do not complain about work. I believe this is because children in healthy nations find their education deeply meaningful and engaging, and thus there is no drudgery to it.

Apache man Geronimo said, "When I was about eight or ten years old I began to follow the chase, and to me this was never work."[33] Ohiyesa wrote, "I hardly think I was ever tired in my life until those first days of boarding-school."[34] Ohiyesa also noted, "The Indian boy enjoyed such a life as almost all boys dream of and would choose for themselves if they were permitted to do so."[35]

Ohiyesa described his upbringing:

> From childhood I was consciously trained to be a man; that was, after all, the basic thing; but after this I was trained to be a warrior and a hunter, and not to care for money or possessions, but to be in the broadest sense a public servant. After arriving at a reverent sense of the pervading presence of the Spirit and Giver of Life, and a deep consciousness of the brotherhood of man, the first thing for me to accomplish was to adapt myself perfectly to natural things–in other words, to harmonize myself with nature. To this end I was made to build a body both symmetrical and enduring–a house for the soul to live in–a sturdy house, defying the elements. I must have faith and patience; I must learn self-control and be able to maintain silence. I must do with as little as possible and start with nothing most of the time, because a true Indian always shares whatever he may possess…I was…alert and alive to everything that came within my ken.[36]

Nootka girls would learn many skills, including basketry, weaving, or making raincapes. They also had strong physical education. One Nootka storyteller described how "every day we had to get our bodies ready. So that when the time came to go from bein' a girl to bein' a woman, we'd be ready."[37] They would swim, even while tied to logs, and run down the beach, even running backwards without kicking up sand.

Nootka girls knew they were preparing as children for a special life in adulthood. Once they'd learned what they needed to learn and experienced menarche, friends and family would gather for a huge celebration on the beach with singing and dancing and food. Then the young woman would dress up in fine clothes and someone would take her far out into the ocean. The woman would undress and jump into the water and swim home alone.[38]

Her family and friends would light fires in anticipation of her return, and begin singing victory songs when they spotted her swimming to shore. After this, women were welcomed to marry and have families if they wished.

Wikis was a member of a healthy nation from the American Great Plains, and his uncle made him a bow and arrow when he was 5-6 years old and told him that "I should hunt little birds, and should learn to kill food, to help support my mother and sisters, as a man ought to do." Soon he began hunting little birds to sharpen his skills. Wikis said, "This was a happy time for me. We little boys played together all the time. Sometimes the older boys allowed us to go with them, when they went far from the village, to hunt rabbits…"[39]

After her time with the Yequana, Jean Liedloff wrote, "I found the complete absence of pressure by persuasion, by the imposition of one individual's will upon another, difficult to believe or understand, despite the Yequana's perseverance in showing me examples of it."[40]

Liedloff described a story of incredible non-coercion from the Yequana. A 10-year-old boy named Tadehah joined 5 Yequana men, Liedloff, and two other outsiders on an expedition. His mother did not stop him. A week later, a disagreement occurred and the Yequana men suddenly marched out of camp to return home. One turned to Tadehah and said, "Mahtyeh!" ("Come along!"). Tadehah said softly, "Ahkay" ("No"). The men turned and left, not even trying to persuade him to come home rather than stay with three strangers half-way up a river. Young Tadehah did not return home for months. Liedloff described him as always up for any adventure, and "never anything but helpful and always happy."

Kids can have a very strong sense of what matters. I once sat around a big dining table in a cafeteria with about eight people. A five-year-old boy whom I'll call Jerry sat to my left, and his grandmother sat to his left. The grandmother loved to speak about superficial things, often with selfish attitudes, and I felt a mounting stress. I wanted to interrupt her and save my soul from this interminable conversation, but I didn't know how to do it without being rude. Finally, Jerry looked up at me with wide eyes and said, "Why are you talking about things that don't matter?!"

I will always feel grateful to Jerry for breaking the spell I was under. A five-year-old taught me how to stand up for myself! I looked at Jerry and said, "Great question! Want to go play outside?" Jerry said, "Yeah!" I invited a few other boys at the table out with us, and we all had a great time playing nature connection games while the adults continued their pointless conversations.

These stories showed me how capable young people can be if raised to reach their fullest potential, and how deeply meaningful every day can be, including the time of youthful education. Teenage years especially don't have to be a time of awkwardness and rebellion when adults raise children to live a meaningful life every day. When adults treat children respectfully, there is nothing to rebel against!

Healthy Boundary-Setting and Non-Coercive Education in an Unhealthy Nation

I was once teaching some adult friends a jiu jitsu technique in an open field. I was visiting a community with many notoriously unruly 4-7 year old boys, and they were roaming about with no adult supervision. As they entered the field, I turned to wave and say hello. The boys were making a ruckus, laughing and rough-housing like usual. They were focused on each other and did not wave back.

I turned towards my adult friends to demonstrate the technique, and after it was complete, I glanced at the boys again. Every single one of them was seated cross-legged on the ground, leaning forward silently in rapt attention. Their parents and teachers would never have believed me if I told them how completely still and quiet the boys were. But without any external pressure, these young boys decided that my self-defense lesson mattered, and they took in every detail.

Coercive schooling makes it difficult for children to recognize for themselves what they care deeply about. However, I have found examples where adults hold strong boundaries around education to bring out the best in their children. One jiu jitsu instructor, whom I'll call Ben, is very grateful for his father's boundary-setting. Ben loved to fight, so his father signed him up for classes as a boy and told him he had to spend every weeknight there from 5-9pm and not to come home early. His father said he didn't care about school so long as Ben passed his classes. Ben said, "I learned that a D is waaaay better than an F." When Ben wanted to play video games or learn to ride a bike, his father made him choose: fighting classes or video games? Fighting classes or bike riding? Ben kept choosing fighting. To this day he doesn't like video games and can't ride a bike. But he became a professional fighter at the age of 18 and now teaches what he loves.

Another friend, Janey, loved music as a little girl and wanted her father to let her take piano lessons. Her father said not yet, not until she was ready to really focus and consistently practice. She kept begging, and he kept saying no until she was 10 years old. She started playing piano and practiced consistently for years, falling in love and becoming an award-winning professional musician. She strongly credits her father with helping her on that path to being a professional musician who now gives lessons online to people around the world.

Both Janey's and Ben's parents held them to a high standard and expected their best. Janey knew she loved music, and Ben knew he loved fighting, so this boundary-setting was a gift. Both of them knew it and still feel grateful to their fathers decades later.

When Natural Desires Go Unmet, Deep Healing Becomes Difficult

Martín Prechtel related the Tzutujil Mayans' perspective on evil, and it describes the consequences of deep self-repression: "We see evil as a form of negative creativity with a vengeance. Its parents are simple, natural desires who, because they have gone unfed, become frustrated, unnatural hungers. These hungers begin to put together things that don't go together, creating monsters, which are personified unnatural hungers that eat everything and never get full."[41]

What do these monsters look like?

These monsters look like people who feel anxious at the thought of choosing their own life path as if money were no object. They look like men who think rape and making love are the same thing. There are infinite ways people can behave disrespectfully towards children, and infinite ways people can respond, and thus monsters can take on an infinite number of forms as people cope with growing up in an abusive nation.

But these monsters aren't who we really are as humans. These behaviors are a pathology, a disease. When an animal gets caught in a trap, it may gnaw off its own leg to help it escape the trap to safety. Similarly, many people learn to close their heart, in many ways and different degrees, as a way to survive and minimize suffering in their unhealthy nation. Heart closure is a common and tragic coping mechanism.

Children can internalize all manner of tragic beliefs from different forms of child abuse. Each child can develop their own perspective, but common examples include all the attitudes explored in Chapter 17, including "I don't deserve love," "I'm not good enough," "I can't trust others and I have to put myself first to be ok," "nothing matters," "life is basically bad," or "people are basically bad." People can develop hurtful associations, seeing some things as threatening or bad that aren't necessarily so – like deep relationships.

Unfortunately, these monsters become very difficult to empathize with, and people who have different kinds of wounds often struggle to relate to each other. When Hannah Arendt described Nazi leader Adolf Eichmann as a spineless follower with no internal sense of meaning or direction, many people disagreed. Arendt's friend, novelist Mary McCarthy, expressed her disbelief: "it seems to me that what you are saying is that Eichmann lacks an inherent human quality: the capacity for thought, consciousness – conscience. But then isn't he a monster simply?"[42]

Sadly, unhealthy nations train people to close their hearts, and some people close them so tightly that they rise to the level of monsters like Adolf Eichmann, who actually wasn't very remarkable according to Arendt. He was just a normal monster given a huge amount of authority in an unhealthy nation.

When I read the vast number of disorders and odd behaviors that psychologists have cataloged, many of them seem to be coping mechanisms. Humans are born expecting a healthy nation of solidarity, pleasure, sharing, integrity, meaningful work, strong mentorship, and deep connection, and it is challenging to grow up in a nation without them.

Rulers do many terrible things, but there has to be something besides rulers that keep people stuck in abusive nations for centuries and millennia. Parents and other lower authorities in children's lives commonly pass these deep wounds on. Each generation, knowingly or not, works to close the hearts of the next, and some people get wounded so deeply that they reject their own healing. This contributes to that larger pattern where unhealthy nations reject their own healing. This helps explain how tragically stable unhealthy nations are even while so many people feel unsatisfied.

Anyone can heal any spiritual wound and thus treat their children better than they were treated. Unfortunately, this is tricky in an unhealthy nation. After all, if a child learns "I can't trust anybody" and grows up around people of low integrity, how are they supposed to learn to trust?

If a child grows up with disconnection from an early age, then grows up in a nation with divisive racism, sexism, and privilege, how can they learn to form deep connections with others?

If a child learns to "shut down" or "hold back" parts of themselves, and then grows up in a nation where almost everyone does this somehow so that it seems normal, how can they learn to give their love fully?

If a child who receives little loving touch develops the attitude "I am bad or undeserving of love" and grows up in a religious culture that preaches they are inherently bad and separated from God, how are they supposed to release that attitude, recognize their own divine nature, and give their love freely?

Of course, anything is possible, but history shows that unhealthy nations make deep healing very challenging.

The Greatest Challenge We Will Ever Face

Spirituality is how a person relates to themselves and the world. Is there an authoritarian god-figure scaring everyone into obedience? Or is the world just a bunch of molecules moving around aimlessly? Or are we each divine beings, and it really matters how each of us shows up in life? The three core spiritual practices are spiritual because they teach people how to relate to the world: with gratitude, by giving their love, and living in reciprocity.

How children are raised affects their spiritual relationship with themselves and the world. Does the world welcome their love and invite the best out of them? Or is it uncaring and painful, with authoritarian gods and adults demanding obedience no matter how the child feels?

When a child's world is uncaring, painful, or meaningless, is it any wonder so many kids learn to close their hearts? And when they become adults, is it any wonder that so many pass on this pain to their own children?

Child abuse or deprivation are not all-or-nothing. Many examples described in this chapter are especially cruel, making it easier to clearly recognize the hurtful patterns children can learn in response. However, there are a vast number of ways of depriving, abusing, or dominating children, and in response children can learn to close their hearts in many ways and to different degrees. Children whose parents offer a little loving touch may still struggle, but less than the soldiers in the True Americanism study. Even seemingly less intense forms of abuse can have very hurtful effects, perhaps more subtle internally or more difficult to notice externally.

In 1980, James Prescott spoke to a US congressional committee and said, "we are producing more criminals… by the manner in which we are raising our children… than we will be able to house in all the prisons that we can build."[43]

In any given moment, transforming or ending an authoritarian nation may not be possible. But in each moment, the present generation can lay the groundwork for a future transformation. An essential way of laying the groundwork is treating children with a deep respect so they grow up recognizing respect and connection as normal and disrespect and disconnection as abnormal.

Children raised with disconnection or disrespect grow up unsurprised to live in an abusive nation because it feels normal. Children raised with deep connection and respect will grow up knowing there is something deeply wrong with their abusive nation.

One Nootka storyteller said, "When I was young they told me if a generation of people got pushed to killin' other people, it took four generations of peace to get people's heads fixed afterward."[44] Even people in healthy nations can struggle when they experience violence for too long, and many people of unhealthy nations have experienced violence for dozens of generations. This will either continue until humans are extinct, or it will continue until a generation frees itself from this terrible unhealthy-nation trap.

I want to be part of the generation who frees itself. But if I cannot help a generation find freedom, I want to at least help lay the groundwork so a future generation can.

This challenge is summed up by Michael Mendizza of the Touch the Future organization: "The way we treat children is the way our children will treat the world. Acting on this insight is the greatest challenge we will ever face."[45]

How can children and adults begin to heal the hurt caused by countless generations of emotional and physical deprivation and abuse? Next, *Chapter 43: Good Contact vs Poor Contact* offers practices that can generate deep healing and connection.

Chapter 43: Good Contact vs Poor Contact

Many sicknesses at the cultural level manifest in people at the individual level. Authorities encourage ignorance and disconnection across millions of people. How can these same patterns impact a person's sensory experience of the world around them? And how can anyone heal, allowing them to fully experience the beauty of life and deep connection with other people?

Discovering that I Could Notice My Own Experience

In late 2016, I found an amazing book called *Gestalt Therapy: Excitement and Growth in the Human Personality*. The authors described how people can learn not to notice parts of their own experience or resist parts of their experience. They offered many experiments that readers could do by themselves to notice these emotional blocks or resistances. As I did these experiments, I realized the authors were describing my own emotional blocks perfectly. It seemed like the book was written specifically for me!

For the first time, I realized that I wasn't noticing many aspects of my own experience. If someone suddenly asked me to close my eyes and point to where the sun is shining, I might not be able to. I would need to look, because even though sunlight was shining on me, I'd learned not to notice it. I'd learned not to notice certain sounds and smells. I did not notice how deeply I was breathing, or which parts of my abdomen and chest I was using to breathe and what effects different ways of breathing had on my mental clarity or the people around me. I didn't notice how balanced I sat in my chair, or how slight changes in my posture had large effects on my body's soreness and emotional state.

Some of my blocks or resistances were conditional. For example, I might remain calm and composed if a friend became angry, but then I might become stressed and lose my composure if an authority figure or romantic partner became angry at me.

I hadn't even noticed that I had a voice in my head that was running a lot, keeping my attention occupied so that I didn't notice my sensual experience much. When I was alone, I didn't notice very much of what I was seeing, feeling, or hearing in part because my attention was on the voices in my head. When I was with other people, I had the sense that I took in their words, thought of an answer, and then spoke it back out, but I didn't continually notice them while we spoke.

I kept practicing awareness and eventually noticed that I'd never really studied how to live in my body well. I hadn't deeply learned how to walk, run, stand, breathe, sit, observe, remember, have sex, feel, climb, fight, stalk, hide, or many other things. I could do these things at a basic level and I was athletic and basically healthy. But, for example, I had thought I knew how to walk once I could move on two feet. I'd never learned to walk gracefully with a firm connection to the ground and without stressing my knees and lower back.

In short, my consciousness was pretty disconnected from my body and my sensual experience of the world. I had learned not to notice many aspects of my own experience. This was basically how I had learned to handle many unpleasant situations earlier in life that I couldn't escape or fix, like being stuck eating unsatisfying school food or smelling smog somewhere or hiding from fears. I'd simply learned not to notice tastes and smells or certain fears much. Even after I learned to have more control of my life, these patterns of disconnection remained subconscious habit that stayed with me until I learned how to notice them again and respond differently.

These are all aspects of contact, and it helped me to think of contact in this way:

- *Good contact*: A person with good contact remains sensually aware of reality around and within them, and energetically connected to other people and nonhumans.

- *Poor contact*: A person with poor contact is somehow ignoring or resisting part of their own experience and thus remains unaware of some aspects of reality.

A person's contact isn't black-and-white, where it's always strong or always poor. A person's contact might be strong in some circumstances and weak in others. For example, a person might be relaxed and sensually present with an old friend, but less sensually present during a job interview or some other stressful moment. Or, a person might pay close attention to a boss's feelings and ignore a servant's or nonhuman's feelings.

Growing up, I had only heard the word "contact" used to describe when two things are physically touching each other. For example, an electrical contact is only strong if two wires firmly contact each other. The contact described in this chapter goes beyond physical connection, exploring how two people can feel energetically connected even when they are not physically touching. *Two people with good contact can be energetically connected without physically touching.* When both people have good energetic contact, they can each be attuned and emotionally responsive to the other.

When one or both people have poor contact, they will not have a very strong energetic connection, and the person with poor contact will not be very responsive to the other.

This showed me how deep disconnection can go. While authorities can physically separate people from the Earth and each other, it is also possible for people's consciousness to become disconnected from their body and sensual experience of reality. It is possible for people to stand right next to each other and, if both have poor contact, for them to feel isolated and unconnected with each other.

This also explains one reason why so many people feel disconnected from nature: many people have simply learned not to be sensually aware of the nonhumans around them and not consider their needs, and so they have a weak energetic connection with nonhumans.

Luckily, just as people can learn to have poor contact, anyone can also learn to improve their contact by practicing noticing their surroundings and their own sensual experiences more and more. Over time, all it takes to grow is for a person to start noticing what they were not noticing before, and practice staying present and aware. This is the best way I have found to heal triple inhibition: learning to notice the aspects of my experience I previously learned not to notice. In the past, I may have learned to hide from some feeling or urge or perception, or make hurtful or incorrect associations or assumptions about things in my life, but I can choose to respond differently now by becoming aware of these things in myself.

Good Contact, Poor Contact

Unfortunately, I had plenty of experience with poor contact!

A few years before finding the Gestalt book, I had decided to learn to dance. I wanted to salsa dance because it looked like such a fun way to connect with women even without words. So I signed up for dance classes and learned a few patterns. The trouble was, I had no understanding of the masculine leadership role in salsa dancing, and I also had pretty severe anxiety at the prospect of dancing with women and little experience consciously responding to anxiety. I hoped that taking classes would help me overcome this anxiety.

I was wrong.

One Saturday night, a pair of friends invited me out to my first social dance at a club in Washington DC. After a little group dance lesson, I invited a lady out on the dance floor. I held her hands in the way I had learned in class, and the music started, and then I froze. I was flooded with such strong feelings that I didn't even notice how I felt, except that I was extremely uncomfortable. I was so uncomfortable that I didn't even notice her. If someone had asked me, "what color top is she wearing?" I would have had to focus again to notice. My breathing constricted. I totally froze and my awareness curled inwards; all I could sense was my own discomfort. I stood there for several awkward seconds, motionless.

The woman pushed my hands away and got angry with me. I cannot quote her words for obvious reasons, but how could she enjoy dancing with a man who had such poor contact with her? It might have been fun and connecting if I had acknowledged and laughed at my own nervousness, for then we could have at least laughed together. My newness at dancing was not the problem. My emotional withdrawal was the problem. It took a long time before I decided I was ready to work through these feelings as they arose, and return to salsa dancing.

This was poor contact. I had a strong emotional response and I did not know how to remain conscious throughout. I became disconnected from my own experience, something I probably first began learning to do as a young child.

Luckily, anything that can be learned can be unlearned. And it turns out that nature connection practices also helped me connect with myself. The most helpful practice was the sit spot as taught in the Kamana program.

In one sense meditation, I practiced having big sensitive eyes with strong peripheral vision like an owl. While looking forward, I practiced noticing how much I could see all around. Then I practiced having a sensitive nose like a dog, and I noticed all the slightest smells that I could. Next, I imagined I had big sensitive ears like a deer, and I practiced listening for the slightest sounds around me. Then I imagined having really sensitive hands and skin like a raccoon, and I practiced feeling the tiniest details in everything, like little gusts of wind or the movement of fabric on my body.

I also noticed how my thoughts could distract me. My thoughts were stuck in my head, but my sensing mind could reach out into my environment. In other words, the more I activated my senses and sensually noticed the world, the less my thoughts distracted me. Every day I went to my sit spot with a clear goal, as Jon Young described: "Your intent is to be fully aware with all of your senses fully engaged at all times."[1]

Joseph Campbell summarized the goal this way: "Use your mind, don't let your mind use you." The Kamana program notes, "when you reach the level of awareness that native people possess when they live close to the land, you don't think at all, except when you choose to." This state, where a person remains sensually present and thinks only when they choose to, is called the Sacred Silence. This is the baseline or standard for human consciousness.

Thus I developed a certain routine for going out to my sit spot. I would take a few deep breaths and relax, offer the Thanksgiving Address, tune into my senses, and quiet the mind. For a long time, I quickly started thinking again! I could not maintain the Sacred Silence for long. Sometimes I spent a whole hour trying to get through the Thanksgiving Address, feeling stressed and having trouble focusing. But my mentors taught me that as I cultivated gratitude and tuned into my surroundings, I would start to learn lessons from the nonhumans. It didn't take long. I was soon learning lessons from animals, as described in Chapter 2.

In time, these practices that connected me with my sensual experience and the nonhuman world began to transform all parts of my life for the better. The awareness perspectives I learned from the nature connection exercises complemented the awareness practices from the Gestalt or Reichian perspectives I was studying. I learned to notice when I had strong feelings arise, when my breathing or posture changed, and what exactly caused these things. This trained me to remain conscious rather than feel overwhelmed by big feelings even in difficult situations, and this allowed me to respond consciously no matter what challenges arose.

As one example, I invited a lover named Cadence to my home one morning. After laughing and flirting, we soon began having sex. I was on top of her, and she was on her back facing me, and for a few minutes we both seemed to enjoy it. Suddenly her face began to scrunch up and her body started convulsing and she started crying. Her crying grew more and more intense and she seemed totally overwhelmed.

Initially I thought that I had unknowingly done something to hurt her, but I didn't see anything immediately to change to help her feel better. She had lost contact with me; she wasn't looking at me at all. I began to feel a strong inner stress as if I had done something wrong, and in the past I might have withdrawn inward too, but I managed to remain present and in good contact. I told her I was going to come out of her which I did, and then I held her, and gently let her know it was ok and I was still there with her. Since I couldn't think of anything else to do, I kept holding her, mostly in silence, while waiting patiently for whatever came next.

Eventually she relaxed a little, and she looked at me again while her crying continued. Eventually the intensity of her crying diminished. Through tears, she looked at me and said, "you're still here!" I nodded, and she started saying over and over that she was sorry, and she told me she was surprised that I hadn't pushed her away somehow. She did not put it in these terms, but she seemed to be surprised that I maintained good contact and did not leave or emotionally withdraw or get angry when she had an unexplainable-to-me emotional moment.

After she calmed down further, Cadence told me what happened: out of nowhere, she had suddenly remembered a very unpleasant moment during sex with someone else years earlier, and something about it brought up huge feelings that had nothing to do with me. She told me it meant a great deal to her that I stayed with her through her feelings.

This was the opposite of how I had responded during salsa dancing. Instead of losing contact when strong emotions arose, I remained sensually present, and so I was able to show up in a better way.

The Freedom of Unconditionally Good Contact

Good contact is essential to human connection. When two people have good contact, they both notice each other and can respond to each other's needs and perspectives. When one person emotionally withdraws, they no longer attune to the other person. That disconnection can be really disturbing, as I saw in that salsa dance.

I think a big part of what makes a person trustable is whether they maintain good contact in a difficult moment. In a romantic relationship, will my partner only stay connected when we get along? Or can I trust her to stay energetically connected in good contact even when emotions get strong?

I was sitting across the couch one afternoon from a woman I'll call Mina. We had been lovers many years earlier and this afternoon we were discussing our past experience together as we considered whether to restart a romantic relationship.

At one point, she began to tell a story of something that happened in the past between us which she was unhappy about. I noticed she became anxious and irritated and she hesitated. I told her I wanted to hear what she had to say. She began to relate the story and told me how upset she had been, and as she told the story she got angry. Her voice intensified, she rose up on the couch and faced me directly, and she very clearly described what she was upset about.

In the past, I would have gone "into my head" somehow. I might have tried to soothe her anger to bring us back to pleasantness, or gotten angry at her for getting angry with me, or frozen awkwardly. Any of these responses assumes anger was a problem to be dealt with instead of a legitimate symptom of a problem.

Luckily I had learned a helpful technique: whenever big feelings arise, especially anger, breathe the energy in and circulate it through the body with my attention. This allows the energy to move without causing stress or feeling overwhelmed.

So, I breathed deeply and maintained good contact, meaning I remained sensually present and aware. When she hesitated again I told her I wanted to hear what she had to say. She finished speaking her piece, and we worked through our past misunderstanding.

A few minutes later, she thanked me for staying with her while she was angry and for even welcoming her anger. She told me no one had ever done that with her before, and it was incredibly freeing to be able to express her anger and know I would stay present with her. This meant a lot to hear, because earlier in life I wasn't able to keep my composure so well when others became angry towards me, and I hadn't even realized how my difficulty maintaining composure in the midst of strong feelings made it hard for others to feel comfortable with me.

This was also an example of receiving another person's gift. Her anger was a gift, as it indicated there was a problem we needed to address. I didn't know at the start what the trouble was – it might have been a mistake on my part, or a misunderstanding on her part, or miscommunication. But the anger itself was a gift because it indicated some trouble that needed addressing. By receiving her anger, I made space for it and made space for her to feel that way. I believe that's why she described how free she felt: she was free to be herself with me, knowing that no particular feeling would cause me to disconnect from her.

Good Contact and Human Connection

Good contact is what allows people to feel energetically connected with each other. Even people in a crowd can feel isolated and alone if no one is paying attention to anyone else, whether they're focused on a TV, their own thoughts, or anything else. But when people can deeply notice and sense each other, this brings a very satisfying sense of togetherness.

I learned this in a very difficult situation I once faced. I had bought some land and invited a mother and two children to live there for a few months whom I did not know very well. I quickly encountered the strangest pattern of domestic violence I had ever witnessed. The younger child, a six year old girl I will call Layna, would commonly say she was hungry while her mother Rachel and I were talking. Rachel would tell her, "not now, I am busy, I will get you food later."

In these moments, Rachel often would not look at her daughter, but just say her response as she continued to look at me. Layna would interrupt again, more loudly this time. Again her mother told her, "no, not now." And her mother would continue to focus on me as she had before our conversation was interrupted.

After several back-and-forths, the young girl would erupt in violence and start beating her mother viciously, often for 30-40 minutes at a stretch. This would only stop when her mother held her tight and pinned her gently but firmly on the ground till she calmed down.

I kept wondering what was going on. Why was Layna behaving this way? Finally I observed an even stranger incident. The mother Rachel and I were seated across from each other having a conversation face-to-face about land projects. Layna came up and put her hand on her mother's arm. The mother ignored her, continuing to focus on our conversation. Layna bent over and draped herself over her mother's arm, and Rachel looked doggedly at me and leaned away from her daughter as if trying not to acknowledge her.

Rachel tried to maintain her conversation with me. Then Layna stood up and moved around her mother and draped herself on her mother's opposite shoulder. Again the mother leaned away and tried to maintain our conversation. Rachel told me later that she was trying to learn to set good boundaries with her children by not responding to them just whenever they asked. After a few minutes, Layna erupted in anger again and fully interrupted our conversation.

It was not until I saw the mother actively lean away from her daughter that I realized what was happening: the only time I had seen the mother hug the daughter was when the daughter was throwing a fit and the mother needed to hold her tight and pin her down just to keep from being hit by her own child.

I remembered being around women who were very comfortable with children. I remembered how at a party one evening, a little girl ran up to my adult friend Leia while we spoke. Leia lifted her up and smiled at her, then held the girl on her hips and swayed with her while we continued our conversation. She welcomed the little girl energetically without diverting her attention from me such that we became a group of three even as we adults continued our conversation. I wondered: was that physical and emotional contact all that little Layna had wanted when she came up and tried to nuzzle her mother?

I found one way to help reduce the number of tantrums. I began consistently making eye contact with Layna whenever she came up to a conversation between her mother and me. With a soft, warm glance, I tried to convey the message, "I see you, and now we're a group of three people instead of two because you're here."

During conversations with the mother, if Layna was present, I would glance at her occasionally to continually include her energetically in the group. When there was a decision to make and it seemed appropriate, I would ask Layna what her preference was. I believe Layna simply wanted good contact with the people around her, and when I energetically included her by maintaining good contact, she relaxed and her tantrums noticeably reduced.

Confusing the Feeling and the Substance of Good Contact

Just as people can feel like they're being loving when they're actually acting hurtfully, people can feel like they're connected with others when they're actually disconnected.

I once visited some friends at an intentional community a few days after they hosted a big dance party with about 30-60 people. I first visited one female friend who had lived there for years and was deeply integrated into the community. She told me how great the dance party had been, and how everyone had loved it. She told me she felt totally connected with everyone, and how blissful and ecstatic that connection was.

A few hours later, I visited another female friend who had lived in the community only a few months. She'd gone to the same party and felt really disconnected from others and uncomfortable. She told me she'd spoken with a half-dozen other women who likewise felt uncomfortable at the party.

I believe my first friend definitely felt bliss and ecstasy at the dance, but I don't believe she was as connected as she thought. If she'd been totally connected as she said, she would have noticed a substantial number of the women were uncomfortable. I believe she had feelings that she associated with connection, such as bliss, but she didn't have good contact as she believed.

This taught me the importance of noticing my own contact. Do I merely "feel connected" with someone? Or do I actually have good contact, where I am deeply aware of them and myself?

Shaming or Dismissing Certain Feelings

Growing up, I learned that hatred was bad, and people shouldn't hate. As an adult, I began hearing people claim that anger was also bad, and people should avoid feeling angry. I even heard one therapist and teacher claim that anger isn't a legitimate feeling, but instead is just misunderstood fear.

Eventually I realized that any feeling can be appropriate. Inappropriate feelings cause trouble, and they can occur when a person doesn't notice something important about themselves or their situation. This can happen if a person has learned to hold back a feeling, urge or perception somehow, and instead some other feeling arises to consciousness as reviewed in Chapter 17. These inappropriate feelings generally cause confusion because they don't respond to the situation as it is.

Of course, feelings might be inappropriate for other reasons. For example, if I were a parent, I might become angry if I notice a person tackling my child to the ground. But if I then notice that my child is at wrestling practice and a coach is merely demonstrating a technique in a consensual way, then I stop feeling angry as I realize there was no disrespect. In this case, my anger would be inappropriate because I misunderstood the situation, but not because I'd learned to hold a part of myself back.

One of the biggest lessons I ever learned is this: love is not a feeling. Any feeling can be offered with love, and that includes anger.

Anger is a key manifestation of a person's power. Anger is the normal, healthy response a person feels when they receive disrespect, or if someone they care about receives disrespect. The energy behind the anger is the motivating force that causes people to heal disrespect. Anger is an individual response that can lead to cultural healing so that nobody disrespects anybody else.

Anger is like a fire. It is a tool that can be channeled for good or ill. And even with good intention, anger can be channeled skillfully or unskillfully.

Hatred is a very bright fire, and appropriate hatred is what helps people fight or escape existential threats – challenges that really deserve fight or flight.

Sometimes people may express their anger unskillfully and don't get a satisfying response. Instead of learning how to express their feelings more skillfully, sometimes people learn the wrong lesson and learn to withhold their anger. This is tragic.

Expressing feelings is a skill that can be practiced and improved just like any other skill. When I feel angry, do I continue to stand for mutual respect, or do I get selfish or belittling towards other people? Do I become foggy or remain clear-headed?

When people, especially children, are shamed for having certain feelings like anger or sadness, people can effectively learn to repress entire types of responses. For example, if a person learns to completely repress anger, how are they supposed to respond to disrespect? If the healthy response of anger and its motivating energy are stifled, whatever other response the person musters is unlikely to be effective.

Ultimately, a person can give love through any feeling. A person can give love through feeling grief, anger, curiosity, frustration, or anything else, channeling any feeling skillfully to somehow make the world a better place. All these feelings are simply a person's relationship to reality. An open-hearted person feels all their feelings, and practices channeling them skillfully for the greatest good.

Healthy Nations Train Children for Good Contact

I commonly read that healthy nations encourage children to develop good contact, developing a deep comfort in their bodies and a sensual awareness of the world around them.

One common pattern is that healthy nations train their young women to feel comfortable in their bodies during their menstrual cycle or moon time. One Nootka storyteller described how the women would often have their moon time at the same time each month, and they would go to a special house and enjoy a four-day party. They would sit on special soft moss and give their blood back to the Earth and play games and talk. Women would rub each others' back and make special tea if someone had cramps. Young women also learned the special Frog posture that could help relieve cramps, where they would tuck their knees under their belly, put their head down like a cat, breathe deep, and then straighten their head back. She said, "Looks funny, but it works. It's good when you first start havin' your baby, too, makes everythin' shift into the right place."[2]

Nancy Basket described how the traditional Cherokee likewise had special lodges for women on their moon time, and women often went together. When a young woman had her first moon, she would get a tattoo, and she would go to a lodge and the old women would celebrate her. Basket said, "you are [in the lodge] for a while. You learn about how thin the veil is for a woman, between the other side, and receiving intuition. There would be practices, you'd have different skill sets with different women that would be able to see beyond more so than others." The women would stay for 5-7 days each month, and the men and grandparents would watch the kids while they were gone.[3]

Instead of the body-shame or ignorance that many girls in unhealthy nations grow up with, women in healthy nations celebrate each others' bodies, and men support this.

Lakota man Gilbert Walking Bull offered an example where the Lakota trained children for good contact. His parents helped him avoid the Catholic boarding schools where so many other children had their mouths washed with soap for "talking that dirty Indian language."[4] He grew up with elders who had lived in a traditional way before entering government reservations. He said that as a little child, the elders always shushed him, urging him to remain silent and listen.[5]

The elders didn't quiet the kids to discourage their exuberance. Rather, they recognized that the wilderness is a cathedral, a sacred place that should be disturbed as little as possible. Tom Brown Jr, who was trained by Apache man Stalking Wolf, echoed this, saying to never disturb a singing bird, as singing birds are giving their Thanksgiving.

Even when several Lakota kids came together, they were often silent since they were being taught to listen. Walking Bull said that as a young child, "I never knew what I was listening to. But still I listened. I learned from a young age to silence myself and to always listen."

He had a grandmother who would send him and other children off to different nearby hills to look for a particular plant. She would ask for different plants which were located in different areas, and in this way, she introduced him and other children to different regions and flora. Walking Bull said that even when seven kids walked together, they did not speak, but they all knew where each other were. They never walked in a group and chatted aimlessly, as do many kids of unhealthy nations.

Even if the little children could not see each other, they could hear each other from disturbances in the leaves or sounds of birds responding to their presence. If they needed to come together, they could signal each other with little sounds.

This illustrates one way that traditional Lakota trained their children to maintain Sacred Silence and very good contact with each other and the Earth.

Ohiyesa also described how children walked with silence, dignity, and deep awareness: "The Indian youth was a born hunter. Every motion, every step expressed an inborn dignity and, at the same time, a depth of native caution. His moccasined foot fell like the velvet paw of a cat – noiselessly; his glittering black eyes scanned every object that appeared within their view. Not a bird, not even a chipmunk, escaped their piercing glance."[6]

Many healthy nations teach children to walk in a sacred way, generating children and adults with strong sensual contact with the Earth and life around them. Different nations teach variations of the same attitude that the Earth is sacred and alive. Tom Brown Jr. said, "Learn to walk making every step a prayer that blesses the landscape. This is walking in a sacred manner."[7]

Oren Lyons, an Onondaga man of the Haudenosaunee Confederacy, said, "When we walk upon Mother Earth, we always plant our feet carefully because we know the faces of our future generations are looking up at us from beneath the ground."[8]

Lakota man Tony Ten Fingers described how he had been reminded countless times in youth to always walk as if he were walking among elders. He recognized the stones, trees, and rivers as his elders, and so he saw that he was indeed walking among his elders.[9]

All of our ancestors returned to the Earth when they died, and all of our progeny will come from the Earth someday. Seeing past generations in the Earth like Tony Ten Fingers, or seeing future generations in the Earth like Oren Lyons are simply ways to acknowledge the reality of humans' connection with the Earth. No abstract mysticism is needed. Each of us belongs here on this Earth, surrounded by the spirits of our ancestors and progeny who want us to give our sacred gifts, just like our ancestors did and just like future generations will in their time.

Walking in a sacred manner is very different from how I learned to walk growing up. It starts with feeling gratitude. Then students practice activating all their senses, including seeing, hearing, smelling, and especially feeling through the feet. One seeks to walk with minimal disturbance, unlike many people who walk without even noticing the Earth below them. In this way, every step is aware and respectful of the Earth and all beings, past, present, and future.[10]

The Kamana program offers many more details and practices for those who wish to learn to connect with the Earth and walk in a sacred manner.

These practices of good contact have helped me in countless more seemingly-mundane ways. For example, I grew up running and playing a lot of sports, and I considered myself athletic. I spent countless hours practicing how to shoot a basketball or dribble in soccer. But it wasn't until my late 20s that I realized that I'd never learned how to breathe properly!

Even now, a decade later, I'm still learning how to breathe better. For example, I used to think I could build endurance only by intensive training, and this would strengthen muscles like the heart. But as I developed better awareness of my body, I realized that my breathing actually became weaker as I got more tired. At the beginning of a long run, I would "belly-breathe," breathing through my nose downward to my pelvic floor, and this was relaxing. As I got tired, I would unthinkingly breathe more shallowly into the chest.

As I practiced belly-breathing no matter what, I noticed how much anxiety and unnecessary exhaustion had been caused just by the shallow breathing. I felt amazed that I could increase my endurance and the joy I felt just by focusing on my breathing technique.

These breathing and walking practices are beautiful, but ultimately my goal is not to do isolated activities in a sacred way. I want to live life in a sacred way. It will be different for each person, but I believe when someone fully embraces the three core spiritual practices in every moment, they'll live life in a sacred way.

To get better at basketball, I trained specific skills in isolation like shooting or dribbling, and then I had to incorporate those skills to improve my overall game. Likewise, practicing specific skills like sacred walking or breathing helps, but the big shift comes from incorporating them into a sacred way of life based on the three core spiritual practices.

Relating to the Subconscious in a Good Way

When I first started reading about the subconscious, I felt a little scared. It was like there was something inside me that controlled me and controlled my feelings that I couldn't perceive. Sigmund Freud called it the Id. I heard people talk about animal instincts that needed to be repressed so people could live in a civilized way. I didn't like having some part of me supposedly driving my behavior that I couldn't perceive. How can a person relate to the subconscious in a good way?

It helped me to realize that there are multiple different things that people call "subconscious":

1. *Unconscious – things I don't need to know*: My body does lots of things I don't normally need to think about, such as cleaning blood in my liver or moving food through my intestines. My body does these things, but I don't consciously think about them unless something goes wrong, such as an injury. This is healthy.

2. *Subconscious – things I have learned not to notice*: Everybody is born experiencing all their feelings and urges, but many of us learn not to notice certain feelings or urges as we grow up. This is triple inhibition, when a person *learns 1) not to react to their own experience, 2) not to notice parts of their own experience, and then 3) not to notice that they are not noticing*. For example, perhaps they learned to ignore the feeling of the ground beneath their feet, or learned not to notice their own breathing in stressful moments, or learned not to attune to other people or nonhumans. Instead of noticing whether each person is trustable or untrustable, and then deeply trusting the reliable ones, a person may not notice anyone's trustworthiness and just not trust anyone.

A person may also learn to ignore certain feelings or urges if they were punished enough for expressing them earlier in life. Often this is situational. For example, a person might feel their anger easily when it comes up with friends and subordinates, but perhaps they learned not to notice their own anger whenever a higher-ranking person is involved.

This is why the subconscious can seem scary – it's just the part of a person's experience that they have learned not to notice, perhaps because they were repeatedly punished for expressing certain feelings or urges in certain situations early in life. For example, conventional schooling trains children to ignore their own curiosity and urges to play and explore the nonhuman world around them. This is simply the training that happens when children learn to tolerate boredom day-in and day-out in school.

The feelings and urges that a person learns to ignore still occur in the body though, and that energy has to go somewhere, and often it comes out in unproductive or hurtful ways. I believe that these repressed feelings and urges are the evil monsters that Martín Prechtel described as "simple, natural desires… [that] have gone unfed." They're feelings and urges that, if they were directly experienced and expressed, would be beautiful. When a person holds back subconsciously, the energy comes out in ugly, hurtful ways, as illustrated throughout this book.

3. *Heart – each person's connection with divinity*: A person's sacred gifts, sacred urges, and feelings all come from the heart, which is each individual's personal connection with divinity. The Spirit That Moves Through All Things moves us and speaks to us through our heart. When a person has a wide open heart, their feelings and urges move directly from the heart to their consciousness, and from that consciousness, the person expresses that energy to make the world a brighter place. The more closed a person's heart is, they less aware they are of these divine messages, and the more they act out selfishly or hurtfully instead.

With this understanding of unconscious, subconscious, and heart, I became less worried about my own subconscious because at least I understood what was going on. All the awareness practices in this book can also be helpful in accessing the subconscious – that is, remembering how to feel the things a person learned not to feel. The same practices that have deepened my awareness of the Earth have also deepened my awareness of myself, helping me notice things I long ago learned not to notice.

For anyone who wishes to open their heart and deepen their awareness of themselves, other people, and nonhumans, I strongly recommend the nature connection practices explored throughout this book.

An Essential First Step for Deep Change: Feel the Dissatisfaction!

As I practiced noticing what I smelled, tasted, saw, heard, and felt, I often didn't like what I found. I practiced smelling the air, and I noticed it sometimes smelled of smog. I practiced tasting food and noticed it sometimes tasted rancid. The more I practiced careful listening, even for the quietest sounds, the more I noticed sound pollution from cars. The more I looked around, the more I noticed that I spent a lot of my life in a room or vehicle, and even when nicely decorated, it wasn't visually very interesting.

In other words, blocking off my sensual awareness of the world had helped me cope with living in a nation of toxins, restrictive land ownership, offensive noise, and other troubles. As a kid, I must have learned that if I'm not going to do anything about these troubles, I might as well not notice them. Instead of feeling my dissatisfaction, I learned to feel numb.

It was painful to start noticing all these troubles I had learned to ignore. But every time I notice my boredom at being inside, I feel motivated to go outside and explore the nonhuman world. Every time I hear vehicle sounds, it reminds me that cars are producing huge amounts of toxins in the air, soil, and water, in addition to sound pollution. Whenever I notice rancid food, it reminds me that a lot of food in unhealthy nations is poisonous, and I need to take care to find good food. I notice my own dissatisfaction, and it motivates me to seek meaningful change in my nation in a way that I never did when I had learned to sensually ignore the problems.

There is an important balance between feeling dissatisfied about all these terrible things on one hand, and not fixating on them and getting depressed or permanently angry on the other. If I ignore the troubles, then I won't feel upset and won't help make things better. But if I pay attention to them continuously, it would be easy to feel continuously angry and sad, and not enjoy life. I would not have much energy, and I would burn out and not do much good. I have often struggled to find this balance!

Finding this balance is important for each person. Notice the dissatisfaction – the anger, or sadness, or the sense that "No, what I see around me is not ok." Then decide what you are willing to do about it, and let the hard feelings go.

I think back to the men in the New Mexico State Penitentiary in 1980, described in Chapter 23. They built up a huge amount of frustration and anger, and they finally relaxed when they collectively committed to taking a stand for themselves – that was when those grins spread across their faces. Likewise, Chapter 16 showed how Harriet Tubman felt upset about slavery, made a plan, and did her best, trusting that God would take care of her until He decided otherwise.

This is the best way I have found to balance the hard feelings about my unhealthy nation with finding joy in life: I feel the dissatisfaction, decide what I'm going to do about it, and then stop worrying. So long as I'm doing my best in service of what matters, and enjoying life along the way, what else is there to do?

Next, *Chapter 44: Training Children to Give or Withhold Love, Part 2* shows how adults can unknowingly train children to close their hearts, and how anybody can encourage children to open their hearts and give their love instead.

Chapter 44: Training Children to Give or Withhold Love, Part 2

Many troubles at the cultural level also play out at the family level.

Unhealthy nations forbid good boundary-setting, because whenever groups of people try to hold boundaries and stand up to abuse, the riot police come out. Thus many adults do not learn how to set healthy boundaries in their lives, and so as parents they can struggle to maintain healthy boundaries in their families. Poorly trained adults with weak boundaries of their own may not respond well when challenges arise.

What is it like when families make space for everybody, welcoming each person to give their gifts and be themselves? And what happens when parents embrace many of the controlling, closed-hearted patterns so common in unhealthy nations?

The Beauty of Receiving Others' Gifts

A gift is a beautiful thing.

It would be tragic if flowers made their fragrances and there were nobody alive to smell them and feel a deep calm, or no pollinators around to spread the flowers far and wide. It would be tragic if no one received the gift of yummy chestnuts and helped spread chestnut trees. It would be tragic if no one received the gift of a baby's laughter and got to feel their own heart melt.

Robin Kimmerer described how sweetgrass is a gift which benefits by being sustainably harvested. When buffalo sustainably harvest sweetgrass and move on before overgrazing, eating the grass actually stimulates new growth. The Potawatomi who likewise receive the sweetgrass's gifts through sustainable harvest help stimulate new growth as they gather it for basketmaking. Kimmerer's research showed that the sweetgrass population had actually declined in areas where respectful basketmakers had stopped harvesting it. The sweetgrass benefited when buffalo and humans received its gifts.[1]

Every gift has two sides, the giver and receiver. Both play an important role. The giver offers something that makes the world a better place, and the receiver makes space in the world for the gift.

I am the giving-of-my-sacred-gifts; I am the giving-of-my-deepest-love, which are the same thing. If my gifts or my love are rejected, then I am rejected.

Receiving a person's love/gifts actually makes space for them in the world. Receiving a person's love makes space for who-they-are.

As infants grow into children, they commonly desire to start taking care of themselves and contributing to their family. Children's urge to learn to take care of themselves and others is a great gift, inviting the gift of mentorship and guidance from adults and older children. It also reduces the burden on adults to take care of them.

I got to live with a family that did not welcome these childhood gifts from a little girl, and I saw how unhappy she was. I then watched the girl's beautiful transformation when the family began to make space for her gifts.

Receiving People's Gifts Makes Space for Them

I once shared a house with a man I'll call Daniel and his 4-year-old daughter Marina. She spent every other week with Daniel and alternate weeks with her mother.

Daniel certainly loved and cared for his daughter. He played with her, cooked for her, bought her toys, and helped her spend time with friends. He helped her understand her feelings and shared his feelings with her. As long as Marina was not hungry, she was generally a joy to be around: she was bright, vibrant, observant, playful, and she laughed easily. But when she became hungry, she became an absolute terror.

Sometimes she would complain continuously until she was fed, which sometimes took an hour or more from when she started to complain till the food showed up in front of her. Other times she would complain, and Daniel would say he would cook by a certain time. Marina would leave and come back after the agreed time, and sometimes Daniel began cooking and sometimes he broke his promise. Either way, Marina would not stop nagging and complaining when he got up to cook. The nagging would only stop when Daniel placed the food in front of her.

Daniel had a job and school and sometimes came home exhausted and did not always wish to cook immediately when Marina demanded. Sometimes he tried to set boundaries for himself and tell his daughter that he was tired and would cook soon. However, she would often escalate, screeching and yelling and stomping around and pouting until he caved in. She would accuse him of not loving her, or of lying even when I knew he was telling the truth. It seemed like she would say whatever she could think would help her get food, regardless whether it was true or false, and regardless how hurtful it was.

After observing this every other week for a few months, I asked myself: what on Earth is going on? Why does Marina behave this way?

After observing for a while, I noticed some curious things. The design of conventional homes in the United States where I live makes it very difficult for children to learn to take care of themselves. Four-year-old Marina was unable to get snacks for herself, unable to cook for herself or even watch her father cook, all because the storage and food preparation areas were higher than her eye level. She could not easily access the dishes, glasses and so on which were kept in cabinets above the counters which were themselves about as tall as Marina was. She could not pull out the drawer with silverware and easily look inside. She could not easily access the sink to clean up after herself or even get some water. For these and other reasons, the kitchen situation forced young Marina to remain totally dependent on her father for food, even when she was old enough to begin taking care of herself in various ways if the environment had permitted it. This dependency was only reinforced by her father who did not teach her how to use knives or cook safely.

I saw several troubles. Marina was totally disconnected from the process of food preparation. She was dependent on a father who loved her but who didn't always have integrity, so she could not trust his promises. Daniel often set poor boundaries, allowing his daughter to nag him until he caved in and cooked, which rewarded her nagging behavior.

Daniel also showed conditional emotional contact (see Chapter 43 to review good contact). When Marina would scream, Daniel would sometimes demand she stop, and when she wouldn't, I saw him emotionally withdraw. His head would drift slightly, his eyes would glaze, his face tightened. I recognized these symptoms because I sometimes emotionally withdrew in the face of challenges, and I was learning that I responded similarly. I happened to look at Marina's face once when she was nagging and Daniel withdrew, and her face was filled with terror. I have never seen so much fear in a child.

Children feel safe in the world in part by maintaining good contact with adults, and when Daniel emotionally withdrew, she lost this contact and felt very afraid. Daniel was essentially showing *conditional love* in the sense that he only remained fully emotionally present with his daughter in certain circumstances. This wasn't intentional, and I do not believe he was aware of his withdrawal and its negative impact on Marina. But she certainly was aware of it, and I believe her desire to maintain at least some contact fueled a lot of her hurtful behavior.

Likewise, I do not think young Marina consciously reflected on her father's attunement and logically considered the best response. I think she had a more emotional or instinctual response to do whatever she could to maintain at least some kind of emotional connection when he withdrew. Even nagging or screaming generated some emotional contact which was better than nothing.

What to Do About All This?

I remembered my time with the Ashaninka, and I remembered how the mother whose family I stayed with prepared all the food over a fire on the ground. The family ate together on the ground too. Everything was visible and accessible to the children.

The relationship between Marina's dependency on her father, her disconnection from the cooking process, and Marina's emotional manipulation finally dawned on me. I approached Daniel with an idea: what if we rearranged the kitchen so that it was as accessible as possible for Marina so that she wasn't so dependent anymore?

In some ways she would be able to take care of herself, and in other ways, where she still required help, she would at least be more connected with the food preparation process. Daniel was willing to try my very unconventional scheme.

I did everything I could think of. We bought wash basins and learned to wash dishes outside on the ground. All silverware and plates and cups got moved to the bottom cabinets where Marina could reach them. Common snacks and ingredients moved down as well.

I couldn't move the gas stove, but I set up a chair so Marina could participate. She was scared at first, but then learned to control the heat and stir food. I consistently placed the cutting board on the ground or a low table so Marina could see it, and I invited her to chop vegetables with me. At first she was scared of the knife, but I told her she could do it, and I showed her how to hold the vegetables and properly cut using her whole body for maximum knife control.

I noticed a profound transformation in response. Marina's nagging noticeably diminished. Even when Marina nagged Daniel to eat, the nagging stopped the moment food preparation began, not when the food arrived. Dinner preparation was no longer a mysterious process apparently motivated solely by her nagging; she could see it in action and even participate. She could verify for herself that dinner was indeed coming and not merely take her father's word for it, and she could appreciate how much work went into it even when she did not participate. Her self-confidence grew as she got better with the knife and learned to give the cooking-fire the respect it deserved without undue fear.

Marina's gift was not merely helping to prepare dinner. Her gift was her desire to learn to cook. More generally, her gift and desire was to learn to take care of herself and contribute to the family life in meaningful ways. This invited the gift of mentorship from her father and me. When Daniel and I began welcoming her gifts, she could have a reciprocal relationship with her father that she did not have when he just cooked for her. She also gave the gift of joyfulness during cooking, and while cooking did take longer when she was around, it was also way more fun. Her gift of joyfulness brought out our gift of joyfulness too. The kitchen became peaceful.

This showed me that gifts are like puzzle pieces that fit together just right. Marina's gift of curiosity and desire to contribute matched her father's and my gift of mentorship and inclusion. Her gift of joyful laughter matched our gift of joyful laughter. Before the transformation, the adults weren't welcoming her gifts, and so none of us felt satisfied. Satisfaction only arrived when we started to *receive everyone's gifts*.

I later learned that this childhood family participation is also common in healthy nations. Martín Prechtel described how Tzutujil Mayan girls developed many skills early, including beginning weaving at the age of four or five. Boys left their mothers' sides around seven or eight and worked with their fathers. By the age of 12, both girls and boys were essentially carrying their weight in the household.[2]

Strong Followers Encourage Strong Leaders

The first two core spiritual practices are cultivating a practical aware gratitude and giving one's sacred gifts. The first practice is receiving graciously, and the second practice is giving. Giving and receiving are complementary practices, and it takes both to make a healthy nation.

Much cultural research focuses on leaders like kings, presidents, and business executives. However, followers and leaders play equally important roles, and any individual can be a leader in one situation and a follower in another. Strong leaders cannot exist without strong followers. Gracious givers need gracious receivers.

Gracious receiving makes space for others' gifts. Daniel and I had to graciously receive Marina's gifts to make space for her. In that context, she was the giver, and we learned to receive Marina's gifts of curiosity and desire to learn.

Everyone plays the role of follower or receiver in countless ways, and if we play this role graciously, we encourage others to give their gifts. When a person plays this role poorly, they discourage the gifts.

Consider two people discussing some trouble. The "giver" is the speaker and the "receiver" is the listener. Both have a responsibility to ensure they develop a shared understanding of reality. The speaker's responsibility is to speak honestly. The listener's responsibility is not to make assumptions.

In a normal conversation, two people take turns, and each is responsible for speaking honestly and listening with an open mind. But these responsibilities also exist when people spread rumors about an event they did not witness. Do listeners falsely assume that what they hear is true without verifying? Or do listeners go to witnesses to find out the truth directly?

False rumors wouldn't spread if people didn't make thoughtless assumptions. I know several people, including myself, who have had false rumors spread to dozens of people in a community, and it can generate a sense of deep insecurity. There is little any individual can do to keep others from making foolish assumptions and believing hurtful rumors. Each individual needs to accept that "receiver" responsibility to either seek the truth or accept their own ignorance.

When people consistently avoid making assumptions, everyone can feel secure knowing that their neighbors won't propagate hurtful misunderstandings about them.

Another important receiver or follower responsibility is acknowledging excellent behavior. Practical, aware gratitude is a core spiritual practice in part because giving gratitude encourages people to continue doing good things.

Consider Martín Prechtel's summary of the Tzutujil Mayan system for choosing leaders:

> Traditional Tzutujil loved to get more than someone else, just so they could dress fancily and give it all away to be big. To get anywhere in traditional Mayan society, you had to work really hard to get wealth, get appointed to office without campaigning, and then give it all away.[3]

The Tzutujil Mayans encouraged giving by recognizing the givers. For that to work, people had to notice each others' giving and honor it.

How could a society possibly have leaders who don't seek office? This required people to notice the givers and name them as leadership candidates. They couldn't have strong leaders without strong followers who looked out for the best leadership candidates and lifted them up.

A nation that wants humble leaders must have strong followers who notice excellent behavior and highlight it so that everybody sees.

The same works for any quality that a nation wants to encourage. Consider bravery. Wikis' uncle gave him this advice: "When you are at war you may do brave things, and other people will see what you have done, and will tell of it. If you should chance to perform any brave act, do not speak of it; let your comrades do this; it is not for you to tell of the things that you have done."[4]

Wikis' uncle encouraged a deep humility in him, training Wikis not to brag. But how will a person's reputation grow if they don't brag about themselves? Wikis' uncle said that other people would tell of his brave feats. In other words, they would share each others' great stories, rewarding and honoring each others' gifts. When people can trust that others will tell of their good deeds, they will feel less pressure to brag.

Black Elk described a Lakota ceremony they held after a battle where people were "having kill talks all over the village, remembering brave deeds done in the fight…"[5] Warriors could die knowing that they and their contributions would not be forgotten, but celebrated and remembered. The Lakota encouraged the gift of brave sacrifice by receiving it graciously with gratitude.

Wikis described a similar ceremony. After one battle, people blackened their faces, and the "old men and old women shouted the names of those men who had been the bravest in the fight."[6]

Ohiyesa described how gracious receiving was a normal part of child-rearing in his Sioux nation. Parents constantly celebrated their children's progression into adulthood, both praising and modeling the qualities they wanted their children to embrace. He wrote, "[the child's] first step alone, the first word spoken, first game killed, the attainment of manhood or womanhood, each was the occasion of a feast and dance in his honor, at which the poor always benefited to the full extent of the parents' ability."[7] The parents honored their children's gifts by graciously receiving them with celebration.

This shows me the power each person has to build a beautiful culture as a follower, receiver, or witness. Practice noticing and praising excellent behavior. Give thanks at least in private, and also in public when appropriate.

Systems of accountability are the boundary-setting that discourage unwanted behavior. Praise, gratitude, and sharing stories of others' good deeds are ways of giving positive reinforcement to encourage more excellent behavior. Anyone can receive graciously and encourage the kind of behavior they want to see in the world.

Watching a Child's Heart Close – "This is the Sickness That Runs Through My Family"

All children are born with wide open hearts. Tragically, many people have learned to close their heart somehow by the time they reach adulthood in unhealthy nations. Different people close their hearts in different ways and to various extents, but this is a common problem.

This transition from open heart to closed heart is what some people call the loss of innocence. The transformation looks different for different people, but often involves a transition from basically generous to basically self-centered, basically trusting to basically untrusting, thoughtful towards others to careless, relaxed to stressed, deep-breathing to tensed or shallow breathing, graceful movement to jerky movement, and more. Children start out life believing that people are basically good and trustable, and over time may begin to believe that people are basically untrustable and bad or conditionally good. Children who initially approach life as an adventure may learn to approach life as a series of chores. Children who are bright and vibrant and expressive may learn to hold back, and somehow not be themselves.

It is misleading to call this the loss of innocence. Innocence is only lost in the sense that people forget their divine nature and the divinity of all life. Instead, I believe people can *forget their innocence*. Innocence is still there in all of us – we need only remember, and remember how to give our love fully, and find people to do this with.

What would it be like to watch two little girls go through this tragic transition from heart-openness to heart-closure?

A friend whom I'll call Alison visits her sister, brother-in-law, and their three children every six months or so.

Alison described eight-year-old Tina, saying, "all through her life she's been really empathetic, such a joyful spirited kid but also sensitive. Really affected by things that she saw that hurt her [or] hurt other people and really in tune and empathetic." Young Tina was very engaging, and when Alison felt sad, she would notice and ask, "Aunt Alison, what's wrong?"

Alison described how easily Tina shared her feelings in previous visits: "A year ago, we were in bed and she's telling me about this boy that she liked… [Tina said,] 'I haven't told anyone this'… it was… so sweet… She really opened up to me."

Noticing the Big Shutdown

In Alison's most recent 6-month visit, she noticed upsetting changes: "[Tina] doesn't look people in the eyes as much. She doesn't really know how to engage as much." Alison would ask Tina questions, and she noticed big differences: "It's a look in her eyes. There's a feeling she doesn't want to look at people… I see a lot of pain in her eyes now. A lack of empathy and connection."

Tina was often mean to her younger brother. Before this visit, Tina would get frustrated with her brother sometimes, and Alison would help her work through her feelings. Alison would say, "we have to be a little more flexible with him because he's learning how to be." With Alison's help, Tina had embraced her older-sister mentoring role and empathized with her brother's experience. In this visit, she noticed Tina seemed to give up with an attitude of "I don't care." She would not look at Alison who said, "[Tina] is shut off… I feel like she's disassociated because she's so sensitive and at home things are really intense."

The parents commonly yelled at the children. The kids often behave hurtfully towards each other, which the parents unknowingly reinforce. Alison said, "most of the time [the kids are] trying to take things from each other and yell at each other… And then the parents yell at them about it and model anger and frustration and then the kids have anger and frustration… You can't yell at the kids and teach them to be compassionate. [They can't] be like, 'be nice to your brother' while they're being mean to the kids."

Alison told of changes in Tina's older sister Eliza as well, describing, "a big shutdown." Eliza was commonly grumpy and easy to get into a bad mood, and never surprised when things went poorly. However, Eliza began to have fun as soon as Alison took her out of her house, saying, "She opened up out of her shell and she was like, oh, I'm not going to be yelled at. She was just great." Alison said how much of a relief it would be "just to have a whole day where she wasn't going to be yelled at! … she just really glowed at someone actually taking interest in her hobbies and things."

Poor Boundary-Setting

The parents sometimes set boundaries by responding violently when the children misbehaved. Eliza would say hurtful things, and Alison's sister, Eliza's mother, would hit Eliza sometimes, or grab her by the face hard. Alison said, "My sister definitely gets angry and just lashes out… it's really chaotic…"

When Alison took Eliza out, Eliza sometimes behaved disrespectfully, and Alison held healthy boundaries in a respectful way, saying, "I'm not going to do whatever you want. I'm not going to let you disrespect me… but it's your birthday. And we're gonna do some fun stuff!"

Alison noticed a lot of troubles in the family when she visited. The father was a weak presence, playing a lot of video games and doing what his wife told him. His wife would nag him, and he would complain and accept it. Alison acknowledged how hard it is for even two parents to raise three children. But that can't be an excuse for acting hurtfully towards the kids.

Hurtful Attitudes – Favoritism, Assuming the Worst, Laughing at Misery

Alison noticed that the parents would scold the children like many people scold dogs: "Bad! No, bad!" Alison said, "It sounds like [the mother is] talking to an animal. Not [that] we should talk to animals this way."

The parents would play favorites. The mother would only scold Eliza this way, but never Tina. Tina had learned to manipulate this, finding ways to lie or behave inappropriately while getting Eliza blamed for it.

The mother acts or assumes that Eliza is always disrespectful and rude, and "she treats her like she's not redeemable. And then Eliza is that way with [her mom]." In other words, Eliza lived down to her mother's expectations.

For example, "[The mother would say] 'good luck with her' when I take her out. And [the mother is] always just exasperated. Just never saying a nice thing about [Eliza]. Expecting her to always be bratty. Instead of [asking] why is she acting like this? What needs of hers are not being met?" But when Alison took Eliza out of the house, she noticed, "she's great. She's emotionally intelligent. She's maturing. She's really excited that I'm interested in her."

Tina would cry a lot in the past, and the adults would laugh at her and not be very kind. Alison said, "I think it just made her kind of shut down that part of herself." The parents also overreacted to minor troubles, yelling at the girls for getting clothes dirty when they could just clean it or put on another layer over the dirty one.

Unnecessarily Controlling

The parents were controlling as well, focusing heavily on how the girls looked and what they wore and forcing them to wear certain things. Alison believes that "Tina learned it's more important how you perform and how you look."

Even dinner time would be controlling, with the parents forcing the kids to eat unhealthy things like chicken nuggets and ketchup and a yogurt tube with sugar: "[the mother would say], you've got to eat it. And then when they're done, [the mother] nags them for an hour to finish everything. It's so painful watching these kids eat. Because she [says], take another bite. Eliza, focus. [But] I [can see that] they're not hungry…" After dinner they would get sugary candy.

Alison described how she does her best when she visits to influence her nieces for the better. Sometimes Alison would cook lunch the kids didn't want, and she would say ok but there would be no sugary snacks later. Alison asked the kids what they wanted and gave them options. The kids would help her cook. Occasionally she would let them have a sugary treat, and she said, "it's hard not to, just because they're so addicted to [sugar]."

I asked Alison how she relates to the kids. She said, "I treat them more like adults and talk to them. They still push things, but I just tell them why I don't like that… I just explain things to them and I think they understand that more. I'm really interested in what they're saying and ask them more questions about it. I think I try to build them up in their confidence [in] things they're doing… [I try] to build them up. [I see when] they did a thing, and I'm watching and I care. I see them growing. [I'm] engaging them, asking questions."

Overwhelmingly, Alison believes the parents don't notice the effect they're having on their children. The parents are commonly exhausted, get angry easily, and are never open to outside feedback, saying, "You can't possibly know what it's like to take care of three kids." However, because the parents behave so hurtfully, they never get to see how beautifully the kids behave when they spend time with an adult who treats them respectfully while holding firm boundaries.

Difficulty Growing Up Without Strong Mentors

Alison noted how hard it is for girls to grow up without strong mentorship: "I think [being really bummed out] is pretty common for girls when they're 11 and 12…" Many Americans act like this is normal and ok, and they expect pre-teens and teenagers to suffer. It is difficult to grow up without healthy role models who are emotionally mature and help young people relate to intense feelings not just with empathy, but with wisdom, maturity, and compassion.

She noted, "Of course [the girls] are lost and sad and bummed out because they've learned… how [their] mom lives and how this culture lives… life is just all about buying clothes and getting this food and this purse. It's all about getting things to feel happy. It's not about growing to be a good person or being in service… Everything they do is about consumption or distraction…"

Alison could see the children's perspective: "I have all these emotional hormones happening and I don't have any guidance. Obviously I feel fucking depressed and I look around coming into being an adult and [thinking], 'this is what life is? I'm a kid and I'm coming into adulthood and adulthood is just more of this for the rest of my life?' Not seeing the options that I now see as an adult where there's so much beauty and so [many] options to live a happy and fulfilling life."

Passing Down the Sickness

Alison believed that her nieces recognized that, "I actually need to protect myself in order to survive… This is really hard to feel so sensitive in this environment." The girls seemed to learn that, "the way to feel good and valuable is by being pretty… and having nice clothes and certain clothes and certain… hairstyles and all this stuff is the way to feel valuable… [Tina] learned to focus on that and shut down to protect herself."

Alison described her father as emotionally abusive and somewhat physically abusive towards her mother. Alison said, "[My sister] was obviously impacted by [her father's hurtful behavior in childhood]. She's very unhappy, very emotionally immature, but I don't think has the self-growth or wisdom to [ask,] where is that coming from?"

Alison noted, "This is the sickness that runs through my family. Obviously if you don't think there's a problem you're not gonna heal it."[8]

This sickness at the family level mirrors the sickness at the cultural level. Unhealthy nations forbid good boundary-setting, because whenever people try to hold boundaries and stand up to abuse, the riot police come out. Thus many people do not learn how to set respectful but firm boundaries in their lives, and so they struggle to relate to their children with respect and appropriate firmness. Unhealthy societies that tolerate violence internally will always have some percentage of families that are emotionally or physically violent with each other. Societies that focus on the wrong things – like consumerism, obedience, appearances, and make-believe – will encourage families to focus on the wrong things too.

Alison illustrated so many patterns of deep love in this story. She had good emotional contact with the kids. She treated them with an open heart as good people making mistakes rather than bad people being themselves. She received their gifts, hearing their intimate stories, taking interest in their hobbies, and praising them and showing she cared. She acted in service by holding strong boundaries and helping the kids find better ways of behaving.

Alison sadly only visited twice per year, and the kids were stuck in a household that embraced the opposite patterns. They had parents who did not receive their gifts or model healthy boundaries. Alison said she watched her two nieces shut down. In spiritual terms, I believe she was watching their hearts close in various ways as they learned to hold parts of themselves back.

Even in the most terrible unhealthy nations, some people manage to keep an open heart. And some of those who close their hearts in childhood may learn to reopen them later. But heart-closure is simply a common pattern in unhealthy nations where a few people rule over everybody else. Heart-closure will stop being a common childhood experience when we generate nations that welcome everyone to set healthy boundaries. In other words, when we generate a way of life where *everybody stands for a culture of mutual respect, and nobody rules over anybody else.*

Experience Love by Giving Love

In unhealthy nations that train people to close their hearts, it can seem like there isn't enough love. If a person was deprived or hurt in childhood, this can easily create a sense of something missing, or the feeling of a gap in the heart where there ought to be something.

This can lead to a sense that the person isn't good enough, or needs love from others to feel ok. It's as if such a wounded person can only experience love when they're validated by others' affection. But what happens in moments of conflict or isolation, when that validation is not there? When a person is dependent on others' validation, on receiving others' love to feel ok, they become vulnerable and fragile. Deep insecurities can come to the surface whenever that validation disappears.

Getting love from others doesn't bring the deepest satisfaction – *giving love* does. Rich people can receive all manner of kind words, favors, affectionate touch, and other gifts, and yet how many seem deeply satisfied with life? In contrast, Jesus Christ received relatively little, and yet he has been widely portrayed for centuries with a glowing heart. I believe that Christ, like so many spiritual leaders, found his deepest satisfaction in giving love.

Giving one's deepest love is the second core spiritual practice, and *giving love is actually the way to experience love*.

Babies are born giving their love with a wide open heart, and the process of heart closure is actually the child *learning not to give their love*. Thus, learning how to give love again is the way to an open heart and deep healing.

Anyone can experience love by giving their love, no matter how others act. When a person gives their love no matter what, they can feel a deep confidence in themselves regardless how others treat them.

When I do not have enough love in my life, I sometimes have a reflexive response to seek love from others. But I've learned that seeking love from others actually doesn't help me feel better. I've found that when I don't have enough love in my life, it's because I'm not giving enough.

To anyone who thinks there isn't enough love in their life, I suggest this: give your own love fully in service of what matters to you. Giving love is the way for anybody to open their heart and experience love again.

Troubles With Love When People Learn to Hold Themselves Back

One of the most beautiful and most sad songs I know is the Beatles' "She's Leaving Home."

The song tells the story of a daughter who runs away from home, leaving only a note for her parents to find. Her parents are devastated. The mother cries while reading the note. The parents feel so upset, having "sacrificed most of our lives" to give her "everything money could buy." They had "never a thought for ourselves" and "struggled all our lives to get by," and yet the daughter feels unsatisfied, and she only finds freedom by finally running away. The singer cryptically notes there was "Something inside, that was always denied, for so many years…"

How many people have found themselves in relationships like this, where one person cares about another and does their best, but ends up acting in hurtful ways? If I love my parent or spouse or child, and I do my best to serve them, how can things work out such that they still feel trapped in the relationship? In this song, the parents are caught by surprise that their daughter did not like the life they made for her and felt the need to escape in secrecy. How is it that some people who truly care, like the parents in this song, can not notice when they're acting hurtfully or ignorantly, and do not even notice that the other person feels little gratitude for their giving?

In this song, the parents cared about their daughter and did their best by her, and yet all their loving sacrifices led to a very dissatisfying result for everyone involved. Why? What were they missing?

Their troubles are common in unhealthy nations. When a person learns to withhold their love and block parts of themselves in childhood, they may grow up struggling to love others in the deepest ways possible. A person with poor contact may not notice the impact they have on other people. A selfish person may focus only on their own feelings and not others', or not take others' needs into account. People who internalize rules of good or moral behavior can follow these internal rules and not notice the hurtful effects on others. People can think they're feeling love or acting in loving ways while they're actually acting hurtfully. I believe this is the rulers' intended goal in every unhealthy nation: for each generation to close the hearts of the next, knowingly or not, with minimal oversight by authorities.

This was made vividly clear in the True Americanism study explored in Chapter 42. The 25 soldiers who struggled to have deeply pleasurable and connecting relationships, and who were willing to be cogs in a corrupt machine, also described their parents' profound unawareness. Many soldiers told stories describing how, in childhood, their parents had imposed many moralistic commands about being good, but broke many of those commands themselves. They hit their kids while saying violence was bad. They scolded and screamed at their kids while forbidding any emotional release in their children. They ignored their kids' feelings while demanding courtesy in return.[9]

As the interviewer summarized, "The parents regarded their own behavior and its acceptance by their children as self-evidently correct." The parents did not have to say "might makes right" for the kids to learn it. The kids learned that it was ok for the powerful to be angry or violent, and this behavior by the weak is morally wrong. People who learn to withhold their own love can easily treat and train their children in ways they don't understand, unknowingly passing on deep emotional and spiritual wounds to their children.

The kids who experienced chronic disrespect at home were the ones most likely to grow up willing to follow the orders of corrupt politicians. I believe the Catholic boarding schools described in Chapter 21 were so abusive precisely because the rulers wanted to start this cycle of child abuse, knowing that abused children would likely grow up and pass on hurtful patterns to their own children later, intentionally or not, and thus generate future generations of adults without the internal strength to stand up to corrupt rulers and lower authorities. In contrast, the True Americanism study also described how the kids who grew up in respectful households were the ones most likely to stand up to corrupt politicians.

I believe acting in a loving way involves many of the patterns explored in this book, including good contact, acting in service, receiving the other person's gifts, judging behavior and not the person, integrity and trust, loving touch, showing gratitude, avoiding assumptions, encouraging authentic passion and personal growth, and healthy boundary setting. The more a family or community embraces these patterns, the more love-gifts will flow, and the more nourishing it will feel.

There are many ways people can be deprived in both childhood and adulthood, and they can easily develop tragic or hurtful attitudes in response. Next, explore how things as fundamental as eating and breathing differently can cause people to have very different outlooks on life, in *Chapter 45: The Spiritual Impacts of Physical Deprivation*.

Chapter 45: The Spiritual Impacts of Physical Deprivation

The first core spiritual practice is to feel a practical, aware gratitude for the gifts of life. A person can live from this place of gratitude even when times are hard, but children who experience chronic deprivation can find it difficult to feel gratitude as their baseline, default approach to life.

In Chapter 42, I defined spirituality as how a person relates to themselves and the world. From this perspective, *everyone experiences spirituality*. It does not necessarily have anything to do with supernatural gods or mysticism. Each person relates to themselves and the world around them in certain ways, and they can approach life from a basic sense of abundance and trust or deprivation and fear.

Unhealthy nations train people to experience life from a place of chronic deprivation, with each person experiencing this in their own way. Authorities commonly train people to believe that obedience and selfishly accumulating money are the best way to acquire abundance in the face of scarcity. But when practically everyone obeys authorities and profits from their neighbors, they do not generate shared abundance, only a further sense of chronic lack as they reinforce the worst aspects of their unhealthy nation.

This book has described a few ways that children and adults can be kept in a state of chronic deprivation:

- *Financial deprivation*: Chapter 10 reviewed how families can be kept in a state of chronic financial desperation. When adults in a child's life are constantly anxious or scared, a child can easily learn to "do whatever it takes" not to experience that in their own adulthood, including by taking exploitative or dissatisfying jobs.

- *Deprivation of loving touch*: Chapter 42 reviewed ways that children can be raised with chronic deprivation of loving touch, and how this lack of abundance trains the opposite of gratitude and reciprocity – it trains selfishness and pain. Different children may respond differently, but these hurtful attitudes are common outcomes of raising children without loving touch.

- *Peace deprivation*: Parts 6, 7, and 8 reviewed how authorities keep people divided and afraid or angry towards others in their own nation. This makes it very difficult to experience a deep relaxation and peace. Stress, worry, or anxiety can easily become normal attitudes.

- *Self-worth deprivation*: Chapters 17, 18, and 30 reviewed how authorities can train people to believe that they are, in a very basic way, "not good enough" and thus undeserving of a life of abundance and respect.

- *Sexual deprivation*: Chapter 25 reviewed how unhealthy nations deprive many people of life-long, satisfying, uncoerced sexual fulfillment.

- *Deprivation of trustworthy people*: When a person is surrounded by untrustworthy or inauthentic people, it can be difficult to cultivate deep relationships and a deep gratitude for life.

- *Deprivation of meaningful work*: Chapter 41 reviewed how people are forbidden from standing up to the abuses and exploitation at the heart of their unhealthy nation. When people learn to ignore the biggest problems and ignore their own dissatisfaction, they can learn to focus on lesser problems instead, and life can seem meaningless as a result.

In unhealthy nations, different people are deprived in different ways and different amounts. Some people have many sexual partners but have few trustworthy friends and work relationships; other people have parents that gave them plenty of loving touch but also grow up in extreme poverty. When people have such very different experiences and develop different spiritual attitudes as a result, it can become very difficult to empathize with neighbors and resolve big political problems.

How else could different people physically experience the world, so that life seems either basically abundant or basically lacking?

Food

Growing up, I had the vague sense that food gave me energy. If I ate enough I would have energy, and if I didn't eat enough, my energy would flag. I had a vague sense that eating nutritious food was important, but I did not really understand why.

It turns out, food provides people with much more than energy. How each person eats, and how their parents ate before, during, and after pregnancy, can profoundly impact how they experience life, including how their body develops, how easily they heal from injuries, and whether they experience chronic pain and disease.

Similar patterns of nutritional deficiency play out in both humans and nonhumans.

Nutritional Deficiency in Nonhumans

Nutritional deficiencies have been well-studied in nonhumans.[1]

In one study, pregnant rats were fed a diet that lacked vitamin E, and researchers noticed a much longer gestation. The baby rats later developed slowly and became either very thin or very fat. Either way, the young rats were frail and had thin skulls.

When mother rats were fed a diet deficient in vitamin A, they experienced a very long gestation and both the mother and child rat would often die. The rats recognized what was missing in their diet. In one instance, rats gnawed their way into a box holding rabbits and consumed only the part of the rabbit that contained the highest levels of vitamin A – the eyes. They left the rest of the rabbits behind.

Cows can also suffer eye soreness and even blindness from vitamin A deficiency. During a drought, when a herd of cows was forced to eat a diet low in vitamin A, researchers found that almost 30% developed eye soreness or even blindness. Approximately half the calves born during this time were deformed or somehow not healthy. Many cows' health improved after they could eat a nutritionally complete diet again.[2]

Vitamin A deficiency can diminish a dog's balance as well as hearing ability. One researcher encountered total deafness in dogs who were heavily deprived of vitamin A.[3]

Nutrients provide the basic building material of the body. Consider the analogy of a house. When a house's siding is damaged, even if a skilled person is present, without new siding, they will not be able to properly fix the house. Likewise, when a body lacks nutrients, without the right material, it will not be able to heal or grow properly. Without nutrition, the necessary building material simply isn't available.

What does nutritional deficiency look like in humans?

Weston Price Learned About Nutrition by Studying Healthy Nations

By the early 20th century, many physicians were very concerned about people's declining health.

Sir Arbuthnot Lane, a distinguished English surgeon, said, "Long surgical experience has proved to me conclusively that there is something radically and fundamentally wrong with the civilized mode of life, and I believe that unless the present dietetic and health customs of the White Nations are reorganized, social decay and race deterioration are inevitable."[4]

Dr. Earnest A. Hooton wrote in his book *Apes, Men, and Morons*, that "human teeth and the human mouth have become, possibly under the influence of civilization, the foci of infections that undermine the entire bodily health of the species… degenerative tendencies in evolution have manifested themselves in modern man to such an extent that our jaws are too small for the teeth which they are supposed to accommodate… as a consequence, these teeth erupt so irregularly that their fundamental efficiency is often entirely or nearly destroyed."[5]

In other words, people's bodies were developing so poorly that, in some cases, the pieces did not even fit together properly, with the underlying jaw being too small for the teeth it was supposed to hold. What could cause such fundamental problems?

Weston Price was an American dentist in the early 20th century who wondered why dental cavities were so incredibly common. Most dentists endlessly studied the various dental diseases and injuries without discovering the root cause, but Price took a different approach: he went around the world studying healthy nations to learn how people lived without developing cavities.

While Price's research focused on nutrition and individual physical health, he also noticed the same deeper patterns so many other observers have noticed too. After studying healthy nations around the world, he wrote that "few impressions can be more vivid than that of the absence of prisons and asylums." In contrast, he described how "serious and disturbing" it was in unhealthy nations to see a widespread "increase in the percentage of individuals with unsocial traits."[6]

With healthy nations serving as his control groups, he studied what healthy humans are like and learned many ways that people in unhealthy nations are predisposed to dental and many other health problems.

Racism and hatred were major obstacles to understanding widespread health problems in the United States. Chapter 22 described how Christians had been trained to look down on "primitives" and "savages." Price warned his readers to avoid "prejudice against the wisdom of so-called savages." Likewise, ideologies of racial purity intended to make poor whites side with rich whites had trained people to believe that racial mixing was the cause of the worsening health that physicians observed.[7]

Price found something different: as people of all "races" switch to poor diets, they show similar health problems regardless of their skin color. In Price's words, "primitive races share our blights when they adopt our conception of nutrition."

Dental Cavities are an Unhealthy-Nation Disease

Weston Price went all around the world, visiting Australia, Pacific Islands, South America, Africa, North America, and Europe. In each region, he studied two types of groups: people of healthy nations who maintained their traditional diets, and people who lived nearby – often just a few miles away – who had adopted diets of unhealthy nations. He documented his findings in his book *Nutrition and Physical Degeneration*, including pictures of the people he encountered.

Prior to encountering European unhealthy nations, the Maori of New Zealand showed a level of health almost unheard-of in Europe.[8]

They ate a large diversity of seafood as well as grubs and roots. Analysis of ancient Maori skulls showed that about 1% showed any sign of cavities. About one out of every 2,000 teeth had a cavity. All of these pre-contact skulls showed normally-formed dental arches.

These healthy people showed physical abilities that astounded the Europeans. One night, a Maori person and European were looking at Jupiter in the sky. The Maori person was able to distinguish the individual moons of Jupiter with their bare eyes. They could tell when a moon became eclipsed by Jupiter, something the European could only see with their telescope.[9]

Everywhere Price visited, he took pictures of the people living on their traditional diets as well as locals and white people who were living on the unhealthy diets of highly processed foods.

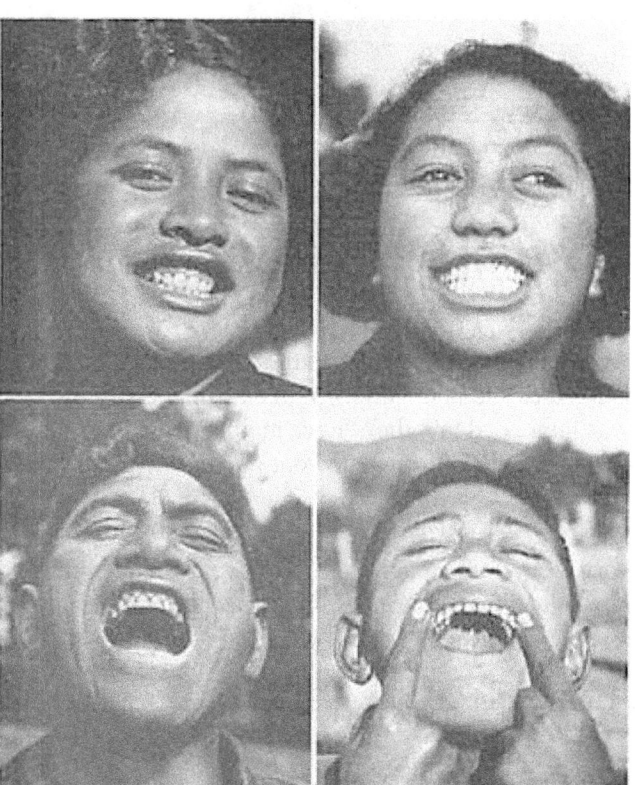

Pictures of Maori living on their traditional diet. Notice the wide arches and well-aligned, healthy teeth. They had no dentists and clearly didn't need them.[10]

When the British took over New Zealand, they forced many Maori to eat diets based on sweetened and canned foods, white flour, and syrup. Price described how these Maori and local white people developed similar deformities in their dental arches, as well as similar rates of cavities.

One researcher informed Price that approximately 86-98% of white people in this region had cavities, as did 95% of Maori who lived on a similar diet. This was plainly visible in the photos that Price took:

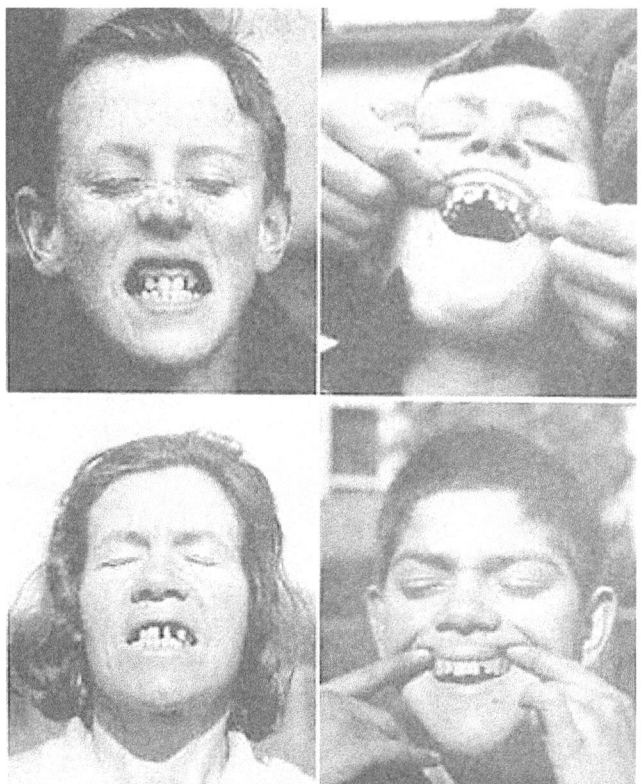

Pictures of Maori and white New Zealanders living on European diets with processed foods. Reduced dental arches meant teeth did not have space to grow normally. Tooth cavities were widespread.

Price encountered the same pattern when he visited Australia. He noticed that the people of healthy nations, "have been able to build good bodies and maintain them in excellent condition" despite living in a region with extremely low rainfall. He was impressed that they "have maintained a vigorous existence in districts in which the white population which expelled them is unable to continue to live. Among the white race there, the death rate approaches or exceeds the birth rate."[11]

Price was again impressed with their physical abilities. He described young men who were able to hunt kangaroos and wallabies, animals that could even outrun Europeans on horseback. They could see animals move from a mile away that white people could not see at all.

When people of healthy nations maintained their traditional diets, they had very healthy teeth and skull development:

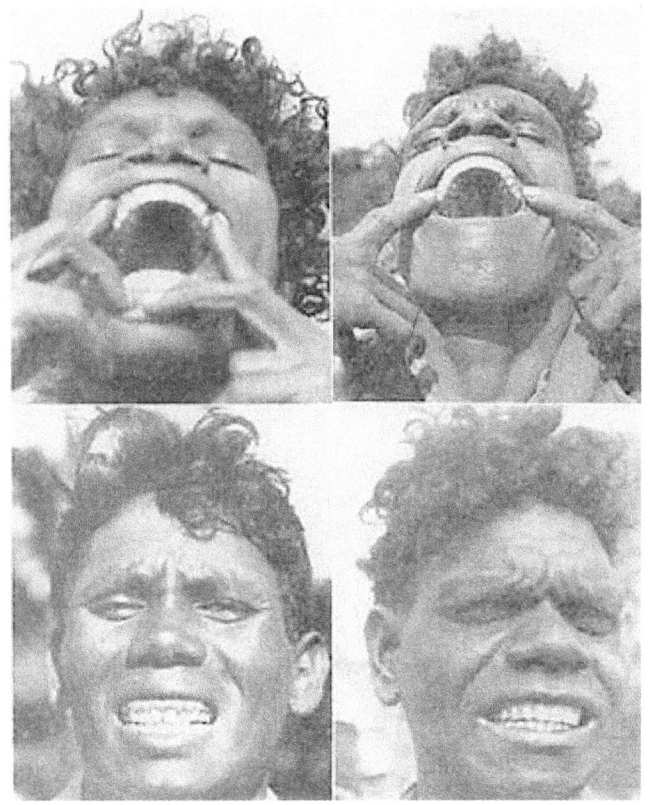

People of Australian healthy nations who lived on their traditional diets.

Unfortunately, like people around the world, when they transitioned to nutrient-poor diets, their teeth and bones suffered dramatically:

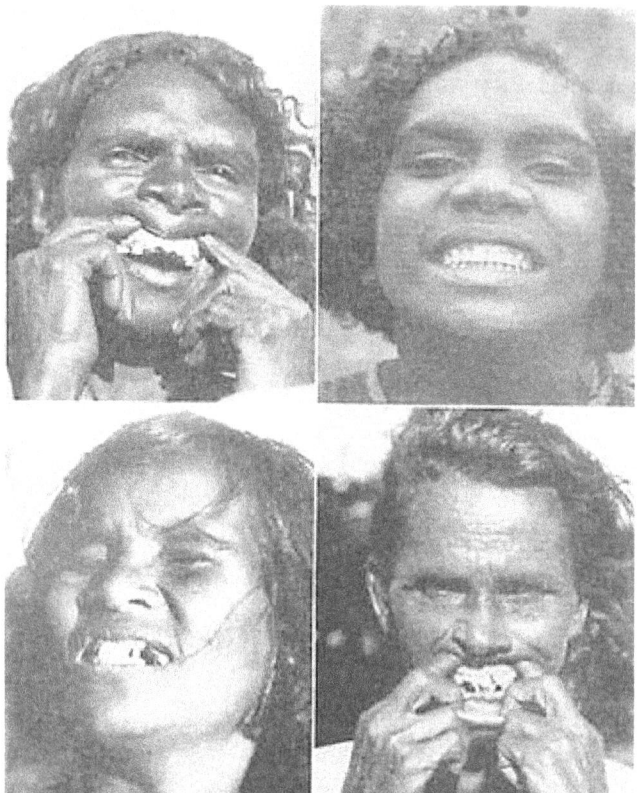

Top-left and bottom: Photos of people of Australian healthy nations who had transitioned to eating heavily-processed foods. Top-right: a woman maintained her nation's traditional diet.

One study of people of healthy nations who had been forced onto the LeParouse reservation near Sydney, Australia and fed processed food showed that 100% had dental cavities. Price found many whites and native Australians who had such large deformities that breathing through the nose was difficult.

Price's research exposed major gaps in American dentistry that persisted decades after his work. For example, many dentists continued to ignore the role of nutrition while focusing on other causes of dental problems, such as the build-up of tartar.

However, Price found many people of healthy nations with strong teeth and healthy gums and no dentists to remove any tartar that built up. He especially described the Eskimos of North America, many of whom had teeth worn down almost to the gum line, but who still had very healthy gums and no periodontal disease.[12]

Amazingly, Price was not the only person to notice the radical change in dental health in recent centuries. Many anthropologists had already learned that a skull without cavities was more likely to be ancient. An anthropologist named Dryer said, "caries [cavities] is a comparatively modern disease and that no skull showing this condition can be regarded as ancient."[13]

Clearly, people of unhealthy nations struggle to eat well, and this has had huge impacts on people's health for centuries or, in some regions, millennia. Unfortunately, the problems are not limited to dental health.

Other Impacts of Nutrition Deprivation

Nutrients such as calcium and phosphorus are crucial for bone development, and when these are missing in nutritionally-poor diets, people's skeletons suffer as a result, manifesting in many different ways.

Two Maori women. The woman at left was raised on her traditional Maori diet. Note the much narrower head of the woman at right raised on processed foods.[14]

A mother and her daughter in Polynesia. The mother was raised on a traditional diet, and the daughter was not. Note the daughter's narrower head.[15]

These are Quichua people from South America. The mother was raised on a traditional diet, while her child was raised on processed food. People's skeletons are strongly affected within a single generation after adopting nutrient-poor diets.[16]

These pictures of people's heads make it obvious how strongly people's bodily development can be affected by nutrition.

Bones can soften without proper minerals, predisposing people to a variety of structural problems. Among other troubles, Price found that people on poor diets can develop bowed legs.[17,18]

Other aspects of people's development can be harder to observe, but still have profound influences on people's lives.

Childbirth

When skeletons do not grow to their full size, with all the pieces in their proper proportion, childbirth can become much more challenging. Dr. Kathleen Vaughan studied people of healthy nations in southern Asia along with people who ate heavily processed foods. In her book *Safe Childbirth*, she acknowledged that a woman's physical development, rather than race or other factors, determines her ability to safely and comfortably give birth.[19]

Many stories of people of healthy nations show that childbirth was not particularly stressful for the women. During Price's travels, he noted, "With several of these tribes… the ease with which childbirth is accomplished is so great that it is looked upon as quite an insignificant experience."[20] Chapter 13 reviewed De Las Casas' comment about the Arawak women: "pregnant women work to the last minute and give birth almost painlessly; up the next day, they bathe in the river and are as clean and healthy as before giving birth…"[21]

While I'm sure women of healthy nations living in their traditional way still sometimes experience difficult births, many stories show that this is the exception rather than the rule.

Weston Price found many stories of women of healthy nations struggling with childbirth after adopting unhealthy nations' diets. Price described the "evidence of a rapid decline in maternal reproductive efficiency after an abandonment of the native foods and the substitution of foods of modern civilization."[22] When he visited the Six Nation Reservation at Brantford, Ontario, he spoke with a doctor who had worked there for 28 years and said the hospital had come to be used largely for "young Indian women during abnormal childbirth."[23]

Price also met a doctor in Anchorage, Alaska who worked with Eskimo women. The doctor said he had never arrived in time to help with the birth of an Eskimo woman who lived on her traditional diet, and he told the story of one Eskimo woman who gave birth to 26 children. Several times, she had given birth during the night and decided not to wake up her husband, letting him meet the infant in the morning. After the Eskimos' diets changed, the doctor reported that women commonly needed to be carried to the hospital where they would be in labor for days.

Difficult births are much more common in unhealthy nations. Poor nutrition has many impacts, including making the hips constricted, making the physical act of birthing more difficult and painful than it otherwise would be.

Other patterns show that, even when a person starts out with sufficient health, long-term nutritional deficiency can lead to long-term problems with pregnancy. For example, researchers found that miscarriages, stillbirths, and premature births were not randomly distributed among a given woman's pregnancies. Rather, they were much more likely to happen immediately before a pregnancy leading to the birth of a child with severe mental disabilities. In other words, the poor nutrition manifested in difficulties with multiple, back-to-back pregnancies over years as the poor food took its toll on the women.[24]

In unhealthy nations, many older girls and young women are trained to feel chronically insecure about their appearance and weight, and this too can have tragic consequences. Weston Price noted that when girls and young women starve themselves to stay thin, they deprive themselves of nutrients at exactly the time when they are physically developing into womanhood. Since the body prioritizes the development of new growth, when girls and young women starve themselves, their bodies will take minerals out of existing bones in order to grow, weakening themselves in the process.[25]

Many healthy nations have recognized that the father's health is also important, and if he is unhealthy, the baby may also suffer.[26] As one example, a full-blooded Eskimo woman married a white man, and she ate her own diet but prepared his imported foods for him. Thus her children had a mother who ate well but a father who ate poorly. Several of her children had incomplete facial development and restricted dental arches. Studies of sheep and pigs also show that the father's health strongly influences the offspring's health.[27]

The Christian Bible and Jewish Torah both contain a passage where God supposedly condemns women to experiencing painful childbirth: "To the woman [God] said, 'I will surely multiply your pain in childbearing; in pain you shall bring forth children.'"[28] For years, I thought this was simply the statement of a mean-spirited patriarchal god, propagated by religious authorities that wanted to perpetually keep women at a lower privilege level than men. However there may be a deeper meaning: childbirth very likely became much harder after the transition to an unhealthy nation, as both women's and men's diets worsened, producing girls who grew up with less fully-developed skeletons and thus struggled to give birth.

Chapter 8 showed how the transition out of the "Garden of Eden" was not a one-off event but a repeating pattern, and difficulty in childbirth may be part of that pattern. When people are forced out of a healthy nation and trapped in an unhealthy nation, it becomes more difficult to eat well, and more-difficult childbirths are one tragic result.

Mental and Social Effects

Weston Price found many examples of people who developed mental disabilities, likely due to nutritional problems during pregnancy and childhood. One example shows the strong influence of nutrition on people's mental and physical development.

Price described a 16-year-old man who had the genitals and mental capacity of a 4-year-old. This boy-like man commonly played on the floor with blocks. He had frequent, long-lasting nausea.[29]

He also showed several skeletal problems. Some bones in his hands had not fused properly, limiting his hands' functionality. His maxillary arch (above the upper row of teeth) was so much narrower than his mandibular arch (lower row) that it fit entirely inside, meaning he could not chew food. Price believed his pituitary gland had not been stimulated sufficiently due to his deformed skull structure, limiting the gland's activity and his physical and mental development.

Even worse, this young man's left nostril was entirely blocked and his right nostril nearly blocked, severely impacting his breathing. He had likely mouth-breathed his entire life out of necessity. At night, he had to sleep with a rolled-up coat under his neck to prop his mouth open. Whenever his mouth closed, he would begin suffocating and wake up.

Price offered the young man a surgery where he widened the upper dental arch by 1/2." Just by changing this aspect of his facial bone structure, Price noticed "a very great change in his physical development and mentality." In a short time, he passed through developmental stages that usually take years. He grew 3" in the following four months, and a mustache started growing immediately. Within 12 weeks, he had a man's genitals.

The mental changes were also distinct. He began playing pranks and calling people with the telephone. At home, his mother could send him to the grocery store with money, and he could know whether he had received the correct change from the clerk. He could travel 90 miles by train to visit Price, including switching between multiple trains and streetcars without trouble. This showed how even a single aspect of skeletal development – the reduced upper arch size – severely impacted the boy's overall development.

Price found many other signs that nutritional deficiency was negatively impacting society. He visited the Ohio State Penitentiary which had 4,000 inmates. He asked the prison's doctor if he'd noticed any strange patterns with the inmates' mouths which weren't observed in people outside of prison. The doctor said that the mouths were often too small, so that the tongue did not fit well inside. Price observed more than half of the prison population, and everyone he observed showed some sign of deformity in the face or dental arches.

While this prison population showed some effects that were not common in the general population, nearly all Americans at the time had severe nutritional deficiencies. Using estimates from his own patients as well as data from the United States Department of Agriculture and Department of Labor, Price calculated that people's calcium intake was 44%-74% of the government-recommended amount, and their phosphorus consumption was 23%-45% of the government-recommended level.[30] However, many governmental dietary recommendations still set a low standard. Price found that healthy-nation diets often had 1.5x – 50x the nutrition of unhealthy-nation diets.[31]

Bone Fragility and Healing

Many people take for granted that elderly people develop frail bones that break easily and, after breaking, heal poorly if at all. Weston Price said, "We look upon this as one of the inevitable consequences of advancing age."

However, Price believed that fragile and poorly-healing bones can be attributed more to diet than to age.

In one story, a 4-1/2-year-old boy broke his leg after falling in the kitchen. He suffered from persistent convulsions, "rampant" tooth decay, and a bad cough. At the time Price was called, the leg had been broken for 2-3 months but had not healed at all.[32]

The leg had not broken because the impact was hard, but because the boy's diet included so few minerals that his bones had little structural strength. The body essentially removed minerals from the bone to maintain the needed mineral levels in the bloodstream. Price also found that the convulsions were due to low calcium-content in the food. To heal the broken bone, Price knew the child needed minerals, including calcium, phosphorus, and magnesium.

Price quickly adjusted the boy's diet, which had mostly consisted of white bread and skim milk. Instead, Price had the family feed him wheat gruel from freshly-ground wheat, whole milk, and a teaspoon of very high-vitamin butter with each meal.

The boy showed immediate signs of improvement. The night after he ate this meal for the first time, he had no convulsions. His health rapidly improved in the coming weeks, and convulsions never returned. Six weeks later, the mother called for the little boy but couldn't find him. He was climbing up the downspout and had reached the second story of the house! After he came down and his mother scolded him, he proceeded to jump across a fence. With better nutrition, he was able to recover good health and energy.

Price often found that people physically shrank as their bodies' nutritional needs went continuously unmet. He witnessed many people who lost 2-6" within 10-20 years.[33] He estimated that, in the communities he studied, between 25-75% of Americans were affected by nutritional deficiencies which led to physical and mental disabilities, including childhood trouble in school. About these struggling children, he said, "their I.Q.'s are generally lower than normal and they readily develop inferiority complexes growing out of their handicap."[34]

Breathing

Air is the most important resource that the universe provides for humans. In a safe environment and with a little training, healthy humans can live several days without water and many weeks without food. I have personally gone more than 90 hours without water and never felt thirsty, and I once went two weeks without food without feeling hungry. But no one can last more than several minutes with air.

In his book *Breath*, James Nestor explored how to breathe properly, and why so many people breathe poorly. Building on Weston Price's research, he found that nutrient deficiency didn't fully explain why people's heads and airways had shrunk over the past few centuries. It turns out, a core aspect of eating is chewing, and chewing too little prevents teeth, tongues, faces, mouths, and throats from fully forming.[35]

Processed foods like white bread and cooked white rice are soft, and most unhealthy-nation foods require little chewing. Instead of chewing and significantly exercising the jaw muscles, many people in unhealthy-nations chew very little, and most "chewing" is relatively easy with soft, low-fiber foods that offer little exercise for the jaw. For over a century, researchers including Scottish doctor James Wallace and American anthropologist Robert Coruccini have noticed that a population's airways and faces would narrow when they switched to processed food and did not need to chew much. This was observed with humans as well as nonhumans like pigs.

Thus, eating nutrient-rich food and exercising the jaw muscles by chewing well are both important for a person's development.

Nestor also shared research by George Catlin, who lived with many North American healthy nations in the 1830s, including the Lakota, Pawnee, Omaha, and Blackfeet. He encountered people who seemed extremely physically healthy, with teeth "as regular as the keys of a piano." Nobody seemed sick, and chronic health problems or deformities were rare or non-existent. He learned the same practice from all of them: nose-breathing.[36]

Catlin wrote, "The air which enters the lungs is as different from that which enters the nostrils as distilled water is different from the water in an ordinary cistern or a frog-pond." He learned from the people of healthy nations that mouth-breathing reduced a person's strength, deformed the face, and caused stress and disease. On the other hand, nose-breathing had the opposite effects.

Catlin found that mothers in all these nations trained their babies to nose-breathe. They would carefully close the baby's mouth with their fingers after breast-feeding. While sleeping at night, the mother would close the baby's lips if they opened. Some groups strapped their babies to a straight board and propped a little pillow behind the child's head to encourage the mouth to stay closed at night.

These studies were not merely theoretically interesting for Catlin. He had severe sleep problems, sometimes even coughing up blood. He snored heavily. He wrote, "I became fully convinced of the danger of the habit [of mouthbreathing], and resolved to overcome it." He intentionally nose-breathed while awake and bandaged his head to keep his mouth closed while asleep to develop new habits. His aches, pains, and bleeding stopped, and he reported feeling healthier than at any time in his life. Another approach to prevent mouth-breathing is to carefully tape the lips closed before sleep.

Chronic poor breathing, whether due to bad habits, congested airways, or developmental problems, can easily create a sense of chronic deprivation or lack. Chapter 25 noted how humans are like fire, and just like fires need oxygen to live, so do people. Restricted breathing reduces a person's vitality.

In his book, Nestor provides many techniques for improving one's breathing. Many structural problems that restrict airways can be improved, though the easiest problems to fix are bad habits. Problems like sleep apnea, snoring, unrestful sleeping, and others can sometimes be resolved simply by learning to breathe properly.

Takeaways: Build and Share Physical Abundance while Cultivating Gratitude

It Takes a Village

It can be challenging to eat well in unhealthy nations. In some cases there is little nutritious and affordable food available, and in other cases the trouble stems from social isolation or a lack of solidarity. A pregnant woman is especially in need of a high-nutrition diet right at the time when it can be most physically difficult for her to work. Especially if the mother-to-be has no reliable partner or savings, or if her income is not very high, eating well during pregnancy can be difficult.

One story from Fiji shows how a whole community can act to support pregnant mothers and the next generation. In one healthy nation which Price did not name, women would tell the chief immediately when they became pregnant. He would then organize a feast in honor of their community's newest member that would arrive in a few months. At this feast, other members of the community pledged to adopt the child if the parents should die, ensuring that the children would be taken care of no matter what. Furthermore, at this feast the chief would appoint one or two boys to go to the sea daily and harvest high-nutrition crabs for all the expectant mothers. Showing deep solidarity, the entire community took responsibility to ensure that the next generation was as healthy as possible. They did not expect the pregnant women to fend for themselves.[37]

Price also found healthy nations who helped the father-to-be eat well too, recognizing the impact of his health on the child's wellbeing.[38]

Any present-day community can adopt a similar way of *supporting pregnant families*. Where I live in western North Carolina, often a family's close friend will host a *meal train*, where people can sign up to bring a home-cooked meal to the family on a particular date after the birth. By itself, this does not support the parents' nutritional needs before birth, but it does strongly support young families for weeks or even months after the pregnancy, a time that can be stressful. Everyone benefits from the meal trains too. The receiving family is grateful for the support, and contributing friends are happy for the opportunity to meaningfully help them.

Spiritual Implications of Poor Diets and Poor Breathing

All these aspects of physical health can heavily impact a person's spirituality, that is, they can impact how a person relates to themselves and the world around them. Attitudes of entitlement, explored in Chapter 30, are examples of spiritual patterns. An entitled person believes they deserve their lot in the world they were born into, whether good or bad. An unentitled person does not.

Unhealthy nations commonly train people to believe that their life situation, whether good or bad, is due to some inherent quality when this often is not the case. For example, Price observed that many poorly-fed American children underperformed at school and developed beliefs in their own inferiority. Would the children have thought so little of themselves if they learned they had just been eating poorly? Would their self-esteem have risen if they were helped to eat better?

Many doctors and religious authorities teach heart-closing beliefs in people's inherent badness or conditional goodness, as discussed in Chapter 18. Medical authorities can promote beliefs about hereditary defects, when the truth is that not all multi-generational problems are genetic. While some diseases may be genetic, in many cases, parents simply pass on their habits to their children, including their attitudes, how they eat, how they breathe, and more. Religious authorities can promote belief in inherent badness due to inherent sin, when the simple truth is that people who are trapped in poverty often cannot feed themselves adequately. Political authorities may propagate the belief that "racial mixing" causes problems, or certain social classes or religions are inferior, when all humans are subject to similar negative consequences if they eat or breathe poorly.

Thus, authorities can train people to see inherent deficiencies in themselves, when really the problems are quite concrete and often fixable if only the nation didn't trap so many people in poverty and isolation. Unfortunately, people's health can also have other consequences for their spiritual attitudes.

If a person consistently struggles to heal from injuries or disease, are they more likely to relate to themselves as basically strong or basically weak?

If a frail person becomes injured easily due to their parents' and their own poor diet, could they more easily see the world as a dangerous, risky place and prioritize keeping life safe and comfortable?

If a woman feels an urge to give birth but consistently finds it painful, difficult, and dangerous, and her children are weak or disabled, how might that impact her attitude towards life?

If a person feels chronic pain, are they more inclined to see life as basically abundant and joyful, or basically miserable and unpleasant?

If a person constantly breathes poorly and suffers from low energy, anxiety, and other troubles, is life for that person more likely to seem basically abundant or basically deprived?

These spiritual troubles due to chronic pain, poor diet, poor breathing, fragility, and so on can compound with other aspects of a closed heart. For example, people may develop chronic muscular tension as they learn to hold back certain feelings and urges, as described in Chapter 25. People can easily feel "stressed" and "pressured" by life as a normal, default state, and this has a physical basis: many people's chronically tensed muscles indeed create very real stressors and pressures on their body, often including their head and heart. Thus, simply learning to relax can change a person's outlook on life.

This book has explored many ways that authorities intentionally divide people, including with racism, sexism, privilege, synthetic hate, class, propaganda, and many other techniques. When each person or group lives in chronic deprivation in their own ways, whether from a lack of loving touch, safety, sexual intimacy, nutrition, or even air, this itself can create division, as different people develop different attitudes and beliefs about "how life is" and whether it's possible to live a life of pleasure and solidarity with other people. These are spiritual differences, as people within the same unhealthy nation can relate to themselves and the world around them in very different ways.

Different kinds and degrees of deprivation can encourage people to adopt different attitudes. Thus, even if they could agree on the "facts" of a social or political issue, they might still make very different choices about how to respond. This makes political unity very difficult to achieve.

I believe this is one reason why sharing is so important to building and maintaining a healthy nation: a gift economy allows everyone to experience abundance or scarcity together. Even if scarcity lasts a long time, perhaps from a drought, at least everyone can know that people in their community will take care of each other. This avoids all the political divisions and manipulations so common in unhealthy nations.

Experiencing deprivation can also make it hard to practice that first core spiritual practice of practical, aware gratitude. For example, I find it difficult to feel grateful for my food when I'm eating poorly. I rarely feel grateful to be alive when I'm breathing poorly.

I learned another spiritual lesson that helped me: *gratitude is a relationship, not just a feeling*. It has been really helpful for me to develop relationships with the things I feel grateful for, rather than just practice thankfulness as an abstract, isolated feeling. When I receive the gift of abundant air by breathing properly, it's easy to feel grateful for the air. Feeling thankful for my food is a lot easier when it actually tastes good and feels nourishing. When I garden, forage, or hunt the food myself, and when I find ways to give back to the nonhuman communities I harvest from, the food tastes better still. In other words, when I develop a relationship with the air and food, it is a lot easier to cultivate that practical, aware gratitude.

Anyone can choose their spirituality at any time – that is, anyone can choose what attitudes to adopt towards themselves and the world around them. And, people's physical experiences of the world can predispose them to embracing attitudes of abundance or attitudes of scarcity and deprivation. Unhealthy nations deprive people in countless different ways to encourage people to close their hearts and approach life from a place of scarcity, distrust and fear rather than abundance, trust and gratitude.

Food Recommendations

Weston Price gave many dietary recommendations in his book *Nutrition and Physical Degeneration*. While no one needs to study nutrition for years to eat well, there are some nutritional facts many people find surprising when I bring them up.

The biggest discovery I made is this: a nutrient may be present in a food, but that doesn't necessarily mean that the body will process it. In some cases, one nutrient may need a second nutrient to be present in order to be absorbed by the body. In other cases, *anti-nutrients* may be present such as phytates. These are naturally-occurring chemicals that inhibit nutrient absorption when eaten. Anti-nutrients are commonly found in seeds, grains, and legumes.[39]

A seed contains many nutrients and calories, enough for the plant to grow underground and push up little leaves before receiving any new energy from the sun. Why doesn't the seed start growing the moment it comes into being in the mother-plant? Why does it wait until it is in the moist ground to grow? The anti-nutrients prevent the seed from using up its nutrients and calories before it's ready. When a seed is exposed to water in the soil, this moisture deactivates the anti-nutrients, unbinding them and allowing the seed to sprout.

Likewise, if humans want to access the nutrients in seeds, they need to deactivate the anti-nutrients by soaking them.

Many healthy dietary practices are as simple as soaking seeds. Eat a variety of colors of nutritious food. Eat hard and soft foods when it's safe to do so. Eat minimally-processed foods not treated with chemical pesticides. Avoid processed sugars. Eat dark leafy greens and healthy fats. Enjoy how your food tastes rather than just gulping it down or ignoring it while watching TV. Enjoy fermented foods. Listen to your body and notice what foods in which combinations feel good, and which don't.

People of healthy nations around the world have lived on a wide variety of diets. When humans tune into their own sense of what their body needs, and they are not oppressed by a ruling class, they will find a diet that works for them. For those of us still in unhealthy nations, there is still much we can do.

I've never been interested in food chemistry. Although discussions of the huge range of vitamins, fats, proteins, carbohydrates, and other things may be helpful, I want to learn how to sense the foods I eat and figure out a diet that works for me without having to mentally understand the dozens or hundreds of different nutrient needs. Luckily, humans have been eating well without chemists or dentists for hundreds of thousands of years. In addition to the book *Nutrition and Physical Degeneration*, for those who want to learn more about healthy eating, I recommend Sally Fallon's book *Nourishing Traditions* as well as Sandor Katz's book *Wild Fermentation*. For those who want to eat wild foods, I recommend Sam Thayer's foraging books, including *The Forager's Harvest*.

The Spiritual Implications of Mistreating the Earth

Weston Price did his research in the 1920s and 1930s, a time before chemical pesticides were widespread. Even much of the unprocessed food was nutritionally deficient because soils had been depleted due to poor farming practices. Processing removed much of the remaining nutrition, leaving little left.

Even back then, dozens of government officials from around the United States confirmed that they had seen soil productivity diminish by 25-50%.[40] In the century since then, many chemicals and fertilizers have been developed to allow crops to grow in depleted soils, though they often have not increased the nutritional value of those crops. Widespread eating of low-nutrient crops continues to yield malnourishment around the world as I write in 2024.[41]

Unfortunately, in many ways, food quality has further deteriorated since Price's time. Many soils are contaminated with heavy metals and other toxins. For example, much modern rice is heavily contaminated with arsenic. Rice easily absorbs arsenic, a poison that can affect a person's whole life if they are exposed during pregnancy or as a young child. The rice plant's affinity for arsenic wasn't a problem until the past few centuries, when arsenic seeped into the soil due to pollution from heavy industries around the world. In 2019, American researchers noted that rice commonly has arsenic levels exceeding the US Environmental Protection Agency's legal limit for arsenic in water.[42] Arsenic and many other human-produced poisons are making food even less healthy over time than it was during Price's time.

This arsenic is only one example of a widespread problem. Toxic chemicals known to cause fertility issues, cancer, liver damage, and diabetes have been found in rainwater in Europe and the United States that exceed Environmental Protection Agency levels, which are already too forgiving.[43] Any amount of poison is too much. No one can protect themselves from polluted rainwater, as it becomes part of our drinking water and even organically-grown food cannot be protected from poisons in the rain.

In every nation, humans treat the soil the same way they treat each other. Healthy nations treat the Earth well, and they eat well and maintain their health as a result. Unhealthy nations commonly treat the Earth poorly, both the farm animals and the soil in which the plants grow. The results of this poor treatment of the Earth show up in our bodies in countless ways, as Weston Price documented.

All this teaches me that treating ourselves better and treating the Earth better are one and the same. We cannot achieve one without achieving the other, because humans and the Earth really are one being together. *We are what we eat*. While I am grateful for organic farmers who seek to protect their little patches of soil, there is only so much people can do in isolation.

Ultimately, protecting ourselves and protecting the Earth will require taking the same stand: creating a nation where *everybody stands for a culture of mutual respect, and nobody rules over anybody else*.

Next, dive deeper on the path to a healthy nation in *Chapter 46: Embracing the Sacred Feminine*.

Chapter 46: Embracing the Sacred Feminine

Unhealthy nations treat women abusively. Depending on the nation, women are offered either one or two ways of responding to the abuse, neither of which addresses the problem at the heart of the nation.

The list of abuses which women suffer is long. Domestic abuse, sexual assault, lower pay compared to similarly productive men, restricted opportunities to work, sexism in the workplace, and disrespect in courts of law regarding sexual assaults are just a few of the common ways women experience disrespect in many unhealthy nations around the world (reviewed in Chapters 24-25).

Sometimes sexism manifests in official ways, as when countries like Saudi Arabia severely restrict women's ability to dress as they wish or choose their marriage partner.

In other cases, the hurtful behavior of selfish men may cause some women to hold themselves back in various ways. For example, some sexual assault victims may purposely gain weight in order to feel invisible and therefore safer.[1] Other times, sexism seems to stem from negligence, as when doctors misdiagnose women at higher rates than men and are more likely to claim women's symptoms stem from anxiety rather than disease.[2]

Every unhealthy nation promotes sexism and gives males higher privilege compared to females. Countless women have suffered in countless ways for thousands of years in these oppressive societies.

The first response which authorities often encourage is to accept that the abuse is normal and legitimate. In some unhealthy nations, like Saudi Arabia in 2024 CE or the United States in 1800 CE, women are given little opportunity to change their situation. Instead, women are encouraged to adopt low-privilege entitlement (discussed in Chapter 30), which is a common trap where someone believes some variation of "I must somehow deserve this abuse." However, no one deserves abuse, and no one is better than anyone else. Everyone is worthy of respect. Believing otherwise just perpetuates the abuse.

Many unhealthy nations encourage these self-limiting beliefs and low self-worth as explored throughout this book, and this has been deeply hurtful for many women. However, some unhealthy nations lay an even more devious trap for many women as they respond to the sexism they encounter.

Faux Freedom That Stems From Selfishness

An unhealthy nation is like a bus, where a tiny number of seats are luxurious, a few seats are comfortable, and most of the seats are miserable. Rulers trick low-privilege people into believing that the best way to escape their misery is to fight their way "up" to the comfortable or luxurious seats – to become a professional, or even rich. But then previously low-privilege people merely begin playing a different role in the abusive nation. Arguing over who gets to be the oppressor or the oppressed doesn't generate freedom for anyone.

I call this *faux freedom*. On a personal level, a person with more money can buy a house and avoid abusive landlords. A person with more money can live in cleaner areas and avoid pollution, or buy more nutritious food. The more money a person has, the more they are able to protect themselves from predation by others.

Unfortunately, this path of faux freedom just encourages people to take higher-paying, more-important roles in exploitative corporations or governments. The individual increases their personal safety and comfort, but only by playing an increasingly exploitative role in their exploitative nation.

The best way I know to describe this faux freedom trick is to compare women's situation in the United States with what's happened with black people in the same country.

In the early 1800s, race-based chattel slavery was legal in the United States. After the US Civil War ended chattel slavery, black people remained horribly oppressed, with Jim Crow laws in the south and other "separate but equal" (but not really equal) racism imposed throughout the country. Huge numbers of black people showed tremendous courage seeking meaningful change, and various civil rights acts were eventually passed in the mid-20th century.

Now fast forward 70 years. What is the position of black people today? America has had a black president, Barack Obama, and he even got reelected. There are black billionaires, black police officers, black business executives, and black judges. But what's the situation for the vast majority of black people? By any measure – life expectancy, disease, income, education, home ownership, employment, and incarceration – black people are generally in a significantly lower-privilege position compared to white people in the US.[3] The rise of prison slavery was reviewed in Chapter 29, and the huge amount of prison sexual assault was reviewed in Chapter 24. This is a degree of oppression that few people even realize exists.

Nonetheless, unlike 100 years ago, some black people have managed to change seats on the bus, moving "up" to positions of power over others. Black police officers can now carry out racist policing, and black judges can impose racist sentencing. Black president Barack Obama's administration launched far more drone strikes overseas on black and brown people in support of US imperialism than his predecessor, white president George W Bush.[4] The United States has essentially allowed some black people to hold key positions in a society that is still fundamentally exploitative. The United States may seem more free than it was 70 years ago, but the exploitation at the heart of the nation lives on, offering the faux freedom of selfish personal "advancement" at the expense of so many others.

While black people in the United States still have lower privilege overall than white people, they are actually being offered the same deal as white people: If you don't like poverty and misery, then you should seek a better-paying, more influential role in an exploitative economy.

This is faux freedom, where individuals look after themselves at the expense of the whole. This is the second path that authorities in some unhealthy nations encourage women to walk.

The United States has offered the same faux freedom to women. Women have become executives of major corporations and top level politicians, including speaker of the house in Congress, secretary of state, vice president, and national security advisor. Hillary Clinton was almost elected president in 2020. Women have become prison guards, judges, doctors, lawyers, accountants, and many other roles previously denied to them. Some women have changed seats on the bus.

Still, what is the status of women overall? US women still face systemic sexism in countless ways, as explored in Chapters 24 and 25. Sexual assault is still rampant, and the courts still promote rape myths. Women can get more jobs than ever before, but I have yet to encounter a mother who thought her maternity leave was long enough, or avoided stress due to fears of potential hospital bills.

Nowadays, women can get high-paying jobs – if they're willing to act as selfishly as men. Marillyn Hewson was ceo of weapons manufacturer Lockheed Martin Corporation from 2013-2020, a company that consistently lobbies for more war and more war spending.[5,6] As I write in 2024, Rebecca Liebert is president and ceo of Lubrizol, a chemical company that manufactures many toxic chemicals that act as endocrine disruptors as explored in Chapter 37.[7] Madeleine Albright was a US ambassador and later first female US secretary of state during the 1990s when the US placed economic sanctions on Iraq. These sanctions killed about 500,000 defenseless Iraqi children, and when an interviewer asked how she felt about those children's deaths, she said, "the price is worth it."[8]

Many women are encouraged to fall for this faux-freedom trap with the message that, "if women want more security or dignity or influence, they need to be more like men." But why would any woman want to be like men who hoard their wealth instead of sharing deeply? Who exploit the Earth instead of generating abundance? Who protect the wealthy and powerful instead of standing for justice?

Women with stressful and meaningless jobs are increasingly showing many of the same health troubles as men who have had stressful and meaningless jobs for a long time. Symptoms include depression, high blood pressure, strokes, and heart attacks.[9]

This trap represents the same privilege-responsibility tradeoff that men face. Anyone who accepts their privilege in an unhealthy nation must give up responsibility for the wellbeing of the nation. The more responsibility a person takes – such as by standing up to the worst abuses – the more one risks their privilege, including career, avoidance of legal persecution, and so on. This is true for both men and women.

We don't need equal numbers of women and men chemical company executives; we need to stop producing toxic chemicals. We don't need equal numbers of men and women prison guards; we need to shut down abusive prisons. We don't need more leaders like Spanish queen Isabella who funded Columbus's conquering of the Arawaks, or British prime minister Margaret Thatcher, who heavily oppressed labor unions.[10] We need a nation without rulers of either sex.

The same is true at all levels of society. Nuclear power plants are not less toxic because women work there. Pesticides are not less toxic because women engineers designed them. SSRI antidepressants are not less dangerous because women doctors prescribe them.

Even women activists can adopt the same hurtful attitudes they say they oppose in men. I once sat in a conflict mediation where a woman announced that she was upset with how women are treated in the broader patriarchal culture, and thus she would only listen to the woman's perspective in this dispute and not listen to me. Instead of avoiding sexism, she merely embraced a different sexism. Women have told me multiple times that there is not and cannot be sexism against men. Clearly they were ignorant of the invisible but vast sexual assaults and genital mutilations men face in many unhealthy nations, as seen in Chapters 24 and 25.

Women are indeed equally capable as men in countless ways – and women are also just as capable of selfishness and ignorance if they follow the path of privileged men. These are simply common qualities people adopt if they prioritize the personal comfort and safety of their privilege instead of taking deep responsibility for the health of their nation.

Obviously it is better to have some resources than none, especially in profit economies that discourage deep sharing and reward selfishness. I support anybody of any sex or skin color in considering the tradeoffs of all their options and then generating income in some way that allows them to live. In economies based on exploitation, it is sadly difficult to make money without participating in exploitation somehow, just as it's difficult to find transportation that does not pollute, or houses made without toxins.

Once again, I look to the Zapatistas and Black Panthers for inspiration. They didn't necessarily stop working normal jobs while they sought deep change; they just knew that each person individually "getting a better job" in an exploitative economy was not the path to collective freedom.

The Loving Way Out of the Trap

Authorities in unhealthy nations often label many feminine qualities as weaknesses rather than strengths.

I once shared my perspective on gift economies with a mother, and she said that mothers already know about gift economies. Children can never repay their mothers for all the energy and resources mothers give them. Embracing that beautiful gift economy attitude, many mothers recognize that the gifts they give their children will keep passing on. This is one way many women create healthy subcultures in their lives.

I notice feminine qualities of nurturing and deep inclusiveness show up not just in many families, but also social movements where women play a prominent role. Many women activists have been clear that they're not just fighting for their own betterment, but they're working to make things better for everybody – that is, they're standing for everybody's needs.

One example comes from doctor Dazon Diallo, president and founder of the Sister Love organization. She has worked to help people with AIDS. She described sexism women have encountered as they deal with AIDS, but she's clear that she is not just focusing on women when she said, "For this epidemic, men opened the door. But what I'm clear about, is that it will be the women who close the door on this epidemic. Because once women own it, we change things. And when we change things, we change things for everybody."[11]

Women's nurturing and tending qualities are strengths, not weaknesses. These qualities are part of every healthy nation there has ever been. A woman's radiant beauty is a blessing everywhere she goes, not an invitation to assault. Women's sensitivity is a gift that shows when things are not quite right and something needs addressing; it is not a sign of irrationality. Women's anger is likewise a core part of healthy nations, as anger can point to trouble that needs addressing.

Embracing the sacred feminine in an unhealthy nation is an act of courage, healing, and love. It is strong to embrace being female, not weak. There is nothing more powerful or revolutionary than being yourself and giving your deepest love.

The Haudenosaunee and Zapatista men and women founders knew they needed strong women to play a strong role in their healthy nation. Without strong women, the nation might not last. Women who try to be "like men" or "as good as men" are not simply being themselves. Yet this is where real strength comes from – from *being yourself, by giving your deepest love*. Healthy nations need strong women being themselves.

Whether a particular woman sees her role as tending children or being a military commander, healer, teacher, administrator, or something else or a mix, women who give their deepest love can contribute in countless ways, as the Zapatista women show.

But sexism will not end and freedom will not come just because women succeed in holding the same exploitative jobs as men. Sexism and male privilege are universal features of every unhealthy nation there has ever been. Deep freedom and the end of sexism will come when everybody stands for a culture of mutual respect, and nobody rules over anybody else.

Let's turn now to *Chapter 47: Embracing the Sacred Masculine* to explore how men can become spiritually lost, and how lost men can find their way again.

Chapter 47: Embracing the Sacred Masculine

Beginning in early adulthood, I occasionally heard women ask, "where are all the good men?"

For a long time, I didn't wonder where all the good men were. I didn't know what a good man was, so I didn't think anything was missing.

As I delved into feminist literature, I found variations on this question constantly. I found Muslim women who saw similar sexism in English, Greek, and Arab men.[1,2] I found British women giving up on educating men.[3] In her book *Caliban and the Witch*, Silvia Federici acknowledged Jonathan Cohen for his "love, courage and uncompromising resistance to injustice," which "helped me not lose faith… in men's ability to make the struggle for women's liberation their own."[4] This statement implied how close Federici was to losing that faith in men.

As I studied healthy nations, I kept encountering stories of really good men, and I noticed two themes repeatedly came up: bravery and integrity. Nez Perce chief Joseph led his people on an epic journey to escape American military subjugation and very nearly succeeded. Later his advice to a young American boy was simple: "Be brave and tell the truth."[5]

Wikis' uncle likewise taught him there was "one thing more important than anything else, and that is to be brave… If you do that, the people will all know of it, and will look on you as a man." He also said, "always be truthful and honest with all your people."[6]

Other men showed me how far they took integrity and bravery. Apache man Geronimo described how each young man was trained to prove "beyond question that he can bear hardships without complaint, and that he is a stranger to fear."[7] Sioux man Ohiyesa hinted at his deep training for Integrity of Service when he said he was "trained to be a warrior and a hunter, and not to care for money or possessions, but to be in the broadest sense a public servant."[8]

As I repeatedly encountered this advice to cultivate integrity and bravery, and I repeatedly encountered men in healthy nations showing these qualities, I noticed how often I showed up without integrity or bravery. As I began intentionally cultivating these qualities in myself, I started to notice how few men embrace them.

Finally I also asked, "Where are all the good men?"

Where are All the Good Men?

After seeing the huge differences between healthy and unhealthy nations, the answer is clear. In unhealthy nations, healthy masculinity is forbidden, and toxic masculinity is encouraged and rewarded. The vast majority of men in unhealthy nations are profoundly spiritually lost.

Each of us has sacred gifts to give, life purposes or ways of making the world a better place. Giving one's gifts is how a person gives their love in life, and if a person's gifts are rejected, their love is rejected.

While each person has their own unique gifts, there are common masculine and feminine gifts too. While everybody has both masculine and feminine energies, most humans align more closely with one or the other.

A core masculine gift is that of setting boundaries, especially protecting one's people from threats. In all nations, few things inspire men more than the need to protect their people from danger. And yet, in unhealthy abusive nations, the rulers are the greatest threat to the people. The greatest threat is not from outside; it is within the nation itself.

As a result, abusive nations raise boys not to honor their innate spiritual calling to protect their people from threats as a gift of love, without any compensation or orders. Instead, men commonly grow up learning to tolerate, ignore, or perpetuate abuse.

Some men go into the police or military, but they are only allowed to follow orders. Thus they protect the threat from the people, rather than protecting the people from the threat.

The vast majority of boys are trained to obey authority figures, conditioning them for an adulthood in which they obey abusive authorities who pose the greatest threat to their people. This is the opposite of being raised to stand up for one's people against any threat. The sacred masculine gift of boundary setting, and especially protecting one's people from the greatest threats, is not welcomed in abusive nations. In fact, it is systematically discouraged and severely punished.

It is not legal to be a good man in an unhealthy nation, because good men stand up against any injustice or threat to their people, and authorities forbid this. Men like Jesus Christ or Martin Luther King Jr who bravely stand for what's right show how authorities respond to good men. In any unhealthy nation, only the police are legally allowed to address threats or inappropriate behavior, and as explored in Chapter 32, they are required to follow orders. Any police officer with integrity who violates their orders and stands up against injustice by the rich and powerful is fired or otherwise punished. Men's deepest love is thus unwelcome in unhealthy nations.

Some men are able to be a strong positive male presence in their family. Many men find this difficult, as it is challenging for a man to stand for what's right in his family but essentially ignore huge injustices and lies outside the family as the law requires. This is a very unnatural division, and navigating it requires a great deal of internal clarity and strength, qualities not cultivated in those boys who are threatened, shamed, and bribed into obeying authority figures from a young age.

In healthy nations, when a threat approaches, men come together to discuss a shared response and build up each others' integrity and bravery, but in unhealthy nations people can be severely punished for even discussing how to effectively stop corporate or political corruption. When the most meaningful conversations are legally forbidden, and police infiltrators are common, it becomes difficult for men to come together and support each other in finding a meaningful response and staying true to themselves rather than hiding in fear.

Spirituality is simply how a person relates to the world and themselves, and every man has a deep, primal urge to stand up to injustice or confront any threat in their own nation. This urge is part of who-a-man-is, part of how he innately wants to relate to the world around him, and in healthy nations men are not just free, but expected to act on this urge in service of their people. Unfortunately, when men's deepest love-gift of boundary-setting is unwelcome in their unhealthy nation and men are shamed, threatened, tricked, or bribed to not stand for what's right from early childhood, many men become deeply spiritually lost. In other words, it becomes difficult to know how to relate to oneself and the world.

As a result, instead of protecting their people from the greatest threats out of love, most men either passively tolerate or actively support the threat of their own abusive authorities. When boys are raised to deny or twist this deep love-gift of boundary-setting and protection, unhealthy nations wind up with deeply spiritually confused men who ask questions like "When does life become meaningful?" or "Why am I even here?"

Unhealthy nations generate men who decide that if nothing matters, they might as well get rich, or get lost in alcohol, TV, work, or other distractions, or try to please everyone to keep life comfortable. Such nations produce men who struggle to act as loving leaders who stand against abuse in their family and community. I believe this ultimately is the spiritual reality behind Henry David Thoreau's comment that "The mass of men lead lives of quiet desperation."[9] It also explains the famous statement that "Every man dies. Not every man really lives."[10] Living a life where a person has learned to hold back their love and tolerate humiliation is deeply unsatisfying.

Obviously women can set boundaries as well, and often I observe women holding boundaries better than men. Men are often so spiritually lost and wounded that many of them are of little help when trouble arises, especially if the man's ability to provide for his family is threatened. In general, women seem less spiritually lost. Around the world, many women are waiting for men to wake up.

If Women Were Subject to the Same Confusion as Men

Writing about "sacred gifts" can seem abstract. An analogy may help clarify the depth of masculine spiritual confusion when men are trained to ignore their innate desire to protect others from the greatest threats and are blocked or punished if they try.

Everyone has many ways they contribute to the world. Each individual person has countless gifts which, when given fully, brighten the world around them. This gift of boundary-setting, and especially protecting one's people from threats, is a primal masculine urge. And when this primal urge is blocked or denied in some way by the nation, men can feel deeply unfulfilled, frustrated, or lost.

To understand better what many men experience, let us imagine a theoretical scenario in which a nation systematically blocked and discouraged one of women's primal urges. For example, how disturbed might women feel if they were taught from earliest childhood that giving birth was evil, or that supporting someone else in pregnancy or childbirth were unacceptable? What if women who did this were severely punished and locked away in prisons for decades? What if merely mentioning childbirth or supporting others' childbirth were so forbidden that women learned not to even think about it?

Not all women choose to have children, or even feel an urge to give birth, and that is fine. But in this imagined unhealthy nation that forbids childbirth, even these women would be discouraged from recognizing their heart's desire and consciously choosing whether to give birth or not. All women would be strongly pressured to simply obey authority and not even notice their true feelings.

Childbirth might still happen of course: in this imagined unhealthy nation, authorities could claim that God only allows a few chosen women to give birth without sinning, and so these few approved women are allowed to give birth while the rest are not allowed to even think about it. In this way, the nation fulfills a core need to propagate itself but in a profoundly distorted, unsatisfying, hurtful way.

Now imagine if any woman who openly considered giving birth or assisting anyone else with pregnancy or childcare were forbidden from having a good job ever again, shamed and shunned from polite society, locked away in a prison cage, and heavily abused while in that cage. She might be locked in that cage for the rest of her life where she faces possible isolation, rape, malnutrition, disconnection from nonhumans, and more. If she were ever allowed out of that cage, her family and previous friends may be afraid to associate with her, as she had done something so forbidden that people were afraid to even think about it. After all, she did the unthinkable thing by conceiving a child, or supporting someone else's childbirth.

How would women growing up in such a nation cope with this reality? Would some of them learn to pretend that they don't really want to give birth, regardless of their real feelings? Would some start to believe that women who get involved with birth are all harlots and devil-worshippers? Would some percentage of women learn to punish those few who secretly choose to give birth somehow? Might some women take drugs to suppress their urges, or drink heavily, or become workaholics, or become abusive to those around them, or suicidal?

This sounds apocalyptic to me, and I am glad I do not live in such a nation. But this is exactly how unhealthy nations treat anybody who takes a stand against the greatest threats their community faces: the abusive authorities in their unhealthy nation. Anyone who seeks to protect their people from their greatest threats is killed or locked in prison where they are subject to rape and malnourishment and disconnection. They are also subject to surveillance, poverty, social isolation, shame, reputation sabotage, and even murder.

This primal masculine urge to set appropriate boundaries and protect his people from threats is absolutely unwelcome in unhealthy nations, and this urge is commonly blocked or distorted from early childhood. Men who insist on protecting their people from danger may join the police or military where they are expected to follow orders. Unfortunately, these organizations protect the threat of abusive authorities from the people, rather than protecting the people from their greatest threat.

Why is alcoholism so common among men? Why do so many men pretend things are fine when they are not? Why do so many men struggle to love passionately their whole lives, or focus on superficial or selfish pursuits? A major factor is that many men learn from early childhood to withhold a deep love-gift of boundary-setting, and especially protecting their people from the greatest threats, and many men become profoundly spiritually lost as a result.

Men in Healthy Nations Set Strong Boundaries and Earn Women's Trust

Many stories from healthy nations illustrate the masculine boundary-setting quality.

Pretty Shield described how her village would move between sites with all their homes and gear packed on horses. They could be attacked at any time, so male Crow scouts would travel ahead, around and behind the main group to give warning if enemies approached. They called these Crow scouts "wolves," and she said, "we women visited while we traveled… The men were ever watching these wolves, and we women constantly watched the men."[11] The women trusted the men to organize themselves into a protection force and pay attention to each other to collectively protect the village, all without pay or threat of punishment by a commanding officer.

In one battle, Black Elk described how his people were short on both food and ammunition while being constantly driven by the American military. The Americans attacked during a blizzard, and he said, "We could not stop the soldiers coming up, because we had not much ammunition. The soldiers had everything. But our men used spears and guns for clubs when the soldiers got there, and they fought hand to hand a while, holding the soldiers back until the women could break camp and get away with the children and ponies."[12]

As I write, there are a large number of women kidnapped and trafficked around the world, often to be abused as domestic servants or sexual slaves. Men of healthy nations do not allow this. On January 7, 1877 a force of 435 soldiers led by American colonel Miles captured a small group of Cheyenne women and children. The very next day, Crazy Horse and Dull Knife led 500 Lakota and Cheyenne warriors in an attack on Miles' force to try to retrieve them.[13]

Many other stories from the Lakota, Cheyenne, and others show men engaging in battle so that women and children had time to escape danger.

Men Warriors Welcome Women Warriors

Of course, there are many stories of women warriors protecting their people too. In one Crow story, Pretty Shield described how Crow woman Strikes Two fought off a Lakota attack[14], and she described how Crow women fought with the Americans against Lakota who had killed their relatives.[15]

In a battle between the American military and a coalition of the Cheyenne and Lakota on June 17, 1876, the Cheyenne and Lakota had succeeded in breaking apart the main American force. Cheyenne Chief-Comes-in-Sight attacked an American flank when his horse was shot out from under him, and immediately someone dashed out on a horse of her own to shield him from enemy fire and take him to safety. His savior was his sister Buffalo-Calf-Road-Woman who had been tending the Cheyennes' herd of horses. Her bravery inspired the Cheyenne to remember the battle as the Battle Where the Girl Saved Her Brother. The American soldiers called it the Battle of Rosebud.[16]

Women can make fearsome fighters. When I write about the masculine responsibility to protect their people, I do not mean to imply anything about women's roles. In dangerous moments where someone must stay to fight so that others may live, it's the masculine role to stay and fight, either together with women or without them. In healthy nations, I observe that women either fight or escape depending on whatever seems most appropriate to them at the time.

Whereas women in many authoritarian militaries face sexism or even sexual assault from some fellow male soldiers, I commonly notice that men of healthy nations welcome these women warriors' presence. For example, Sioux man Rain-In-The-Face described how a war cry went out through the village one day as the American military approached. Warriors from the Ogallala, Minneconjou, Cheyenne, and Unkpapa nations went out together, and Rain-In-The-Face noticed a woman in their midst while the rest were all young men. This woman was Tashenamani, or Moving Robe. Her brother had just been killed protecting his people from the American military.[17]

Rain-In-The-Face said: "Holding her brother's war staff over her head, and leaning forward upon her charger, she looked as pretty as a bird. Always when there is a woman in the charge, it causes the warriors to vie with one another in displaying their valor." He used Tashenamani's presence as a gift to build up the men's courage when he shouted: "Behold, there is among us a young woman! Let no young man hide behind her garment!"

Rain-In-The-Face told his interviewer, "I knew that would make those young men brave." He used Tashenamani's presence to boost the men's bravery without belittling her in any way.

Brave Men Inspire Women's Trust, and Trusting Women Inspire Men's Bravery

During moments of great danger, women may help their people by fighting or by helping people escape. There are also many beautiful stories of women intentionally inspiring bravery in their men.

Wikis was a boy of five or six years old when his village was attacked. He remembered seeing the men instantly jump on their horses and ride towards the danger while the women gathered the children. He said, "My mother rushed out and caught me by the hand… and then she stopped and in a shrill, sweet voice began to sing; and other women that were running about stopped too, and began to sing songs to encourage their husbands and brothers and sons to fight bravely; for enemies were attacking the camp."[18]

The warriors were heavily outnumbered, and so they repeatedly engaged the enemy and retreated to avoid being overwhelmed. Wikis said, "there were many of these strangers, while our people were only a few. But still my people kept stopping and turning and fighting. Now the noise was louder. The women sang their strong heart songs more shrilly, and I could hear more plainly the whoops of men…" Wikis' mother then ran away with the children across a river. Help came from a larger nearby village and pushed the attackers away. Four warriors died that night protecting their people.

Women's beauty and trust can be deeply inspirational to men who have trained to give their love in service to their people. Black Elk described how the Lakota women would cheer on their men both during preparation and during battle. In the Battle of Little Bighorn in 1876, Black Elk described an attack by the American military led by lieutenant colonel George Armstrong Custer. As the attackers approached, they kicked up a huge dust cloud. Women and children ran into their village while the warriors ran out. Warriors shouted war cries and Black Elk described how he once ran to a group of women: "When I got to the women on the hill they were all singing and making the tremolo to cheer the men fighting across the river."[19]

Lakota man Fire Thunder described the battle where he first encountered Americans with repeating rifles, and how the women inspired the men to action: "Our women were watching us from the hills and we could hear them singing and mourning whenever the shooting stopped."[20]

These women knew they inspired their warrior men, and in one case a woman warrior was quite explicit. During the Battle of Little Bighorn, a group of warriors arrived which included a woman, and she sang to the men who were already fighting, "Brothers, now your friends have come! Be brave! Be brave! Would you see me taken captive?"[21]

Sioux man Standing Bear told how women sometimes sang after men brought food: "All over the flat… there were men butchering bison now, and the women and the old men who could not hunt were coming up to help. And all the women were making the tremolo of joy for what the warriors had given them."[22]

These stories show me that it's possible for all the men of a nation to live with integrity and bravery. The women would not have sung for untrustworthy men. These stories showed me what men are capable of, and how women's trust in men need not be misplaced. Men can be trustworthy. Unfortunately, unhealthy nations encourage and even require low-integrity and low-bravery in their men. If men fully offered their sacred gifts of bravery and integrity, unhealthy nations could not exist.

In desperate situations where everyone in a group must stay and fight for the group's survival, then so be it. In situations where everyone must escape, then everyone escapes together. But if someone must stay and confront a threat so that others may escape, it's the male warriors' responsibility to stay and fight. This boundary-setting is a core masculine responsibility in healthy nations. Women may fight, inspire the fighting men, escape with the children and elders, or take any other actions depending on how they believe they can best serve the group.

This gift of boundary-setting is necessary for healthy-nation gift economies to thrive. Gift economies where everyone shares abundantly must be able to protect themselves from predation. Otherwise the selfish take from the generous. Violence is neither inherently good nor bad; it is simply one option to consider when choosing how to establish boundaries and forbid inappropriate behavior.

Good Men Offer Boundary-Setting as a Gift of Love in Service of Their People Without Entitlement

I notice something beautiful in many nations where men give their love by upholding boundaries that the whole group finds satisfying. I do not know if this is so in every healthy nation, but in several nations I notice that women do special favors for the men. Huron women would commonly feed the men first as a way to honor the family's protectors.[23] When I first read this, I wondered if I was encountering some kind of unhealthy sexism, but I remembered how the Ashaninka men would travel between villages with guns so that they were always ready to protect their people, and I remembered how women graciously shared food with them.

Finally I found a passage in *When Buffalo Ran* that changed my life, where Wikis' uncle taught him why women treated him specially:

> "It is a good thing to be a member of our tribe, and it is a good thing to belong to a good family in that tribe. You must always remember that you come of good people. Your father was a brave man, killed fighting bravely against the enemy. I want you to grow up to be a brave man and a good man. You must love your relations, and must do everything that you can for them. If the enemy should attack the village, do not run away; think always first of defending your own people. You have a mother, and sisters, who will depend on you for their living, and for their credit. They love you, and you must always try to do everything that you can for them. Try to learn about hunting, and to become a good hunter, so that you may support them. But, above all things, try to live bravely and well, so that people will speak well of you and your relations will be proud.

> "You are only a boy now, but the time will come when you will be a man, and must act a man's part. Now your relations all respect you. They do not ask you to do woman's work; they treat you well. You have a good bed, and whenever you are hungry, food is given you. Do you know why it is that you are treated in this way? I will tell you. Your relations know that you are a man, and that you will grow up to go to war, and fight; perhaps often to be in great danger. They know that perhaps they may not have you long with them; that soon you may be killed. Perhaps even to-night or to-morrow, before we get back to the camp, we may be attacked, and may have to fight, and perhaps to die."[24]

Of course anyone, male or female, could die at any moment. But if enemies attacked Wikis' nation, the women would be much more likely to survive than the men because the men would stand between the danger and the women and children. I see no evidence that the men had entitled attitudes, or acted as if they deserved any sort of special attention. I don't believe the women offered men special comforts due to masculine domination or sexist control. I believe the women of Wikis' nation, like the Huron, were grateful for the men who consistently trained to give up their lives at a moment's notice to protect the women and children.

Wikis' uncle described a division between men's work and women's work. This division of labor does not necessarily imply sexism or restrictive gender roles. The Huron also had some work that was more commonly done by women and other work more commonly done by men.[25] The Ashaninka seemed to have some work that only women or only men did. People don't have to do the same work to receive equal respect. So long as everyone feels satisfied, dividing up the work can be a beautiful way for people to complement each other.

When the women sang their songs to inspire bravery in their husbands and sons, I believe they knew that their men were offering their lives so that the women and children could live. The women knew that the men cultivated this bravery every day as a normal part of life. This brave boundary-setting was simply a masculine gift that the men offered the women. Like all sacred gifts, it was offered freely.

This passage from Wikis' uncle showed me what it's like for a masculine mentor to teach a young man to offer his bravery in service of others. Wikis' uncle taught him to never feel entitled to special treatment. He wasn't inherently better than the women. I believe women gave Wikis special favors because they knew he was growing up to be the sort of brave man who would reliably risk his life and comforts to save theirs, and I believe these women felt gratitude and found ways to show it without any coercion.

I don't know how many healthy nations have this pattern where women offer men special little comforts or favors in gratitude for their bravery. This is not important, and I believe a nation could be quite healthy even if women did not do this. These stories simply showed me what it's like when men bravely offer their love without holding back. They showed me what it's like for women to deeply trust men and feel grateful for the men who honor that trust.

Men Transitioning Into Unhealthy Nations

People of healthy nations noticed how men changed when they were forced into unhealthy nations.

Sioux man Red Cloud hinted at the loss of masculine wisdom when he described the time before being forced into the unhealthy American nation: "Their children were many; herds, large; young men and women, vital and beautiful; old men, wise."[26]

Crow woman Pretty Shield described this masculine transition in painfully vivid terms: "Our men had fought hard against our enemies, holding them back from our beautiful country by their bravery; but now, with everything else going wrong, we began to be whipped by weak foolishness. Our men, our leaders, began to drink the white man's whisky, letting it do their thinking. Because we were used to listening to our chiefs in the buffalo days, the days of war and excitement, we listened to them now; and we got whipped. Our wise-ones became fools, and drank the white man's whisky. But what else was there for us to do? We knew no other way than to listen to our chiefs and head men. Our old men used to be different; even our children were different when the buffalo were here."[27]

Rain-In-The-Face described what it was like to experience this transition to a life of submitting to authorities: "I have lived peaceably ever since we came upon the reservation… I fought for my people and my country… Rain-In-The-Face was killed when he put down his weapons before the Great Father [US president]. His spirit was gone then; only his poor body lived on, but now it is almost ready to lie down for the last time."[28]

Every transition into unhealthy nations required this deep spiritual wounding in men. Rain-In-The-Face could at least recognize his wound because he had grown up in a nation that welcomed his deepest love. He knew what giving his love and setting boundaries was like, so he knew something was wrong when these gifts were unwelcome in the unhealthy nation. Boys in unhealthy nations are raised to submit to authority and thus withhold their deep love starting in early childhood, leading many boys and men to become spiritually lost.

When Men Become Lost

The exploitation in unhealthy nations generates legitimate anger in many men. However, when men see no clear path to constructively channel that anger, and no people to fight for, it can become difficult to know what to do.

Martín Prechtel described how disturbed he was by the unhealthy American nation that was mining, polluting, cutting up, and otherwise destroying the land he loved. His ancestors fought to protect the land, but this was difficult now. He noticed he was "becoming a one-man culture, a lonely young man with a lot of grief, excessive principles, and a mission. I became a renegade..." He sensed he was feeling the same way Geronimo or Victorio must have felt when "they returned from a major cattle raid, bearing food for their tribe, only to discover the impaled hearts and ruined lives of their people numbed and scattered by these unfeeling forces. Like them, I had no one to bring my 'cattle' to, nowhere to give my gifts. When there is no village to hunt for, nothing to come home to, then the self-governing laws of our souls and lives are discarded. That's what makes a person into a careless renegade."[29]

Angry men with no clear cause to fight for and no clear way to stop the disrespectful behavior can become renegades and engage in meaningless or self-destructive behavior. When Malcolm X was killed in 1965, black American Bobby Seale started angrily throwing bricks at passing police cars, and he said that he "cried like a baby. I was righteously crying. I was pissed off and mad... I was ready to die that day." His friends had to come and stop him. It would have been tragic if he had been imprisoned or killed for throwing bricks. Fortunately, Bobby Seale learned to channel his anger better and later co-founded the Black Panthers.[30]

Prisons provide one of the most extreme examples of people feeling appropriate anger and being forbidden from expressing it productively. Prisoners are forbidden from holding good boundaries while they are abused.

Edward Kuznetsov witnessed much disturbing behavior in Soviet prison colonies in 1971, with some prisoners swallowing barbed wire, sewing their mouths shut, swallowing toxins, nailing their genitals to the bed, bleeding themselves and drinking it, cutting off their limbs, and more. Kuznetsov explained that these prisoners were "in a permanent state of depression... The destructive element within them boils over in a rage of impotence and is transformed into fits of hatred and feverish dreams of revenge on the prison governor; as soon as they realize that they can't get their teeth into his throat, they finally turn on themselves."[31]

These are examples of what Prechtel described as "simple, natural desires who, because they have gone unfed, become frustrated, unnatural hungers... that eat everything and never get full." (reviewed in Chapter 42) Without solidarity with others, a passionate and frustrated man can easily become a careless renegade. Without a meaningful way to channel his anger and take a stand, a man can wind up directing his energy in unhelpful ways. This taught me the importance of somehow channeling my anger productively. Anger never stays repressed; it always goes somewhere. *Find a productive way to channel anger*.

Rejecting Inspiration – One Reason Why So Many Men Resist Feminine Gifts

This book has explored how people can adopt authoritarian ideologies if trapped in abusive situations for long enough. By creating and maintaining societal structures and systems in which some people have more privilege and power than others, authorities create and perpetuate the reality of sexism and racism, and then many people adopt beliefs that rationalize the ruler-imposed discrimination.

Still, this hardly explains the depth of many men's fear and anger towards women. Chapter 24 reviewed examples of men stating that women are devils, or myths stating that women's sex organs are toothed monsters. Yes, authorities throughout history have put men in charge of women, and many men have adopted sexist attitudes. Yes, child abuse can cause very deep disturbances. But there has to be something else going on that explains these kinds of strange, resentful or fearful attitudes towards women.

There is another common pattern: I believe many men learn to reject in themselves some of the feelings and urges that beautiful and trusting women inspire.

Chapter 42 explored how people can learn to reject or ignore their own urges which have led them to feel pain or fear from a young age. For example, a person may fear their urge to bravely speak up when an authority breaks a promise, or they may ignore their urge to trust someone after they've been disappointed many times. A person may even associate negative feelings with pleasure and thus learn to resist pleasure.

People can likewise learn to fear or become angry at the people or things that inspire those unsafe feelings or urges. This helps explain why many men act hurtfully towards women in unhealthy nations.

If a beautiful and trusting woman inspires a man to feel pleasure just from her presence, but he grew up associating pleasure with fear, shame, anger, or revulsion and then practiced not noticing these feelings, how will he respond to her? If a man has learned from earliest boyhood to submit to authority rather than bravely stand up for what's right, and if he fears or feels deep shame about his own bravery, how will he respond to a woman who inspires bravery?

In addition to all the other kinds of authoritarian training explored in this book, I believe this is another factor driving many men to behave in manipulative ways, either controlling or submissively placating their women partners. Men and women can inspire each other to give our deepest love, not just with each other but everywhere in life. But when certain feelings or urges get repressed from early childhood because the feelings themselves seemed threatening or bad (because acting on those feelings led to abuse by adult authority figures), anything that inspires those dangerous feelings may likewise seem bad or threatening. Tragically, I believe many women throughout history have suffered because they inspired feelings in men that the men couldn't handle because they'd learned to fear and repress those feelings from early childhood.

Recall that each person is the giving-of-their-deepest-love, or the giving-of-their-sacred-gifts, which is the same thing. Spiritually, this is who we are.

A nation that does not welcome a person's deepest love does not welcome them. While almost all men in unhealthy nations are trained to withhold their love in various ways, I believe the most abused among us may learn to hate life and hate the world they were born into that rejects their love.

This is another factor that explains much abusive male behavior towards women. The feminine quality is life itself. The life force is feminine. I believe Black Elk hinted at this when he said, "behind the woman's power of life is hidden the power of man… The woman is the life of the flowering tree, but the man must feed and care for it."[32]

What happens when "life" (meaning an abusive family and nation) rejects a man's love so strongly that he blocks pleasure, struggles to trust others, dishonors his own feelings and urges, has no connection with nonhumans, and utterly smothers his own sense of dignity and integrity as he learns to submit to abusive authority figures? This could happen due to more commonly-recognized forms of child abuse such as physical or sexual violence. However, common child-rearing patterns produce men who tolerate humiliation and discard their own integrity and bravery. Being raised as a child to obey authorities regardless whether they behave appropriately is humiliating. Young men are expected to pretend that this situation is ok, only humiliating themselves further. Many other child-rearing patterns discourage strong integrity such as religious or sexual shaming, deprivation of loving touch in early childhood, excusing inappropriate behavior with sayings like "boys will be boys" and much more.

The most abused boys and men can easily learn to hate life – and to hate parts of themselves. In some ways, women embody some qualities that many men learn to hate or reject in themselves. In other ways, women may inspire some men to feel certain feelings or urges that they long ago associated with shame, anger, revulsion, or other negative qualities. This helps explain not only some men's disgust towards women, but also some hurtful male behavior towards women. Women are the embodiment of the feminine life force itself, and when "life" seems to totally reject abused men's love – and when these men then learn to withhold their love – such men who hate life can likewise learn to hate and abuse women.

How can such men love passionately when their own love was strongly rejected from early childhood and continually rejected into adulthood? How can such men honor other people's boundaries when they were trained to be obedient rather than set good boundaries, and thus they never learned what healthy boundary-setting is like?

None of this excuses any man's inappropriate behavior. However, this perspective does explain much inappropriate male behavior in unhealthy nations. I believe anyone can heal from such trauma in the right conditions, but clearly this is challenging and many men throughout history have not been able to heal.

Different boys suffer different amounts of hurtful behavior or abuse. Different boys may learn to give or withhold their love to varying degrees and cope with this in different ways. However, all authorities reject men's love-gift of boundary-setting and protecting their people from the greatest threat because abusive rulers are themselves the greatest threat. All men in unhealthy nations must struggle with this reality in one way or another. This is the root cause of toxic masculinity, as many boys and men learn a variety of hurtful patterns when being themselves and giving their sacred gift of boundary-setting is unwelcome.

Jesus Christ, Martin Luther King Jr, and many others show that even men who grow up in abusive nations can cultivate their integrity and bravery and do great things. Other men, sadly, are unable to heal or even recognize their spiritual wounds and act out hurtful patterns instead.

Stand for the Needs of Everybody in the Group

Weak men do not stand for anything or set any boundaries, or only take a "stand" with authorities' approval.

Selfish or self-centered men stand only for their own needs. For example, in the US before 1873, nearly all male-dominated labor unions barred women from membership, based in part on the fear that women workers would compete for jobs and thus reduce pay levels. Even after some women were allowed to join, they often faced sexist comments and other discouragement.[33]

Even men leaders that have explicitly sought shared abundance and equality have sometimes left women out. For example, when Gerrard Winstanley and the Diggers published their pamphlet about their radical gardening work at St. George's Hill in 1649 called *The True Levellers Standard Advanced*, it included many beautiful words about equality, abundance and people's relationship with the Earth. However, the title page listed 15 people who participated in the St George's Hill gardening, and it only listed men. No women were listed, even though women participated from the beginning. Names of women were excluded from many Digger publications.[34]

Unhealthy nations and profit economies train people for selfishness or self-centeredness, and these stories showed me how deep that training can be. How many failed social movements in history might have succeeded if men had fully included women, standing in solidarity and accounting for everyone's needs?

Masculine leaders of healthy subcultures and healthy nations stand for the needs of the whole group, including children and women. Cherokee woman Rebecca Adamson described how the traditional Cherokee sought a balance of men and women in leadership. That balance requires strong men willing to stand for the wellbeing of the group. It also requires male leaders who welcome female leaders.

In healthy nations, leaders are selected based on whom people trust to lead. Martín Prechtel gave one example when he described spiritual leadership: "A shaman simply had to become something worth seeing, a vision that inspired life in an authentic way."[35] In 1727, Cadwallader Colden observed, "There is not a Man in the Ministry of the [Haudenosaunee], who has gain'd his Office, otherwise than by Merit… Their Authority is only the Esteem of the People, and ceases the Moment that Esteem is lost…"[36]

Good leaders make decisions based on the needs of the group. That's why I believe people follow leaders in healthy nations and healthy subcultures: people simply like the leader's direction. To lead women, men, and children without abusive coercion requires *standing for the needs of everyone*.

Core aspects of leadership include knowing what questions to ask, being able to observe and listen, and standing for the needs of the group. I believe this is why women of healthy nations could commonly trust the male leaders, and why Crow woman Pretty Shield would say, "We knew no other way than to listen to our chiefs and head men. Our old men used to be different…" The Crow didn't have coercive leaders; I believe they listened to the men because the men had something valuable to say in service of the whole. In an unhealthy nation, the women might listen to male authorities out of fear of punishment. In healthy nations, women listen to those men whose perspective they value.

Masculine boundary-setting does little good when a man only protects himself and his own boundaries. The gift of boundary-setting serves the community when the man stands for the needs of the whole. Whether someone disrespects a woman, man, or child, it is equally unacceptable, and in a healthy nation or healthy subculture disrespect of anyone brings an equally strong response. This is how healthy nations maintain their internal baseline of mutual respect.

Integrity and bravery are clearly qualities which both men and women can embrace. I do not mean to imply that they are solely qualities for men. They are simply the two qualities which I notice that men in healthy nations emphasize and which are also the most lacking in unhealthy nations, or are only allowed in the context of obedience to authority figures.

Words to Men

I have a message for boys and men readers. I welcome girls and women to read this too, but the message is directed at boys and men raised in unhealthy nations.

My message is this: we've been raised in a nation that trained us not to be good men. Different men are poorly trained in different ways: some are trained to focus on their job or career or following orders or seeking safety and superficial pleasures. Some have been trained to avoid trouble and avoid deep questions, or think they're inherently superior somehow. For the vast majority of us, we weren't trained for deep wisdom, good judgment, bravery in service, humility or strong integrity. Very few of us were raised to walk the most meaningful path imaginable no matter what, and stand for a culture of mutual respect.

We've been misled a lot. Men may be taught that they are better than women, or one race is better, or the rich are better, or selfishness is ok, or nothing matters, or humans are better than nonhumans, or that leadership involves giving orders rather than taking a stand for what's right. There is a lot for most of us to unlearn.

All that life asks of you is your love, even if some people are not able to receive it. And the Earth, and me, and millions of other people want your deepest, most courageous love. You matter, and how you show up in every moment matters. Somewhere in your heart, you know what's important for you to do, and what's a waste of your precious life. If you can't tell what your heart says, take some time alone and practice listening. I promise that divinity is speaking to you through your heart. If you've forgotten how to listen, you will learn to hear it again with practice.

Life can be an adventure, or it can be dull. Prioritizing safety and comfort above all else generates a dull life. When you walk a meaningful path, risking failure and living on your edge, life becomes an adventure again. Failure does not make life dull, but boredom, depression, meaninglessness, and excessive comfort do.

If you're not living that most meaningful life in every moment, or if you're tolerating humiliating subservience, meaningless distractions, or selfish pursuits, it's because you've somehow learned to hold back. Inside every one of us is a loving warrior that doesn't tolerate such bullshit. A loving warrior who takes deep responsibility for the wellbeing of his people and the Earth. A loving warrior who wasn't welcomed from his earliest days, or who was tricked into serving abusive authorities or serving himself or dreaming small. But I'm calling for that loving warrior inside you. Now is the time.

We can cultivate integrity and bravery at any age, and we can offer these in service to the people and nonhumans around us. We can insist on a meaningful life and a culture of mutual respect. We can do this even if it costs us dearly – even if it costs some of us our lives.

There's a reason healthy nations train men to prefer a brave death to a humiliating long life. Tolerating humiliation leads to all the troubles of abusive nations.

I was inspired by the story of the enslaved man named Joe (reviewed in Chapter 17). When his master demanded that he submit, Joe recognized that in his situation, there wasn't much he could do, so he took the whipping without fighting back. But he knew in his heart that slavery wasn't ok, and he stood up for himself when he could by escaping a while later.[37]

Anyone who lives in an abusive nation may need to show some submissiveness just to survive. And, like Joe, each of us can have that courage and integrity to choose when and how to submit, and where to take a stand to do the most good in the world. This is the same attitude that Martin Luther King Jr showed when he paid his taxes, and which Jesus Christ showed when he said, "render to Caesar the things that are Caesar's" while he continued to work to free his people from the predatory priests, moneylenders, and Roman authorities.[38]

I look to men and women heroes in American and European nations like Harriet Tubman, Malcolm X, Eugene Debs, Rosa Luxemburg, Wilhelm Reich, and Martin Luther King Jr to model that courageous love for me. I also look for mentors outside my nation who model integrity and bravery, including Black Elk, Ohiyesa, and others. Nonhumans like hawks and wolves have much to teach as well.

Find your heroes and mentors and elders who model how you want to move through the world, and cultivate yourself so you can stand for what's right. Build relationships with men and women likewise willing to give their deepest love, who take responsibility for their people, who build each other up and hold each other to a high bar, who enjoy life, and who live with courage.

I also strongly recommend that you find or start a men's group where the men consistently hold each other to a high bar of integrity and bravery. I have grown alone and I have grown with mentors or male friends holding me to a high bar, and it is much easier and more fun to grow with other men's help while helping them too.

Anyone can train bravery. Coming up next, *Chapter 48: Bravery and Cowardice* offers a guide for those who want to cultivate their courage.

Chapter 48: Bravery and Cowardice

Starting around age seven, I learned in school about pre-Civil War chattel slavery in the United States. I remember having fantasies of being a rich man back then, and I would buy people to free them. In other fantasies, I would go on daring raids to save enslaved people, some who were friends and some strangers.

Later, as a young adult, I still had an unquestioned belief that if something as terrible as slavery ever occurred around me, I would surely do something about it.

Then it hit me. I commonly drove by prisons in full awareness that 98% of trials end in plea-bargains, and many inmates accepted a years-long prison sentence even though they were entirely innocent.[1] They plea-bargained out of fear of losing at trial and going to jail for decades. And I knew full-well that many people would not be in prison at all if private prison corporations didn't bribe government officials with payments called "campaign donations" to arbitrarily extend prison sentences.[2]

Yet I had not done a thing to help imprisoned people.

I also knew that the destruction of forests and the life that lives there was a major cause of climate change, mass extinction, soil erosion, and other environmental problems humanity faces. I commonly drove past clear-cut logging operations which turn whole hillsides of trees into fields of orange clay. Yet, I always just kept on driving.

Finally I realized that if I had been alive 200 years ago when chattel slavery existed in my country and coffles of chained humans were regularly marched down my street, I would have responded to such injustices then the same way that I did now. Up to the time of this realization, all I'd ever done was feel bad about such injustices. I had never taken any concrete steps to stop them.

I had to face the fact that I had never taken any risks, and I had not grown up with the bravery that I fantasized about as a child. I had stood up for friends or family at times, but I realized I mostly just tried not to think about all the things I felt upset about.

This sparked an internal question: If I really wanted to protect the forests or stop prison slavery or do anything else that I care about, what would I do? And what kind of person would I need to be?

Noticing where one lacks bravery is a great first step on the path to cultivating it.

A Deeper Perspective of Bravery

For years I thought of bravery as the ability to aggressively face danger without fear.

I was puzzled at first by the story of Crazy Horse and his mother (shared in Chapter 9). After Crazy Horse gave away the family's food and felt hungry the next day, his mother urged him to be brave. But why would a person need to be brave if there was no danger or enemy or fighting? Crazy Horse wasn't near death; he was merely uncomfortable.

Finally I found a deeper understanding of bravery offered by Ohiyesa:

[An Indian's] own conception of bravery makes of it a high moral virtue, for to him it consists not so much in aggressive self-assertion as in absolute self-control. The truly brave man, we contend, yields neither to fear nor anger, desire nor agony; he is at all times master of himself; his courage rises to the heights of chivalry, patriotism, and real heroism.

"Let neither cold, hunger, nor pain, nor the fear of them, neither the bristling teeth of danger nor the very jaws of death itself, prevent you from doing a good deed," said an old chief to a scout who was about to seek the buffalo in midwinter for the relief of a starving people. This was his childlike conception of courage.[3]

I think of bravery this way: *A person showing bravery remains fully conscious and acts in service of what matters under any challenge.*

I like this perspective for several reasons:

- *Brave even when afraid:* I can be brave even if I feel fear. The question is: do I still do the right thing, whatever that means in my heart, even when I feel afraid? With training I may learn not to feel afraid at all, but in the meantime I can still be brave even while I feel afraid.

- *Brave even when seemingly helpless*: People can be brave even if they are seemingly helpless. For example, Siddique Hasan has been trapped in an Ohio State prison for decades while advocating for prisoner resistance and solidarity against abuses they face. When prison staff feared his activism, they moved him to solitary confinement and took all of his things. He communicated through air vents to pass messages. After his continued activism, prison staff barricaded his cell with sandbags to further prevent interactions with anybody else. This showed me that even when a person is unable to stop something terrible, they can remain conscious and do their best, whatever that is. This is brave.[4]

- *Brave without an enemy*: A person can be brave even when there's no human enemy. When Crazy Horse gave away his family's food during a hungry winter, it was his mother who was brave. Her hunger was suddenly imposed by her young child after a period of hardship which she believed was at least temporarily over. Even as she watched her food disappear into the community, she took the opportunity to bring the best out of her son and build him up, saying, "you must be brave." She acted in service of her son in difficult circumstances and so modeled bravery for young Crazy Horse.[5]

The Trouble With Cowardice

This perspective on bravery also clarifies the meaning of its opposite, cowardice. A coward behaves appropriately when it's easy or comfortable, and they behave selfishly or inappropriately when doing the right thing would lead to scary consequences, or make them uncomfortable, or other excuses.

Integrity and bravery are closely connected. In any relationship, people want to be able to trust each other, and that requires each person to consistently act with integrity. Chapter 28 contains the story of Daniel who lied to me, and one of his excuses was, "I was busy."

When I heard Daniel say that, I knew that our future conversations would be difficult. Every time I heard him make a statement, I would wonder just how busy he was, and was he too busy to tell me the truth? Or, was he under some other kind of stress, such that I couldn't trust what he was saying?

This is the trouble with cowardice. When someone only acts with integrity when they feel like it, or when it's easy, there can never be deep trust. Fortunately, if a person makes a mistake and acts dishonestly, trust could potentially be recovered with the return-to-integrity process or in some other way.

When everyone in a relationship or group is brave, they can trust each other to do the right thing – that is, behave with all three forms of integrity – no matter the situation. Whether in two-person partnerships or larger groups, deep trust is one of the big benefits when everybody cultivates their bravery.

Deliberately Training Bravery

Like gratitude, authenticity, and many other qualities, bravery can be trained. A person can practice bravery, and that means that a person can also practice cowardice.

This is the truth behind Julian Assange's observation: "Every time we witness an injustice and do not act, we train our character to be passive in its presence and thereby eventually lose all ability to defend ourselves and those we love."[6]

People practice cowardice merely by repeatedly tolerating inappropriate behavior around them. Unhealthy nations forbid people from standing up to authorities' and corporate owners' injustices, because this is supposedly the police's job, meaning that *unhealthy nations actually forbid the most meaningful acts of bravery and solidarity and thus train people for cowardice*. Training people for cowardice is how unhealthy nations train people to embrace the comfort and safety of their privilege rather than stand for a culture of mutual respect.

Because unhealthy nations train people for cowardice, a key step towards generating healthy nations and healthy subcultures involves cultivating bravery. When everyone is brave, people can trust each other to behave appropriately even when it's scary or uncomfortable.

Practice Facing Fear and Discomfort

In a really scary or uncomfortable situation, an untrained person can feel overwhelmed and their consciousness becomes clouded. Such a person may act selfishly or hurtfully, not out of clear, calm decision-making, but out of an untrained, instinctual response to overwhelming feelings.

Thus a major aspect of training bravery is to train myself not to feel overwhelmed when I'm scared or uncomfortable. I practice remaining conscious and clear-minded even in very scary or uncomfortable moments. I call this *feeling comfortable in the midst of discomfort*.

The best way to practice remaining conscious when I feel afraid or uncomfortable is to intentionally put myself in situations in which I feel afraid or uncomfortable, and practice remaining conscious. In other words, I intentionally cause myself to feel fear or discomfort so that I can practice relating to them in a good way.

The Yequana challenged their babies, and carefully noticed when the baby was ready for a challenge and when they had enough. Jean Liedloff described how they would slowly help the baby feel comfortable in dangerous waters: first they would just dip the baby's feet, then their legs, then their whole body. The adults would then move the baby to faster waters, then to rapids as the baby's confidence grew. Before the child could even talk, they were very capable of judging water's direction, depth, and force by sight, and as adults they are some of the world's best white-water canoeists.[7]

Sioux man Little Crow's mother was a chief's daughter and widely recognized for her spirit and beauty. Shortly after Little Crow was born, she would take him to an ice covered lake, find a hole in the ice, and plunge her baby into the water. Then she would rub him with snow afterwards to strengthen his nerves. However, Little Crow remained completely safe in his loving mother's arms. Thus Little Crow learned to associate a sense of safety and comfort with the discomfort of severe freezing cold. She also took him out into the deep woods for days at a time so that he would feel comfortable with solitude and not fear being alone in the wilderness. At a young age, she threw a feast for Little Crow and announced that he would fast for two days. She did these things because she wanted him to be a worthy leader of his people.

She said, "My son, if you are to be a leader of men, you must listen in silence to the mystery, the spirit."[8]

Many great spiritual leaders have cultivated their power by going into the wilderness alone.

Martín Prechtel spent days at a time in the wilderness as a young man, even as his friends and parents became worried. He said, "Spirit beings began to visit me in those places, teaching me little lessons, revealing their natures to me."[9] Jesus Christ spent 40 days fasting in the wilderness facing his fears and temptations, and thus cultivated the bravery he showed in his later ministry.[10] Ohiyesa said that Crazy Horse spent a great deal of time fasting alone in prayer. Ohiyesa noted that this was not unique, but rather it "was customary with the best young men."[11]

I commonly notice healthy nations intentionally training their children to bravely give away their possessions as Jesus Christ recommended. Ohiyesa wrote that Sioux children were taught to give away what they prized the most. One young boy named Hakadah was even challenged by his grandmother Uncheedah to bravely sacrifice the dog to whom he felt closest as an offering to the Great Mystery. The little warrior bravely rose to the challenge.[12]

Vanuatu men cultivate courage with a practice called land-diving. They build huge scaffolds up to 100' in the air. With many friends and neighbors cheering them on from below, the diver will climb the scaffold, attach vines to his ankles, and dive towards the ground. Young divers jump from lower platforms, and older divers jump from the top. The diver's goal is to brush the ground with his shoulders. The vines are not elastic, so if they are too short, he stops above the ground, and if they are too long, he faces injury or death.[13]

I have grown a lot from extended water-only fasts, no-water/no-food fasts in the woods, self-defense jiu-jitsu, physical training, salsa dancing, and cold training. The key is to start easy and find my edge. A person's edge is the level of difficulty where, if the challenge gets any harder, the person might get hurt, exhausted, or otherwise have to stop.

Take cold training, for example. I recommend Wim Hof's cold training program, where participants take on a slightly bigger cold challenge each week. Participants start with a warm shower followed by a 30-second cold shower each day for the first week. For each day in the second week, participants take a 30-second cold shower, a normal warm shower, and then a 30-second cold shower. Each following week becomes a little harder. Eventually I was taking 20 minute long ice baths and stayed comfortably in near-freezing ocean water for 90 minutes while harvesting seaweed.

This careful progression is essential. Consistently facing one's edge helps cultivate bravery, as well as whatever other skill is being practiced. Increasing difficulty too fast could cause injury or demotivation, and too little difficulty does not improve bravery or the other skills. The descriptions of the Vanuatu and Yequana show how they use progression to slowly but steadily build up their courage and abilities. This steady progressive approach works for all skills and any kind of personal growth.

Often I make amazing discoveries by pushing myself. One of my favorite lessons is how often I can actually feel invigorated in the midst of shocking cold water. I'm not the only one; many people take ice baths or polar plunges in lakes and oceans to feel enlivened and sharpen their senses.[14]

Training to feel comfortable in the midst of discomfort doesn't have to mean ignoring my feelings or pain. Discomfort can actually feel invigorating. I have found that this applies to many things. I've learned to feel relaxed and calm while not eating for days, or while self-defense sparring with someone much bigger than me. And these experiences help me know what kinds of discomfort are actually ok, and what kinds really aren't ok and need to stop.

Another big bravery practice I know is simply to always face one's fears. In romantic relationships, friendships, work, or anywhere else, I practice noticing when I feel afraid, and I practice facing the fears.

Having mentors or peers can be very helpful. When I train alone or without any guidance, sometimes I push myself too hard or take it too easy. I've noticed I can be so used to hiding from a fear, especially in some social situations, that I don't even notice it. It can be helpful for others to offer me feedback, and who likewise receive my feedback too. I strongly recommend being part of a group that brings the best out of each other in this way.

The biggest bravery practice I know is to practice caring. Practice giving love fully with a wide open heart. Ultimately, even a brave person has to decide they care enough to take a big risk to serve some people or cause that matters. Many brave people throughout history have never intentionally practiced bravery as far as I can tell; they just cared so much about something that to shy away out of fear was unthinkable.

Jesus Christ illustrated these last two patterns. I am unaware of any Biblical passages showing that Christ intentionally practiced bravery. But he did consistently face his fears and temptations in the wilderness. And he did care deeply about the people around him, choosing again and again to lead and protect people despite knowing that authorities would eventually kill him.

Similarly to how a mother would face great danger to protect her child simply because she loves the child so much, Christ was willing to consistently face his fears and face death in service of the people he loved. Deep love makes cowardice disappear.

This shows how the second core spiritual practice – giving one's love, one's sacred gifts fully – is the foundation of bravery.

My Personal Journey Towards a More Satisfying Life

Before 2014, I had a life that was comfortable but not satisfying. I had a comfortable career and home, predictable income and expenses and extra savings, and physical safety. I had a little free time to have fun with friends. Sometimes I felt bored or unfulfilled, but I had felt bored for years in school and even that feeling was comfortable, like someone I'd known for a long time.

In this life I was comfortable and even happy at times, but I wasn't very satisfied. As long as I kept that old way of life, I was always going to be coping with that dissatisfaction somehow – with escapist books or TV, or worrying about politics, or social drama. As long as I prioritized comfort when I made my major life decisions, I was never going to feel deeply satisfied.

Later I realized that I could have a life that is comfortable but not satisfying, or I could have a life that is satisfying even if it's sometimes uncomfortable. And when I began walking a more satisfying path in 2014, the switch was super uncomfortable. But I've never regretted it for a moment.

My definition of bravery is remaining fully conscious and acting in service of what matters under any challenge. One of my biggest challenges has been the temptation of superficial comforts over walking a deeper path, even after I made the change in 2014.

It took me years to recognize a good balance between having a satisfying life and enjoying comforts. Whenever I find that I've prioritized comforts, I also notice I've gotten off the good path. I aim to *walk a satisfying path and enjoy comforts along the way*.

Benefits of Bravery

One of the big benefits of this training is that I get to learn my limits. When a challenge arises, knowing my limits helps me know whether I'm actually in danger or not.

Tom Brown Jr noted, "Most people underestimate their abilities because they have never had a chance to test their limits." Many people panic when they face a survival situation in the wilderness because they think they face insurmountable obstacles. Those who survive almost always avoided panic, finding that they could survive far past what they believed to be their limits.[15]

This panic is related to cowardice, as panic occurs when a person feels overwhelmed with fear and thus behaves inappropriately or foolishly. Thus training for bravery helps people avoid panicking as well.

Stories from people of healthy nations show how far they take this training. Pretty Shield described how, if a person fell into icy water in winter, they would take off their clothes and roll in the snow and rub snow onto their body to get warm. Afterwards, they would wring the water out of their clothes, put them back on, and forget about being wet. After integrating with the American unhealthy nation, she said, "Now my people wear gloves, and too many clothes. We are soft as mud."[16]

American colonel RI Dodge encountered the fantastic physical training that Apache warriors endured when he wrote, "The tenacity of life of an Indian, the amount of lead he will carry off, indicates a nervous system so dull as to class him with brutes rather than men… I myself have seen an Indian go off with two bullets through his body, within an inch of his spine, the only effect of which was to cause him to change his gait from a run to a dignified walk."[17]

This illustrates how easily people of unhealthy nations can make foolish assumptions. Colonel Dodge was fighting against warriors who trained to run as much as 75 miles per day for days in a row, intentionally cultivated bravery, and were heavily motivated to protect the land and people they loved.[18] Instead of noticing the warriors' deep love, bravery and physical capability, Dodge thought they were unfeeling brutes because they kept going even when he shot them repeatedly.

Bravery doesn't just help in extreme moments; it's made a huge difference in my day-to-day life. I'm honest with friends or coworkers in moments where, in the past, I might have told a half-truth or remained silent instead. I'm more comfortable speaking up when I'm dissatisfied, and a friend recently confirmed feeling relaxed knowing that I'll speak up if I'm unhappy with something instead of silently building up resentment. I'm better able to work through conflicts with others because I'm better at keeping my composure.

Release False Assumptions and Cultivate Faith

I have found it helpful to release false assumptions and cultivate faith instead.

An assumption is an unexamined belief. Having faith means believing without evidence. Harriet Tubman taught me the difference.

Any false assumption could have cost Tubman and her escapees their lives. Tubman's stories show that she avoided assumptions through carefully observing the people and environment around her. In other words, she had no unexamined beliefs. She did her very best to avoid trouble while serving the people she cared about, and then had faith that God would provide as long as he supported her work. I don't believe she had direct physical evidence of God in the way a scientist would recognize. She clearly had a wide open heart and felt a vivid connection with divinity, and her faith gave her tremendous bravery.

Assumptions can also directly hold someone back from bravely taking on a big challenge. One of the most common false assumptions I see involves talent. Many people seem to believe that top athletes, musicians, leaders or other high-performing people have a special talent, meaning some inherent quality that allowed them to reach their high level of performance. Research consistently shows this is wrong.

I don't believe in talent. I believe in confidence, desire, and consistent high-quality training. Research into world-class swimmers shows that desire, consistent high-quality training, resilience to setbacks such as injuries, and lack of external pressure such as from parents are strongly present in top world-champion-level athletes, and less so in lower-level athletes.[19]

Everyone has great potential, and some people seem to have special interests or abilities, but these don't make anybody high-achieving. What allows people to succeed is a willingness to keep doing their best even in the face of obstacles. Just like high-privilege entitled people believe they deserve their high social status because of their supposed inherent superiority and low-privilege entitled people believe they deserve their inferior status because of supposed inherent inferiority, "talent" likewise justifies people's performance based on supposed inherent qualities that simply don't show up in research.[20]

Why is this assumption about talent a problem? Believing in talent discourages effort. After all, if a person wants to play piano and believes success is determined by natural talent, and if they don't notice any musical abilities in the beginning, should they even bother trying? If the person believes talent dictates success, and they don't already show talent, then why bother trying?

When I notice how I've held myself back in life, holding false assumptions has been a big factor. All my assumptions were self-limiting. Each assumption discouraged effort, and since I feared I would fail, why try? What helped me was releasing those assumptions and cultivating faith instead.

Deep self-confidence is based on believing without evidence. Before a world-champion athlete achieves their first championship, why would they think they could become a champion? They had never won a championship before!

When Tubman first imagined helping people escape slavery, did she have clear evidence that she would succeed? The most Tubman could do was give her best effort and face the consequences as they came. She had to go on her first mission before she had proof that she could succeed. She had to have faith.

I think of faith as a deep acceptance that, as long as I do my best, the universe will provide. It's an attitude of trust that the world welcomes my deepest love, and *as long as I'm doing my best in service of what matters to me, I don't have anything else to worry about.* There is no evidence for this – it is simply a deep knowing.

That's faith.

Recognize Bravery in Others and Build a Library of Inspiring Stories

I learn a lot about bravery and cowardice by observing other people. I look for people who show integrity when they could get away with lying, or who acknowledge their own mistakes even when they feel uncomfortable. I like to encourage these people by privately letting them know that I admired their behavior.

In healthy nations, parents and elders commonly tell stories that reinforce qualities they want their child to adopt. Thus between the child's brave neighbors and stories of bravery, he or she is surrounded by bravery.

I surround myself with bravery, and I find this helpful. I take care to nourish friendships with people who show bravery in their lives. I commonly read and reread stories of bravery such as those from Harriet Tubman, Martin Luther King Jr, Crazy Horse, and Geronimo. I also hold on to present-day stories of bravery from people like Julian Assange or Chelsea Manning who risk a lot to protect people from predatory rulers. Whenever I feel weak or unsure, I reread some of these stories and it helps me find strength.

I recommend to anybody that they *build a collection of stories about admirable people.* It is an excellent antidote to news stories full of superficiality or selfishness.

Enjoy Life

Growing up, I thought a person already had to be brave to laugh at danger. It turns out, laughter helps a person generate bravery in scary or difficult moments.

Laughter also helps heal shame, feelings of inadequacy, and more. Whenever I feel ashamed or inadequate, I practice noticing these feelings and laughing at how silly they are.

For example, many times while writing this book, I've felt stressed that I'm upset about so many things in the world, and in one sense, all I'm doing about it is sitting at a desk typing. What a silly response to serious problems!

I can imagine, many years in the future, sitting around a fire with children. They might ask, "what did you do in the early 2020s to respond to all the big challenges you saw?" I could say "Well, I sat around typing on a computer. I basically spent many hours a day thinking and pushing buttons while sitting somewhat comfortably at a desk."

I can imagine those children of future generations looking at each other, remarking sarcastically on my "obvious" bravery in difficult times!

I believe that writing this book is the best thing I can do right now to address the challenges I see in my nation, so that's what I'm doing. And, it's very silly that my response to all my frustrations is to sit at a desk alone and type words that no one will read for months or years, if ever. That's simply what it means to write a book.

Occasionally, over the years it took me to write this book, I had to stop and laugh out loud at the silliness of sitting at a comfortable desk alone while I write about privilege and isolation. Otherwise, I'd have gotten too depressed to finish the book. Then I wouldn't have done any good at all!

Joy isn't a privilege or a distraction, and it's not something to feel guilty about. Joy is how I feel when I'm remembering to notice how beautiful life is, and how excited I feel to change things for the better.

Onondaga chief Lyons understood the importance of enjoying life: "Two things were told to us: to be thankful… And … enjoy life. That's a rule, a law – *enjoy life* – you're supposed to. I know you can only do as much as you can do and then… you're supposed to get outside and enjoy life."[21] (emphasis added)

Laughing in the face of danger can help a person feel brave when they didn't already. Choosing to find joy while walking a meaningful path instead of falling into depression can help build bravery too.

Cultivate a Healthy Relationship with Death

One thing that builds bravery is for a person to recognize how they would want to die, and how they wouldn't. What sort of death is acceptable and even admirable? And what kind of death should be avoided at all costs?

While he was mentored by Apache man Stalking Wolf, Tom Brown Jr nearly died because of drunken people shooting randomly in the woods. He described how unhappy he felt at the thought of dying due to other people's foolishness. He wrote about what sort of death he wanted instead: "I wanted a death that would be an omen to anyone who saw it. I wanted a spectacular death, full of final insights. I did not care if it was a painful death as long as it was one from which something could be taken… I wanted a death where the signs of my going would say to whoever read them that if there was nothing beyond life but the abyss, I had gone into it taking the best of myself with me in one joyous leap."

Brown also described what death he wanted to avoid, including being "Killed by boredom and the tiny, unconnected insignificance of civilized life… Cancer, Heart attack. Stroke. Emphysema. Any number of insults to the body…useless death…"[22]

This perspective helped me recognize that there are some ways worth dying. Which causes are worth risking my life or freedom for, and which not? This helps me prepare to face certain dangers and avoid others.

Black Elk and another Lakota man named Protector taught me how powerful people can be when they are willing to choose to die in service of what they love. Lakotas had entered the Pine Ridge reservation and encountered continual abuses and broken promises from the Americans. One day, fighting broke out and one man yelled, "Black Elk, this is the kind of a day in which to do something great!" Black Elk decided to fight and dashed on his horse up a hill through a hail of bullets. Finally he reached the top and was shot.

Black Elk described how Protector came to him and helped bandage him "so that my insides would stay in." Black Elk wanted to fight, and he said, "Help me on my horse!… It is a good day to die, so I will go over there!" Protector responded, "No, young nephew! You must not die today. That would be foolish. Your people need you. There may be a better day to die."[23]

I had never heard men debate the best time to risk death in service of their people. But this showed me what bravery is like.

Choose What to Believe About Death

Black Elk described how he and others expected to die once after being captured by the Americans. They dressed for death and began singing death songs as they wished to end life bravely even if they could not escape. He said, "if it was the end of our lives and we could do nothing, we wanted to die brave. We could not fight this that was going to kill us, but we could die so that our spirit relatives would not be ashamed of us."[24]

Black Elk acknowledged that spirits live on after death, and he wanted to die in a way that his spirit relatives would not be ashamed of him. Chapter 25 explored how healthy nations can have understandings of pregnancy and family that encourage healthy, satisfying relationships. Likewise, healthy nations can have understandings of death that encourage a healthy relationship with it too.

Another perspective likewise shows how death need not be something to fear, but merely another step in an ongoing journey. Nancy Basket described how the Cherokee reincarnate "until everybody gets it right and nobody's left behind… Isn't that cool? Until you achieve what you need to be doing. Each lifetime you come with a medicine, a purpose that only you can get done…"[25] In this view, death is not the end, but another step in a collective adventure where everyone helps each other give their love fully. And we just keep reincarnating until everyone's fully giving their love together.

Different healthy nations have very different perspectives on death and reincarnation. But these perspectives showed me that I don't have to believe the perspective on heaven and hell I learned growing up, and I don't have to believe the secular scientific understanding of death as the final end of a person's life. Black Elk's perspective acknowledged an ongoing connection with ancient ancestors whom he wanted to make proud, and I can feel such a connection myself. Likewise, Basket's perspective on reincarnation reflects a view of life as an ongoing cycle of birth, growth, death, and new birth, which certainly describes life as I see it play out around me. These perspectives make deep sense to me.

Ultimately, anybody can choose what to believe about death. Why not relate to death in a way that makes it seem less scary, and motivates you, in the words of Black Elk, to "[want] to die brave?"

The Need for Bravery

There were only about 32,000 white French colonists in French St. Domingue in 1789, but they collectively treated the approximately 500,000 enslaved people abominably. Unfortunately, they also had a powerful security and surveillance system geared towards keeping the workers at work and the masters in comfort. The enslaved people faced a choice: they could keep on suffering endless tortures, sexual assaults, family separation, overwork, disease, and other humiliations, or they could risk their lives and revolt. The Haitians succeeded, but it came at a steep price. During the Haitian revolution from 1791-1804, the total population of French St. Domingue dropped to ~250,000.[26,27]

No one guaranteed the rebels that they would succeed. No one can ever know the future. This shows the power of choosing how to die and wanting to die bravely. I believe many Haitians decided they would rather die than continue to live under their masters. Hundreds of thousands had to die bravely with an uncertain outcome so that the survivors could live in freedom.

Once people are trapped in abusive relationships, it can be very dangerous to take a stand against the abuse. Few revolutions are peaceful, and many revolutions don't succeed. But every successful revolution I've studied involved people who showed deep bravery in service of each other, and deep bravery in the face of uncertainty.

There are many ways to help achieve meaningful change. Let us turn now to the last big question of this book, in *Part 10 - What Can I Do?*

Part 10 - What Can I Do?

Sometimes I worry that healing my nation seems impossible. But the Zapatistas showed me that it's not impossible – it's just hard. And there's a world of difference between impossible and hard!

What paths might lead to that deepest cultural healing, where nobody rules over anybody else, and everybody stands for a culture of mutual respect?

Chapter 49: What to Keep and What to Let Go

For millennia, people have debated what kind of governance systems they should have. What kind of government would guarantee people freedom? I have heard debates about monarchies, democracies, republics, sociocracies, theocracies, and dictatorships. Some people prefer to focus on the economy, and they will endlessly debate socialism, capitalism, communism, and many other -isms.

Unfortunately, these debates ignore a profound truth: *no system of government will save people from themselves*. If people are afraid to stand up for what's right, no government will impose justice. If people are afraid to stand in solidarity when a neighbor is disrespected, no legal system will guarantee everyone is treated equally. If people are afraid to hold their leaders accountable, they will get unaccountable leaders.

People will get the kind of nation they're willing to stand for. For example, the Nootka didn't have a beautiful nation because they got lucky, or because they knew about some secret governance system. As the story of the clown and preacher showed in Chapter 3, they had a beautiful nation because the moment anyone was disrespected, the entire nation immediately addressed it. When the preacher attacked the clown, no one said, "it's not happening to me, so it's not my problem" or "the woman was naked in public, what do you expect?" When they saw disrespect to one of their own people, they took a stand to stop it.

Different systems of self-governance have different benefits and drawbacks, but the truth is that *any system of governance can work as long as everyone is willing to stand for a culture of mutual respect*, and *no system of governance will work if people are too afraid*. The key is not the particular form of government, but the foundation on which it is built.

Some healthy nations, such as the Huron, have even had hereditary chiefs.[1] This shows me that even self-governance systems that are superficially similar to monarchies can be part of a respectful way of life – if everyone stands for a culture of mutual respect.

There is so much room for creativity in deciding how to get along. For example, it may seem obvious that everyone should speak for themselves in a council. Those who don't speak for themselves lose their chance to influence the decision. But then how does a community respond to voices that cannot be present? The Okanagans recognized this and trained people to respectfully speak on behalf of those who could not always speak for themselves, including mothers, elders, the land, and so on.

I believe that the Okanagans first committed to having a respectful nation that took all perspectives into account; then they figured out a system to accomplish this that worked for them. Other healthy nations could make this same commitment and then figure out different decision-making systems that likewise accommodate everyone's needs. But without the commitment and then the willingness to actually follow through and stand for a culture of mutual respect, no form of governance can work.

I have been asked, "how did the Zapatistas keep their government from deteriorating and eventually having rulers?" The answer is simple: they continuously stand for a culture of mutual respect. They did not pick the perfect kind of government at the beginning and then just hope for the best. They *continuously* stand for that respectful culture, and thus the government adjusts over time to meet the needs of the people, not the other way around.

Once an entire group of people is willing to stand for a culture of mutual respect, they will figure out a respectful system of self-governance. As long as people are too afraid to take a stand in solidarity with their neighbors, no system of governance will ever generate a healthy nation.

Discussing Freedom vs Discussing Improvements to a Slave Society

Sioux man Sitting Bull said "The life of white men is slavery. They are prisoners in their towns or farms."[2] He was speaking about Americans, but this is true of any unhealthy nation. Everyone in an unhealthy nation is a slave, even the rich. Everyone is expected to support the exploitative rulers, and those who don't comply get punished. The rich and soldiers get exploited, as explored in Chapter 38. Police with integrity get punished, as explored in Chapter 32. Prisons offer a great example: the warden is far more comfortable than the prisoners, but he or she would be punished if they tried to release the prisoners who had been unjustly imprisoned. Of course, some slaves are much less comfortable than others. That's why if a person had to choose whether to be a prisoner or a prison warden, most would choose prison warden – but neither wardens nor prisoners are free.

Many political discussions essentially explore how to improve life while remaining "prisoners in [our] towns or farms." For example, many political debates discuss how to have a more comfortable profit economy. Should there be more public transportation or more bike lanes? Should there be better vehicle fuel efficiency, or more school funding and higher education standards? I support all these improvements, but it's helpful to me to remember that none of these questions address the exploitation at the heart of the nation. None of these changes will end the widespread financial desperation inherent in a market economy, or create a way of life where the economy rewards generosity rather than selfishness.

In other political debates, people discuss the most efficient way to arrange their exploitative economy. Is it better to live in a capitalist or libertarian society, where individuals can own lots of property and the government protects their private property rights? Or should we live in a socialist or communist society, where the government controls more wealth directly and hopefully provides more public services? Some people prefer capitalism because they see how exploitative and unfree life could be under a heavy-handed government, and some people prefer socialism or communism because they see how exploitative and unfree life would be with rich private landlords and unfettered corporate greed. All their fears are valid: none of these economic systems generates a free society without rulers. Capitalism, communism, libertarianism, and socialism are all variations on a profit economy that, in practice, encourage and reward selfishness, and all of them allow rulers and the rich to exploit everyone else.

As long as people only debate how to have a more efficient or comfortable slave society, nothing will fundamentally change. Real transformation will be possible once enough people discuss how to create a truly healthy nation among themselves, where everyone stands for a culture of mutual respect, and nobody rules over anybody else.

Honor Healthy Nation Traditions

One source of friction between people of healthy nations and people of unhealthy nations is cultural appropriation. For example, some outsiders like to wear certain clothes or sing songs associated with healthy nations. Almost always, people who copy things like clothes or songs miss important context.

However, the debate about cultural appropriation shows that most outsiders deeply misunderstand healthy nations. People of healthy nations know or remember what it's like to live in a way where everyone stands for a culture of mutual respect, and nobody rules over anybody else.

Every living human today had ancestors who lived in healthy nations at some distant time. Most people today in unhealthy nations have forgotten this; that memory has been lost. This is true for me; I know almost nothing about any generation older than my grandparents. I suspect my ancestors have been trapped in unhealthy nations for many generations.

Nations like the Cherokee in North America or Mosuo in Asia are not fully sovereign, as the US and Chinese militaries impose their laws. However, people of healthy nations retain a memory of what it was like to live in actual freedom.

Many Americans believe they live in the "land of the free," but most Americans have been trapped in authoritarian nations for generations. They don't know what freedom is like, while people of healthy nations do. They remember what it's like to live in reciprocity with the Earth. They remember integrity and bravery. They remember how to raise children to walk in a sacred way, give thanks for life's gifts, and have balanced leadership.

There is a reason the Zapatistas were the ones to lead a successful revolution in Mexico: they maintained some amount of cultural cohesion even after centuries of abuse. They remembered what a healthy nation was like, so when they launched their revolution, they created laws that actually allowed them to live without rulers. Even so, it took them 10 years of preparation.[3]

Many Mexicans, like many other people around the world, have lost that cultural cohesion and cultural memory of how to live in a good way. But I suspect that whenever a chance for a successful revolution arises, it will be healthy nations who are most likely to have the cultural cohesion and memory needed to reestablish fully sovereign, healthy nations.

Revolutionaries who don't know what freedom is like will make the same mistakes as the American and Soviet Union founders: they will simply create a different unhealthy nation.

Each healthy nation's clothing, songs, and other visible effects are important in the context of that nation. But I'm not as interested in nations' clothing and songs because copying them won't help me generate a healthy nation. It's the healthy nations' wisdom, attitudes, and core practices that make them healthy, and embracing these is the key to generating healthy nations. That is why this book focuses specifically on qualities that anybody can embrace, including balanced leadership, respect for children, solidarity, sacred circles, sharing, bravery, joy, integrity, deep nature connection, gracious receiving, an open heart, the three core spiritual practices, systems of accountability, and more. To review all the healthy-nation patterns explored in this book, see Appendix 2.

Everything changed for me when I realized I did not need to just learn from my biological elders or people in my own nation. I definitely have learned from my family and other Americans and I will keep learning from them, but I am not limited to them. I can seek wisdom anywhere. Anyone can be my elder, my mentor, if I let them.

Nancy Basket described how important it is to *seek out other elders* when she said, "if you don't look anywhere except one place, one set of elders, then you're not getting other perspectives to add to your understanding. When you ask deep questions, you'll be given other stories that feed in through the root system of our spiritual growth process. And that's what we need to be doing…"[4]

This points to some big questions: what should I learn from the past, what should I learn from other nations, and what do I need to create anew to generate a healthy nation?

Every nation, healthy or not, has wisdom worth keeping. I grew up Christian, became atheist, and then later went back and pulled the useful lessons from Christianity while discarding elements that seem hurtful and unhelpful. Christianity, Islam, and other authoritarian religions often train people to think of religion as all-or-nothing; one either believes the whole thing or one is cast out as an unbeliever. But the truth is that there is wisdom everywhere, and also any nation can adopt hurtful patterns and make mistakes. I say, *accept the lessons and wisdom from any nation, and leave behind the hurtful or unhelpful parts.*

Much healthy-nation wisdom has been lost over centuries and millennia of oppression. The wisdom that remains is a treasure that may form the seeds of healthy nations yet to come.

People who have lost that ancestral memory can work together with people of healthy nations to bring about deep change. People born into unhealthy nations can potentially play important roles. Subcommander Marcos was a military leader of the Zapatistas, with large responsibilities for planning and supporting their revolution in 1994 – but he wasn't from any of the local healthy nations. He acknowledged not being "Indian" at all! He wasn't even from that region.[5]

Major Ana María described Marcos's total commitment and humility when she said how he came to be so deeply trusted: "He was born eleven years ago in the Lacandon jungle and since then he has lived, eaten, drank and slept alongside us, the indigenous people of Chiapas. Marcos, like all the members of the [core planning committee], knows nothing and is nothing. Marcos is just another representative, like the [committee], of the indigenous people and of the people of Chiapas."[6]

There does not need to be any artificial separation between people born into healthy nations and people born into unhealthy nations. We're all humans who want dignity, clean food and water, meaningful work, and satisfying relationships. Marcos' role with the Zapatistas shows that people of very different backgrounds can work together to generate deep change.

Many Paths, One Cure

Sometimes solutions that work well in one place don't work in another. Or cultural practices that work for one group don't work for another.

For example, the Gumbaynggirr people in Australia want to stop logging. While they physically work to block the logging, they also want the government to create specially designated heritage sites to protect the land.[7]

In contrast, in India, so-called conservationists have tried to evict the Jenu Kuruba from their ancestral land in the name of protecting the endangered species, and the Jenu Kuruba have fought back. In practice, the conservationists have tried to create tourist industries and open mines where the Jenu Kuruba have been displaced.

Superficially, it might seem like the Gumbaynggirr and Jenu Kuruba are pushing in different directions. The Gumbaynggirr in Australia want the government to help conserve land, and the Jenu Kuruba in India are fighting government "conservation" efforts that are actually subtle attempts to open new territory for exploitation.

People of both healthy nations want to protect the land, and each group is following the best path they see to do that in their particular circumstances. Each nation is acting on that third core spiritual practice – living in reciprocity – and doing their best to serve the land that serves them.

Unhealthy nations around the world have a lot in common, and in some ways each one is unique. The path to protecting the Earth and generating new healthy nations may look different in different places. The voice in each person's heart will help them know the best path if they can open their heart and listen.

When people can come together, open their hearts, and connect so deeply that they have "one body, one heart, one mind," as the Haudenosaunee say, they will do great things.

Why Did Unhealthy Nations Form? Does it Matter?

Some people ask, why did unhealthy nations originally form?

My current response is: Does it matter?

Unhealthy nations formed independently on several continents over the past few thousand years. Some healthy nations may have transformed without external pressure, but I suspect many healthy nations transformed after either winning or losing a war. If two healthy nations went to war and the winners incorporated the losers as servants or chattel slaves, the winners gained a life of greater comfort at the cost of no longer living in a healthy nation without rulers.

"Why did unhealthy nations start?" and "why do unhealthy nations persist so long?" are different questions. I imagine two healthy nations going to war long ago where the winners chose to integrate the losers as an underclass. The losers knew what a healthy nation was like even as they adapted to their underclass status. But over the centuries, many people from around the world have forgotten what it's like to live in a healthy nation, or even forgotten healthy nations exist. Many exploited people actively support their rulers when the rulers are threatened.

Unhealthy nations formed for one set of reasons, but they have persisted for other reasons. Unhealthy nations are so durable because of all the techniques explored in this book – child abuse, desperation management, money dependency, privilege, systemic sexism, hate campaigns, economies that reward selfishness, systemic racism, encouraging people to ignore or fight healthy nations, training or forcing people to believe falsehoods, and more.

All these things make deep solidarity difficult, and none of them existed at the moment when one early healthy nation won out over another thousands of years ago and they became an unhealthy nation together. The emotional and spiritual wounding came after any initial military victory. Why unhealthy nations started and why they are so persistent seem very different.

Thus I do not think much about why unhealthy nations first formed. I am interested in why they are so durable and what I can do to heal the unhealthy nation in which I live.

How Much Do People Really Want Freedom?

I have spoken with so many people who are upset about our current troubles, including pollution, discrimination, imperialism, and much more. But when I talk about what life would be like in a nation without these troubles, they often admit they wouldn't want that life.

For example, in the United States, all kinds of exotic foods are available year-round because chemical pesticides allow large scale farming at the expense of the soil, fossil-fuel-driven ships move food around the world, and huge numbers of people are kept in financial desperation, from overseas migrant farmers to dock workers to accountants to grocery store clerks.

What would life be like without fossil fuels, toxic chemicals, and keeping people in financial desperation? It would mean gardening, foraging, and otherwise taking responsibility for one's own food. People who are used to "working" by sitting in a chair all day would have to learn practical skills and find the joy in meaningful work with other people.

This extends to every aspect of life. Without exploitative economies, cell phones could not exist, so people used to communicating at long distances would no longer be able to. People would be more present with each other, and enjoy each others' company more. Without exploitation, huge houses wouldn't exist, and people would need to work with neighbors to make houses. I can attest that working with many friends to build one friend's home can actually be fun. But for many people, it would require an attitude shift to see these changes as good.

In profit economies, many people's whole way of life depends on continuous exploitation. How many people really want a world without exploitation, including all the practical consequences that would entail?

For example, phasing out plastics, just to choose one type of profitable poison, would entail massive change. Vehicles, houses, phones, computers, toys, food packaging, medical equipment – so many products would be radically altered or disappear entirely without toxic plastics. And of course, the change would raise the product's purchase cost, if it could still exist at all. This is simply the reality of unhealthy nations' dependency on toxins.

The Four Horsemen of the Apocalypse from ancient times were conquest, war, famine, and death. All of humanity now faces so many more threats – pervasive toxins that are diminishing humans' and nonhumans' health and reproductive abilities, climate change dramatically affecting temperature and rainfall patterns, a mass extinction leading to huge biodiversity loss, resources like groundwater disappearing faster than they recharge, and much more.

And yet, how many people with comfortable jobs who have all their purchases delivered to their front door would give this up? How many people who get excited about the latest car or bigger house would seek the beauty of small, simple and sufficient? I have spoken with many good-hearted people who speak eloquently about the troubles with racism in their country, but when I tell them what it would be like to live without the goods and services of an exploitative economy, I rarely encounter a willingness to make that tradeoff.

People in unhealthy nations have been trapped in catastrophes for millennia, and the catastrophes are getting worse. But when I speak with a variety of people, including a variety of skin colors, I find that many prefer the catastrophe rather than relinquish their privilege in their unhealthy nation. People might not like the exploitation, but few are willing to give up their way of life that so thoroughly depends on it. They will put signs in their yard saying "Black Lives Matter" and talk about peace and love, but how many would want the changes they would face if exploitation actually ended?

Of course, this is simply part of the trap, and part of why unhealthy nations have been so resilient for millennia. When a whole nation's way of life depends on exploitation and profiting, it is difficult for those who believe they benefit from it to give it up. This is why revolutions are generally begun by the poorest, with the least to lose and the most to gain.

And in truth, everyone would gain more than they know.

It becomes much easier for people to take care of each other in gift economies when everybody lives in a simple way. As I write in 2024, many young people in the United States struggle to make enough money to buy a house and start a family. The cost of land makes this difficult, as does the size and cost of houses. But when Wikis married his wife Standing Alone, his relatives gave them everything they needed to have a home – including the home! After their marriage, Wikis said, "[Our families] brought us a lodge and much lodge furniture–robes and bedding, backrests, mats and dishes–all the things that people used in the life of the camp… as husband and wife, Standing Alone and I began our life well provided with all that we needed."[8]

Only very wealthy parents can afford to give their children an entire furnished home in unhealthy nations. European colonial traders called people of healthy nations poor in the 1600s-1700s, but Wikis' and his wife's families could give them a fully furnished house without worry when they chose, and Wikis did not say this was unusual. Which nations are truly poor and which have abundance?

This is a beautiful benefit of living simply: deep generosity and mutual aid become much easier. I cannot help pay my friends' mortgages, but I can help them build cabins to live in. I cannot extract and refine oil to run oil heaters, but I can chop wood for heating a home. I cannot chop enough wood to heat a large home, but I can chop enough wood to heat a home big enough to live comfortably and simply.

I suspect there would be lots of pleasant surprises too. For example, as I walk around my neighborhood, I see a lot of trash on the ground, including lots of trash that people leave on their own lawns. Many people seem to not care much about the beauty of their space or the impact they have. This is a direct consequence of living in a nation that trains people to withhold their love. When people are forbidden from stopping abusive and exploitative behavior, they can easily learn not to care about anything, even themselves, and one way that this shows up visually is trashy neighborhoods. Nations that welcome people's deepest love – that is, nations without rulers – don't have this problem because everyone is free to act on any concerns they have.

And really, litter shouldn't be a problem in the first place. All humans litter, and this is normal. When a little girl carves a spoon out of a wooden stick, what does she do with the wood shavings? She lets them fall to the ground – littering! When a little boy makes a basket out of vines, what does he do with the unused vines at the end? He leaves them on the ground somewhere – littering! When a family is done with a fire and puts it out, where do they leave the burned coals? On the ground!

The ground is simply the place people leave things they don't need anymore. This is perfectly appropriate when people only use non-toxic, biodegradable materials. Littering isn't the problem. The problem is that unhealthy nations produce toxins like plastic which are either expensive or impossible to dispose of without poisoning the environment. Healthy nations would never produce something like plastic in the first place, and thus it would be ok to litter, knowing one's refuse wouldn't poison the soil and look ugly.

To anyone who feels deeply upset by the sexism, racism, hatred, pollution, dishonest and selfish political leaders, wars based on lies, manipulative law, prison slavery, child abuse, and more, I ask you: how much do you really want to get rid of these and be part of building a healthy nation? Are you willing to give up the comforts and predictability you would need to give up in order to be part of actual, deep change? Are you willing to find joy in deep connection with other loving people and the Earth, in sharing food and planting trees and saying "no" to some people's really inappropriate behavior?

Deep change won't be easy, but it is definitely possible. For practical suggestions on next steps to take, join me in *Chapter 50: What Can I Do?*

Chapter 50: What Can I Do?

Growing up, I learned that the United States was the best country in the world, and I felt proud to live in a capitalist democracy. I looked forward to contributing to the United States' progress in many ways throughout my life. As a church-going Christian, I bowed my head every night before dinner and prayed.

Over time, as I learned all the things that I share in this book, I had to give up a lot of beliefs – beliefs about the society I live in, beliefs about history, beliefs about myself, beliefs about the future, beliefs about what matters and what doesn't matter.

For years I felt really ungrounded. I grew up with medium-privilege, so I had a deep sense that the government would treat me fairly and that I would be safe as long as I worked hard and followed the rules.

But the more I read about low-privilege people and activists being persecuted, the more insecure I felt. I studied environmental problems, unsustainable resource usage, and imperialism, and everywhere I looked I saw that the future could not be like I had thought it would be. And through my job and my spending, I realized I had unknowingly been contributing to a lot of the problems I saw in the world.

Confronting difficult truths and dramatically changing one's worldview can be really difficult.

Bogaletch Gebre described how difficult it was for her. She had undergone female genital mutilation in Ethiopia, and she was taught this made her a "whole woman." One day she discussed it with a friend who felt horrified, and Gebre felt outraged at her friend's horror. She said, "How dare she question the most sacred, the most precious part of my life?" But even as she tried to defend her culture, she "experienced an incredible awakening, then a tidal wave of anger, as I began to comprehend all that had been taken from me in ignorance… Tears of understanding flooded from me as I allowed the scientist in me to see, to examine in a new light, all that I remembered…"[1]

Don Cox described his own transformation. He went to a conference in 1967 where black people openly discussed their social and political situation in the United States and what to do about it. They spoke of returning to Africa, protecting themselves from oppression, and revolution. Cox heard Black Panthers speak. He said, "I was drunk with this new world I had not even known existed. Pieces started falling into place. It was a cascade, a snowball rolling down the mountainside."[2]

Then he described how hard this was: "Everything I had heard during the weekend helped me understand that all the efforts I had made up until then to be acceptable to mainstream society had just made me a 'good nigger.' I was simultaneously ashamed and furious. All I could do was cry."

In September 2014, about 100 French forest protectors gathered to stop corporate and government leaders from clear-cutting the Sivens Forest and installing a dam. Activists risked their personal safety in countless ways as they sought to protect the trees from destructive machines and obedient police.

As the destructive machines approached, activists stayed in trees, barricaded roads, confronted police, and faced arrest. One activist named Verdun was asked why he felt so upset, and he said, "Because they are just killing the fucking forest. I have just become aware of our powerlessness, in the face of capitalism. How it devours the Earth, over and over…"[3]

The first step to address any challenge is to acknowledge the truth of the situation. This is the first step in a sacred circle, a process that helps people collectively address their shared challenges and respond together.

Cox, Verdun and Gebre show that deep acceptance can be hard. But in order for them to walk a better path, deep acceptance had to happen. Cox would not have meaningfully stood for dignity for black people if he had not first realized that trying to live up to white people's standards was a waste of time. Verdun would not have taken a stand for the forest in France if he hadn't accepted the destructive truths of capitalism. Gebre would not have worked to end female genital mutilation in Ethipia if she had not first questioned its legitimacy.

Acknowledging bitter truths can be hard. But there is something beautiful on the other side of the transformation that comes from deep recognition and acceptance: the basic principles of life start to make sense. When Ohiyesa learned about Christian principles, he noticed that they did not fit in with the core principles of life: "I [tried] to fit the new ideas like so many blocks into the pattern of my philosophy, while according to my untutored logic some did not seem to have straight sides or square corners to fit in with the cardinal principles of eternal justice."[4]

Systems of morality and ethics in unhealthy nations can never make sense if they justify some people ruling over others. Unhealthy nations do not generate deep justice, so religious and political teachings don't perfectly "fit in with the cardinal principles of eternal justice."

But the teachings of healthy nations do fit with these principles. Their basic perspectives on spirit, love, boundary-setting, dignity, solidarity, sharing, personal autonomy, collective action, respect for other people and nonhumans, reciprocity and much more all fit together in a beautiful and cohesive way.

Recognizing the power of these deeper truths helped me feel much more grounded than I ever had before. I no longer saw myself as a cog in a massive machine doing my part to help it supposedly progress a little further. I left behind my identity. In fact, I stopped identifying as anything. Instead, I simply asked the questions: *What do I care about? And how am I acting in service of what I care about?*

In other words, what truly matters to me, and how can I give my deepest love?

I didn't have to worry about "who I am" or how the unhealthy nation identified me. Focusing on what mattered to me and how I could act in service helped me release shame and guilt about my past, and it kept me from worrying too much about the future.

Personal Healing, Collective Healing

Sometimes I feel stressed because I imagine I need to solve all the world's troubles. What can I do to end exploitation everywhere? Climate change, profit economies, and other troubles are globe-spanning. Does that mean I need to act on a global level in order to make a difference?

The Zapatistas show me the scale I can work at. Humans address shared challenges in sacred circles where they can see each other face-to-face. This can scale well, as the Zapatistas' system of tiered self-governance shows. But it still means that deep change starts with working with the problems and people around me.

I often hear, "Ok, I agree with your perspective, but what should I do?"

I do not have all the answers, but after experiencing and studying healthy nations so much, I do have suggestions.

Notice Your Dissatisfaction

If you are displeased with your world in some way, the first step is to acknowledge it. None of us can fix what we don't face. For me, this eventually entailed a huge break with my former life. But it doesn't have to begin with a radical change. Fixing a problem always begins with noticing it. When you feel the dissatisfaction for long enough, without distraction, you'll find the next step to take to begin making things right.

Start on a Personal Level

I strongly suggest taking the time to purposely adopt the *three core spiritual practices* shared by healthy nations (offered in Chapter 2):

- Cultivate a practical, aware gratitude for the gifts of life, and practice living from gratitude.

- Figure out your sacred gifts and practice giving your deepest love.

- Practice living in reciprocity with the humans and nonhumans who bless you with their gifts.

These are non-trivial practices, and they are not theoretical. Reading about them is only the first step; for them to have a positive effect, they have to be put into practice. They have opened my heart, and I believe they will open anyone's heart. Many chapters offer practical suggestions for how to embrace these practices.

On a Collective Level

Next, I suggest finding other caring people and holding sacred circles with them. "Sacred circle" is just a fancy name for people sitting together and addressing the three questions (reviewed in Chapter 23):

1. What is the challenge we face?

2. What are we going to do about it?

3. How are we going to take care of each other along the way?

Whether it's a group of parents seeking to hold school leaders accountable, a neighborhood seeking to prevent the construction of a dirty factory, friends who want to protect a forest, or any challenge, this sacred circle process can help. As challenges keep arising, hold more circles and address each challenge together.

On a Community Level

If a group that holds sacred circles wants to form its own distinct nation or subculture, I suggest addressing these three questions (offered in Chapter 4):

1. *External boundaries*: how are we going to protect ourselves from disrespect by outsiders?

2. *Internal boundaries*: what rules and systems of accountability do we want to have to ensure that, within our group, everyone treats everyone else and the land respectfully?

3. *How people live within the boundaries*: once we've established that baseline of mutual respect among ourselves, how do we want to live together? How will we share and take care of each other in the face of great challenges? How will we account for the needs of the Earth?

Protect Each Other

Find your tools of self-defense and train with them. Self-defense is the ultimate act of self-respect, both individually and collectively. Decide as a group when and how people will coordinate to protect each other, whether verbally or physically.

When Lakota chief Big Foot's band surrendered to the US cavalry in 1890, the first thing the military did was take everybody's weapons and separate the men from the women.[5] In other words, they made it impossible for the Lakota to protect each other from any predation by authorities of the conquering nation. Since then, the Lakota have worked to protect themselves and the land in countless ways, but that initial disarming showed me the importance of being able to protect myself and the people and land I care about.

Fools use weapons to puff themselves up, waving them around to cover for their own insecurity. Warriors use weapons to establish healthy boundaries and forbid outsiders from exploiting their people. Healthy boundary-setting is necessary for any healthy nation or healthy subculture to protect itself from predators. Each group must use wisdom and good judgment to decide on their own rules for when and how to set their boundaries. Each armed person must take deep responsibility for their actions, a responsibility every warrior must accept in order to serve their people.

Learn to Receive the Gifts of the Earth

I strongly suggest learning how to receive the gifts of the Earth. Learn to make friction fire with wood that you gather, or how to find and clean water, or what plants and animals to eat, and how to responsibly harvest them. These are often called "earth skills," "survival skills," or "primitive skills."

Sometimes when I study plants and animals, I focus too much on learning their names and studying them in books. It's important to learn how to receive their gifts too. When I go walking through a suburban neighborhood, and I see yucca plants and basswood and cedar trees, I feel an excitement and gratitude because I have made fire from these plants before, and I know I could do it again if I ever needed to. Oaks, chestnuts, beeches, blueberries, persimmons, and many other plants offer me food. I have even used plants like miscanthus grass to make a watertight thatched roof.

One reason people of healthy nations can feel gratitude for the gifts of life is that they learn how to receive those gifts. They learn how to live with the Earth - to make fire and shelter, gather food, learn life lessons, make ceremonial items, and more, all from the plants and animals around them. They also learn how to responsibly harvest so that the plant and animal communities are not harmed by the taking, as discussed in Chapters 9 and 34.

When I first seriously studied foraging, I saw the forest around me as a "green wall." I couldn't tell any of the trees or other plants apart. I enjoyed being in the forest, but I didn't feel particularly grateful for anything in it.

Now, as I walk through the forest, I see gifts everywhere. I see animals that provide sustenance and show me where I can find water, and plants that offer fire, food, medicines, and materials for shelter, among many other things. I don't just see plants and nonhuman animals as resources for the taking, but I do recognize the ways they can benefit me. I recognize their gifts, and I know in a really practical way what I feel grateful for. I probably only know one ten-thousandth as much about the Earth as someone who grew up in a healthy nation, but I can imagine what it would be like to see all of life as a gift, in part because I'd learned about many gifts each creature offers.

Learning to recognize and receive life's gifts has lots of benefits.

Comfort in the wilderness: I feel more comfortable in the wilderness than I used to. It also makes me less dependent on my unhealthy nation. Unhealthy nations train people to depend on abusive authorities and make people financially desperate (see Chapters 10 and 14), so learning to receive the Earth's gifts directly and harvesting responsibly is an important part of finding some degree of freedom from those abusive authorities.

Cultivating a practical, aware gratitude: Learning survival skills helps me feel not just gratitude, but a practical and aware gratitude. Sometimes when I try to practice feeling grateful for the life around me, the gratitude feels hollow. The gratitude becomes practical when I remember all the practical gifts I receive that give me warmth, sustenance, joy, protection, or other benefits.

Desire to serve the Earth: Another great benefit is that I feel a real desire to serve the Earth. When I stayed with the Ashaninka and I received gifts all the time, I started continuously looking for ways to give back because I felt so grateful. Receiving gifts from the Earth can have a similar effect – but only if a person learns how to receive them, and receives them with gratitude. Economic "development" that cuts down forests and paves over fields only started to really seem detrimental to me when I realized how many gifts wild creatures have to offer. The more I learned to connect with the Earth and receive life's gifts, the more I wanted to protect it.

Resilience: The idea of "economic collapse" isn't as scary as it used to be, and it even sounds like an adventure. Indeed, learning these survival skills is a core part of generating healthy nations. What would happen if our unhealthy nation disappeared or collapsed? Or on the bright side, what would happen if people intentionally created their own healthy nation so that they did not depend on the old unhealthy nation's laws and money? Either way, the grocery stores and building supply stores would empty out, and then we would need to survive by receiving the gifts of the Earth.

Many TV shows make this seem like a frightening prospect, but receiving the Earth's gifts directly is actually the normal way for humans to live. If it seems scary, that is because many of us in unhealthy nations have removed ourselves so thoroughly from the Earth that we think of the real world as "outside," someplace different from where we live our lives.Many people even call the wilderness "the middle of nowhere." But immersing ourselves in the natural world and learning to receive the Earth's gifts doesn't have to be stressful or scary. It just takes training. It may also seem scary if people imagine going through collapse alone, but being part of a group with deep solidarity would make it an entirely different experience.

Fun: Another major benefit is that learning to receive the gifts of the Earth is fun. It's *super* fun. When a group of friends gather for dinner and a kid is misbehaving, and I invite the kid to rub sticks together to make fire to prepare for dinner, everything changes. The kid goes from being unhelpful and annoying to making an important contribution to the group's dinner. All of a sudden, the kid had a meaningful role to play, and they developed a skill that really matters. Doing important work together helps people of all ages get along, whether they are making fire, gathering firewood, repairing someone's home, foraging, or anything else.

Whether you learn to receive the Earth's gifts for resilience, for fun, to connect with other people or nonhumans, to maintain ancient wisdom, or all of these reasons, I highly recommend it.

Accept Deep Responsibility – Don't Fear It

I commonly encounter a fear that it's wrong to "play god." A common riddle goes as follows: imagine a train is inbound and you notice a person is stuck on the track. The train is going too fast to stop, but you have a switch you can pull that would redirect the train. However, when you look at the detour route, you see three people on the other track who would die when the train hits them.

Do you pull the switch and divert the train to save the one stuck person and kill the three others? Or do you let the one person die, even though you could save them?

I've often heard people speak of this as an unsolvable conundrum, and I have never heard anyone give a serious answer. And yet, this is simply a life-and-death decision, and many people take responsibility for life-and-death decisions on a regular basis. Whenever medics triage injured people at a disaster scene, they prioritize who gets treatment and who is left to die. Military leaders know some number of their soldiers will likely die in every battle, and when they consider what battles to fight, they simply ask whether the expected deaths will be worth the gains. Parents make this decision when they choose whether to abort or give birth.

People who accept deep responsibility accept that sometimes, life-and-death decisions need to be made. Anyone can accept this level of responsibility. Anyone who hides from this responsibility simply lets others make life-and-death decisions for them.

Currently, chemical company executives are making life-and-death decisions to pollute the Earth, fossil fuel companies are making the decision to increase climate change, and weapons companies are choosing to lobby for more war. These corporate leaders are making life-and-death decisions in a deeply selfish way.

To anyone who seeks deep change, I say: do not fear taking deep responsibility for life-and-death decisions. Each individual can cultivate the judgment and strength to do it, ideally with others' input and support.

If generating a truly healthy nation seems very hard, I actually consider that good news. Many people are in despair, believing that humans are supposedly inherently selfish or violent, and thus it seems impossible to build a nation that can maintain mutual respect internally. But the message of this book is simple: it's not impossible. It's just very hard because of the trap so many of us are stuck in. And "very hard" and "impossible" are very different!

Dream Big and Take Risks

Growing up, I learned that a prophet was someone who could predict the future. Eventually I learned the truth: a prophet is someone who sees the present so clearly that, if nothing changes, the future is easily predictable. Anybody can know their present path is intolerable, and if things don't change, the future will be intolerable too. In her youth, Cherokee woman Rebecca Adamson's mother warned her, "if you don't change directions, you're going to end up where you're headed."[6]

A huge number of people recognize at some level that their unhealthy nation is not ok. But too few people are willing to take meaningful risks. I have encountered plenty of white people who feel upset about discrimination towards black people but are afraid to take a meaningful stand because that would entail personal risk.

Instead, many people either do nothing or they waste time and energy on campaigns that don't help much even when they succeed. Compare Harriet Tubman with the people who fought for a Juneteenth US federal holiday or for capitalizing "B" when writing about black people. Harriet Tubman took significant risks, but when she succeeded in her mission, she made a very big difference in the lives of the people she served.

In contrast, the people who pushed for a Juneteenth US federal holiday or capitalizing "B" succeeded, but what do they have to show for it? Prison slavery continues, as do all the other forms of discrimination black people still endure in the United States today.

Picking fights that don't matter is a major coping mechanism for surviving in unhealthy nations. It's one way that people go through the motions of seeking meaningful change. Picking low-risk, low-reward fights is how people can spend huge amounts of time and energy on a project while protecting their own safety and comfort.

Tubman showed me a different way. She taught me to dream big and risk failure. She picked fights that she might lose, fights that might even cost her her life. But when she succeeded, she made a huge difference. And if she lost a fight and were caught, at least she would have died doing her best, giving her deepest love.

Become Comfortable with Uncertainty

Even if a nation could successfully transform so that it didn't have rulers, and it replaced its profit economy with a gift economy, there would still be many challenges left.

If many people are used to living with polluting plastics, how can they learn to live without them? How could people reorganize their villages and jobs to live without polluting fossil fuels? If local soils are poor after years of extractive farming, how could the soils be regenerated again? If prisons are full of people, what should be done with them? If most people are used to just voting and then letting political leaders make the important decisions, how could communities organize where everyone has a say and everyone's needs are met? Could the group still live with electricity? What could be done to support injured or chronically ill people who depend on certain medications or expensive technologies to live?

How could a young healthy nation resolve these thorny questions?

While certainly not easy, I think the answer is simple: without rulers, *people would figure it out*. There would be trial and error and mistakes, and eventually the group would figure out how best to take care of everyone's needs.

Zapatista major Moisés described big changes the Zapatistas were going through and said that "we are just learning and... it will take a while to get going well."[7]

When Leia described how the Rainbow participants addressed challenges, she said they were "dancing with the awkwardness of it. We're not going to get everything right. We're just a group of people trying our best."

Both Moisés and Leia embrace a confidence that, even if they don't know all the right answers at first, they and their nation or subculture will figure it out if they keep trying.

I don't believe in talent, and I don't believe in destiny. I believe in initiative, desire, bravery, and all the other qualities reviewed in this book. Harriet Tubman didn't wait for a perfectly safe plan before taking any action. She just decided she wasn't ok with her people being enslaved so she went and freed many slaves, learning as she went. Jesus Christ wasn't ok with people being sick and hungry, so he healed and fed many people.

Subcommander Marcos wasn't ok with endless oppression, so he helped the Zapatistas lead a revolution. Each person simply saw a problem and figured out how they could help address it. No matter what a person feels upset about or what they want to do about it, anyone can take similar initiative with their own abilities and resources.

I've had people ask me how social change happens. What's my "theory of change?" It's simple: I commit to a goal before I know how to accomplish that goal, and then I figure out how to achieve it, learning from mistakes along the way. If I want to protect a forest, I commit to preventing logging and *then* figure out how to keep my commitment. If I want to protect a river or co-found a community, I commit first and *then* figure out how to reach my goal. Anybody who waits for certainty or a "perfect" plan will wait forever.

Great fighters throughout history know that a person has to commit to a goal, prepare the best they can, and then expect their plans to change. General Helmuth Von Moltke was the top Prussian military commander in the 1870s, and he described his attitude towards planning battles: "no plan survives contact with the enemy's main [army]."[8] Champion boxer Mike Tyson said, "Everybody has a plan until they get punched in the mouth."[9] Mike Tyson, Leia, Jesus Christ, Helmuth Von Moltke, Harriet Tubman, Moisés and Marcos could not tell the future. I believe they simply committed to doing something important and then figured out how to do it.

That is how change happens. Deep cultural healing occurs when people come together in the face of uncertainty, acknowledge their dissatisfactions, and commit to addressing their problems together.

My Dream: Instead of Fighting Symptoms Separately, Activists Address the Root Disease Together

There is sexism in every unhealthy nation, and countless feminist movements have worked throughout history to fight sexism, and yet not a single feminist movement has ever ended sexism in their unhealthy nation.

The rich exploit the workers in every unhealthy nation, and countless labor activists have worked to stop exploitation of workers, and yet not a single labor movement has successfully ended the exploitation of workers in their society.

Some feminist groups have improved the treatment of women, just like some labor movements have improved wages or working conditions, at least somewhat. But no group in history has ever fully ended sexism or oppression of workers in their unhealthy nation.

The same is true for almost any cause:

- *Child sexual abuse*: Countless people have worked to end child abuse, and no social movement has ever ended child sexual abuse in their unhealthy nation.

- No *environmental movement* has ever completely ended pollution or environmental destruction within their nation.

- No *anti-poverty movement* has ever ended poverty in their society.

- No *nature connection movement* has ever helped everyone in their society live in deep connection with the Earth.

- No *peace activists* have ever made authorities permanently stop pushing for wars that serve the rich, or caused politicians to stop spreading lies and hate in support of war.

- No *anti-racism activists* have ever fully ended racism in their unhealthy nation.

Activists may occasionally see some positive changes after years or decades of effort, but what would it take to have big, enduring victories and deep cultural change? The racism, sexism, disconnection from nature, widespread child abuse, environmental destruction, wars that serve the rich, and many other troubles are not actually different problems. They are merely symptoms of the same root cultural disease, where *a few people rule over everybody else*.

This makes it clear why so many social movements have only seen minor or temporary changes, at best, in their unhealthy nation throughout history. As every doctor knows, treating a symptom will never actually lead to deep healing because the underlying disease persists.

As long as activists treat racism, sexism, greed, child abuse, and political corruption as different problems, and allow rulers to persist, all these big troubles will tragically persist too and meaningful, enduring change will be elusive.

My dream is for feminists to join forces with people fighting racism, and for them to work with environmentalists, labor activists, and others. What if all these different activists didn't just fight separately against the symptoms, but also addressed the root cultural disease together and created a new healthy nation?

This book offers case studies on how to do this. Chapters 31 and 40 explored how the Haudenosaunee and Zapatistas created a healthy nation with leaders who responded to the will of the people. Chapter 40 reviewed how the Zapatistas redistributed rich peoples' excess wealth at the beginning of their revolution, ensuring rich people did not undermine their nation from within. Chapter 40 also showed how the Zapatistas didn't try to take control of the government and impose their laws on all of Mexico. Instead, they created their own laws so they could live in a good way, and protected themselves when authorities tried to retake control. Many chapters have explored other key patterns, including how to take the Earth's needs into account as a normal way of life, or have economies that reward sharing rather than hoarding.

Deep cultural change is possible, but it will never come as long as activists treat discrimination, greed, poverty, environmental destruction, political corruption, disconnection from nature, and child abuse as separate problems. I encourage activists to *join forces and address the root cultural disease together*, creating nations where everybody stands for a culture of mutual respect, and nobody rules over anybody else.

Generating Healthy Nations: the Solutions to Humanity's Seemingly Intractable Problems

Unhealthy nations have created a lot of trouble in the world.

Problems like climate change, loss of freshwater, pollution, soil degradation, slavery in all its forms, mass species extinction, resource overconsumption, and many more threaten many humans and nonhumans right now. All these things are the result of rulers dominating and manipulating everyone else in their nation, and too many people accepting this as ok.

People in profit economies have gotten themselves stuck in a seemingly intractable situation. Many people have accumulated wealth to protect themselves from future risks and live in comfort, but much of that "wealth" is unsustainable at best and often actively destructive. Many people own houses or cars that require fossil fuels or electricity to be usable. How many people could cook or heat their houses only with local materials?

In all unhealthy nations, wealth in stocks or bonds are tied to the stability of the banking system and government that encourage ever more destruction of the living world. Many companies underlying these stocks and bonds in some way exploit people or the Earth, usually both.

Even if an unhealthy nation's rulers didn't put up any obstacles, how can groups of people change when seemingly all their incentives motivate them to stay on their current self-destructive but comfortable path?

Unhealthy nations have no good answers to these problems because each individual is incentivized to get more resources to protect themselves from an uncertain future. Profit economies encourage an attitude of needing to always get more to feel safe. But that pattern where people take more than they need is exactly what's causing so much trouble.

I believe the only way to address unhealthy nations' deepest troubles is for more people to *adopt the healthy-nation patterns* explored in this book (compiled in Appendix 2).

Giving up industrial civilization and protecting the Earth is going to require many individuals to give up some of their wealth. In other words, many people will have to give up more material wealth than they receive – the essence of a gift economy. People will need to act in service of future generations even if that means a sacrifice now. However, people who do this will receive so much more than they know. The essence of that gift economy – giving as needed, where needed – actually creates far more security for everyone involved, no matter what the future brings, because no one is left to fend for themselves. Jeannette Armstrong described it as the *most secure feeling in the world* – who doesn't want that?

Transitioning out of a profit economy and into a gift economy may seem impossibly hard. A person who trained to become a professional oil engineer or corporate businessman may have to give up their career. Factory owners get to give up their factories, bankers forgive their loans, and politicians stop obeying their donors. People whose ideologies and self-images are attached to a resource-rich life get to give these up. Jesus Christ and Martin Luther King Jr showed what it's like to even give up one's life.

This is what it would look like for people to adopt healthy-nation gift economies: people feeling satisfied to only have as much as they really need, intentionally giving up their excess wealth and transferring it to other people or to the nonhuman world, or destroying it so it cannot be used by others to exploit the Earth.

It's amazing to me that all humanity needs to do to escape its current terrible path is for enough people in unhealthy nations to adopt healthy-nation practices.

It is easy, in unhealthy nations, to feel alone or unable to depend on neighbors if times get difficult. It's easy to feel as if nothing can ever change. But the healthy-nation practices of sacred circles, living in reciprocity, deep sharing, and solidarity can address these troubles.

Many people will likely continue to support their profit economy and privilege no matter what, even as others choose to stand in solidarity with each other and the Earth. This conflict exists now, and I expect it will continue. Healthy-nation practices of bravery and integrity will be needed to protect each other and the Earth in dangerous moments. Warriors can seek the deepest truth and fight in service of what matters, not just fight to make money or fight in service of authorities to stay out of trouble.

Notice your own dissatisfaction and commit to personal and collective healing. Even in unhealthy nations, *anyone* can adopt healthy-nation patterns at any time. Anyone can cultivate integrity or move resources where they're most needed. Anyone can notice and develop a personal relationship with the nonhumans around them. Any group can use sacred circles and set good boundaries.

Healthy nations are not some leftist, new-age, cult-driven fad. Millions of people have lived in healthy nations all around the world for millions of years! Some still do today, and I doubt if any of these suggestions would seem strange to them. In fact, I believe they would consider it strange that anyone would live as so many people in unhealthy nations live.

Personal Growth is Essential for Collective Healing

Any individual can practice these healthy-nation patterns. I see each individual as a little potential healthy-subculture bubble. As these individuals find each other, they can form healthy subcultures together. The healthy-subculture bubbles can then grow and merge and grow even more, as open-hearted people keep finding each other, opening their hearts together and creating the kind of culture they want to have.

Healthy-nation practices and unhealthy-nation practices do not mix well. I have personally witnessed low-integrity people in an organization drive out a woman leader with high integrity. I have witnessed people excuse their own sexist and dishonest behavior because doing the right thing would feel scary. A person who demonstrates cowardice, self-centeredness, poor contact, and other unhealthy qualities will only be part of a healthy subculture as they grow out of them.

Rulers train people to tolerate being ruled. In practice, this includes training people for selfishness, cowardice, ignoring reality and living made-up lives, isolation, discrimination and privilege, forgetting, ignorance, normalizing abuse, rejecting pleasure, shame and more. All these have been explored throughout this book. A nation is unhealthy when a few people rule over others, and this cultural disease manifests in individuals as these hurtful qualities, with different people exhibiting them to different degrees. The leaders who least exhibit these hurtful qualities and embrace bravery, service, awareness, and so on risk being killed or imprisoned, as discussed in Chapter 41.

Knowingly or not, people who exhibit hurtful qualities and do not work to heal them will support abusive rulers and help maintain their unhealthy nation. This is why rulers encourage these qualities. For example, 18th century American slaveowners didn't just propagate racism and lazy thinking because they were mean; training people to have foolish and hurtful attitudes was an essential part of perpetuating their rule.

In present-day United States and many authoritarian democracies around the world, rulers and oligarchs propagate different nonsense to justify their rule. For example, they pretend that merely holding elections causes the government to respond to the people. Every unhealthy nation has its own make-believe stories and falsehoods that will need to be released.

Thus the training runs deep, and it runs so deep that even when a ruling class has fallen and people have had the opportunity to create a new society, many times they've chosen new rulers instead. But it doesn't have to be this way.

If ignorance supports unhealthy nations, then deep awareness supports healthy nations instead. If selfishness, isolation, and holding back one's love generate unhealthy nations, then deep sharing, solidarity, and giving love fully can generate healthy nations instead.

This is Who We Really Are

Remember in Chapter 33, during the prisoner exchanges, when countless captured Europeans had to be bound and physically dragged away from their healthy-nation hosts by their European "rescuers?" They were free to go but they did not want to leave!

Why?

Because it turns out that being treated with care and respect, feeding others and being fed, meeting life's needs with meaningful work, and living closely with open-hearted people feels wonderful. And it feels so incredibly wonderful because this is who we really are.

All these healthy-nation qualities are in each of us right now. We are healthy nations; each one of us has the same universal sacred urges towards gratitude, integrity, sharing, and all the other beautiful qualities explored in this book. Every one of us has deep love to give. Every one of us can embrace and live these qualities at any time, generating healthy nations or healthy subcultures everywhere we go.

And it turns out, what's good for the individual is also good for the group. As Robin Kimmerer wrote, "in order for the whole to flourish, each of us has to be strong in who we are and carry our gifts with conviction, so they can be shared with others."[10]

What are your gifts? What can you give or do or be that would open your heart and let it sing?

Chapter 51: We Are the Promised Land

I have my blindspots, and I continue to learn every day. But there are a few things I know beyond any doubt.

Some people say the arc of history bends towards justice. I say the arc of history bends whichever way people bend it.

Ultimately, we remain in an abusive nation because we tolerate it. Yes, there has been a massive amount of shame, violence, broken promises, lies, and spiritual wounding that make deep change really hard. Rulers and their servants use so many tricks and traps to get us to continue to tolerate our own abuse, to accept our own humiliating submissiveness as legitimate and "just the way life is."

I believe the only way to end abuse is to stop tolerating it. That's what deep revolution is: when enough people take a stand together and take care of each other even at great personal risk in order to create a new way of life. The arc of history bends when enough people choose to give their divine love fully, right now, rather than holding back in hopes of avoiding abuse for another day.

The night before his assassination, Martin Luther King Jr said, "I've seen the promised land. I may not get there with you. But I want you to know tonight, that we, as a people, will get to the promised land."[1]

I'm telling you I've BEEN to the promised land. I've lived with a whole healthy nation where people routinely have integrity, generosity, respect for men, women and children, deep connection with the Earth, strong leaders, and no rulers.

The promised land is real, and I'll tell you what else I learned – **WE are the promised land**. Every single person can be one of our messiahs, one of our liberators as we free ourselves from the biggest trap in human history. And the more messiahs, the more liberators, the better. *Living with rulers has been a multi-millennia catastrophe. Now is the time to end it.*

Heaven is not someplace off in the sky. We're living in paradise right now. In Christian, Muslim, or Jewish terms, we're living in the Garden of Eden. We never left! Many of us just forgot who we were and where we are when we got trapped in unhealthy nations. We and the Earth are one, and the Earth is waiting for us to remember. We are in paradise right now. We are the promised land. We are our own saviors.

As Jesus Christ, Harriet Tubman, and other spiritual leaders around the world have proven, this is no easy path. Never has been. But now is the time. People are suffering as prison slaves. Pollution is causing all manner of diseases and destruction. Racism and sexism persist. Genocides and hate continue, as do the wars that kill the poor and profit the rich. Nonhumans are dying in large numbers. And nuclear apocalypse threatens all of us.

Kings and billionaires of unhealthy nations threaten, bribe, trick, and trap countless people to support all these terrible things and more. I believe the only solution is to transform or end these nations of abuse.

I don't know how to achieve the transformation I want, but I know where I stand. I stand with the Earth, and I stand for a culture of mutual respect. And I'm not the only one.

Millions of people are standing for the Earth and standing for cultures of mutual respect right now. Some of us were born into healthy nations, and some of us were born into unhealthy nations. In countless different ways, all around the world, we are taking this stand together.

And I'd love for you to join us.

For future updates, opportunities, and connections, I invite you to sign up here:
https://thedeepestrevolution.com/signup

* * *

Dear Reader,

At the time of finishing this book, I did not clearly see a way to build a new healthy nation where justice is pervasive because everyone stands for a culture of mutual respect. Since then, I have found more stories from people who have done this, and they show a practical path. To learn about this path, I welcome you to read my second book, *The Deepest Revolution,* available at https://thedeepestrevolution.com. It is free to download and less than 200 pages, and a physical version is available as well.

Sincerely,
The Author

Appendices

Appendix 1: Acknowledging Contradictions

I believe healthy nations and unhealthy nations are fundamentally very different. In this book, I make the case that unhealthy nations, no matter how seemingly different from each other, all share one foundational characteristic: they each have rulers that impose laws that exploit and manipulate people, while in healthy nations everyone stands for a culture of mutual respect and nobody rules over anybody else. Healthy nations in which no one person or group rules over everyone else are commonly able to maintain an internal baseline of respect that eludes people in unhealthy nations.

However, while researching and writing this book, I sometimes came across stories from healthy nations that seemed to contradict this core difference. For example, the female Nootka storytellers and Crow woman Pretty Shield both talked of having "slaves." Haudenosaunee talked of having "governments" with "laws." The Tzutujil Mayan nation had "Lords and Ladies."

In this appendix, I want to explore various contradictions I found, how I interpret them, and what lessons I learned.

Seemingly Contradictory Stories From Healthy Nations

Here are some examples of stories I found during my research that seem to contradict the book's core message that nations where no one rules over anyone else can maintain a baseline of mutual respect. In the following section, I offer different ways I interpret these apparent contradictions.

- *Speaking of slavery*: Both the Nootka storytellers and Crow woman Pretty Shield acknowledge slaves who lived with them. How could a nation be healthy if people say they have slaves?[1,2]

- *Calling some people "lords"*: Martín Prechtel described how Tzutujil Mayan chiefs were called Xuojá, either "man lord" or "woman lord." Does this imply they had some superior status to the others?[3]

- *Describing "governance" and "laws"*: For example, Cree woman Priscilla Settee described her nation as having systems of governance. However, Chapter 31 described how Seneca man Segwalise said, "The national Councils of Chiefs do not govern the people; instead they act as representatives…" When Settee speaks of governance, does that mean the nation is unhealthy?[4,5]

- *Practices of seeming masculine control*: Apache man Geronimo described needing to pay Alope's father for his blessing to marry his daughter. Lakota man Black Elk tells the story of High Horse who paid a father a huge amount to be allowed to marry his daughter.[6,7] Did men in these nations control the women?

- *Sexual coercion and restriction*: Whereas many unhealthy nations strongly discourage sex outside of marriage, some healthy nations would have special ceremonies or events where they prohibit sex between married partners and instead only allow sex outside the marriage. Doesn't this represent some people imposing laws or sexual restrictions on each other?

- *Some cited sources are classified as fiction*: Books labeled as fiction include *Wolf Totem* and *Daughters of Copper Woman*.

- *A lot of quotes about unhealthy nations reference white people*: Is the problem really just with white people?

Exploring the Seeming Contradictions

For some of these apparent contradictions, I have a clear response. For others, I do not. I have only spoken with people of a few healthy nations, and most of what I know comes through books, which is not ideal. I had to make judgment calls about what stories and patterns to include and what to exclude in *One Disease One Cure*. I was unable to contact people associated with many of the healthy nations discussed in this book, so I had to judge which observers or writers were honest and open-minded, and which ones were not.

I want to share how I made these judgment calls so that you can weigh the evidence fully yourself. While this appendix doesn't contain a complete list of the contradictions I found, it includes enough to show how I approached studying nations very different from my own, especially when I was not able to speak with someone from every nation.

Racism and Foolish Assumptions by Observers

Chapter 22 showed how unhealthy nations have been generating hatred and racist attitudes towards healthy nations for literally millennia. Even when British colonists spoke positively of the healthy nations they encountered, they often insulted them. Ben Franklin, for example, called the Haudenosaunee "ignorant savages" while he admired some of their nation's practices so much that they became a model for the United States (as reviewed in Chapter 31).

This racism became so universal that even people of healthy nations could refer to themselves as savages, as when Ohiyesa wote, "During the summer, when Nature is at her best, and provides abundantly for the savage, it seems to me that no life is happier than his!" (from Chapter 9).

A huge amount of scholarship and news stories about healthy nations, especially prior to the 1900s, is either deliberately deceitful propaganda or so ridden with racist assumptions that it is of little value.

I always prioritize stories from people who grew up in healthy nations and can speak about them from first-hand experience, such as Black Elk or Pretty Shield. I also welcome stories from respectful, thoughtful observers from unhealthy nations.

I always pay attention to the writer or observer's attitude. Do they seem respectful and self-aware? Do they question their own assumptions? US president John Adams assumed the Haudenosaunee had kings and nobles when, in reality, nobody ruled over anybody else. This shows that it takes a lot of discretion to decide which sources to trust and which to discard.

In contrast, Jean Liedloff showed a deep willingness to question her prior beliefs when she wrote, "I found the complete absence of pressure by persuasion, by the imposition of one individual's will upon another, difficult to believe or understand, despite the Yequana's perseverance in showing me examples of it." Liedloff showed this kind of humility, open-mindedness, and insightfulness throughout her book *Continuum Concept*, which makes it seem very credible to me.

Drawing from Books Labeled as Fiction

In this book, I reference some books classified as fiction, including *Daughters of Copper Woman* and *Wolf Totem*.

Daughters of Copper Woman contains the Nootkas' creation story and the history that followed, comparable to the Christian *Bible* or Jewish *Torah* which contain their creation stories and following history. I consider *Daughters of Copper Woman* no more or less fiction than the *Bible* or *Torah*. I consider the detailed historical narratives in *Daughters of Copper Woman* accurate and therefore I chose to reference them as nonfiction in this book.

In the case of *Wolf Totem*, the author Jiang Rong spent 11 years in Mongolia, experiencing many of the stories conveyed in the book.[8] As with *Daughters of Copper Woman*, I decided to reference parts of Wolf Totem which I believe are true and worth sharing.

Are White People the Problem?

Throughout this book, many people who complained about unhealthy nations specifically referred to white people. Are white people the problem?

Sadly, no. Skin color really is irrelevant. Anyone can embrace patterns of selfishness, low awareness, and other negative qualities explored in this book.

"White supremacy" is not real; it's simply another cover story for encouraging poor white people to side with rich white people so the poor people remain divided. Even in nations where white people specifically talk about white supremacy, the rich obviously don't mean it. There is no global unity among white people; some of the most brutal wars in history were World War I and World War II, and while many non-white people died, a huge amount of the fighting and killing was between nations of white people. White people have been anything but united in a quest for supremacy. And whenever white workers try to unionize, wealthy white business owners commonly oppose them viciously, showing there's no such thing as white solidarity.

Consider that the word "slave" stems from the word "Slav," a reference to the white Slavic people of eastern Europe. These white eastern Europeans were enslaved in such vast numbers in the 9th and 10th centuries that their ethnic name became the word Europeans used to describe slavery for a thousand years, up to the present day.[9] White western Europeans enslaved white eastern Europeans for centuries before they enslaved Africans and hauled them to the Americas. So much for white supremacy!

Furthermore, the richest slaveowner in human history was black: Mansa Musa, king of the Mali empire in Africa in the 1300s. One historian said, "Contemporary accounts of Musa's wealth are so breathless that it's almost impossible to get a sense of just how wealthy and powerful he truly was." This black man was Muslim, and on his pilgrimage to Mecca he brought 60,000 people, including 12,000 chattel slaves. He brought thousands of pounds of gold and gave so much away during a three-month stay in Cairo that the price of gold plummeted and the region's economy became depressed for 10 years. This black man was quite willing to accumulate massive wealth and enslave huge numbers of black people.[10]

Whenever a nation allows rulers to take hold and impose an economy that rewards selfishness, terrible things result. People of any skin color can fall into this trap.

Looking Deeper Than the Words

Another trouble comes with words like "slave," "government," "laws," and "lord." How can a nation be healthy if it has these things?

I have seen a few different explanations for this.

Often, the English, Spanish, French, or other colonists simply had no vocabulary to describe the healthy nations they encountered, so I believe people often just chose the nearest words they could find. The Haudenosaunee, for example, don't have governments that impose laws in the way unhealthy nations do, but they do have councils that manifest the will of the people in the form of agreements that everybody lives by, and to which people are held accountable (see Chapter 31).

But the Europeans could hardly comprehend a nation without rulers where sharing was the norm, and so they had no vocabulary for it. Thus they used words like "government" and "law" to describe healthy nations. The Zapatistas also use the terms "governance" and "laws," but again, these governments and laws routinely manifest the will of the people, not the will of rulers.

In *Secrets of the Talking Jaguar*, Martín Prechtel talked about a clear leadership hierarchy and "Lords and Ladies." And yet, every time a chief achieved a new layer in the hierarchy, he or she ceremonially gave up all their wealth until they were equally as impoverished as everyone else. Prechtel wrote that the entire hierarchy of leaders was "composed of people who'd regularly and ritually distributed all their wealth to the village."[11,12]

Just because the word "lord" or "government" means something to me, doesn't mean that other people use the term the same way.

The simplest way to address questions like this would be to directly ask people of healthy nations, such as the Cherokee or Haudenosaunee. Not everyone wants to discuss their nation with outsiders, but someone who grew up in these nations could address questions better than trying to speculate based off of unclear text.

That said, sometimes the written stories are clear enough to show whether there was disrespectful coercion in a nation or not. Even apparently-controlling cultural practices need not actually be disrespectful upon deeper investigation. Black Elk described the Lakota man High Horse who found a particular young lady very attractive and wanted to marry her. Her father demanded many horses which High Horse could not pay. Many unhealthy nations have men who restrict their daughters' lives, so at first glance this father's behavior seemed inappropriately controlling.

However, the Lakota traditionally had three routes to marriage. Couples could elope if they wished in one form of marriage, but in another the man gave the bride's father many things.[13] High Horse asked the young woman to elope, but she refused, saying she wanted to be "bought like a fine woman." Black Elk said, "you see, she thought a great deal of herself too."

High Horse proceeded to raid an enemy nation and returned with a huge number of horses. He rode them up to his bride's family home. Black Elk described what happened: "The old man did not wave him away that time. It was not the horses that he wanted. What he wanted was a son who was a real man and good for something."[14]

As I interpret this, both the daughter and father wanted High Horse to prove himself. The father was standing for his daughter's best interests by ensuring he only gave approval to a capable man. She could have eloped, but she wanted to be bought. Even though a man had to pay his bride's father to marry her, this is not a case of abusive masculine control. It also does not imply that the woman was someone's property, even though she was "purchased." I don't see any sign that she was coerced in any way.

The word "slave" provides another example where the meaning of language can be confusing. In unhealthy nations, a "slave" can mean someone who is legally owned by another person, or someone with no legal rights at all or other terrible status. Universally these people are treated terribly.

However, I commonly find people of healthy nations refer to war captives as "slaves," and they still treat captives respectfully while demanding that they stay. Pretty Shield described a Lakota woman named Good-trader who was captured by Pretty Shield's father. She said, "My father captured her, giving her, as a slave, to his brother-in-law, Warm-robe… She lived with Warm-robe and his woman and learned to love them. I liked this slave-woman very much… Finally, when there came peace between the Lakota and the Crows, Good-trader's Lakota man came here to get her. But she would not listen to him now. She said, 'Look at my lodge, and then think of your own. Go away from here.' I remember how glad I felt when Good-trader spoke these words to her Lakota man. I liked her even more when I heard them."[15]

In other cases, healthy nations may forbid behavior that most people I know would find perfectly ok. Chapter 25 explored the Kulina practice of women choosing men with whom they would have sex that night if the man was successful hunting. In this case, women were allowed to choose any man except their husband. Some people might consider this coercive, but observers noted that all the women and men seemed very satisfied with the arrangement. And the whole nation benefited, as this reinforced norms of sharing and deep connection across the nation, not just within nuclear families.

It seems strange to me to write about healthy nations and how they do not coerce each other within the nation, and then notice that they keep war captives who might prefer to go home. However, there are a few ways healthy nations can relate to war captives without being exploitative. In many cases, when healthy nations take captives, the captives are treated with the same dignity and respect as anyone else, even if they're forbidden to leave. Sioux man Ohiyesa wrote, "It was a point of honor in the old days to treat a captive with kindness." He told the story of Sitting Bull who captured an Assiniboin boy and adopted him as a brother named Hohay. They became close and later Hohay said many kind things about Sitting Bull.[16]

I believe these stories of healthy nations treating captives benevolently are true because my research uncovered many stories of captured European-American colonists who wanted to stay with their captors even after the war was over. They preferred the nation that maintained a baseline of mutual respect over the one they were born into (as reviewed in Chapter 33). Alternatively, if healthy nations do not wish to keep the captive or allow them to return home, they can kill the captive.

Either treating captives with equal dignity or killing them allows the nation to maintain that baseline of mutual respect within the nation. Pretty Shield described this equality when she said, "[slaves] were treated well; they never tried to get away. They had the same rights as Crow women, and worked no harder."[17]

The only relationship with captives that would cause a nation to become unhealthy is forcing them to work extra hard as an underclass. I did find an example where captive women in one otherwise healthy-seeming nation were made to tan hides of bear, beaver, wolf, or coyote that the non-captive women did not tan.[18] The observer was told this was a newer practice, and previously these hides were tanned by men.

Sometimes even people in healthy nations may embrace practices that make it easier for the nation to succumb to having rulers and embracing selfishness. Making captives do extra work for a brief period might not immediately threaten that internal baseline of mutual respect in a healthy nation. But if captives are treated as inferiors indefinitely, in time the nation will become unhealthy, with a few people exploiting the rest becoming a normal way of life.

As another example, some healthy nations have practiced male circumcision.[19] Diminishing people's capacity for pleasure is clearly associated with profoundly unhealthy nations, as explored in Chapters 25 and 42. Circumcision by itself does not spontaneously cause people to start controlling each other, but any practice that diminishes people's capacity for pleasurable connection makes the nation susceptible to becoming unhealthy.

Going through long stretches of violence doesn't have to make a nation unhealthy either, but extended violence can be hard to deal with. One Nootka storyteller said she was told as a child that when a generation starts becoming violent, it can take four generations of peace to for the nation to really recover.[20]

History offers examples of healthy nations transitioning into nations of control and imposed law over time. The Nootka storytellers described how some Nootka men had already begun controlling women even before the Europeans arrived, and the women collectively threatened to leave. The storyteller said, "The men stopped arguing and began to talk. The women said why they had wanted to leave. The men listened. The women listened. They went home together, to try to live properly again."[21] The Nootka were able to recognize their cultural trouble and heal it. Other healthy nations throughout history have not been able to heal when they go down a bad path, and now the world has many unhealthy nations.

Some healthy nations changed over time after coming under continual pressure from unhealthy nations' militaries, missionaries, traders, colonists, and more. For example, if I wanted to investigate how the Cherokee live, I would get very different answers depending on whether I look at 1700 CE, 1800 CE, or 2024 CE.[22] The same applies for many other healthy nations that have been overrun by unhealthy nations in recent centuries.[23] I have to be careful to ask the right questions and understand the full context of a nation before drawing big conclusions based on one piece of information.

All this teaches me something simple: there is nothing inherently different about people of healthy nations. They are simply humans who maintain a baseline of mutual respect within their nation. Any group of people can make mistakes and go down a bad path. There were already some unhealthy, authoritarian nations in Africa, Asia, North America and South America long before the Europeans arrived. But people can recognize their mistakes and choose a better path too – a path that allows people, in the Nootka storyteller's words, to "live properly again."

Appendix 2: Healing Practices

Below are practices that I associate with healthy nations, as well as the chapters where they are discussed in the book.

Foundation

- Three Core Spiritual Practices (practical, aware gratitude; giving one's sacred gifts; and living in reciprocity): *Chapter 2: Discovering Three Core Spiritual Practices of Healthy Nations*

Individual

- Bravery: *Chapter 48: Bravery and Cowardice*

- Integrity: *Chapter 6: Blind Belief 1 - When People Ignore Reality to Maintain Safety and Comfort, Chapter 28: The Three Integrities*

- If you see something that needs doing, do it: *Chapter 19: Creating a Culture of Remembering*

- Find love by giving love: *Chapter 44: Training Children to Give or Withhold Love, Part 2*

- Be yourself by giving your deepest love: *Chapter 46: Embracing the Sacred Feminine*

- Keep laughing: *Chapter 18: The Great Scam of Heart-Closing Cultural Narratives, Chapter 22: Imposing And Maintaining Hatred*

- Walk a satisfying path and welcome comforts along the way: *Chapter 48: Bravery and Cowardice, Chapter 17: Heart-Opening vs Heart-Closing*

- Become comfortable with uncertainty: *Chapter 50: What Can I Do?*

- Choose your elders: *Chapter 50: What Can I Do?*

- Have faith: *Chapter 16 - Courageous Solidarity in Action, Chapter 48: Bravery and Cowardice*

- Build a collection of stories about admirable people: *Chapter 48: Bravery and Cowardice*

- An open heart: *Chapter 17: Heart-Opening vs Heart-Closing*

- Do your best: *Chapter 48: Bravery and Cowardice*

- Seek the truth / avoid assumptions: *Chapter 28: The Three Integrities, Chapter 39: Even More Propaganda Techniques*

- Get inspired by other people's stories and then find your own way to do it: *Chapter 35: Guerilla Gardening: Generating Abundance Without Permission*

- Feel the dissatisfaction that motivates change: *Chapter 22: Imposing And Maintaining Hatred, Chapter 43: Good Contact vs Poor Contact*

- Enjoy life: *Chapter 48: Bravery and Cowardice*

Collective

- Deep sharing: *Chapter 9: Gift Economies, Chapter 11: Cascading Generosity vs Cascading Selfishness, Chapter 25: Sexual Freedom vs Sexual Repression*

- Loving touch: *Chapter 42: Training Children to Give or Withhold Love, Part 1*

- Gracious receiving: *Chapter 44: Training Children to Give or Withhold Love, Part 2*

- Lead by standing for the needs of everybody: *Chapter 47: Embracing the Sacred Masculine*

- Hold everyone accountable to the same standards: *Chapter 4: Shared Accountability vs Abusive Law Enforcement*

- Send generosity cascading through your nation: *Chapter 11: Cascading Generosity vs Cascading Selfishness*

- Make room for everyone's gifts: *Chapter 44: Training Children to Give or Withhold Love, Part 2*

- Support pregnant families: *Chapter 45: The Spiritual Impacts of Physical Deprivation*

- Deep respect for children: *Chapter 42: Training Children to Give or Withhold Love, Part 1, Chapter 44: Training Children to Give or Withhold Love, Part 2*

- Equal respect for everyone while acknowledging people's differences: *Chapter 24: Sexual Discrimination vs Sexual Equality*

- Acknowledge excellent behavior: *Chapter 44: Training Children to Give or Withhold Love, Part 2*

- Generate abundance without permission: *Chapter 35: Guerilla Gardening - Generating Abundance Without Permission*

- Balanced leadership: *Chapter 24: Sexual Discrimination vs Sexual Equality, Chapter 31: The Story of the Peacemaker, Chapter 40: Enough! - The Zapatistas' Successful Revolution*

- Lovingly hold everyone to high standards: *Chapter 24: Sexual Discrimination vs Sexual Equality, Chapter 28: The Three Integrities*

- The golden rule of healthy nations (stand with others the way I would want them to stand with me): *Chapter 3: Shared Agreements vs Imposed Laws*

- Join forces and address the root cultural disease together: *Chapter 50 - What Can I Do?*

- Create a healthy subculture within an unhealthy nation: *Chapter 7: When Children Learn to Take Responsibility, Chapter 19: Creating a Culture of Remembering*

- Create a healthy nation: *Chapter 4: Shared Accountability vs Abusive Law Enforcement, Chapter 31: The Story of the Peacemaker, Chapter 40: Enough! - The Zapatistas' Successful Revolution*

Nature Connection

- Gratitude: *Chapter 20: Imposing And Maintaining Racism vs Generating Unity*

- Deep awareness: *Chapter 20: Imposing And Maintaining Racism vs Generating Unity, Chapter 43: Good Contact vs Poor Contact*

- Sit spot: *Chapter 2: Discovering Three Core Spiritual Practices of Healthy Nations, Chapter 20: Imposing And Maintaining Racism vs Generating Unity*

- Take the nonhumans' needs into account in everything you do: *Chapter 9: Gift Economies*

Addressing Trouble

- Sacred circles: *Chapter 23: Addressing Shared Challenges With the Sacred Circle*

- Boundary-setting: *Chapter 4: Shared Accountability vs Abusive Law Enforcement*

- Collective self-defense: *Chapter 4: Shared Accountability vs Abusive Law Enforcement, Chapter 23: Addressing Shared Challenges With the Sacred Circle, Chapter 50: What Can I Do?*

Going Deeper with Nature Connection

For anyone who wants practical, friendly guidance on how to embrace the three core spiritual practices as a routine part of life, I suggest the Kamana program and associated books and audio programs such as *Advanced Bird Language* and *Seeing Through Native Eyes*. Kamana is a self-study program designed to be done at home as part of a person's regular life. It is discussed in chapters 2, 20, and 43.

As I write in July 2024, the Kamana Program is currently unavailable while it is being redesigned and renamed. Some used Kamana material may be available on the internet. Interested readers may find updates about the redesigned Kamana program at https://www.livingconnection1st.net/pages/kamana-naturalist-training-program.

Appendix 3: Healthy Nations Discussed in this Book

Following are the healthy nations discussed in this book, listed alphabetically by continent.

Africa
Akamba	Mbuti	San

Asia
Evenk	Jenu Kuruba	Khangar	Kunjur	Maghyar Dom
Mongol	Mosuo	Nivkh		

Australia
Gumbaynggirr

Europe
Sami

Central America
Guaymi

Central and North America
Mam	Maya

North America
Anishinaabe	Apache	Arikara	Assiniboin	Blackfeet
Cayuga	Cherokee	Cheyenne	Chippewa	Chol
Cree	Creek	Crow	Dakota	Eskimo
Haudenosaunee	Hopi	Huron	Lakota	Minneconjou
Mohawk	Montagnais-Naskapi	Muscogee	Navajo	Nez Perce
Nootka	Ogallala	Ojibway	Okanagan	Omaha
Oneida	Onondaga	Pawnee	Pequot	Potawatomi
Pueblo	Sac and Fox	Seneca	Sioux	Tojolabal
Tzeltal	Tzotzil	Unkpapa	Zapatista	Zoque

Pacific Islands
Maori	Trobriand	Vanuatu

South America and the Caribbean Islands
Arawak

South America
Ashaninka	Aymara	Bari	Kulina	Lenca
Quichua	Shuar	Tchimane	Yequana	Yuracare

Image Credits

Cover: *Credit: Sophia Mueller and Author*

Chapter 2: Illustration: Hawks Hunting. *Credit: Chelsea Spitzer.*

Chapter 3: Diagram: Triangle - Circle - Boundaries. *Credit: Author.*

Chapter 6: Illustration: The Emperor's New Clothes. *Credit: Sophia Mueller.*

Chapter 10: Diagram: Triangle - Circle - Resources. *Credit: Author*; Graph: Comparing Unemployment, Non-cyclical Rate of Unemployment, Federal Funds Effective Rate. *Credit: Federal Reserve Economic Data.*[1]

Chapter 14: Illustration: Same Planet, Different Worlds. *Credit: Sophia Mueller.*

Chapter 15: Illustration: Rulers and Other Authorities Manipulate Huge Numbers of People and Lie About It. *Credit: Chelsea Spitzer*; Poster: "We Will Annihilate Kulaks as a Class!". *Credit: Soviet Union; Moscow-Leningrad: Gosudarstvennoe izdatel'stvo.*[2]

Chapter 17: Illustration: Glowing Heart, Chained Heart. *Credit: Sophia Mueller.*

Chapter 19: Illustration: People Carrying a Tree. *Credit: Sophia Mueller.*

Chapter 29: Chart: Cumulative Probability of Male Incarceration by Age 34. *Credit: Bruce Western, Brent Orrell.*[3] Reprinted with permission; Chart: Drug Arrest Rates for White and Black Americans. *Credit: Jeremy Travis, Bruce Western, Steve Redburn.*[4] Reprinted with permission; Chart: Rise in US Prison Population. *Credit: Bruce Western, Brent Orrell.*[5] Reprinted with permission; Illustration: Mouse on a Wheel. *Credit: Sophia Mueller.*

Chapter 32: Illustration: Police Protect the Rulers and the Rich from the People they Exploit. *Credit: Sophia Mueller.*

Chapter 35: Illustration: Guerilla Gardening. *Credit: Sophia Mueller.*

Chapter 36: Illustration: Sabotaging Efforts at Deep Cultural Healing. *Credit: Chelsea Spitzer.*

Chapter 37: Illustration: The Result of Culture Jamming. *Credit: Chelsea Spitzer.*

Chapter 41: Painting: Cursed Field. *Credit: Fyodor Bronnikov*[6]; Image: Riot Police in Venezuela. *Credit: (AP Photo/Ariana Cubillos).*[7] Reproduced with permission; Image: Riot Police in China. *Credit: AP Photo/Eugene Hoshiko.*[8] Reproduced with permission; Image: Riot Police in the United States. *Credit: Graeme Sloan/Sipa USA.*[9] Reproduced with permission.

Chapter 42: Image: Monkeys Reared in Isolation and Together. *Credit: James Prescott*[10]

Chapter 45: All images taken from *Nutrition and Physical Degeneration*. *Credit: Weston Price*[11]

Citations

Important Notes on Sensitive Topics

1. (Eastman (Ohiyesa), 2013, "Chief Joseph")
2. (kswheeler, 2011)
3. ("Sioux"/Lakota, n.d.)
4. (Standing Rock Sioux Reservation, n.d.)
5. (Cheyenne, 2018)
6. (Nelson, 2008, "An Okanagan Worldview of Society")
7. (Questions and Answers for Census 2000 Data on Race, 2001)
8. (Nelson, 2008, "Peace Technologies from the San Bushmen of Africa")
9. (Prechtel, 1999, 209)
10. (kswheeler, 2011)
11. (Notes, 2005, 105)
12. (Top 10 Indian Indigenous Defence Weapons, 2020)

Chapter 2: Discovering Three Core Spiritual Practices of Healthy Nations

1. (Young, n.d.-b, 84)
2. (Kimmerer, 2013, "Allegiance to Gratitude")
3. (Brown Jr, 1988, 80)
4. (Nelson, 2008, "An Okanagan Worldview of Society")
5. (Kimmerer, 2013, "Skywoman Falling")
6. (Young, n.d.-a, 14)
7. (Young, n.d.-a, 15)
8. (N. Basket, personal communication, August 5, 2023)
9. (Weston, 2017)
10. (Debunking the Idea of Protected Areas, 2023)
11. (Jenu Kuruba, n.d.)
12. (Gauthier & Pravettoni, 2016)
13. (Kenyon, 2020)
14. (Skerk, 2022)
15. (Solon, 2017)
16. (Russia: Sakhalin Island Indigenous Peoples Protest Oil Development, 2005)
17. (Kimmerer, 2013, "Allegiance to Gratitude")
18. (Nelson, 2008, "Introduction")
19. (Nelson, 2008, "First Nations Survival and the Future of the Earth")
20. (N. Basket, personal communication, August 5, 2023)
21. (N. Basket, personal communication, August 5, 2023)
22. (Nelson, 2008, "An Okanagan Worldview of Society")
23. ("Dunbar's Number: Why the Theory That Humans Can Only Maintain 150 Friendships Has Withstood 30 Years of Scrutiny," 2021)
24. (Malinowski et al., 1999, 244)
25. (Ho-de-No-Sau-Nee-Ga (Haudenosaunee), n.d.)
26. (Malinowski et al., 1999, 244)
27. (Trigger, 1969, 26)
28. (Trigger, 1969, 71)
29. (Johansen & Mann, 2000, vii)

Chapter 3: Shared Agreements vs Imposed Laws

1. (Saudi Arabia Bans Trade Unions and Violates All International Labour Standards, 2012)
2. (1947 Taft-Hartley Substantive Provisions, n.d.)
3. ("2 May 1933: Dissolution of German Trade Unions," n.d.)
4. (Shenker et al., 2011)
5. (Hertsgaard, 2016)
6. (Guidelines for Law Enforcement Whistleblowers, n.d.)
7. (Air Force Whistleblower George Sarris Prevails in Settlement, n.d.)
8. (Bates, 1995)
9. (Tsoi, 2023)
10. (Macolo, n.d.)
11. (LaPierre, 2012)
12. (The Cato Institute, 2009)
13. (Grove, 2013)
14. (McDonough, 2015)
15. (Callegari, 2023)
16. (Regent University School of Law, 2012)
17. (Cameron, 1981, 109-112)

Chapter 4: Shared Accountability vs Abusive Law Enforcement

1. (Young, 1996, Track 27)
2. (Nelson, 2008, "Definition of Indigenous Knowledge")
3. (Nelson, 2008, "Peace Technologies from the San Bushmen of Africa")
4. (Kimmerer, 2013, "Windigo Footprints")
5. (N. Basket, personal communication, July 1, 2023)
6. (Trigger, 1969, 87)
7. (N. Basket, personal communication, July 25, 2024)
8. (Eastman (Ohiyesa), 2013, "Red Cloud")
9. (Trigger, 1969, 71)
10. (Price, 1939, "Physical, Mental, and Moral Degeneration")
11. (Loewen, 2007, 108)
12. (Kaiman, 2013)
13. (Baurick et al., 2019)
14. (Gopal, 2023)
15. (Ackerman, 2011)
16. (Ehrenreich & English, 2010, "The Suppression of Women Healers")
17. (Umbra, 2011)
18. (Declaration of Independence: A Transcription, 1776)
19. (Zinn, 2002, "In Court: 'The Heart of the Matter'")
20. (Barrett, 2010, "Preparation of a Warrior")
21. (Barrett, 2010, "Tribal Amusements, Manners, and Customs")

Chapter 5: Encouraging Healing vs Discouraging Healing

1. (N. Basket, personal communication, August 5, 2023)
2. (King Jr, 1963)
3. (Diamond, 2012, "Compensation for the Death of a Child")
4. (Grimmett & Ward, n.d., p. 18)
5. (Pattern of Violations (POV), 2021)
6. (Department of Labor Conducted Second Pattern of Violations Screening to Protect Miners in 2023; Identifies Chronic Violator, 2024)
7. (Berkes et al., 2014)
8. (Morford, 2010)
9. (Department of Labor Conducted Second Pattern of Violations Screening to Protect Miners in 2023; Identifies Chronic Violator, 2024)
10. (Wang, 2023)
11. (Balmforth, 2021)

Chapter 6: Blind Belief 1 - When People Ignore Reality to Maintain Safety and Comfort

1. (Pharr, 1952, 440)
2. (What Is Islam?, n.d.)
3. (The Quran, 4:59, Translated by Mustafa Khattab)
4. (Brooks, n.d., "Islam and The Caliphates")
5. (The Torah Devarim (Deuteronomy), 17:9-13, Judaica Press)
6. (Cartwright, 1851)
7. (Sublette & Sublette, 2016, "A Literature of Terror")
8. (Opara et al., 2022)
9. (van Voren, 2010)
10. (Munro, 2000)
11. (van Voren, 2010)
12. (van Voren, 2012)
13. (Prisoners of Conscious in the USSR: Their Treatment and Conditions, 1975, 104)
14. (Prisoners of Conscious in the USSR: Their Treatment and Conditions, 1975, 69)
15. ("Report of the U.S. Delegation to Assess Recent Changes in Soviet Psychiatry," 1989, 5)
16. (Munro, 2000)
17. (Golichenko & Chu, 2018)
18. ("It Is Difficult to Get a Man to Understand Something When His Salary Depends Upon His Not Understanding It," 2017)
19. (Richter, 2021)
20. (Agrawal, 2021)
21. (Llana & Davidson, 2022)
22. (Medical Evidence, n.d.)
23. (Alba, 2021)
24. (Fung, 2021)
25. (COVID-19 Vaccine Development, n.d.)
26. (Tahir, 2022)
27. (Pettypiece et al., 2021)
28. (Strozewski, 2022)
29. (Boucau et al., 2022)
30. (Myths and Facts, 2023)
31. (Alden & et al, 2022)
32. (Hansen & Et al, 2021)
33. (Shrestha et al., 2023, "Effectiveness of the Coronavirus Disease 2019 Bivalent Vaccine")
34. (Shrestha et al., 2023, "Risk of Coronavirus Disease 2019 (COVID-19) among Those Up-to-Date and Not Up-to-Date on COVID-19 Vaccination")
35. (Tindle, 2024)
36. (Vogel & Couzin-Frankel, 2023)
37. (Understanding COVID-19 mRNA Vaccines, n.d.)
38. (Thacker, 2021)
39. (Goodman, 2023)
40. (Guzman, 2020)
41. ("Moderna Meets Forecast with $18.4 Billion in COVID Vaccine Sales in 2022," 2023)
42. (Kimball, 2023)
43. (Doshi, 2023)
44. (Thacker, 2021)
45. (Piller & You, 2018)
46. (Weiss, 2024)
47. (North Carolina Lawmakers Approve Mask Bill That Allows Health Exemption After Pushback, 2024)
48. (Suskind, 2004)
49. (Interns at M/s. Black Robes Legal, n.d.)
50. (Hubs, 2024)
51. (Eastman (Ohiyesa), 2016)
52. (Eastman (Ohiyesa), 1916, "Civilization as Preached and Practiced")
53. (Eastman (Ohiyesa), 1916, "College Life in the East")
54. (Barrett, 2010, "Introductory")
55. (Vestal, 1955, "Introduction")
56. (Wood, 1936, 336)
57. (Grinnell, 2005, "Lessons of the Prairie")
58. (Ballantine & Ballantine, 2001, 233)

Chapter 7: When Children Learn to Take Responsibility

1. (D'Amore, 2022)
2. (Definition of A-, n.d.)
3. (Definition of -ARCHY, n.d.)
4. (Private Interview with "Jordan," 2024)

Chapter 8: Blind Belief 2 - Multi-Millennia Misunderstandings

1. (Lohnes, 2024)
2. (Matthew 2:2, English Standard Version Bible)
3. (Luke 1:52, King James Version Bible)
4. (Luke 1:53, English Standard Version Bible)
5. (Luke 4:18, English Standard Version Bible)
6. (Mark 1:15, English Standard Version Bible)
7. (Gaster & Dimitrovsky, 2024)
8. (Denova, 2022)
9. (Mark 2:23-27, English Standard Version Bible)
10. (Mark 10:17-26, English Standard Version Bible)
11. (Mark 11:15-18, English Standard Version Bible)
12. (Luke 9:22, English Standard Version Bible)
13. (Luke 9:43-45, English Standard Version Bible)
14. (Luke 23:2, King James Version Bible)
15. (Mark 14:56-64, English Standard Version Bible)
16. (Denova, 2022)
17. (Matthew 19:21, King James Version Bible)
18. (Matthew 4:8-10, English Standard Version Bible)
19. (Eastman (Ohiyesa), 1916, "Civilization as Preached and Practiced")
20. (Jackson, 2016, "Black Robe Days")
21. (Prechtel, 1999, 248)
22. (Prechtel, 1999, 209)
23. (Eastman (Ohiyesa), 2016)
24. (Eastman (Ohiyesa), 2013, "Sitting Bull")
25. (Genesis 2:25, English Standard Version Bible)
26. (Genesis 2:19-20, English Standard Version Bible)
27. (Genesis 3:23-24, English Standard Version Bible)
28. (Genesis 3:16-19, English Standard Version Bible)
29. (Genesis 3:17, English Standard Version Bible)
30. (Linderman, 1932, 248)
31. (Carlson & Becker, 2021)
32. (Brink, n.d. "The Buffalo")
33. (War is Boring, 2014)
34. (King, 2012)
35. (Wooster, 1988, 171)
36. (American Bison, n.d.)
37. (Eastman (Ohiyesa), 2013, "Sitting Bull")
38. (Linderman, 1932, 249)
39. (Linderman, 1932, 251)
40. (Linderman, 1932, 248)
41. (Linderman, 1932, 249)
42. (Neihardt, 2014, "Early Boyhood")
43. (Neihardt, 2014, "The Offering of the Pipe")
44. (Eastman (Ohiyesa), 1916, "On the White Man's Trail")
45. (Jackson, 2016, "Black Robe Days")
46. (Barrett, 2010, "Subdivisions of the Apache Tribe")
47. (Nabokov, 1987, 153)

Chapter 9: Gift Economies
1. (Utopia, 2024)
2. (Notes, 2005, 104)
3. (N. Basket, personal communication, August 5, 2023)
4. (Eastman (Ohiyesa), 2008, "Early Hardships")
5. (Kimmerer, 2013, "The Gift of Strawberries")
6. (N. Basket, personal communication, August 5, 2023)
7. (Kimmerer, 2013, "The Gift of Strawberries")
8. (Mann, 2006, "Fire Place")
9. (Neumann, 2015)
10. (Mann, 2006, "The Rise and Fall of the American Bottom")
11. (Ballantine & Ballantine, 2001, 236)
12. (Kimmerer, 2013, "The Gift of Strawberries")
13. (Nelson, 2008, "An Okanagan Worldview of Society")
14. (Eastman (Ohiyesa), 1916, "Civilization as Preached and Practiced")
15. (Nelson, 2008, "Introduction")
16. (Trigger, 1969, 40)
17. (Trigger, 1969, 93)
18. (Eastman (Ohiyesa), 2013, "Crazy Horse")
19. (Eastman (Ohiyesa), 2013, "Two Strike")
20. (Eastman (Ohiyesa), 2016)
21. (Eastman (Ohiyesa), 2013, "Crazy Horse")
22. (Neihardt, 2014, "The Fight With Three Stars")
23. (Prechtel, 1999, 210)
24. (Prechtel, 1999, 248)
25. (Mark 10:26, English Standard Version Bible)
26. (Cox, 2019, "Use What You Got to Get What You Need")

Chapter 10: Profit Economies
1. (Kimmerer, 2013, "Windigo Footprints")
2. (Lumbanrau & Hankin, 2023)
3. (National AIDS Memorial, 2019)
4. (Green & Isaacson, 2012)
5. (Gardner, 2018)
6. (Berbard, 2021)
7. (von Clausewitz, 2021)
8. (Koehler, 1999, "The Sword of Repression")
9. (Trudeau, 2022)
10. (Vlamis, 2023)
11. (PK, 2023)
12. (Callegari, 2023)
13. (Gurner, 2023)
14. (The Federal Reserve's Dual Mandate, 2020)
15. (The Non-Accelerating Inflation Rate of Unemployment (NAIRU), n.d.)
16. (Meeting of the Federal Open Market Committee, 1996)
17. (Mena, 2023)
18. (Kashkari, 2023)
19. (U.S. Congressional Budget Office, 2024)
20. (Storm, 2023)
21. (Wiener-Bronner, 2022)
22. (Storm, 2023)
23. (Private Interview with "Jon," personal communication, May 24, 2023)
24. (Zinn, 2021, "A Kind of Revolution")
25. (Schogol, 2010)
26. (Shane III & Winkie, 2022)
27. (Cartwright, 2018)
28. (Kalecki, 1943)
29. (1936 Constitution of the USSR Article 118, n.d.)
30. (Davies, 1998)
31. (Solzhenitsyn, 2018, "The History of Our Sewage Disposal System")
32. (Weisberg, 1974)
33. (Davies, 1998)
34. (Baptist, 2014, "1805-1861")
35. (Loewen, 2007, 54)
36. (Mark 10:26, English Standard Version Bible)

Chapter 11: Cascading Generosity vs Cascading Selfishness
1. (Eastman (Ohiyesa), 2013, "Crazy Horse")
2. (Nelson, 2008, "An Okanagan Worldview of Society")
3. (Trigger, 1969, 40)
4. (Ballantine & Ballantine, 2001, 231)
5. (Eastman (Ohiyesa), 2013, "Red Cloud")
6. (Seo, 2018)
7. (Parenti, 2003)
8. (Graeber, 2014, "On the Experience of Moral Confusion")
9. (Strong, 1976, 181)
10. (Kimmerer, 2013, "The Gift of Strawberries")
11. (Smokestack, n.d.)
12. (Kropotkin, 1902, "Mutual Aid in the Medieval city")
13. (Hardship Fund FAQ, n.d.)
14. (Srinivasa et al., 2022)

Chapter 13: An Endless Nightmare Descends on a Healthy Nation
1. (Loewen, 2007, 53)
2. (Sale, 1991, 96)
3. (Zinn, 2021, "Columbus, the Indians, and Human Progress")
4. (Sale, 1991, 100)
5. (Zinn, 2021, "Columbus, the Indians, and Human Progress")
6. (Loewen, 2007, 54)
7. (Zinn, 2021, "Columbus, the Indians, and Human Progress")
8. (Loewen, 2007, 54)
9. (Zinn, 2021, "Columbus, the Indians, and Human Progress")
10. (Zinn, 2021, "Columbus, the Indians, and Human Progress")
11. (Loewen, 2007, 54)
12. (Zinn, 2021, "Columbus, the Indians, and Human Progress")
13. (Loewen, 2007, 55)
14. (Loewen, 2007, 56)
15. (Arawak, n.d.)
16. (Zinn, 2021, "Columbus, the Indians, and Human Progress")
17. (Loewen, 2007, 57)
18. (Zinn, 2021, "Columbus, the Indians, and Human Progress")
19. (Ellsberg, 2012)

Chapter 14: Same Planet, Different Worlds
1. (X, 1965, "Nightmare")
2. (Kinealy, 1997)
3. (Backhouse & Et al, 2024)
4. (Eastman (Ohiyesa), 2008, "An Indian Sugar Camp")
5. (Rong, 2008, Chapter 1)
6. (Rong, 2008, Chapter 2)
7. (Liedloff, 2004, "The Beginning of Life")
8. (Rong, 2008, Chapter 2)
9. (Eastman (Ohiyesa), 2008, "Winona's Childhood")

Chapter 15: Unhealthy Nations Shape the Worlds of Millions of People
1. (Chakravorti, 2016)
2. (Rowlatt, 2016)
3. (Economic Survey 2016-17, 2017, 2)
4. (Suresh, 2017)

5. (Kaul, 2017)
6. (Scofield, 2016)
7. ("Government's Demonetisation Shock Has Hit the Poorest the Most," 2016)
8. (Narayan, 2016)
9. (Rowlatt, 2016)
10. (Chakravorti, 2016)
11. (Purohit, 2016)
12. ("6 More Deaths; Man Tries to Set Himself on Fire at Bank," 2016)
13. (Banerjee, 2016)
14. (Purohit, 2016)
15. (Economic Survey 2016-17, 2017, 2)
16. (Parent, Jr, 2003, 27)
17. (Parent, Jr, 2003, 34)
18. (Parent, Jr, 2003, 26)
19. (Parent, Jr, 2003, 107)
20. (Parent, Jr, 2003, 110)
21. (Parent, Jr, 2003, 124)
22. (Parent, Jr, 2003, 109)
23. (Parent, Jr, 2003, 121)
24. (Parent, Jr, 2003, 118)
25. (Parent, Jr, 2003, 127)
26. (Parent, Jr, 2003, 130)
27. (Parent, Jr, 2003, 124)
28. (Parent, Jr, 2003, 115)
29. (Parent, Jr, 2003, 121)
30. (Parent, Jr, 2003, 119)
31. (Parent, Jr, 2003, 128)
32. (Parent, Jr, 2003, 123)
33. (Parent, Jr, 2003, 116)
34. (Parent, Jr, 2003, 117)
35. (Sublette & Sublette, 2016, "Wake Up Rich")
36. (Bradford, 2020)
37. (Parent, Jr, 2003, 112)
38. (Parent, Jr, 2003, 113)
39. (Parent, Jr, 2003, 114)
40. (Sublette & Sublette, 2016, "Little Shadows")
41. (Snyder, 2010, 21)
42. (Snyder, 2010, 22-23)
43. (Martin, 2024)
44. (Snyder, 2010, 14)
45. (Kulak, n.d.)
46. (Snyder, 2010, 25)
47. (We Will Annihilate Kulaks as a Class / Kukryniksy., 1930)
48. (Snyder, 2010, 28)
49. (Snyder, 2010, 26)
50. (Snyder, 2010, 29)
51. (Snyder, 2010, 33)
52. (Snyder, 2010, 34)
53. (Snyder, 2010, 35)
54. (Snyder, 2010, 37)
55. (Snyder, 2010, 30)
56. (Snyder, 2010, 55)
57. (Snyder, 2010, 39)
58. (Snyder, 2010, 41)
59. (Andriewsky, 2015, 33)
60. (Andriewsky, 2015, 29)
61. (Snyder, 2010, 43)
62. (Snyder, 2010, 45)
63. (Snyder, 2010, 46)
64. (Snyder, 2010, 47)
65. (Snyder, 2010, 49)
66. (Snyder, 2010, 50)
67. (Private Interview, personal communication, March 2015)

Chapter 16: Courageous Solidarity in Action
1. (Larson, 2016)
2. (Larson, 2016)
3. (Larson, 2016)
4. (All material in this chapter not from (Larson, 2016) is from (Bradford, 2020))
5. (Larson, 2016)
6. (Larson, 2016)

Chapter 17: Heart-Opening vs Heart-Closing
1. (Trigger, 1969, 71)
2. (Trigger, 1969, 84)
3. (Cox, 2019, "Joe Cox's Grandson")
4. (King Jr, 1968)
5. (Bradford, 2020)
6. (Prechtel, 1999, 206)
7. (Nabokov, 1987, 100)
8. (Nabokov, 1987, 101)
9. (Prechtel, 2012, "Always a Place at the Table")
10. (Nabokov, 1987, 138)
11. (Baptist, 2014, "1805-1861")
12. (Bettelheim, 1943)
13. (Bradford, 2020)
14. (Jacobs, 2000, "The New Master and Mistress")
15. (Sublette & Sublette, 2016, "Little Shadows")
16. (Kenyon, 2020)
17. (Daly, 2004, 6)
18. (White, 2018)
19. (Arendt, 1963)

Chapter 18: The Great Scam of Heart-Closing Cultural Narratives
1. (Malleus Maleficarum, 2024)
2. (Ehrenreich & English, 2010, "Witches as Healers")
3. (Catechism of the Catholic Church, 1997, 405)
4. (Catechism of the Catholic Church, 1997, 416-418)
5. (Catechism of the Catholic Church, 1997, 408-409)
6. (Brown, 2021)
7. (Romans 5:8, English Standard Version Bible)
8. (Isaiah 53:5, English Standard Version Bible)
9. (Ephesians 1:7, English Standard Version Bible)
10. (The Quran, 2:218, Translated by Mustafa Khattab)
11. (The Quran, 2:220, Translated by Mustafa Khattab)
12. (The Quran, 2:224, Translated by Mustafa Khattab)
13. (The Quran, 2:216, Translated by Mustafa Khattab)
14. (Landon, 1905, 350)
15. (DeBakcsy, 2013)
16. (Gelder & Gelder, 1964, 127)
17. (Eastman (Ohiyesa), 1916, "Civilization as Preached and Practiced")
18. (Ryan & Jethá, 2010, "The Tragedy of the Commons")
19. (Hardin, 1968)
20. (Ryan & Jethá, 2010, "The Tragedy of the Commons")
21. (Reich, 2013, "Biology and Sexology Before Freud")
22. (Gatto, 2017, 15)
23. (Young, 1996, Track 44)

Chapter 19: Creating a Culture of Remembering
1. (Prechtel, 1999, "Acknowledgments")
2. (Prechtel, 1999, 107)
3. (Prechtel, 1999, 209)
4. (Prechtel, 1999, 107)

5. (Private Interview with "Leia," 2024)

6. (Kimmerer, 2013, "The Three Sisters")

Chapter 20: Imposing and Maintaining Racism vs Generating Unity

1. (Haitian Revolution, n.d.)
2. (Bucciferro, 2013)
3. (Forbes Billionaires 2020, 2020)
4. (Correcting Course, 2022, xiii)
5. (The Attica Liberation Faction Manifesto of Demands and Anti-Depression Platform, 1971)
6. (Robinson, 2022)
7. (Strong, 1976, 54)
8. (India's Caste System: Brahmins, Kshatriyas, Vaishyas and Sudras, n.d.)
9. (Mitra, 2017)
10. (Hou & Truex, 2020)
11. (Lymperopoulou, 2022)
12. (Shankley & Williams, 2020)
13. (Reeves & Et al, 2023)
14. (Hinton et al., 2018)
15. (Bradford, 2020)
16. (Cox, 2019, "Long Way From Missouri")
17. (Oltermann, 2019)
18. (Solzhenitsyn, 2018, "Hand Over Your Second Skin Too!")
19. (Kimmerer, 2013, "Allegiance to Gratitude")
20. (Young, n.d.-b, 1)
21. (Kimmerer, 2013, "Allegiance to Gratitude")

Chapter 21: Training People to Adopt Authoritarian Ideologies

1. (Mantell, 1974, 27)
2. (Bettelheim, 1943)
3. (kswheeler, 2011)
4. (Jackson, 2016, "Vanishing Americans")
5. (Horwitz & et al, 2024)
6. (Jackson, 2016, "Vanishing Americans")
7. (Cameron, 1981, 62)
8. (Sublette & Sublette, 2016, "A Snake Biting Its Tail")
9. (Getty, 1991)
10. (Thom, n.d.)
11. (Beardsley, 1976)
12. (White, 2019)
13. (Harari, 2014, "Imperial Visions")
14. (Klippenstein, 2023)
15. (Lichtblau, 2015)
16. (Ballantine & Ballantine, 2001, 274)
17. (McKee, 2024)
18. (General Secretariat Organization of American States, 2007)
19. (Lentz-Smith, 2009, 42)
20. (Book Addict, 2023)
21. (Williams, 2023)

Chapter 22: Imposing and Maintaining Hatred

1. (Hirliman, 1982, "Chapter 1")
2. (Hirliman, 1982)
3. (Colvin, 1992, 151)
4. (Hett, 2018, 21)
5. (von Thaer, n.d.)
6. (Kershaw, 2015, "The Great Disaster")
7. (von Thaer, n.d.)
8. (Mikics, 2017)
9. (Grady, 2017, 167)
10. (Grady, 2017, 30)
11. (Grady, 2017, 168)
12. (Grady, 2017, 169)
13. (Grady, 2017, 168)
14. (von Thaer, n.d.)
15. (Mikics, 2017)
16. (Hilmar & Sachweh, 2022)
17. (Newton & Newton, 1991, 191)
18. (Flynn, 2021)
19. (Olsen, 1962, 342)
20. (Ideals of the Ku Klux Klan, n.d.)
21. (Olsen, 1962, 342)
22. (Olsen, 1962, 346)
23. (Olsen, 1962, 353)
24. (Olsen, 1962, 361)
25. (Overy, 2005, "Total War")
26. (Gilbert, n.d.)
27. ("Have You All Lost Your Minds?". Amazing and Terrifying Speech by @SWagenknecht, 2024)
28. (Judah, 2014)
29. (Khatib et al., 2024)
30. (Horton et al., 2024)
31. (Dismantle Israel's Carceral Regime and "Open-Air" Imprisonment of Palestinians: UN Expert, 2023)
32. (Lyons, 2023)
33. (Dismantle Israel's Carceral Regime and "Open-Air" Imprisonment of Palestinians: UN Expert, 2023)
34. (Kubovich, 2024)
35. (Government press office, 2023)
36. (Scahill, 2024)
37. (Scahill et al., 2024)
38. (Ginsberg, 2024)
39. (Khatib et al., 2024)
40. (Solomon, 2024)
41. (Ehrman, 2019, 80)
42. (Pharr, 1952, 440)
43. (Bailyn, 2012, "Abrasions, Utopians, and Holy War")
44. (Piecuch, 2008, 375)
45. (Pittenger, 2020)
46. (The American Heritage Dictionary Entry: Civilized, 2022)
47. (The American Heritage Dictionary Entry: Savage, 2022)
48. (The American Heritage Dictionary Entry: Barbarian, 2022)
49. (Webster, 1828)
50. (Dunbar-Ortiz, 2014, "Bloody Footprints")
51. (Holmes, 2014)
52. (Johnson, 2023)
53. (Snyder, 2010, 55)

Chapter 23: Addressing Shared Challenges With the Sacred Circle

1. (Krauss & Bradsher, 2015)
2. (Cox, 2019, "Just Another Nigger")
3. (Cox, 2019, "Mystery Phantom Sniper")
4. (Hirliman, 1982, "Chapter 1")
5. (Barrett, 2010, "KAS-KI-YEH")

Chapter 24: Sexual Discrimination vs Sexual Equality

1. (Anderson, 1985)
2. (Prechtel, 1999, 202)
3. (Nelson, 2008, "First Nations Survival and the Future of the Earth")
4. (Ballantine & Ballantine, 2001, 156)
5. (Nelson, 2008, "A Democracy Based On Peace")
6. (Johnston, 2003, 1)

7. (Anderson, 1985)
8. (Trigger, 1969, 28)
9. (N. Basket, personal communication, August 5, 2023)
10. (Blackstone, 2014)
11. (United States v. Yazell, 382 U.S. 341 (1966), 1966)
12. (Blackstone, 2014)
13. (Spousal Rape Laws: 20 Years Later, 2004)
14. (Saudi Arabia: 10 Reasons Why Women Flee, 2019)
15. (Strong, 1976, 329)
16. (Rees, 2014)
17. (Zechariah 5:5-8, King James Version Bible)
18. (Malleus Maleficarum, 2024)
19. (Ehrenreich & English, 2010, "The Crimes of Witches")
20. (Denova, 2021)
21. (Genesis 3:16, English Standard Version Bible)
22. (Definition of Bishop, n.d.)
23. (Denova, 2021)
24. (Bai et al., 2022)
25. (Atencio & Posadas, 2015)
26. (Kochhar, 2023)
27. (Weiss, 2009)
28. (Biswas, 2017)
29. (Reese, 2014)
30. (Gottipati, 2014)
31. (Reese, 2014)
32. (Everyone Blames Me, 2017)
33. (Murray et al., 2023)
34. (General Secretariat Organization of American States, 2007)
35. (Etienne & Leacock, 1980, 113-125)
36. (Anderson, 1985)
37. (Thomas & Kopel, 2023)
38. (Rape Addendum, 2017)
39. (Abkowitz & Lin, 2015)
40. (Rand, 2009)
41. (Proposed National Standards to Prevent, Detect, and Respond to Prison Rape Under the Prison Rape Elimination Act (PREA), 2011)
42. (Sabol et al., 2010)
43. (Proposed National Standards to Prevent, Detect, and Respond to Prison Rape Under the Prison Rape Elimination Act (PREA), 2011)
44. (Proposed National Standards to Prevent, Detect, and Respond to Prison Rape Under the Prison Rape Elimination Act (PREA), 2011)
45. (Ilyina, 2021)
46. (Prosvirova & Boldyrev, 2022)
47. (Szczepanski, 2019)
48. (Thompson, 2021)
49. (Feminism and Gender Equality around the World, 2017)
50. (Everyone Blames Me, 2017)
51. (Weiss, 2009)

Chapter 25: Sexual Freedom vs Sexual Repression

1. (Ryan & Jethá, 2010, "Who's Your Daddies?")
2. (Ryan & Jethá, 2010, "Making a Mess of Marriage, Mating, and Monogamy")
3. (Ryan & Jethá, 2010, "Paternity Certainty: The Crumbling Cornerstone of the Standard Narrative")
4. (Trigger, 1969, 118)
5. (Anderson, 1985)
6. (Trigger, 1969, 67)
7. (Anderson, 1985)
8. (Thwaites, n.d.)
9. (Eastman (Ohiyesa), 1916, "The Soul of the White Man")
10. (Malinowski, 1932, 61)
11. (Reich, 1971, "The Problem of Social Sex-Economy")
12. (Malinowski, 1937, 87)
13. (Ryan & Jethá, 2010, "Love, Lust, and Liberty at Lugu Lake")
14. (Trigger, 1969, 26)
15. (Barrett, 2010, "The Family")
16. (The Quran, 2:228, Translated by Mustafa Khattab)
17. (The Quran, 4:34, Translated by Mustafa Khattab)
18. (The Quran, 43:70, Translated by Muhsin Khan)
19. (Carland, 2017, "Journey to the Fight")
20. (1 Corinthians 14:34, King James Version Bible)
21. (Ephesians 5:22, English Standard Version Bible)
22. (1 Timothy 2:12, King James Version Bible)
23. (1 Corinthians 11:3, King James Version Bible)
24. (Barr, 2021, "The Beginning of Patriarchy")
25. (The Quran, 24:2, Translated by Mustafa Khattab)
26. (The Quran, 17:32, Translated by Mustafa Khattab)
27. (Deuteronomy 22:13-21, King James Version Bible)
28. (Deuteronomy 22:28-29, King James Version Bible)
29. (Worth et al., 2018)
30. (Wafula & Ford, 2023)
31. ("Iran Sentences a Woman to Death for Adultery, State Media Say," 2023)
32. (Beauvais, n.d., 10.45)
33. (Denova, 2021)
34. (Romans 8:13, New International Version)
35. (Proverbs 14:12, English Standard Version Bible)
36. (Graham, Billy, 2004)
37. (Denova, 2021)
38. (Ehrenreich & English, 2010, "The Crimes of Witches")
39. (Mark, 2019)
40. (Madden & Baldwin, n.d.)
41. (The First Discourse of the Buddha, n.d.)
42. (Female Genital Mutilation (FGM), 2024)
43. (Female Genital Mutilation, 2024)
44. (Female Genital Mutilation Dashboard (Table View), n.d.)
45. (Female Genital Mutilation, 2024)
46. (World Population Prospects 2022 Summary of Results, 2022)
47. (Nelson, 2008, "Ethiopian Women: From Passive Resources to Active Citizens")
48. (Answers To Your Questions About Your Young Son's Circumcised Penis, n.d.)
49. (Circumcision by Country 2024, 2024)
50. (Morris et al., 2016)
51. (Khan, n.d.)
52. (Diamont, n.d.)
53. (Green, 2007)
54. (Female Genital Mutilation, 2024)
55. (Denova, 2021)
56. (Reich, 1971, "Sex-Economy in Matriarchal Society")
57. (Ryan & Jethá, 2010, "What Is Evolutionary Psychology and Why Should You Care?")
58. (Reich, 2013, "The Development of the Orgasm Theory")
59. (Malinowski, 1932, 284)
60. (Reich, 1971, "Sex-Economy in Matriarchal Society")
61. (Reich, 2013, "The Development of the Character-Analytic Technique")
62. (Ehrenreich & English, 2010, "Conclusion")

Chapter 26: Privilege 1 - Lift-and-Turn

1. (Kwiet, 2021)
2. (Baptist, 2014, "1805-1861")
3. (Solzhenitsyn, 2018, "Tearing at the Chains")
4. (Snyder, 2010, 50)

5. (Eastman (Ohiyesa), 1916, "The Ghost Dance War")
6. (McCormack, 2024)
7. (Haitian Revolution, n.d.)
8. (Perowne, n.d.)
9. (Gonzalez, 2022, "Central Americans: Intervention Comes Home to Roost")
10. (Llewellyn & Et al, n.d.)
11. (Colvin, 1992, 152)
12. (Solzhenitsyn, 2018, "The Bluecaps")

Chapter 27: Privilege 2 - Social Class and Promise Keeping

1. (Cox, 2019, "Just Another Nigger")
2. (Mark 3:24, New International Version)
3. (Federici, 2004, 42)
4. (Savage, 1990, 14)
5. (Hand, 2015)
6. (Williamson, 2024)
7. (Savage, 1990, 15)
8. (Savage, 1990, 56)
9. (Savage, 1990, 57)
10. (Zernova, 2012)
11. ("Beat Him, Take Everything Away": Abuses by China's Chengguan Para-Police, 2012)
12. (Ayer, 2018)
13. (Tremlett, 2002)
14. (Corriher, 2008)
15. (Index to SSRI Stories, n.d.)
16. (Private Interview with "Alison," 2023)
17. (Bettelheim, 1943)
18. ("What Is India's Caste System?" 2019)

Chapter 28: The Three Integrities

1. (Cameron, 1981, 18)
2. (Solzhenitsyn, 2018, "Or Corruption?")
3. ("The Importance of Structural Integrity in Engineering," 2024)
4. (Guzman, 2024)
5. (Wel, 2024)
6. (Koehler, 2023)
7. (United States Code, n.d.)
8. (US Case Law, 2024)
9. (Linderman, 1932, 173)
10. ("I Disapprove of What You Say, But I Will Defend to the Death Your Right to Say It," 2015)
11. (Martin Niemöller: "First They Came for the Socialists…," 2023)

Chapter 29: Privilege 3 - Going Through the Motions

1. (Mote, 1999, 9)
2. (Johnson, 2023)
3. (An Offer You Can't Refuse: How US Federal Prosecutors Force Drug Defendants to Plead Guilty, 2013)
4. (Kennedy, 2012)
5. (An Offer You Can't Refuse: How US Federal Prosecutors Force Drug Defendants to Plead Guilty, 2013)
6. (Chawla, 2019)
7. (Ataman et al., 2013)
8. (van Voren, 2010)
9. (van Voren, 2015)
10. (van Voren, 2010)
11. (The Growth of Incarceration in the United States: Exploring Causes and Consequences (2014), 2014, 89)
12. (Western & Orrell, 2020)
13. (The Growth of Incarceration in the United States: Exploring Causes and Consequences (2014), 2014, 61)
14. (Western & Orrell, 2020)
15. (13th Amendment to the U.S. Constitution: Abolition of Slavery (1865), 2021)
16. (Sawyer & Wagner, 2024)
17. (Anguiano, 2022)
18. (Baptist, 2014, "1805-1861")
19. (Definition of ACADEMIC, 2024)
20. (Notes, 2005, 68)
21. (Notes, 2005, 69)
22. (Graeber, 2014, "The Axial Age (800 BC - 600 AD)")
23. (Funding and Financial Overview, n.d.)
24. (Tax Form 990 - World Wildlife Fund, 2022)
25. (Funding and Financial Overview, n.d.)
26. (Rating for World Wildlife Fund, n.d.)
27. (Environmental Defenders, Human Rights and the Growing Role of IUCN Policy: Retired, Red-Tagged or Red-Listed?, 2021)
28. (Korten, 2023)
29. (Lawsuit Accuses Oregon Police Department of Illegally Monitoring Progressive Activists, 2024)
30. (Hicks, 2023)
31. (Torrella, 2024)
32. (U.S. Beef Industry Sustainability Framework, 2019)
33. (Torrella, 2024)
34. (People Don't See Industrial Meat as a Key Cause of Global Warming – Poll, 2023)
35. (Torrella, 2024)
36. (Barwick, 2024)
37. (Daley, 2015)
38. (Salvador Allende, 2024)
39. (Covert Action in Chile 1963-1973, 1975)
40. (Augusto Pinochet, 2024)
41. (National Foundation for Cancer Research (NFCR), n.d.)
42. (Cavalier et al., 2023)
43. (LaMotte, 2024)
44. (Dewan, 2023)
45. (Bagenstose, 2022)
46. (Crenshaw, 2019)
47. (Scheer and Moss, 2011)
48. (Alengebawy et al., 2021)
49. ("Pesticide Industry Lobbying Congress with Misinformation to Prohibit Local Pesticide Policies," 2023)
50. (Sayki, 2023)
51. (Varangis, 2019)
52. (Nash-Hoff, 2017)
53. (Kimball & Scott, 2014)
54. (Vergun, 2021)
55. (McCarthy, 2024)
56. (Tegler, 2024)
57. (Kube & Gains, 2023)
58. (Eisenhower, 1961)
59. (Hartung & Fisher, 2023)
60. (Eastman (Ohiyesa), 1916, "My First School Days")
61. (Notes, 2005, 68)
62. (June 30, 1876: Peter Kropotkin Escapes from Prison: A Tale of Derring-Do on the Occasion of His Birthday, 2021)
63. (Munro, 2000)

Chapter 30: Privilege 4 - Entitlement

1. (Parenti, 2003)
2. (Carland, 2017, "Journey to the Fight")
3. (Strong, 1976, 174)
4. (Loewen, 2007, 211)
5. (Barr, 2021, "Making Biblical Womanhood Gospel Truth")
6. (Carland, 2017, "Journey to the Fight")
7. (Weiss, 2009)
8. (X, 1965, "Forward")
9. (Barr, 2021, "Making Biblical Womanhood Gospel Truth")
10. (Carland, 2017, "One Beyond the Harem")
11. (Padierna Jiménez, 2013)
12. (Mujeres 45% de Las Bases Zapatistas, 2011)
13. (Loewen, 2007, 211)
14. (Mantell, 1974, 27)

Chapter 31: The Story of the Peacemaker

1. (Cameron, 1981, 121)
2. (Notes, 2005, 265-267)
3. (Johansen & Mann, 2000, 269)
4. (Johansen & Mann, 2000, 270)
5. (Notes, 2005, 31)
6. (Notes, 2005, 37)
7. (Notes, 2005, 35)
8. (Notes, 2005, 35)
9. (Notes, 2005, 38)
10. (Notes, 2005, 26)
11. (Notes, 2005, 35)
12. (Notes, 2005, 27)
13. (Notes, 2005, 38)
14. (Notes, 2005, 104)
15. (Utopia, 2024)
16. (Notes, 2005, 104)
17. (Notes, 2005, 38)
18. (Notes, 2005, 39)
19. (Notes, 2005, 85)
20. (Notes, 2005, 81)
21. (Notes, 2005, 38)
22. (Notes, 2005, 34)
23. (Notes, 2005, 27)
24. (Notes, 2005, 24)
25. (Notes, 2005, 104)
26. (Notes, 2005, 105)
27. (Notes, 2005, 37)
28. (Notes, 2005, 38)
29. (Nelson, 2008, "A Democracy Based On Peace")
30. (Miller, 2015)
31. (Engels, 2010, 18)
32. (Engels, 2010, 40)

Chapter 32: A Study in Privilege and World-Shaping - the Police

1. (Black, 2010)
2. (Loftsgordon, 2024)
3. (Wollan & Harris, 2011)
4. (de Sousa, 2019)
5. (Anti-Austerity Protesters Clash with Police in Rome, 2014)
6. (Paris Police Swoop on Occupy La Défense Protest, 2011)
7. (Duret et al., 2021)
8. (Levenson, 2021)
9. (Dunkle, 2021)
10. (Stamper, 2016, 193)
11. (Moran, 2023)
12. (Taibbi, 2019)
13. (Goldstein, 2018)
14. (Valencia et al., 2021)
15. (Goldstein, 2018)
16. (Moran, 2023)
17. (Goldstein, 2018)
18. (Burnham, 1970)
19. (Duret, 2021)
20. (Kamil Warraich v. Asbury Park, 2020, 22)
21. (Kutnjak Ivković et al., 2020)
22. (Burnham, 1970)
23. (Rodriguez, 2020)
24. (Kuzmarov, 2023)
25. (Schwartz, 2023)
26. (FBI Whistleblower Testimony Highlights Government Abuse, Misallocation of Resources, and Retaliation, 2023)
27. (Duret, 2021)
28. (Burnham, 1970)
29. (Vice News, 2014)
30. (Western & Orrell, 2020)
31. (The Growth of Incarceration in the United States: Exploring Causes and Consequences (2014), 2014, 61)
32. (Drug Arrests Stayed High Even as Imprisonment Fell From 2009 to 2019, 2022)
33. (Fellner, 2000)
34. (Baum, 2016)
35. (More Imprisonment Does Not Reduce State Drug Problems, 2018)
36. (Binswanger et al., 2007)
37. (Western & Simes, 2019)
38. (Volkow, 2021)
39. (Drug Abuse Treatment Evaluation: Strategies, Progress, and Prospects, 1983)
40. (Principles of Drug Addiction Treatment: A Research-Based Guide (Third Edition), 2018)
41. (Webb, 1996)
42. (Kuzmarov, 2022)
43. (Duret et al., 2021)

Chapter 33: It All Starts with Justifying or Ignoring Exploitative Rulers

1. (Divine Right of Kings, n.d.)
2. (Denmark: Heads of State: 1863-2024 - Archontology, n.d.)
3. (Monaco: Sovereign Princes: 1814-2024 - Archontology, 2023)
4. (United Kingdom: Heads of State: 1801-2024 - Archontology, n.d.)
5. (Netherlands (The): Heads of State: 1945-2024 - Archontology, n.d.)
6. (Harari, 2014, "Imperial Visions")
7. (Wheelan, 2014)
8. (Davies, 1998)
9. (Fukue, 2024)
10. ("Pharaoh," n.d.)
11. (Pharr, 1952, 440)
12. (Kakel III, 2011, "Introduction")
13. (Snyder, 2012, 54)
14. (Schneider, 2014, "Stars Appearing in the Sky")
15. (Loewen, 2007, 284)
16. (Turner, 1994, "Possession")
17. (Eastman (Ohiyesa), 2013, "Sitting Bull")
18. (Linderman, 1932, 173)
19. (Turner, 1994, "Possession")
20. (Loewen, 2007, 107)
21. (Loewen, 2007, 108)

Chapter 34: Who Controls the Land?

1. (Kimmerer, 2013, "Wisgaak Gokpenagen: A Black Ash Basket")
2. (Brown Jr, 1988, 80)

3. (Eastman (Ohiyesa), 2013, "Chief Joseph")
4. (Linderman, 1932, 21)
5. (Eastman (Ohiyesa), 2008, "The Faithfulness of Long Ears")
6. (Grinnell, 2005, "The Attack on the Camp")
7. (Trigger, 1969, 27)
8. (Eastman (Ohiyesa), 1916, "My First School Days")
9. (kswheeler, 2011)
10. (Prechtel, 1999, 267)
11. (Neihardt, 2014, "Early Boyhood")
12. (Fairlie, 2009)
13. (Volin, 1953)
14. (Eisenman, 2018, "Institutional Origins and Evolution")
15. (Eisenman, 2018, "Economics: Super-Optimal Investment")
16. (Grinnell, 2005, "My Marriage")
17. (Neihardt, 2014, "Early Boyhood")
18. (Neihardt, 2014, "Walking the Black Road")
19. (Neihardt, 2014, "The Dog Vision")
20. (Neihardt, 2014, "Walking the Black Road")
21. (Perdue, 1998, 135)
22. (Perdue, 1998, 157)
23. (Nelson, 2008, "First Nations Survival and the Future of the Earth")
24. (N. Basket, personal communication, August 5, 2023)
25. (Perdue, 1998, 156)
26. (Perdue, 1998, 157)
27. (Perdue, 1998, 158)
28. (Kimmerer, 2013, "A Council of Pecans")
29. (Skerk, 2022)
30. (Dunbar-Ortiz, 2014, "Bloody Footprints")
31. (Peckham, 1947)
32. (Eastman (Ohiyesa), 2013, "Sitting Bull")

Chapter 35: Guerilla Gardening - Generating Abundance Without Permission

1. (Tracey, 2007, 207)
2. (Gurney, 2013, "Winstanley the Digger")
3. (Miles, 2023)
4. (Tracey, 2007, 24)
5. (Tracey, 2007, 206)
6. (Tracey, 2007, 11)

Chapter 36: Sabotaging Efforts at Deep Cultural Healing

1. (Bettelheim, 1943)
2. (Stuchbery, 2019)
3. (Hertzgerg, 2021)
4. (Introduction - Ministry for State Security, n.d.)
5. (Stuchbery, 2019)
6. (Oltermann, 2019)
7. (Nelson, 2023)
8. (Bumiller, 2010)
9. (To see the video: Smith, 2024)
10. (Bumiller, 2010)
11. (Cook, 2020)
12. (Johnstone, 2019)
13. (Cook, 2020)
14. (Manglona & Said-Moorhouse, 2024)
15. (Munsi, 2023)
16. (Dembicki, 2022)
17. (Evans & Lewis, 2012)
18. (Daly, 2004, 8-10)
19. (Daly, 1998, 85)
20. (Daly, 2004, 75)
21. (Hertzgerg, 2021)
22. (Bailey, 1957)
23. (Hingley, 2021, "The Okhrana in the Age of Assassinations 1901-1908")
24. (Daly, 1998, 126)
25. (Palat, 1986)
26. (Bailey, 1957)
27. (Hingley, 2021, "The Okhrana in the Age of Assassinations 1901-1908")
28. (Hingley, 2021, "The Decline and Fall of the Okhrana 1908-1917")
29. ("George Floyd: Timeline of Black Deaths and Protests," 2021)
30. (Wimpee, 2020)
31. (Director of Central Intelligence, Assistant Director, Research and Reports, 1951)
32. (The Editors of the Encyclopedia Britannica, n.d.)
33. (Ford Foundation Announces $180 Million in New Funding for U.S. Racial Justice Efforts, 2020)
34. (2021 Tax Form 990-PF Chan Zuckerberg Initiative Foundation, n.d.)
35. (Toh, 2020)
36. (2021 Tax Form 990-PF for Omidyar Network Fund, Inc, n.d.)
37. (2020 Tax Form 990-PF for Democracy Fund, Inc., n.d.)
38. (Zilber, 2023)
39. (Impact, n.d.)
40. ("About Us," n.d.)
41. (Daniszewski, 2020)
42. (Coleman, 2020)
43. (For example: 10 Microaggressions Companies Must Avoid, n.d.)
44. ("Koch Industries: Secretly Funding the Climate Denial Machine," n.d.)
45. (Mayer, 2019)
46. (Mizelle, 2023)
47. (Anguiano, 2022)
48. (Hirliman, 1982)
49. (The Attica Liberation Faction Manifesto of Demands and Anti-Depression Platform, 1971)
50. (Gage, 2019)
51. (Sammon, 2020)
52. (Anguiano, 2022)
53. (Selective Draft Law Cases, 245 U.S. 366 (1918), 1918)
54. (Cox, 2019, "The Split")
55. (Sweet, 2021)
56. (Gaiter, 2017)
57. (Sweet, 2021)
58. (Ganeva, 2019)
59. (Fred Hampton (August 30, 1948 - December 4, 1969), n.d.)
60. (Sweet, 2021)
61. (Lennard, 2022)
62. (Memories of Tort, 2023)

Chapter 37: Culture Jamming

1. (Snyder, 2010, 39)
2. (Gallagher, 2024)
3. (Gilbert, n.d.)
4. (Lewitzke, 2014)
5. (Wilber, 2019)
6. (Çınar & Arıkan, 2002)
7. (Lopez, 2016)
8. (Francis, 2012)
9. ("How I Responded to AIDS in the 1980s," 2015)
10. (What It Was Like to Live with HIV During the '80s and '90s, 2023)
11. (National AIDS Memorial, 2017)
12. ("How I Responded to AIDS in the 1980s," 2015)
13. (Fanon, 2004, "Colonial War and Mental Disorders")
14. (Fox et al., 2024)

15. (Gun Violence Archive, 2024)
16. (Fox et al., 2024)
17. (Gun Ownership in America: 1973 to 2021, 2022)
18. (Wilkinson, 2004)
19. (Blanchet et al., n.d.)
20. (Gøtzsche, 2017)
21. (Akathisia, 2022)
22. (ResponsibilityLive85, 2023)
23. (Akathisia, 2024)
24. (Montejo et al., 2001)
25. (Fisher & Thomson, 2007)
26. (BBC Stories, 2017)
27. (SSRI Stories, n.d.)
28. (Baum et al., 2001)
29. (Mojtabai, 2008)
30. (Pratt et al., 2017)
31. (Hillhouse & Porter, 2015)
32. (Antidepressant Discontinuation Syndrome, n.d.)
33. (Colborn et al., 1996, 9)
34. (Colborn et al., 1996, 8)
35. (Colborn et al., 1996, 3)
36. (Colborn et al., 1996, 5)
37. (Colborn et al., 1996, 6)
38. (Colborn et al., 1996, 83)
39. (Colborn et al., 1996, 44)
40. (Colborn et al., 1996, 85)
41. (Colborn et al., 1996, 182)
42. (Breast Cancer Causes and Risk Factors, 2023)
43. (Colborn et al., 1996, 182)
44. (Impact of EDCs on Reproductive Systems, n.d.)
45. (Lucaccioni et al., 2020)
46. (Brehm & Flaws, 2019)
47. (Ritchie et al., 2023)
48. (Colborn et al., 1996, 113)
49. (New EPA Data Confirm Widespread 'Forever Chemicals' in Drinking Water, 2024)
50. (Johansson & Et al 2022)
51. (Zurada et al., 2018)
52. (Turley, 2021)
53. (Attacks on Gender Affirming Care by State Map, n.d.)
54. (Lawther & Luffy, 2024)
55. (Lawther & Lee, 2023)
56. (Lawther & Wallace, 2022)
57. (Gilead Sciences, Inc. (GILD) Stock Price, News, Quote & History, n.d.)
58. (Bustos et al., 2021)
59. (Bickerton, 2023)

Chapter 38: Endless Predation When the Root Disease Goes Unhealed
1. (The Global Scale of Child Sexual Abuse in the Catholic Church, 2021)
2. (Cox, 2008)
3. (The Global Scale of Child Sexual Abuse in the Catholic Church, 2021)
4. (Liu, 2013)
5. (Tsering et al., 1997, "Chapter 3")
6. (Ball, 2022)
7. (Smith, 2016, 3-4)
8. (Smith, 2016, 49)
9. (Tremlett, 2010)
10. (Tremlett, 2002)
11. (DeCamp, 1996, 4)
12. (DeCamp, 1996, 12)
13. (DeCamp, 1996, xvii)
14. (Knight, 2021)
15. (Satter, 2016)
16. (The Editors of the Encyclopedia Britannica, n.d.)
17. (Bergen, 2024)
18. (Bush Delivers Ultimatum, 2001)
19. (Witte, 2024)
20. (Bergen, 2024)
21. (Architects & Engineers for 9/11 Truth, n.d.)
22. (NIST WTC 7 Investigation, 2022)
23. (NIST NCSTAR 1, 2005, 146)
24. (MacQueen, 2006)
25. (Explosive Features | Twin Towers, n.d.)
26. (Joint Chiefs of Staff, 1962)
27. (September 11 Hijackers Fast Facts, 2013)
28. (FBI Releases Declassified Documents about Investigating Ties between Saudi Government and Sept. 11 Attacks, 2021)
29. (FBI Releases Newly Declassified Record on September 11 Attacks, 2021)
30. (Coll, 2004, "I Loved Osama")
31. (Unger, 2018)
32. (Marcetic, 2024)
33. (Edwards, 2006, 105)
34. (Boissoneault, 2017)
35. (Mandal, 2011)
36. (Boniface & Glaze, 2013)
37. (Sayare, 2010)
38. (LaFleur, 2016)
39. (Johnston, 2005)
40. (Kessler, 2011, "Secret Files")
41. (Chulov, 2020)
42. (Goldman, 2020)
43. (Wood, 2022)
44. (Cameron, 1981, 71)
45. (Cameron, 1981, 74)

Chapter 39: Even More Propaganda Techniques
1. (Herman & Chomsky, 2008, "Worthy and Unworthy Victims")
2. (Eastman (Ohiyesa), 2013, "Chief Joseph")
3. (First Debate: Ottawa, Illinois, n.d.)
4. ("Foreign News: Consecrated Press," 1933)
5. (Bernays, 2005)
6. (Cohen, 1963)
7. (Chomsky, 1998)
8. (Pope, 2018)
9. (Blitzer, 2016)
10. (Fox, 2024)
11. (Clinton, 2014, "Latin America: Democrats and Demagogues")
12. (Varela, 2016)
13. (Generals Who Led Honduras Military Coup Trained at the School of the Americas, 2009)
14. (Blitzer, 2016)
15. (Luke 23:34, New International Version)
16. (Biden, 2022)
17. (Johnstone, 2023)
18. (Farge, 2022)
19. (Broad, 2022)
20. (B, 2023)
21. ("Pickett's Charge – 12 Remarkable Facts About Gettysburg's Deadly Climax," 2016)
22. (Maté, 2022)

23. (JAR, 2024)
25. (Joseph Goebbels On the "Big Lie," n.d.)
27. (Solzhenitsyn, 2018, "The History of Our Sewage Disposal System")
29. (Karnasiewicz, 2023)
24. (Bridgen, 2024)
26. (Demm, 2017)
28. (Carini, 2020)
30. (Breitman, 1965, 93)

Chapter 40: Enough! - The Zapatistas' Deep Revolution

1. (Marcos, 1994)
2. ("First Declaration of the Lacandon Jungle," 1994)
3. ("Mayor Moisés: We Will Not Allow Anyone to Talk about Peace without Justice and Dignity.(Google Translate, Trans.)," 1995)
4. (Moisés, 2023)
5. ("Mayor Moisés: We Will Not Allow Anyone to Talk about Peace without Justice and Dignity.(Google Translate, Trans.)," 1995)
6. (Las Mujeres En El EZLN y Su Ley Revolucionaria; Por La Rebeldía, Autonomía y Libertad, 2023)
7. ("Everyday Heroism Makes the Sparkles Possible (Google Translate, Trans.)," 1994)
8. (Rull, 2021)
9. ("Interview with Mayor Ana María (Google Translate, Trans.)," 1995)
10. ("Justice Law (Google Translate, Trans.)," 1993)
11. ("Interview with Mayor Ana María (Google Translate, Trans.)," 1995)
12. (Indigenous Clandestine Revolutionary Committee, 2005)
13. (Marcos, 2014)
14. ("Interview with Mayor Ana María (Google Translate, Trans.)," 1995)
15. (Johansen & Mann, 2000, 272-280)
16. ("Everyday Heroism Makes the Sparkles Possible (Google Translate, Trans.)," 1994)
17. (Marcos, 2014)
18. ("Everyday Heroism Makes the Sparkles Possible (Google Translate, Trans.)," 1994)
19. ("Ley Revolucionaria de Mujeres," 1993)
20. ("Everyday Heroism Makes the Sparkles Possible (Google Translate, Trans.)," 1994)
21. (Marcos, 2014)
22. ("Revolutionary Agriculture Law (Google Translate, Trans.)," 1993)
23. ("Labor Law (Google Translate, Trans.)," 1993)
24. (Gonzalez, 2022, "Central Americans: Intervention Comes Home to Roost")
25. ("Urban Reform Law (Google Translate, Trans.)," 1993)
26. ("War Tax Act (Google Translate, Trans.)," 1993)
27. ("Industry and Commerce Law (Google Translate, Trans.)," 1993)
28. ("Law on the Rights and Obligations of Peoples in Struggle (Google Translate, Trans.)," 1993)
29. ("Justice Law (Google Translate, Trans.)," 1993)
30. ("Social Security Law (Google Translate, Trans.)," 1993)
31. ("Ninth Part: The New Structure of Zapastista Autonomy (Google Translate, Trans.)," 2023)
32. (Nelson, 2008, "Return of the Ancient Council Ways: Indigenous Survival in Chiapas")
33. ("Ninth Part: The New Structure of Zapastista Autonomy (Google Translate, Trans.)," 2023)
34. (Marcos, 1994)
35. ("Everyday Heroism Makes the Sparkles Possible (Google Translate, Trans.)," 1994)
36. (Rebrii, 2020)
37. ("Ninth Part: The New Structure of Zapastista Autonomy (Google Translate, Trans.)," 2023)
38. ("Twentieth and Last Part: The Common and Non-Property," 2023)
39. (Nelson, 2008, "Return of the Ancient Council Ways: Indigenous Survival in Chiapas")
40. (Vásquez, 2023)
41. (Rull, 2021)

Chapter 41: The Deepest Lessons From Thousands of Years of Spiritual Leaders

1. (Neihardt, 2014)
2. (Matthew 4:1-11, King James Version Bible)
3. (Matthew 2:2, King James Version Bible)
4. (Joseph, 2022)
5. (Mark 3:1-6, King James Version Bible)
6. (Mark 8:31, English Standard Version Bible)
7. (Mark 9:31, King James Version Bible)
8. (Mark 10:32-34, King James Version Bible)
9. (John 12:7, English Standard Version Bible)
10. (Mark 11:18, King James Version Bible)
11. (Luke 23:2, New International Version Bible)
12. (Mark 14:56-64, New International Version Bible)
13. (Bronnikov, 1878)
14. (Cubillos, 2018)
15. (Hoshiko, 2012)
16. (Sloan, 2020)
17. (History.com editors, 2023)
18. (King Arrested for Speeding; MIA Holds Seven Mass Meetings, 1956)
19. (Kirk, 2020)
20. (MLK Saw New Level of Hatred When He Took Fight into the North, 2016)
21. (Gage, 2014)
22. (Pressman, 2012)
23. (King Jr, 1967)
24. (Theoharis, 1999, 123)
25. (King & Pierre, 2018)
26. (King Jr, 1968)
27. (Douglass, 2000)
28. (Hoover, n.d.)
29. (Messiah, n.d.)

Chapter 42: Training Children to Give or Withhold Love, Part 1

1. (Struble & Riesen, 1978)
2. (Ardiel & Rankin, 2010)
3. (Prescott, 1976, 435)
4. (Mantell, 1974, 25)
5. (Mantell, 1974, 139)
6. (Mantell, 1974, 137-139)
7. (Mantell, 1974, 151)
8. (Mantell, 1974, 137)
9. (Mantell, 1974, 24)
10. (Prescott, 1975)
11. (Philbrick, 2010, "The Crow's Nest")
12. (Boswell, 1980, 164)
13. (Wax, 2014)
14. (O'Donnell, n.d.)
15. (Gemme & Wheeler, 1976, 434)
16. (Prescott, 1975)
17. (Liedloff, 2004, "Deprivation of Essential Experiences")
18. (The Real News Network, 2013)
19. (Bos, 2024)
20. (Weiss, 2024)
21. (Liedloff, 2004, "How My Ideas Were So Radically Changed")
22. (Prescott, 1977)
23. (Prescott, 1977)
24. (Prescott, 1975)
25. (Mantell, 1974, 50)
26. (Mantell, 1974, 3)
27. (Mantell, 1974, 141)
28. (Mantell, 1974, 147)

29. (Saunderson, 2022)
30. (The Attica Liberation Faction Manifesto of Demands and Anti-Depression Platform, 1971)
31. (Neihardt, 2014, "The Bison Hunt")
32. (Eastman (Ohiyesa), 1916, "On the White Man's Trail")
33. (Barrett, 2010, "The Conquered Weapon")
34. (Eastman (Ohiyesa), 1916, "On the White Man's Trail")
35. (Eastman (Ohiyesa), 2008, "Early Hardships")
36. (Eastman (Ohiyesa), 1916, "The Way Opens")
37. (Cameron, 1981, 101)
38. (Cameron, 1981, 102)
39. (Grinnell, 2005, "The Attack on the Camp")
40. (Liedloff, 2004, "Growing Up")
41. (Prechtel, 1999, 232)
42. (White, 2018)
43. (Innes, 1983)
44. (Cameron, 1981, 121)
45. (Mendizza, n.d.)

Chapter 43: Good Contact vs Poor Contact
1. (Young, n.d.-b, 88)
2. (Cameron, 1981, 103)
3. (N. Basket, personal communication, August 5, 2023)
4. (Kimmerer, 2013, "Learning the Grammar of Animacy")
5. (Young, 1999, Track 35)
6. (Eastman (Ohiyesa), 2013, "The Boy Hunter")
7. (Young, n.d.-a, 49)
8. (Welker, 2019)
9. (Young, n.d.-a, 62)
10. (Young, n.d.-a, 61)

Chapter 44: Training Children to Give or Withhold Love, Part 2
1. (Kimmerer, 2013, "Mishkos Kenomagwen: The Teachings of Grass")
2. (Prechtel, 1999, 99)
3. (Prechtel, 1999, 210)
4. (Grinnell, 2005, "The Way to Live")
5. (Neihardt, 2014, "The Rubbing Out of Long Hair")
6. (Grinnell, 2005, "The Attack on the Camp")
7. (Eastman (Ohiyesa), 2013, "Crazy Horse")
8. (Private Interview with "Alison," 2023)
9. (Mantell, 1974, 24)

Chapter 45: The Spiritual Impacts of Physical Deprivation
1. (Price, 1939, "Prenatal Nutritional Deformities and Disease Types")
2. (Price, 1939, "Primitive Control of Dental Carries")
3. (Price, 1939, "Prenatal Nutritional Deformities and Disease Types")
4. (Price, 1939, "The Progressive Decline of Modern Civilization")
5. (Price, 1939, "The Progressive Decline of Modern Civilization")
6. (Price, 1939, "Physical, Mental, and Moral Degeneration")
7. (Price, 1939, "Why Seek Wisdom from Primitive Races")
8. (Price, 1939, "Isolated and Modernized New Zealand Maori")
9. (Price, 1939, "Isolated and Modernized Australian Aborigines")
10. (Price, 1939, "Isolated and Modernized New Zealand Maori")
11. (Price, 1939, "Isolated and Modernized Australian Aborigines")
12. (Price, 1939, "Physical, Mental, and Moral Degeneration")
13. (Price, 1939, "The Progressive Decline of Modern Civilization")
14. (Price, 1939, "One Origin of Physical Deformities")
15. (Price, 1939, "Isolated and Modernized Polynesians")
16. (Price, 1939, "One Origin of Physical Deformities")
17. (Price, 1939, "Characteristics of Primitive and Modern Dietaries")
18. (Price, 1939, "Physical, Mental, and Moral Degeneration")
19. (Price, 1939, "Physical, Mental, and Moral Degeneration")
20. (Price, 1939, "Practical Applications of Primitive Wisdom")
21. (Zinn, 2021, "Columbus, the Indians, and Human Progress")
22. (Price, 1939, "Isolated and Modernized New Zealand Maori")
23. (Price, 1939, "Prenatal Nutritional Deformities and Disease Types")
24. (Price, 1939, "One Origin of Physical Deformities")
25. (Price, 1939, "Physical, Mental, and Moral Degeneration")
26. (Price, 1939, "One Origin of Physical Deformities")
27. (Price, 1939, "Prenatal Nutritional Deformities and Disease Types")
28. (Genesis 3:16, English Standard Version Bible)
29. (Price, 1939, "Physical, Mental, and Moral Degeneration")
30. (Price, 1939, "Characteristics of Primitive and Modern Dietaries")
31. (Nestor, 2020, "Chew")
32. (Price, 1939, "Characteristics of Primitive and Modern Dietaries")
33. (Price, 1939, "Physical, Mental, and Moral Degeneration")
34. (Price, 1939, "Introduction")
35. (Nestor, 2020, "Chew")
36. (Nestor, 2020, "Nose")
37. (Price, 1939, "Practical Applications of Primitive Wisdom")
38. (Price, 1939, "Practical Applications of Primitive Wisdom")
39. (Arnarson, 2017)
40. (Price, 1939, "Soil Depletion and Plant and Animal Deterioration")
41. (Gaikwad et al., 2020)
42. (Karagas et al., 2019)
43. (Pelc, 2022)

Chapter 46: Embracing the Sacred Feminine
1. (Johnstone, 2023)
2. (Friedman, 2024)
3. (Quarshie & Et al, 2020)
4. (Purkiss & Serle, 2017)
5. (Auble, 2021)
6. (Lockheed Martin Board Elects James D. Taiclet as Chairman; Marillyn A. Hewson to Serve as Strategic Advisor and Gregory M. Ulmer as Executive Vice President of Aeronautics, 2021)
7. (Rebecca Liebert, n.d.)
8. (Jackson, 2022)
9. (Job Stress? It Could Strain Your Heart, 2012)
10. (Laybourn, 2022)
11. (National AIDS Memorial, 2017)

Chapter 47: Embracing the Sacred Masculine
1. (Carland, 2017, "Journey to the Fight")
2. (Abbas, 2020)
3. (Cox, 2021)
4. (Federici, 2004, "Acknowledgements")
5. (Wood, 1936, 336)
6. (Grinnell, 2005, "Lessons of the Prairie")
7. (Barrett, 2010, "Preparation of a Warrior")
8. (Eastman (Ohiyesa), 1916, "The Way Opens")
9. (Thoreau, 2021, "Economy")
10. (Gibson, n.d.)
11. (Linderman, 1932, 22)
12. (Neihardt, 2014, "Walking the Black Road")
13. (Neihardt, 2014, "Footnotes")
14. (Linderman, 1932, 202)
15. (Linderman, 1932, 230)
16. (Brown, 2012, "The War for the Black Hills")
17. (Eastman (Ohiyesa), 2013, "Rain-In-The-Face")
18. (Grinnell, 2005, "The Attack on the Camp")
19. (Neihardt, 2014, "The Rubbing Out of Long Hair")
20. (Neihardt, 2014, "Early Boyhood")
21. (Neihardt, 2014, "The Rubbing Out of Long Hair")
22. (Neihardt, 2014, "The Bison Hunt")

23. (Ballantine & Ballantine, 2001, 156)
25. (Trigger, 1969, 26)
27. (Linderman, 1932, 251)
29. (Prechtel, 1999, 20)
31. (Prisoners of Conscious in the USSR: Their Treatment and Conditions, 1975, 99)
33. (Porter, 2014)
35. (Prechtel, 1999, 200)
37. (Bradford, 2020)

24. (Grinnell, 2005, "Lessons of the Prairie")
26. (Jackson, 2016, "Black Robe Days")
28. (Eastman (Ohiyesa), 2013, "Rain-In-The-Face")
30. (Seale, 1970, 3)
32. (Neihardt, 2014, "The Powers of the Bison and Elk")
34. (Gurney, 2013, "Winstanley the Digger")
36. (Loewen, 2007, 108)
38. (Mark 12:17, King James Version Bible)

Chapter 48: Bravery and Cowardice

1. (Johnson, 2023)
3. (Eastman (Ohiyesa), 2016)
5. (Eastman (Ohiyesa), 2013, "Crazy Horse")
7. (Liedloff, 2004, "The Beginning of Life")
9. (Prechtel, 1999, 18)
11. (Eastman (Ohiyesa), 2013, "Crazy Horse")
13. (Ronca, n.d.)
15. (Brown Jr, 1978, 102)
17. (Nabokov, 1987, 139)
19. (Poirier-Leroy, n.d.)
21. (Nelson, 2008, "Listening to the Natural Law")
23. (Neihardt, 2014, "The End of the Dream")
25. (N. Basket, personal communication, August 5, 2023)
27. (Haitian Revolution, n.d.)

2. (Valentin, 2021)
4. (Nam-Sonenstein, 2018)
6. (Assange, 2007)
8. (Eastman (Ohiyesa), 2013, "Little Crow")
10. (Matthew 4:1-11, King James Version Bible)
12. (Eastman (Ohiyesa), 2008, "Hakadah's First Offering")
14. (Holland, 2020)
16. (Linderman, 1932, 84)
18. (Nabokov, 1987, 138)
20. (Chambliss, 1989)
22. (Brown Jr, 1978, 149)
24. (Neihardt, 2014, "Across the Big Water")
26. (Richardson, 1992, 166)

Chapter 49: What to Keep and What to Let Go

1. (Trigger, 1969, 45)
3. (Marcos, 1994)
5. (Marcos, 1994)
7. (Kenyon, 2020)

2. (kswheeler, 2011)
4. (N. Basket, personal communication, July 25, 2024)
6. ("Interview with Mayor Ana María (Google Translate, Trans.)," 1995)
8. (Grinnell, 2005, "My Marriage")

Chapter 50: What Can I Do?

1. (Nelson, 2008, "Ethiopian Women: From Passive Resources to Active Citizens")
3. (Vice News, 2014)
5. (Neihardt, 2014, "Appendix 3: Drawings by Standing Bear")
7. ("Ninth Part: The New Structure of Zapastista Autonomy (Google Translate, Trans.)," 2023)
9. (Mike Tyson Explains One of His Most Famous Quotes, 2021)

2. (Cox, 2019, "Just Another Nigger")
4. (Eastman (Ohiyesa), 1916, "The Way Opens")
6. (Nelson, 2008, "First Nations Survival and the Future of the Earth")
8. (Vandergriff, 2013, 10)
10. (Kimmerer, 2013, "The Three Sisters")

Chapter 51: We Are the Promised Land

1. (King Jr, 1968)

Appendix 1: Acknowledging Contradictions

1. (Cameron, 1981, 11)
3. (Prechtel, 1999, 111)
5. (Notes, 2005, "The Haudenosaunee: A Nation Since Time Immemorial")
7. (Barrett, 2010, "The Family")
9. (Slave (n. & Adj.), Etymology, 2024)
11. (Prechtel, 1999, 210)
13. (Neihardt, 2014, "Footnotes")
15. (Linderman, 1932, 44)
17. (Linderman, 1932, 173)
19. (Male Circumcision: Global Trends and Determinants of Prevalance, Safety, and Acceptability, 2007, 4)
21. (Cameron, 1981, 58)
23. (Notes, 2005, 10)

2. (Linderman, 1932, 44)
4. (Nelson, 2008, "Definition of Indigenous Knowledge")
6. (Neihardt, 2014, "High Horse's Courting")
8. (About the Book - Wolf Totem: A Novel, n.d.)
10. (Mohamud, 2019)
12. (Prechtel, 1999, 260)
14. (Neihardt, 2014, "High Horse's Courting")
16. (Eastman (Ohiyesa), 2013, "Sitting Bull")
18. (Grinnell, 1972, 198)
20. (Cameron, 1981, 121)
22. (N. Basket, personal communication, August 5, 2023)

Image Credits

1. (U.S. Congressional Budget Office, 2024)
3. (Western & Orrell, 2020)
5. (Western & Orrell, 2020)
7. (Cubillos, 2018)
9. (Sloan, 2020)
11. (Price, 1939)

2. (We Will Annihilate Kulaks as a Class / Kukryniksy., 1930)
4. (The Growth of Incarceration in the United States: Exploring Causes and Consequences (2014), 2014, 61)
6. (Bronnikov, 1878)
8. (Hoshiko, 2012)
10. (Prescott, 1976, 435)

Bibliography, Copyright, and Further Reading

To reduce printing and shipping costs, the physical edition of this book does not contain the bibliography. The full bibliography is available in the free epub and pdf versions of this book, available at https://thedeepestrevolution.com

Copyright

One Disease One Cure: Ending Our Multi-Millennia Catastrophe. Copyright 2025 William Randolph

This book is copyrighted under the Creative Commons CC BY-NC-ND 4.0 license. Readers may copy and redistribute the material in any medium or format. To view a copy of this license, visit https://creativecommons.org/licenses/by-nc-nd/4.0/

I want the messages of this book to reach as many people as possible, so if you want to use material from this book in a way not supported by the license, whether commercially or non-commercially, please contact me through the book's website: https://thedeepestrevolution.com/contact/

The physical book contains black and white versions of all images. The digital version contains the original color images.

Nothing in this book is intended to substitute for personalized advice from trusted practitioners in health, nutrition, law, or any other field.

Physical Book ISBN: 979-8-9920652-0-6

Further Reading

For a concrete, practical path to building new healthy communities and healthy nations, based on the stories of people who have done this before, see my second book *The Deepest Revolution* at https://thedeepestrevolution.com. It is less than 200 pages and 6"x9". The ebook is available for free or donation, and a physical version is available as well.

Praise for *The Deepest Revolution:*

"This was really intriguing, really powerful and inspiring. It's going to change the way a lot of people think. It gives them actionable things that they can do to change their daily life, which people are craving right now. I think it's awesome. – Nina R

"Very hard-hitting... This is poignant. It's beautiful." – Chris W.

"I've always wanted to believe that reform could solve our problems but this book makes it clear that a fundamental reset is needed." – Bob B

Index

AIDS 97, 384, 491

Abundance begets abundance 116

Abuse
... begets abuse: 116, 242
... consenting to: (see coercive consent)
... multigenerational abusive relationships: 133, 201
... child: (see child abuse)
... ignoring or justifying: 29, 53-67, 204-206, 294, 344

Accept responsibility 529

Accountability
... lack of in unhealthy nations: 37-40, 48-51
... present in healthy nations: 35-37, 46-48
... and using hate campaigns to avoid: 211

Adopting authoritarian attitudes 120, 166, 198-209, 433-447

Allende, Salvador 306, 405

Antidepressants
... and depression: 173-177
... and gun violence: 387-389

Arbenz, Jacobo 405

Arendt, Hannah 168, 446

Armstrong, Jeannette 5, 21, 25, 90, 109, 532

Assange, Julian 1, 370, 507, 512

Attakullakulla 233

Avoiding history's deepest lessons 220-223, 329-331

Awareness
... of nonhumans: 21-24, 90, 182, 454-456
... good contact, poor contact: 448-459
... practices: (see kamana)
... teaching children: 68-74, 454-456

Banality of evil 169

Basket, Nancy 1, 23, 25, 36, 46, 86, 234, 455, 514, 518

Bear Bull 36

Become Comfortable with Uncertainty 530

Being part of nature 90

Bettelheim, Bruce 163, 198-201, 204, 280, 368

Bhutan 26, 315

Biesele, Megan 36

Black Elk 1, 4, 14, 82, 92, 201, 355, 358, 425, 431, 464, 495, 497, 501, 504, 513, 537, 540

Black Panthers 93, 160, 229, 379, 490, 500, 523

Blind belief 166, 345, 408
... in China: 57, 65
... in Russia: 58, 65
... in the United States: 55, 59-64, 213-216, 225
... in the Soviet Union: 56, 65, 216-218, 225
... in Christianity: 54, 75-84
... in Islam: 54, 79-84
... in Judaism: 54, 79-84
... in Nazi Germany: 216-218, 225
... and going through the motions: 292-298
... forming in real time: 63
... and hate campaigns: 225
... in the legal system: 398
... in the face of severe abuse: 406

Bolivia 3, 14, 24

Boundaries 71, 129-131, 322-327

Bravery
... nature of: 505
... and its opposite, cowardice: 506
... training: 507-514
... benefits: 510
... and healthy relationship with death: 513
... need for: 514
... and faith: (see faith)
... and spiritual leaders: 425-432

Breathing 107, 258, 448, 456, 465, 477, 481-483

Bronislaw Malinowski 221, 249, 257

Brown Jr, Tom 1, 20, 351, 455, 510, 513

Build abundance to share it 91

Bullshit 174, 178, 299, 504

CONAIE 228

Capitalism 95, 172, 193, 270, 278, 330, 345, 347, 371, 516, 523

Cartwright, Samuel 55

Caste System 191, 273

Catholic Church
... mysogeny: 39, 237, 254, 256
... scams: 55, 105, 170, 178
... oppression: 124, 255
... rampant, centuries-long, worldwide child abuse: 201-204, 396, 404
... Nootka first encounter with: 404
... boarding schools: 201-204, 455
... Malleus Maleficarum: 170, 237, 254

Censorship 57, 59, 61, 145, 211, 216, 219, 369, 412, 417

Child abuse
... as part of subjugation: 201
... as way to normalize abusive nation: 202
... lacking in healthy nations: 404
... impact on politics: 440
... lack of loving touch: 433-441
... training people to reject healing: 440
... lessons for prisons: 441
... and coercive schooling: 441
... and monsters: 445
... watching a child's heart close: 465-468

Children
... everyone's responsibility: 180
... child abuse: (see child abuse)
... sexism against: (see sexism)
... Raising powerful: 16, 68-74, 245-247, 442-445, 452-456, 461-470

China 3, 8, 10, 31, 37, 50, 56-58, 84, 106, 125, 191, 222, 227, 240, 242, 245, 248, 253, 269, 278, 294, 308, 313, 356, 415, 429, 502, 506

Christ, Jesus 1, 39, 48, 75-78, 84, 92, 108, 122, 141, 169, 171, 221, 253, 266, 270, 292-294, 319, 341, 365, 411, 425-431, 433, 469, 493, 502, 504, 508, 529, 532, 535

Christianity 10, 21, 24, 33, 37, 54, 66, 75, 78-80, 83, 91, 123, 138, 141, 152, 157, 159, 163, 171, 179, 197, 201, 206, 215, 220-223, 237, 239, 248, 251, 253-256, 292-294, 314-316, 344, 347, 385, 437, 441, 473, 480, 519, 523, 535, 539

Class (see privilege)

Coercive consent 97, 108, 112

Collective self defense 32, 42, 162, 180, 230, 269, 354, 526

Columbus, Christopher 81, 106, 111, 122-124, 222, 490

Communism 57, 95, 278, 516

Comparison of results of anti-sexism and anti-racism movements 489, 531

Concentration camps
... compared to normal life in unhealthy nations: 199-201
... and racism towards inmates: 205
... to compel obedience of people outside the camps: 105
... train people to close their hearts: 163, 198-201, 204
... and lift-and-turn privilege: 263
... and middle-class privilege: 280

Contact (see awareness)

Controllable world 126, 134, 135-150

Cortés, Hernán 111

Covid vaccine 59-61, 65, 415

Cox, Don 93, 158, 229, 270, 414, 523

Crazy Horse 91, 495, 505, 508, 512

Cultural appropriation 517

Culture jamming
... caricaturing thoughtful people: 383
... love it or leave it: 384
... victim-shaming: 385-387
... creating controversies that ignore deep problems: 387-396

Custer, George Armstrong 497

Cycles of "normality" and protest 204

De Las Casas, Bartolome 123

DeChristopher, Tim 39, 341

Debt
... market: 104, 106, 112, 271, 421
... command: 99, 111, 190, 421
... unforced: 112
... forced: 111

Dependency
... on profit economy: 97, 111
... on gift economy: 110
... on uncaring people: 127, 262
... on the Earth and caring people: 128
... on money: 94-108, 135-137
... on law: 137-142
... on corporate or government-provided water: 149
... on corporate or government-provided food: 127, 142-149

Disconnection from nature 107, 133

Divinity 25, 93, 155, 158-160, 163, 166, 169, 178, 196, 205, 220, 294, 347, 458, 465, 504, 511

Dominance display 31, 77, 427-429, 432

Drapetomania 55

Dream Big and Take Risks 529

Drug laws
... unequal sentencing: 191
... as form of persecution: 338
... in policing: 338-342

Dystopia 94

Earth skills 526

Economy
... gift: 15-19, 86-93, 109-113, 115, 179-187, 405
... profit: 94-108, 405
... market: 96-106
... command: 96, 106
... incompatibility of sharing and selfishness: 109-114, 405

Ecuador 10, 14, 149, 228, 370, 395

Egypt 10, 30, 84, 108, 131, 255, 346

Eichmann, Adolf 168, 446

Elections
... as illegitimate ways for some to impose law on others: 205
... well-managed: 306

Embracing the responsibilities of living in healthy nation 51, 62, 226

En'owkinwiwx

Enclosure (see land)

Engels, Friedrich 329

Enjoy life 44, 121, 440, 459, 504, 512

Entitlement
... high-privilege and low-privilege entitlement: 313
... and spiritual leaders' efforts to end it: 313-318

Ethiopia 255, 523

Evil 13-18, 47, 51, 54, 58, 85, 97, 108, 110, 113, 115, 122, 139, 145-147, 165, 168-172, 178, 205, 221, 231, 233, 236, 246-248, 251-254, 256, 258, 269, 283, 289, 317, 344, 347, 353, 356, 411, 415, 422, 426, 437, 441, 444, 458, 464, 494-496, 498, 500, 540

Externality 114

Faith 151-155, 185, 510

Fasting in the wilderness to cultivate strength 426, 508

Fearing the urge, feeling, or perception
... and heart closure: 164
... and training people for authoritarian ideologies: 198-209
... and rejection of pleasure and connection: 433-440
... as cause of many men's hurtful behavior towards women: 493, 500-502

Feel the dissatisfaction 226, 458, 525

Feelings
... appropriate vs inappropriate: 166, 210, 453

Felicie, Jacoba 39

Feminity
... and balanced leadership: 232
... and faux freedom: 488
... and manipulation and shaming by patriarchal religious authorities: 235
... and equal respect for different gifts: 242, 498

Fernandez de Oviedo y Valdes, Gonzalo 221

Financial desperation 7, 94-105, 107, 109-112, 116, 173, 361, 470, 521

Financial whipsaw 100, 108

Find love by giving love 468

Forgetting 3, 5, 179, 313-318, 418

France 3, 26, 37, 39, 115, 157, 163, 189, 192, 206, 239, 248, 254, 264-266, 287, 290, 329, 331, 338, 344, 349, 356, 359, 385, 396, 402, 514, 523, 540

Freedom
... authoritarian views of: 205-208
... how much do people desire freedom?: 520
... scams: (see scams)
... training people not to notice or understand free societies: 220
... faux freedom: 488

Garden of Eden 75, 79, 83, 239, 480, 535

Generosity
... among the Ashaninka: 14-19
... among the Arawaks: 122
... economies that reward generosity: 86-93
... as prerequisuite for Haudenosaunee leadership position: 327
... Jesus Christ's generosity seems normal to men of healthy nations: 78
... and indian givers: 89
... cascading generosity: 109-117, 185
... in healthy communities, mutual aid societies: 115

Genital mutilation 255

Germany 10, 30, 67, 98, 105, 168, 175, 198-201, 211-213, 216-218, 227, 242, 263, 280, 283, 290, 348, 368, 372, 375, 382, 396, 402, 408, 410-412

Geronimo 42, 66, 83, 162, 230, 251, 443, 492, 500, 512, 537

Gilbert Walking Bull 1, 20, 455

Ginés de Sepúlveda, Juan 221

Going through the motions (see privilege)

Golden rule of healthy nations 34, 37

Good governance requires a solid foundation 516

Governance
... self-governance only works when everyone stands for a culture of mutual respect: 516
... Zapatista self-governance: 422
... Haudenosaunee self-governance: 322-328

Green, Sam 153

Grigoryev, Grigory Ivanovich 283

Guerilla gardening
... history of: 365
... how to: 366

Hampton, Fred 379

Harney, William 36, 443

Hatred
... appropriate and inappropriate: 210
... synthetic hate campaigns (propaganda that generates hate): 211-217
... scapegoating, to avoid accountability: 211
... to prevent solidarity: 213
... prisons as hate factories: 441
... to motivate support for war: 216
... dehumanizing: 216
... towards patriots, peace activists, and truth-tellers: 218
... towards healthy nations: 220
... forced hatred with blind beliefs:
... sources of abusers' hate: 224

Healthy nations (see nations)

Heart-closing cultural narratives 170-178, 384-386

Heart-closure 121, 155-158, 163, 166, 169, 172, 178, 203, 225, 251, 255, 258, 293, 319, 344, 384-386, 433, 438, 445, 465, 468, 484, 543

Heart-openness 121, 155-161, 163, 166, 169, 181, 187, 204, 225, 283, 344, 367, 432-434, 455, 458, 465, 468, 509, 511, 518, 533, 543

Ignoring the first strike 222

India 10, 30, 37, 108, 127, 135, 180, 182, 191, 238, 242, 281, 365, 519

Indian giver 87

Ingwe 1, 20, 37, 72, 80, 139, 162, 199, 207, 235, 259, 269, 282, 289, 346, 353, 387, 400, 409, 422, 431, 435, 463, 482, 486, 508, 510, 529

Innocence 65, 146, 211, 225, 255, 267, 294, 416, 465, 505

Instead of fighting symptoms, address the root disease together 531

Integrity
... and the three integrities: 282-291
... of service: 282
... examples in healthy nations: 19, 66, 283, 288, 495
... and the three core spiritual practices: 283
... of word (honesty): 284
... of action (promise-keeping): 284
... return to integrity: 284, 287
... and shared responsibility for understanding reality (avoid assumptions): 285, 463
... and boundaries: 285-287, 322-328
... and conflict resolution: 288
... especially when it's scary: 289-291
... deliberately maintaining a culture of low integrity to corrupt people: 331-338

Islam 5, 10, 25, 54, 75, 79, 84, 171, 220, 252, 256, 294, 313, 315-317, 401, 492, 519, 535, 539

Isolation 30, 48, 50, 96, 107, 170, 175, 193, 202, 225, 227, 235, 265, 268, 278, 302, 333, 371, 377, 433-435, 440, 449, 452, 457, 469, 483-485, 487, 494, 512, 533

Jacobs, Harriet 164, 224

Judge behavior, not the person 43, 160, 181, 268

Kafala System 190

Kamana 20-23, 194-197, 353, 450, 456

Kapos 263-265

Kimmerer, Robin 1, 21, 24, 36, 88, 94, 113, 185, 196, 351, 360, 460, 534

King Jr, Martin Luther 1, 46, 159, 169, 425, 429-431, 493, 502, 504, 512, 532, 535

Kolchak, A. V. 168

Land
... benefits of avoiding land ownership: 352-354
... concerns about no land ownership: 355
... enclosure - individual ownership: 356
... enclosure - collective ownership: 357
... enclosure - enclosing healthy nations: 358-361
... land ownership is sacrilege: 364

Law
... manipulative/abusive: 29-32, 37-41
... terrible even if perfectly enforced: 40
... and systemic discrimination: (see sexism, hatred, racism)
... vs shared agreements: 29
... learned from nature: 35

Leadership
... balanced: 233
... take everyone's needs into account: 502
... without coercion: 502
... untrustworthy leadership in a disaster in an unhealthy nation: 61

Learning from nonhumans 21, 132, 186, 194-196, 294, 363, 439, 472

Lee, Bobby 379

Liedloff, Jean 1, 131, 438, 444, 507, 539

Lift-and-turn (see privilege)

Linderman, Frank 80

Love
... withholding: 93, 163-168, 178, 201, 251, 257, 424-430, 433-447, 460-470, 495, 521
... giving fully: 92, 161, 169, 204, 251, 258, 310, 312, 432, 469, 509, 514, 535
... same as giving one's deepest gifts: 23
... and divinity: 93, 158, 166, 178, 457
... scared into withholding love as adults: 425-431
... training children to withhold love: 433-447, 460-470
... experience love by giving love: 468
... family troubles when people learn to withhold love: 460-470
... and innocence: 465

Malcolm X 1, 127, 316, 415, 431, 500, 504

Malleus Maleficarum 170, 237, 254

Manning, Chelsea 1, 370, 512

Mantell, David 1, 198, 318, 435

Manufacturing Consent 408

Marx, Karl 329

Masculinity
... and common sexual confusion: 256
... and common spiritual confusion: 492-495
... healthy masculinity forbidden, toxic masculinity encouraged: 492-495
... setting good boundaries and earning womens' trust: 495-498
... men transitioning into unhealthy nations and becoming lost: 498-500
... words to men: 503

McDonald, Mike 35

Mental health 54-58, 173-177, 337

Missionaries 26, 37, 66, 78, 91, 157, 163, 172, 179, 206, 234, 237, 239, 248, 287, 292, 355, 360, 407, 441, 542

Mutual aid 115, 180, 262, 521

Nabokov, Peter 161

Nation
... defining differences of healthy vs unhealthy nations: 27, 41, 44
... and boundaries: 42-44, 285, 322
... military: 42
... and healthy community: 37, 108, 116, 186, 287, 491, 502, 507, 525, 533
... creating healthy nations: 41, 524
... unhealthy nations as a bus: 208, 488
... formation of unhealthy nations: 519
... and economies that reward generosity or selfishness: (see economy)

Nature connection practices 71-74
... with children: 71-74
... and cultural unity: 194-197
... and deep empathy: 194-197
... take the Earth's needs into account: 90
... see also Kamana

Nepal 242

No system of government will save people from themselves 516

North Korea 278

Nutrition 471-482
... and nonhumans: 472
... and cavities: 474-477
... and childbirth: 479
... mental and social effects: 480
... and fragility and healing: 481

Ohiyesa 1, 3, 36, 44, 65, 78, 81, 83, 86, 90, 93, 109, 128, 132, 249, 265, 309, 349, 352, 358, 408, 442, 456, 464, 492, 504, 508, 524, 538, 541

Partible paternity 245

Peru 10, 14, 18, 66, 92, 295, 335, 505, 510

Plea bargain 7, 225, 274, 295, 376

Pleasure
... anti-pleasure propaganda: 254-256
... denial in children: 433-441
... changes when people feel pleasure and connection again: 258
... a normal part of child-rearing among Yequana: 438

Politics
... effects of deprivation on: 439, 485
... effects of child abuse on: 439
... of selfish leaders in gift economy and generous leaders in profit economy: 405
... instability of sharing and selfishness in: 109-113, 405
... that ignore the important issues: 382-395

Pontiac's Rebellion

Possessions 17, 66, 76-79, 88, 90-93, 108, 111, 292, 330, 358, 443, 492, 508

Prayer
... submissive posture, with closed senses, to an abstract god: 196
... compared with Haudenosaunee Thanksgiving Address: 196

Prechtel, Martín 1, 78, 92, 161, 179, 233, 355, 445, 458, 463, 499, 503, 508, 537, 540

Predation at a large scale
... authorities sexually abusing children: 397-399
... treasonous rulers: 399-403
... nobody is safe: 403
... Who are the rulers? Can we tell?: 404

Pregnancy 38, 123, 142, 245, 248, 256, 296, 380, 390, 479, 484, 487, 494

Pretty Shield 1, 5, 80-82, 84, 234, 288, 349, 352, 495, 499, 503, 510, 537, 541

Price, Weston 1, 37, 473, 479-482, 485-487

Prisons
... and pretending inmates deserve to be there: 294
... as hate factories: 210, 441
... unneeded in healthy nations: 157, 441, 473
... and sexual abuse: 240-242
... slavery: (see slavery)
... low trial rate in USA: 225, 294
... and nutritional deficiencies: 480
... blind beliefs and: 225, 294
... resistence efforts: 229, 506

Private property 87, 324, 327, 329, 360, 517

Privilege
... lift-and-turn: 262-269
... solidarity despite: 266-269, 310
... privilege-responsibility tradeoff: 264, 336, 341, 490
... rise-and-turn: 269
... and cowardice and selfishness: 269
... and class: 270-281
... and promise-keeping: 270-281
... and the middle class: 271-281
... and entitlement that makes superficially makes sense: 277
... and luck and skill: 281
... and going through the motions: 292-309, 341, 357
... and deep confusion: 309
... police have high-privilege: 338
... deliberate adjustments in Colonial Virginia: 137-142

Propaganda
... and divine support for rulers: 344
... and wishful thinking: 345-348
... and false narratives of progress: 348
... encouraging assumptions and modeling the conversation: 409
... feel good cover stories: 410
... big lie and selective reporting: 411
... defeaning silence: 412
... power of propaganda: normalizing inappropriate behavior: 413
... successfully dealing with: 414-417
... see also pleasure, culture jamming, hatred, blind beliefs, racism, sexism, privilege

Quakers 69, 154
Racism
... covert: 191
... overt: 190
... see also Three core drivers of deep division, racism, sexism, class, privilege, hate
Rainbow gathering 179-187, 379, 529
Receive the gifts of the Earth 527
Red Cloud 36, 44, 83, 111, 358, 499
Reich, Wilhelm 1, 173, 250, 256, 504
Releasing false beliefs and confronting the truth 278, 524
Remembering 12-27, 120, 179-187, 457, 465, 513
Return to integrity (see integrity)
Revolution
... different ruler, same problems: 78, 125, 347
... and getting rid of rulers: 161, 418-423
... and Jesus Christ as revolutionary: 76-80, 292, 426
... and destroying debt records: 112
... as act of dignity and self-respect: 312
... backed by authorities or wealthy people: 340, 345, 347
... Algerian: 385
... Pueblo: 161
... how to build towards: 490
... Haitian: 224, 514
Russia 3, 5, 10, 24, 31, 37, 50, 58, 63, 65, 97, 106, 108, 148, 168, 199, 212, 216, 218, 227, 237, 241, 264, 273, 306, 310, 347, 356, 371, 373, 377, 382, 398-401, 403, 406, 411, 415, 530
Sabotaging Social Movements
... arresting activists: 369
... reputation sabotage, blackmail, sexual shaming: 370
... infiltration and subversion: 372, 381
... astroturf social movements: 374-380
... murder: 380
Sacred Circle 227-232, 374, 386, 389, 394, 410, 417, 518, 524, 532

Saint Augustine 254, 437
Scams
... profit economies: 9, 95, 105, 412
... racism: 142, 193
... turning public against patriotic peace activists and truth-tellers: 218
... sexism: 243
... hate campaigns: 227
... heart-closing cultural narratives: 170-178
... to avoid healthy nations: 220
... general: 83
... prisons: 441
... laughing at: 178, 227
... police participation in: 334
... culture jamming: 382-395
... war on drugs: 338-342
... pretending people are free when they're not: 54
... pretending revolutionaries are bandits: 78
... training people to misunderstand freedom: 207
School
... assuming coercive school is appropriate: 177
... coercive vs non-coercive: 441
... nature connection: 68-74
Sekaquaptewa, Wayne 83
Selfishness
... cascading: 109-113
... doesn't mix with generosity: 109, 405
... specifically avoided in healthy nations: 37, 43, 269
... trained through child abuse, among other ways: 433-447, 461-463, 465-468
... symptom of root cultural disease: 27
... systemic: 94-108
... unproductive violence and: 36
... even fair laws would be inadequate when people behave with selfishness: 40
... property rights not needed when selfishness is avoided: 41, 355
...energetic boundaries that block selfishness: 42
... and private property 'rights': 88
... opposite of: 89

Selfishness (con't)
... train bravery to avoid selfishness: 91
... unnatural behavior and: 90
... and how to relate to possessions: 93
... and corruption are the same thing: 292
... can motivate selfishness in others if not addressed: 94
... are people basically social or selfish: 157, 170
... what people call evil: 169
... boys supposedly inherently selfish: 242
... and disturbed sexual behavior: 257
... solidarity even when tempted by: 266
... violence without: 268
... opposite of integrity of service: 289
... going through the motions when people are trained for selfishness: 292-310
... and high-privilege entitlement: 313
... and inability to recognize gift economies: 328
... hope as false antidote to: 347
... avoiding after a revolution: 421, 531
... and poor contact: 469
... and deprivation: 471
... and faux freedom that stems from: 488
... deep training for: 502
... when afraid: 507
... antidote to: 512

Serfdom 111, 115, 172, 191, 313, 356

Settee, Priscilla 35, 537

Sex
... economy: 251
... sexual freedom: 245-248
... sexual sharing: 247
... sexual repression: 252-260, 440
... masculine sexual confusion: 256, 500-502

Sexism
... against women: 235-239, 252-255, 488
... against men: 239-242, 256
... against children: 242
... systemic: 259
... end of: 491

Single inhibition 164, 199, 204, 269, 318

Sitting Bull 3, 6, 79, 81, 201, 354, 363, 517, 541

Slavery
... military: 7, 98, 207
... prison: 7, 98, 298-302, 376-378, 489
... wage: 7, 98
... chattel: 6, 7, 56, 98, 106, 137-142, 151-156, 300-302, 344, 376, 489
... coerced labor: 7, 207, 377

Snowden, Edward 1, 30

Social class (see privilege)

Socialism 95, 147, 345, 374, 516

Solidarity
... with the land: 24, 83
... with integrity of service: 282-284
... with other people: 25, 32, 35, 51, 62, 151-155, 159, 226-235, 266-280, 283-291, 310, 324-326, 338, 418-423
... with Earth means being in solidarity with God: 25, 197
... seeing as a threat; preventing or forbidding: 29-32, 115, 120, 137-142, 163, 165, 189-194, 198, 211-225, 235-243, 262-266, 270-281, 368-395, 425-447
... and golden rule of healthy nations: 33, 37
... laws to prevent: 29
... definition of: 89
... especially when difficult: 158
... trained by three core spiritual practices: 170
... humans struggle growing up without: 173

Solzhenitsyn, Aleksandr 106, 266, 283

South Korea 242

Soviet Union 29, 31, 56-58, 63-66, 98, 106, 127, 142-148, 170, 193, 202, 205, 216, 225, 227, 265-267, 272, 283, 287, 298, 312, 328-330, 345, 347, 350, 369, 382, 395, 402, 407, 413, 500, 518

Spain 3, 14, 17, 80, 111, 122-124, 128, 161, 166, 221, 228, 270, 354, 383, 390, 404, 418, 420, 422, 433, 436, 447, 459, 490, 540

Spiritual leaders
... anyone can be a spiritual leader, and the more the merrier: 161, 535
... walk meaningful paths: 169
... raise people's self-worth and dignity: 313-318
... welcomed in healthy nations: 327, 425, 431
... targeted for opposing oppression in unhealthy nations: 425-432
... messiah, liberator, savior mean the same thing: saving people from oppression: 75, 431
... deepest lessons can be ignored by followers in abusive nations: 294, 425
... deepest lessons from: 431
... shamans, real and fake: 92

Spirituality
... Three Core Spiritual Practices: 20-24, 90, 113, 170, 197, 208, 283, 446, 456, 525
... What makes a practice sacred or sacriligious: 231
... as how a person relates to the world: 446, 471
... and impact of physical deprivation: 471
... and living life as a gift: 161-163

Spreading abundance 86-93, 234

Stalking Wolf 20, 351, 455, 513

Stop Cop City 380

Story of the Peacemaker 320-323

Strong followers encourage strong leaders 463

Strong leaders and no rulers 17, 19, 27, 37, 43, 78, 84, 125, 193, 198, 292, 328-330, 463, 535

Swamp, Jake 1, 20

Switzerland 26, 302

Symptoms of the root cultural disease 27, 107, 531

Taiwan 26

Talawema 161

Ten Fingers, Tony 20, 22, 456

Theodosius 220, 293, 347

Three core drivers of deep division 190, 225, 259

Three integrities (see integrity)

Tibetan Buddhism 25, 112, 171, 236, 315, 396, 404

Tragedy of the Commons 172

Triple inhibition 164-167, 199, 203, 223, 269, 318, 338, 449, 457

True Americanism study 435-447, 470

Tubman, Harriet 1, 93, 151, 155, 159, 164, 169, 310, 319, 433, 459, 504, 511, 529, 535

Uncle Tom's Cabin

Unhealthy nations (see nations)

United Kingdom 4, 14, 25, 30, 36, 59, 86, 104, 127, 137, 166, 191, 205, 217, 221-223, 228, 236, 240, 256, 260, 270, 272, 302, 306, 319, 328, 344, 347, 349, 355, 358, 361, 365, 370, 386, 397, 402, 473, 490, 492, 538, 540

United States 3, 6-10, 14-18, 20, 26, 30-32, 37-39, 49-51, 55-57, 59-64, 66, 74-83, 87, 89, 91, 97, 99, 102, 105, 108, 111, 117, 119, 121-123, 126, 133, 135, 139, 141-143, 146, 151, 157, 160, 163, 169-175, 177-179, 187, 191-194, 197, 202, 206, 210, 212-214, 217-221, 223, 225, 231, 236-242, 248, 255, 260, 265, 268, 270, 273, 278, 285, 290, 292, 294-297, 299-303, 306-308, 310, 314-316, 319-321, 325, 328-341, 344, 347-350, 355, 358-360, 363, 370-372, 374-376, 378, 383-393, 395, 397-399, 401, 407, 410-412, 416, 419, 425, 427, 429, 431, 436, 441, 445, 450, 452, 458, 461, 473, 478, 480, 483, 486, 488, 496, 505-507, 510, 512, 514, 518, 520, 522-524, 527-529, 532, 538-540

Universal sacred urges 53, 115, 157, 163, 166, 168, 199, 203, 224, 231, 284, 338, 342, 458, 534

Utopia 86, 92, 94, 200, 325

Vietnam 39, 159, 266, 383, 391, 430, 435, 437, 440

War
... and authoritarian and non-authoritarian militaries: 42
... and financial desperation: (see financial desperation)
... in self-defense, from a place of awareness: 230
... and responsibility of civilians: 361
... and avoiding conquering others even after winning the war: 327
... and being satisfied with enough, vs constantly taking more than necessary: 360
... and the root cause of endless violence: 362

War on Drugs 338-341

We are the promised land 536

Webb, Gary 1, 340

Whiteness isn't the problem 3, 539

Windigo 94

World Bank 172, 375

Young, Jon 1, 20, 177, 194, 450

Zapatistas
... and collective self-defense: 418
... initial policies to end sexism: 419-421
... other initial policies: 421
... creating a government that actually responds to the will of the people: 422
... setting their own boundaries instead of taking over gov't: 531

Zinn, Howard 1, 39

www.ingramcontent.com/pod-product-compliance
Lightning Source LLC
Chambersburg PA
CBHW081212170426
43198CB00017B/2595